Archaeology of the Southwest

SECOND EDITION

Bowl of dipper, Tularosa Black-on-white (UCM 9494, courtesy of the University of Colorado Museum).

Archaeology of the Southwest

SECOND EDITION

Linda Cordell
University Museum
University of Colorado
Boulder, Colorado

Academic Press, Inc.
San Diego London Boston New York Sydney Tokyo Toronto

Front cover: Betatakin Ruin, Navajo National Monument (photo by H. F. Robinson, courtesy of the Museum of New Mexico, neg. no. 37394). See Chapter 10 for details.

This book is printed on acid-free paper. ∞

Academic Press
a division of Harcourt Brace & Company
525 B Street, Suite 1900, San Diego, California 92101-4495, USA
http://www.apnet.com

Academic Press Limited
24-28 Oval Road, London NW1 7DX, UK
http://www.hbuk.co.uk/ap/

Library of Congress Card Catalog Number: 97-80320

International Standard Book Number: 0-12-188225-X (case)

International Standard Book Number: 0-12-188226-8 (paper)

PRINTED IN THE UNITED STATES OF AMERICA
97 98 99 00 01 02 EB 9 8 7 6 5 4 3 2 1

CONTENTS

CHAPTER 3

The First Southwesterners, Paleoindian Archaeology 67

CHAPTER 4

The Archaic Period: The Hunting and Gathering Spectrum 101

CHAPTER 5

Agricultural Beginnings: Last Hunters, First Farmers 127

CHAPTER 6

Systematics of Southwest Culture History 153

CHAPTER 9

Expansion (AD 800 to 1000) 261

CHAPTER 10

Integration (AD 1000 to 1250) 303

CHAPTER 11

Abandonment: A Complex Social Phenomenon 365

CHAPTER 12

Reorganization 399

PREFACE

The purpose of this book, like that of its 1984 predecessor, *Prehistory of the Southwest,* is to provide an up-to-date synthesis of southwestern archaeology for students, scholars, and other interested readers. The literature of southwestern archaeology is enormous and continues to be augmented at an accelerating pace. This book does not provide a catalogue of the literature or a guide to known archaeological sites. Rather, I hope to give readers a familiarity with the vocabulary of southwestern archaeology, an introduction to primary sources, and the context for and a guide to questions being pursued and debated in the field today. I am pleased that the first edition of the book was able to do many of these things for more than a dozen years. Of necessity, this book goes beyond a simple update and minor revisions of the 1984 edition. The book has been retitled, reorganized, and expanded with the addition of two new chapters. Every chapter has been rewritten.

I am of the generation that was taught that history must be written to be history. This view is considered offensive by many Native Americans, who believe that it denigrates the value and validity of oral history. In deference to this position, I use "archaeology" in the title of the book and "history" or "culture history" throughout the text. If something is ancient or pre-Columbian, I say so.

As in the first edition, Chapter 1 introduces the southwestern landscape, the cultural heterogeneity of its modern inhabitants, and, briefly, the archaeologically defined ancient cultures. The chapter includes Native American perspectives on modern cultural diversity and expands the scope of the book to incorporate somewhat more discussion of northwest Mexico than the previous edition. The second chapter concerns the natural environment today and in the past. Southwestern paleoclimatic and paleoenvironmental reconstructions have been advanced significantly in the past 10 years. Hence, I have devoted more attention to the new reconstructions than to the methods used to prepare them. There should be adequate citations, however, so that interested readers can pursue the methods on their own.

The organization of this book departs from its predecessor with Chapters 3, 4, and 5. Respectively these concern Paleoindians, the Archaic period, and the beginnings of agriculture. I have placed these chapters ahead of the discussion of the systematics and frameworks for southwestern culture history that apply primarily to the archaeology of peoples who made ceramics and lived in relatively durable structures. The tremendous amount of new data on the early periods of Southwest occupation necessitated complete revision of the contents of Chapters 3 and 4. Chapter 5 was extensively rewritten to focus on data pertaining to and explanations for the adoption of agriculture rather than on the diversity of agricultural techniques used in the Southwest.

This book contains two chapters on systematics, Chapters 6 and 7, rather than one as in the first edition. My reasons for expanding these discussions are to provide a more detailed human and historical context for the pioneering studies and key issues of southwestern archaeology and to bring the reader up to date on the questions being asked today. Fortunately, many of the chronological problems that were so salient in discussions of systematics in 1984 have been resolved. For this reason, I have eliminated lengthy discussion of specific dating techniques and debates about chronology to focus instead on what the important questions are and why. I hope readers will be interested in the personal histories included and gain an appreciation for the significance of the important discoveries described.

In Chapters 8–12, I have tried to provide a chronological overview of cultural developments throughout the Southwest with topical issues addressed as they come up. Two aspects of these chapters are very different from the 1984 book. First, I have tried to give more even coverage to the southern deserts and the "intenational four corners" in recognition of the vast amount of new research in these areas. I acknowledge that more could be added. Second, I have tried to separate observations of archaeological phenomena from inferences made from and about them particularly with regard to social organization. For example, archaeologists can observe that a site consists of three or four houses. Whether or not these were occupied simultaneously, year round or seasonally, or by members of the same kin group is a matter of inference made with more or less confidence. I hope this will clarify the process of archaeological reasoning and the basis of debate where it exists. As in the previous edition, I do not hesitate to address controversy.

Chapter 8 considers the earliest southwestern sites that indicate more residential permanence than camping places. The process of settling down, the reasons for it, and its differential pace, pattern, and consequences throughout the Southwest are explored. Chapter 9 covers the expansion of agricultural communities throughout the region and the diversity of farming strategies and subsistence options that made the expansion possible. Chapter 10 focuses on the regionally integrated systems in the low deserts and on the Colorado Plateaus that flourished in the 11th and 12th centuries, as well as neighboring areas that were apparently little affected by them. The revised chronologies that are available for this edition correct some of the horrendous problems of the first one; the extent of the Chacoan system of the Colorado Plateau and its permutations over time are explored here in Chapter 10, while the system that developed at Casas Grandes, Chihuahua, is considered in its appropriate centuries in Chapter 12.

Chapter 11 focuses on the documented changes in the distribution of populations across the Southwest between about AD 1150 and 1450. A tremendous amount of new data on this period allow discussions of a variety of models and causes for the changes seen in the archaeological record of this time. I discuss these at length and, I hope, provocatively. Finally, Chapter 12 explores the landscape of the Southwest after large areas had been deserted by their original inhabitants. New centers of population in the Rio Grande and new centers of regional organization, especially in Chihuahua, developed and are discussed. Chapter 12 also considers some traditional Native American histories and their implications for archaeology. I hope that this and other research directions suggested in the text will be useful to my colleagues and students.

Over the years, a few of my colleagues have been particularly encouraging to me to do this revision. I thank Peggy Nelson of Arizona State University, Alan Sullivan of the University of Cincinnati, Patty Jo Watson of Washington University, and members of the Arizona Archaeological Society for their enduring interest, and Scott Bentley of Academic Press for his. I am greatly indebted for detailed comments on the manuscript to my colleagues Michael Adler of Southern Methodist University, Suzanne and Paul Fish of the Arizona State Museum, Judith Habicht-Mauche of the University of California, Santa Cruz, Barbara Mills of the University of Arizona, and Harry J. Shafer of Texas A&M University. I am responsible for all errors in fact and interpretation, but the manuscript was immeasurably improved by their thoughtful suggestions. I thank Steve Lekson and Cathy Cameron of the University of Colorado for helpful clarification and "road testing," respectively. I thank June-El Piper of the University of New Mexico, and Tracey Beserra, Lori Jensen, and Lisa J. Spiegel of the University of Colorado for technical assistance. David Underwood of the University of Colorado Graphics Center and Marjorie Leggitt of Leggitt Design were invaluable in developing the comprehensive maps and illustrations for this edition. It was a great pleasure to work with them both. I am also grateful to Diana Leonard of the University of Colorado Museum for her patience and assistance with archival photographs. I thank Karin Burd for being the best graduate assistant in the universe. I am forever grateful to Eden Welker and Inga Calvin for organizing "the crew" and to "the crew" for all their work. This book could not have been written without the support and encouragement of my colleagues and my students. I hope both will find it useful.

Linda S. Cordell
Boulder, Colorado

CHAPTER 1

Introduction: The Place and Its Peoples

The North American Southwest is a culture area encompassing diversity in land forms, modern Native American societies, and past indigenous cultures. This chapter provides a brief introduction to the land and its modern and ancient inhabitants.

INTRODUCTION

The North American Southwest (Figure 1.1) is a land of contrasts and diversity that is united by an arid climate. The physical landscape includes extensive mesas (table lands), rugged mountains, and low-lying deserts. The mesa country is generally high, above 1524 m, and is bisected by steep-walled, narrow canyons. Much of the mesa country is sparsely covered with vegetation, and there are extensive areas of bare rock. Piñon and juniper woodlands occur on mesa tops where soils have developed and not eroded away. Many of the mesas are composed of layers of sandstone and shale. Weathering of the softer sandstone creates caves and rock shelters in which some ancient inhabitants built their homes, as did the cliff dwellers of the Mesa Verde in Colorado. At the contact zone, where sandstone overlies less permeable shale, seeps and springs can form that provide important water sources.

The mountains of central Arizona, northern New Mexico, and southern Colorado rise majestically from the mesa country. A few peaks are snowcapped year-round, but

FIGURE 1.1 The Southwest culture area, which includes portions of the United States and Mexico (illustrated by Charles M. Carrillo).

most of the mountains have alpine meadows or ponderosa pine and Douglas fir forests at their highest elevations. Below these are stands of piñon and juniper. Winter snows in the mountains provide water that feeds the great Southwestern rivers: the Colorado, Rio Grande, and San Juan. Although vegetation along the banks of rivers is lush, it is sparse elsewhere. At low elevations, there may be only desert grasses, stands of yucca, or strangely shaped desert plants such as ocotillo and saguaro. Except for a few weeks of the year, when golden aspens light the mountainsides in fall or when desert cacti bloom in spring, the landscapes of the Southwest are not colorful. They are impressive landscapes of shape, mass, form, and light.

Summer daytime temperatures are commonly 80° to 90°F. In winter, the high mesas and mountains are bitterly cold and often deep in snow. In spring, strong winds carry sand and dust, which can obscure the landscape for days. Most of the time,

FIGURE 1.2 A series of Check dams across a small arroyo at Hopi traps soil and slows and channels runoff allowing corn plants to grow. Note wide spacing of plants that decreases competition for water. (Photo taken in 1931 courtesy of the University of Colorado Museum.)

though, the air is remarkably clear and immense vistas the rule. Residents of Albuquerque, for example, can usually see the peak of Mount Taylor on the western horizon, a distance of nearly 100 km. Despite the variety of land forms and vegetation, the entire Southwest is dry. Everywhere, water is the critical resource for life. Yet despite the harsh climate, the temperature extremes, and the aridity, the indigenous peoples of the Southwest developed a way of life dependent on farming native American crops: corn, beans, and squash. They used a variety of ingenious techniques to cultivate the soil and conserve moisture (Figure 1.2) and are responsible for some of the most spectacular architecture in the Americas north of the Valley of Mexico. Native peoples built the still impressive cliff dwellings of Mesa Verde in Colorado and Canyon de Chelly, Arizona (Figure 1.3); the stark, stone towers of Utah's Hovenweep; the formal, multistory stone towns of New Mexico's Chaco Canyon; and the multistory adobe buildings, mounds, and ball courts of Paquimé (Casas Grandes) in northern Chihuahua.

Precise boundaries for any culture area are usually difficult to specify. It is the agricultural adaptation that most clearly defines the Southwest as a culture area. In a brief and useful way, archaeologist Erik Reed (1964) noted that the Southwest can be described as extending from Durango, Mexico, to Durango, Colorado, and from Las Vegas, New Mexico, to Las Vegas, Nevada (Figure 1.4). The Native peoples in this area are diverse in language and culture, but the cultivation of corn, beans, and squash sets this region apart from the gathering-and-hunting peoples of California and the Great Basin and the bison-hunters of the western Great Plains.

FIGURE 1.3 Cliff Palace, Mesa Verde, Colorado (courtesy of the University of Colorado Museum).

The southern boundary of the Southwest is perhaps the most difficult to define, for the pre-Columbian peoples of Mesoamerica also depended on farming the same crops. Mesoamerica, however, was one of the centers of American civilization, with urban centers, such as Teotihuacan; organized state governments; and empires, such as those of the Toltec and Aztec. Developments of this scale did not occur in the Southwest. Among indigenous Southwestern peoples, there was little differentiation in wealth and living conditions. Culturally, then, the Southwest is defined both by what was present at the time Europeans first arrived there and by what was absent. Practices that were present include agriculture; the use of digging sticks, flat *metates* (grinding stones) and *manos* (hand stones); the manufacture and use of excellent pottery; the construction of aggregated multiroom *pueblos* (villages) as well *rancherías* (dispersed settlements); and the occasional development of more complex towns with some unique forms of public architecture. Absent were state-level governments with social classes, well-developed systems of writing and notation, large urban centers, and public architecture on the scale of the pyramids of Oaxaca or central Mexico.

The Native peoples of the Southwest developed their basic cultural patterns through a combination of their own invention and acceptance of some aspects of Mesoamerican culture (especially the basic crops, possibly pottery, and perhaps some religious beliefs), adapting these to the environmentally diverse and risky agricultural

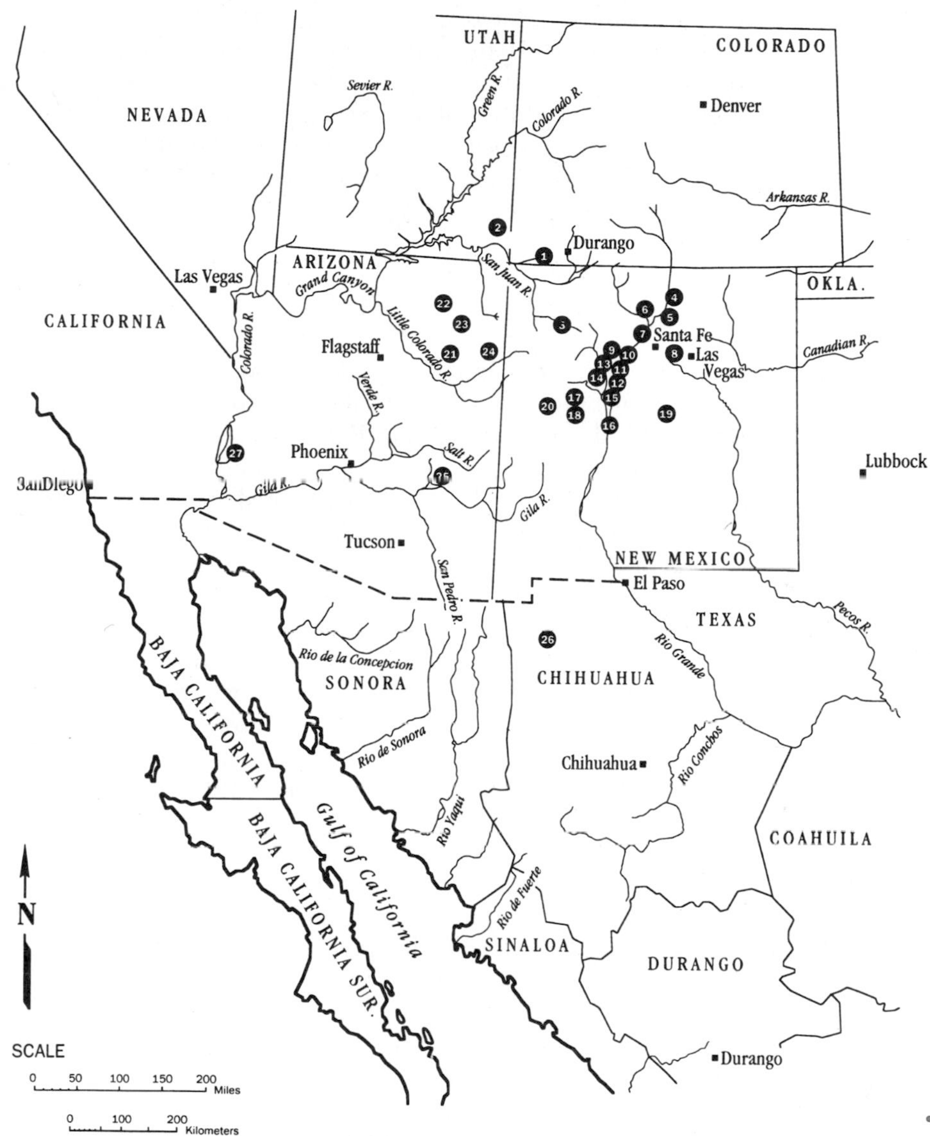

FIGURE 1.4 The sites located on this map are discussed in this chapter. Key: 1 Mesa Verde, Colorado; 2 Hovenweep, Utah; 3 Chaco Canyon Culture Center, New Mexico; 4 Taos; 5 Picuris; 6 San Juan Pueblo; 7 Santa Clara Pueblo; 8 Pecos Pueblo; 9 Jemez Pueblo; 10 Cochiti Pueblo; 11 Santo Domingo Pueblo; 12 San Felipe Pueblo; 13 Zia Pueblo; 14 Santa Ana Pueblo; 15 Sandia, New Mexico; 16 Isleta; 17 Laguna Pueblo; 18 Acoma Pueblo; 19 Fort Sumner; 20 Zuni; 21 Hopi; 22 Black Mesa, Arizona; 23 Antelope Mesa; 24 Fort Defiance/ Window Rock, Arizona; 25 San Carlos Reservation; 26 Casas Grandes; 27 Colorado Indian Reservation. (Map by David Underwood.)

settings of the Southwest. Throughout their histories, the people moved between periods of sedentism and mobility. At times they depended more on hunting and gathering and were therefore relatively mobile. At other times, periods of regional integration occurred, when very large areas of the Southwest seem to have been incorporated into one social, economic, or belief system, but these always had a tenuous hold. Eventually large centers were deserted as places of habitation by their builders and the populace returned to village life.

PRESENT-DAY PEOPLES

The descendants of the precontact inhabitants of the Southwest live among the ethnically and linguistically heterogeneous Native American groups of the region. It is a tribute to these people that despite incursions of Europeans, religious persecution, cultural prejudice, and periods of forced acculturation, much of their Native culture has remained intact. Of all the regions of the contiguous United States, it is the Southwest that holds the largest number of indigenous peoples who continue to occupy their original homelands, retaining their languages, customs, beliefs, and values. The same is not true of the Native peoples of the north coastal plain of Mexico, who were largely overrun in the wake of the Spanish conquest and subsequently absorbed into other cultural groups both Hispanic and indigenous. There is an enormous ethnographic literature about Southwestern peoples. Because this book is about archaeology, only a cursory overview of modern native peoples is given as an introduction to the past. (Useful bibliographies about the modern peoples may be found in Dutton 1983; Laird 1977; Ortiz 1979, 1983; Riley 1987; Saunders 1944; Spicer 1962; Vogt 1969; and Whiteley 1988.)

In the United States and Mexico, Native peoples are most often classified by "tribe," a political unit imposed by the modern federal governments. It is unlikely that such tribes normally constituted an indigenous organization. Yet the use of the tribal name provides a reference to the historic and ethnographic literature. Anthropologists often use a people's language or language family as an important element in classification because a shared tongue often indicates a group's origin or particularly close relationships among peoples. By emphasizing either language, modern tribal boundaries, elements of social organization, or other cultural characteristics, somewhat different groupings of the Native peoples will emerge. This very brief overview presents cultural traditions according to their geographical location within the Southwest, except for the Navajos and Apaches, whose settlements are interdigitated among other peoples. For each geographic sub-area, some of the historical factors responsible for present-day groupings and distributions are discussed. It is also true that in what follows, the northern groups are described in disproportionately greater detail than the southern and western peoples. This reflects the amount of archaeological attention and literature available and the fact that the northern groups retain their lands, customs, and languages to a greater extent than do most other peoples indigenous to the region.

In some of what follows below, I use both the official tribal designation and the people's self-designation if different. In the United States, Native Americans are increasingly concerned about the negative political implications of official tribal names. Some groups, such as the Tohono O'Odham (former Papagos), have requested that their own self-designation become their official tribal name. Other groups use both terms. For example, the Navajos call themselves Diné but as yet have not asked for an official change, in part because they believe that would further confuse their Anglo-American neighbors. The major Native cultural traditions of the Southwest are those of the Tohono O'Odham (Papagos) and Pimas of southern Arizona and Sonora; the Yaqui, Mayo, Cahita, Rarámuri (Tarahumara), Tepehuan, Tahua and related peoples of northern Mexico; the Yuman-speaking peoples of the Colorado River Valley and Baja California; the Pueblo Indians of Arizona and New Mexico; and the Athapaskan-speaking peoples (Apaches and Navajos) (Figure 1.5).

Southern Peoples

Most of the vast land area of northwestern Mexico and adjacent southern Arizona is the traditional homeland of agricultural peoples who speak languages of the Uto-Aztecan family. These peoples include the Upper Pimas and Tohono O'Odham of Arizona; the Lower Pimas, Opata, Yaqui, and Seri of Sonora; the Cahita and Mayo of Sinaloa; the Tepehuans of Durango; and the Concho, Suma, Rarámuris (Tarahumaras), and Zacatec of Chihuahua. This enormous territory was the most populous subregion of the Southwest at the time the Europeans arrived. It includes relatively fertile river valleys, such as the Yaqui, Mayo, Salt, and Gila; the coastal plain of northwest Mexico; inhospitable deserts; and rugged mountainous uplands. Some of the major differences among the Native peoples relate to their particular environments. Other differences can be ascribed to variations in their interaction with Western European cultures (Erikson 1994; Sheridan and Parezo 1966). According to Carpenter (1996), no region of Mexico was so thoroughly and quickly decimated by the Spanish conquistadors as the northwest Mexican coastal plain. Consequently, our knowledge of even basic linguistic and other cultural information for many groups is meager. Today, the only indigenous peoples remaining on the coastal plain north of Nayarit are the Seri, Mayo, and Yaqui.

The basic crops planted in this region, as throughout the Southwest, were corn, beans, and squash, and where possible, cotton. Documentary sources (cited in Carpenter 1996) indicate that central Mexican crops such as chile and guavas were planted south of the Rio Mocorito. Canal irrigation was practiced in a few locations, but flood plain irrigation was practiced by most riverine communities and could be very productive. The Yaquis, for example, obtained two crops a year and enjoyed access to abundant wild plant foods such as various species of agave, mesquite seeds, prickly pear, pitahaya, and other cactus fruit. Desert groups, such as the Tohono O'Odham, generally planted *ackchin* fields, which are fields located on the outwash fans of arroyos (ephemeral drainages), and gathered substantial amounts of wild plant foods. Mountain dwelling groups generally relied on rainfall for farming, supplementing their crops with substantial amounts of wild plant foods and game.

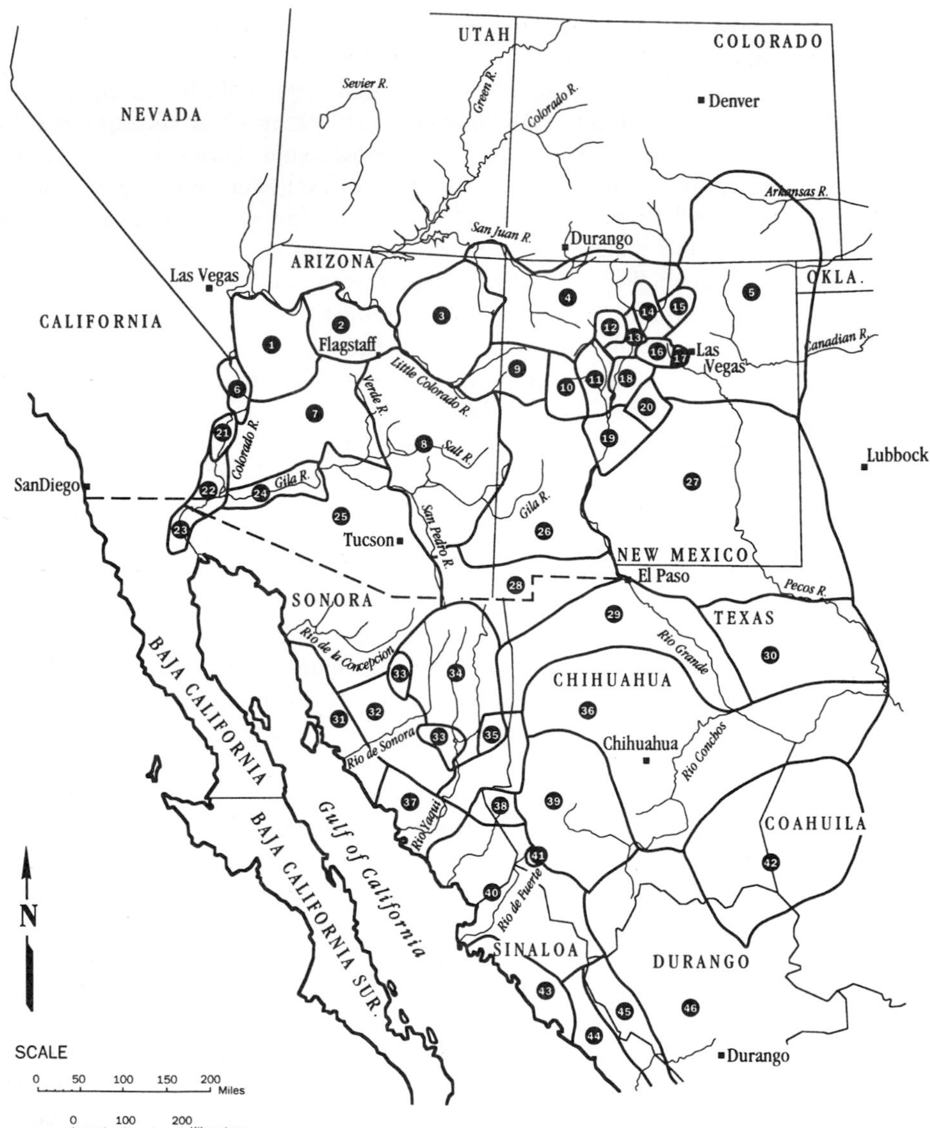

FIGURE 1.5 Historic tribal territories of Southwestern peoples. The Upper Pima, Tohono O'Odham, Lower Pima, Tarahumara, Yaqui, Mayo, and Northern Tepehuan constitute the traditional southern Uto-Aztecan speaking peoples. The Maricopa, Cocopa, Quechan, Halchidoma, Mohave, Yavapai, Walapai, and Havasupai speak Yuman languages of the Hokam language family and are tribes of the western tradition. The Rio Grande Pueblos and Laguna, Acoma, Zuni, and Hopi are the traditional northern peoples. They speak diverse languages. The Apaches and Navajos entered the Southwest late in pre-contact times and speak Athapaskan languages related to those of interior Canada. Key: ❶Walapai; ❷ Havasupai; ❸ Hopi; ❹ Navajo;

Hunting and, locally, fishing were important. Deer, peccary, rabbits, iguanas, and quail and doves were hunted for food. Coastal groups fished, collected shellfish and mollusks, planted some crops, and traded for others.

All of these people lived in rancherías, that is, settlements composed of spatially separated dwellings of nuclear or extended family units. Among those groups inhabiting river valleys (e.g., Pimas, Yaquis, and Mayos), individual houses were closer together and communities were larger than among either mountain or desert settlements (e.g., Rarámuris, northern Tepehuans, Tohono O'Odham). Where water sources and agricultural production were relatively secure, residential groups were sedentary throughout the year; however, various patterns of residential movement characterized other groups. For example, Rarámuri families maintained fields in several different locations and, since contact with Europeans, have kept herds of goats. During the agricultural season, families may move from one agricultural plot to another, while in winter, they take their goats to sheltered canyon locations. Rarámuri residential moves and the make-up of the household group are extremely variable and flexible over even short periods of time. Many local groups of Tohono O'Odham engaged in biannual residential moves, living in greatly dispersed farmsteads near washes during the summer rainy season and moving to foothill villages in fall, when water was available only at the village reservoir.

House types and other structures within the rancherías varied considerably. For example, Rarámuri rancherías might consist of five or six one-room log houses with adjacent stone or log grain-storage cabins and a flat, open patio for outside work space. Tohono O'Odham settlements consisted of several dome-shaped brush structures with slightly excavated floors, separate ramadas (sunshades), outdoor cooking areas, and a small house used as a menstrual seclusion hut. Traditional Yaqui rancherías are composed of several flat-roofed, rectangular, *jacal* (wattle-and-daub) houses with separate ramadas and outdoor cooking areas all enclosed by a high cane fence.

Families living in the same ranchería are usually related. Among the Yaquis and Mayos, residence patterns are bilateral (married couples reside near either the husband's or wife's natal family), as they tend to be among the Rarámuris. The residence patterns of the northern Tepehuans, Pimas, and Tohono O'Odham are generally patrilocal (married couples reside near the husband's natal family). Extended families are not usually economically self-sufficient, and communal work parties are a common feature of most of these peoples. Craft production of domestic items such as pottery

---

FIGURE 1.5—*Continued* ❺ Jicarilla Apache; ❻ Mohave; ❼ Yavapai; ❽ Western Apache; ❾ Zuni; ❿ Acoma; ⓫ Laguna; ⓬ Jemez; ⓭ Rio Grande Keresans; ⓮ Tewa; ⓯ North Tiwa; ⓰ Tano; ⓱ Pecos; ⓲ South Tiwa; ⓳ Piro; ⓴ Tompiro; ㉑ Halchidhoma; ㉒ Quechan; ㉓ Cocopa; ㉔ Maricopa; ㉕ Papago and Upper Pima; ㉖ Chiricahua Apache; ㉗ Mescalero Apache; ㉘ Jocome and Jano; ㉙ Suma; ㉚ Jumano; ㉛ Seri; ㉜ Lower Pima; ㉝ Eudeve; ㉞ Opata; ㉟ Jova; ㊱ Concho; ㊲ Yaqui; ㊳ Guarijio; ㊴ Tarahumara; ㊵ Mayo; ㊶ Tubar; ㊷ Toboso; ㊸ Guasave; ㊹ Tahue; ㊺ Acaxee; ㊻ Tepehuan. (Map by David Underwood.)

varies in organization as well as technology. For example, although all Rarámuri women learn to make pottery, in practice some villages are known to produce especially good vessels and these are exchanged through barter. The way pottery vessels are made varies throughout the Southwest. The variation is important to archaeologists because pottery fragments are virtually indestructible, and they are a major component of archaeological sites. Throughout the Southwest, pottery is made without the wheel, by building up the vessel walls with coils of clay. The Tohono O'Odham, Rarámuris, and Yaquis use a paddle (a flat object held outside the vessel) and anvil (a stone held inside the vessel) to shape and finish pottery, whereas the Pimas and formerly the Opatas (who are now ethnically extinct) produced pottery by the coil-and-scrape technique (shaping and finishing the vessel by smoothing the coils and scraping inside and out with the edge of a fragment of gourd or pottery sherd). Craft specialization in pottery production or other items is not noted. Nevertheless, there was considerable trade in shell, turquoise, salt, cotton textiles, hides, feathers, and foodstuffs.

Political organization beyond the level of the individual ranchería is highly variable and reflects interactions with Europeans. Most groups seem not to have had indigenous patterns of supra-village organization, except in times of war when villages would unite under the leadership of the hierarchy of leaders of warrior societies. However, warfare seems to have been endemic in some areas, and among the Yaqui may have served as an integrative factor that was sufficient to support the development of a class of leaders able to extract wealth and labor in addition to obedience in battle. As a result of contact with the Spaniards, and especially of the efforts of the Jesuit missionaries, a structured organization of officials served to unite several rancherías and provide an interface between them and the Spanish Colonial government. This village organization typically includes a *gobernador*, with *capitanes*, *'tenientes* (lieutenants), and subsidiary officials.

As described by Spicer (1969), the contrasting histories of the Mayos and Yaquis are illustrative of the influence of European contact. The two Indian groups, speaking dialects of the same language and living much the same way, were at war with one another at the time of initial contact with the Spaniards. The Mayos allied themselves with the Spaniards, whereas the Yaquis fought and defeated the Europeans. The Yaquis requested Jesuit missionaries, and both groups had peaceful relations with the missionaries for more than 100 years. From 1740 until 1887 both Mayos and Yaquis (often in combination) staged a series of revolts. The fighting escalated after Mexican Independence from Spain in 1821. After severe native defeats in 1886 and 1887, the Mexican government attempted to pacify the Mayos by offering them work on the Mexican haciendas and to pacify the Yaquis by giving them plots of land along the Yaqui River. The Mayo resistance was broken. Mexican residents moved into Mayo villages and took political power from them. Although the Mayos participated in a messianic religious movement, much of their ethnic distinctiveness has been lost.

After 1886, the Yaquis were forcibly dispersed throughout Sonora, and to Oaxaca and Yucatan. Many fled to southern Arizona, where their descendants still reside. Those Yaquis remaining in their homeland continued to fight intermittent guerrilla warfare against the Mexican government. Many Yaquis were again forcibly deported under the Diaz regime, which ended in 1910. Those Yaquis remaining in Sonora retain a tremendous cultural pride and a sense of Yaqui nationalism, as do those Yaquis in Arizona. Their allegiance is to Yaqui religion and also to the "traditional" eight Yaqui pueblos, which were in fact established by the Jesuits. In contrast, few Mayos retain an ethnic identity that is unlike their Mestizo neighbors.

Religion among these groups is a combination of syncretisms, or blendings of native Yaqui and Catholic beliefs, and some compartmentalization, where borrowed and native elements are conceptualized as belonging to different realms. There is also considerable variation among the groups, although all but the most isolated are nominally Catholic. Holy Week ritual, summer Saints' Day celebrations, and *Matachine dances* (a masked, all-male dance performance dedicated to the Virgin Mary) are virtually universal. At the local level, rainmaking rituals and dances are held among the Raramuris and the Tohono O'Odham, and deer dances are important features of Yaqui ritual. Shamanism and witchcraft are prevalent. In widely shared beliefs, serpents are associated with springs and other water sources, there are sun and moon deities, and deer and flowers are ritually important. Much of this symbolism occurs throughout native communities in modern Mexico and reflects very ancient Mesoamerican belief systems. At the time of contact, some groups, such as the Cahita and some of their neighbors, played various ball games involving squads of players, special flat courts, and a solid rubber ball.

Western Peoples

Since the arrival of European peoples, various tribes speaking Yuman languages occupied the lower Colorado River Valley; the lower Gila River Valley; and adjacent uplands in California, Baja California, and Arizona. The Yuman languages are thought to belong to the Hokan language stock. Within Baja California, the Cocopahs occupied the delta of the Colorado River and the Tipais, Kiliwas, and Paipais lived in the neighboring highlands. (*Pai* means "people" in Yuman. Here it refers to all Yuman-speaking peoples.) Northwest of the Cocopahs, in the state of California, the groups were the Kiliwas, Paipais, and Diegueños. North of the Cocopahs, along the Colorado River, the groups were the Halyikwamais, Kohwans, and Quechans (Yumas) at the confluence of the Gila and Colorado rivers, and the Halchidhomas, Mohaves, and Havasupais of the Grand Canyon. The Walapais and Yavapais occupied uplands in the vicinity of the Grand Canyon. The Cocomaricopas and the Opas lived along the lower Gila. In the nineteenth century, the Halyikwamais, Kohwans, Halchidhomas, Kavelchadomas, Opas, and Cocomaricopas merged to form the Maricopa tribe, and the Chemehuevis moved to the Colorado River from central California.

Despite brief contacts with Spanish explorers and with the famous Jesuit missionary Father Eusebio Kino, the Pais were not missionized or conquered by the Spaniards. The presence of Europeans had major effects on the Yumas through the introduction of horses and wheat and through slaving. It was not until the California gold rush of the 1850s, however, that Euro-Americans regularly entered Pai territory and not until the 1880s that the Pai accepted various reservations. Since the 1700s, and possibly in pre-Columbian times as well, the Pai area was one in which there were numerous wars, population movements, migrations, and alliances of tribal groups. The Maricopas, for example, allied themselves in warfare with the Pimas, and their culture reflects considerable blending of Yuma and Pima traits. Today, some of the reservations are not occupied exclusively by only one official tribe or ethnic group. The Colorado River Indian Reservation, which lies along both the Arizona and California sides of the lower Colorado River, is occupied by Yuma, Mohave, Chemehuevi, and Cocopah peoples as well as a few Navajo families. The Gila River Reservation in Arizona is occupied by both Pima and Maricopa.

The peoples living along the Colorado River practiced agriculture on the river's flood plain. In spring, the Colorado River overflowed its channel, inundating an area that could be as much as 0.80 km (½ mile) wide. When the flood subsided, in summer, this area was planted. However, the Colorado has always been unpredictable. In some years the spring flood could be a month late, and in some years no flood occurred. In addition, the river frequently changed course along its lower reaches, sometimes creating lakes in the Mojave Desert. The riverine Pais made biannual residential moves, living in temporary shelters or ramadas on the flood plain during the summer and moving to the foothills of neighboring mountains at the end of the harvest. In addition to growing domestic crops, the Yumas practiced semicultivation of six species of native wild grasses, and all groups depended to a great extent on hunting, gathering, and fishing. Mesquite may have constituted as much as 50 percent of the Pai diet. Because of variations in the flood plain, fields were rarely located in the same place each year, and structures on the flood plain were ephemeral. The Maricopas, in part a result of their extensive contact with the Pimas, came to use canal irrigation to divert water from the Gila. Winter villages in the mountain foothills were composed of a loosely arranged series of rectangular pithouses (houses with floors sunken below ground level). They were very large and accommodated several nuclear families. During the nonagricultural season, these houses served as bases for hunting and gathering.

Upland groups generally practiced some rainfall farming and a great deal of hunting and gathering. House forms were variable. In Baja California, *jacal* structures were built; elsewhere, combinations of stone and jacal were used in house construction. The use life of even the more permanent Yuma houses was not very long because at the death of an individual, the house as well as all possessions were burned as part of an elaborate death and mourning ritual. The Yuma generally expressed a preference for patrilocality, and villages were inhabited by members of named, totemic patrilineal descent groups (groups that trace their relationship through males and are named for a putative, usually animal or spirit, ancestor). Village leadership was frequently in the hands of a particularly charismatic and spiritually powerful male, and some villages had additional councils of elders. Shamans had great religious power but were not headmen of villages. Among some groups, such as the Quechans (Yumas), village leadership may have been hereditary, but leaders ruled through their authority as respected persons rather than through their inherited right to exercise power.

Leadership was very important in times of war. From at least the eighteenth century, warfare seems to have been pervasive in the Yuman area. Yuman war organization was similar to that of the Yaquis. Tribes could mobilize hundreds of warriors and move them over great distances. In addition, the Yumas formed alliances among themselves during periods of warfare. Eventually, these spread to incorporate some of the Pimas. A major alliance was formed that included the Mohaves, Quechans, Yavapais, Kamias, and Chemehuevis. Allied against this group were the Cocopahs, Halchidhomas, Paipais, Diegueños, Cocomaricopas, Opas, Gila River Pimas, and Tohono O'Odham.

The Yuman-speaking peoples produced a number of craft items, including mats, baskets, blankets, and pottery. The latter was finished by the paddle-and-anvil technique and was generally a plain buff or brown ware. The Maricopas, however, traded with the Pimas for the red slips and clay the Pimas themselves used to make their own ceramics. At the turn of the twentieth century, heirloom pottery collected from the Mohaves was also painted with red designs on a buff background. In addition to being recognized as exceptional in warfare, the Yumans were also respected as active traders. They maintained an elaborate network of trails throughout their territory, with many trails crossing the Mojave Desert—the most extreme desert in the United States.

Among the Colorado River groups, all males were believed to be endowed with sacred religious power. Individual dreams were important in order to attain this power. Public religious ceremonies involving sponsorship included curing rituals and initiation rites for both males and females. The death ritual was particularly elaborate. Individuals were cremated and, as noted, personal property and houses were burned during the mortuary ceremonies.

Northern Peoples

The Northern peoples are the Pueblos of Arizona and New Mexico, whose ancestors have been in the Southwest for thousands of years. All Pueblo peoples live in the compact communities of stone or adobe that the Spanish call *pueblos*.

Traditional Pueblo villages are composed of contiguous rectangular rooms of one or more stories, arranged around open plazas. Extended family households use a series of interconnecting rooms for living and storage. In multistory pueblos, ground-floor rooms are often used for storage, and in all pueblos, the flat roofs are used as additional work areas. All pueblos also have special ceremonial rooms (some of which are called *kivas*) in which some rituals take place. Among the Western Pueblos (Hopi, Zuni, Acoma, and Laguna), kivas are rectangular and incorporated into roomblocks. Among the Eastern Pueblos, kivas are separate, round structures.

Agriculture is of great importance to all Pueblos. The Hopis, lacking perennial streams, divert some water from washes but rely on rainfall for farming. They plant fields in diverse topographic settings to ensure that at least some of the fields obtain enough moisture to produce a crop. Other villages rely on both stream-irrigated and rainfall-watered fields. Among all the Pueblos, hunting and gathering were historically important methods of supplemental subsistence. Although villages were occupied year-round, family members might spend large parts of the agricultural season at field houses near their crops, and work parties would use temporary camps, such as piñon-collecting and hunting camps, at other times.

There is great cultural similarity among Pueblo peoples that goes beyond the basic agricultural economy. Anthropologists usually expect that such homogeneity reflects deep historical roots and close interactions. Under such conditions, similarity in language would also be expected. In fact, that is not the case. Pueblo languages and language families suggest divergent origins. Hence, anthropologists have emphasized differences among Pueblos speaking unrelated languages and have sought historical reasons for the linguistic diversity. The Pueblos of modern Arizona are all Hopi who live in villages clustered on and around three small mesas that form the southern edge of the large Black Mesa landform. Until the eighteenth century, there were Hopi villages on Antelope Mesa, east of First Mesa, but these were abandoned as a result of interactions with the Europeans. The First (east) Mesa communities are Walpi, Sichomovi, and Tewa Village. The communities of Second (middle) Mesa are Shongopavi, Sipaulovi, and Mishongnovi. The Third (west) Mesa communities are Oraibi, Moenkopi, Hotevilla, Kyakotsmovi (New Oraibi), and Bacavi. With the exception of the residents of Tewa Village, which was founded in the seventeenth century by migrants primarily from the Rio Grande region, the Hopi speak the Hopi language, which is within the Uto-Aztecan family of languages. The people of Tewa Village speak both Hopi and Tewa, which is related to other languages spoken among the Rio Grande Pueblo Indians (see following).

The New Mexican Pueblos speak five different languages (Figure 1.6). The westernmost Pueblo in New Mexico is Zuni, the only Pueblo village today where the Zuni language is spoken. At the time of European contact, the Zunis occupied six villages near the Zuni River in western New Mexico. The Zuni language is not closely related to other Pueblo languages but has been linked to Penutian, a language spoken by some native California peoples. East of the Pueblo of Zuni, the people of Acoma occupy their ancestral village on a high mesa-top above the Rio San Jose and Acoma Creek, and two villages (Acomita and McCartys) below Acoma mesa. The Acoma speak the Keresan language, which is divided into eastern and western dialects. Western Keresan is spoken at Acoma and at the Pueblo of Laguna, their immediate neighbors to the east. Keresan is not related to any other known Native American language. The Pueblo of Laguna occupies six villages (Old Laguna, New Laguna, Seama, Encinal, Paguate, and Mesita) on both sides of the Rio San Jose. The Pueblos of Zia, Santa Ana, San Felipe, Santo Domingo, and Cochiti also speak Keresan, but the eastern Keresan dialect. Zia and Santa Ana are located on the Jemez River west of Albuquerque. San Felipe, Santo Domingo, and Cochiti are located within the Rio Grande Valley, where they form a wedge between Pueblo villages speaking Tanoan languages.

Three related languages in the Tanoan language group are spoken today. Tiwa is spoken at Isleta and Sandia, the southernmost Pueblo villages of the Rio Grande Valley, and at Taos and Picuris, the northernmost Pueblo villages. Tewa is the Tanoan language spoken at San Juan, Santa Clara, Pojaque, San Ildefonso, Nambe, and Tesuque, as well as at Tewa Village on the First Hopi Mesa. Towa is a Tanoan language that today is spoken only at the Pueblo of Jemez, north of Zia. Towa was spoken at Pecos Pueblo, on the upper Pecos River, until that town was abandoned in 1838. The Tanoan languages are part of the Kiowa-Tanoan language family, which is related to other

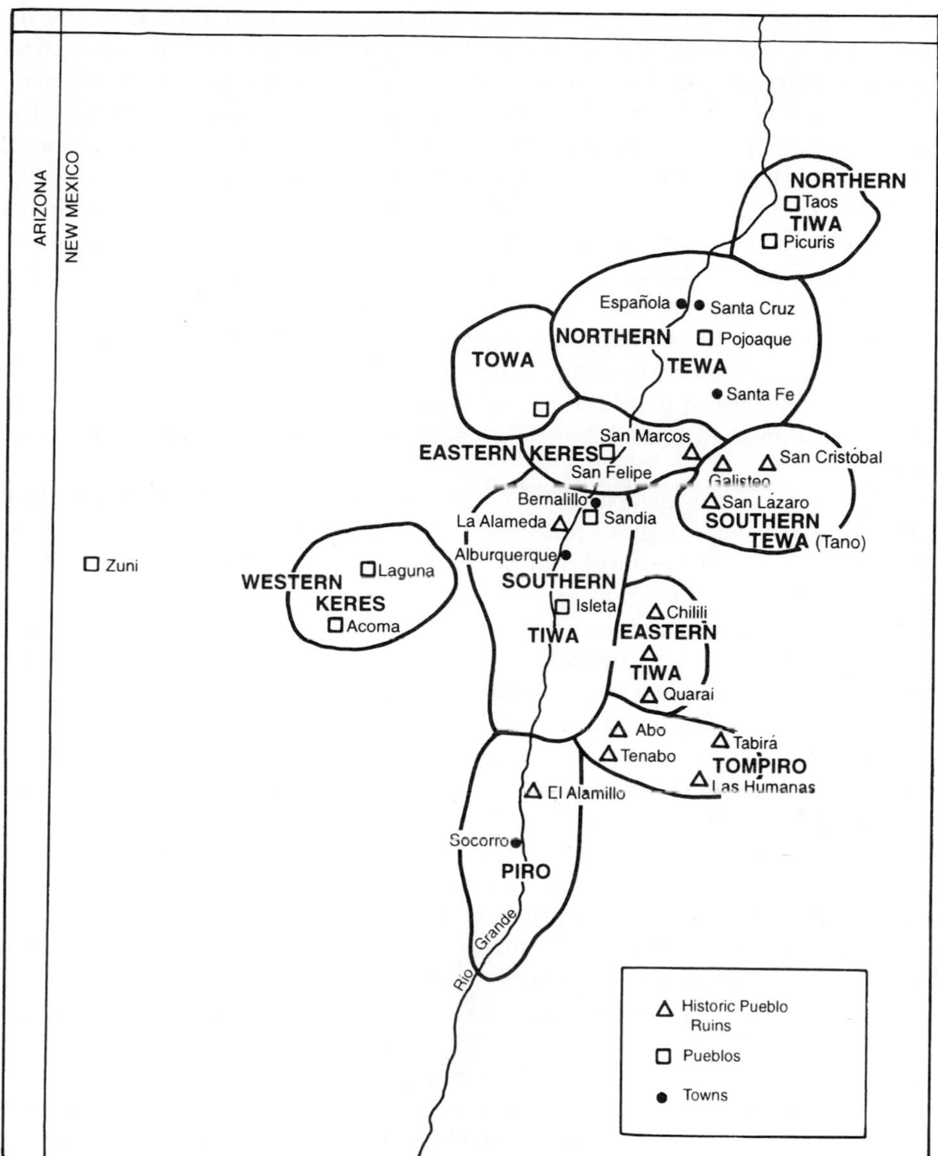

FIGURE 1.6 This map shows the Rio Grande Valley of New Mexico with the modern Pueblos and languages spoken. (Map by Marjorie Leggitt, Leggitt Design.)

languages spoken by some peoples of the Great Plains. In addition to these languages, Pueblo speakers of Piro and Tompiro lived along the Rio Grande south of Isleta and east of the Sandia and Manzano Mountains until they were abandoned in the wake of events related to the European conquest. Although descendants of these groups live among some of the modern Pueblos, their languages are no longer spoken. Given the diversity of languages spoken and the fact that interaction among Pueblo villages is very old, the Pueblos have been multilingual, of necessity, throughout most of their history. Nevertheless, villages that share a single language have particularly close ties and the people think of themselves as closely related.

Of the peoples living in the northern portion of the Southwest, the Rio Grande villages bore the brunt of early and continued contact with the Spaniards. Coronado visited Zuni and the Rio Grande Pueblos in 1540, and the first Spanish Colonial capital in New Mexico was established near modern San Juan Pueblo in 1598. Missionization was pursued most ardently among the Rio Grande Pueblos during the seventeenth century, and the repressive activities of the friars was a major factor leading the Rio Grande Pueblos to unite and revolt against the Spaniards in 1680. Reconquest was not accomplished until 1692–1693 under Diego de Vargas, and even then it was incomplete.

Differences among the Pueblos, besides language, relate to social organization, political organization, religious practices, and different histories of interaction with other Native Americans and with Europeans and Euro-Americans. Among the Western Pueblos, the matrilocal household (married couples residing near the wife's natal family) is generally the basic unit of social organization. Above the level of the household, the Western Pueblo organization is dominated by named, matrilineal, exogamous clans. Western Pueblo leadership is often described as theocratic, in that the leaders are the male heads of the specific lineages responsible for the religious obligations of each clan. In addition to the clan rituals, the katcina society has tribewide membership among the Western Pueblos, and there are other tribal ceremonial associations. In the Hopi villages, the katcina ritual involves representation of a series of supernatural beings who are associated, in a general way, with ancestors and with bringing rain and well-being to the pueblo. The katcinas are represented by men in dramatic, masked performances. Other important tribal associations are concerned with social control, hunting, curing, and warfare. Some ritual performances occur at specific times during the year (e.g., at the solstices). Other ritual activities occur at an appropriate time, such as when a series of retreats, prayers, and other activities have been completed. The ceremonies may initiate or conclude certain economic tasks, such as the planting of the crops. The timing of these events and their orderly progression throughout the year are therefore crucial to maintaining village life. Individuals gain positions of leadership and knowledge by assuming obligations and by being initiated into ceremonial groups. The process of education and initiation to greater responsibilities continues throughout much of a person's life. For ceremonies to be effective, there must be enough knowledgeable elders drawn from the leadership of different associations to contribute each of the necessary aspects of the ceremony. The actual organization of clans, the katcina ceremonies, and other associations vary among the Western Pueblos. For example, the coordination of activities is most diffuse among the Hopis and most centralized at Zuni. Nevertheless, it is difficult to overestimate the degree of coordination that must be achieved.

The organization of the Tanoan Rio Grande Pueblos contrasts most markedly with that of the Western Pueblos. Among the Tanoans, the bilateral extended family is the basic household unit of organization. Above the level of the household, the Tanoan organization is dominated by non-exogamous dual divisions (moieties). It is most common for children to belong to the moiety of their father, but there are exceptions, and individuals sometimes change moiety affiliation during their lifetimes. In general, it is the moiety leadership that is responsible for coordinating activities. For example, among the Tewa, one moiety is responsible for leadership during the late fall, winter, and early spring, whereas the opposite moiety assumes leadership for the agricultural portion of the year. In addition to the moieties, there are also ceremonial associations whose membership crosscuts moiety lines. These are concerned with the same types of activity as those mentioned for the Western Pueblos. It has been noted, however, that whereas assuring rainfall is more important in the west, the concerns of curing, hunting, and warfare are more important in the east.

The katcina ceremony and beliefs are also important among the Eastern Pueblos, except at the Pueblo of Taos, where they are absent. (The Taos perform a Turtle Dance that is similar to katcina performances in all respects except that the participants are not masked.) In contrast to those of the Western Pueblos, however, Eastern Pueblo masked katcina dances are not performed in public. These and other rituals are maintained in secret among eastern groups, in part because the Eastern Pueblos were subjected to the most extreme and sustained religious persecution during Spanish Colonial times. In addition to the native religious hierarchy, the Eastern Pueblos are governed by a series of "outside" leaders, that is, the *gobernador*, *capitanes*, and *'tenientes* established during Spanish hegemony. The Keresan-speaking pueblos and the Pueblo of Jemez have been described as organizationally intermediate between the western and eastern patterns because their organizational systems contain elements common to both west and east. These pueblos have named, exogamous, matrilineal clans that are characteristic of the Western Pueblos, as well as patrilineal moiety divisions associated with the kivas.

In addition to the pursuits involved in agriculture, gathering and hunting, the ceremonial concern for rainfall, curing, social control, and increasing the supply of game and to the compact nature of their settlements, the Pueblos share other aspects of culture. For example, among all Pueblo Indians the cardinal directions, the zenith, and the nadir are associated with specific colors, and color and directional symbolism is important. The Pueblo origin stories are also similar, involving a female creator and the emergence of people from a dark, wet underworld, after which they move through a series of settlement locations until they eventually find their central place, where they locate their modern village. Pueblo craft items include finely made ceramics that are finished by coiling and scraping and painted with well-executed designs; well-made textiles; stone and shell jewelry; and the more prosaic items such as stone arrowheads, manos, and metates.

Notable differences among groups of Pueblos also reflect differences in recent interactions with outsiders. For example, as historian Joe Sando (1992), who is from the Pueblo of Jemez, points out, the northernmost villages were strongly influenced by non-Pueblo tribes, especially the Jicarilla Apache and various Plains peoples. The influence is seen in such features as the wearing of beaded moccasins and braids. Most Pueblo men wear their long hair tied back in one *Chongo*. Men from Taos and Picuris, especially, wear braids. The Taos and Picuris and their Jicarilla Apache neighbors also run foot races on their annual feast days. All of the eight northern Pueblos (and Zuni) perform what they call the Comanche Dance—an adaptation of a Plains Indian war dance—as one of their social dances. There was a good deal of trade between the northern Pueblos and Plains Indians. During the seventeenth and eighteenth centuries, this trade became quite formalized.

The southern New Mexican Pueblos have had more interaction among themselves in the past 300 years than they have had with outsiders, according to Sando (1992). For example, their dances and dance costumes do not show borrowing from Apache or Plains groups. The Western Keresan-speaking Pueblos of Laguna and Acoma have been greatly affected by Euro-American culture, perhaps because the Santa Fe Railroad was built through their lands. Many Acoma and Laguna worked for the railroad, accepting assignments in Barstow and Richmond in California as well as in railroad towns in Arizona and New Mexico. Such distant employment meant that although people would come home for traditional feast days and dances, they could not be in their home villages for the long periods of preparation that precede these occasions. Traditional dances are performed, uninfluenced by Apache or Plains dances, but costumes are decorated with store-bought materials that can be assembled quickly rather than with items that must be gathered over a period of time.

According to Sando (1992) many Pueblos, historians and anthropologists, consider that the Hopis represent a "purer" version of Pueblo traditional life than do other Pueblos. In part, this is a result of the fact that the Hopis were never successfully missionized or governed by the Spaniards. Thus, unlike many of the Rio Grande Pueblos, the Hopis have not incorporated Spanish loan words into their everyday speech. While it may be true that Hopis do retain a more traditional form of aspects of Pueblo culture, none of the Pueblo communities have remained static for the last 400 years of interaction with outsiders of European descent and for considerably longer with other non-Pueblo Native Americans. The various Pueblo peoples have reached different accommodations with the changing human and political landscape they inhabit. The same must be true of other native Southwestern peoples as well. The late anthropologist Edward Dozier, from the Pueblo of Santa Clara, used the term compartmentalization to characterize the Rio Grande Pueblos' relationship to Spanish culture. In this view, the Rio Grande Pueblos practice traditional and European customs but keep them conceptually distinct (Dozier 1970). Hopi scholar Hartman Lomawaima (1989:97) describes the accommodation the Hopis have made as one of "Hopification," which he defines as "the synthesizing process by which an idea or thing became imbued with Hopi values . . . a process by which Hopi view, test, analyze, and make decisions about the actions or impositions of alien cultures or elements." Hopification is not restricted to the fairly recent encounter between the Hopi people and Euro-American culture but includes the diverse Native American societies with which

Hopis have interacted for many centuries. Hopification then is described as a process which has allowed Hopi culture to change but, at the same time, to remain traditionally Hopi.

Interjascent Peoples

The Southwest is also home to modern tribes speaking Navajo and Apache, the southern Athapaskan languages. Dutton (1983) refers to the Navajos and Apaches as "interjascent" people, a term that appropriately describes their current geographic distribution. These southern Athapaskan-speaking peoples occupy land surrounding and lying in between groups with longer histories of residence in the region. The Navajos and Apaches customarily live in dispersed, ranchería settlements and make their living as herders and stockmen. Both Navajos and Apaches speak Athapaskan languages that link them to peoples in central Canada and Alaska, the region from which they migrated, reaching the Southwest less than 1000 years ago. The distribution reflects their history as relative newcomers in that they have land that is generally less well watered or higher in elevation than land that can be more reliably farmed with traditional agricultural technology. The distribution also reflects the requirements of the herding economy Navajos and Apaches adopted in the eighteenth and nineteenth centuries. Today, it is impossible to discuss Navajo or Apache economy without discussing herding. Navajos consider sheep herding an essential aspect of living a traditional Navajo way of life. Yet, domestic livestock were introduced into the Southwest by Europeans, beginning with the Spaniards.

Linguists, using a method of dating called glottochronology, suggest that the Navajos and Apaches spoke a single language when they separated from other Athapaskan speakers in the Mackenzie Basin region of Canada, perhaps 600–1000 years ago. What series of events occurred in the north is not known, but other groups of Athapaskan speakers moved to the west and as far south as modern California. The route by which those who would become Navajos and Apaches reached the Southwest is contested by scholars of the subject. There is agreement that they made their living as hunters and gatherers and must have been highly mobile of necessity. Linguistic data again indicate that divergence of the single Apachean language occurred over a period of time. By 1600, historic documents suggest that the Navajo language was no longer the same as that spoken by the Jicarilla Apaches.

When the Spaniards arrived in the Southwest, the Navajos were planting some corn, and likely other crops; the name applied to them, Appaches de Nabahu, refers to fields. Nevertheless, they depended on hunting and trading. They traded meat, hides, and salt to Pueblo peoples for corn, cotton textiles, and pottery. Until the Pueblo Revolt of 1680, Navajos and Apaches either traded with or raided neighboring Pueblos depending on a variety of factors including climatic and political fluctuations. Navajos and Apaches participated with the Pueblos in the Pueblo Revolt. After the Reconquest, some Pueblo refugees joined ancestral Navajos and Apaches in the Dinetah, the traditional Navajo homeland on the northern San Juan River. Change and borrowing characterized cultural interactions among peoples within the Dinetah. Among the most pervasive of outside forces was slave raiding on the part of the Spaniards and later New Mexicans.

In 1846, as a result of the Mexican-American War, Navajo, Apache, and Pueblo country became subject to the United States. The California gold rush of 1849 soon brought countless Anglo-Americans through the Southwest, and U.S. Army troops to ensure their safety. While Navajos and Apaches asked the United States government for protection against slave raids, the Pueblos and colonial settlers asked for protection against raids by Navajos and Apaches. Finally, in 1860, after the Navajos attacked Fort Defiance, which had been established in their territory, the U.S. military planned the evacuation of the Dinetah, and forced resettlement of Navajos and Apaches at the Bosque Redondo (Fort Sumner), where the Native Americans were to be taught how to become farmers. The plan and subsequent Long Walk, of more than 500 km (270 miles), were carried out between 1863 and 1864.

The forced acculturation at Fort Sumner was a disaster because the land was unsuitable for farming and sheep herding, there were inadequate sources of water and fuel, and not enough supplies had been assembled to feed those who had been forced to be there. Finally, in 1867 those held captive at Fort Sumner were allowed to leave. The death toll among Navajos and Apaches from what has been called the "experiment at the Bosque Redondo" had been terrible. The reservation created for the Navajos in 1868 contained less than 10 percent of the land they had originally used. Over the subsequent years, reservation land has been greatly expanded, removed, renegotiated, exchanged, and disputed.

Today, the Navajo Nation occupies contiguous land in Arizona, Utah, Colorado, and New Mexico. Navajo Nation headquarters is in Window Rock, Arizona, and there is an eastern administrative center in Crown Point, New Mexico. The territorial expansion from the 3.5 million acres of the original reservation to the 16 million acres of the 1930s represents a gradual confirmation of land the Navajo were using as their population increased (from 9,000 in 1870 to nearly 166,500 in 1981). Since their return from the Bosque Redondo, Navajos have made their living as sheep herders and stockmen. Farming has been supplemental and more common in the eastern half of their reservation than in the west. Navajos have long been regarded as expert weavers of wool blankets, which were highly regarded trade items among Indian groups. With their return from the Bosque Redondo and the completion of the transcontinental railroad in 1880, the Navajos were encouraged to develop a livelihood based on raising sheep. The U.S. military served as a customer for meat while traders and trading posts became customers for wool and textiles. The traders were also providers of flour, sugar, coffee, and manufactured goods. The influence of the trading post on Navajo economy cannot be underestimated and has only begun to decline following World War II.

In the United States, Apaches are currently organized into six official tribes: Chiricahua, Jicarilla, Kiowa-Apache, Lipan, Mescalero, and Western Apache, with reservations or allotments in Arizona, New Mexico, and Oklahoma. Not all tribes have separate reservations. For example, about two-thirds of the Chiricahua were relocated to the Mescalero Reservation in the early 1900s. Somewhat less than one-third live on allotments near Apache Oklahoma, and some live with the Western Apache on the San Carlos Reservation in Arizona. Most Apaches have made their living as stockmen, practicing less agriculture than the Navajos. Some groups of Chiricahua Apaches traditionally did no farming at all. Today, forestry, tourism, and the recreation industry are economically important to the Apache tribes.

Traditional Navajos and Apaches live in matrilocal-residential groups consisting of a few nuclear families related to an older woman, or mother. Individual dwellings (called hogans in Navajo and wickiups in Apache) are made of a variety of materials, such as logs, pole and mud, and stone. The distinctive traditional hogan is a polygonal structure of horizontal log walls with a cribbed, mud-covered roof. Traditional wickiups are nearly conical dwellings made of upright poles covered with mud plaster. Houses are dispersed so that the residence pattern in general is of the ranchería type. Residence groups were associated with a traditional locality, for which they were sometimes named, but there was no traditional political organization above the local level. Among the Navajos and Western Apaches, there are named, matrilineal clans. Among many of the groups, especially those like Navajos who are herders, families move seasonally between the winter home and summer sheep camps, where the only structures are ramadas. Navajos and Apaches also exploited a variety of wild food sources that entailed preparing camping areas that might be used for a few days or weeks. Camps where piñon nuts were harvested and roasted and other camps where agave was harvested and roasted are examples.

Important, traditional crafts include woven textiles among the Navajos and baskets among the Apaches. The Navajos have made pottery at least since the aftermath of the Pueblo Revolt, and this craft is being revived today. The oldest Navajo pottery vessels are unpainted gray ware with nearly pointed or rounded bases. The exterior of some traditional Apache baskets are covered with pitch to make them waterproof. Among some groups, such as the Jicarilla, women made pottery of micaceous clays for domestic use.

Ceremonial life is described as a combination of standardized rituals and shamanistic practices. Even the shamanistic practices could be taught to others, eventually becoming standardized ceremonies. An elaborate girl's puberty ceremony is held among Navajos and Apaches. Masked dances are performed by most groups and deities appear as masked personages. Witchcraft and sorcery are also common, and spirits of deceased individuals are greatly feared. Imbalances among people, deities, and other natural agents are seen as causes of sickness and emotional distress. Chants and ceremonies lasting several days are done to restore balance, order, and harmony among these forces.

The southern, western, northern, and interjascent peoples occupied landscapes ranging from low, hot deserts to verdant river valleys, cool, high plateaus, and rugged mountains. Within the large area of the Southwest and its diverse environments, people practiced traditional ways of maintaining themselves. Some peoples practiced only limited cultivation of crops, deriving most of their food from wild plant and animal resources. Other groups engaged in irrigation agriculture supplemented by hunting and gathering. Settlement patterns were and are equally diverse. Some people occupy small hamlets composed of only a few houses. Elsewhere, compact villages of a few hundred people are the usual settlement type. It is apparent in examining the ancient past of these peoples that there has also been great diversity in material culture, subsistence economy, and settlement patterns over time. For example, some locations with the highest density of ancient town sites have been abandoned by town-dwellers for centuries. At some other locations where compact villages exist today, there were thinly dispersed settlements over most of the archaeological past. This book concerns the changes in economic strategies, community organization, and aspects of material culture that have always been important features of the Southwest.

CULTURES OF THE PAST

The living native peoples of the Southwest have been briefly described in terms of their similarities and diversity. Some of the characteristics they display today are the result of a very recent phenomenon: contact and interaction with Western European culture. Over the millennia before this contact, events and gradual processes occurred that also greatly affected people's ways of life: The acceptance of the basic cultigens from Mesoamerica, trade and interaction with the state-level societies of Mesoamerica, and natural events such as changes in rainfall patterns all had impacts to which local populations responded in diverse and innovative ways. The goal of this book is to trace the development of the indigenous cultures of the Southwest through archaeology, a tool that is useful in studying the ancient history of all societies, including our own. In the absence of written records that might provide information about the symbolic, religious, and intellectual aspects of cultures, archaeologists define cultures on the basis of material remains—houses, ceremonial structures, stone and bone tools, ceramics, etc. It is probably only rarely that any archaeological culture corresponds directly to descendant living societies.

The oldest archaeological remains in the Southwest date to the end of the last major Pleistocene glaciation. These artifacts were made by people living as hunters and gatherers at a time before agriculture was practiced anywhere in the world, a time when the landscapes of the Southwest were quite different from those of today. Archaeologists refer to these first inhabitants of the Americas as Paleoindians. The Paleoindians were undoubtedly ancestral to later Southwestern peoples, but their way of life was so remote and their material remains so scant that no very direct relationships can be documented. Following the end of Pleistocene and until about the first century AD, people living in the Southwest continued to pursue a hunting and gathering way of life but one into which they integrated the cultivation of domestic crops. Archaeologists use the word Archaic to refer to this time period. The Paleoindian and Archaic periods are discussed in Chapters 3, 4, and 5 of this book.

Archaeologists working in the Southwest have defined three major Southwestern archaeological cultural traditions, and a number of minor ones, that follow the Archaic and that are considered generally ancestral to the modern indigenous cultures. Given that archaeological cultures are defined on the basis of material remains and that pottery and architecture are among the most obvious relics preserved in the Southwest, it is not surprising that these two classes of artifacts are important components of the definitions of the archaeological cultures. Archaeological traditions show continuity in material culture over time. It cannot be assumed that an archaeological tradition corresponds to a language group, ethnic group, or political entity such as a tribe. The major archaeological traditions of the Southwest are the Anasazi, Hohokam, and Mogollon. The Patayan tradition is less well-known. Each of these is defined here and more fully described in Chapters 6 and 7. Archaeologists working in the border region between the United States and Mexico, an area referred to as the International Four Corners (Carpenter and Sanchez 1997; Kelley and Villalpando 1996) find that their data do not fit well within the previously defined cultural traditions. Rather than propose an additional cultural tradition, they discuss several subregional variants appropriate to the vast area in which they work. These are briefly described following the discussion of the Anasazi, Hohokam, Mogollon, and Patayan (Figure 1.7).

Remains of the Anasazi tradition are found within the northern portion of the Southwest, from northern Arizona and New Mexico into southwestern Colorado and southeastern Utah. The Anasazi tradition is ancestral to Pueblos from the Hopi mesas to the Rio Grande region. The name "Anasazi" has come to mean "ancient people," although the word itself is Navajo, meaning "enemy ancestors." It is unfortunate that a non-Pueblo word has come to stand for a tradition that is certainly ancestral Pueblo. The term was first applied to ruins of the Mesa Verde by Richard Wetherill, a rancher and trader who, in 1888–1889, was the first Anglo-American to explore the sites in that area. Wetherill knew and worked with Navajos and understood what the word meant. The name was further sanctioned in archaeology when it was adopted by Alfred V. Kidder, the acknowledged dean of Southwestern archaeology. Kidder (1936b) felt that it was less cumbersome than a more technical term he might have used. Subsequently some archaeologists who would try to change the term have worried that because the Pueblos speak different languages, there are different words for "ancestor," and using one might be offensive to people speaking other languages. My own preference is to use Ancient Pueblo or Ancestral Pueblo, where possible, but this too is problematical. Such usage obscures the observation that the Mogollon tradition is also considered by many to be ancestral to Pueblo peoples. Further, archaeologists are themselves tradition bound and would not be dissuaded from continuing to use the term Anasazi, which features so prominently in their professional literature.

In any case, although rancherías are typical of some parts of the Anasazi area at some time periods, the Anasazi were the first in the Southwest to adopt villages of contiguous rectangular rooms. Early in their development, the Anasazi lived in semisubterranean structures that archaeologists call pithouses. The hallmark of Anasazi culture, however, is settlement in compact, well-made, one- or two-story dwellings with open work-areas and special ceremonial rooms (kivas). Anasazi pottery was finished by coiling and scraping and generally fired to a gray or white core color. Painted ceramics throughout most of the area were decorated with black designs on a white

FIGURE 1.7 Ancient cultural traditions of the Southwest. The Patayan area includes the Colorado River and adjacent uplands, the home of the Yuman-speaking tribes. The Anasazi area of the Colorado Plateau is the traditional homeland of Pueblo peoples. The Mogollon area of southcentral New Mexico and northern Mexico was also occupied by Pueblo peoples. The Hohokam area of southcentral Arizona is the traditional homeland of Pima and O'Odham peoples. (Map by David Underwood.)

FIGURE 1.8 Anasazi pottery on display at the Wetherill Trading Post in Chaco Canyon. Generally black-on-white painted ware (top two rows) was used for serving and storing and unpainted, corrugated ware (bottom row) for cooking. (Photograph from the collection of Fay-Cooper Cole. Courtesy of Lewis R. Binford.)

slip (Figure 1.8). Much of the northern portion of the Anasazi area was abandoned as a place of intensive occupation before Europeans arrived in the region. The ruined cliff dwellings of Mesa Verde and the austere towns of Chaco Canyon are attributed to the Anasazi. Today, Anasazi descendants live among all the Pueblo villages.

The Hohokam tradition centered in the middle Gila and lower Salt River drainages and lower Sonoran Desert regions of Arizona and adjacent Chihuahua and Sonora. Although Kidder (1962:298) remarked on how different remains in this region are from those of the Anasazi area, it was the work of Harold S. Gladwin that explicated the distinctiveness of the Hohokam. The word "Hohokam" is Piman, meaning "ancestors" (Haury 1976). Throughout much of their development, Hohokam settlements were of the ranchería type. Early houses were large, nearly square structures with slightly excavated floors. House shape and size changed slightly over time, but it was not until very late in the Hohokam sequence that structures of contiguous surface rooms were built. Hohokam ceramics were finished by paddle and anvil and fired to a buff color. Decorations were made with red paint. Some archaeologists view the Hohokam tradition as ancestral to the modern Pimas and Tohono O'Odham, but discontinuities between the fourteenth century Hohokam and modern Pima and Tohono O'Odham are so great that others argue for more complicated scenarios of descent (see Chapter 12 of this book).

The Mogollon tradition occupied an extensive area in what is today southeastern Arizona and southwestern New Mexico. (Some archaeologists have used the term to refer to archaeological remains that extend far to the south into modern Mexico.) The term Mogollon (pronounced muggy-own) derives from the major mountain range along the Arizona-New Mexico state line that was in turn named for an eighteenth century Spanish Colonial governor of New Mexico. The name Mogollon was applied to the archaeological tradition by Emil W. Haury (1936), who had been working with Gladwin and later became a towering figure in Southwestern archaeology. Typical Mogollon settlements were composed of loosely arranged pithouses. Like Anasazi pottery, Mogollon pottery was finished by coiling and scraping. Mogollon pottery was generally fired to a brown or red-brown color. After about AD 1000, however, some portions of the Mogollon area saw the development of compact villages of contiguous rectangular rooms, with roomblocks arranged around plazas. Also, after AD 1000, painted ceramics in parts of the Mogollon region were decorated with black paint on a white slip. One such area was along the Mimbres River, where pottery was made that today is known throughout the world for the beauty and technical skill in its painted designs. Much of the Mogollon area was abandoned long before Europeans arrived in the area. Archaeologists suggest that the descendants of the Mogollon are incorporated within some of the modern Western Pueblos.

The Patayan tradition is represented by sites in the Colorado River Valley, from the Grand Canyon to the delta and adjacent uplands. Archaeologically, the Patayan area is still poorly known; however, upland settlements are generally of the rancheria type. Ceramics were finished by paddle and anvil, and most were unpainted. Patayan ceramics were apparently somewhat casually fired, and surface colors range from buff to gray. Most archaeologists agree that, in a general way, the Patayan tradition was ancestral to the modern Yuman-speaking tribes.

The International Four Corners-Northwest Mexico

Until quite recently, the ancient cultures of Northwest Mexico have been viewed as peripheral to the civilizations of the Valley of Mexico and the cultures of the U.S. Southwest. Now although the cultures are beginning to be understood in their own terms, the archaeology of this vast region suffers from two dilemmas. First, there has been relatively little recent archaeological research there compared with neighboring regions. Second, native populations were decimated in the wake of the Spanish conquest so that there are discontinuities between the archaeological and modern cultures. Nevertheless, four probably interacting regional traditions have been described (Kelley and Villalpando 1996). One of these developed in north-central Chihuahua culminating in the fourteenth century site of Paquimé (Casas Grandes) with multistory adobe architecture, I-shaped ball courts, platform/effigy mounds, craft specialization in shell and turquoise, production of polychrome pottery, and breeding and raising macaws. A second tradition, the Trincheras tradition, developed in the region west of the Casas Grandes, in northern Sonora and southern Arizona. It is best known for elaborately terraced, steep hillsides, some of which were in use from Archaic times. Eventually, the tradition may have merged with the Hohokam. A separate tradition has been defined along the Rio Sonora (Pailes 1990), where there were sizable communities of sedentary agricultural peoples from about 1000 AD. The northern half of this region developed close interactions with Paquimé that may have involved considerable economic exchange in pottery and other items.

Extending from southern Chihuahua to the southeastern edge of the region in Zacatecas and Durango, the Loma San Gabriel culture has been defined extending from perhaps as early as 200 BC to the modern Tepehuan. Loma San Gabriel sites reflect small, dispersed settlements and a ceramic tradition that Foster (1985) suggests relates the sites to the Mogollon. North of Loma San Gabriel sites, in the Bustillos Basin, there were similar, small agricultural settlements dating back to perhaps AD 600 that are geographically close to Casas Grandes and contemporary with periods in the early development of Casas Grandes yet which Kelley (1992) sees as distinct from Casas Grandes. Throughout northwest Mexico, especially in desert areas, there were some groups that depended on hunting and gathering, while for agricultural peoples wild resources were also critical. Along the West Coast, a long-term tradition of fishing and foraging peoples was ancestral to the modern Seri.

In the past, the various archaeological remains of northwest Mexico have been viewed as generalized Mogollon with overlays of "more advanced" traditions deriving from the Valley of Mexico. The information presented here, while greatly abbreviated, indicates that there were local developments, distinct from the Mogollon. Some of these developed into important regional centers that influenced ongoing traditions in other parts of the Southwest. As yet, archaeologists have not developed a single scheme for northwest Mexico, and it is likely that as both understanding and appreciation for the time depth of local diversity in the region increases, no single scheme will emerge.

CONCLUSION

The kinds of information brought to bear on the history of the Southwest includes the traditional history of the native peoples living there today; eyewitness accounts by the first Spanish explorers, religious officials, and colonists; descriptions written by ethnographers; and interpretations by archaeologists, assisted by other scientists such as zoologists, paleobotanists, geologists, and paleoclimatologists. Each of these sources is influenced by cultural patterns of thought and perspective. Each one also pictures the world at slightly different scales, with different degrees of precision and resolution peculiar to their way of understanding. For example, traditional native histories often include migration narratives that are rich in metaphor, symbolism, and ethical and philosophical considerations, but are usually not specific with regard to places and the timing and duration of events. Some traditional histories are wonderfully informative regarding details about sites and artifacts that would otherwise be meaningless to archaeologists.

The writings of the Spanish chroniclers are a rich source of information about the general nature of the country and its inhabitants, yet often silent about the daily lives of the people themselves. Further, we often lack the cultural context to interpret the chronicle accounts. For example, distances are invariably given either as days-march or in measures (such as *varas*) with which we are unfamiliar. The writings of trained anthropological ethnographers are invaluable resources, yet these too are of necessity mute with respect to time periods so remote from the present that there are no ready analogs or even regard for processes that occur over several generations. Nevertheless, all of these sources, when used critically and cautiously, are invaluable references for a broad range of interpretations.

The archaeological record is one made up entirely of physical objects and their context. These bones, sherds, and stone tools reveal a great deal about the most common activities of past lives and virtually nothing about unique events or the words used to communicate them. The artifactual record can sometimes be astonishingly precise about the date on which an event occurred, climatological conditions, meals eaten, fuels burned, building materials used, and distances over which items were obtained in trade. The same record will say nothing directly about the thoughts, motivations, or feelings of the individuals who tended their crops, traded, and prayed so long ago.

Most of these fields of study, especially archaeology, are in a period of both critical assessment of method and development of appropriate bodies of theory. As archaeology develops, our confidence in the narratives produced by its practitioners increases. Over the past dozen years, since the publication of the first edition of this book, our knowledge about the past in the Southwest has increased tremendously. In this edition, I have tried to include a great deal of the new information that has resulted from literally hundreds of small excavation and survey projects, and the far fewer large-scale efforts. All of this work has changed what we know about the ancient Southwest. For example, chronological problems were much more salient 12 years ago than they are today. Also, we have learned a great deal about settlement distributions throughout huge portions of the Southwest that until recently were poorly known. In addition to new field research, the past dozen years have seen important topical syntheses that provide new insights into the past. These play an important role in this revision. Finally, much recent research has seen a focus on issues that transcend localities, particularly for the later periods in the major Southwestern traditions. I have tried to bring these into this edition as well.

There are many reasons for scholarly interest in the antiquities of the Southwest. Four, in particular, continue to motivate my own interest and appear as recurrent themes throughout this book. First, material remains from the past are relatively well preserved in the Southwest. Resulting in part from a natural aridity that favors preservation, this is also due to the low density of modern population and the lack of industrial development. There are very real and immediate threats to the archaeological resources of the Southwest, particularly where urban populations are established and growing and where fossil fuels are being mined. Nevertheless, the abundance and variety of materials that have been preserved permit a much richer view of the past than is often possible elsewhere.

Second, and probably in part because of the fine preservation conditions, the Southwest has long been an area in which students receive their first training as archaeologists. Students often bring innovative ideas to their work and explore these in the Southwest. Thus, the Southwest has benefited from the application of new techniques and methods.

Third, many issues of concern to anthropology in general have been and can be readily examined in the Southwest. For example, understanding the various conditions under which agricultural crops are adopted can be examined in the Southwest. Similarly, there is a general interest in the development of regional systems of trade and exchange, which can be explored with Southwestern data. Anthropologists are also interested in the processes involved in the development of complex social systems. The Southwest offers insights into these processes because complex social systems did emerge at certain times but were not sustained. As a result, another set of inquiries focuses on the disruption of regional systems or the collapse of systems of political integration and abandonment of large areas. Many theoretically derived explanations for these phenomena can be productively examined in the Southwest, where the data from the past are well preserved and where innovative techniques have been employed.

Finally, the archaeology of the Southwest is important because it is a large part of the cultural heritage of the native peoples who live there. All the native peoples, of course, have strong traditions of oral history, but archaeologists should provide their own information and a clear understanding of how they have derived their interpretations. With this archaeological context then, the information from archaeology may be of use to the native peoples of the region.

Chapter-opening art: Bowl of dipper, Tularosa black-on-white (UCM 9494, courtesy of the University of Colorado Museum).

CHAPTER 2

The Natural Environment

This chapter examines the natural environments within which ancient cultural developments took place. Modern environments are baselines from which past environmental changes are extrapolated. The geology, climate, vegetation, and fauna of the modern Southwest are presented, followed by discussion of various methods of interpreting past environmental conditions.

INTRODUCTION

The natural environment imposes a set of conditions to which any society must adapt or must modify if it is to survive. Compared with many areas of the world, the environmental constraints of the Southwest are relatively harsh. The entire region is arid. The lack of moisture restricts the abundance of vegetation and game animals, and the locations and sizes of areas suitable for agriculture. Water sources are extremely important to the contemporary peoples of the Southwest, as they were to peoples in the past. Additional constraints of the natural environment include short growing seasons in some areas and poorly developed soils in others. The range of behaviors societies use to cope with environmental conditions will depend, in part, on population size and available technological knowledge. Nevertheless, an understanding of the general configuration of the natural environment, and problems associated with it, is basic to an appreciation of the kinds of adaptations made.

Some cultural solutions to environmental problems have short- and long-term effects on the natural environment, and they may condition future adaptations. For example, ancient timber-cutting for building material, firewood, or simply to clear agricultural land may have increased surface erosion, eventually lowering the water table and rendering continued farming impossible. Prolonged irrigation of poorly drained soils may have led to instances of irreversible mineralization and salinization damage.

In addition to defining limiting conditions, the natural environment provides the resources that are crucial for social survival; that is, those used for food, medicines, tools, shelter, and/or items of exchange. The distribution of arable land is, of course, critical for crops, but throughout the history of human occupation of the Southwest, people depended to some extent on wild plant foods and game. At certain times, the availability of wild foods may have been the key to survival. Some materials with limited natural occurrences were widely traded in pre-Columbian times, including obsidian, high-quality cherts, and petrified woods that are useful for tools, and luxury items, such as shell and turquoise, that were important to the culturally defined network of social interactions. The distribution and relative abundance of various resources significantly affect the ways societies are organized.

The natural environment also determines preservation of the archaeological record of the past. Specific environmental characteristics are important to the kinds of materials that are likely to be preserved and those that are not. In many parts of the Southwest, the preservation of perishable items such as wood, seeds, and animal bones enables a richness of interpretation of ancient lifeways that is not possible in other parts of the world. There are, nevertheless, some places in the Southwest where conditions are not favorable to the preservation of organic remains. In these areas, cultural historical and basic chronological questions are very difficult to resolve. The use of the natural environment by our modern society is frequently critical to the recovery of archaeological remains as well as to their destruction. It is not coincidental that a great deal of the recent information on the San Juan Basin became available in the 1970s when uranium exploration and coal mining were of major importance in the economy of the United States. Federal law requires assessment of historic cultural resources prior to mining or otherwise modifying public land. Intensive archaeological surveys have been conducted in the San Juan Basin, a major producer of energy resources. In the nineteenth century, grazing throughout enormous areas of the Southwest precipitated erosion that exposed many archaeological sites and destroyed countless others.

Finally, interpretations of past events in the Southwest rely heavily on climatic and other environmental changes. For example, regional abandonments have been attributed to major droughts in some areas, to destruction of trees needed for firewood in others, and to salinization of fields in still other areas. In part, reliance on climatic factors as underlying causes of regional abandonment seems to reflect modern concerns and the limits of our own technological abilities. Nevertheless, evaluation of these and other interpretations requires an understanding of how past environments are reconstructed and the means by which the magnitude of change is discerned.

There are many ways of describing natural environments. Landscapes may be characterized by landform types (mountains, plateaus, etc.), weather patterns (cold deserts, hot deserts, etc.), vegetation zones (Transition, Upper Sonoran, etc.), or dominant plant and/or animal communities (short grass prairie, shadscale-kangaroo rat association, etc.). In general, the natural environment of the Southwest is best characterized by its diversity, with respect to land forms, temperature regimes, precipitation patterns, vegetation, fauna, and mineral resources. Dean and others (1994) suggest that the environments of the Southwest may be characterized by three overlapping classes of variability: stable, low frequency, and high frequency processes. Stable factors show change over space but have remained the same over long periods of time, essentially the last 2000 years. Their current states reflect past conditions. Stable factors include bedrock geology and climate type. Low frequency variability includes processes that occur over periods of time that are longer than a human generation. Cycles of erosion and deposition are examples. High frequency variability is controlled by processes with periodicity less than about 25 years. Among those that are most familiar are seasonal, annual, and short-term changes in precipitation or temperature. Because the characteristics of any natural environment are the result of interactions between the stable processes of the atmosphere (including climate type) and the lithosphere, it is reasonable to begin a discussion of the environments of the Southwest with these.

THE MODERN ENVIRONMENT

Physiographic Provinces

The culturally defined Southwest does not correspond to a single physiographic province, but rather includes portions of four major provinces. These are described here and illustrated in Figure 2.1. The western and southern portions of the cultural Southwest lie within the Basin and Range Physiographic Province, but are not coincident with it. The Basin and Range extends from about Agua Caliente and San Luis Potosi in Mexico to portions of Idaho and Oregon. In general, the Basin and Range Province is characterized by a series of narrow, rugged, usually north-south trending parallel ranges of mountains interspersed with structural basins. In the southern section of the Basin and Range Province in the United States, which includes part of the cultural Southwest, mountains compose less than half the surface area. As one moves south into Mexico, the massive range of the Sierra Madre Occidental composes far more surface area. Although the mountains generally rise abruptly from the basin floors, the ranges are usually not so vast as to impede travel. The province depends primarily on winds from the Pacific to bring essential moisture over the high California Sierra to the west, which trap most of this moisture so the province itself is dry. Internal drainage, frequently resulting in ephemeral lakes or playas (termed *barriales* in Mexico), is characteristic of much of the province. The southern section, however, is drained in part by the Rio Grande, and the Gila, Colorado, Yaqui, and Conchos rivers. Most land surfaces within the province are underlain by deep detrital sediments and consist of gravel fans, gentle slopes (*bajadas*) rising from valleys to the base of the surrounding mountains, either dry lake beds or river flood plains in the central portions

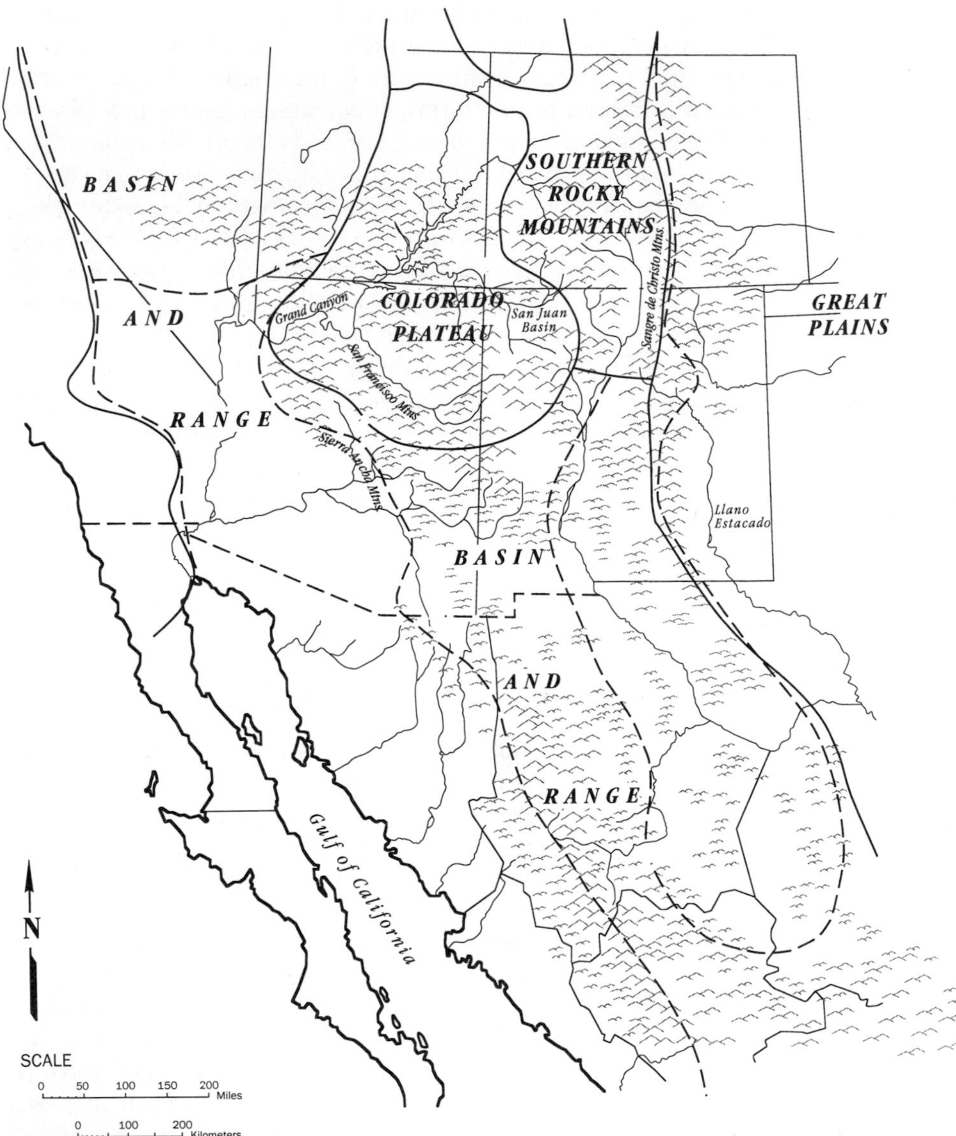

FIGURE 2.1 Physiographic provinces and regional climatic divisions of the Southwest. The Southwest includes portions of the Basin and Range, Southern Rocky Mountains, Colorado Plateaus, and Great Plains physiographic provinces. (Map by David Underwood.)

of the basins, and rugged mountains. Deposits of salt, copper, and lead are among the resources commercially exploited today in the southern section of the Basin and Range and important to ancient populations as well.

The central and north-central part of the cultural Southwest lies within the Colorado Plateaus Province, although the province extends north beyond the Southwest. This province is characterized by relatively high elevations—most of the land surfaces are higher than 1524 m and some mountain peaks reach elevations of more than 3657 m. The plateaus manifest extensive areas of nearly horizontal sedimentary rock formations, but there are also down-warped basin structures such as the San Juan and Gallup-Zuni basins, and elevated igneous structures, particularly along the plateau margins. Examples of the latter are the rock formations of the Grand Canyon section (including the San Francisco Mountains of Arizona), the Datil volcanics of central Arizona and New Mexico, and the San Juan Mountains of southern Colorado and northwestern New Mexico.

Aridity is also a feature of the plateaus province. The principal drainage is through the Colorado River system, including important tributaries such as the San Juan and Little Colorado rivers. Most of the rivers within the province are deeply entrenched and have high gradients. Land surfaces may consist of nearly flat plateau segments (referred to as mesas) and tilted plateau segments (termed cuestas) with steep-walled canyons and escarpments. The volcanic areas contain obsidians that were important ancient lithic sources. Much of the spectacular stone architecture of the Anasazi is made of the local sandstones of this province. Today, coal and uranium are extensively mined in a few areas of the plateaus. Although certainly not of major economic importance, coal was used in pre-Columbian times in some locations as a fuel for firing ceramics.

The cultural Southwest extends into the southernmost portion of the Southern Rocky Mountain Province, which includes the San Juan Mountains on the west slope and the Sangre de Cristo Mountains on the east. Between the two groups of ranges are the San Luis Valley in the north and the Rio Grande Valley in the south. The southern Rocky Mountains are primarily composed of metamorphic rock, but there are extensive areas of igneous inclusions in the San Juan ranges. Elevations within the province range from about 1524 m in the valleys to peaks of more than 4267 m. The Southern Rocky Mountains greatly influence weather patterns (discussed below). Generally though, the mountains themselves are quite well-watered. The mountains provide a significant watershed for large areas of the Southwest. The major drainage to the east is the Rio Grande and its tributaries; the Dolores and San Juan rivers and their tributaries drain the area to the west. The province is well-known for its mineral resources; however, few of these were used in pre-Columbian times. Those that were include igneous rock, primarily basalts and obsidian, fine-grained chert, galena (lead ore), turquoise, and malachite.

At times during the pre-Columbian period, the cultural Southwest extended short distances onto the Great Plains Province; thus, portions of the Raton Section, the Pecos Valley, and the Llano Estacado were occupied, visited, or used extensively by Southwestern peoples. Elevations generally range from about 1828 m to 2133 m in the Raton Section to between 609 m and 1524 m in the Llano Estacado. Topographic relief is slight. Most of the rocks are flat-lying sedimentary deposits overlain by silts, sands, and gravels that were washed eastward from the Rockies. The Raton Section is exceptional in having high mesas capped by lava flows. Past climatic changes enabled southwestern agriculturists to establish communities on the margins of the plains. The important drainages within the area are the Cimarron and the Pecos rivers. The generally arid southwestern plains contain extensive salt deposits that were used in the precontact period. Other resources Native peoples procured from the Great Plains included bison and cherts from the Edwards Plateau of Texas.

In sum, the Southwest encompasses a tremendous amount of physiographic diversity. Elevations range from about 30.4 m above sea level in the basins of the western Basin and Range Province to peaks up to 4267 m high in the Southern Rocky Mountains. Rugged mountains, mesas, narrow canyons, and broad valleys all occur within the area, as do formations of sedimentary, igneous, and metamorphic origin. The physiographic provinces of the Southwest extend far beyond the area included within the cultural boundaries. In general, the cultural boundaries in the west, north, and east are defined by the limits of indigenous farming. These limits, as well as the diversity of natural vegetation found, are largely conditioned by the regional climate.

Climate

At the broadest, most inclusive level, subcontinental areas of related climates are grouped in the same domain (Bailey 1980). At this very general level, the entire Southwest falls within the Dry Domain. Occupying about one-fourth of the earth's land surface, dry climates are characterized by water deficits; that is, the rate at which water is lost annually through evaporation is greater than that gained through precipitation. Beyond this very general characterization, diversity is, once again, the rule.

By definition, moisture is a limiting factor for vegetation in all of the earth's dry areas. Precipitation derives from cyclonic, orographic, and convectional storms, each of which is described below. Cyclonic rainfall patterns are the result of large air masses of low pressure moving across a path determined by the jet stream. Because of the large size of these low-pressure systems, they influence precipitation in a general way over large areas. The Southwest has cyclonic rainfall patterns of two different types: a biannual pattern characteristic of the west and rainfall with a single maximum in the east (Figure 2.2). The biannual pattern centers in Arizona and extends into southern Utah, Nevada, southwestern Colorado, eastern California, and Sonora, Mexico. The primary maximum precipitation in the western area occurs in July and August and derives its moisture from the Gulf of Mexico. The secondary maximum occurs in winter, from December to March, usually peaking in February. The moisture for the winter storms, originating from the Pacific Ocean and the Gulf of California, consists typically of soaking rains or snowfall in the higher elevations. This moisture is absorbed by the soil and encourages early greening of rangeland. The winter precipitation is followed by a very dry period from April through June. The summer maximum may account for 50 percent of the annual precipitation, but the storms are of a different type. Summer rainfall is produced largely by high-intensity thunderstorms of generally short duration. Partly a result of the intensity of the storms, and also because the ground has dried out during the spring, the summer rains do not penetrate the soil

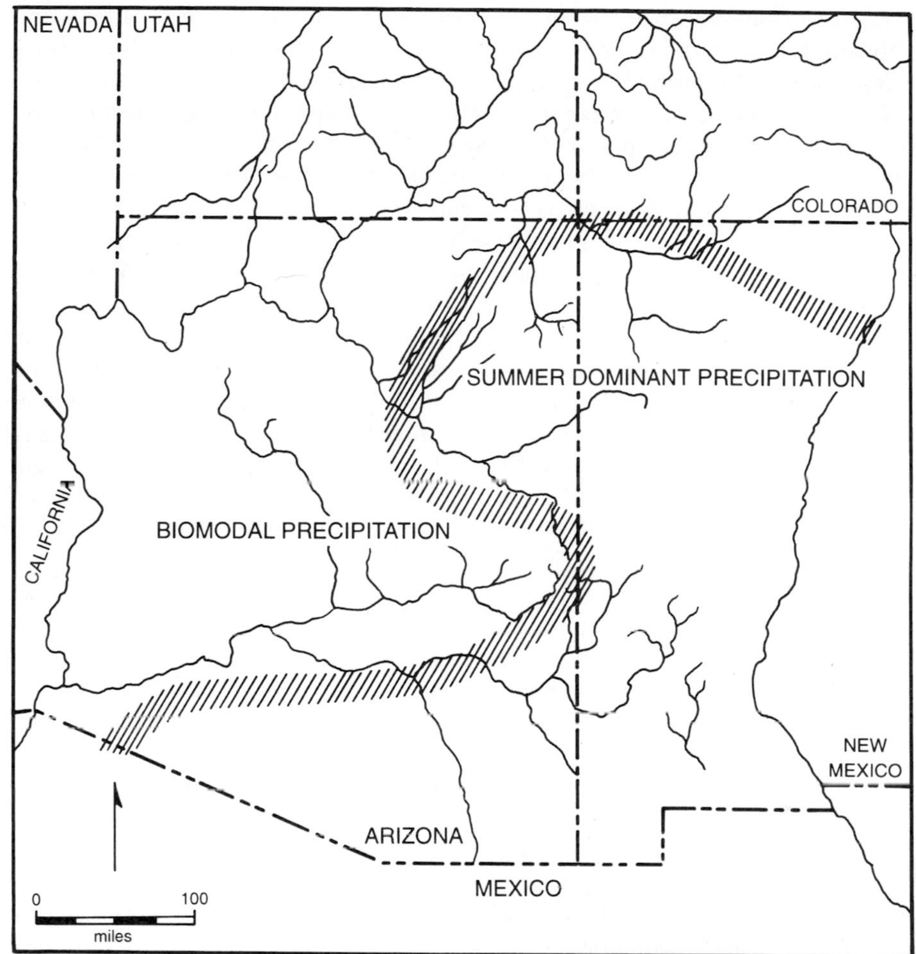

FIGURE 2.2 Spatial distribution of seasonal precipitation in the Southwest over the last century. (Illustrated by Marjorie Leggitt, Leggitt Design; adapted from Dean 1988a.)

as well as the winter precipitation. Much of the summer moisture is lost to runoff (Comeaux 1981; Trewartha 1966).

The eastern portion of the Southwest, including most of New Mexico and Colorado, westernmost Texas, and much of Chihuahua, Mexico, has a different pattern of cyclonic rainfall. In this area, there is a single maximum in the late summer months of June and July. These storms derive their moisture from the Gulf of Mexico in the same way that summer storms are produced in the west, and like the western storms they are of high intensity and short duration. Because cyclonic storms are conditioned by the jet stream, shifts in that stream can have a great impact on storm patterns in the Southwest. Of note, though, such changes will affect the western and eastern parts of the Southwest differently. For example, a northward shift in the jet stream would deprive the western area of important winter precipitation but have little effect in the east. This observation is important because paleoclimatic reconstructions (discussed in detail below) that are derived from one part of the Southwest cannot be generalized across the entire region. Also, it has been suggested that at some specific times in the past, this subregional patterning may have broken down, an issue that is also discussed below. The differences in local precipitation patterns are emphasized by examining the distribution of convectional and orographic storms.

Convectional storms occur in the summer when the ground surface receives maximum solar radiation. Heat from the ground is transferred to the air, which rises rapidly above the earth's surface, cooling quickly. This type of air movement produces violent thunderstorms of a local nature. The high-intensity storms generally begin in the afternoons when the ground has had sufficient time to heat. A great deal of rain is generated by these storms, but the velocity is also high and crops may be damaged, washes flooded, and soil eroded. In general, the storm tracks of convectional rainfall are not very predictable and areas just outside the track receive no precipitation.

Orographic precipitation occurs when winds carrying moisture are forced upward to cross a mountain barrier. The amount of precipitation depends on the moisture content of the air and the height and mass of the mountains. Generally, large mountain masses act as catchment areas for precipitation. The Southern Rocky Mountains, the Mogollon Mountains, and the central mountains of Arizona (the Bradshaws, Sierra Anchas, and Gilas) receive more orographic precipitation than the small mountain ranges of the southern Basin and Range country. Orographic precipitation may occur at any time of year when there are moisture-bearing winds. At times, during the winter, winds from the Gulf of Mexico predominate over the eastern portion of the Southwest. The orographic winter storms provide the snowfall for the Southern Rockies. Also in winter, moisture-bearing winds originating in the Gulf of California occasionally enter Sonora and Arizona, causing orographic snowfall in the high mountains. Orographic precipitation, of course, occurs primarily on the windward side of mountains. The ranges themselves are barriers to precipitation on their leeward sides. Thus, the northeastern portion of Arizona receives very little winter precipitation because it is on the leeward side—or in the rain shadow—of the central mountains.

It is common to discuss the distribution of precipitation in terms of average yearly amount. From this perspective, the Southwest is divided into two regional climatic divisions (Figure 2.3). The desert division is characterized by fewer than 20 cm of annual precipitation. The steppe division receives generally fewer than 50 cm of precipitation annually. It should be obvious, given the foregoing discussion, that average precipitation is misleading. Yearly deviations from the average may be extreme, and not all precipitation is useful for vegetative growth. For example, although the mean annual precipitation in Santa Fe, New Mexico, is 35.9 cm, recorded deviations since 1950 have ranged from 16.9 to 51.2 cm. The annual timing of precipitation is more critical for crops than the average amount. Throughout the higher elevation steppe

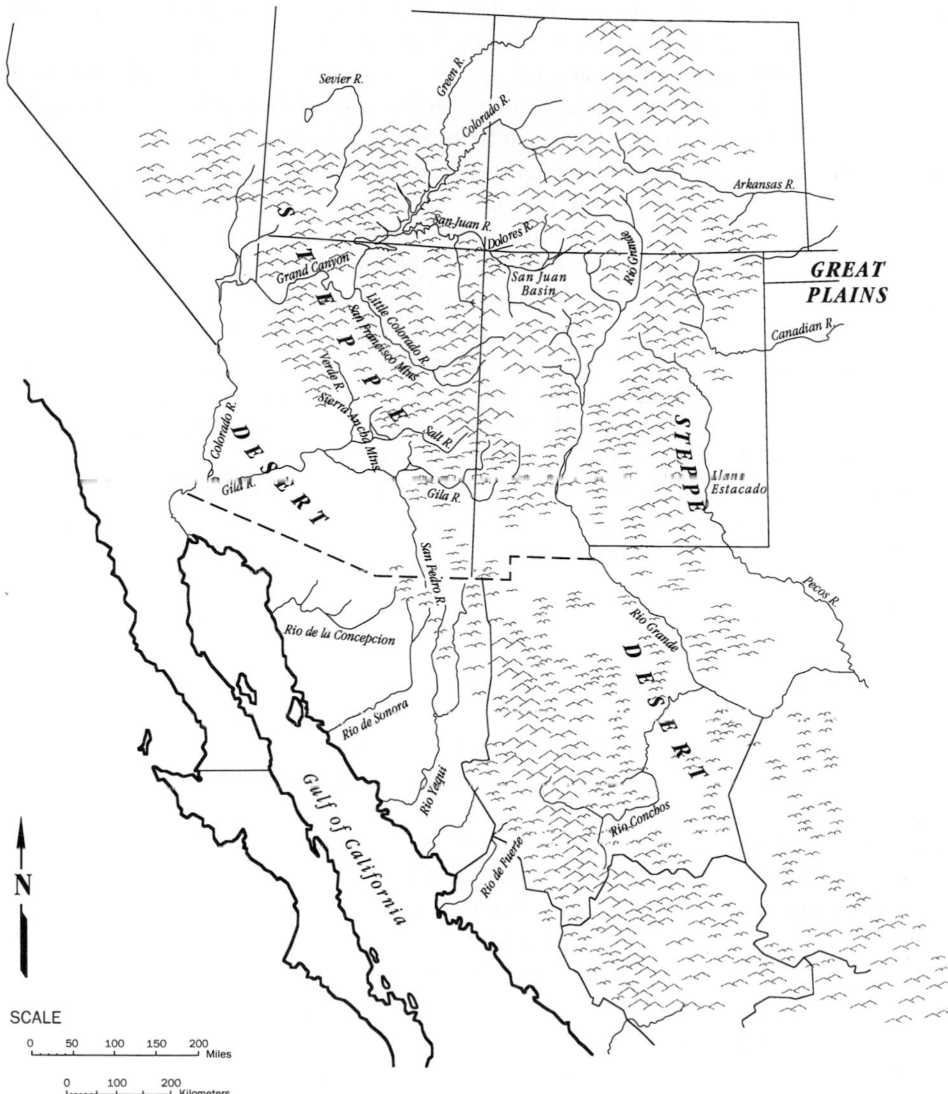

FIGURE 2.3 This map locates the major rivers in the Southwest and shows two broad climatic divisions, the Steppe Region which has an average of 50 cm annual precipitation and the Desert Region with an average of 20 cm annual precipitation. (Map by David Underwood.)

division, winter snows melt and penetrate the soil, allowing wild seeds and crops to germinate during the generally dry spring. In the low, desert division, the scant winter precipitation is inadequate for crops. In the absence of irrigation technology, it is summer precipitation that is crucial for desert agriculturalists. As noted, however, the particularly high-intensity summer thunderstorms in either steppe or desert setting may damage natural ground cover and crops. The most precise methods of paleoclimatic reconstruction available generally are better indices of winter than summer moisture. Given the generally dry climatic regime of the Southwest as a whole and the erratic nature of the distribution of precipitation, reliable sources of water are of critical importance to contemporary and ancient populations.

The major rivers of the Southwest (Figure 2.3) are clearly important; however, not all of them are either completely useful or beneficial for crops. For example, most of the northern portion of the San Juan is so deeply entrenched that its waters are not useful for irrigation. Irrigation using water from the Rio Grande was and is extremely important to contemporary peoples of the area; however, flooding does occur and can be disastrous. In 1886, for example, floods destroyed not only the fields but also much of the village of Santo Domingo, New Mexico, and the town of San Marcial, New Mexico, was destroyed by floods in 1886 and again in 1929. Seeps and springs may be more important sources of water for domestic use (and for hand-watering crops) than the rivers. Over much of the Colorado Plateaus, where many drainages are entrenched, this is especially true. The presence of seeps and springs is conditioned by overlying rock of differential permeability. For example, at Mesa Verde relatively permeable sandstones overlie impervious shales. The seeps and springs that occur at the contact zone of the two formations were an important source of water for the indigenous population. The differences in permeability at the contact zone are also responsible for the formation of rock shelters and cliff overhangs under which the native peoples built their stone dwellings.

In addition to precipitation, the length of the growing season and the temperature and humidity ranges are critical for successful agriculture. Modern hybrid corn requires about 40 to 60 cm of water during the growing season. Water deficiencies at specific times during the growing season, such as the period during which corn tassels, can decrease yields between 50 and 75 percent (Classen and Shaw 1970; Minnis 1981). The high temperatures and low humidity of the Southwest create the characteristic water deficit. The unpredictability of summer rainfall can dramatically decrease yields of maize. In addition, the frost-free period, which is that portion of the year during which vegetation will normally grow, presupposing an adequate amount of moisture, can be quite a bit shorter than the 120 days required by modern corn. Experiments with indigenous varieties of maize suggest that some may have been selected for their ability to tolerate somewhat shorter growing seasons. Growing seasons that are frequently too short even for these varieties are especially likely in locations above 2000 m in elevation (Snow 1991).

In general, temperature range is determined primarily (not exclusively) by latitude and altitude. In the Southwest, temperature decreases northward from 1.5 to 2.5 degrees F for every degree of latitude. Temperatures also generally correlate inversely with elevation, but this is conditioned by several factors related to local and regional topography. The direction of exposure is important for the amount of insolation received and, therefore, for temperature. Contrasts are marked, especially in deep, narrow valleys and canyons with east–west orientations. Canyons of this sort are common on the Colorado Plateaus and in mountainous country. For example, temperatures recorded at the same elevation on the north and south walls of Frijoles Canyon, New Mexico, differed by 13 degrees F. Temperature differences are also noted between the east and west flanks of north-south oriented mountains, with temperatures on the west flanks generally being higher. Other well-known factors of topography that influence temperature are air drainage and wind shifts that cause temperature changes in narrow valleys. Especially on clear, still evenings, cool, heavy air drains into canyon bottoms so that temperatures at these locations may be several degrees below those on the sides of canyons. For example, at Mesa Verde the shortest growing season is in canyon-bottom settings, at elevations of about 1920 m and not on the mesa top, at an elevation of about 2590 m (Erdman *et al.* 1967).

Two other general observations about temperatures are important to germination and the growing season of crops. In many areas of the Southwest, daily temperature changes are greatest in spring, which may endanger the germination of seeds. For example, in New Mexico the daily average range in temperatures in April may be as much as 39 degrees F (Houghton 1959:70–71). Also, variability from year to year in the length of the growing season, particularly in mountainous areas, may be extreme; thus, although the mean length of the growing season at Taos, New Mexico, was recorded as 138 days over a 10-year period, variations of more than 30 days occured from one year to another during the same period (Houghton 1959; Tuan *et al.* 1973).

Over much of the Southwest, particularly in the low-elevation areas of the Basin and Range Province, the growing season is adequate for corn and other crops. The limiting condition for crops in these areas is moisture. Over the portions of the Southwest that consist of mountains and high-elevation mesas, the growing season is frequently not sufficient for corn, and the annual variability in the length of the growing season and the amount of precipitation work together to make agriculture risky. As noted, the combination of high temperatures and direct solar radiation, most marked in the low-elevation areas of the western and southwestern Basin and Range Province, conditions evaporation and evapotranspiration rates. For example, the average evaporation and evapotranspiration rates (combined) at Phoenix, Arizona, are 381 cm, but Phoenix receives an average of only 17.8 cm of precipitation (Comeaux 1981). The general aridity in the Southwest and the ranges in temperature are important factors affecting the natural vegetation found in the region. The varieties and distribution of natural vegetation are discussed below.

Natural Vegetation

A consideration of the plant life found in the Southwest is important for two reasons. First, many of the plants were sources of food, medicines, and raw materials for the indigenous population. Second, the natural vegetation provides habitat for animals that were equally important resources.

Most models of ecosystems describe paths of energy flow because radiant energy from the sun is the limiting factor for life. In dry climates, however, water is the critical variable, and models that reflect this situation are more useful (Noy-Meir 1973).

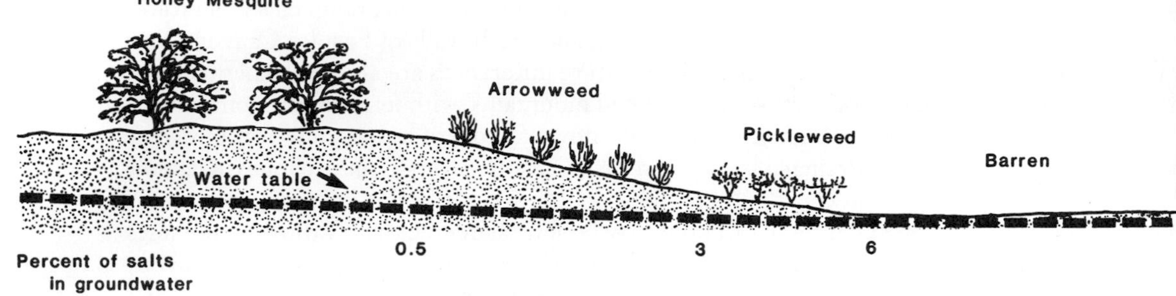

FIGURE 2.4 Edge of salt pan: The plant distribution reflects salt tolerance. Desert plants such as pickleweed and arrowweed tolerate higher percentages of salt in soil than does mesquite. (Adapted from Charles B. Hunt [1967] by Charles M. Carrillo.)

Vegetation in dry regions must be adapted to using moisture that enters the system in short duration "events" (such as a thunderstorm), which occur unpredictably in any one area. In addition, edaphic factors, such as soil depth, friability, moisture-retention characteristics, and mineral composition, are important.

A number of adaptive mechanisms are found in plants that enable them to withstand arid conditions. Some plants (drought-evaders) remain inactive during dry periods and photosynthesize only when moisture becomes available. These include desert annuals that produce seeds that remain viable for long periods of drought, and perennial plants that store water and nutrients in bulbs and rhizomes. Drought-persistent plants (xerophytes) maintain some photosynthesis throughout dry periods. Many desert shrubs persist through drought by shedding most of their leaves, stems, and rootlets, which reduces their activity level and water requirements. Other desert plants maintain nearly constant levels of photosynthesis but have evolved adaptive structures that minimize water loss. For example, some have waxy substances on their leaves that retard transpiration. Others, such as the succulents and cacti, store water internally. Still other plants (phreatophytes) develop specialized root systems and long tap roots that enable them to use ground water (Comeaux 1981; Hunt 1967; Noy-Meir 1973).

Soils form as a result of the interaction between weathering rock and decaying organic matter. Because organic matter is sparse in deserts, soils are generally poorly developed. Soil types have a marked effect on vegetation. With respect to soil texture, clayey, silty, and loamy soils retain moisture near the surface. Where these soils predominate, shallow-rooted plants, such as desert grasses, are common. Sandy, gravely, and rocky soils allow percolation of water to deeper levels. On these soils, deep-rooted perennial shrubs predominate. Yucca is a common deep-rooted Southwestern plant that prefers gravely soil. Plants also have different capacities for tolerance of salts and other minerals that accumulate in desert soils, particularly along the edges of playas, which are characteristic features of the southern Basin and Range country. Salt grass, arrowweed, and pickleweed are among plants that tolerate considerable salinity and

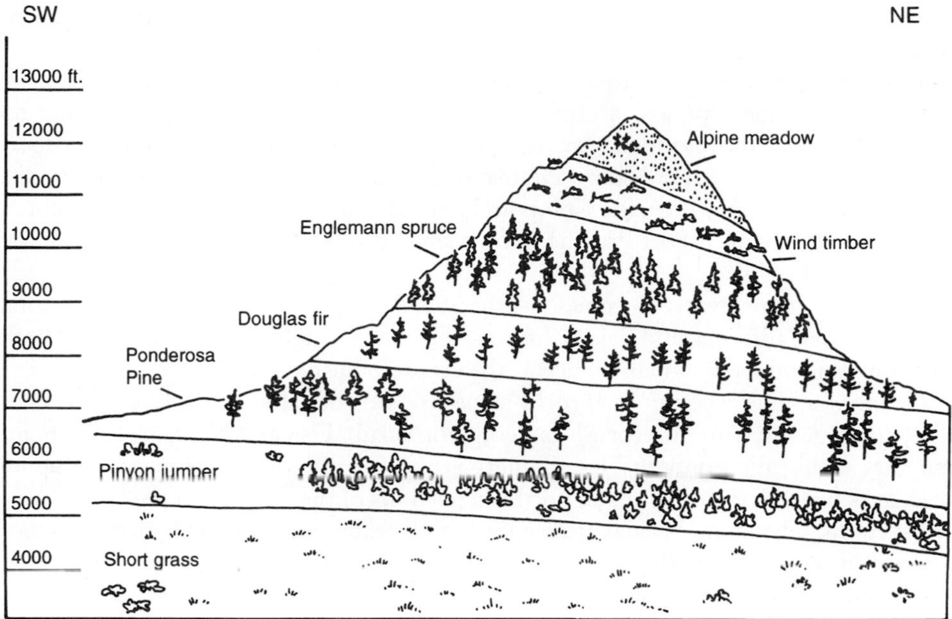

FIGURE 2.5 This schematic diagram of plant communities at the San Francisco Peaks, Arizona changes due to elevation and the direction of exposure. (Adapted from C. H. Merriam [1890] by Marjorie Leggitt, Leggitt Design.)

are found in zones along the edges of saline playas, according to the amount of salt present in the soil (Figure 2.4).

The direction of exposure is important for the moisture-retention capabilities of soil and will, therefore, influence vegetation cover. Generally, north- and east-facing slopes are wetter than south- and west-facing slopes. North slopes may support stands of trees and shrubs, whereas south-facing slopes at the same elevation may support only desert annuals and cacti. Any areas within the Dry Domain that contain fresh water, such as spring-fed ponds, rivers, and streams, will support riparian plant communities that might consist of cottonwoods, willows, reeds, and ferns.

Overviews of the southwestern environments usually present vegetation patterns as if they were determined exclusively by latitude and elevation. A common, and useful, characterization is provided by Merriam's (1880) famous diagram of plant communities at the San Francisco Peaks in Arizona (Figure 2.5), which reflects the direction of exposure in addition to elevation. While it is certainly true that broad vegetation zones exist and are a useful shorthand for characterizing plant communities, they obscure some of the diversity found at any one elevation and latitude, which is conditioned by soil type and water availability as well as by exposure. Zonal characterizations also minimize some of the comparability among disparate latitudes and elevations that are conditioned by the same factors of soil type and water availability.

Plant Provinces The system of description used here follows Bailey's (1980) descriptions of provinces, modified by Spaulding and others (1983) floristic delineation of North American deserts. A province is a contiguous geographic area characterized by a broad vegetation type and a uniform regional climate. The provinces making up major portions of the Southwest are the Sonoran and Chihuahuan deserts of the American Desert Province, the Mexican Highlands Shrub Steppe Province, the Upper Gila Mountains Forest Province, the Colorado Plateaus Province, the southern segment of the Rocky Mountain Forest Province, and a small portion of the Great Plains Shortgrass Prairie Province.

The Sonoran Desert occupies nearly 300,000 square km in Arizona, Sonora, southeastern California, and Baja California. The most widely distributed plant in both the Sonoran and Chihuahuan deserts is the creosote bush. Cholla, a type of cactus, is also common. The vegetation on rocky slopes consists of paloverde, agave, sotol, ocotillo, and saguaro, with bitterbrush as a common shrub. Fish and Nabhan (1991) point out that within the Sonoran Desert, there are major differences between the upper bajadas (slopes) in the eastern and northern portions of the desert and the lower western sections. The upper bajadas are relatively well-watered compared with the western desert and are covered with plants of the paloverde-cacti mixed scrub series. This series is structurally complex, consisting of the giant saguaro, tree-legumes, annuals, and root perennials. In the western Sonoran Desert, there are fewer perennials but more ephemeral plants. Although there is less diversity of both plants and of animals at the lower elevation western Sonoran Desert, many of the ephemeral plants produce abundant high-calorie seeds. Low-elevation playa margins and areas subject to flooding and salinization support stands of salt-tolerant plants such as mesquite, saltbush, arrowweed, and pickleweed.

The Chihuahuan Desert Province consists of short grasses and shrubs, with creosote again covering extensive areas. Mesquite dominates in places where soils are deep, while ocotillo, agave, yucca, and sotol occur on slopes. Mountains within the province will, if they are high enough, support a belt of oak and juniper woodland; on some of the highest mountains, piñon grows interspersed with oak. Along the southeastern margin of the Sonoran Desert and the northern edge of the Chihuahuan Desert are highlands that support a variety of grasses, piñon, and oak. At the highest elevations (above 1900 m), there are quite extensive stands of Douglas fir. An important point made by Fish and Nabhan (1991) is that from virtually anywhere in the habitable Sonoran Desert, one can access coniferous forest within 200 km.

Freshwater streams and oasis marshes are rare in both the Sonoran and Chihuahuan deserts. Fish and Nabhan (1991) estimate that far less than 0.1 percent of the Sonoran Desert consists of wetland areas. Nevertheless, in these deserts, as elsewhere in the Southwest, wetlands contribute disproportionately to habitat heterogeneity. Wetlands support riparian forests (termed *bosques*) that may include cottonwood, willows, cattails, and a variety of shrubs and grasses.

The Upper Gila Mountains Forest Province covers more than 93,000 square km in Arizona and New Mexico. Within the province, vegetation is zoned primarily by elevation. Below 2100 m, mixed grasses, chaparral brush, and mixed woodlands of oak, juniper, and piñon occur. From about 2100 m to about 2400 m, the vegetation is an open forest of ponderosa pine with piñon and juniper on the south-facing slopes. On dry rocky ground above about 2400 m, Douglas fir and aspen occur with limber pine.

Throughout the Colorado Plateaus Province are extensive areas of bare rock, devoid of vegetation. At low elevations arid grasslands are extensive, though not dense. Sagebrush is common in locations with fairly deep soils. The most extensive vegetation zone in the province, the piñon-juniper woodland, is generally quite open with grama and other grasses, herbs, and shrubs occurring among the trees. Above the piñon-juniper woodland is a montaine zone. In the southern part of this zone, ponderosa pine is dominant and may be associated with Douglas fir, although the latter generally occurs in more sheltered sites or at higher elevations. In the northern part of the province, lodgepole pine and aspen are the dominant trees of the montaine zone, while at the highest elevations, Englemann spruce and subalpine fir are characteristic. In the San Francisco Mountains of Arizona, bristlecone pine is associated with spruce. San Francisco Peak is the only mountain within Arizona that contains alpine meadowlands; however, a few more northern mountains in the province have small areas of alpine meadows above timberline.

The southern Rocky Mountain Province is also characterized by well-marked altitudinal zones. The woodland zone adjacent to the Colorado Plateaus has extensive areas of piñon and juniper, often alternating with ponderosa pine, depending on the direction of the exposure. Rocky slopes may host dense stands of mountain mahogany and scrub oak, with sagebrush and grasses covering large areas extending to the ponderosa pine and Douglas fir forest. Above this forest, a zone of subalpine vegetation is dominated by Englemann spruce and subalpine fir, succeeded finally at even higher elevations by areas of treeless alpine meadows.

Only a small portion of the Great Plains Shortgrass Prairie Province occurs within the Southwest. The characteristic grasses (grama and buffalo grass) are a ground cover for sunflower and locoweed, the typical plants. Scattered piñon and juniper occur over some of the area, particularly on slopes near the foothills of the Southern Rockies. Riparian plants are found along the limited watercourses.

A comparison of the plants characterizing each of the provinces indicates that many are found throughout the Southwest, although they may be more abundant in one province than another. For example, cholla, bunchgrass, and chenopodium (goosefoot) are virtually ubiquitous. Widespread distributions of understory plants associated with the woodlands and forests are also characteristic. Some widely distributed understory plants are hackberry, serviceberry, and mountain mahogany. The density of the understory plants and their particular configurations vary with elevation, direction of exposure, and soil conditions.

Economic Uses of Plants A great many plants of the Southwest have edible parts and were used as sources of food by both modern native peoples and their ancestors. Some of the more important are mentioned here. (The interested reader is referred to Castetter 1935; Fish *et al.* 1985; Harrington 1967; Minnis 1989, 1991; Nabhan 1985; Spielmann and Angstadt-Leto 1995; Wetterstrom 1986.)

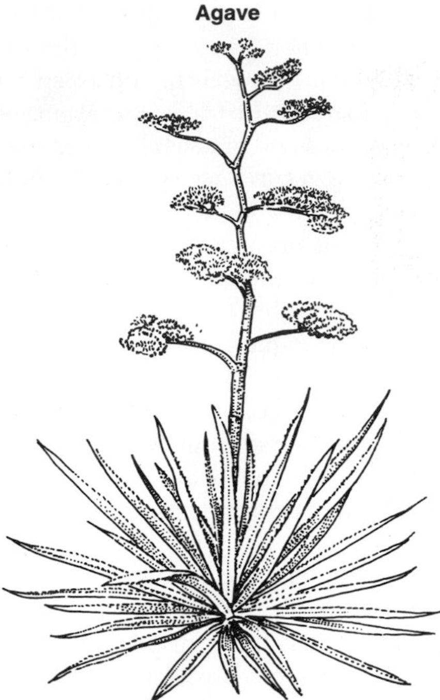

FIGURE 2.6 Agave is found throughout the low desert areas of the Southwest and was used for fiber as well as food. (Illustrated by Marjorie Leggitt, Leggitt Design.)

Agave (Figure 2.6) was an important food source throughout the low desert areas. The leaves and centers (crowns) of the plant are roasted and may be stored. Sotol hearts were used in a similar way. The young stems and hearts of saltbush and yucca were eaten, as was yucca fruit, which could also be boiled and stored. Cactus fruits from the prickly pear cholla, hedgehog cactus, and saguaro were made into a variety of foods. In addition, cholla joints were roasted and stored. The bulbs of wild onion were eaten, and wild potato tubers were eaten fresh or stored and later made into a gruel. The fruits and pods of various plants were eaten alone or mixed with other foods. Among the more important were evening primrose, lamb's quarter, Rocky Mountain bee plant, bunchgrass, Indian ricegrass, sunflowers, paloverde, oak, and piñon. In addition, many varieties of plants were used as greens and, importantly, as medicinal herbs.

In addition to being eaten, plants served a wide variety of other economic uses in ancient times. Timbers for building were made from piñon and Douglas fir; fibers for baskets and sandals from yucca, agave, and apocynum (Indian hemp); paint pigments from Rocky Mountain bee plant; roofing thatch from riparian grasses and reeds; and firewood from the woody portions of shrubs and from woodland and forest trees. In general, Southwestern peoples possessed an intimate knowledge of the plant resources available in their environments, using most of them for food, medicinal purposes, clothing, shelter, or fuel.

In conclusion, the characteristics of vegetation distributions in dry regions cannot be overemphasized. First, as noted, many species either are dormant entirely (the drought evaders) or limit the production of seeds (xerophytes and phreatophytes) until moisture conditions are adequate for successful reproduction. Hence, the most nutritious parts of plants, and the parts most often used for food, are the reproductive parts —the fruits, seeds, and nuts—which are not available at all times of year or even every year. Also, because the weather conditions that trigger plant reproduction are erratic, the ability to predict—on a long-term basis—when and where plant foods will be available is very low. For example, although piñon nuts are a highly nutritious source of food and piñon is widely distributed throughout the Southwest, good nut crops are not available in any one area from one year to the next. Second, because the distributions of plants are controlled by microenvironmental factors such as soil depth, soil salinity, direction of exposure, and soil composition, very large stands of a single plant type in one area are rare. For this reason, it is often difficult to gather sufficient quantities of wild plant food without moving over great distances. For example, Wetterstrom (1986) estimates that if the archaeological site of Arroyo Hondo (a large Pueblo ruin in the Galisteo Basin of New Mexico) housed 400 people, slightly less than 2 percent of the caloric needs of the population could have been satisfied by seeds of wild plants growing within 1 km of the site. The potential harvest of the fruits of prickly pear cactus from within 1 km of the pueblo could have supplied 0.4 percent of the required calories and 6.6 percent if cactus fruits were collected within a radius of 4 km of the site. On the other hand, Sullivan (1995) has suggested that other groups of Anasazi increased the abundance of wild plant foods by controlled burning of piñon-juniper woodland. Yet, both the unpredictability of wild plant foods and small areas of pure stands affect the density and mobility of game animals, discussed below. Finally, compared with other parts of North America, the overall productivity of the Southwestern environments is relatively low. The average annual net above ground productivity in arid regions varies between 30 and 200 g/m^2 (Noy-Meir 1973). For human populations dependent on plant resources, the Southwest is a low productivity, high-risk environment.

Fauna

Animals not only require food and water for survival, they must maintain their body temperatures within tolerable limits. In dry climates, animals generally display considerable flexibility in behavioral patterns, which, combined with their mobility, allows them to use the temporally and spatially heterogeneous resources available. In part resulting from the sparse nature of nutritious plant food in arid climates, most dryland herbivores are indiscriminate feeders, subsisting on a variety of less desirable foods as preferred foods disappear (Noy-Meir 1974). This dietary flexibility allows these animals to colonize a wide variety of vegetation zones. It therefore is not surprising that the larger herbivores, those that are particularly important game animals for humans, may be found in virtually all parts of the Southwest. For example, although mule deer are most abundant in the ponderosa pine forests, they are nearly ubiquitous in the Southwest and may be encountered regularly among the paloverde and cactus shrub land of the desert provinces, the piñon-juniper woodlands and slick rock areas of the Colorado Plateaus, and the grassland communities characteristic of the lower elevations of the Southern Rocky Mountains. There are two generalizations about the differential distributions of animals within the Southwest that are useful to consider. First, there is generally more diversity in larger animals in the mountain and plateau areas and more diversity in small animals in the lower desert areas. Second, the differences in the distributions of animals may relate more to their specific behavioral responses to predators or to key climatic factors, such as amount of winter snowfall, than to their food requirements (see Osborn 1993 for a discussion of ungulate ecology).

The three most common southwestern game animals—with very extensive distributions—are mule deer, pronghorn antelope, and Rocky Mountain bighorn sheep. As noted, mule deer occur throughout the Southwest. They are not selective browsers, but prefer oak, piñon, juniper, Douglas fir, ponderosa pine, and the understory plants associated with these trees. They are usually found most abundantly in broken country and along the borders of dense forest areas. They are found less frequently in more open settings. Pronghorn antelope occur at a variety of elevations from northern Colorado through northern Mexico and from the Shortgrass Prairie to the Chihuahuan Desert. Despite the variety of elevations they inhabit, they prefer open plains and open valleys and avoid rough terrain. This preference relates primarily to their defensive strategy of outrunning predators. Rocky Mountain bighorn sheep, in contrast, require steep, rocky terrain for protection; it is the terrain rather than the elevation that is critical. Bighorn sheep are relatively rare today (except where herds have been reintroduced into areas and are protected). The archaeological record suggests that in the past, they occurred virtually throughout the Southwest.

Four fairly large game animals are important but have more restricted distributions in the Southwest. White-tailed deer occur in the Chihuahuan Desert, although their numbers there are not as great as those of the mule deer. Elk are today of local importance only in the Colorado Plateaus, the Southern Rocky Mountains, and the Upper Gila Mountains, although they may have had more extensive ranges in the past. Bison were, of course, very abundant on the shortgrass plains. In the very remote past (see Chapter 3), their range extended west into south-central Arizona. Bison require extensive grasslands. In the past 300 years, their range has been coincident with the grasslands on the easternmost margins of the Southwest. Finally, the collared peccary, occurring primarily in the desert areas of the southern Southwest, are fairly common in the paloverde communities of the southern portions of the Chihuahuan Desert Province, although its range may extend farther north.

Large predators are generally not important sources of food for people because, although they are of large body size, they usually hunt singly or at night, which increases the difficulty involved in searching for and pursuing them. Nevertheless, large predators are more numerous, and more diverse, in the highlands and mountains that also support the more abundant herbivore populations. Mountain lions and bobcats occur in the Southern Rockies and the Upper Gila Mountains. Black bears are found primarily in the Southern Rockies. The smaller carnivores are more numerous and more widely distributed throughout the Southwest: The coyote is found everywhere in the region and foxes are common.

Smaller animals generally account for the bulk of the animal bones found in archaeological contexts. Jackrabbits and cottontail rabbits proliferate throughout the Southwest and are frequently the major components of archaeological assemblages of fauna. The ranges of these two animals overlap considerably. Nevertheless, jackrabbits prefer open terrain that allows them to escape predators by outdistancing them, whereas cottontails prefer dense vegetation in which they escape predators through concealment. In addition to rabbits, animals such as pocket gophers, prairie dogs, kangaroo rats, wood rats, squirrels, and voles are abundant in the Southwest and are frequently encountered in archaeological sites. Some of these animals burrow into abandoned rooms and trash, but most were probably sources of food.

Within the Southwest, the low desert areas generally have the fewest large and medium-size animals. In the desert provinces, there are few large mammals, but kangaroo rats, pocket mice, and ground squirrels are common, and there is considerable variety in reptiles such as snakes and lizards. These small animals, as well as the jackrabbits and cottontails, were important sources of food in the remote and more recent past. For example, Szuter (1991) argues that rodent-size game animals were essential to the agricultural populations in the Sonoran Desert.

Along water courses, muskrats and beavers are locally significant. The remains of fish and turtles occur in archaeological sites, and fish are depicted on some kinds of pottery. These animals were probably eaten, but their contribution to human diet is not known and is likely not to have been great even among people living near rivers. Insect remains have been found in human coprolites from Southwestern archaeological sites. Most of these were probably accidentally incorporated into food and ingested (Elias 1994:125–127). In one case, however, Stiger (1977) argues that cicadas and grasshoppers were food sources for some Mesa Verde populations.

Various birds are important to the contemporary and ancient peoples of the Southwest. The feathers of certain species of birds are required for items of religious paraphernalia, such as dance costumes, prayer plumes, and katcina representations (see Tyler and Ormsby 1991). Among the more important birds are various raptors: species of hawks, owl, and eagles. Bones of these birds occur in archaeological contexts, as do those of turkeys and various waterfowl. Throughout the arid Southwest, rivers and ponds continue to be the important habitat areas for migrating waterfowl that they were in the past. It also has been suggested that ancient agricultural practices, such as the diversion of floodwater from streams to fields, may have created larger areas of wet habitat for these birds (Emslie 1981). Turkeys were domesticated by some groups in the Southwest and seem to have been used for their feathers as well as for meat. The only other ancient North American domestic animal is the dog.

In sum, the arid and semiarid conditions of the Southwest encourage generalized feeding strategies in animals. For this reason, most of the fauna are able to colonize and adapt to diverse habitats. The modern distribution of game animals and the archaeological record both reflect considerable homogeneity in fauna represented.

Mule deer, pronghorn antelope, jackrabbits, and cottontails are the most characteristic southwestern food animals. Locally, other animals are important. In the southern desert areas, reptiles and small rodents are more abundant. In the mountains and the high plateau country, elk, mountain lions, and bears occur. The archaeological record indicates that throughout the Southwest a great diversity of animals were hunted, including birds. Largely because agriculture is a risky strategy in much of the region, gathering and hunting were always of economic importance. As noted, gathering would not consistently provide secure sources of food in sufficient quantity to feed very many people. Hunting may have been similarly risky as an economic base. In the very early periods of southwestern history, when human population density was low and groups were highly mobile, hunting and gathering were sufficient for subsistence. Later, with higher population densities, agriculture became critical, although gathering and hunting always retained important subsistence roles.

Some of the practices for agriculture may have had adverse effects on some game animals. Clearing woodlands and forests for agricultural fields and for firewood may have reduced the amount of habitat preferred by elk and wild turkey. It has also been noted that in areas of dense human occupation, overhunting may have greatly reduced the availability of game such as bighorn sheep. On the other hand, agricultural fields themselves are important habitat for smaller animals, such as rabbits, that are hunted for food. As noted, agricultural practices, such as irrigation, would have expanded the habitats of some animals, particularly several species of birds. The diverse effects of agricultural production are discussed in Chapter 5. Here it is important to note that the general aridity of the Southwest and the erratic patterns of rainfall limit the natural productivity of the entire region. Even relatively minor changes in climate can have rather marked effects on the landscape and concomitantly on the flora and fauna. Southwestern climates have not been stable throughout either the recent or very ancient past. As noted, many interpretations of change in the archaeological record are attributed to environmental fluctuation. In order to evaluate these interpretations, it is necessary to understand how paleoenvironmental reconstructions are derived. This is the topic of the following section.

PALEOENVIRONMENTAL RECONSTRUCTION

The intent of the following paragraphs is not to describe a series of past climatic events. Rather, it is to present the kinds of data used to infer past environments, the information that each data source provides, and particular interpretive problems associated with specific data sources. Throughout the history of Southwestern archaeology, changes in climate and environment have been invoked as causes of human behavior. For example, sites and regions are said to have been abandoned because of drought, flood, or erosion. This is in part a reflection of our modern American attitude toward the difficulties in making a living from the harsh landscape. Nevertheless, because of the importance of climate as an explanatory variable, methods of paleoenvironmental reconstruction are extremely well developed and continuously refined. This allows evaluation of the methods of reconstruction themselves as well as their applications. All the techniques of paleoenvironmental reconstruction ultimately depend on the principle of uniformitarianism developed by geologists of the eighteenth century. This principle states that the geological record is the result of processes that continue and may be observed today. Hence, understanding the contemporary environment is crucial to reconstructions of the past.

In the Southwest, five sources of paleoenvironmental data are widely used by archaeologists: geomorphological, palynological, dendroclimatological, macrobotanical, and faunal studies. Each of these provides data appropriate at different levels of precision and each has inherent strengths and weaknesses. Ideally, generalized schemes should include information from many sources, and attempts along these lines are the most promising (e.g., Euler *et al.* 1979; Dean 1988a; Gumerman 1988; Nials *et al.* 1989; Wendorf and Hester 1975). The sources of data are discussed separately here to contrast their unique features.

Geomorphology

Geomorphological studies in the Southwest have focused primarily on documenting past episodes of arroyo cutting and filling. In the latter part of the 1800s and in the early 1900s, there was great concern among southwestern farmers and ranchers, geologists, and government agricultural personnel because erosion was occurring, arroyos were cutting deep channels, ground water levels were falling, and vegetation along arroyos was dying. Many people attributed these phenomena to overgrazing. In a series of articles, geologist Kirk Bryan (1925, 1929, 1941) discussed erosion caused by changes in vegetation on southwestern landscapes. Bryan demonstrated that soil profiles in modern arroyos revealed fossil arroyos that had been cut during erosion cycles of the past and were separated from the modern arroyo by observable geologic disconformities that indicated periods of alluviation during which the arroyos had been filled. It was important to the political arguments of the time that some of the fossil arroyos contained the bones of extinct fauna and others were associated with ancient pottery. These observations supported Bryan's belief that episodes of erosion and arroyo cutting could be attributed to climatic change in addition to overgrazing, since there were no domestic livestock prior to their arrival with Europeans.

Relationships among arroyo cutting and filling, increases and decreases in vegetation cover, and climate changes are not straightforward and continue to be debated (e.g., Cooke and Reeves 1976; Hall 1977; Karlstrom 1988; Love 1980; Waters 1986). According to Bryan (1941) and others, erosion would occur during dry periods when vegetation is reduced and runoff is not slowed or spread by plant roots. Arroyo cutting should take place because during a dry period although rains would be infrequent, the intensity of individual storms would not be diminished. Conversely, a wet period would encourage vegetation and periods of alluvial deposition or channel filling. Others argue that arroyo cutting is more commonly associated with periods of increased precipitation, which increases runoff and the amount and velocity of water carried in arroyos, or that changes in the seasonal distribution of rainfall underlies arroyo cutting (Hall 1977; Love 1980; Martin 1963). At present, it appears that several factors are instrumental to arroyo formation, including drainage-basin size and morphology, the type and density of vegetation within the drainage system, and the characteristic intensity of rainfall events (Waters 1986). Karlstrom (1988) argues that even when these factors are considered, there is a general original correlation of arroyo cutting and drought.

The precision with which past episodes of arroyo cutting and filling may be dated varies considerably, depending on local conditions. In some cases, resolution is only on the order of hundreds or thousands of years. For example, an episode of arroyo cutting may be associated with the bones of Pleistocene fauna or with a Pleistocene soil horizon. In such cases, the formation of the arroyo could probably not be dated with accuracy beyond a bracketing interval of a few thousand years. Under unusual conditions, dating may be much more precise. For example, at Black Mesa, Arizona, a number of "fossil forests" (Figure 2.7), where trees were buried in alluvium, have been exposed by recent erosion (Euler *et al.* 1979; Gumerman 1988). In these instances, it is possible to obtain tree-ring dates for the germination and death of the trees that are accurate to within 25 years. In this instance, the alluvial deposits can be dated accurately by correlation with the tree-ring dates. In many cases, ancient arroyos in the Southwest are dated by reference to archaeological materials (primarily ceramics) found within them. The accuracy and precision of these dates depend on how well the archaeological materials have been dated in other contexts and on an understanding of how they were introduced into the geological record. For example, an arroyo forming in AD 1500 may cut through an archaeological site that was occupied between AD 900 and 950. Ceramics from the site found in the arroyo would not date its formation but would provide the earliest date after which it could have developed.

Beginning with Bryan's work and continuing to later studies, attempts have been made to correlate episodes of arroyo cutting and aggrading across the entire Southwest or large areas of it (Bryan 1925; Euler *et al.* 1979). The reasoning here is that if changes in arroyo patterns are associated with climate change, as they appear to be, they should reflect global climatic events. As noted earlier, changes in the cyclonic storm pattern, influenced by the jet stream, would affect large portions of the Southwest, though the implications will be different for the eastern and western rainfall regimes. On the other hand, changes that are the result of convectional storms should be local. This situation may introduce considerable complexity. For example, one study (Love 1980) of sedimentation in Chaco Canyon showed that parts of Chaco Wash were being cut at the same time that other parts of the wash were being filled. This occurred because streams emptying into Chaco Wash originate in two different mountain areas, each with a different rainfall regime.

Clearly, past episodes of arroyo cutting and filling must be related to climate change. The formation of deeply entrenched arroyos and the headward expansion of arroyos would have had great impact on the land available for ancient farming and the kinds of farming strategies that would have been effective. A modern example is shockingly informative. Between 1905 and 1906, one third of the best farmland used by the

FIGURE 2.7 Tree buried in alluvium at Black Mesa, Arizona. The alluvial deposits can be dated by determining the germination and death dates of the tree through dendrochronology (tree-ring dating). (Photo courtesy of George J. Gumerman.)

Hopi Third Mesa village of Oraibi was lost to arroyo cutting (Bradfield 1971). Careful dating of episodes of arroyo cutting could provide considerable insight into local archaeological sequences. The better local patterns are understood, documented, and, if possible, precisely dated, the clearer the regional interpretations should become.

On a rather different scale, a temporally broader one, geomorphologic studies of a different nature are important to paleoenvironmental reconstructions. Studies of the geological deposits within which the sites of the earliest inhabitants of the Southwest (the Paleoindians, see Chapter 3) are found are keys to understanding the environmenttal contexts of the late Pleistocene. These studies are primarily concerned with describing the kinds of sediments at Paleoindian sites and, based on the principle of uniformitarianism, inferring the processes responsible for their deposition. For example, at Blackwater Draw (discussed in Chapter 3), the occurrence of artifacts within a layer of mudstone indicated that the implements had been deposited when a pond was present. The presence of waterworn gravel and sands is an indication of the earlier existence of a stream where none may be present today. The different kinds of sediments deposited in one locality are good indices of climatic change. Hence, transition from water-abraded gravel to mudstones to wind-deposited sand would indicate a change from stream to pond to an absence of water at the site. The precision with which such sediments can be dated varies, but it is generally not great. Frequently the deposits are dated on the basis of correlation with artifactual or faunal remains, using the latter as index fossils. If faunal remains are present, these may be dated directly through the application of radiocarbon dating. Although early in the history of the investigation of late Pleistocene archaeological sites in the Southwest it was common to describe climatic changes in broad, regional terms and to infer synchroneity in change, later studies are more conservative. Again, it is important to develop an understanding of changing environmental conditions within rather limited areas and to date these as precisely as possible before generalizing.

Palynology

Palynology is the branch of science concerned with the study of fossil pollen. Plants produce pollen, some of which is buried and preserved. Pollen can be extracted from soil samples through a combination of chemical and mechanical procedures. Once extracted, individual pollen grains are visible under magnification, and because pollen of different genera and sometimes different species of plants have different morphological characteristics, it is possible to identify the plants represented in the sample (Figure 2.8). By knowing the climatic and edaphic tolerances of the plants in the pollen recovered, the environmental conditions prevailing when the pollen was deposited can be reconstructed. The pollen grains themselves cannot be dated directly, therefore dates are assigned on the basis of geomorphological studies, radiocarbon dates from associated materials, or dates obtained from archaeological sites. Palynology has a long history in Europe. In the Southwest, palynological research was stimulated largely by the work of Paul Schultz Martin (1963) and his students (e.g., Bohrer 1962, 1970; Hevly 1964; Schoenwetter 1966).

Pollen, by reflecting vegetative communities of the past, should be a sensitive indicator of climatic change; however, there is always a discrepancy between the present plant cover and the surface pollen rain. That is, the relative frequencies of pollen types found on the surface of the ground do not mirror the frequencies of the plants growing in the vicinity. One reason is that some species, such as piñon, are overproducers of pollen, whereas other species, such as gourds and cacti, produce relatively little pollen. Also, some pollen is particularly light and is wind-transported over considerable distances. For example, pollen samples from the surface at Mesa Verde

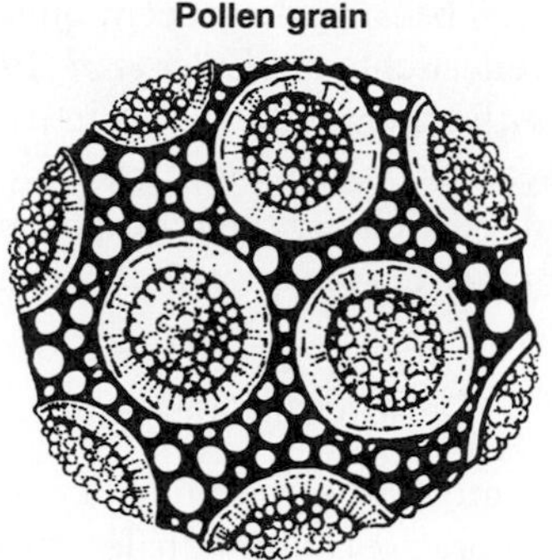

FIGURE 2.8 Illustration of an individual pollen grain as visible under magnification. Pollen of different species and genera are identified by shape, size and surface features. (Illustrated by Marjorie Leggitt, Leggitt Design.)

contain small amounts of spruce pollen, although the nearest spruce trees are about 80.5 km away (Martin and Byers 1965:125). There seem also to be some soil conditions that differentially preserve pollen. For example, pine pollen is more abundant in fine-grained than in coarse-grained sediments (Euler *et al.* 1979). These conditions make it difficult to infer the past vegetative communities directly from the pollen frequencies represented; but because these sources of variations are known, they can be tested for systematic biases.

It is difficult to make direct inferences about climate from pollen that is recovered from most archaeological sites, and the relative precision with which these pollen samples can be dated is less than is desirable. The difficulty is that pollen is differentially introduced into sites by human activities, such as plant processing (Cully 1979 provides a classic example of an ancient room in Chaco Canyon). To minimize interpretive difficulties, pollen analysts suggest using a variety of specific sampling and analytic strategies (Bohrer 1981; Gish 1991). Changes in pollen frequencies may also be difficult to interpret. For example, one significant change in the pollen at Mesa Verde (Martin and Byers 1965:122) was an increase in tree pollen following the residential depopulation of the mesa in about 1300. Such a rise in tree pollen frequency could be interpreted as indicating either increased precipitation or a regeneration of the natural forest allowed by the discontinuation of clearing land and cutting firewood. In another example, modern pollen samples from stock tanks near Cienega Creek, Arizona (Martin 1963), showed that local aggrading of the creek flood plain provides increased suitable habitat for grasses that then deposit proportionately more pollen, locally masking the tree pollen blown in from higher elevations. An increase in grass pollen in relation to tree pollen is often cited as an indicator of general drying conditions. But in this case, a local development produced the same pollen profile as that produced by widespread climatic change. In part because of these difficulties in interpretation, some studies of pollen that attempt to measure climatic change, rather than cultural activity for example, use ratios of pine pollen to juniper pollen or of willow pollen to ponderosa pine pollen because these seem quite consistently to identify the plant community types that reflect climate (Euler *et al.* 1979; Gumerman 1988). Palynology, used in conjunction with other methods of paleoenvironmental reconstruction, is certainly an important research tool. As is the case with geomorphological studies, ongoing research will undoubtedly clarify the mechanisms responsible for changes in pollen spectra and enable a higher degree of confidence in interpretation.

Dendroclimatology

In many ways, dendroclimatology, or the study of past climates through tree rings, is the best-developed and most precise source of paleoclimatological information available in the Southwest. The astronomer Andrew E. Douglass, who established the Laboratory of Tree-Ring Research at the University of Arizona, is generally considered to be the founder of the science of dendrochronology (tree-ring dating), of which dendroclimatology is a subfield. Douglass was not the first to discover that trees could be cross-dated (Dean, in Fritts 1976); however, his work established the scientific discipline. Douglass's primary interest was sunspot activity and the influence it might have on weather patterns. Initially working at Lowell Astronomical Observatory in Flagstaff, he noted that the variations in tree-ring width in tree stumps in the area were regularly patterned. Although he knew that ring width in trees of the eastern U.S. forests was conditioned by shading and competition for nutrients, he reasoned that the differences in ring width in Southwestern trees might reflect variation in available moisture, because moisture is the limiting condition for plant growth in arid areas. The tree rings themselves might then allow him to reconstruct past climatic conditions, which could be tied to cycles of sunspot activity (Fritts 1976).

Some trees produce annual, observable, cortical rings as the result of a growth spurt in early spring that terminates in late summer or fall. The cell structure produced at the beginning of the growing season is different from that at the end, so a sharp boundary generally separates yearly rings. Starting with living trees, from which a small core may be taken, or newly cut trees, it is possible to count back from the present and observe the variation in the width of rings produced each year (Figure 2.9). One of the primary advantages of dendroclimatology for the archaeologist, as well as for the astronomer, is that precise dating to a specific year is possible. The correlation of a single ring with one year is not always possible, however. If conditions are severe at the beginning of a growing season, no ring may be formed that year. If stress occurs within one growing season, two rings may be formed. For these reasons, it is necessary to examine and cross-date many specimens. It is also essential to examine trees that are growing under climatically stressed conditions. Trees thriving in locations where water is abundant, for example, along a stream or where the water table is high, will not manifest variations in ring width that can be attributed to climatic change. In the Southwest, deciduous trees that normally grow in riparian settings cannot be used for paleoclimatic reconstructions. Cottonwood is a good example. Fortunately, trees that were often used in ancient building, such as piñon and Douglas fir, are appropriate for extrapolating past climates.

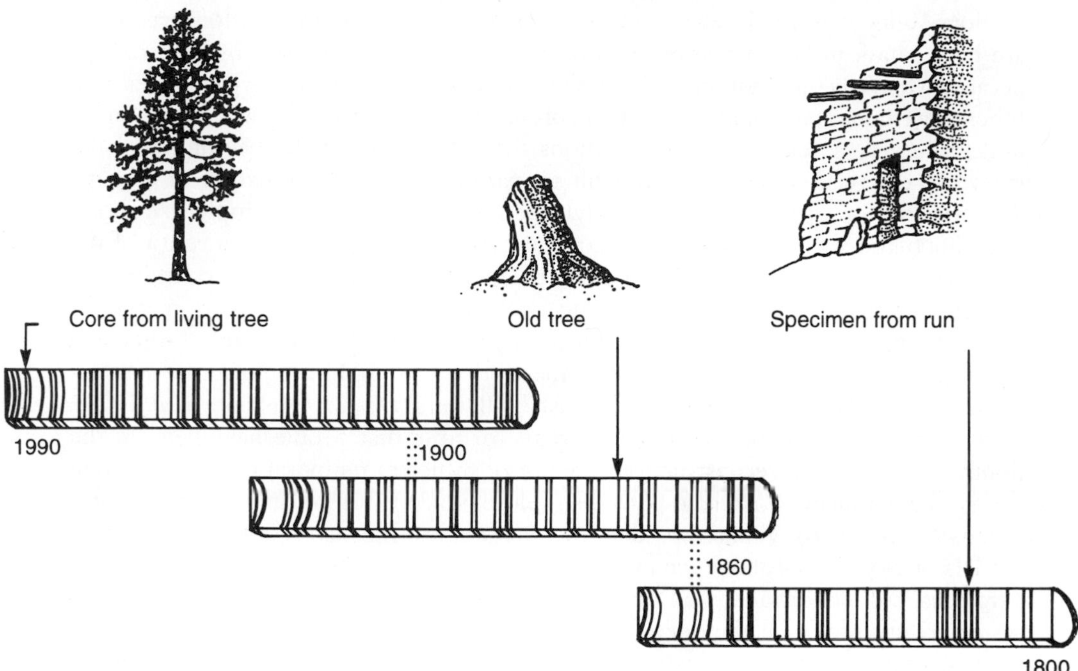

FIGURE 2.9 Dendrochronology is the science of tree-ring dating. The annual variation in tree-ring width in some species that grow in arid regions corresponds to the degree of moisture available for tree growth. In wet years, trees produce wider rings than in dry years. The pattern of wet and dry years can be matched from living trees through sequentially older specimens, allowing dating of timbers used in ancient buildings. (Illustrated by Marjorie Leggitt, Leggitt Design.)

The width of any tree ring depends on factors other than climate: age of the tree, height within the stem, species, etc. Dendroclimatologists correct for these factors by estimating their effects on ring growth and removing these from the measurements. This procedure is referred to as *standardization*, and the resulting values are *ring-width indexes*. "The standardized indices of individual trees are averaged to obtain the mean chronology . . . for a sampled site" (Fritts 1976:25). Generally, deviations from mean ring width are not plotted for every year because ring growth is, in part, conditioned by moisture conditions over the preceding 3 years (Fritts *et al.* 1965:120; Schulman 1956:40). Usually, 5- or 10-year means are plotted as standard deviants from the mean chronology (Figure 2.10). It is important to remember that a tree-ring index chronology or master chronology is derived from trees growing within the same area and therefore is influenced by the climate of that area. Each master chronology has a unique variance and cannot be directly compared with other master chronologies (Euler *et al.* 1979). The master chronology from Mesa Verde, which was derived from Mesa Verde trees, cannot be directly compared with the master chronology from Hay

Hollow Valley or directly with any other master chronology. In addition, tree rings are better indicators of situations of low rainfall than of conditions of high rainfall because when trees are not under the stress of low precipitation, ring width varies with other environmental conditions such as soil nutrients. Also, no ring will be produced under the very severe or harsh conditions that may occur at the beginning of the growing season; therefore, it is difficult to extrapolate the actual extent of climatic depreviation for very bad years. Finally, tree-ring reconstructions emphasize short-term fluctuations and suppress low frequency, long-term variations as a result of the standardization procedures that are used to compile the indexes from several individual trees. Most other sources of archaeological paleoenvironmental information are sensitive to long-term rather than short-term fluctuations, so it is sometimes difficult to correlate dendroclimatological data with these other studies. Finally, accurate dendroclimatological data are available for the past 2000 years (Dean 1983; Euler *et al.* 1979); they are not appropriate for the entire range of time that people have been in the Southwest. Tree-ring reconstructions are not of sufficient temporal depth to be used for the Paleoindian or Archaic portions (before AD 1) of the archaeological record.

As Fritts (1976) emphasizes, dendroclimatological reconstructions are based on models or hypotheses about the influence of various climatic factors (moisture, temperatures, soil conditions, etc.) on the development of tree rings. Fortunately, the systematic maintenance of modern meteorological records in many parts of the Southwest facilitates continual evaluation of the models and has led to exciting refinements in dendroclimatological reconstruction. Advances include the application of multivariate statistical analyses to dendroclimatological problems, which has, for the first time, enabled quantitative rather than simply qualitative paleoclimatic reconstruction. For many locations in the Southwest it is now possible to reliably reconstruct seasonal and annual values of temperatures, in degrees, and precipitation, in centimeters (Fritts 1976; Rose *et al.* 1981:4).

Using the new models of tree growth, it is possible to extract information about environmental conditions other than temperature and precipitation. For example, one can estimate past surface runoff or atmospheric pressure anomalies (Rose *et al.* 1981). It should be noted that to apply modern meteorological data to living and archaeological tree specimens it must be demonstrated that the trees belong to the same statistical population. This may be difficult in some cases, particularly those in which archaeological wood is recovered from areas where no trees (or very few trees) are currently growing—a common situation. On the other hand, the new techniques, because they allow reconstruction of past surface runoff, are allowing expansion of tree-ring based data into parts of the Southwest that lack appropriate tree species. The key case in point is the Sonoran Desert of Arizona, the ancient Hohokam heartland. Since the headwaters of major rivers of the Sonoran Desert, the Salt and Verde, are located in areas where there are tree-ring master chronologies, the calculation of surface runoff enables reconstruction of the past stream flow and discharge rates in these rivers. This information, in turn, has been used to reconstruct episodes of flooding that are likely to have been disastrous for Hohokam agriculture (Nials *et al.* 1989). In addition, careful, systematic archaeological recovery and the development of tree-ring chronologies

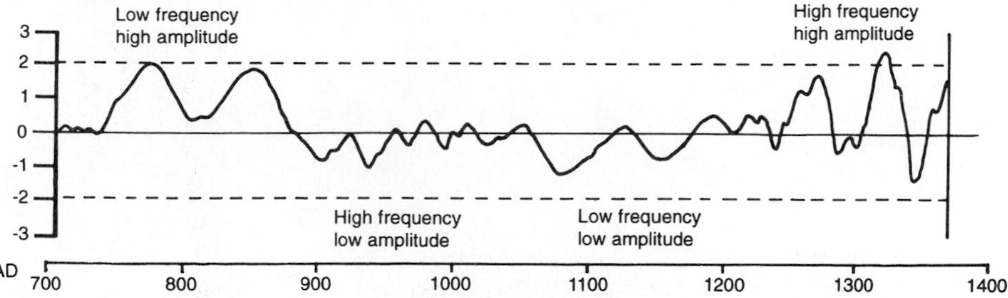

FIGURE 2.10 Tree-ring charts plot the deviation from mean ring width for any one area. Dendroclimatologists usually plot 5- or 10-year average deviation from the mean ring width for composite charts. On this chart, amplitude or the amount of variation above and below the mean is shown as is the frequency or the number of oscillations over time. In the chart, the years from AD 900 to 1050 show high frequency, low amplitude variation. The years from AD 750 to 850 show low frequency, high amplitude variation. (Illustrated by Marjorie Leggitt, Leggitt Design.)

for the mountain ranges of the Sonoran and Chihuahuan deserts have allowed the first pre-Columbian tree-ring dates for sites in the Sonoran Desert (Dean *et al.* 1996).

Without a doubt, paleoclimatological data from tree-ring studies are the most temporally precise and accurate information currently available. As discussed below, the research commitment of the Laboratory of Tree-Ring Research at the University of Arizona, and its dedicated archaeological research staff, has proved the long-term value of devoting an institution and adequate resources to understanding tree growth in relation to climate.

Southwestern paleoclimatologists distinguish two kinds of environmental processes. Low frequency processes (LFP) are those with periodicities longer than a human generation (25 years). LFP underlie episodes of arroyo cutting and deposition and raising and lowering water tables. High frequency processes (HFP) are responsible for annual variations in climate. Variation in rainfall and growing season reflect HFP (Dean 1983). Although some HFP do interact with local topographic features to initiate LFP, the relations among processes are complex so that identical conditions rarely occur. Further, the different temporal natures of the processes are such that most human adaptive strategies are geared toward coping with HFP rather than LFP (Dean 1988).

Tree rings are the most precise indicators of HFP and can yield information about three kinds of variability. First, tree rings indicate the amplitudes of departures or the relative amounts of precipitation. The amplitude can be seen as the distance above or below the mean plotted on tree-ring charts (Figure 2.10). With the caveats mentioned above, amplitude indicates how dry or how wet a year or series of years was. Second, tree rings provide frequency information observable in the number of oscillations from high to low values within temporal periods. Generally, this is interpreted as how many years in a row it was very wet or very dry. Figure 2.11 is a composite chart of tree-ring values from the Colorado Plateaus, plotted at 10-year intervals. The periods

FIGURE 2.11 This fossil packrat midden is preserved within a rock overhang at Chaco Canyon, New Mexico. (Photo courtesy of Julio Betancourt.)

AD 310–380, 750–1000, 1350–1560, and 1730–1800 are intervals during which there were relatively rapid oscillations from high to low values. In the intervening times, the prevailing patterns persisted for longer periods (Dean 1983). Archaeologists must consider whether human strategies that may have been appropriate for high frequency oscillations may not have been so for changes of much lower frequency. For example, storing corn to eat for seed for periods of two to three years will not be adequate if poor climate conditions persist for six to eight years. Dean (1988) discusses various options and strategies in this regard. Finally, the existence of tree-ring stations and master chronologies for large parts of the Southwest allow us to use tree rings to examine variation across space as well as in time (Plog *et al.* 1988). For example, there were times when precipitation was more varied throughout the Colorado Plateaus than at other times when whatever the pattern (high, medium, or low precipitation), it was the same everywhere.

The observation about spatial variability has had exciting implications that Dean (1995) has begun to explore. At the beginning of this chapter, it was noted that two different precipitation patterns characterize the Southwest and that the overall pattern is conditioned by the location of the jet stream. In fact, the situation is slightly more complicated than that. Nevertheless, Figure 2.2 indicates the two different regimes of precipitation distribution throughout the year. Over time, with the oscillation of the jet stream, the two patterns have shifted slightly. For example, one or a few stations that currently lie within the bimodal pattern would at times in the past have had a unimodal pattern. Using the reconstructed paleoclimate data, Dean (1995) found that despite these minor fluctuations, the two patterns and their spatial distributions, were remarkably stable for the past 1200 years with one major exception. Between 1250 and 1450, there was a complete disruption of the pattern. If human populations worked successfully with the long-term situation of two different precipitation patterns, they might have depended upon strategies of mobility or exchange of foods, as appropriate for their regional population densities. Whatever strategies these were, they would not have been effective during the key 200 year period when the entire structure of precipitation patterning broke down. More details and some implications of Dean's (1995) research are discussed in Chapters 11 and 12.

Macrobotanical Studies

Studies of macrobotanical remains (seeds and plant parts) provide another source of paleoenvironmental information. The archaeological recovery of plants in the Southwest has a long history. The remains of corn and other cultivars were often recovered to provide information on the history of plant domestication (see Chapter 5). To recover smaller fragments of plant material, one of various water-flotation techniques is generally used (Watson 1976). Water flotation depends on the principle that particles of plants, particularly if they are carbonized, are lighter than soil particles and less dense than water. Consequently, when the soil matrix is submerged in water, organic materials float to the surface and can be trapped in fine mesh, sorted, and identified under 10- or 20-power magnification. This technique was reportedly used by Volney Jones in 1936 to recover plant remains from adobe bricks of the Franciscan mission at the Hopi Pueblo of Awatovi, and by Hugh Cutler in the 1950s to recover charred seeds from the screened dirt from Higgens Flat Pueblo, a Mogollon site near Reserve, New Mexico (Cutler, in Watson 1976:79). Despite these early efforts, flotation was not used consistently in the Southwest until the mid-1960s (Streuver 1979).

Generally, macrobotanical (as opposed to pollen, which is termed microbotanical) information is relevant to interpretations of past subsistence and economic practices rather than to paleoenvironmental studies. This is because seeds and other small plant fragments are introduced into archaeological sites by their former inhabitants, who may have obtained them at varying distances from the site, either directly or through exchange. These remains therefore do not necessarily provide information about the vegetative composition of the environment in the immediate vicinity of a site. One type of macrobotanical study, that of fossil packrat middens, is used for paleoenvironmental reconstruction.

Packrats gather plant materials within a restricted area of about 30–100 m from their dens (Figure 2.11). They are apparently not selective, and the plants gathered by them provide a representative sample of plants in the immediate vicinity (Betancourt and Van Devender 1981; Van Devender and Spaulding 1979). "In protected perch areas, crystallization of packrat urine through desiccation cements waste debris containing plant fragments, animal bones, fecal pellets, dust, and pollen" (Betancourt and Van Devender 1981:656). In the laboratory, this material is segregated in water, screened, dried, and identified by standard techniques. There are not many studies of fossil packrat middens that specifically relate to the Southwest (see Betancourt and Van

Devender 1981; Van Devender *et al.* 1978; Van Devender and Spaulding 1979). Major efforts have so far been made in the Great Basin but some results are appropriate for both regions (Spaulding *et al.* 1990).

There are important advantages of these studies, for, unlike pollen, which can be transported over great distances by wind, the limited foraging radius of packrats ensures that the vegetation in their middens is local. Also, a portion of the entire midden can be dated by radiocarbon techniques, so it is possible to date accurately the vegetation sample it contains. Finally, packrat middens preserve remarkably well in rock shelters and other sheltered locations in the Southwest, and the time span for which they are relevant is longer than that for dendroclimatological studies. For example, two packrat middens from Chaco Canyon, dated to an age of 8600–7400 BC, contained material indicating that Douglas fir, Rocky Mountain juniper, and limber pine were dominant plants in the area at that time. Middens from the same area, dated to between 3550 and 2480 BC, show that the vegetation pattern had shifted to one in which piñon-juniper woodland is characteristic (Betancourt and Van Devender 1981).

The identification of animal bones from archaeological contexts is sometimes used in paleoenvironmental reconstruction, especially when species are found outside their present ranges or habitat areas. Particularly with respect to the larger animal species, the paleoenvironmental inferences are not always convincing. As noted above, most of the medium and large body-size animals of arid and semiarid areas are not choosy feeders, and finding them outside areas in which their preferred food occurs may mean relatively little. Also, when these animals are found in archaeological sites, it cannot be inferred that they were living in the immediate vicinity. Southwestern peoples travel considerable distances on hunting expeditions, and their ancestors probably did as well. For example, hunting parties from the New Mexico Pueblo of Laguna are reported to have traveled up to 258 km from their villages on hunting expeditions (Cordell 1979; Ellis 1974a, 1974b). Also, since the sixteenth century, game was frequently obtained through trade.

Recovery of very small animals, including invertebrate fauna and insects, from archaeological contexts in which they may or may not be intrusive can provide valuable paleoenvironmental information. Some species of small rodents seem to have rather narrow environmental tolerances, and this can be informative. In one study, the remains of two species of mice (*Microtus mexicanus* and *Peromyscus leucopus*) were recovered from archaeological sites in a part of the Jemez Mountains of New Mexico, which is too dry today for these animals. On this basis, it has been suggested (Holbrook 1978; Holbrook and Mackey 1976) that the climate in the vicinity of the sites was wetter in about AD 1200, when the sites were occupied.

Small rodents, invertebrate fauna, and insects are useful in paleoclimatic reconstructions of quite remote time periods. Masked shrews and meadow voles recovered from deposits dating to between 9500 and 9200 BC on the southern plains of New Mexico indicate that considerably cooler summers characterized the area at that time (Wendorf and Hester 1975; also see Chapter 3). A variety of snails retrieved from the same area support the interpretation of relatively cooler summers, and some species indicate the presence of more moisture at that time as well (Wendorf 1961). Elias

(1994:130–134) discusses insect fauna and climate interpretations for several late Pleistocene sites on the southern Plains and in the Rocky Mountains. Insect remains from anthropogenic contexts in the Southwest are useful with respect to determining the season of the activities at the sites rather than the general climate.

DISCUSSION

In sum, geomorphological, palynological, dendroclimatological, macrobotanical, and faunal studies are all used in paleoenvironmental reconstructions in the Southwest. These techniques are frequently complementary in the data they provide, but they differ in the time periods for which they are useful, the chronological precision they afford, the accuracy with which they can be used to retrodict climate and past vegetation patterns, and the interpretive issues they raise.

The Southwest is characterized by considerable environmental diversity. A variety of resources was available for ancient populations to use for food, medicines, building material, firewood, tools, and other items. Nevertheless, the aridity that is characteristic limits the natural productivity and affects the reliability with which some resources occur. The aridity poses, and has posed, a challenge for people living in the Southwest. Yet, it has also been an important factor in the preservation of archaeological remains. Some of these remains, such as wood, plant seeds, and the bones of small rodents, are useful in helping archaeologists reconstruct past environments of the Southwest and the economies of its peoples.

In addition to preserving archaeological remains, some characteristics of the arid Southwest promote their destruction. Desert and semidesert environments are relatively fragile in that small and short-term disturbances can have disproportionately great effects. The rate at which the environment recovers from a disturbance is slow. Erosion may be initiated by a short drought or overgrazing, either of which destroys plant cover, or by the wind as it carries thin layers of sand and soil from an archaeological site. Arroyo cutting, gullying, and aeolian deflation also destroy countless acres of soils and frequently the archaeological remains contained in these soils.

By far the greatest impact on the archaeological resources of the Southwest results from human activity. The ancient inhabitants of the Southwest mined some archaeological sites for building materials. The practice of using timbers from old, abandoned sites in newer construction is well-documented throughout most of the pre-Columbian period. Yet, the level of disturbance to sites before the modern period was certainly minor.

Today, the archaeological resources of the Southwest are most in danger of being destroyed by resource development and by the enormous population growth in the region. As noted, parts of the Southwest are mineral-rich, containing fossil fuels and other resources that are actively mined today. Coal is strip-mined from huge areas of the Colorado Plateaus, and subsurface drilling is done for gas, oil, and uranium. Although drilling disturbs a smaller area of surface than does strip-mining, there are associated land-modification activities, such as construction of access roads. These activities permanently alter much of the surface and immediate subsurface of the ground. Any archaeological sites between the drag lines of a strip-mine will, of course, be destroyed. Public law requires that the adverse impacts on cultural resources (including archaeological sites) be mitigated, generally through a program of systematic recording, data recovery, and analysis conducted prior to site destruction. In practice, this legal requirement has meant that archaeologists have surveyed, tested, and excavated thousands of sites that they might not otherwise have seen. A great deal of information has accrued on the basis of this work; however, the ultimate value of much of the information, in terms of increasing our general understanding of Southwestern archaeology or archaeological method, or culture change, will probably be debated for some time to come. The ultimate result, though, is that the cultural resource base is destroyed. Observations cannot be reexamined or confirmed at a later time, nor can new information be extracted at a later date. This situation puts a very great burden on the researchers conducting archaeological salvage.

In addition to mining, two other land-modifying activities currently ongoing in the Southwest, inundation projects (the construction of reservoirs) and timber cutting, have a great impact on archaeological resources. Reservoirs are constructed in the Southwest for flood control, irrigation, recreation, or to provide hydroelectric power. There have been several studies designed to document the effects that flooding has on different kinds of archaeological sites and archaeological materials (e.g., Lenihan *et al.* 1977). Archaeological surveys and research programs designed to extract information from sites scheduled to be inundated are among the few recent, very large-scale projects in the Southwest. Results of this work are reported throughout the chapters that follow.

Very large areas of public land in the Southwest are used for the commercial production of timber. The activities associated with timber harvesting (creating access roads, pushing trees, chaining and removing timber) disturbs the surface and immediate subsurface of the ground. There is potential destruction of archaeological materials; consequently, surveys to locate cultural resources and research programs designed to recover information from these resources prior to timber cutting are initiated. Although some aspects of timber harvesting damage archaeological materials, it is not clear that the activity completely destroys all archaeological resources. As with inundation, research is currently evaluating the long- and short-term effects of commercial lumbering on archaeological remains.

Finally, the Southwest as part of the national "sun belt" is receiving a relatively enormous influx of populations. Urban areas, such as Phoenix, Tucson, Albuquerque, El Paso, and Salt Lake City, are among the fastest growing areas in the country. Simple increases in population and the spread of urban areas virtually ensures the destruction of cultural resources. The destruction occurs as housing is built, roads are paved, water lines are put in, and as individuals and groups become involved in "recreational" pot hunting. The impact of these activities can be devastating; not only are the contents of sites removed from their context, but in some cases large sites are entirely destroyed. Although it is nearly a certainty that pot hunting will have particularly devastating effects on Southwestern archaeological resources, some archaeologists are hopeful that educational programs aimed at developing public awareness and respect for cultural resources may help to reduce the anticipated damage.

This very brief discussion of current activities that are having a great impact on archaeological resources should be sobering. Southwestern archaeology has long enjoyed a distinctive role in American archaeology in part because ruins were "so abundant" that the area could serve as a major training ground for generations of archaeologists. The climate and the low population density virtually ensured excellent preservation of archaeological resources that are not often preserved in other kinds of settings. Some of these materials, such as fiber baskets, netting, sandals, painted wood, cotton textiles, and fur and feather blankets allow archaeologists an unusual view of the richness of the daily life of southwestern people. The preservation of building timbers and macrobotanical and microfaunal remains enables great detail in reconstructing the environments in which the ancient peoples lived and in documenting changes in the natural environment over time. The degree to which archaeologists have used these resources to provide an understanding of the cultures and culture change in the Southwest must be critically examined because in the near future, the resources needed to answer fundamental questions will be much reduced in number or eliminated entirely.

Chapter-opening art: Colorado Plateau landscape near Cove, Arizona, 1931 (photo courtesy of the University of Colorado Museum).

CHAPTER 3

The First Southwesterners, Paleoindian Archaeology

The term Paleoindian refers to late Pleistocene Native Americans, people ancestral to modern Native Americans but living at a time remote from our own and in an environment unfamiliar to us today. The natural environments of the late Pleistocene in North America, from the last glacial advance, termed Wisconsinan in North America, until about 8000 years ago were characterized by glacial or periglacial climates, great fluctuations in climate, unusual distributions of plants and animals by today's standard, and the presence of some 35 now extinct species of Pleistocene animals (Grayson 1993; Martin and Klein 1984). The cultural environment was one in which only hunting and gathering peoples occupied the hemisphere.

INTRODUCTION

Neither the artifacts nor key issues of Paleoindian archaeology are unique to the Southwest. Artifacts of the Clovis complex, the oldest undisputed Paleoindian remains, have a nearly ubiquitous distribution throughout those regions of North America that were unglaciated during late Wisconsinan times. Folsom and later Paleoindian complexes that followed Clovis in portions of the Southwest are distributed throughout the Great Plains. Artifacts of the Cochise, San Dieguito, and other complexes that succeeded Clovis in the low deserts of the Southwest are extensions of Western Stemmed point industries that are also characteristic of the Great Basin and Desert West in general.

The key issues of Paleoindian archaeology concern dating the earliest human occupation of North and South America and understanding the ways of life and changes in adaptation that occurred during the terminal Pleistocene. The matter of dating the oldest Paleoindian sites is contentious and controversial for archaeologists and Native Americans. Some archaeologists stake their professional reputations on either finding or discrediting purportedly pre-Clovis sites. Some Native Americans propose their own traditional histories as equally valid accounts of their origins in part because they do not want their claim to being the first inhabitants to be ignored or diminished. These are also general issues that are not limited to the Southwest. Yet, the Southwest is a key area for researchers interested in Paleoindians. There are a great many known Paleoindian sites exposed in the Southwest, but in large part, the focus is the result of an event of great intellectual consequence for American archaeology: the discovery of stone spear points associated with a now extinct variety of bison outside the town of Folsom, New Mexico.

THE DISCOVERY OF FOLSOM

The Folsom site holds a deservedly important place in the history of American archaeology because it provided the first incontrovertible evidence of humans in North America during the late Pleistocene (Figure 3.1). Ever since the 1860s, when Boucher de Perthes' finds of European Paleolithic tools were accepted as genuine, American scientists had been looking for equally crude and ancient remains on this continent. Such artifacts were eventually found, and some exaggerated claims for human antiquity in North America were made on very shaky evidence (Dall 1912; Hrdlička 1926).

Ales Hrdlička, one of the most prestigious anthropologists of the early 1900s, expressed skepticism about crude tools being ancient, realizing that they were probably unfinished items. He was also concerned by the fact that humans usually bury their dead and that skeletal remains associated with very ancient geological deposits may have been introduced long after the geological deposition. Finally, as a physical anthropologist, he was aware that no evidence for premodern man, such as Neanderthals, existed in the Americas. In addition to this healthy skepticism, Hrdlička was a stubborn man, and having made up his mind that humans were not in the New World during the Pleistocene, he consistently rejected finds, some of which have since proved to be quite old (Wilmsen 1965). Before the advent of radiocarbon dating or the routine use of precise stratigraphic controls, it was extremely difficult to conclusively prove the antiquity of archaeological remains (as it still is today). However, Hrdlička was one of a very few prestigious men in the small field of anthropologists of his day, and his attacks against those who would disagree with him were so "increasingly personal" that few men wished to risk their reputations by going against his pronouncements (Wilmsen 1965:179).

In 1908, following a disastrous flood that nearly destroyed the small town of Folsom, New Mexico, George McJunkin (Figure 3.2), a largely self-educated African-American cowboy and foreman of the Crowfoot Ranch, discovered the bones of an

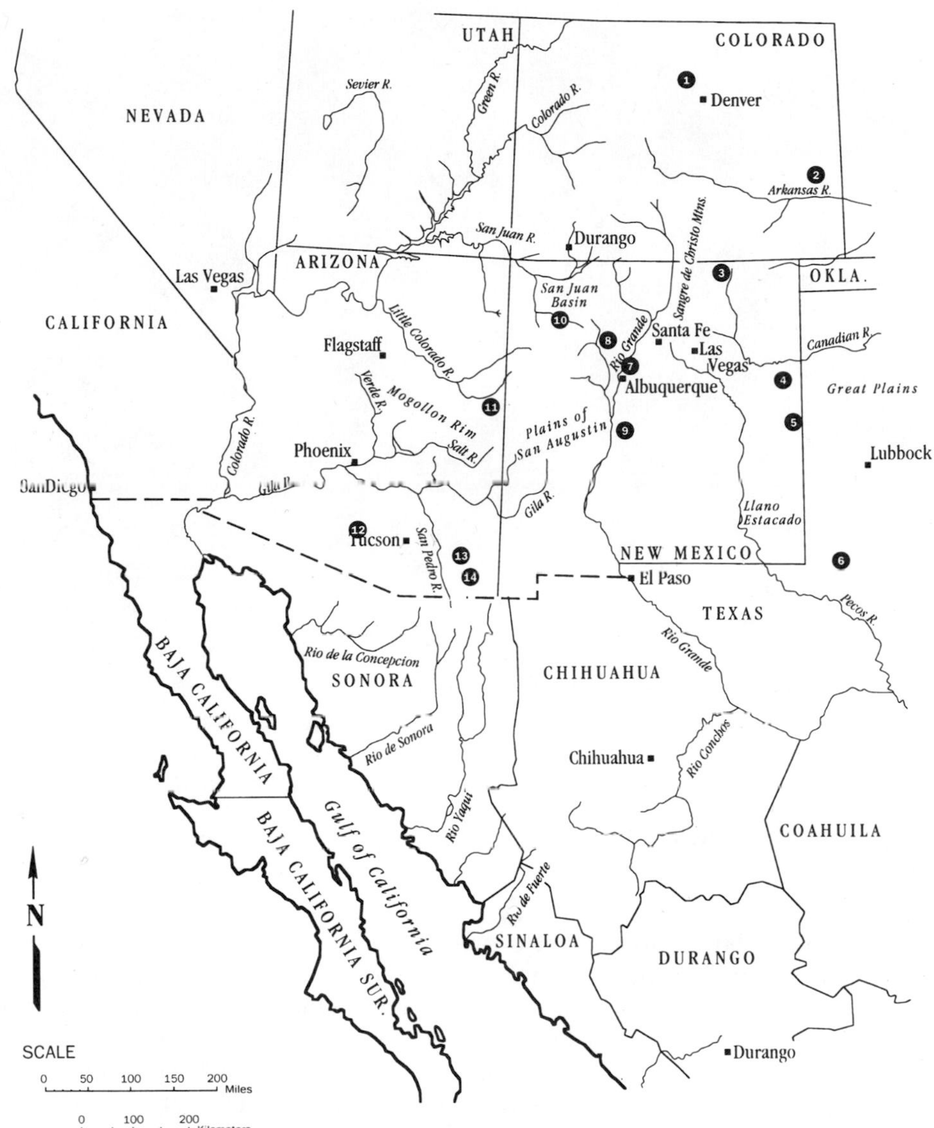

FIGURE 3.1 Paleoindian sites of the Southwest. Key: 1 Lindenmeier Site; 2 Olsen-Chubbock Site; 3 Folsom; 4 Clovis Site; 5 Blackwater Draw; 6 Midland; 7 Sandia Cave; 8 Arroyo Cuervo; 9 Mockingbird Gap; 10 Chaco Canyon; 11 St. Johns; 12 Ventana Cave; 13 Whitewater Draw; 14 San Pedro River Valley Sites (Escapule, Lehner, Naco, Leikem, Murray Springs). (Map by David Underwood.)

FIGURE 3.2 George McJunkin (1851–1922) is rightfully credited as the discoverer of the Folsom site when he found and recognized the bones of an extinct form of bison eroding out of an arroyo near Folsom, New Mexico after torrential rains in 1908. He brought his discovery to the attention of others who eventually interested archaeologists from the Colorado (now Denver) Museum of Natural History in the location. (Colorado Historical Society photo with the permission of George Agogino.)

extinct form of bison eroding out of the deeply cut bank of Wild Horse Arroyo. McJunkin was familiar with the bones of bison and of cattle and knew these very large bones were different. He apparently tried to interest others in his find but was unable to do so until 1912 when he met Carl Schwachheim, a blacksmith, and six years later, Fred Haworth, a banker, both of Raton, New Mexico. Schwachheim and Haworth were interested in the discovery but were unable to make the trip out to the Crowfoot Ranch. McJunkin died on January 21, 1922. In December of that year, Schwachheim and Haworth followed the directions McJunkin had given them, located the site, and excavated "a sackfull" of bones, which they took to J.D. Figgens and Harold J. Cook of the Colorado (now Denver) Museum of Natural History in 1925 (Folsom 1973; Folsom and Agogino 1975). Figgens sent a party, under the supervision of his son, to the site in the summer of 1926. During that summer two point fragments were found in loose fill. Although a third fragment was found in matrix associated with the rib of an extinct form of bison, the find had been removed to a laboratory in Denver, so its original context could not be proved. In fact, there was "a definitely hostile attitude

FIGURE 3.3 Folsom point as found embedded in matrix between rib bones of an extinct form of bison at Folsom, New Mexico in 1927. The find helped establish the Pleistocene antiquity of human beings in the Americas (photo courtesy of the Denver Museum of Natural History).

toward suggestions that the occurrence might be of importance worthy of further investigation" (Roberts 1938:533).

Nevertheless, the Colorado Museum again sent a field party to Folsom in 1927. Fortunately in that year when another point was found imbedded in matrix associated with bison ribs (Figure 3.3), all work ceased and telegrams were sent to notable archaeologists inviting them to examine the find *in situ.* Among those who responded were Frank H. H. Roberts Jr., Barnum Brown, and Alfred V. Kidder, all highly respected scientists. These three were convinced of the association of man-made tools and the fossil bison, and they reported to that effect at the annual meeting of the American

Anthropological Association. It is indicative of the philosophical climate of the times that "in spite of the convincing nature of the evidence, most of the anthropologists continued to doubt the validity of the discovery" (Roberts 1938:533).

In 1928 a cooperative expedition to Folsom was organized by the American Museum of Natural History and the Colorado Museum. The American Museum staff included Barnum Brown and Clark Wissler, in addition to several graduate students. Finally, with the continued appearance of points associated with bison bones, various prominent specialists, including archaeologists, geologists, and paleontologists, became convinced of Folsom's authenticity (Roberts 1938).

George McJunkin is rightfully credited with the discovery of the Folsom site. It is unfortunate that he did not live to see the site become a focus of national scientific interest. The acceptance of the discoveries at Folsom was of broad significance for at least two reasons. First, as Roberts (1938:534) noted, it legitimized further research in Paleoindian studies. Second, the Folsom site was evidence for the great antiquity of Native American occupation of the continent. The find provided a temporal framework of sufficient length to allow for indigenous development of the diverse languages, customs, and traditions of Native Americans.

PALEOINDIAN ARCHAEOLOGICAL RESEARCH

Following the acceptance of the Folsom finds, the intensity of Paleoindian research increased. Stone projectile points that we now call Clovis points (Figure 3.4) for the type site in southeastern New Mexico, were found with remains of mammoth (Figgens 1933). It is not surprising that scholars were drawn to the Southwest. Although sites of late Pleistocene age are still relatively rare in the Southwest, as they are elsewhere in North America, a few areas have yielded abundant Paleoindian material. The San Pedro River Valley in southeastern Arizona has yielded more mammoth remains in association with Clovis points than any other locale in North America. Blackwater Draw, on the Texas-New Mexico border, has produced an abundance of Paleoindian sites of different ages. Other areas that have been closely examined by archaeologists, such as the San Juan Basin, have produced relatively little of late Pleistocene age. These differences relate both to the geological contexts of the material and to characteristics of Paleoindian assemblages.

Given the great antiquity of Paleoindian remains, they will most often be covered by more recent geological deposits. Only those areas that have been subject to recent, quite severe erosion will expose late Pleistocene strata. For example, Blackwater Draw is in one of the most badly eroded locations in New Mexico. The remains found in the San Pedro River Valley were exposed in arroyo cuts that began to form in the 1880s. Further, with the exception of cave sites, which afford special protection, all known Paleoindian sites in New Mexico are located within areas currently undergoing moderately severe to extreme erosion (Cordell 1979:132). Intervals of erosion in the past have likely destroyed many deposits of appropriate late Pleistocene antiquity. Only recently have archaeologists developed search strategies that are particularly sensitive

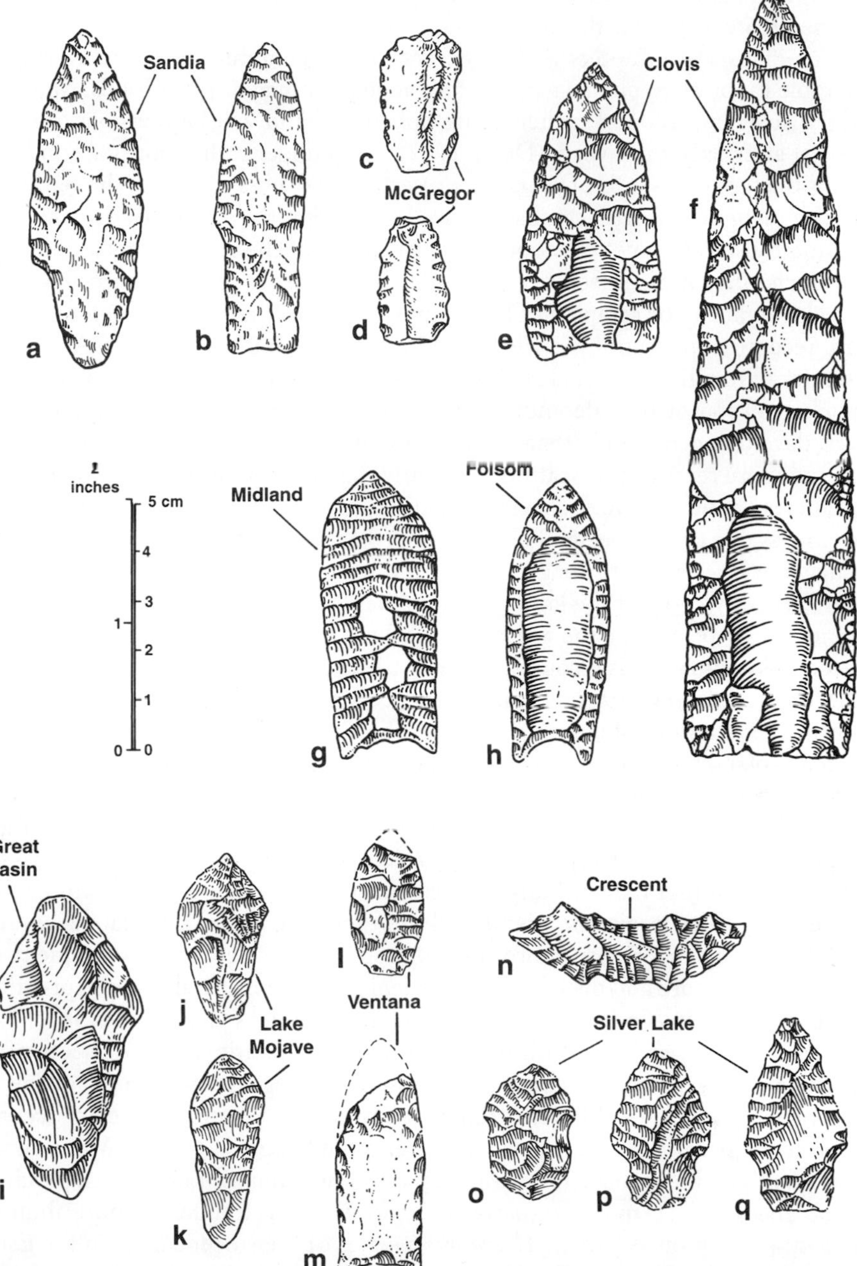

FIGURE 3.4 Diagnostic Early Paleoindian point types include (a and b) Sandia; (c and d) McGregor; (e and f) Clovis; (g) Midland; (h) Folsom; (i) Great Basin; (j and m) Lake Mojave; (k and n) Ventana; (l) crescent; (o, p, and q) Silver Lake (illustrated by Marjorie Leggitt, Leggitt Design).

to these specific issues of geological context (see Butzer 1991; Collins 1991), with as yet no immediate payoff for the Southwest.

Paleoindians were hunters and gatherers. This economic base usually requires considerable mobility to pursue game and to acquire sufficient plant foods. Most sites left by transient hunters and gatherers are ephemeral and will be invisible to the archaeologist after only a few years (Deetz 1972). Only under rather unusual conditions are camps that are thousands of years old preserved, and when they are, their antiquity may not be recognized. Artifacts that survive the millennia are made of durable materials, primarily stone, sometimes bone or ivory. Most of the stone items are debitage (the products of tool manufacture) or nondistinctive items such as sharp flakes that were used for cutting or scraping. These simple, effective items continued to be used by more recent peoples until the widespread introduction of metal tools. An isolated lithic scatter of nondiagnostic debris could have been produced by recent peoples on a foraging expedition or by Paleoindians thousands of years ago. Although archaeologists are developing methods that are appropriate for distinguishing between very ancient and more recent lithic scatters, presently the only widely recognized unambiguously ancient tools are very specialized, distinctive, and relatively rare projectile points. Unless one of the specific Paleoindian projectile point types is found at a camp site, it may not be possible to assign the site to the appropriate time period.

Until recently, most of the known Paleoindian sites in the Southwest were kill or processing sites—places like the Folsom site, where large game animals were killed or butchered. This situation is a consequence of the archaeological record and the state of archaeological survey methods. Kill and processing sites are most often found and brought to the attention of archaeologists, as the Folsom site was, because bones are discovered protruding from arroyo banks. Further, because the sites represent activities of the hunt, they are most likely to contain the distinctive projectile point types that allow them to be assigned to Paleoindian times. However, intensive archaeological surveys, conducted for a variety of reasons, have located many Paleoindian camp sites at which activities other than hunting were carried out. Although a great many of these sites have not yielded projectile points and are therefore difficult to date accurately, they are beginning to provide more information about Paleoindian settlement and technology. The nature and distribution of Paleoindian materials allow interpretations about the ways humans first used the environments offered by the Southwest.

The Southwest was well south of the limits of the continental ice sheets of the Wisconsinan, but, even so, the climates and associated vegetation patterns of the late Pleistocene were markedly different from those of today. Mountain glaciers occurred as far south as the Mogollon Rim of Arizona and the Sangre de Cristo Mountains of New Mexico. Late Pleistocene temperatures were lower but average annual precipitation was higher than it is today, so that surface moisture was frequently more abundant than it is now (Grayson 1993:84). There was a series of Pleistocene lakes in the Estancia Basin and in the Plains of San Augustin. Paleontological studies (Axlerod 1967; Slaughter 1967) indicate that during the late Wisconsinan there was less seasonal variability in temperatures, a situation referred to as climatic *equability.* At least in the Sonoran Desert, summer temperatures would have been far cooler than they are today but winter temperatures similar to those of the present (Van Devender 1990). Palynological data suggest that the boundaries of vegetation zones may have been considerably lower in elevation, and local vegetation patterns quite different from those known at present. For example, a boreal pine forest with occasional spruce developed in the Llano Estacado at about 8400 BC (Wendorf 1970), and a ponderosa pine forest was present in the vicinity of Chaco Canyon before 5000 BC (Hall 1977; Webb and Betancourt 1990).

As paleoclimatological data accumulate and analytical sophistication increases, it becomes apparent that generalized models of gradual climatic change (e.g., Antevs 1955, 1962) may not be appropriate characterizations of late Pleistocene-early Holocene transitions. Rather, the available evidence suggests that quite rapid changes in climate separated a series of "quasi-stable climatic episodes" (Bryson *et al.* 1970:72). The biotic response to such episodes may be very fast, occurring in just a few decades. Even gradual, global climatic changes (such as a gradual increase in solar radiation) will produce rapid and *diverse* climatic changes, depending on local and regional conditions. As an example of diverse effects from the same cause, the annual southern shift in the jet stream produces an increase in rainfall in California but a decrease in rainfall in eastern Colorado (Bryson *et al.* 1970:55–56).

Very few areas of the Southwest have been the subjects of detailed environmental studies of the late Pleistocene and early Holocene; however, the data that have accumulated since 1927 allow interpretations of human social and technological adaptations to a variety of climatic changes. These interpretations are of interest to quite general issues of cultural evolution.

CHRONOLOGICAL OVERVIEW OF PALEOINDIAN COMPLEXES

Paleoindian complexes of the eastern Southwest are distinguished primarily on the basis of distinctive projectile point styles (Table 3.1). Although the point forms included within a single complex may be technologically or stylistically different, they are grouped together because they are not spatially or temporally separable and therefore probably represent the workmanship of a single group of people. For example, Folsom points and Midland points resemble each other in outline, but Folsom points are fluted (Figure 3.5). The fluting process involved an elaborate technology not associated with the manufacture of Midland points (Judge 1970). The two point types are included in the same complex because they have been recovered from the same components at the Scharbauer site near Midland, Texas (Wendorf and Hester 1975), and at the Hanson site in north-central Wyoming (Frison and Bradley 1980). In fact, some of the point types in some complexes show so much variation that the variation requires thoughtful explanation. For example, in some cases, one projectile point style may be a resharpened version of another, such as Meserve and Milnesand points (Figure 3.5). In other cases, the significance of the variations are less clear.

Clovis is the oldest undisputed Paleoindian complex in North America, although there are assemblages that may be older. Of the several finds in the Americas that may

TABLE 3.1 A Guide to Some Southwestern Paleoindian Complexes

	Late	
Early	East	West
Sandia Two point types Clovis Two point types: Bone: end points, batons, punches, foreshafts, scrapers; Stone: scrapers, gravers, backed blades Ventana Complex (?) Two point types; side scrapers, gravers, choppers McGregor Complex	Folsom Folsom, Midland points; end scrapers, denticulates; bone: needles, disks, flakes Plainview Plainview, Milnesand, Meserve, Belen points Agate Basin Agate Basin points; scrapers, notched flakes Firstview Firstview, San Jon points Cody Eden points, Scottsbluff points (two types); Cody knife Jay Jay points	Western Stemmed Point Tradition Lake Mohave, Silver Lake Great Basin, etc. points, Crescents

be of greater antiquity, the most promising are those from Meadowcroft Rock Shelter near Pittsburgh, Pennsylvania (Adovasio 1993; Adovasio *et al.* 1978, 1990), and Monte Verde, in south-central Chile (Dillehay *et al.* 1992). Materials from Meadowcroft may date to between 14,000 BC and 9350 BC based on radiocarbon dating (Adovasio 1993). Radiocarbon dates for Monte Verde place the site at 10,550 BC. In the Southwest, pre-Clovis age has been inferred for the Sandia Complex from the lowest levels of Sandia Cave, New Mexico, and for different materials from Pendejo Cave in southern New Mexico (MacNeish 1994). Claims of great antiquity for both sites are disputed.

Sandia Cave

Sandia Cave (Hibben 1941, 1946, 1955) is in Las Huertas Canyon, 15 miles northeast of Albuquerque, New Mexico. The site yielded Folsom and later artifacts in addition to those termed Sandia. The diagnostic Sandia artifacts consist of two types of single-shouldered points, some of which show basal fluting and wear patterns restricted to one lateral edge (Figure 3.4) (Wormington 1957). In addition to the points, tools associated with the Sandia levels consist of blades with wide striking platforms, keeled scrapers, choppers, and leaf-shaped points. Considering the unilateral wear observed on some of the Sandia points, the Sandia "points" may have been Clovis knives (Judge n.d.). Haynes and Agogino (1986) propose that Sandia points were specialized tools

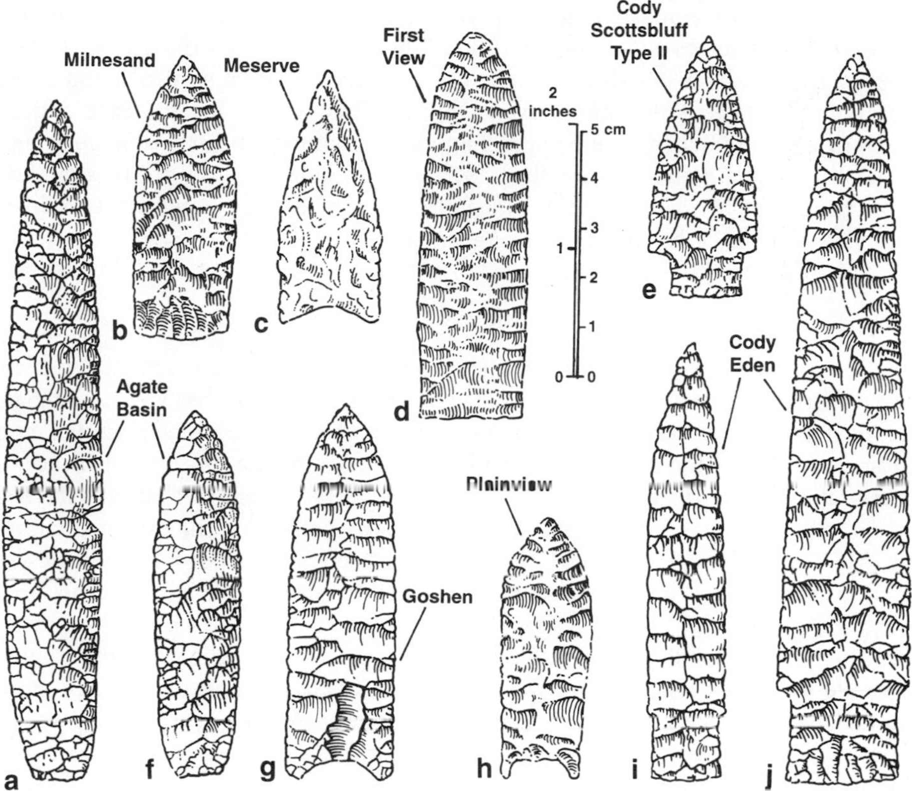

FIGURE 3.5 Late Paleoindian point types, known from the eastern portion of the Southwest include (a,f) Agate Basin; (b) Milnesand; (c) Meserve; (d) Firstview; (e) Scottsbluff Type II; (g) Goshen; (h) Plainview; and (i, j) Eden (illustrated by Marjorie Leggitt, Leggitt Design).

used in cutting out blocks of limonite ocher, a prominent feature of the cave stratigraphy.

Although radiocarbon dates ranging from 33,000 to 15,000 BC were reported for the Sandia complex (Crane 1955, 1956; Hibben 1955), questions arose about the association of the cultural material and the fossil bone that was used for radiocarbon dating, the interpretation of the stratigraphic position of the Sandia artifacts within the cave, and other problems (Bryan 1965; Irwin 1971; Stevens and Agogino 1975). Sandia points have been reported from many areas, but the only other known Sandia site is the Lucy site, in the Estancia Basin of New Mexico (Roosa 1956a, 1956b). Unfortunately, the Lucy site has been subject to aeolian deflation and has produced a mixed assemblage including Sandia, Clovis, and Folsom points as well as Archaic artifacts.

In a long-term effort to more fully evaluate the Sandia material, Vance Haynes and George Agogino conducted additional excavations at Sandia Cave, studied the cave environment, performed chemical and other analyses of cave deposits, obtained

18 additional radiocarbon dates, and prepared a detailed report on the geochronology of Sandia Cave (Haynes and Agogino 1986). They conclude that the archaeological context of the Sandia materials had been subject to bioturbation so that it contained materials from most of the other cave deposits. They argue that the cave and its deposits of limonite ocher were open to humans and animals from 14,000 years ago and that the Sandia points are less than 14,000 years old. They do not rule out the possibility that the Sandia material is older than Clovis but they state that it could as well predate Folsom or be contemporaneous with it.

Pendejo Cave

Pendejo Cave is a deeply stratified site near Orogrande, in southeastern New Mexico (Christman *et al.* 1996; MacNeish *et al.* 1994). The cave has yielded Archaic materials in its upper levels, a Clovis component, possibly older cultural materials, and 52 radiocarbon dates for the cave as a whole. The dates for the Paleoindian zones of the cave range from greater than 55,000 years ago to two dates of 11,300 and 11,900 years ago for the Clovis component. The Clovis dates are within the expected Clovis range. MacNeish (MacNeish *et al.* 1994) proposed a series of names for complexes he defined in strata below the Clovis levels. From the lowest upward, these are the Orogrande, McGregor, and North Mesa. Three of the 52 radiocarbon dates—one of which MacNeish considers improbable—relate to the zones of the cave from which Orogrande artifacts have been recovered. Because these dates were obtained from organic materials and not from the artifacts themselves, a number of archaeologists are skeptical about the dates applying to the artifacts and especially of MacNeish's assertion that the only relevant date is the one of older than 55,000 years ago (MacNeish *et al.* 1994:11, 35). The McGregor complex contains pointed prismatic unifaces (Figure 3.4) that MacNeish suggests resemble Ayacucho points similar to those he excavated at Pikimachay Cave, Peru (MacNeish 1979) and to the Mingo points from Meadowcroft Rock Shelter (Adovasio *et al.* 1978). Although one of the 20 dates is older than 51,000, 19 other radiocarbon dates for the McGregor complex cluster fairly tightly at about a remarkable 32,000 years ago. The McGregor complex levels are the ones that have also yielded the publicized and skeptically received fingerprints on burned clay and three rock-lined hearths (Christman *et al.* 1996; MacNeish *et al.* 1994: 38). The North Mesa complex was first identified at an open site, the North Mesa site, excavated by MacNeish in 1988 and 1989, as well as at Pendejo Cave, where it was also stratigraphically below Clovis (MacNeish *et al.* 1994:42–45). MacNeish compares this complex with several other sites in North America, including the Sandia complex artifacts from Sandia Cave. Sandia points themselves have no counterparts at Pendejo Cave. There are 21 radiocarbon dates for the North Mesa complex at Pendejo that range from 12,970 to 33,830 years ago.

Both Sandia Cave and Pendejo Cave yielded some artifacts that are arguably older than the well-dated Clovis complex. Skeptical archaeologists raise objections to the suggested ages of the proposed pre-Clovis materials. As Meltzer (1995:22) comments, "there is universal agreement only that the first Americans were *Homo sapiens*, who were in North and South America by Clovis times, 11,200 years ago." On all other points, there is substantial disagreement. The criteria archaeologists use to evaluate claims of great antiquity include clear evidence of the presence of humans. That is, there must be either skeletal material or undisputed artifacts or features that can be dated (such as a hearth containing charcoal), rather than pseudo-artifacts that can be produced by natural processes or dates from nonartifactual materials that have been inappropriately cited. The relevance of the radiocarbon dates for the Orogrande complex was questioned because they came from dispersed charcoal rather than hearths or artifacts. The artifacts must be in their original depositional context in undistrubed deposits, where their stratigraphic position and minimum age can be determined, rather than like Sandia Cave, where there has been bioturbation or other mixing (Grayson 1993:53–56; Haynes 1969). Finally, results must be published so that they may be evaluated by others, as is the case in any other science.

Based on these criteria, the most promising of the complexes is the North Mesa. It alone is documented from two sites in southern New Mexico and possibly the Sandia levels of Sandia Cave. The assemblage includes a variety of artifacts that are distinctive enough to compare with other assemblages. The dates given overlap with the chronological interpretation of Sandia Cave by Haynes and Agogino (1986). It is also possible, however, given the dates, that the complex is within the time range of Clovis. The stratigraphically lower, and possibly earlier, McGregor complex seems a less likely candidate as long as the hearths are considered questionable human constructs. Should additional evidence of the McGregor complex come to light at other sites or additional McGregor-associated human material be dated, its acceptance is more likely.

Clovis

As a whole, the Clovis complex is characterized by the manufacture of tools on or from bifacial flakes through a unique process of biface thinning and flake removal and the use of high-quality stone raw material. Flakes were removed from alternate margins of first one face and then the other, each flake traveling across the entire face and removing some of the opposite margin. Tools were then made on these long flakes. The biface, however, eventually also served as a core that was then systematically shaped into one of the two forms of Clovis points (Bradley 1993). The diagnostic Clovis tools are the two projectile point types. In the first type (Figure 3.4) the point is fairly large (7 cm average length), lanceolate in shape, fluted, and concave based. Fluting generally occurs on both faces, occasionally on one face, but extends for only a short distance along the length of the point to the location of maximum biface width. Flutes frequently terminate in hinge fractures, and multiple flutes are common. The ends of basal thinning flake scars were removed from the lateral margins of the points. Heavy basal and lateral grinding are typical of finished points. The second type (Figure 3.4) is similar to the first, but is generally smaller, with a triangular blade that is widest at the base (Bradley 1993; Hester 1972; Judge n.d.; Sellards 1940; Worming-

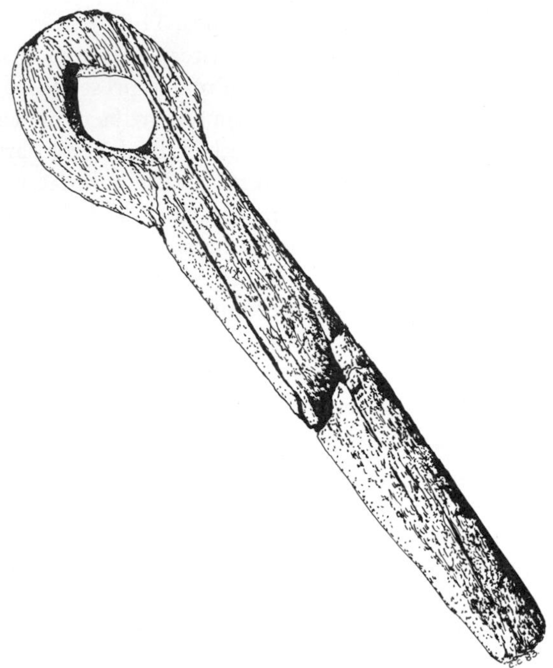

FIGURE 3.6 Shaft wrench or baton of mammoth bone. Tools such as these are known from European Upper Paleolithic deposits where they are referred to as *bâtons de commandemant.* This specimen was found at the Murray Springs Clovis site in Arizona. It is 259 mm long and 21 mm thick and believed to have been used to straighten wood or bone spear shafts (illustrated by Charles M. Carrillo).

ton 1957:57–58). As Frison (1993:241) notes, a Clovis point "is a well-designed piece of chipped stone weaponry that is capable of repeated, predictable, and dependable use in killing large mammals." Other Clovis artifacts include the following morphological types: spurred end-scrapers, large unifacial side scrapers, flake knives, some backed worked blades, gravers, perforators, and bone tools—points, foreshafts, awls or punches, scrapers, fleshers, and shaft wrenches or batons (Figure 3.6) (Haynes 1970, 1980).

Ten sites with stratigraphic integrity have produced radiocarbon dates for the Clovis complex (Figure 3.7). These have been reevaluated and those dates that are most reliable because they are based on charcoal, bone collagen, or amino acids dated by accelerator mass spectrometry (AMS) have been averaged. The resulting dates fall

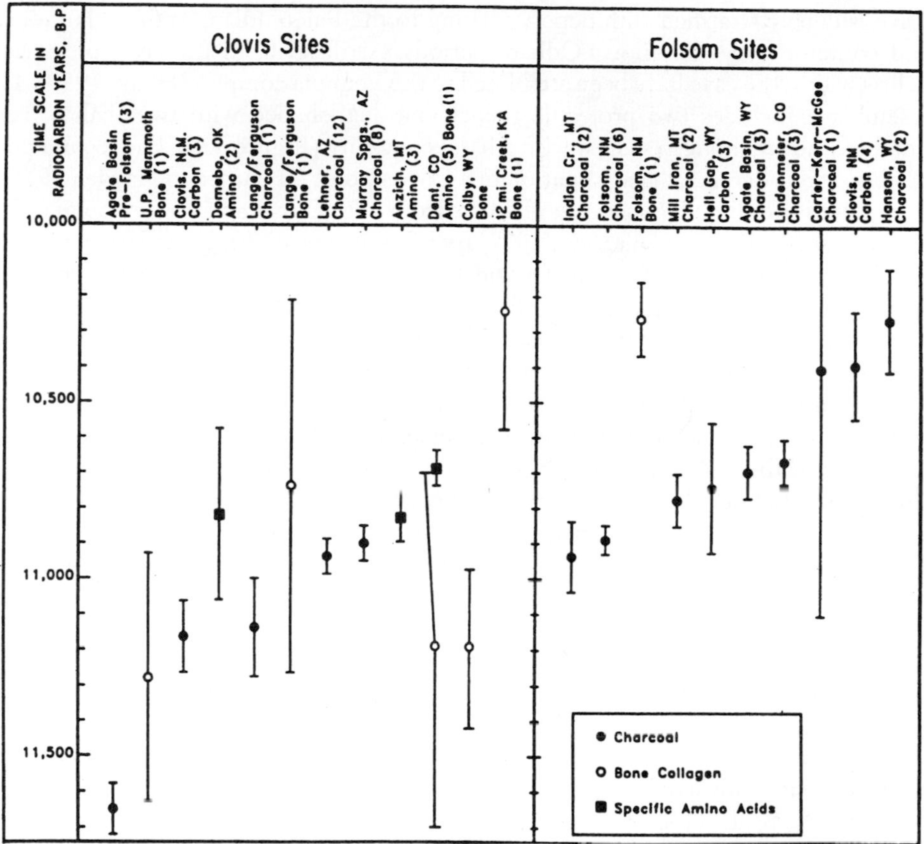

FIGURE 3.7 Chart of Clovis, Folsom, and related radiocarbon dates. Bone apatite dates and radiocarbon dates younger than 10,000 BP are not plotted (adapted from Haynes, 1993).

between 11,650 and 10,250 years ago, with a tight cluster between 11,200 and 10,800 years ago (Haynes 1993:220–224). Although this tight cluster of Clovis dates is earlier, the dates as a whole overlap somewhat with dates from Folsom complex sites (Haynes 1993:224). The Clovis dates are consistent with geological interpretations of stratigraphy and with the association of Clovis and Pleistocene fauna. Virtually all excavated Clovis sites have yielded the remains of mammoth. Bison, horses, camels, cervids, tapirs, canids, antelope, bears, and jackrabbits are also reported (Frison 1993; Haynes 1980; Haynes and Hemmings 1968; Hester 1972; Judge n.d.:22–27).

The Ventana complex identified at Ventana Cave, near Sells, Arizona, appears to be as old as Clovis and could possibly be included within the Clovis complex. Ventana

Cave is deeply stratified with deposits dating to the Paleoindian, Archaic, Hohokam, and contemporary Tohono O'Odham periods. Artifacts from the layer of volcanic debris within the cave have been attributed to the Ventana complex (Haury 1950). This assemblage includes two projectile points, one leaf-shaped with two shallow basal notches, the second leaf-shaped with a basal concavity (Figure 3.4). The second point has been considered "a local imitation of a Clovis point" (Haury and Hayden 1975:v). The point is not fluted, however, and differs from both Clovis and Folsom points (C. V. Haynes, personal communication, 1977; Irwin-Williams 1979). New data suggest the Ventana component may be early Archaic. Other artifacts included in the Ventana complex are irregular side scrapers, long flakes with retouch on one (termed side scrapers), dischoidal and core scrapers, gravers, choppers, planes, hammerstones, and a grinding stone (Haury 1950). The associated fauna included bison, horse, sloth, and tapir (Colbert 1973; Haury 1950). A radiocarbon date of 11,350 ± 1200 years ago has been reported from the cave layer yielding the Ventana complex artifacts (Haury and Hayden 1975).

Most of the western Clovis sites are interpreted as kill sites or meat processing sites. At the Lehner Ranch site in the San Pedro River Valley, bones of 13 mammoths were found with 13 Clovis points, stone scrapers, knives, and a chopper (Haury *et al.* 1959). Murray Springs, also in the San Pedro River Valley, consists of a camp site in addition to two kill locations that yielded remains of a mammoth and 11 bison. There are a few burial sites, including Anzick, a site in Montana (Lahren and Bonnichsen 1974) or cache sites (Bradley 1993). At the San Pedro River Valley site of Naco (Haury *et al.* 1953), a mammoth was found with eight projectile points but no other tools, signs of butchering, or evidence that the points had been resharpened. Naco, Escapule (also in the San Pedro River Valley), and the Domebo site in Texas each produced a mammoth and Clovis points but no other signs of human activity. The sites are considered unsuccessful kill sites, locations where, perhaps mortally wounded, mammoth died without their meat being recovered by hunters. In addition to Murray Springs, camp sites include the Aubrey Clovis site near Denton, Texas (Hall 1996); Blackwater Draw El Llano, interpreted as a redeposited camp site (Hester 1975); and the incompletely reported site of Mockingbird Gap near Socorro (Weber and Agogino 1968; R. Weber, personal communication, 1983).

The Clovis complex was defined on the basic of the kill and processing sites. Therefore descriptions of the complex do not generally include the range of tool types characteristic of more diverse activity settings. Sandia, Ventana, and Pendejo are cave sites that seem to have been used as camping places. If these sites are the same age as Clovis, as has been suggested by some, they may reflect activities that did not entail the use of the diagnostic Clovis projectile point type.

Western Stemmed Point Tradition

The Western Stemmed Point Tradition includes a variety of named complexes, phases, and regional projectile point styles of the Great Basin and adjacent far western United States (Willig and Aikens 1988), including those of the San Dieguito and Lake

Mojave complexes (Warren 1967; Willig and Aikens 1988). Diagnostic artifacts are stemmed projectile points, generally with slightly rounded bases, such as Lake Mojave and Silver Lake types, crescents (Figure 3.4), and less distinctive artifacts such as leaf-shaped knives, ovoid large-domed scrapers, rectangular end and side scrapers, engraving tools, occasional manos, and metates (Grayson 1993:240–241; Warren 1967:177; Willig and Aikens 1988). The points have thick stems that contract to a rounded or square base. Many points are also distinctly shouldered. The edges of the point bases are heavily ground. Crescents are either steeply retouched or ground at their midsections. The way crescents were used is unclear. The central grinding suggests that they were hafted at midsection. Proposed uses include scrapers, knives, drill bits, sickle blades, or bird-stunning points (Grayson 1993:240–241). Although most Western Stemmed Point Tradition sites are open sites or surface scatters, 22 radiocarbon dates are available from sites with stratigraphic integrity. These dates fall between 11,200 and 7,500 years ago (Grayson 1993:240; Willig and Aikens 1988). Fauna associated with Western Stemmed Point Tradition components include artiodactyls (deer, antelope, and mountain sheep), jackrabbits, and freshwater mollusks. The mollusks, in particular, indicate the use of marshes and shallow lakes that were present in large areas of the Great Basin until about 7,500 years ago.

Folsom

The Folsom complex, which follows Clovis in the eastern Southwest, includes both the distinctively fluted Folsom point and the unfluted Midland point (Figure 3.4), and possibly the Goshen or Mill Iron point, which is also not fluted (Frison 1992, 1993). Folsom points are fluted on both faces for nearly the entire length of the point, requring careful preparation of the point preform, which also frequently resulted in breaking the point during manufacture. Fluting of this quality is a lost art, and archaeologists have attempted to reconstruct the process in a variety of ways, including replication studies and piecing together fragments of points broken while they were being made (Bradley 1993:254). Of two reconstructions of the process, one is based on collections from the central Rio Grande Valley (Judge 1970), the other on collections from the Hanson site in Wyoming (Frison and Bradley 1980).

Following a detailed analysis of all the lithic materials recovered from the Hanson site, Bradley (1993) proposes that the initial stages of Folsom preform preparation were, like Clovis, intended to produce flakes for subsequent modification into tools. He notes that this core-reduction technology, generally on dischoidal bifacial cores, shows continuity with Clovis. Midland points resemble Folsom points in outline but are not fluted (Figure 3.4). Although Folsom points were undoubtedly used as projectile points, Midland points were also used. Frison (1993:242–43), comments that "fluting may allow somewhat easier hafting of the point to a split shaft but nonfluted points are not difficult to attach to a split shaft so that they will not fail during use."

The difficulty in actually producing finished fluted Folsom points, with a failure rate Judge (1973) estimated at 25 percent, provides a context for interpretations of the utility of the points as weapons. Judge (1973) regards the manufacturing process itself as valuable in providing useful tools at nearly every stage. Hence, before fluting, the preforms were used as knives. Subsequently, the channel flakes, snapped tips, and other byproducts of the fluting process were also used as tools. He states that the Folsom points "can be considered part of a complex implement system in which efficiency in material utilization was maximized" (Judge 1973:178).

Bradley (1993:255) notes that in the Folsom component of the Agate Basin site in Wyoming (Frison and Stanford 1982), the points recovered from the area of the site where several bison had been killed and butchered were not fluted Folsom points. The bison kills were associated with three bone points, a Clovis-like point, and a small trimmed flake. Yet the same site yielded abundant evidence of successful preform fluting in the form of channel flakes that could be refitted into discarded preforms. In addition, well-fluted but unfinished preforms are characteristically recovered from nearly all Folsom sites and as surface finds. Bradley (1993:255) also describes a case in which one preform was successfully fluted at least three times before having been intentionally smashed.

With these examples in mind, Bradley (1993:255) suggests that producing the completed Folsom projectile point may not have been the most important objective of the fluting process. Rather, he suggests that fluting may have begun as an expedient way to thin the base of a projectile point but it came to be an integral part of pre-hunt predictive ritual. He states, "because the fluting of an already thin preform was a risky business, the failure of the attempt may have been considered a prognostication of the success of an upcoming event such as a hunt" (Bradley 1993:255–56). He also considers the care, skill, and artistry that is expressed in many Paleoindian projectile points to be symbolic of the power invested in them. Other artifacts associated with the Folsom complex include a variety of scrapers, especially end scrapers, bifacially prepared cores, bifacial knives, denticulates, backed flake tools, composite tools, burins, and gravers (Frison and Bradley 1980; Irwin and Wormington 1970). Bone and antler items include tine flakers, points, needles, beads, and incised disks.

Folsom sites are well documented in the eastern Southwest, in part because the points are easily recognized. Sites are reported in the central Rio Grande area (Judge 1973), on the Plains of San Augustin (Beckett 1980; Berman 1979), in the San Juan Basin (Judge 1982), and near St. Johns, Arizona (Longacre and Graves 1976). Most of the sites within the area appear to be camps rather than kill sites. In part, this reflects recent intensive site surveys (Judge 1970, 1982).

Plainview

The Plainview complex (Johnson and Holliday 1980; Knudson 1973; Sellards *et al.* 1947; Wheat 1972) is defined somewhat ambiguously. Here (following Johnson and Holliday 1980; Judge 1973, 1982; Wheat 1972), the complex includes Plainview, Milnesand, Meserve, and Belen points (Figure 3.5). Plainview points are parallel-sided with slightly concave bases. Thinning was accomplished through transverse parallel bifacial flaking. Milnesand points are formally similar but have straight bases and more small, vertical, basal, thinning flake scars. Meserve points have transverse blades; some are resharpened Plainview points. Belen points are laterally thinned with a slight basal concavity and may represent a Rio Grande variant of either Plainview or Milnesand points (Judge 1973). Plainview sites occur primarily on the Llano Estacado and adjacent areas of Texas. Belen sites, as noted, occur in the central Rio Grande Valley. The Plainview complex is considered part of a southern Plains tradition.

Agate Basin

The Agate Basin complex is characterized by a single point type. Agate Basin points (Figure 3.5) are long and slender with slightly convex sides. They are basally constricted with either straight or nearly pointed bases. Other Agate Basin stone tools include scrapers, notched flakes, perforators, and retouched flakes (Irwin-Williams *et al.* 1973). Agate Basin complex sites are not reported for the Southwest proper. Except for their occurrence at Blackwater Draw, they seem to be concentrated on the northern Plains.

Firstview

The Firstview complex, as defined by Wheat (1972), includes points recovered from the Olsen-Chubbock site in Colorado and from those previously identified as Portales from Blackwater Draw and as San Jon from the San Jon site on the Llano Estacado. The points (Figure 3.5) resemble Milnesand in outline and are transversely flaked. Final edge grinding was done perpendicular to the long axis of the point (Judge 1973: Wheat 1972). Firstview complex points are not well represented in the Southwest outside of the Llano Estacado. Irwin-Williams (n.d.:16), among others, considers the Firstview complex to be a variant of the Cody complex.

Cody

Traditionally, the Cody complex (Bradley 1993; Bradley and Frison 1987; Wormington 1957) includes Eden points, three types of Scottsbluff points, and the Cody knife. Intermediate types have also been defined, making the Cody tradition even more heterogeneous in projectile point styles than other Paleoindian complexes. Scottsbluff points are shouldered points with transverse parallel flaking and broad stems. The Type II Scottsbluff point (Figure 3.5) has a more triangular blade than that of Type I (Figure 3.5). Type III are intentionally much thinner. Eden points, long and narrow with only slightly constricted bases, are collaterally flaked with a pronounced median ridge (Figure 3.5). Cody knives have transverse blades and sometimes may have been fashioned from Scottsbluff points.

Scottsbluff Types I and II and Eden points were likely produced by the same technological sequence with the differences being the stage at which the sequence is ended and the formation of the hafting element. Bradley (1993; also see Bradley and Stanford 1987) proposes that Cody points were made by percussion shaping and thinning of a biface, followed by selective pressure shaping, and finished by one or more series of pressure-flaking sequences, generally one that was comedial. This pattern produces a distinctive medial ridge. Eden points represent the most complete pressure flaking sequence. If the point maker terminated the sequence after fewer stages of pressure flaking, one or another of the Cody point types is produced (cf. Bamforth 1991:315). Finishing the point was accomplished by fine pressure retouch and grinding of the stem and base. Bradley (1993:260) suggests that next to Folsom, Eden and Scottsbluff Type III consistently exhibit exceptional skill in their manufacture.

Other Cody complex artifacts include end scrapers, raclettes, denticulates, notched flakes, and knives (Irwin-Williams 1973). Cody complex sites are quite well represented in the eastern Southwest and adjacent areas of the Plains. In addition to Cody components at Blackwater Draw, Cody sites have been found in the central Rio Grande Valley (Judge 1973; Judge and Dawson 1972), the Arroyo Cuervo area (Irwin-Williams 1979), the plains of San Augustin (Berman 1979), and the San Juan Basin (Wait 1976). Cody complex points, as isolated finds, have an even wider distribution throughout much of the Southwest.

Jay

Irwin-Williams (1973, 1979) defined the Jay complex as Archaic. In other discussions (Stuart and Gauthier 1981; Wait 1981), Jay is attributed to late Paleoindian times. The latter determination is based in part on the general resemblance of Jay points to late Paleoindian points of the Great Plains. The diagnostic Jay artifact (Figure 4.3) is a fairly large, shouldered point that is similar to Hell Gap points in outline. Other Jay complex artifacts include well-made leaf-shaped knives and a variety of scrapers (Irwin-Williams 1973). Jay materials are known from the central and northern Rio Grande area, the Arroyo Cuervo area, the San Juan Basin, and the Plains of San Augustin.

VARIETY OF PALEOINDIAN COMPLEXES AND CHRONOLOGY

The Clovis complex is the oldest widely accepted, well-documented, and widespread evidence of Paleoindian occupation in the Southwest and in fact in North America. Nevertheless, new radiocarbon dates demonstrate that Clovis is not a synchronous horizon across the continent. Clovis assemblages from Alaska and the northeastern United States are about 1000 years later than those from the Southwest. As would be expected, there is recognized regional variation in Clovis assemblages as well (Meltzer 1993:304).

The traditional literature recognizes formal similarities between Clovis and Folsom point types (both are thinned by fluting) and considers these as having been sequential and followed by non-fluted complexes arranged in a generally accepted order, also based on form. This order is Plainview, Agate Basin, Firstview, and Cody. If Jay is included, it follows Cody. New radiocarbon dates from Folsom sites range from 10,980 ± 150 years ago from Indian Creek in Montana to 10,080 ± 330 for the

Hanson site in Wyoming (Haynes 1993:222). These dates slightly overlap dates for Clovis sites (Figure 3.7) and also dates from later Paleoindian assemblages (Frison 1993:240). As Haynes (1993:225) states, the temporal differences among these complexes is too short to resolve using radiocarbon dating given the different materials used to obtain the dates (carbon vs. bone collagen, for example) and the statistical limitations of the radiocarbon technique.

The sequential order of complexes obtained in stratified archaeological deposits differs from the order derived from form. The Hell Gap site in Wyoming (Irwin-Williams *et al.* 1973) is a geologically complex site, and the sequence of Paleoindian point types is based on material recovered from four separate localities. The sequence is as follows: Goshen, Folsom, Midland, Agate Basin, Hell Gap, Lusk, Alberta, and Cody. (Hell Gap and Alberta complexes are northern Plains manifestations.) Goshen points (Figure 3.5) are not fluted. They are formally similar to Plainview. It therefore appeared as though at the Hell Gap site, Plainview preceded Folsom, an order that is contrary to one expected based on form. The recently excavated Mill Iron site in Montana (Frison 1988) contains a variety of unfluted types that confirm Goshen as a type distinct from Plainview and as predating Folsom (Frison 1992, 1993; Haynes 1993). At the southern Plains site of Blackwater Draw, Locality 1 (Haynes and Agogino 1966; Wendorf and Hester 1975), the sequence is Folsom and Agate Basin (considered contemporary), Firstview, and Cody. In essence, new information suggests more variety in Paleoindian point forms than is expressed in standard point typology. Not surprisingly, there is temporal overlap among point types based on both radiocarbon dating and stratigraphy. As a whole there is some contradiction among the sequences represented at stratified sites that is not resolved by radiocarbon ordering.

Another approach to chronology is in the paleontological literature, which suggests that there were genetic changes in bison populations over time. However, while the overall trend was toward a decrease in bison size, this change was not uniform over time or over space. Diminution seems to have occurred earlier in the north than in the south (Guthrie 1980; Wilson 1980) and overall change was accelerated during the Altithermal (Frison 1974:242–243). Frison (1992:339) notes that by 5000 years ago, bison were of modern form.

Marked change can be rapid and can produce diverse local or regional conditions. The paleontological data for bison suggest long-term trends with accelerated rates of change that may have been triggered by abrupt climatic change. The cultural responses to changed conditions are, of course, potentially much more rapid than the genetic changes reflected in the bison populations. If Paleoindian populations pursued bison wherever the animals were present in sufficient numbers, it would be expected that the ranges of various Paleoindian groups would expand and contract as conditions on the western margins of the Plains became more or less able to support bison herds.

The rapidity with which relatively minor fluctuations may have taken place, as well as their marked ecological and cultural effects, is suggested by a study of a well documented, rapid, recent climatic change on the Great Plains (Bryson *et al.* 1970). A shift in the pattern of westerly winds occcurred about AD 1160, resulting in a migration of agriculturalists to the Texas-Oklahoma Panhandle by AD 1220 and ending agricultural occupation of areas farther to the west at the same time. By about AD 1550, agriculture on the Panhandle had once again become impossible.

It seems likely that most of the ambiguities in the radiocarbon and stratigraphic sequences for the Paleoindian period reflect an inability to isolate rapid cultural changes with appropriate precision. A great many more radiocarbon determinations are necessary, as are detailed studies of the expansion and contraction of range-land during Paleoindian times. Given the present state of the chronological record, Clovis and Cody are excellent horizon markers within the Paleoindian period, whereas the other complexes are less so. It should also be noted that Clovis, Folsom, and Cody have the widest spatial distributions in the Southwest. This may be an artifact of archaeology itself in that Clovis and Folsom are easily recognized and Cody is both easily recognized and broadly defined. On the other hand, the wide geographic distributions of Clovis, Folsom, and Cody suggest that they reflect hunting strategies that could have spread because of particularly favorable environmental circumstances. Alternatively, the distributions may indicate economic strategies that were flexible enough to have been appropriate across a range of environmental conditions. A preliminary evaluation of the alternatives may be made by examining current information pertaining to the paleoenvironmental record and studies relating to the economic bases reflected by the complexes.

VARIETY OF PALEOINDIAN COMPLEXES AND PALEOENVIRONMENTAL FACTORS

A few areas in the Southwest and adjacent portions of the Great Plains provide the kinds of detailed paleoenvironmental studies that are useful for the Paleoindian period. Among them are Blackwater Draw, a broad, shallow valley in the Llano Estacado of eastern New Mexico and western Texas; Lubbock Lake, Texas (Johnson and Holliday 1981); and the San Pedro River Valley, Arizona. Additional data are available for portions of the Great Basin (Grayson 1992; Haynes 1993; Willig *et al.* 1988). Recently, Haynes (1993) has correlated some paleoclimatic indicators among some of these areas.

Wendorf and Hester's (1975) synthesis of the late Pleistocene environments in the Blackwater Draw area draws on geology, palynology, and vertebrate and invertebrate paleontology. The results of these studies are discussed here in somewhat simplified form. The earliest geological deposits exposed are of Pleistocene age, but they antedate the presence of Paleoindians. A pine and spruce forest extended to the southern edge of the Llano at the end of this period (about 11,500 BC). A discontinuous layer of mudstone was formed in ponds that were present in the area. The Clovis remains occur near the base of a wedge of brown sand and silt that was deposited by a spring. The change from pond-deposited to spring-deposited sediments is interpreted as indicating reduced water flow as the result of a general drying trend. The pollen recovered from the brown sand showed a decrease in pine and an increase in composites and grasses consistent with the interpretation of drying conditions. The vertebrate fauna from the Clovis deposits are remarkably diverse. Some species, such as meadow voles and masked shrews, occur today in areas where it is cooler than it is on the Llano Estacado. The presence of cotton rat and armadillo negates the possibility that winters were much cooler than they are today. These fauna suggest a fairly equable climate with mild winters and cool summers. Some of the species recovered, especially muskrat, indicate more surface moisture in the past than at present.

Haynes (1993) suggests that similar drying conditions preceded Clovis in the San Pedro River Valley and in the Far West, at lake margin sites in Utah, California, and Oregon. In all three areas, climatic equability is reflected by disharmonious distributions of warm-loving and cool-loving animals. The San Pedro River Valley has the greatest concentration of Clovis sites in North America: the Escapule, Lehner, Naco, Murray Springs, and Leikem sites (Haynes 1970). The Lehner Ranch site, which was discovered after heavy rains in 1955, has provided geological, paleontological, and palynological data relevant to the Clovis period (Antevs 1959; Haynes 1970; Mehringer and Haynes 1965). The invertebrate fauna and pollen recovered from basal deposits at Lehner Ranch suggest that cooler and wetter conditions existed prior to about 9500 BC. Paleoindian materials are not associated with these deposits. An erosional disconformity, indicating drying, separates these levels from those containing Clovis artifacts and the remains of mammoth, bison, horse, tapir, camel, rabbit, muskrat, and bear. Clovis materials extend from a layer of coarse gravels, interpreted as a stream channel, through various layers of stream- or spring-deposited sediments to the base of a black organic silty clay loam soil. Pollen from these deposits shows a relatively high abundance of pine, oak, and juniper, indicating climatic conditions that are somewhat cooler and wetter than those of today. Pollen samples from the black organic layer above the Clovis deposits, as well as from beds lying conformably above the organic layer, show a decrease in tree pollen. Otherwise, both pollen and invertebrate fauna from the Clovis levels, as well as from the beds above them, indicate desert grassland and riparian communities. The pollen spectra can be duplicated in the vicinity of modern *cienegas* (wet meadows), except for higher frequencies of mesquite pollen in the modern examples.

In sum, from those areas for which we have data, Clovis artifacts were deposited at a time when it was drier than the periods before it or after it but wetter than today. The pattern of seasonal variation was also different than it is today in that temperatures did not vary greatly throughout the year.

Following Clovis at Blackwater Draw, there is an erosional disconformity followed by a layer of diatomaceous earth. The diatomaceous deposit signals a rise in the water table and the presence of the shallow, discontinuous ponds in which the diatoms flourished. About halfway through the diatomaceous earth deposit, the pollen spectra show an increase in pine and the presence of some spruce, indicating a reinvasion of woodlands. Folsom and Midland artifacts are associated with the diatomaceous earth. An erosional disconformity and a change in the pollen spectra indicate that drying conditions marked the end of the Folsom occupation. Deposits above the disconformity are carbonaceous silts, suggesting a return to more mesic conditions. Cultural materials within the carbonaceous silts consist of Firstview complex artifacts and artifacts of the Cody complex. The latter occur on the eroded surface of the carbonaceous silt layer.

A series of deep blowouts similar to those of today indicate that a very clear drop in the water table occurred after the deposition of the carbonaceous silts. Cultural materials deposited above these silts belong to the Archaic and more recent time periods. Unlike the situation at Blackwater Draw, at the Lehner Ranch site in the San Pedro River Valley, there is no evidence of reforestation following Clovis. Rather, conditions approximate those of the modern period but before very recent erosion. A desert grassland with *cienegas* seems to have prevailed.

In the Great Basin sites of the Far West, the situation is similar to that of the San Pedro River Valley. A period of desiccation terminates the Clovis occupation, and continued drying ensues. In the Far West, complexes of the Great Basin Stemmed Point tradition follow Clovis but are found in more diverse environmental settings than Clovis. These observations indicate that the climatic change toward more mesic conditions, which produced the diatomaceous earth at Blackwater Draw, was either a local phenomenon or, more likely, a local response to a global weather change that had different consequences farther west (cf. Wendorf 1970). Importantly, there are no Folsom, Midland, Agate Basin, or later Paleoindian artifacts at Lehner or the other San Pedro River Valley sites. Subsequent manifestations in the area relate to the Chiricahua and later phases of the Cochise tradition.

The paleoenvironmental data available are sufficient to indicate that the earliest specialized Paleoindian points (Clovis) appear slightly after a period of greatly increased effective moisture, but when there was more surface water in the west than there is today. Clovis occupation is ended with an episode of further drought. Following Clovis in the west, including the San Pedro River Valley, the environment becomes drier and there is an increase in diversity of projectile points and they are found in more different kinds of settings. In the eastern portion of the Southwest, Clovis is also ended by a period of drying. This, however, is followed by wetter conditions, and the appearance of Folsom and Midland points. At Blackwater Draw, pollen data suggest a gradual drying after Folsom and Midland, but no marked depositional changes correlate with the introduction or disappearance of any of the other later, specialized Paleoindian complexes. In all three areas discussed, a major period of desiccation seems to coincide with the less-specialized complexes of the Archaic. Importantly, the timing of this desiccation is not synchronous, but seems to occur first in the south and west and later in the east and north.

VARIETY OF PALEOINDIAN COMPLEXES, PALEOINDIAN ECONOMY, AND SETTLEMENTS

As a general characterization, Paleoindians were hunters and gatherers, exercising highly mobile strategies and manufacturing sophisticated hunting tools and a diversity of items appropriate for butchering game and for processing hide, wood, and bone. They lived in the Americas when conditions were unlike those of modern-day hunters and gatherers in three ways: (1) Climate patterns were unlike those of today in having less difference in temperatures on a seasonal basis; (2) Pleistocene megafauna were available as game animals for at least the early part of the period; and (3) there were no farmers whose settlement strategies and population growth patterns differed from and perhaps conflicted with those of hunters and gatherers.

This section provides a more detailed, though in some cases, more speculative, view of the economic activities and settlement distributions of Paleoindian groups. The information presented is based on studies that go beyond descriptions of sites to deal with issues other than chronology. Not all Paleoindian complexes have been examined within this larger cultural context. There has been considerable interest in the economy and settlement patterns reflected by both Clovis and Folsom. Far less attention has been given to the Southwestern manifestations of Plainview, Firstview, and Cody, or to the economy represented by the Western Stemmed Point tradition. The emphasis on Clovis and Folsom in this discussion is therefore an artifact of archaeological interest, reflecting the results of recent studies.

Clovis artifacts are clearly associated with mammoth, but the association has been interpreted in two directly contradictory ways. On one hand, Clovis hunters are seen as having been so effective that they are credited with the extinction of mammoth. On the other hand, Clovis hunters are seen as depending on scavenging mortally ill mammoth. In one popular, though extreme view (Martin 1973), Clovis hunters are characterized as highly efficient, relying nearly exclusively on mammoth, and causing the extinction of mammoth in North America. Paul Martin's (1967) overkill hypothesis of Clovis hunters exterminating mammoth depends on Clovis peoples relying exclusively on mammoth, consuming 10 pounds of meat per day, and consistently wasting meat. It also generally minimizes the difficulties involved in killing mammoth (Agenbroad 1980; Frison 1978; Haynes 1980). In fact, the faunal assemblages from Clovis processing sites indicate a more diverse economy.

On the Great Plains, Clovis fauna from Clovis sites include mammoth, bison, and pronghorn antelope as primary game species. Present but fewer in numbers are camel, horse, musk ox, mountain sheep, and jackrabbit (Frison 1993). At the Lehner Ranch site in the San Pedro River Valley, the calcined and burned bones of bison, tapir, bear, muskrat, and rabbit indicate that these animals were part of the Clovis diet. Knowledge of the degree to which the Clovis economy incorporated wild plant foods is difficult to obtain from the archaeological record because of the problems of preservation of the plants themselves and the lack of specialized, diagnostic equipment used in plant processing (Grayson 1988:114). Nevertheless, in those instances where excavation strategies have been directed toward recovering such evidence, they have been successful (Johnson 1987; Meltzer 1993). Most archaeologists (e.g., Haynes 1980; Hester 1975; Judge n.d.) agree that plant foods must have been an important part of the Clovis economy.

Some Clovis sites are interpreted as "unsuccessful" kill sites. As noted, these include Naco, Escapule, and Domebo. At these locations, there are low frequencies of artifacts, high frequencies of complete Clovis points, which is unusual because they would be recovered by hunters in the course of processing the kill, and no butchering tools. These sites suggest that in some cases, mammoth were wounded by Clovis hunters but were not recovered.

The difficulty of killing mammoth with the tool assemblage available to Clovis hunters has been addressed by George Frison (1988, 1993). Although there are no living mammoth on which to experiment, studies of frozen mammoth and African elephants indicate the two species are comparable in physiology, especially in size and the thickness of their hides. With this in mind, Frison participated in culling elephant herds at Hwange National Park, Zimbabwe, in 1985 and 1986. The purpose of the experiments was to determine whether hunters using replicas of Clovis tools could "deliver a projectile point with sufficient velocity to regularly and predictably inflict lethal wounds on animals of all ages and both sexes. Experiments had to be limited to elephants either mortally wounded or killed in the culling operations. There was no provision for experiments on live animals nor would such activities have been allowed in any of the National Parks in Zimbabwe" (Frison 1988:773).

Frison (1988) determined that Clovis weaponry was reliably effective. Replica Clovis points were hafted to wooden foreshafts that in turn were fitted into wooden shafts. An atlatl (spear thrower) was also of wood. Frison found that the shape of the Clovis point was effective in penetrating the hide and allowing penetration of the foreshaft and shaft. The flutes thinned the point in the location where the point contacts the nock, allowing an adequate sinew binding that secures the point but does not inhibit penetration. The most important problem with the stone Clovis point was unobserved and unanticipated flaws in the stone of which it was made and which appear only under stress. Frison found that replica large biface reduction flakes were appropriate for skinning, removing the flesh from the elephants, and disarticulating major long bones. These operations were accomplished without leaving cut marks on the bone.

The physiologies of African elephants and the mammoth are similar. The behavior patterns of the mammoth can only be based on African elephants; however, in an inferential manner. Nevertheless, Frison's (1988) discussion is illuminating. He notes that Clovis weaponry could be used regularly to inflict crippling and/or lethal wounds on members of African elephant family units. "However, a strategy of direct confrontation of a family of elephants with Clovis weaponry seems highly improbable. Clovis weaponry cannot be depended on to drop quickly and reliably a charging matriarch or even younger and smaller elephants as can be done using high-powered rifles" (Frison 1988:782). This observation surely further weakens the suggestion that Clovis hunters alone were responsible for the annihilation of the mammoth. Finally, the recent radiocarbon determinations, discussed above, demonstrate that Clovis was not the temporally limited "event" required by the Pleistocene overkill model. The archaeological record suggests that Clovis hunters were like most modern hunters and gatherers in being "generalists." This means that they used the game, and probably plants, in their environment in about the same proportions as their natural abundance. This is what nearly all modern hunters and gatherers do, except for those living under very specific constraints that do not apply to the Clovis period (Meltzer 1993). Another observation made about Clovis is that the raw materials used to manufacture Clovis points and other tools was uniformly of very high quality, sometimes, though not always, obtained from very great distances from where it was ultimately deposited. Given

Frison's (1988) observations about the problem of undetected flaws causing weapon failure in Clovis spear points, the efforts required to obtain the best lithic material possible make a great deal of sense.

By the end of the Clovis period, mammoth and other Rancholabrean fauna were extinct in North America. Later Paleoindian sites in the eastern Southwest are associated with now-extinct, large forms of bison and with modern fauna. Paleoindian sites following Clovis in the chronology of the western Southwest are associated exclusively with modern fauna. It is not likely that humans played a key role in exterminating mammoth. Guilday (1967) cites habitat destruction, range restriction, and competition as more likely immediate causes of the extinction of Pleistocene megafuana, including mammoth. Clovis mammoth sites occur stratigraphically above episodes of desiccation and contain evidence of more moisture than do succeeding levels. The apparently very dry conditions preceding Clovis may have stressed populations of mammoth so severely that perhaps only with a very long interval of ameliorated conditions might their numbers have been replenished. It is worth emphasizing that the stress factor of critical importance would have been diminishing abundance of the long grasses that mammoth foraged on, not a lack water *per se*. The paleoenvironmental data indicate that tall grasses did not reestablish themselves over extensive areas of the West after Clovis times. The extinction of mammoth seems to have been a somewhat delayed response to a dry interval and the failure of the appropriate habitat to be reestablished for a sufficient length of time to allow recovery. By the time grasslands (mixed and short) were well established on the Great Plains, the animals that were in a position to benefit from this situation were bison.

Western Stemmed Point Tradition

Following Clovis, there is the first real separation of Paleoindian strategies. In the Far West of the Great Basin and adjacent areas, the next evidence of human beings is the Western Stemmed Point tradition specifically manifest in the Southwest by the San Dieguito complex. Sites of the Western Stemmed Point tradition occur over an enormous area and date to between 11,200 and 7,500 years ago. Obviously, with that much time and space involved, there is considerable variability in site location and evidence of subsistence resources. Only the most generalized overview can be presented here. Grayson (1992:242–247) suggests that following climatic desiccation that ends the Clovis period, most sites occur in valley bottom settings, in locations where there were lakes, marshes, and streams. In these locations, shallow water resources continued to be important to hunters and gatherers. These include fresh water mollusks; bones of small artiodactyls such as mountain sheep, deer, and pronghorn; and cottontail rabbits; jackrabbits; lizards; and small rodents. Western Stemmed Point tradition sites are also found in upland areas. At these slightly higher elevations, fauna remains are much the same, although mollusks are generally lacking. The assemblages invariably contain rabbits, jackrabbits, and small rodents, with artiodactyl bones present but varying in frequency (see also Douglas, Jenkins, and Warren 1988). Given the small size of the fauna, one might expect evidence of plant processing; however, while there are occasional grinding stones found in Western Stemmed Point contexts, they are rare. This is in contrast to somewhat later periods of time.

In Arizona at Whitewater Draw, the archaeological manifestation that postdates the Clovis period is the Sulphur Spring stage of the Cochise cultural tradition. Waters (1986) suggests that it is contemporary with early San Dieguito and other Western Stemmed Point tradition sites. The Sulphur Spring stage artifacts, however, are dominated by ground stone objects, milling stones, and handstones, indicating the importance of plant foods, particularly seeds, in the diet. The flaked stone assemblage, though smaller, consists primarily of unifacial, percussion flaked scrapers, domed or planoconvex scraper cores, cobbles, and a few, rare bifacial point or knife fragments.

In the cases of the Western Stemmed Point tradition sites and the Sulphur Spring assemblages, there is an obvious, early reliance on small game, with plant foods seemingly important at the Sulphur Spring sites. The assemblages seem to reflect ways of life that occur throughout the Americas at the end of the Pleistocene and that archaeologists call Archaic (see Chapter 4), and it has been suggested that the name Archaic be applied. I think it is more reasonable to retain the term Archaic for assemblages that are clearly post-Pleistocene in age but recognize that the generalized economies, in which a variety of small animals, invertebrates, and sometimes plants were used, are very old indeed. In my view, the term *desert culture*, as defined by Jennings (1957, 1973) and meaning a way of life *not* an ethnic or other specific group of people, might be used. For the Southwest as a whole, the pattern in the West and southern Arizona is one in which resource use and mobility would have been completely different than it was to the east where a tradition of big game hunting continued. I suggest that the persistence of two distinct ways of life, with different energetic needs and demographic outcomes, set the stage for the much later adoption of agricultural strategies.

Folsom and Later Hunting Strategies

The Folson complex follows Clovis in the east. Both mountain sheep and American elk have been recovered at Folsom sites, but they were far less important than bison (Frison 1993). At most, but not all, Folsom kill sites, bison were apparently maneuvered into natural traps, such as steep-sided sand dunes or lava tongues, where they were dispatched. The strategy of stampeding bison into jump situations was not widely used in Folsom times. Frison (1974) points out that the successful use of the bison drive and jump depends on the size of the herd rather than the skill of the hunter. Bison are quite agile, and unless there is a mass of animals sufficient to prevent a change in direction, bison confronted with a jump situation will simply turn around. Frison (1980:76) suggested that the larger bison associated with the Folsom complex "may have been more of a solitary or small-herd type than the present-day, smaller, large-herd oriented form" for which "maneuvering of small groups of bison into arroyo and sand dune type of traps may have been more favorable for procurement."

On the other hand, the numbers of bison at Folsom kill sites are not always small. Todd and others (1990) report the minimum number of bison at the Lipscomb site in

Texas was 55 animals, about twice the usual number. Although it is tempting to link the highly specialized Folsom point with a high mobility strategy of bison hunting, it must be remembered that not all aspects of the Folsom complex are equally specialized and that nonfluted points accompany these assemblages, often associated with the bison. Detailed information on other resources used by Folsom hunters comes from the Lindenmeier site, near Fort Collins, Colorado (Roberts 1935a,1936; Wilmsen 1974). Lindenmeier shows use of a diversity of smaller fauna species including rabbits, cervids, canids, and pronghorn.

Following Folsom, there was a bifurcation in hunting strategies on the northern Plains that lasted for about 1000 years. The contrast is between the open Plains and the adjacent foothills and mountains. Frison (1992) argues that on the open Plains, groups were focused on bison hunting, whereas in the foothills and mountains, the hunting and gathering ways of life predominated. On the open Plains, bison was the primary game animal with pronghorn a very distant second. The late Paleoindian complexes of the open northern Plains show an emphasis on large communal kills. For example, at the Olson-Chubbock site in Colorado (Wheat 1972), 191 bison were driven into an arroyo in a single incident kill. Bamforth (1991) suggests that preparation for large communal hunts must have involved the production of a large number of projectile points at a time of the year when there were many other items to make and tasks to accomplish. Under these circumstances, he maintains, the task of making the points may have been allocated to a group of particularly skilled individuals. This, in turn, would produce assemblages of points at communal kills that are more standardized than those in general use in such groups and might, in fact, be the work of only one or a very few individuals.

It is difficult to determine how frequently, either within a year or over decades, such large communal kills took place on the northern Plains. Frison (1978, 1980) has shown, on the basis of the age distributions of the animals killed, that most very large drives took place in the late fall and winter. His examination of butchering practices from several sites indicates that animals were cut into units and stored in frozen ground. Whether or not such events could have been carried out year after year is not known. Grass range that is essential for bison is limited by the amount of water available. Throughout the Holocene, there is evidence that long-term cycles of aridity periodically reduced bison numbers (Guthrie 1980; Reher 1977b), which would have made the mass drives impossible.

On the other hand, in addition to the Olsen-Chubbock site, Clary Ranch and the Lipscomb and Scottsbluff sites were not late fall or winter season kills (Todd *et al.* 1990). Rather, these sites reflect kills in the warm season. At both cold and warm season mass kills, there is no evidence that bison meat was processed for storage, for example by boiling out bone grease (Frison 1982b; Todd *et al.* 1990). This suggests that food processing strategies may have been the same for Paleoindian groups year round. As has been noted, seasonal variation during Paleoindian times was not as marked as it is today. Although modern hunters and gatherers in temperate climate regions of the earth follow seasonal patterns of movement for food resources, movement in the late Pleistocene may have been more responsive to locational variations in food supplies than to seasonal variation (Bamforth 1985; Todd *et al.* 1990). At Olsen-Chubbock and other large Paleoindian kill sites, some animals were partially butchered and others not butchered at all. Frison (1982b) suggests that limited use of many foods available during the warm season is to be expected. However, as a whole, Paleoindian sites reflect more waste of meat than do later Plains Indian hunting strategies, and complete processing for storage is not a feature of even winter kills. Again this suggests that modern hunters are not necessarily appropriate analogs for the late Pleistocene when, despite larger populations of hunters, competition for resources may have been lower on regional scales.

In the foothills and mountains adjacent to the open Plains, the strategy appears to have included about equal amounts of hunting and gathering. It is not until after Folsom that mule deer occur in Paleoindian sites. In the foothills and mountains, mountain sheep, mule deer, and bison occur in about equal frequency. Sites in the foothills and mountains tend to have fewer diagnostic artifacts, more variety in projectile point styles represented at a single site, and more use of local sources for stone for tools than Plains sites.

The southern Plains and the adjacent Southwest in general are much drier than the northern Plains and there another strategy may have developed that was in some ways closer to the foothill and mountain hunting and gathering patterns than to hunting on the open Plains. Some of the lack of diversity in Paleoindian complexes in the Southwest may reflect conditions of local and regional aridity that were not felt further north or east.

Hence, there may have been times when bison hunting was not an appropriate economic strategy on the southern Plains or in the Southwest simply because the animals were not present in sufficient numbers. When archaeologists have more control over the temporal placement of the late Paleoindian complexes, it may be possible to correlate the appearance of complexes such as Plainview and Cody with westward shifts in range-land. Similarly, the absence in the Southwest of Hell Gap, Alberta, and other northern Plains complexes may be correlated with regional cycles of aridity and the contraction of range-land to the north. Further, the organization of hunting in the Southwest should have involved less task-group specialization, probably resulting in fewer highly formal projectile point types.

Looking at the Southwest as a whole, there would have been three different hunting and gathering trajectories followed after Folsom times. One pattern is reflected in the Sulfur Spring and Desert Stemmed Point complexes. This pattern is associated with hunting relatively small game and collecting marsh-dwelling species, especially plant foods. Another pattern, found in the eastern Southwest, resembled the foothill and mountain pattern of the northern Plains. This pattern seems to reflect dependence on about equal amounts of hunting diverse game with some gathering and bison hunting during those times when bison were available. A third pattern, dependent on bison hunting, would have been restricted to the open Plains but was probably only possible intermittently because of aridity on the southern Plains and consequently inadequate numbers of bison.

PALEOINDIAN POPULATIONS

It is tempting to view Clovis as providing the generalized hunting and gathering technology that was basic to later developments in the Southwest. The San Dieguito tradition of the west may represent a continuation and intensification of that aspect of the technology involving emphases on smaller game and plant processing. Folsom and the later Paleoindian complexes would involve specialization in the direction of heavy utilization of large game resources. There is, as yet, no convincing evidence for much human use of the central-southern Southwest after Clovis until the later Archaic cultures, such as the Chiricahua Cochise. The apparent gap in occupation may not be real in that it might reflect failure to recognize a nonspecialized technology as ancient, or an absence of exposed landforms of appropriate age. On the other hand, if the gap in occupation is real, as it currently appears to be, detailed analyses of the paleoclimatic and vegetation structure of the south-central Southwest will be necessary to a preliminary understanding of its cause.

In the foregoing discussion, no mention has been made of population size or population density throughout the Paleoindian period. This reflects the difficulties involved in trying to derive such information from the archaeological record: very few sites are exposed for study; estimates of the numbers of people that may have been camped at a particular site or who may have participated in a bison kill are extremely difficult to derive; and establishing precise contemporaneity among sites is beyond the currently available dating techniques. In most instances, archaeologists rely on ethnographic analogies that may not be appropriate. Except in unusual environmental situations (such as the Aleutian Islands) population densities for modern hunters and gatherers are quite low (not more than one person per square mile) and band size usually does not exceed 50 persons. Because Paleoindian groups were hunters and gatherers, it is generally assumed that group size and population densities were comparable. It must be remembered, however, that modern hunters and gatherers have been circumscribed by the expansion of agriculture and generally occupy environments of low productivity, a situation in which population densities should be regulated at low levels. If equally low population densities are assumed for the Paleoindian period, two interpretive problems arise. First, late Paleoindian kill sites that have been the subject of careful excavation indicate that a tremendous amount of meat was used, and second, we may develop an unrealistic view of population size during that time that agricultural crops were accepted in the Southwest.

Among the best studies, both outside the Southwest, are Wheat's (1972) discussion of the Olsen-Chubbock site and Frison's (1974) analysis of the Casper site. The Olsen-Chubbock site represents a bison jump and Casper a bison trap. Olsen-Chubbock is interpreted as a single incident late spring kill. The Casper site represents a late fall kill that may have taken place over a period of several weeks. The amount of meat recovered in each case is, however, astounding if small group size is also assumed. The amount of meat taken, as estimated from disarticulated bone and butchering marks, is given as 69,000 pounds (31,400 kg) of usable meat, tallow, and internal organs from

Olsen-Chubbock and 42,000 pounds (19,000 kg) of meat, exclusive of hearts, tongues, livers, and some other internal organs for Casper. Even if it is assumed that large communal hunts were relatively infrequent, and that meat was stored in frozen ground for winter supplies, it is nearly impossible to account for the processing and consumption of the amounts of meat indicated using population estimates based on modern hunters and gatherers.

The second problem in accepting small group size and low population density for the Paleoindian period relates specifically to recent discussions of the origins and spread of agriculture, topics that are presented in detail elsewhere in this book. Briefly, however, following a line of reasoning expressed most clearly by Ester Boserup (1965), some archaeologists argue that economic change, particularly change involving intensification of labor, is the result of population pressure (e.g., Binford 1968; Cohen 1977; Spooner 1972) or population/resource imbalances (Cordell and Plog 1979). If population densities are assumed to have been low for late Paleoindian and early Archaic hunters and gatherers, the adoption of agriculture in the Southwest (as well as elsewhere in the world) becomes very difficult to explain. The Southwest is one appropriate laboratory for consideration of this question.

One aspect of the economic data of the Paleoindian period of the Southwest has implications for considerations of population dynamics. Following Clovis, groups in the western Southwest seem to have been dependent on plant foods and nonmigratory, relatively small game, whereas groups in the eastern Southwest depended on bison, supplemented by plant foods and small game. Assuming that economic mainstays have some effect on the rate of overall population growth and levels at which semi-stable population balances are reached, conditions existed for markedly different demographic patterns to have developed and maintained by groups participating in each economic system (see Stuart and Gauthier 1981 for an extended theoretical discussion of this observation). In the west, population growth depended on the availablity of diverse resources, a situation that was conducive to a slow but steady rate of population increase and one in which an equilibrium is reached at quite low population densities. In the east, population growth and expansion was regulated primarily by the presence of bison, which in turn depended on the rather abrupt expansions and contractions of range-land. Population growth may have been slow, but movement into areas attractive to herds would have been immediate. Recall that although expansion and contraction of bison range may be ultimately related to global changes in climate, these have diverse local effects. (That is, whatever conditions seemed to have caused increased moisture on the Llano Estacado, the synchronous development in the San Pedro River Valley seems to have been desiccation.)

These conditions indicate that when the Southwest is viewed as a whole, the heterogeneity in subsistence economy would produce periodic, sometimes very rapidly occurring situations in which regional population growth and density were at great variance with the available, *average* food supply. Further, the size of territories over which particular subsistence strategies were practiced would have fluctuated considerably as well. Although the economic context was markedly different during Paleoindian times, the regional interplay among different economic systems is a feature of the

Southwest. For example, in modern times, Pueblo agriculturalists and Navajo pastoralists, each with different rates of population growth and different territorial and mobility requirements, are interdigitated within the Southwestern landscape. It is most tempting to view the heterogeneity as characteristic with no one strategy being able to dominate either the entire region or portions of it for a great length of time.

The archaeology of the Paleoindian period, beset with problems of low site visibility, poor preservation, and imprecise chronology, nevertheless provides a perspective for understanding the inherent diversity of the Southwest. During Paleoindian times, this diversity was illustrated by the differences among hunting and gathering economies. There were differential emphases, for example, on plants as opposed to game, and a variety of strategies appropriate to the behavioral characteristics of the different animals hunted. The economic strategies had consequences for group mobility and population growth that became increasingly important through time. The diverse natural environment of the Southwest and the human environment characterized by different levels of mobility and population growth provide much of the context for understanding the significant developments of the Archaic and later periods.

CONCLUDING SUMMARY

The historical role of the Southwest in Paleoindian archaeology, the excellent conditions of preservation, and site visibility continue to bring researchers to the area. The earliest undisputed Paleoindian artifacts are those of the Clovis complex, but remains from Sandia and Pendejo caves in New Mexico may be older. There is a sequence of Paleoindian projectile point styles and complexes in the eastern Southwest that is well-documented from about 11,000 years ago to about 7,500 years ago. There is chronological overlap within this sequence and considerable variability in the types and styles of artifacts representative of each complex. In the western Southwest, Clovis is followed by a stemmed point tradition that also lasts until about 7,500 years ago.

Throughout the Paleoindian period, climatic fluctuations and subsequent environmental change produced landscapes that are unlike those of today. These underlie different patterns of surface water, vegetation, and animal distributions across the Southwest. The human responses to these included variety in subsistence strategies, mobility, group size, settlement patterns, and population growth. These, in turn, are reflected in the kinds of sites and tool assemblages found throughout the region as a whole.

Archaeological and experimental data indicate that Paleoindians were effective hunters who used a variety of techniques and sophisticated stone, wood, and bone tools to kill, process, and, where possible, cache stores of meat. In those parts of the Southwest where big game were locally extinct, the people were efficient hunters of smaller game, collectors of nonmarine shell fish, and gatherers of plant foods. Some of the variety in tool kits and assemblages relate to the way they were used, such as the kinds of tasks performed. Other sorts of variety reflect different tool-making patterns that were conditioned to some extent by the requirements of group mobility and locations of lithic source materials. Variety in tool types and styles also reflect some specialization in tool production and ritual behavior.

From nearly the beginning of the archaeological record, the Southwest supported several different large-scale regional patterns of subsistence, mobility, and probably also social organization, group size, and population growth. These provided the bases for changes in succeeding periods.

Chapter-opening art: Folsom point (illustrated by Marjorie Leggitt, Leggitt Design).

CHAPTER 4

The Archaic Period: The Hunting and Gathering Spectrum

In southwestern archaeology, the term Archaic refers to both a period of time and a way of life. The southwestern Archaic dates from about 5500 BC to about AD 200. During this time, the climate and vegetation of the Southwest came to assume their modern patterns. Economies were based on hunting modern game animals and gathering, with an emphasis on small- and medium-sized game animals and some plant foods. Archaic stone tool assemblages are less specialized and less distinctive than those of the Paleoindian period. Archaic archaeological sites are not highly visible. When they lack diagnostic artifacts, they are difficult to place chronologically. During the Archaic, southwestern peoples obtained cultivated crops that had been domesticated far to the south in Mesoamerica. This economic change eventually profoundly altered the course of southwestern culture history. Following a discussion of archaeological research on the southwestern Archaic and the ways that archaeologists classify Archaic assemblages, this chapter explores the environmental contexts—both natural and cultural—within which domesticated crops were acquired.

INTRODUCTION

In American archaeology, the term Archaic refers to a stage in culture history characterized by hunting and gathering in the context of modern environmental conditions (Willey and Phillips 1958) (Figure 4.1). In contrast to the Paleoindian period, there is an increased dependence on plant foods. The game animals hunted are all modern species. The tools used by Archaic hunters and gatherers reflect this economic base; ground stone tools were used for plant processing, and projectile points are less specialized. Woodworking tools, drills, and tools made of locally available materials characterize Archaic assemblages.

This description of the Archaic represents a pan-North American, in fact, a worldwide post-Pleistocene pattern. Throughout the world, as the Pleistocene climates gave way to those of the recent period and vegetation and fauna distributions came to approximate their present form, hunters and gatherers relied increasingly on locally available resources. Depending on the character of the local environment, these resources varied from one area to another. In coastal and riverine settings, the economic base included fish and shellfish in addition to plants and terrestrial game. In the far north, hunting continued to predominate because the short growing season precluded the use of much plant food. In inland, temperate areas of the world, there was a greater reliance on plant foods than on game. In those parts of the world where agriculture developed, Mesolithic or Archaic ways of life end with the appearance of domestic crops. In the Americas, the Archaic is viewed as a prelude to agricultural Formative stage cultures (Willey and Phillips 1958).

ARCHAEOLOGICAL RESEARCH OF THE ARCHAIC

The definition of the Archaic as a stage of development, beginning with the end of the Pleistocene and ending with the development or adoption of agriculture, links a way of life with temporal duration, creating an immediate conceptual problem. At one end of the scale, some archaeologists term the Desert Culture of the Far West that dates as early as 7000 BC as Archaic because the economic base included plant foods and associated ground stone tools (Fowler and Jennings 1982; Willig and Aikens 1988). At the other end of the period, societies throughout the Americas that did not practice agriculture could be considered to bring the Archaic to the modern period.

Irwin-Williams (1967) (Figure 4.2) was one of the first to address this problem, arguing that analysis and synthesis must take place on two different levels. On one level, analysis is what she terms *integrative.* Integrative analysis recognizes material traits that link Archaic southwestern complexes to the Archaic way of life in general and to adaptation to the desert environment of the West. On the integrative level, Desert Culture and the southwestern Archaic reflect similar ways of life. The second level of analysis is termed isolative. Here one attempts to select those traits and patterns of distribution that set the culture history of one area apart from other areas. For example, although the presence of projectile points is indicative of hunting and is therefore important to analysis at the integrative level, a particular form or style of point may have a limited temporal or spatial distribution and so be germane to the isolative level of analysis. Irwin-Williams proposed that by about 3000 BC four interacting traditions had crystallized into a distinct culture area in the Southwest (Irwin-Williams 1979). Collectively, these are referred to as the Picosa culture, an acronym

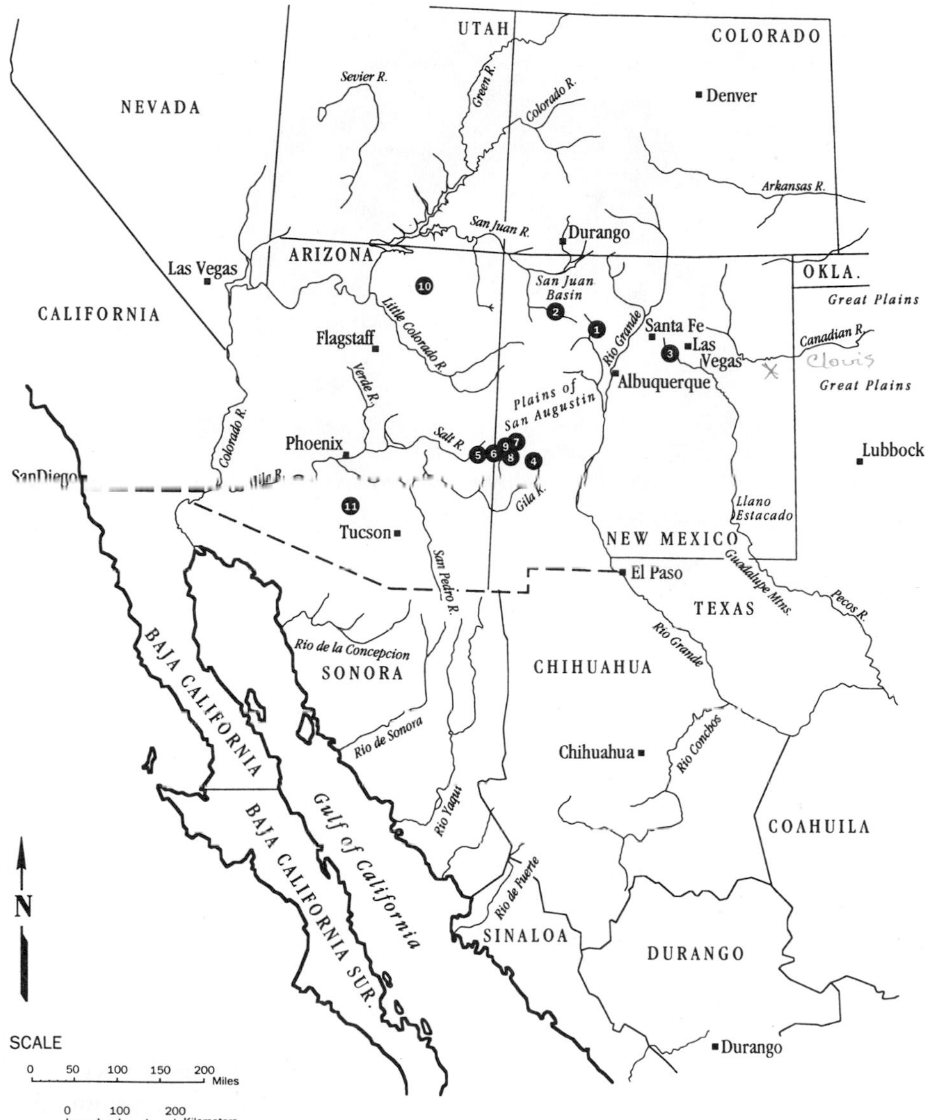

FIGURE 4.1 Archaic sites of the Southwest. ❶ Arroyo Cuervo; ❷ Chaco Canyon (Atl Atl Cave); ❸ Galisteo Basin; ❹ Bat Cave; ❺ Cienega Creek; ❻ Wet Leggett Site; ❼ Tularosa Cave; ❽ Cordova Cave; ❾ Pine Lawn Valley; ❿ Black Mesa; ⓫ Ventana Cave. (map by David Underwood).

derived from the names of three well-known Archaic complexes: Pinto Basin, Cochise, and San Jose. Irwin-Williams concluded that isolative analysis showed that the Southwest could not be subsumed within the general category of Desert Culture. Today, the

FIGURE 4.2 Cynthia Irwin-Williams (1936–1990) conducted important research on every time period in Southwest archaeology. Her synthesis of the Archaic is a landmark achievement. Her interest in the Archaic inspired a generation of young archaeologists (photo courtesy of George Agogino).

term Picosa is not much used but a three or four part culture-historic framework is retained and is discussed below.

A similar way of defining the Archaic depends on distinctive artifact types that have been assumed to be of culture historical, as opposed to functional, significance. In this view, the beginning of the *Late* Archaic is distinguished by the appearance of side-notched projectile points, while the end of the Archaic coincides with the use of pottery (see discussions in Haury 1950; Huckell 1984; Vierra 1994b; Wills 1988). As with the preceding distinctions, this definition also conflates chronology with developmental criteria. In this case, with the additional, sometimes inappropriate, assumption that classes of artifacts or artifact types are primarily *stylistic* rather than functional. On the contrary, in some cases, two projectile point *styles* may be the same tool in different stages of reduction. The relative frequency of one or the other in a particular subregion may have more to do with the distance to sources of raw material than to changes in artifact style over time. The problem of mixing the description of a way of life with criteria that include a period of time has not been resolved in the Southwest. In general, the name Archaic is retained as a stage within which specific cultural historic sequences have been defined (Vierra 1994b; Wills and Huckell 1994).

During the Archaic, domestic crops were first accepted by southwestern peoples. Ultimately these had a tremendous impact on southwestern cultural developments. Because hunting and gathering was a stable economic base for hundreds of thousands of years of human evolution and because agriculture generally requires more labor than hunting and gathering and is also often more risky, there must have been important reasons for the initial cultivation of crops. The southwestern data are applicable to situations in which domestic plants were accepted or acquired rather than to conditions of initial domestication (Minnis 1992); nevertheless, an understanding of the context of agricultural adoption in the Southwest facilitates evaluation of some current theoretical arguments in anthropology that treat the worldwide spread of agriculture.

Before the 1970s, archaeological interest in the southwestern Archaic focused on documenting the history of the use of corn as well as its genetic relation to corn from other parts of the Americas. For this reason, the most intensively studied sites were rock shelters and caves where corn and other perishable items may be preserved. Cave sites sometimes preserved basketry, fiber sandals, rabbit-fur blankets, and split twig figurines. Some of these objects are much like those used by later Native Americans. Consequently, archaeologists attempted to link particular Archaic assemblages with later cultures and with their ethnographically known descendants. It is likely that cave sites reflect only a part of the yearly activities of the peoples using them. It was not until the 1980s that enough radiocarbon dates had been obtained from southwestern sites to demonstrate the contemporaneity of specific assemblages found in cave sites with those from open sites of the same age (Huckell 1984).

Detailed knowledge of the Archaic is critical to the culture history of the Southwest and to general issues of cultural evolution. Nevertheless, the archaeology of the Archaic suffers from many of the same problems as Paleoindian archaeology: sites may be ephemeral because they are remains left by mobile hunters and gatherers; sites are obscured by more recent geological deposition, and many undoubtedly were destroyed by ancient episodes of erosion; the artifactual remains at Archaic camps may include few, if any, temporally diagnostic tool types; and Archaic chronology and paleoenvironmental reconstructions are far less precise than is desirable. In addition, because the fauna associated with the Archaic are modern and because Archaic peoples emphasized plant processing, hence a non-specialized tool kit, the great age of Archaic sites is not generally obvious to casual observers. Finally, there has been somewhat less archaeological interest in the Archaic than in either the Paleoindian period or later periods. This seems to reflect the fact that Archaic sites are not important for establishing the time of the first human occupation of the Americas, which stimulated much of the Paleoindian research, and the fact that the remains are not as rich (in ornamental items or impressive architecture) as are later sites.

Nevertheless, within the last 15 years, archaeologists have obtained a great deal of new information about the southwestern Archaic. Major credit for this must be given to Cynthia Irwin-Williams, whose own interest in the Archaic dated to the 1960s (Irwin-Williams 1994). Not only did she develop the first, still widely used, framework for describing Archaic southwestern assemblages, but she interested generations of her students in pursuing research topics dealing with the Archaic. Abundant new data include many recently excavated sites, many radiocarbon determinations, some refined paleoenvironmental reconstructions, regional syntheses, and novel explanatory frameworks. These are emphasized in the discussions that follow.

SYSTEMATICS OF ARCHAIC CULTURE HISTORY

Isolative Analysis

The isolative level of analysis and synthesis undertakes to organize data in a way that is informative about culture history. Isolative analysis attempts definition of cultural units (ethnic groups or perhaps tribes), and cultural continuities and discontinuities within defined regions, generally smaller than the Southwest as a whole. Archaeologists have little developed theory that permits specifying the range of artifacts appropriate for defining cultural identity. It is sometimes assumed that cultural identity is reflected in artifact styles. Not only are there very few studies and virtually no theory that guides delimiting the conditions under which stylistic behavior does or does not relate to cultural identity, there is little information that is useful for defining purely stylistic attributes of stone tools (Weissner 1983 is a useful beginning in this task).

Southwestern archaeologists working with Archaic data recognize these problems and some others that confound classification and synthesis. These include the fact that within any single area and time period, a diversity of projectile point types were in use, but the range of variation in assemblages is often left undescribed in the literature. In some older studies, temporally diagnostic artifacts were illustrated in outline form for ease of recognition. Using outlines, however it is almost impossible to distinguish artifacts if these are similar in form but of different sizes. Another problem is that many archaeologists, working with surface collections in the context of field surveys (which is often the case in cultural resources management or public archaeology) fit site or artifact descriptions to existing categories without independent radiometric information. An almost uniform failure to consider the stage of reduction represented by artifacts is also a continuing problem. Finally, on a conceptual level, archaeologists have given little thought to the underlying assumption that Archaic hunters and gatherers lived in marked and bounded territorial units, an assumption that is most likely false (Shelley 1994; Vierra 1994b; Wills 1988b).

Definitions of subregional traditions, which is synthesis at the isolative level, allow archaeologists to present descriptive frameworks that encapsulate their ideas about spatial and temporal relations among assemblages. The framework developed by Irwin-Williams (1973, 1979) with subsequent modifications (Beckett and MacNeish 1994; Irwin-Williams 1994; Warren 1984; Waters 1986) is widely used in the Southwestern literature organizing a great deal of previously existing information. The

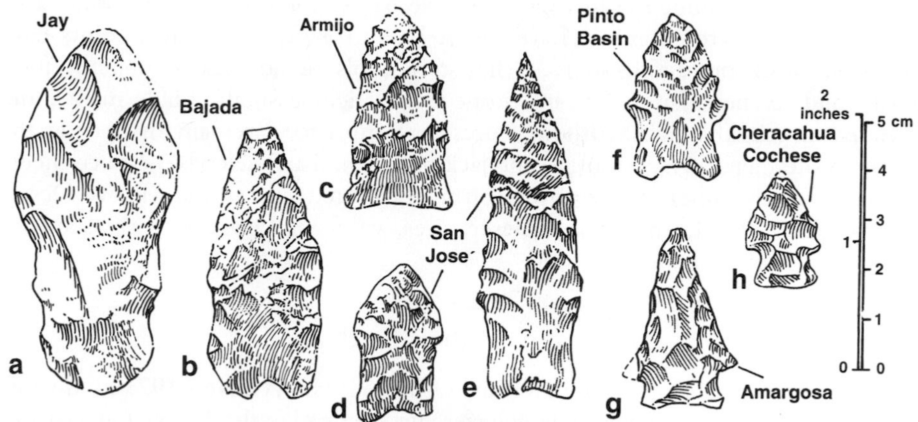

FIGURE 4.3 Archaic points include (a) Jay; (b) Bajada; (c) Armijo; (d and e) San José, of the Oshara tradition; (f) Pinto Basin; (g) Amargosa of the Western tradition; and (h) Chiricahua Cochise of the Southern tradition (illustrated by Marjorie Leggitt, Leggitt Design).

traditions are presented here but with far less detail or precise chronological refinements than might be desirable. Chronologies are being refined nearly continuously, and that refinement is reflected in the fact that a few new syntheses (Huckell 1993; Matson 1991) correlate changes in one subregion of the Southwest with those in other subregions and have moved toward using a simplified scheme—of Early, Middle, and Late Archaic—to refer to the Southwest as a whole.

SUBREGIONAL TRADITIONS

San Dieguito-Pinto, the Western Tradition

The westernmost Archaic tradition is referred to as the San Dieguito-Pinto tradition. The San Dieguito-Pinto tradition includes the Pinto Basin and Amargosa complexes, which seem to have been derived from the San Dieguito tradition discussed in the previous chapter. Materials relating to this tradition are distributed from southern California to southern Arizona and, within the Great Basin, north to southern Nevada. Most of the sites with Pinto Basin points are from the eastern Great Basin, where they are dated between about 6300 and 4300 BC (Grayson 1993:254). Rogers (1958) described the Amargosa tradition in terms of three phases (Amargosa I, II, and III) that as a whole derived out of San Dieguito. The Amargosa sequence does not appear often in southwestern literature today. Rather, a Great Basin tradition that also derives from San Dieguito but features phases labeled Early Death Valley (with Pinto style projectile points) and Late Death Valley (with Gypsum style points) is sometimes used (Warren 1984). The most distinctive artifacts following San Dieguito are Pinto Basin points, Gypsum Cave points, and those of similar styles (Figure 4.3). Pinto Basin points are generally straight-stemmed points with concave bases. Some points are shouldered, and serrated edges are common. Late Death Valley, or Gypsum Cave, points have convex bases with contracting stems. Other stone tools include flake chopperes, flake scrapers, and scraper planes. Ground stone items include small cobble manos and shallow-basin grinding slabs. Although preservation of food remains is poor at the many open sites, leporids (cottontails and jackrabbits) and artiodactyls (bighorn sheep, mule deer, and antelope) were recovered from excavated sites in the Mojave Desert (Douglas *et al.* 1993). In the Mojave Desert sites, artiodactyl remains decreased over time but the variety of fauna increased.

Oshara, the Northern Tradition

The northern Archaic tradition, termed Oshara (Irwin-Williams 1973), is divided into a number of sequential phases, which were first defined in the Arroyo Cuervo area of north-central New Mexico. With the range of dates suggested by Irwin-Williams (1973, 1979), these are Jay (5500–4800 BC), Bajada (4800–3200 BC), San José (3200–1800 BC), Armijo (1800–800 BC), and En Medio (800 BC–AD 400). Oshara sites are also found in the San Juan Basin, the Rio Grande Valley, the Plains of San Augustin, south-central Colorado, and southeastern Utah.

As noted in the preceding chapter, Irwin-Williams considers the Jay complex to be Archaic rather than Paleoindian, and the Jay phase is the first phase of the Oshara tradition. Diagnostic Jay phase artifacts include large, slightly shouldered projectile points, well-made leaf-shaped knives, and well-made scrapers. Other archaeologists (Judge 1982; Wait 1981) consider the Jay materials to be Paleoindian. The issues involved relate, in part, to interpretations of projectile-point morphology and different interpretations of culture history (Vierra 1994b). Irwin-Williams (1973) contended that Cody represents the last Paleoindian manifestation in the northern Southwest and that Paleoindian peoples moved north and east onto the Plains sometime around 6000 BC. She further averred that there was a hiatus in occupation in the Oshara area, followed by a movement into the area of Archaic peoples whose closest cultural affiliation was to the west. This movement was to have occurred at about 5500 BC. Including Jay within the Paleoindian tradition, other authors suggest continuity between Paleoindian and Archaic peoples. The issue has not been resolved in recent discussions (Vierra 1994b), nor is it resolved here. The argument itself, it may be suggested, demonstrates the difficulty of culture historical reconstructions, including differentiation of ethnically distinct groups, by comparing assemblages of stone tool forms and projectile point styles. These will reflect many factors and conditions such as tool function, reduction sequence, distance from lithic source material, kind of lithic source material, numbers of skilled flint knappers, context of use, reuse, and discard. Under circumstances that must be specified (but as yet have not been) one or more or all of these may also serve as markers of cultural identity. It is not appropriate, however, to simply assert or assume which ones do.

The Bajada phase tool assemblage shows general continuity with the preceding Jay phase. Bajada points (Figure 4.3) are distinguishable from Jay points by the presence of basal indentation and basal thinning. In addition, the assemblage contains "increasing numbers of large chopping tools and poorly made side scrapers on thin irregular flakes" (Irwin-Williams 1973:7). Small cobble-filled hearths and earth ovens have been found at Bajada phase sites in the Arroyo Cuervo area. In some areas, such as the Plains of San Augustin, archaeologists have described the presence of Bajada points in assemblages characterized as Chiricahua Cochise (Whalen 1975). Chiricahua Cochise belongs to Irwin-Williams' southern tradition, so it is unlikely that Bajada points represent cultural markers.

The San José phase includes materials previously described as the San José complex (Bryan and Toulouse 1943) and the Apex complex (Irwin-Williams and Irwin 1966). San José points (Figure 4.3) are similar to Bajada points but are more frequently serrated along the edges, smaller in total length, and tend to have a shorter stem-to-blade ratio. The tool kit is dominated by poorly made side scrapers on thin flakes and large chopping tools. Well-made side scrapers and bifacial knives of the earlier Archaic complexes are rare or absent. Ground stone implements include pounding stones, shallow basin grinding slabs, and manos made on small cobbles. Large, cobble-filled subsurface ovens are features that have been found at some sites.

The succeeding Armijo phase includes materials that have been termed the Lobo complex (Bryan and Toulouse 1943), the Santa Ana complex (Agogino and Hester 1953), and the Atrisco complex (Campbell and Ellis 1952). Irwin-Williams (1973:11) describes the projectile points as "evolved late forms of the old serrated San José style with short widely expanding stems and concave or (later) straight bases" (Figure 4.3). Other artifacts that relate to the isolative level are not well-defined, but small bifacial knives, flake scrapers, drills, and choppers or pounders are documented. Most of the discussion of the Armijo phase treats the appearance of maize in the Oshara tradition at this time.

The En Medio phase is characterized as showing considerable continuity with the preceding phases, although there is an increased emphasis on ground stone tools and further stylistic variability in the total assemblage. En Medio phase projectile points are described as "variations of stemmed corner notched forms which trend through time toward the use of increasingly long barbs" (Irwin-Williams 1973:13). The final phase of the Oshara scheme is the Trujillo, which represents a continuation of trends established in the En Medio phase, with the introduction of "limited quantities of plain gray ceramics" (Irwin-Williams 1973:13). The importance of the dating of the En Medio and Trujillo phases is that together they span the transition from Late Archaic to Early Anasazi. The emphasis placed on continuity in artifact inventories indicates that Irwin-Williams sees the Oshara tradition as a development in place from early Archaic to the Pueblo-Anasazi sequence.

Cochise, the Southern Tradition

The southern Archaic tradition in the Southwest, the Cochise, was first identified in southeastern Arizona (Sayles and Antevs 1941). The phases within the tradition are the Sulphur Spring, discussed in Chapter 3, Chiricahua, and San Pedro. Sayles (1983) proposed a "Cazador" phase to follow the Sulphur Spring phase; however, the suggestion has not been generally accepted (Eddy and Cooley 1983; Waters 1985). Although dated to the Archaic in general, more precise dating of the Chiricahua phase is problematic. Matson (1991:139–142) accepts Waters' geological correlation and radiocarbon dates from White Water Draw as evidence for dating the Chiricahua phase to 7500 BC, or 8000 to 6000 BC. Whalen (1975), on the other hand, cites a series of radiocarbon dates from the San Pedro River Valley that would place the Chiricahua phase to between 3500 and 1500 BC (Whalen 1971, 1975). Dates for the San Pedro phase are given as 1500 to 200 BC with the caveat that the upper date is subject to revision (Sayles 1983; Whalen 1971, 1975).

The Chiricahua phase is known from the San Pedro River Valley and Ventana Cave. Chiricahua Cochise assemblages are often dominated by cobble manos and shallow metates and a large number of quite amorphous scrapers and choppers, all of which relate to plant processing and are therefore uninformative with regard to culture historical reconstructions. Projectile points are formally diverse; however, many are side-notched with concave bases. Others are diamond-shaped and may be serrated or unserrated; some have short contracting stems (Dick 1965a; Irwin-Williams 1967, 1979). The types of points that have been labeled Chiricahua Cochise are so diverse that the category is not very useful.

At the time that it was defined, the Cochise tradition was the only available model for most of the Southwest. Assemblages from the Cienega Creek site on the San Carlos Reservation (Haury and Sayles 1947), from the Wet Leggett site (Martin *et al.* 1949) in western New Mexico, and from Bat Cave on the Plains of San Augustin (Dick 1965a) have all been categorized as Chiricahua Cochise. Wills (1988a:12–29) argues persuasively that none of them are. Surface finds have been reported from north-central and northeastern Arizona, the Moquino locality of northwestern New Mexico, and the Galisteo Basin of north-central New Mexico (Irwin-Williams 1979: Irwin-Williams and Beckett 1973; Lang 1977b). Vierra (1994b) suggests that these surface assemblages are precisely the ones that have been "fit in" to existing type names and might as easily have been classified in the Great Basin series (see also Irwin-Williams 1994). Although the distribution of Chiricahua Cochise artifacts has been suggested to extend into northern Chihuahua and Sonora (Irwin-Williams 1967), some illustrated material from northern Mexico (Rinaldo 1974) appears to resemble the succeeding San Pedro Cochise.

Projectile points typical of the succeeding San Pedro phase are large, low-corner or side-notched points with straight to convex bases (Figure 4.3). In some assemblages, points with bulbous convex bases and serrated points occur. Other chipped stone artifacts include a variety of scrapers and denticulates, bifacial knives, and choppers. Ground stone metates have a deeper basin than those of the Chiricahua phase, and mortars and pestles occur, though infrequently (Irwin-Williams 1967).

Chihuahua, the Southeastern Tradition

Beckett and MacNeish (1994) proposed a southeastern Archaic tradition that they call the Chihuahua Tradition, and date from about 6000 BC to about AD 250. The sequence is based on "40 + radiocarbon dates" (Beckett and MacNeish 1994:341), 16 obsidian hydration dates, stratigraphic interpretations of excavation data from rock shelter and open sites excavated by the authors and others, and MacNeish's seriation of 200 Archaic sites recorded from surveys. Their results are very difficult to interpret but are nevertheless presented here. They term the earliest manifestation the Gardiner Springs complex (not phase), which they state is the beginning of a tradition different from others defined in the Southwest. Artifacts from the Gardiner Springs complex include Jay, Bajada, and Abasalo points that resemble Oshara tradition artifacts, and a variety of scrapers, grinding stones, basin milling stones, anvil mortars, and pebble hammers that are unlike Oshara artifacts. The Keystone phase is characterized by a variety of projectile point types, including Pelona, Amargosa, Pinto, Todsen, and Gypsum-Almagre, bifacial side blades, pebble choppers, milling stones, manos, and metates. The Fresnal phase includes Chiricahua, Nogales, and Augustin points along with Armijo and San José points of the Oshara Tradition, but La Cueva, Fresnal, and Maljamar points are dominant types. There are many more manos and metates than mullers and milling stones. Corn and squash are present. Finally, the Hueco phase is similar to that previously defined (Irwin-Williams 1979; Taylor 1966). Projectile points include types with contracting stems and strong barbs, notched and stemmed points, and Hatch and Hueco types. Disk-shaped choppers, wedge-shaped manos, trough metates, and cobble pestles are considered diagnostic.

Beckett and MacNeish (1994) do not include materials referred to as the Coahuila complex (Taylor 1966) from Coahuila and eastern Chihuahua in Mexico and west Texas. A great many diverse wooden objects are characteristic of the Coahuila complex. The lack of similar material from the sites north of the Mexican border (which may be due to preservation conditions) makes it difficult to use these for specific comparisons. Although not numerous in Coahuila assemblages, the projectile points include forms found in New Mexico and Texas (Irwin-Williams 1979; Taylor 1966).

Discussion

In sum, Irwin-Williams (1979) suggested that during the Archaic the Southwest consisted of four interacting cultural traditions: the San Dieguito-Pinto, the Oshara, the Cochise, and an eastern tradition. As a group, the four are considered to differ from Archaic traditions elsewhere in North America (e.g. the Plains Archaic, the Archaic of northern California, the Archaic of the Columbia Plateau). Irwin-Williams also viewed the four as ancestral to later traditions in the Southwest: The San Dieguito-Pinto tradition leading to the later Colorado River peoples, the Oshara tradition as ancestral to the Anasazi of the Colorado Plateaus and the Rio Grande Valley, and the Cochise tradition as leading to the later Mogollon culture (Irwin-Williams 1967, 1979). These specific relationships have been debated (e.g., Haury 1976; Schroeder 1979a).

There are a few attempts to collapse the subregional schemes into a pan-southwestern scheme. As Huckell (1993) points out, there is little agreement about whether to divide the Archaic into two, three, or five time periods. Further, each scheme uses a different set of artifacts as criteria marking chronological divisions. Nevertheless, Huckell expresses hope that the value of a truly regional perspective will grow. Huckell makes an additional important observation. He notes that if the beginning of the Archaic is defined on the basis of the appearance of ground stone milling tools, then the Archaic begins throughout the Southwest by at least 6000 BC. If the end of the Archaic is the last preceramic cultural manifestations in the Southwest, then Basketmaker II and San Pedro are both the final Archaic stages in their areas; they are contemporary and agriculture is present in both.

Given the plethora of terms, projectile point types, complexes, phase names, and disputes about dating, and assemblage similarities and differences, I would applaud virtually any scheme that offers simplification. On the other hand, I believe that archaeologists wrestling with the many-faceted problems of the Archaic will have to pull their categories apart rather than combine them in order to make progress. I do not mean that archaeologists should become category *splitters* as opposed to *lumpers* in the paleontological sense. I suggest that if we archaeologists are to understand variation in projectile points and other artifact categories, we will need to invest in understanding stone tool technology and function.

For example, Bradley (1991) notes that nearly all Archaic point types were produced by the same sequence of percussion thinning, followed by selective, nonpatterned pressure shaping. The complicated sequences of flake removal seen in Paleoindian projectile point types, especially Clovis, Folsom, and Cody, is not characteristic of Archaic assemblages. Throughout the Archaic, at least on the Plains, flake blanks become the more numerous form for production of points, and although bifacial cores continue to be used, unifacial and multidirectional flake cores become more common (Bradley 1991:294–295). These trends indicate that for Archaic knappers, not every part of the production processes ends in a completed tool. What conditions of availability of raw materials, knappers' skill, and time to manufacture stone tools would lead to these changes? Similarly, we know that Paleoindian and Archaic projectile points were hafted on spears, probably thrown with an atlatl. At the same time, most southwestern Archaic sites lack bison as well, of course, as the long-extinct mammoth. Were Paleoindian and Archaic hunting tactics for mule deer and bighorn sheep the same and the same as those used for bison? Were points used to kill bison at Archaic kill sites damaged or broken in the same way as broken points discarded at camp sites that lack bison remains?

Focusing on the technology of only one element of projectile point form—the hafting element—has suggested a model that is very much in agreement with the approach suggested here. Musil (1988) suggests that three major hafting traditions known in North America (fluted/lanceolate, stemmed, and notched) allowed increasingly effective killing instruments to be made that also served to prevent damage to wooden shafts and made for more efficient use of broken projectile points. He suggests that the major change from fluted/lanceolate points to contracting stemmed points involves a change in design to a socketed shaft. Notching is associated with the beginning of the Archaic in some areas of the West. Elsewhere, it came in later but it remained the dominant form into recent times. Notched points allow resharpening in the shaft, as do other hafting traditions; however, "the major advantage of notching is that damage to the haft element usually occurs across the notches on impact, which means there is much less waste of lithic material when the basal fragment is discarded. The recovery of the remaining point and the addition of new notches further up the blade edges allows the point to be re-hafted more frequently and successfully than previous traditions" (Musil 1988:382). Rather than viewing changes in projectile point traditions across North America as the result of movement of ethnically distinct populations or as differences in environmental or economic adaptations, Musil suggests that these may be seen as the adoption of more efficient hafting designs that made previous methods obsolete (Musil 1988:385).

Before attributing changes in tool assemblages to cultural identity or preference, we must also know a great deal more about stone tool technology and patterns of group mobility. This final topic has been considered in the recent literature based on models derived from the distribution of resources and patterned use of resources among ethnographically documented hunters and gatherers (Binford 1980, 1982; also see the papers in Vierra 1994a). The topic is not usually examined in the way that it was presented (Binford 1980, 1994). In essence, Binford (1980) argues that on a global basis, edible resources pattern with Effective Temperature. Latitude is sometimes used as a surrogate measure for Effective Temperature. If such patterning is seen as a continuum, there is extreme seasonality in availability of resources at one end of the spectrum and continuous availability at the other. Put very simply, in the tropics, resources are available year-round, although they may pattern differently spatially from year to year. In Arctic regions, food resources are available for brief seasons on an annual basis. Further, Binford proposed that human economies adapted to these two extremes are organized differently. At the extreme of marked seasonality, human groups are organized in what he terms a collector mode. When resources are continuously available throughout the year, organization follows what he terms a forager pattern.

Group mobility is one dimension along which the differences between collector and forager can be observed. Collectors organize their activities in space so that they are *logistically* situated with respect to the availability of key resources. Throughout a year, this will involve one or a few base camps from which smaller task groups are organized and deployed (Binford 1980). Where resources are not strongly patterned seasonally, groups as a whole move from one resource patch to another, as needed. If all other things are equal, which of course is never true, and our archaeological landscapes include all archaeological sites ever produced, then logistically organized societies would produce and we would find a few base camps and many functionally differentiated sites. The latter would pattern spatially in a consistent way, as long as environmental conditions were relatively constant. Foragers, on the other hand, would produce many similar sites representing base camps with very few patterned sites that result from task groups.

Another dimension along which the patterning of modern hunter-gatherer societies can be modeled, using Binford's (1980) distinction, is with respect to assemblage content. The pure logistic mobility pattern should be associated with what Binford has termed *curated* technologies (Binford 1979). If resources are available at known locations seasonally on a quite predictable basis, then hunters can and do make stone tools for future use, caching them for the time of year in which they are needed. This will involve being able to tailor specific tool types for tasks that are known to be required in the future and planning moves so that raw materials can be obtained and saved for tool production. At the other conceptual extreme are foragers whose moves from week to week are not predictable. In these cases, technologies are expected to take advantage of whatever materials are available that will do the job. There will be no opportunity to cache tools for the future since a return to a cache cannot be predicted. Binford terms this extreme end of the continuum an *expedient* technology.

Binford (1994) proposed these dimensions of resource structure, group mobility, and technology as analytical devices. What one does with any model is vary one or two dimensions at a time and see what the outcomes are with respect to model predictions. In this case, one would first examine the ethnographic record to see how the interacting dimensions are patterned. If this produces interesting results, one would then examine the archaeological record, allowing for and controlling such archaeological problems as site visibility, potential sampling errors, and changes in resource distributions over time. Unfortunately, few archaeologists have used this model as a tool for analysis. Rather, the extremes have become categories into which archaeological sites are fit. Hence, one reads of logistic sites and logistic technologies and perhaps worse, one reads analyses of lithic tool production and discard that were conducted to determine whether assemblages at a given site or sites are logistic or curated.

There are exceptions to the dismal categorizing picture. For example, there are studies that compare the archaeologist's descriptions of site types with artifact data obtained at different sampling intensities (Vierra and Doleman 1994). These studies found that multiple site typologies reflect different sampling intensities, not functionally different sites. There are also studies that are concerned with the fact that models based on ethnographic or even archaeological studies of modern hunters and gatherers document seasonal changes in economy. Whether or not similar responses are used by hunters "in response to long term, aseasonal, climate change" must be determined (Shelley 1994).

In Chapter 3, suggested relations between changes in hunting patterns and changes in climate and environment were discussed. Paleoclimatological data available for the Archaic indicate that, although there were periods of relatively more or less moist conditions, overall climatic perturbations were less severe than they had been during Paleoindian times. Yet, the onset of the Archaic marked a change from relatively large-game hunting, at least in the eastern Southwest, to small-game hunting and more use of plant food. Toward the end of the Archaic, domestic crops were accepted by southwestern peoples. The environmental context of this economic change is of interest in order to evaluate proposed explanations for the acceptance of agriculture.

PALEOENVIRONMENTAL CONSIDERATIONS

The Natural Environment

The same considerations that pertained to environmental reconstructions of the Paleoindian period also apply to the Archaic. In essence, some climatic changes may have been quite rapid, and climatic fluctuations of global or continental scale are expected to produce diverse local effects. Unfortunately, too few areas have been the subject of intensive climatological studies relevant to the Archaic, and major interpretive issues are unresolved. Although lacking ideal precision, studies of hydrology, soil formation, pollen, macrobotanical remains, and faunal material are available for developing characterizations of the environments of the Archaic. One particularly useful source of information is from packrat nests that are fossilized and preserved in rock shelters and caves. The utility of these nests derives from the fact that the animals forage for nesting material within a radius of about 100 m of their nests and the nest itself can be fractionated and radiocarbon dated (Van Devender *et al.* 1987).

Whither the Altithermal? The beginning of the Archaic coincides with environmental changes in many parts of the Southwest and adjacent areas. At one time, initiation of the Archaic was defined by these changes. In an exceedingly influential scheme, geologist Ernst Antevs (1948) correlated postglacial climatic changes on a continental, if not global scale. His three temperature-age scheme (Anathermal, Altithermal, and Medithermal) spans the time from about 7000 BC to the present. While the proposed Anathermal and Medithermal climates are not much referred to, gaps in the geological and archaeological record were and still are interpreted as evidence of an extremely hot and dry Altithermal, dated between about 5500 and 2900 BC. Throughout the Southwest, evidence of past erosion that might be correlated with the suggested time interval for the Altithermal were assumed to date to between 5500 and 2900 BC because of Antevs' scheme.

The nature of the Altithermal climate continues to be debated. Whether an episode of climate change occurred at 5500 BC must be determined independently for subregions. For the Llano Estacado on the southeastern edge of the Southwest, older paleoclimatic reconstructions, based on pollen (Oldfield and Schoenwetter 1975), paleopedology (Holliday 1982), and alluvial stratigraphy (Haynes 1975), have been revised (Johnson and Holliday 1986). The revisions include radiometrically dated Archaic deposits that suggest two episodes of aridity, separated by 500 years during which the local climate was moist, all within the time span of the Altithermal. Shelley (1994) cautions that while these changes are assumed not to be associated with seasonality, the events may reflect a change in the seasonal patterning of rainfall rather than an overall change in precipitation and temperature. Studies of fossil packrat middens from the nearby Guadalupe Mountains (Van Devender *et al.* 1979) show that the juniper-oak woodland that had been present until about 6000 BC was later replaced by desert scrub and grassland communities.

For the Great Basin, at the extreme western edge of the Southwest, studies summarized by Grayson (1993:216–217) show that the 3000 year drought of Antevs' Altithermal did not exist. Rather, dates of the onset of increased aridity vary from one place to another, as do dates for the onset of less arid conditions. The studies indicate high variability within a generally arid period of time. On the eastern margins of the Great Basin in southeastern Arizona, alluvial paleoenvironmental reconstructions are available for the San Pedro River Valley (Haynes 1987), the Cienega Valley (Eddy and

Cooley 1983), and the Sulphur Spring Valley (Waters 1987). These can be examined along with pollen studies (Mehringer 1967, among others), and packrat midden analyses (Betancourt *et al.* 1990). All of these show geological cycles of cutting and filling that are most likely not synchronous. Some are not synchronous for different portions of the same basin. Nevertheless, all of these do show a trend toward filling that began sometime after about 2500 to 2000 BC and lasted until the mid AD 1800s. The record of pollen and macrobotanical remains from the packrat middens reveals a significant change at about the same time: 2400 to 2000 BC. The underlying climatic change is suggested to have been from warm, wet summers and cool, dry winters to warmer, wetter winters and more dry and warm summers.

Several lines of evidence indicate a trend toward increased moisture at times during the later Archaic. However, whether this increase in moisture was synchronous over the entire Southwest (as was suggested by Antevs' proposed Medithermal) is not known. Nevertheless, geological studies (Powers 1939) indicate that the San Augustin Basin reached its maximum depth of about 30.5 m of water at about 1500 BC, followed by a lowering of the level of the lake thereafter. In the Estancia Basin, Lake Meinzer formed at about 2000 BC and became desiccated shortly before 100 BC (Bachuber 1971). Macrobotanical material from packrat middens and microtine rodents from Atl-Atl Cave in Chaco Canyon, New Mexico, indicate wetter and warmer conditions at about 2200 BC. Finally, although these variations in climate should not be ignored, it is worth reiterating Haynes' observation that, "for the Llano Estacado from about 2000 BC to the present, there were cycles of erosion, deflation and dune activity alternating with alluvial deposition and soil development, but amplitudes of the cycles did not approach those of the previous cycles" (Haynes 1975:83). Hence, the cultural events of the Late Archaic, especially the adoption of crops, took place during periods of climatic fluctuations that were less severe than those of preceding periods. As with the Paleoindian period, annual patterning in preciptation and temperature were not always as they are today, and the consequences of these shifts seem to have been relatively great.

Varied Cultural Responses

Obviously, human cultural responses to changes in the natural environment vary. Some of the variation reflects different regional environments and some different human environments. For example, until recently, it was thought that with the onset of a dry interval initiating the Early Archaic there was complete abandonment of the Northern Plains. The discovery and excavation of sites in the adjacent foothills and intermontaine basins demonstrate continuity in occupation from the terminal Paleoindian into the Early Archaic (Frison 1991). In this case, although resources diminished on the High Plains, the foothills continued to provide an adequate setting for big game hunters.

On the very southern margins of the Llano Estacado, the Mustang Springs site also provides evidence of a very dry period beginning shortly after 6000 BC, when surface water became increasingly brackish and springs failed (Meltzer 1991). By 4800 BC, surface water had disappeared. The water table dropped about 3 m in about 200 years, leaving a dry, wind-scoured lake bed. In spite of this, the area around Mustang Springs was not completely abandoned. As the water table dropped, Archaic peoples excavated at least 86 wells over 200 years. The wells range from 0.10 m to 1.65 m in depth. Archaic wells are also known from three neighboring Southern High Plains sites. The wells demonstrate that the region was not abandoned, but as Meltzer (1991) notes, we do not know whether the well diggers were people living year-round in the area or whether they ventured out to the area only episodically to collect local resources.

In similar settings on the southern and southwestern portions of the Southwest, there are a series of low elevation river valleys; the Cienega, Santa Cruz, and San Pedro valleys. These valleys seem to have experienced a period of arroyo formation and erosion between about 4000 BC and 2000 to 1000 BC, reflected in erosion channels and associated deflated surfaces. There is scant evidence of human use of these valleys at this time. At about 2000 BC, however, water tables began to rise and may have risen very quickly. At first, streams were probably intermittent with wet meadows in parts of the valleys. Fine alluvium was deposited on valley floors. With the change in conditions, human occupation increased dramatically. Those peoples settling in the valleys excavated wells and other kinds of pits. They also planted corn (Eddy and Cooley 1983; Huckell and Huckell 1988). In this case, it can be suggested that the river valleys of southern Arizona, like those of the Llano Estacado, may have been visited only occasionally during the Early and Middle Archaic by peoples living at slightly higher elevations in the surrounding areas. When the valleys provided an attractive and new niche for settlement, they were settled very quickly (Huckell and Huckell 1988).

Settlement data are also available for the San Juan Basin and Black Mesa, both in the Colorado Plateaus region. In these settings there is evidence of use during the Early and Middle Archaic but it consists almost entirely of isolated surficial artifacts (projectile points) and a few sites with no storage pits or other evidence of sustained occupation. The lithic materials that were used for tools are frequently obsidians and cherts from relatively distant sources. Limited botanical data suggest the use of seeds of ricegrass, dropseed, and weedy plants such as goosefoot, pigweed, and mustard. Saltbush was used for firewood. The botanical and artifactual data suggest periodic use of these areas only during the summer. At other times, people were presumably elsewhere, at higher elevations and in proximity to the sources of stone from which they made their tools. This picture changes dramatically with the Late Archaic, when there is a dramatic increase in the number of sites, the size of sites, and the number of storage features and well prepared hearths, along with a nearly exclusive use of locally available raw material sources. Late Archaic populations also had corn (Parry *et al.* 1994; Toll and Cully 1994).

In sum, there were changes in climate throughout the Archaic, although these were not as extreme as during the Paleoindian period. Desiccation did occur, as suggested by Antevs' Altithermal, but it was not the uniform "long drought" he described. Human populations seem to have adjusted by shifting their patterns of mobility and using resources when these were available. None of the occupations seem part of an annual seasonal round, so familiar in studies of modern hunters and gatherers in temperate settings. The technology of digging wells, perhaps to extend the length of time a site could be occupied, was widespread. Well digging can be viewed as a pre-adaptation to subsequent farming practices. The size of the territory through which a single group of people might have moved in the course of a decade is not known, of course, but there is every reason to suggest that it was larger than the territories documented ethnographically for hunters and gatherers.

The Cultural Environment

The situations to which human societies adapt include the contexts created by other societies as well as those of the natural environment. The amount of territory through which a particular group moves in order to gather and hunt may in part be determined by the movements of neighboring groups of people. In addition, the cultural environment can provide information relevant to technological change. A cultural environment that includes agricultural communities is qualitatively different from one constituted entirely of hunters and gatherers. The former provides information about alternative sources of food, whether or not these are accepted. This section first examines the general demographic context of Southwestern Archaic adaptations, which has implications primarily for group mobility. Then it explores the qualitative content of the cultural environment.

Demography Although Archaic peoples of the Southwest were hunters and gatherers, there is no doubt that corn was known and used to some extent within all groups by Late Archaic times. Questions about populations in the Archaic are not divorced from theoretical concerns about the conditions under which hunters and gatherers accept domestic crops. Virtually all extant models about plant domestication or the acceptance of crops depend on a developing imbalance between human populations and their food resources. The models are discussed in detail in the next chapter. Here the questions serve to focus interpretations of population dynamics in the Archaic.

Throughout the Southwest, population seems to have increased during the Archaic. There are more documented Late Archaic than Early Archaic sites, and although this may be a consequence of the higher probability associated with finding sites as time depth decreases, Late Archaic sites are also much larger, contain more features that indicate an increase in intensity of occupation, and are distributed throughout a greater range of environmental zones than are Early Archaic sites. It is unlikely that the increased number of sites is a result of greater group mobility because some Middle Archaic sites contain the remains of houses, suggesting somewhat more residential permanence (Cordell and Gumerman 1989). In contrast to this generally accepted view, Wills (1995) suggests that it is the move toward increased sendentism, rather than population growth per se, that makes Late Archaic sites more visible. Nevertheless, without population growth, it is unlikely that a more sedentary population would also have been as widely distributed as Late Archaic sites seem to indicate that they were.

Our understanding of population dynamics as well as of subsistence and settlement has changed considerably in the past decade as a result of new discoveries of open sites (as opposed to cave or rock shelter sites), some with architecture. The new data of open sites are from the Tucson Basin; the Keystone Dam on the Rio Grande Valley near El Paso, Texas; the San Juan Basin; and the Northern San Juan River drainage (Ezzo and Deaver 1996; Gilpin 1992; Huckell 1990, 1995; Huckell *et al.* 1994; O'Laughlin 1980; Reed and Reed 1992; Vierra 1994b; Whalen 1994; Wills 1995). The discoveries have been made primarily in the context of contract or cultural resources management archaeology and the use of innovative testing techniques such as augering, removing massive amounts of overburden with mechanical equipment, and water screening and/or fine screening tremendous quantities of soil.

As a result, small, shallow, circular to oval pithouses (with floors excavated about 0.5 m below the ground surface) are now known from half a dozen Southwestern sites that are dated by radiocarbon to the period between about 3200 and 2000 BC. At most sites, the number of excavated houses is quite small. The imprecision of radiocarbon dating and the lack of super-positioning of houses generally does not allow determining how many houses at a site were occupied simultaneously. In the case of the Keystone Dam sites near El Paso, coring suggested that houses were clustered in groups of two to five units, so that several families may have lived at the site at the same time. Further, although the houses were simple brush huts with mud floors, the floors had been refurbished several times, indicating that the sites were revisited over time (O'Laughlin 1980; Whalen 1994).

Houses at higher elevation sites, on the Colorado Plateau, usually have interior storage pits as well as hearths. By the Late Archaic, about 1500 BC, there are many more sites with shallow pithouses in the low Basin and Range areas and at higher elevations. Corn is present at almost all of these sites and others throughout the Southwest. Archaeological questions that emerge from trying to understand population dynamics during the Archaic concern the degree and kind of residential mobility reflected by pithouse and cave sites. The issues include knowing whether different kinds of sites reflect seasonal occupation or short-term sedentism over several seasons, whether the sites indicate repeated use over time, and the numbers of people who might have occupied a single small house or an entire site. Inevitably, these questions become questions relating to subsistence and settlement systems.

Subsistence and Settlement Throughout at least the early half of the Archaic, southwestern peoples were mobile hunters and gatherers. Between about 1500 and 1000 BC, Archaic peoples thoughout the Southwest incorporated corn in their diets. Information about Archaic subsistence is available from two sources—perishable material that is preserved in rock shelter sites, and carefully extracted plant fossils recovered from open sites. Neither of these two sources of data is entirely unambiguous.

While floral and faunal remains from rock shelters are the more robust evidence of past subsistence, there are problems that should be recognized. Cave sites may represent the loci of seasonal activities or other special uses and therefore not contain the entire range of foods used by Archaic peoples. In addition, not all of the floral and faunal materials recovered at caves are the result of human deposition. Raptorial birds and mammalian carnivores introduce animal bones as well, and special techniques should be employed to distinguish these from cultural deposits (Thomas 1971). Controlled experiments (Gasser and Adams 1981) indicate that differential destruction of plant remains by bacteria and rodents may occur. In general, plants with dense inedible parts, such as corn cobs, have the highest probability of survival. Plants with dense edible parts, such as small seeds, have less chance of being preserved. Plant foods that are not dense, such as greens and tubers, have the least survival potential (Munson *et al.* 1971).

Techniques of processing and cooking also condition the probability of survival and being identified. Plants that are boiled are less likely to be preserved than those that are charred or roasted because boiling increases the water content and destroys cell structure (Minnis 1981:162–164). Finally, archaeological recovery of plant remains may depend on the use of special techniques such as flotation and pollen analysis, which were not commonly practiced in the past. Fortunately, archaeologists now quite consistently use recovery techniques designed to increase the amount of organic material obtained in excavations. In general, however, many of the problems noted are exacerbated in open sites, where plant preservation is poor. Hence, information about the diversity of plant foods is incomplete.

It has long been noted that Archaic sites are frequently located in deflated sand dunes. This is to be expected, in part, because wind erosion removes the overburden from the Archaic remains. After noting that not all deflated sand dunes expose Archaic sites, Reher and Witter (1977) suggest that within dune areas, Archaic sites were associated with locations of relatively high botanical diversity, reflecting the subsistence pursuits of Archaic groups. This suggestion was tested during survey work in a portion of the San Juan Basin (Allan *et al.* 1975) by comparing the diversity of vegetation found on dunes with Archaic remains with that of comparable land forms lacking Archaic sites. Although the test confirmed the association of Archaic sites and dunes with diverse plant cover, suggested causal relations have been questioned. Soil conditions that act to retain water would also produce the observed diversity, and human populations may have been attracted by the availability of water rather than by the diversity of plants. Archaic wells excavated into dune deposits are well-documented from even the Early Archaic at Mustang Springs and other sites. The availability of water could have attracted game animals that would have been important to Archaic hunters. Questions regarding the kinds of resources Archaic peoples were using at dune locations have been answered for many such sites in the San Juan Basin (Toll and Cully 1994).

Excavation and extensive flotation for plant macrofossils have shown that plant resources at the San Juan Basin open dune sites were dominated by seed remains of two kinds of grasses, ricegrass (*Orzyzopsis*) and dropseed (*Sporobolus*), and a very small array of weedy species, goosefoot (*Chenopodium*) (Figure 4.4), pigweed (*Amaranthus*, mustard (*Descurainia*), tickseed (*Corispermum*), and mallow (*Sphaeracea*). Firewood recovered from hearths was mostly saltbush (*Atriplex*). While there is no reason to expect preservation of greens that may have been used at these sites, the ethnobotanists found that abundant charred seeds of ricegrass and dropseed in all contexts point to a clear and consistent emphasis on these two taxa (Toll and Cully 1994). They conclude that the botanical remains point to "short-term occupation of dune sites at intervals during

FIGURE 4.4 Goosefoot (*Chenopodium*) is one of a few weedy species the seeds of which have been recovered from Archaic dune sites. Goosefoot thrives in disturbed ground and may have grown in habitats created by human camping.

the summer months, and to exploitation of a narrow spectrum" of food and fuel species from the immediate vicinity of the sites. These findings were somewhat surprising in that most archaeologists have come to accept the idea that Archaic peoples used a broad spectrum of locally available food resources rather than just a few species. On the other hand, emphasis on a very few grasses and weedy species is now widely reported from other Southwestern Archaic sites (Huckell 1990; O'Laughlin 1980; Wills 1995). Toll and Cully (1983) point out that both goosefoot and pigweed thrive in disturbed ground and may have been semi-cultivated at camps that people used in successive years.

Plant macrofossils are generally not preserved at sites in the higher elevation piñon woodlands. Where they have been recovered, they again consist of the seeds of the weedy plants and grasses noted. A few of the higher elevation sites have yielded ephemeral structures that are dated to the pre-maize Middle Archaic. Yet, even at these sites that might have been expected to serve as storage for a variety of resources, the same suite of grasses and weeds were recovered (Wills 1995).

Cave sites can preserve macrobotanical and fauna remains far better than open sites. Three very well-known cave sites that have yielded quantities of perishable food items are Bat Cave (Dick 1965a; Wills 1988), Tularosa Cave (Heller 1976; Martin *et al.* 1952), and Cordova Cave (Martin *et al.* 1952). All three sites are in the Mogollon highlands along the central New Mexico-Arizona border. Bat Cave is located on the southeast side of the Plains of San Augustin and overlooks the ancient lake bed. Tularosa Cave is situated on the north side of Tularosa Creek, a tributary of the San Francisco River. Cordova Cave is on the west side of the San Francisco River below Pine Lawn. A diversity of wild plant remains is recorded for the Archaic levels of these caves, including pigweed, grasses, hackberry, goosefoot, walnut, juniper, prickly pear, Indian ricegrass, and yucca. Among the larger animals reported from Tularosa Cave and Bat Cave are bison, pronghorn antelope, mountain sheep, Sonoran deer, and mule deer. The remains of numerous rodents, which may have been introduced by non-human predators, were recovered from the caves. As Berman (1979) noted, the plant resources recovered from the cave sites mature in late summer or early fall. She suggests that either the caves were occupied at that time of year or that they were used to store these foods. An alternative interpretation is discussed in Chapter 5. The similarity of food remains among the three caves is expected because they are in similar environmental settings and in fairly close proximity.

Ventana Cave, on the Tohono O'Odham Reservation near Sells, Arizona (Bayham 1982; Haury 1950; Szuter and Bayham 1989), is a classic Archaic site that provides pre-maize Archaic data from the low Sonoran Desert. The site was excavated prior to the routine use of fine screen and water flotation recovery, nor were plant macrofossils well preserved. A recent reanalysis of fauna from Ventana Cave shows a trend from use of small, locally available animals, mostly rabbits, to increasingly specialized hunting in which larger game, primarily deer, were taken. The trend begins in the Middle Archaic but continues steadily. There is no indication of improved conditions locally for the larger game. Rather, there was a change in the use of Ventana Cave in the overall subsistence-settlement system. Similar changes from hunting diverse small game to fewer, larger game animals accompanies increased sedentism documented in ethnographic literature for many parts of the world. As people become more sedentary, possibly exhausting the local small game populations, hunting parties periodically travel considerable distances to obtain larger, higher valued game (Bayham 1982; Szuter and Bayham 1989).

Tool inventories of Archaic sites indicate a mixed hunting and gathering economy. The grinding stones are important for seed processing, and the numerous large scrapers, chopping tools, and scraper planes indicate reliance on plants in general. Other technological Archaic features related to plant processing and the storing of plant foods include roasting ovens, storage pits cut into cave floors, digging sticks, and baskets. Items related to hunting, in addition to projectile points, include various snares and atlatl fragments recovered from cave sites (Martin *et al.* 1952). The technology of excavating wells, known from the Early Archaic, may have been crucial to the acceptance of domestic crops into some areas.

A list of resources found in sites is not a statement about resource procurement strategies, mobility, or the structure of subsistence activities. In the case of the open sites in the San Juan Basin, short, intermittent occupation during the summer and into fall is reasonably inferred because of the timing of seed crop production and the lack of storage facilities and hearths. Elsewhere, the degree of residential mobility is more difficult to determine and may depend in part upon ethnographic models of hunters and gatherers in similar settings. For example, O'Laughlin (1980), the excavator of the Keystone Dam sites suggests that:

> The mud plaster coating of the houses suggests that they were occupied during the colder part of the year, while the small fire cracked hearths and botanical and fauna evidence indicate a spring, summer, and fall occupation. There is reason to suspect that the houses may have been utilized throughout the year, perhaps as infrequently visited cache or storage sites during the late spring, summer, and fall, and as dwellings during the winter and possibly early spring in an economic regime based on central based, wandering pattern (O'Laughlin 1980:234).

Another investigator comments on the same houses:

> These site type and location data, together with ethnographic models of hunter-gatherer behavior, suggest that Late Archaic populations spent much of their time dispersed over the landscape in small groups. Sites like Keystone Dam seemingly represent longer stays by slightly larger groups at well-watered localities. These aggregations most likely took place in the dry winter when water was at a premium (Whalen 1994:627).

Whalen also notes that Great Basin groups moved to areas where seeds could be gathered in the summer and fall. They would cache these seeds for winter use near where they were gathered. These locations "were sometimes miles away from the winter base-camp locations. The stored food was brought from caches to the winter camp as needed" (Whalen 1994:633).

Whalen (1994), like many other archaeologists, applies the Great Basin model of hunter-gatherer mobility derived from Julian Steward's (1938) wonderfully detailed ethnographic descriptions. Very different inferences will be made, however, if the basis of a model for the Archaic is derived from Western Apache (Buskirk 1986), rather than Great Basin. Western Apache practiced agriculture casually, planting a variety of small gardens in different settings. Their winter camps were located at low elevations where they hunted and gathered. Farming was done at higher elevations. Yet another model may be derived from observations of Colorado River Yuman-speaking peoples who stockpiled wild and cultivated plant food at their winter settlements, sometimes inside houses (Whalen 1994:633). Which is *correct*? Perhaps none of them. This is a situation in which all of the analytical tools we have that can help us determine season of occupation should be applied and may, in the long run, tell us more about a kind of world that does not have ethnographic analogs either because climates were less seasonally structured than they are today or population densities were regionally much lower than they are at present. These questions are discussed in more detail in the following chapter.

In sum, the climatological information available for the Archaic indicates that, although moisture conditions varied, overall climatic perturbations were less severe than they had been during Paleoindian times. The faunal and botanical remains recovered from Archaic sites show that Archaic peoples had detailed knowledge of the available wild foods in the Southwest and that they had the technology to obtain the resources they needed. Nevertheless, there is evidence that corn and squash were being cultivated in many locations throughout the Southwest by about 1500 to 1000 BC.

HORTICULTURE: THE QUALITATIVE ENVIRONMENT

Minnis (1992) makes an important point when he reminds us that the Southwest is an area of what he terms "primary crop acquisition," rather than pristine domestication. Primary crop acquisition can occur differently than domestication. For example, those who acquire domestic crops from elsewhere may also know of a variety of crops and techniques for farming them.

Pristine domestication of the most important New World crops—corn (*Zea mays*), beans (*Phaseolus* sp.), and squash (*Cucurbita* sp.)—occurred in tropical and subtropical Mesoamerica. The relevant data are from the semiarid Tehuacán Valley in central Mexico, from Guilá Naquiz in Oaxaca, and from dry caves in interior Tamaulipas, eastern Mexico (Flannery 1973; Hardy 1996; Long *et al.* 1989; MacNeish 1958, 1967). Very early dates originally published for corn from Coxcatlán Cave in the Tehuacán Valley were taken from charcoal and not the corn itself. That corn has now been radiocarbon dated to about 3600 BC using the accelerator mass spectrometer (AMS) technique (Long *et al.* 1989). Long and others (1989) suggested that the discrepancy between the original dates and the AMS dates was a result of mixed deposits, whereas Wills (1988a) proposed the difference derived from sampling charcoal from arbitrary rather than stratigraphic levels. More recently, a detailed study by Hardy (1996) has not been able to verify the stratigraphic sequence or cultural phases proposed for the Tehuacán sites. Nevertheless, the corn does date to 3600 BC and is derived from *teosinte* (*Zea mexicana*), a tropical grass that is its genetically closest extant relative (Beadle 1981) (Figure 4.5). The early Tehuacán corn is a popcorn with cobs only about 2 cm in length. It could have been used only as a supplement to other food resources. Other cultigens from Tehuacán include bottle gourds (*Lagenaria siceraria*), warty squash (*Cucurbita moschata*), the common bean (*Phaseolus vulgaris*), chili peppers (*Capsicum* sp.), avocados (*Persea americana*), green-striped cushaw squash (*Cucurbita mixta*), cotton (*Gossypium* sp.), jack beans (*Canavalia ensiformis*), tepary beans (*Phaseolus acutifolius*), pumpkins, and summer squashes (both *Cucurbita pepo*). The later corn from Tehuácan was larger (cobs of around 10 cm) and more productive than the earlier varieties. In the Tamaulipas area, the earliest cultigens are bottle gourds, chili peppers (*Capsicum* sp.), and possibly squash (*Cucurbita pepo*). The common bean is the next cultigen to be included, but corn does not occur until slightly later. Despite the variety of crops grown in Tamaulipas, gathering and hunting continued to be major subsistence pursuits for another 1000 years.

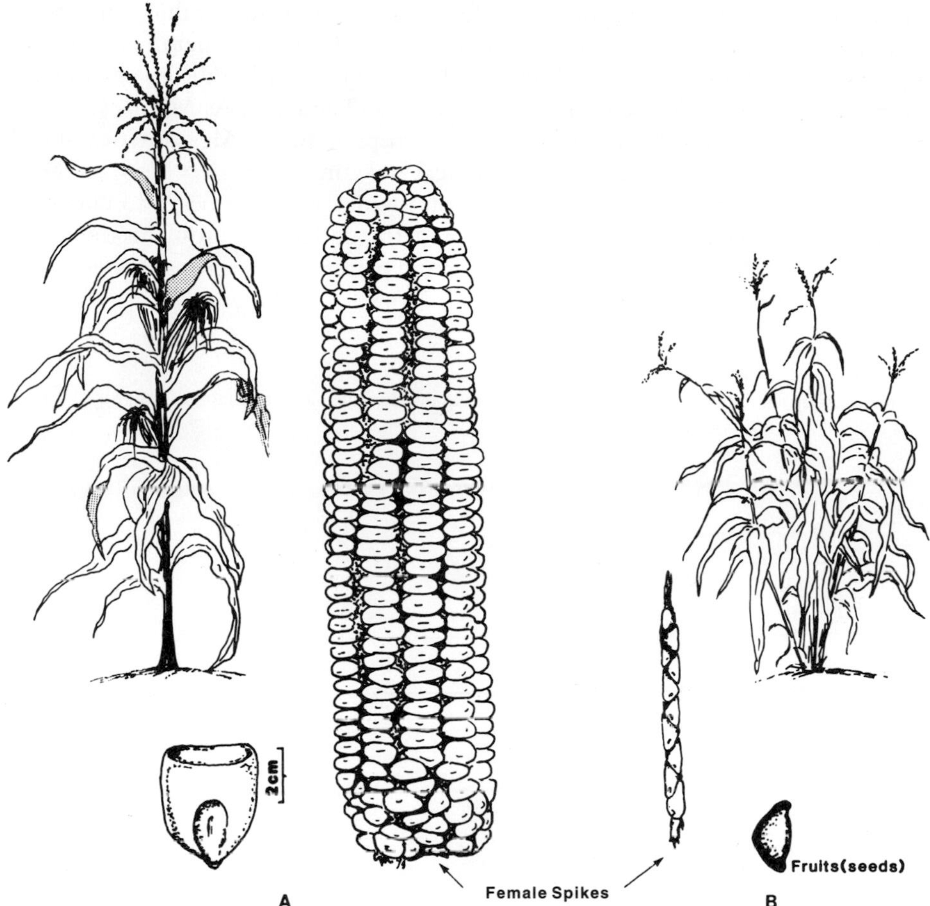

FIGURE 4.5 Modern corn (A) is derived from teosinte (B) its still extant, less productive, but genetically closest relative (illustrated by Charles M. Carrillo).

The presence of corn and other domestic crops in Mesoamerica provided the cultural environment for technological change that would ultimately have a tremendous impact on the Southwest. However, knowing that crops are available to grow is not sufficient to explain their acceptance into a people's economic inventory. Although there must have been continuous information exchange between Mesoamerica and the Southwest, there were differences in the specific plants that were acquired by southwestern peoples. For example, Minnis (1992) comments that although 67 plants were domesticated in Mesoamerica, only 10 were accepted into the Southwest. Even if one excludes plants that will not grow in the Southwest, the ancient Southwesterners were selective. They did not accept chili peppers or, probably, domestic amaranth. Chili peppers were eventually accepted only after Spanish contact. Further, the order of domestication in Mesoamerica was probably different from the order of acceptance of crops in the Southwest. Maize and squash were accepted at about the same time, but cotton, however, is not present until between AD 300 and 500. As Minnis (1991:133) states, in addition to sustained movement of crops between Mesoamerica and the Desert Borderlands, "there were also biological and cultural barriers between the two areas." The Southwest must be considered on its own terms to begin to understand the contexts into which cultigens were accepted, the underlying problems the acquisition of crops resolved, and the new problems and patterns these crops created. This is the subject of Chapter 5.

Chapter-opening art: Goosefoot (*Chenopodium*) (drawing by Marjorie Leggitt, Leggitt Design).

CHAPTER 5

Agricultural Beginnings: Last Hunters, First Farmers

This chapter concerns ancient southwestern agriculture. It describes the crops and contexts into which they were accepted, modified, and adapted. Maize agriculture is so important to the Native peoples of the Southwest that it is nearly impossible to imagine the time in the Archaic when domestic crops were first planted. The chapter also explores theoretical models that attempt to explain the acquisition and use of crops in the Southwest. Most of these models concern the benefits agriculture may have conferred for more successful hunter-gatherer groups.

INTRODUCTION

Before the 1950s and 1960s, the *invention* of agriculture worldwide was seen as the natural outgrowth of humankind's more complete control over the natural environment. As such, agriculture was considered progress and not requiring an explanation. Then, studies of modern hunters and gatherers (Lee and Devore 1968) began to dispel a number of ethnocentric myths about hunting and gathering life-ways. It is now well documented that on average, hunters and gatherers invest less labor in subsistence activities than do agriculturists. Children, even young adolescents, are not typically part of the labor force among hunters and gatherers but they are among agriculturists. Hunters and gatherers are just as healthy, if not healthier, than agriculturists. Studies of skeletal remains (Larsen 1995) document a variety of biological changes in human populations with agriculture. These include higher incidence of dental caries, evidence of poor nutrition including anemia, increased birth rates, and evidence of infectious disease. These patterns co-occur with increasing dependence on agriculture in the Southwest (El-Najjar 1974; El-Najjar *et al.* 1976; Nelson *et al.* 1994). Archaeological evidence indicates that many early domestic crops were not highly productive (Flannery 1968; Harlan 1967). All of these observations lead to the conclusion that rather than being the result of a natural trend, the initial development and later adoption of agriculture require explanation.

Currently, there are two very general theoretical models that attempt to explain the origins of agriculture worldwide, aspects of which may be relevant to situations, like that of the Southwest, in which agriculture was acquired. One model relies heavily on Boserup's (1965) argument that demographic pressure is the independent variable responsible for technological change. In the archaeological literature, this theoretical framework was elaborated by Binford (1968). Briefly, the model depends on documenting a situation of population disequilibrium in an area where potential domestic plants (or animals) exist. Binford (1968) maintained that areas supporting low-density hunting and gathering populations received increments of people displaced from sedentary communities outside the area. The increased numbers of people forced the development of the more labor-intensive strategy of plant domestication. In theory, population disequilibrium might also occur if depleted game resources forced hunters and gatherers to supplement their diets with agricultural crops. In Binford's argument, the initial population disequilibrium occurred at the end of the Pleistocene, when newly available aquatic resources allowed some previously highly mobile populations to become sedentary and abandon cultural practices that had limited their population growth. In a variant of this model, Cohen (1977) severed the link with sedentism, simply arguing that at the end of the Pleistocene the habitable world was full at a density appropriate to hunting and gathering but human populations continued to grow, forcing some groups to increase their food supply by domesticating crops.

Sanders and Webster (1978) raised serious questions about the general applicability of Boserup's thesis. They argue that although population pressure may constitute the primary factor involved in agricultural intensification in stable environments (such as the tropical forest areas of Boserup's original research), in differently structured environments other factors are equally important. Specifically, they contend that in environments that are characteristically variable, because of marked deviations from average rainfall, for example, intensified production may be undertaken in order to reduce subsistence risk. For Binford (1968) and Cohen (1977), the most important feature of agriculture is that it increases the amount of food per unit of land. For Sanders and Webster (1978), the key feature of domestic crops is reduction of risk of starvation because crops can supplement periods of poor yields of collected foods.

In the Southwest the most important food crops were acquired rather than domesticated. Currently, there are four somewhat different theoretical positions that attempt to explain the southwestern acceptance of domestic plants. One position generally follows Binford (1968) and Sanders and Webster (1978) with some modifications

(Cordell 1984; Glassow 1980; Huckell 1990; Wills 1988). This perspective states that increased numbers of people restricted mobility for hunters and gatherers, creating greater subsistence risk by limiting their usual response to climatic variability. Another position (Minnis 1992) emphasizes the opportunities provided by acquiring crops that were domesticated elsewhere. In this case, horticulture might have been a benefit, regardless of stresses related to risky environments or population/resource imbalances. There are also scholars who argue that agriculture was introduced into the Southwest by immigrant peoples who brought with them the crops and the technology for growing them (Berry and Berry 1986; Haury 1976; Huckell 1992). Yet a different perspective is proposed by Matson (1991) who emphasizes the evolutionary ecology of maize and cultivation practices. In his view, maize agriculture spread when genetic changes occurred in the plant that allowed it to survive the environments of the Southwest. Matson's view is compatible with either the in-place or immigration-based model of agricultural acceptance, and as Huckell (1995:13) notes, it is possible that both of these views are correct for the Southwest as a whole with one or the other being appropriate in different subregions.

Today, our understanding of the timing and circumstances of the appearance of crops in the Southwest has been greatly modified through re-excavations of some well-known sites, studies of available radiocarbon determinations, new radiocarbon and accelerator mass spectrometer radiocarbon dates, and a tremendous amount of recent, carefully done, excavation. All of the data we currently have suggest that corn (*Zea mays*) was first planted in the Southwest between 1000 and 1500 BC.[1] At that early date it was being grown in the low Sonoran and Chihuahuan desert basins, in the Mogollon Highlands and on the Colorado Plateaus (Figure 5.1). There is disagreement only about how casually or intensively horticulture was being practiced. By 100 BC, corn is known from sites everywhere from Chihuahua to Colorado and Sonora to Utah, although not all people living in this vast area used domestic crops. In recognition of the fact that the most important characteristic of the archaeological record of the Southwest for the period from 1500 BC to AD 200 is the appearance and spread of farming, Huckell (1995:15–16) suggests substituting the term Early Agricultural Period for the name Late Archaic, a change first proposed by Martin and Rinaldo (1951). Huckell's Early Agricultural Period would span the time from the initial appearance of domesticates at 1500 BC to the first appearance of pottery at about AD 200. It would include the San Pedro Cochise, Basketmaker II, and En Medio Oshara. He maintains that use of the term Early Agricultural Period is "appropriate, for it is with the arrival of agricultural production strategies that significant changes are observed in material culture, settlement occupational intensity, and patterns of land use" (Huckell 1995:16). Yet the name Early Agricultural Period does not preclude continued use of phase designations on the subregional level (i.e. San Jose phase, En Medio phase). Although I have no objection to the more general term Early Agricultural Period, I suggest that because it is applied to a period of time and a subsistence pattern, we risk the same problem as in the use of the term Archaic: There are two, perhaps uncorrelated, dimensions in the definition. It is also crucial to our continued understanding of the processes involved in the acquisition of agriculture that we not assume that domestic

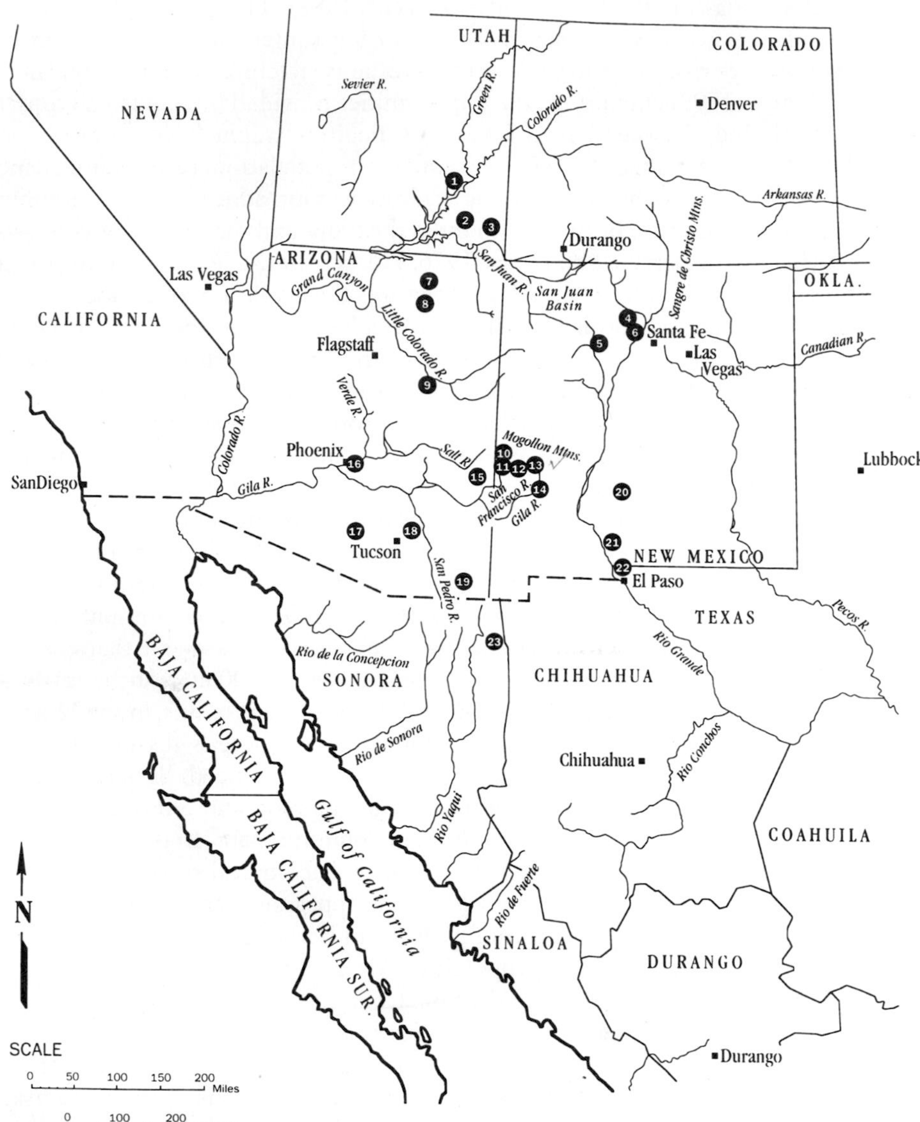

FIGURE 5.1 Sites important to the discussion of early agriculture in the Southwest. Key: ❶ Cowboy Cave; ❷ Turkey Pen Cave; ❸ Cedar Mesa; ❹ Jemez Cave; ❺ Arroyo Cuervo (Armijo and En Medio Rock Shelter); ❻ Bandelier National Monument (Ojala Cave); ❼ Marsh Pass (White Dog Cave); ❽ Black Mesa (Three Fir Shelter); ❾ Chevelon Creek (O'Haco Rock Shelter); ❿ Pinelawn Valley; ⓫ O Block Cave; ⓬ Tularosa Cave; ⓭ Bat Cave; ⓮ Cordova Cave; ⓯ Cienega Valley (Donaldson Site, Los Ojitos Site); ⓰ Pueblo Grande; ⓱ Ventana Cave; ⓲ Tucson Basin (Matty Canyon and Milagro); ⓳ Double Adobe Site; ⓴ Fresnal Rock Shelter; ㉑ Las Cruces (Tornillo Rock Shelter); ㉒ Keystone Dam Sites; ㉓ Swallow Cave (map by David Underwood).

crops were accepted at the same time by all groups living in the Southwest. Hunting and gathering was an option pursued by some peoples at various times.

Not everyone living in the Southwest acquired corn at the same time. Nevertheless, the crop was accepted into diverse environmental settings very rapidly. Squash was acquired at the same time as corn, and common beans arrived a few hundred years later, by 300–500 BC. An additional suite of domesticated plants that includes cotton, sieva beans (*Phaseolus lunatus*), jack beans, possibly scarlet runner beans (*Phaseolus coccineus*), green-striped cushaw squash (*Cucurbita mixta*), warty squash, and amaranth was first planted in the Southwest's Lower Sonoran Desert regions between AD 300 and 500, after their domestication in Mesoamerica. Finally, some plants that are native to the Southwest were domesticated there, while others were cultivated. Of all these crops, corn was of the most dietary importance. The new dates and new data show that corn and squash were accepted into foraging economies that we can now describe in some detail. Explanations for the acceptance of corn especially and other crops are appropriately being phrased from the perspective of societies of hunters and gatherers (Wills and Huckell 1994, Wills 1995), while an understanding of the crops themselves continues to be important to these explanations.

CORN

Corn (*Zea mays*) is a tropical grass derived from teosinte (*Zea mexicana* and *Zea perennis*) (Figure 4.5), its genetically closest relative. Teosinte still grows in parts of Mexico, Guatemala, and Honduras. The two plants are very similar genetically, are completely interfertile, and cross spontaneously when grown close to one another. Of all the world's grains, maize is the most fully domesticated in that it has most completely lost its ability to disperse seed and reproduce without human intervention. The evolution of corn and the societies that domesticated and developed it are truly intertwined.

Botanists divide corn into a number of varieties or races that are thought to reflect its evolution. The differentiation of races is based on morphological criteria such as average row number, size and shape of cob, and shape of kernel. Corn is genetically extremely variable and morphologically plastic. This means that the dimensions used to categorize races are not straightforward indices of genetic relationships. Isozyme studies are helping to clarify the relationships among varities (Doebley 1983). Through isolation and manipulation of maize, people can introduce an enormous amount of phenotypic variation in very short periods of time, often on the order of a few years (Iltis 1983). The extraordinary number of maize races in the Americas is the result of human efforts to grow maize in a variety of soil conditions, climates, and topographic settings. The extreme adaptability of maize is reflected by the fact that yellow flint corn of the Caribbean thrives at sea level, whereas Puño maize is cultivated successfully near Lake Titicaca at an elevation of 3800 m (12,000 ft) above sea level. The Chococeno maize of Columbia grows in wet, coastal areas, while varieties of Hopi corn are planted in sand dunes. The versatility of maize is also reflected by the fact that today, some 300 varieties are grown worldwide (Nabhan 1989).

The races that occur in the archaeological record of the Southwest, some of which are still planted, are proto-Mais de Ocho (also called proto-Harinoso de Ocho), pre-Chapalote, Chapalote, Reventador, Onaveno, Mais de Ocho, Pima, Fremont Dent, Mexican Pyramidal, Mais Blando, and Pueblo (Adams 1994). Maize probably originated in the Balsas River drainage southwest of Mexico City (Doebley 1990). Maize from the Tehuacán Valley of Mexico, which dates to about 3200 BC, is the oldest corn known. The routes over which corn traveled from Central Mexico to the Southwest are not known in detail. There is some agreement among botanists that Chapalote, Reventador, Mais de Ocho, and Onaveno moved through the lower elevations of the Pacific coast of Mexico, through northwestern Mexico, and then into the Southwest. Mexican Pyramidal types passed from the highlands of Mexico either along the Pacific Coast or along the eastern flanks of the Sierra Madre Occidental through Chihuahua and into the Southwest (Adams 1994).

The early maize found throughout the Southwest, from the Chihuahuan and Sonoran deserts to the Mogollon Highlands and the Colorado Plateaus, is proto-Mais de Ocho and pre-Chapalote, both eight-rowed types (Adams 1994). Since morphological changes may reflect environmental factors rather than genetic change, this consistency among early maize is surprising. Wills and Huckell (1994) suggest two reasons for this uniformity. One is that the corn had a stable role in Archaic economies so that there was no need for it to be more productive. The second reason, and in my opinion the more likely, is that high human mobility made it difficult to maintain isolated varieties required for varietal divergence. Wills and Huckell (1994) note that the best evidence for diversification of Southwestern maize without new genetic material occurs after AD 200. The plasticity of maize was not used or exploited in the Southwest for the first 1000 years of its presence there.

Nevertheless, this maize had been selected and modified so that a plant that had originated in the moist tropics of Mesoamerica could withstand the dry climate and short growing seasons of the Southwest. If corn were not so fully domesticated, the genetic changes it must have undergone would have taken many thousands of years. With humans selecting certain characteristics, probably quite unconsciously, change was far more rapid. The corn that eventually became Pima-Papago and Pueblo corn might have been planted by foraging groups living further and further north of the tropics. Those plants that matured early might be harvested with some being saved and used for seed corn in future plantings. Foragers do not spend much time in one area, so that the slower maturing plants would be left for birds, insects, and small animals but not replanted. By means such as this, corn may have been modified rather quickly as it spread.

From the perspective of plant growth, there are two very different environments in the Southwest. One set of environmental conditions exists in the low basin and range country of the Sonoran and Chihuahuan deserts, the second set in the higher elevations of the Colorado Plateaus and Mogollon Highlands. In the low deserts the growing season is generally long and frosts rarely a problem. The availability of water is the limiting condition for plant growth. Many indigenous plants are perennial, flowering and fruiting soon after the annual summer monsoon. The seeds of indigenous annual plants lie dormant until the rains. Most of the time, corn, which requires about 120 to 130 days to mature, can be planted at the time of the summer rains and still reach maturity before there is risk of a killing frost.

On the Colorado Plateaus and in the Mogollon Highlands, precipitation is marginal for farming but there are regions and sequences of years when there is adequate precipitation to farm without irrigation. In addition to periodic droughts, however, the growing season at the higher elevations and at low elevations in narrow canyons and valleys may be too short for crops to reach maturity. Crops planted during or after the summer monsoon will not mature before the first killing frosts. In the absence of irrigation, seeds may be planted in those soils that retain moisture from winter snow melt. If seeds are planted well before the summer rains, they can still reach maturity before the frosts.

Through a combination of strategies involving seed selection (which would emphasize and modify the genetically controlled characteristics of maize), planting decisions, and horticultural practices, the combined problems of deficient moisture and short growing seasons are much reduced. By selecting seed corn from plants showing resistance to dry conditions, structural properties of the corn planted in the Southwest were developed and maintained. For example, the two varieties of Pima-Papago corn that were eventually planted over much of the Southwest differ from other varieties of corn in two respects. First, the mescotyl will grow to 25–50 cm in length, compared with about 10–15 cm in modern hybrid varieties of corn. This allows seed to be planted at considerable depth, where it can use ground moisture retained from winter precipitation to germinate. Second, the corn produces a single long radicle rather than a number of seminal roots, enabling the plant to tap and use ground water for growth (Bradfield 1971; Collins 1914) (Figure 5.2).

Modern hybrid corn requires about 40–60 cm of water during the growing season (Minnis 1981:197). The distribution of moisture at key times during the growing season is equally important. Field studies and experiments indicate that mild water stress at the beginning of the growing season may not substantially damage yields, although there must be enough moisture to ensure seed germination. Similarly, moisture stress at the end of the season, when grains are mature, has little effect on the crop. However, water deprivation when the plant is at the tasseling or silking stage may decrease yields by 50 to 75 percent (Classen and Shaw 1970; Minnis 1981). On the plateaus and in the mountains, corn that germinated in the spring would reach the tasseling stage at the time of the summer rains.

The types of maize that were eventually grown in the Southwest were adapted to a variety of environmental conditions and show diverse morphological characteristics. Reventador is a flint corn (the kernels are soft on the interior but hard on the exterior) grown in the Hohokam area. Pima-Papago corn refers to two types of drought-resistant corn that were widely cultivated in the Southwest and were derived by crossing Chapalote with Mais de Ocho. Onaveno, the flint variety of Pima-Papàgo corn, and Maiz Blando, the flour or soft-kernel variety, differ by the mutation of a

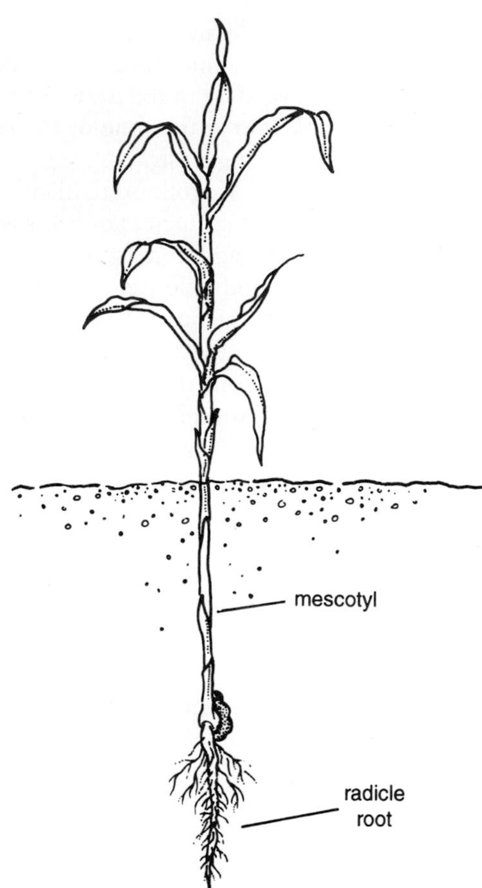

FIGURE 5.2 The varieties of Pima-Papago maize developed in the Southwest can withstand the dry spring. Seeds can be planted deep in the soil and still grow to the surface and the single radicle can tap and use ground water for growth (illustrated by Marjorie Leggit, Leggitt Design).

single gene that could have occurred anywhere (Ford 1981). It is significant that despite the development of new and more productive varieties of corn, Chapalote continues to occur throughout the later archaeological record of the Southwest. Ethnobotanist Karen Adams (1994) points out that while there were marked changes in types of *Zea mays* from the Mogollon Highlands and the Colorado Plateaus, maize from the Hohokam region was more stable through time, probably reflecting more homogenous growing conditions. In the higher elevations, changes in maize did not take place simultaneously. Mogollon Highland corn shifted to a lower cob row number, presumably through the introduction of Mais de Ocho, 400 years before the change occurred on the plateaus.

OTHER CROPS

The earliest squash in the Southwest (*Cucurbita pepo*) is a versatile plant that provides edible seeds and fruit and thick rinds that were used as tools and containers. The remains of squash are known from all the preceramic contexts in which maize has been found, with the possible exception of Cordova Cave in the Mogollon Highlands. The squash from southwestern sites that date before about AD 900 are all of a single variety. After AD 900, several varieties of *Cucurbita pepo* were grown. Whether these reflect local development or the result of further contact with central Mexico is not known.

Bottle gourds (*Lagenaria siceraria*) occur in southwestern contexts, but not as early as corn. Ford (1981) considers dates of about 300 BC for bottle gourds from Tularosa Cave and Cordova Cave to be generally applicable. The bottle gourd was not present at Bat Cave or Jemez Cave. Bottle gourds are also useful containers, and their seeds are edible. The plant does not tolerate short and cool growing seasons. Although it was eventually cultivated in many parts of the Southwest, it was apparently not grown in the more northern latitudes or at high elevations (Ford 1981).

Common beans (*Phaseolus* sp.) include types we recognize as pinto beans, red kidney beans, and navy beans. The common bean occurs at Bat Cave, Tularosa Cave, Cordova Cave, and Fresnal Rock Shelter. Dates for the introduction of the common bean are not as precise as they might be, but Ford (1981) suggests that 300–500 BC is reasonable. They are not found on the Colorado Plateaus before about AD 200. The plant was eventually grown throughout the Southwest, and it may have been the only bean grown at some Pueblo sites (Ford 1981). Following Kaplan (1965), it has often been noted that corn and beans complement each other in two respects. First, beans contain a high level of the amino acid lysine, which enables efficient digestion of the protein available in corn. Second, whereas corn generally depletes nitrogen from the soil, beans, as legumes, return nitrogen to the ground. Consequently, when corn and beans are planted in the same field, problems of nutrient depletion are ameliorated (Castetter and Bell 1942). Because of this complementarity, it has been considered surprising that beans occur later than corn in the archaeological record. However, some native southwestern wild plants may also supply lysine, and we do not know whether southwestern peoples traditionally noted the nitrogen-fixing properties of legumes.

Between about AD 300 and 500 new crops were accepted into the Southwest from Mexico (Ford 1981). Unlike the previous crops, which were probably transmitted initially among mobile hunters and gatherers, the new plants were introduced first to people who had already made some commitment to agriculture, the Hohokam, who practiced irrigation in favorable areas of the lower Sonoran Desert. The new crops were plants that tolerate the high temperatures of the desert but also generally require abundant water. They include cotton (*Gossypium hirsutum* var.), sieva beans (*Phaseolus lunatus*), jack beans (*Canavalia ensiformis*), possibly scarlet runner beans (*Phaseolus coccineus*), green-striped cushaw squash, warty squash (both *Cucurbita* sp.), and amaranth (*Amaranthus hypochondnacus*). Nearly all of these crops are known from the Tehuacán Valley. The exceptions are sieva beans, scarlet runner beans, and amaranth.

The sieva bean has been found only rarely in ancient southwestern archaeological contexts. It is known from a few Hohokam and Anasazi sites dating after AD 1100. The origins of the sieva bean, which resembles the South American lima bean and with which it is sometimes confused (Gasser 1976), are obscure. One variety of the sieva occurs in the Tamaulipas area and in northern Durango, Mexico, in sites that predate AD 1100 (Ford 1981; Gasser 1976). Scarlet runner beans are even more problematic in the Southwestern archaeological record. One such bean was identified in an unprovenienced context from Pueblo Grande. A second example, identified as a possible scarlet runner or sieva bean, was recovered from the same site in a context postdating AD 1100 (Gasser 1976). Ford (1981) concurs with a previous assessment (Nabhan 1977) that there are no uncontested pre-Columbian examples of the scarlet runner bean in the Southwest. Scarlet runner beans are cultivated by the Hopi, but they may have been introduced to them after 1700. The amaranth (*Amaranthus hypochondriacus*) is also presently difficult to evaluate. It is known with certainty from a post-AD 1100 context in central Arizona (Bohrer 1962) and from northern New Mexico (Baker 1996). Although dates of AD 500 for this amaranth have been confirmed from Tehuacán, its putative ancestor (*Amaranthus powelli*) is a native plant in Arizona. It is therefore possible that domestication of the amaranth took place in Arizona (Ford 1981:19).

INDIGENOUS CROPS

Bohrer (1991) and Minnis (1992), among others, recognize a continuum from plants that are tolerated in fields, to those that are encouraged, by watering for example, to those that have undergone morphologic changes indicative of domestication. As with any continuum, drawing a line between wild and domesticated plants may be difficult. Nevertheless, some indigenous southwestern plants show the kinds of morphological changes indicative of domestication. Among them is amaranth, mentioned above. Another is devil's claw (*Proboscidea parviflora* var.) (Figure 5.3), which is used in basket making. Tepary beans (*Phaseolus acutifolius* var.) (Figure 5.4) and panic grass (*Panicum sonorum*) provide edible seeds. Little barley (*Horedeum pusillum*) is known from Hohokam contexts as early as AD 900. As with the Old World variety, the Hohokam barley seed does not adhere well to the enclosing bracts, a characteristic that appears to have been selected—consciously or not. Mexican crucillo (*Condalia warnockii* var. *kearneyana*), a shrub with edible fruit, has been recovered in virtually all periods of occupation of the Hohokam site of La Ciudad, outside its current range and with larger stones or pits than are found in the wild variety (Bohrer 1991). Seeds of a domesticated tobacco (*Nicotiana rustica*) (Figure 5.5) have been identified at Hohokam sites, but since the size range of these may overlap with wild tobacco (*Nicotiana trigonophylla*), domestication is not entirely certain. *Nicotiana rustica* is known from a fourteenth century site in the Rio Grande area (Garber 1979).

Still other plants native to the Southwest were cultivated if not domesticated. *Chenopodium* (lamb's quarters) seems to have been among these in both the lower Sonoran Desert and the Colorado Plateaus. Agave (*Agave murpheyi* or *A. parryi*) is a

FIGURE 5.3 Devil's Claw (*Proboscidea parviflora*) is an example of an indigenous crop that shows the morphological changes indicative of domestication. It is used in basket making (illustrated by Marjorie Leggitt, Leggitt Design).

highly versatile plant that is used for food as well as for fibers. Agave hearts are eaten roasted and fibers can be used for basketry, sandals, and other woven items. Agave has been found growing outside its natural range on archaeological sites above the Mogollon, suggesting that it was used for food or fibers (Minnis 1992). In Hohokam sites in the Tucson basin, very large field systems were devoted to agave cultivation (Fish *et al.* 1992; also see Chapter 9). Minnis (1992) also suggests that Rocky Mountain beeweed (*Cleome serrulata*), which provides edible greens and a pigment used for paint in pottery decoration, was another plant cultivated on the Colorado Plateaus (Minnis 1992).

THE ACCEPTANCE AND SPREAD OF AGRICULTURE

With the archaeological data available to him at the time, Emil Haury (1962) published a highly influential discussion about the entry of maize into the Southwest. Haury's (1962) paper noted that virtually all the pre-ceramic occurrences of maize were in cave sites and all were at relatively high elevations in the Mogollon Highlands and

FIGURE 5.4 The tepary bean (*Phaseolus acutifolius* var.) is indigenous to the Southwest and may have been domesticated here or in northwest Mexico (illustrated by Marjorie Leggitt, Leggitt Design).

the Sierra Madres of Chihuahua. These were the classic sites of Bat Cave (Dick 1965a), Cienega Creek (Haury 1957), Cordova Cave (Martin *et al.* 1952), Swallow Cave (Lister 1958), and Tularosa Cave (Martin *et al.* 1952). Haury proposed that the maize and other Mexican crops were adapted to relatively moist conditions and had been transmitted through a "highland corridor," where rainfall was more plentiful than elsewhere in the Southwest. Since maize appeared much earlier than either pottery or the remains of houses in the high elevations, Haury argued that maize was used casually and had little impact on people's lives. It was only later, he suggested, by about 500 BC when a more drought tolerant maize was introduced or irrigation technology developed, that agriculture spread to lower elevations and permitted sedentary village life.

A tremendous amount of data on early southwestern agriculture has accumulated in the past 20 years. Some sites, such as Bat Cave (Wills 1988a), the Cienega Valley, and Matty Canyon sites (Huckell 1995) have been re-excavated and new radiocarbon dates obtained (Wills 1988a). For other known sites, radiocarbon dates have been obtained for the first time or new dates on corn macrofossils obtained (White Dog

FIGURE 5.5 Nicotiana rustica (wild tobacco) seeds have been recovered through flotation from Hohokam sites and fourteenth century Pueblo sites (illustrated by Marjorie Leggitt, Leggitt Design).

Cave, Jemez Cave). Archaic-age open sites have been excavated in ways that allow recovery of maize pollen and macrofossils (Milagro, Matty Canyon sites, Keystone Dam sites). These excavation strategies include auger testing, removal of enormous amounts of overburden, and water screening and fine screening of literally tons of soil. As a result, quite a long list of well-dated sites is available for early agriculture in the Southwest as a whole. Table 5.1 and Figure 5.1 (a map) provide the names, locations, type of site, and dates of early corn in the Southwest. The sites presented are those that are considered reliable in that corn is present in the form of macrofossils rather than pollen alone and the dates are corrected. Accelerator (AMS) dates are starred where they are given.

Examination of Table 5.1 indicates that the oldest undisputed date is from Tornillo Rock Shelter (Upham *et al.* 1987) in the low basin and range country near Las Cruces, New Mexico. Dates that are nearly as old are from Bat Cave in the Mogollon Highlands, and from Three Fir Shelter and Sheep Camp Shelter on the Colorado Plateaus.

TABLE 5.1 Early Maize Sites in the Southwest[a]

Site name	Location	B.P. Dates	Excavator/ reporter
Bat Cave	New Mexico	4090*[b] 3350[b]	Wills
Three Fir Shelter	Arizona	3890[b]	Smiley
Tornillo Rock Shelter	New Mexico	3460[b]	Upham, MacNeish
Milagro	Arizona	2780 ± 90[c]	Huckell
Chaco	New Mexico	2720 ± 265	Simmons
Jemez Cave	New Mexico	2690 ± 125[b]	Berry Ford
Fresnal Shelter	New Mexico	2540 ± 200[c]	Wills, Wimberly
Tularosa Cave	New Mexico	2473 ± 200[b]	Cutler, Wills
Tumamoc Hill	Arizona	2470 ± 270[bc]	Fish and others
Sheep Camp Shelter	New Mexico	2290 ± 210[bc]	Simmons, Wills Ford
Zuni	New Mexico	2200[c]	Hall
Cordova Cave	New Mexico	300 BC	Cutler
Elsinore	Utah	2140 ± 100[b]	Wilde and Newman
Cowboy Cave	Utah	2115 ± 70[b]	Berry, Jennings, Wilde and Newman
Island Mesa	Utah	2110 ± 70[bc]	Jett
Clyde's Cavern	Utah	1740 ± 100[b]	Winer and Wylie Wilde and Newman

[a]Adapted from Adams (1994) and Smiley (1994).
[b]Calibrated date.
[c]Accelerator date.
*Date may be contaminated.

The dates indicate that there is no clear source of secondary maize dispersal, no one place or kind of environmental setting within the Southwest where maize was used over a long period of time, perhaps genetically modified, and subsequently spread to other locations. Hence one feature of the Haury (1962) model is not supported. The data also fail to support Matson's (1991) contention of a low elevation flood plain corridor of initial maize dispersal.

When Haury's (1962) paper was written, available data suggested a gap of about 2000 years between the oldest record of corn in the Southwest and its more general appearance, along with ceramics and architecture. The dates in Table 5.1 have narrowed that gap considerably, but it has not altogether disappeared. At issue is whether maize was at first planted "casually," as Haury suggested, or whether it was given considerable attention requiring Archaic populations to become seasonally more sedentary than they had previously been. Paul Minnis (1991) currently espouses the view that initial cultivation was casual.

Minnis (1992) terms the spread of agriculture into the Southwest an instance of primary crop acquisition, referring to the first use of crops that were domesticated elsewhere. As such, those acquiring agriculture have access to technological information about planting, cultivating, processing, storing, and cooking, as well as the plants themselves. Minnis contrasts his general theoretical position with those derived from Binford (1968) and Sanders and Webster (1978) discussed above. In their models, agriculture is acquired as a necessity, whereas Minnis sees agriculture in the Southwest as occurring as an opportunity, with little conflict in scheduling activities in the general context of mobile hunting and gathering. Using descriptions of the Western Apache as a model, Minnis (1992) suggests that the early Southwestern agriculture was small scale (fields were small and dispersed) and could be planted and harvested without greatly disrupting the normal foraging schedule. Western Apache winter camps were located in the lower elevations in the southern part of the territory within which they hunted and gathered. Planting occupied three to four weeks in spring when

> few naturally available plant resources would have been ready to collect. . . . If crop harvesting conflicted with the collection of naturally available foodstuffs, then the cultigens could have been left in the field until the other resources had been collected; one characteristic of domesticates is their lack of natural dispersal mechanisms (Minnis 1992:131).

Hence, harvesting of corn could be delayed without appreciably decreasing the yield. Minnis also notes that the focus on wild grasses in the Early Archaic indicates that southwestern peoples would have been familiar with the characteristics of maize: maize could be seen as another, productive, grass. Other crops, such as beans, bottle gourds, squash, and cotton did not disperse from the areas of their domestication as quickly as maize. The pattern of acceptance of crops in the Southwest—maize, cucurbits, and beans before cotton and bottle gourds—suggests, to Minnis, that the need for crops was a need for food, which is not always the case in regions where initial domestication may involve non-food crops.

In contrast to Minnis (1991), Wills (1988b, 1990) proposes that initial use of maize in the Southwest was anything but casual. While both authors acknowledge that their disagreement reflects emphasis at different scales of observation, Wills (1988b, 1990, 1995) and Wills and Huckell (1994) point out that the introduction and spread of agriculture between about 1500 and 1000 BC co-occurred with a major shift to intensive land use and economic reorganization. Agricultural production, they argue, enhanced foraging efficiency, allowing foragers to occupy the land more intensively and to more efficiently exploit a range of economic resources. The evidence for more intensive land use includes the appearance of dwellings (pithouses); a variety of storage facilities including pits, bags, and baskets; and the appearance, archaeologically, of thick, extensive middens and more formalized burial practices. To this list, I would add evidence of intergroup conflict with some indication of violence. That houses and storage pits reflect more intensive land use is intuitively obvious. Foragers, visiting an area for short periods episodically and unpredictably over time, do not construct durable houses and storage features. Thick, extensive middens develop through time with continuous or repeated occupation. Formal burials are human universals, but the use of specific burial areas or cemeteries is correlated with residential sedentism and with rights of access to or stewardship of land (Saxe 1970). Intergroup hostilities are indirectly linked to intensive land use because they suggest competition for resources.

It may be possible to test whether early maize cultivation was casual by examining the maize itself in excavated Early Agricultural Period sites. Generally, high variability in cob size and some other characteristics reflect poor field maintenance (Ford 1991), which would occur when there is little or no effort in cultivation. More uniform maize would suggest the contrary. Such an examination of maize would, of course, be limited to those situations in which preservation is excellent, not all locations in which corn was first grown. This would be a potential inherent sample bias. It also appears likely that maize was accepted into different hunting and gathering contexts, perhaps with different amounts of energy invested in cultivation, among the various regional environments of the Southwest.

In the Early Agricultural Period, patterns of intensive land use are seen in three open sites in the low desert region: Milagro (Huckell 1990; Huckell and Huckell 1988) and the Costello-King site (Ezzo and Deaver 1996), both on the northern edge of the Tucson Basin, and the Keystone Dam site (O'Laughlin 1980), near El Paso, described in Chapter 4. At Milagro the surface of the site was marked only by a low level of lithic scatter. Excavation of only a small portion of the site revealed an extensive occupation surface, three pithouses, storage pits, other pit features, and hearths. Flotation and fine screening permitted recovery of plant macrofossils. Corn was present and ubiquitous throughout the site. Other recovered plants were amaranth, chenopodium (lamb's quarters), horse purslane, walnut, manzanita, creosote, hackberry, cactus, and sedges. Fauna was poorly preserved. The identified taxa were jackrabbit, one artiodactyl long bone fragment, and small rodent bones. The pithouses at Milagro were shallow, oval constructions, about 3.0 m by 2.2 m and 0.25 m deep with circular hearths and large, interior bell-shaped storage pits. Seven large bell-shaped storage pits were also excavated outside of houses. These were of different sizes, but their capacities ranged from 0.39 cubic meters to 0.628 cubic meters. Huckell (1995:120–121) calculates that a storage pit of 0.5 cubic meters could accommodate enough maize to feed one person, exclusively on corn, for 364 days. This exercise demonstrates that the amount of corn that could have been stored is not trivial.

The Costello-King site has yielded radiocarbon dates on maize of ca. 1000–600 BC, among the oldest dated maize in Arizona. Despite the Late Archaic age, intensive occupation and cultivation are documented by the presence of pit structures with storage features similar to those at Milagro. In addition, the Costello-King site yielded evidence of two irrigation canals that would have served to channel runoff into *akchin* (arroyo mouth) fields (Ezzo and Deaver 1996).

The Keystone Dam site pithouses were also small irregular ovals, with interior hearths, storage pits, and pit features. The site yielded corn and other charred plant macrofossil seeds and fruits of prickly pear cactus, mesquite pods, smartweed dock, amaranth, bulrush, and tornillo. As with other open sites, animal bone is not well-preserved. Remains included cottontail and jackrabbit. The similarities of the Keystone site to Milagro are marked. This is particularly interesting in view of the fact that they are in similar settings but at opposite "ends" of the Southwest, on the southwestern and southeastern edges of the Southwestern region.

Two sites in the Cienega Valley of southeastern Arizona further document the pattern. The Donaldson site and Los Ojitos (Huckell 1995) contained small oval houses, a variety of storage pits, burials, and the remains of maize. The remains of wild plants included horse purslane, grasses, mesquite pods, acorns, agave, and yucca. With unusually good preservation at the Donaldson site, the fauna include a wide range of animals. There the largest part of the archaeological sample of fauna was artiodactyls. Huckell (1995:123) suggests that deer were the preferred targets in hunting, with pronghorn antelope second in quantity. The observation that large game increases in the archaeological record with increased sedentism was also noted for Ventana Cave, Arizona, where Szuter and Bayham (1989) view this as an example of a more general phenomenon: Hunting among sedentary peoples can focus on procuring larger and higher value game, which are obtained by small task groups traveling considerable distances to hunting areas. Eventually, however, increased regional population densities can make this impossible so that there is reversion to small game and field hunting.

In the Mogollon Highlands, the pattern is different. There cave sites show little or no use in pre-agricultural times. With corn, there is a dramatic change to intensive use of caves as evidenced by abundant hearths, thick midden deposits, and storage areas. In the Mogollon Highlands, there is as yet no evidence of open-air pithouse sites such as the Keystone Dam sites or Milagro. However, Wills and Huckell (1994) report 17 Late Archaic sites, with aceramic pit structures, located on surveys in the Lower San Francisco and Gila Drainages (Chapman 1985). Wills (1988, 1995) has argued that before the acquisition of maize, use of the mountainous Mogollon Highlands would have been restricted to late summer and fall when piñon, other nut crops, and deer would have been abundant. At other times, there is little human food at these elevations, and foragers would move to lower elevation settings. With corn and other crops, people in the highlands modified their pattern by planting in the high elevations in spring or quite early in summer. Wills suggests that the change might have been a result of some groups establishing year-round residence in the mountains or of changing mobility patterns of some groups so that they were at the higher elevations in both spring and fall and low elevations in between. The reason for the shift in the timing of use of highlands, Wills believes, might reflect people's establishing a base from which to monitor the potential productivity of highland resources in the spring so that they would know where or if they should return in the fall. In either case, the change would have been initiated by regional competition over resources or unusually high population density that restricted movement from the highlands and lower elevations. Wills's emphasis on monitoring resources is prompted by knowledge of the annual unpredictability of piñon and other nut crops and a general acceptance of the notion that agriculture was acquired as a risk reduction strategy for foragers. Osborn (1993) makes a strong case for overwintering, or less likely prolonged use of high elevations, based on animal ecology and the likelihood that the preferred resources for the foragers in question were deer.

Despite the lack of house structures, the high elevation Cienega Creek site in the White Mountains of east-central Arizona was also reoccupied, intensively over a long period of time (Haury 1957). The Cienega Creek site produced 47 cremation burials, 40 in a single pit, that date to between 150 BC and AD 50. As noted in Chapter 4, the Spanish word *cienega* means wet meadow or marsh. I suggest that both the low elevation Cienega Valley and the high elevation Cienega Creek may have provided similar habitat for game animals, and to a lesser extent for plants, in being islands of relatively high water table in an arid region. As such, they would have supported a relatively lush flora and been attractive to game animals as well. Human use of cienegas and the excavation of wells date to the very beginning of the Archaic, as noted in Chapter 4. The high water table, and perhaps the use of wells, might have ensured the germination and maturation of enough corn to allow groups to remain in these settings, where game animals and perennial wild foods were abundant, nearly year-round. Localized sedentary groups within the region would become islands of differential population growth, the impacts of which would be felt far beyond their local areas.

There are also abundant new data about the Early Agricultural Period on the Colorado Plateaus (Matson 1991; Matson and Chisholm 1986; Smiley 1994; Smiley *et al.* 1986). Wills and Huckell (1994:44–46) interpret these as manifesting a more complicated pattern of land use than either the low desert basins or Mogollon Highlands. On the other hand, the apparent complexity may be a function of many, many more well-excavated sites with concomitantly finer chronological control. As indicated, the earliest appearance of maize documented on the plateaus is just as old as it is elsewhere in the Southwest. Three Fir Shelter, on the northern rim of Black Mesa, has produced early radiocarbon dates and shows intensive occupation with the appearance of maize. Within the shelter are slab-lined cists and pits, some with maize, roasting features, hearths, and a possible structure indicated by a clay lens. White Dog Cave and other classic Basketmaker Marsh Pass cave sites, originally excavated by Guernsey and Kidder (1921), yield evidence of intensive occupation and having been recently radiocarbon dated have remains of corn that are as old as Three Fir Shelter. Further north, Cowboy Cave, a Basketmaker II site in Utah (Jennings 1980; Matson 1991), shows the same pattern of early agriculture and intensive use. All of these Colorado Plateau Early Agricultural Period cave sites then are similar in age and use to the cave sites of the Mogollon Highlands. The difference between the regions appears to be in open sites.

As noted, there are as yet no excavated sites with pithouses in the Mogollon Highlands. There are more than 100 Early Agricultural Period sites known on Black Mesa alone. Thirty-five of these have been excavated and 140 radiocarbon dates obtained (Nichols and Smiley 1985; Smiley 1985, 1994). The open sites consist of lithic scatters without structures that are interpreted as places where resource extraction or other special activities took place, sites with one or two shallow structures that are interpreted as warm season camps, and sites with 2 to 12 deep pithouses, storage pits, hearths, and dense middens that are inferred to have been winter camps. Corn has been recovered from all three kinds of sites, although not all of these sites yielded maize. One of the smaller sites, with small hearths and no structures, and one of the larger sites, with three structures and bell shaped storage pits, each produced 25 percent of the maize found in the entire sample of excavated sites (Wills and Huckell 1994). A very similar pattern is documented for Cedar Mesa, Utah, just north of Black Mesa. There Turkey Pen Cave (Matson and Chisholm 1986) was intensively used and its residents seem to have depended considerably on corn. There are also abundant open sites that date to the Early Agricultural Period, and these also manifest a range with respect to intensity of use (Matson 1991).

What Wills and Huckell (1994) conclude is unusual or unexpected about the open sites of the Colorado Plateau is that they demonstrate episodic occupations. Dates obtained from them suggest that they were inhabited during a period of only about 200 years. On Black Mesa, the open sites date to AD 1–200; on Cedar Mesa AD 200–400. Before and after these intervals, Black Mesa and Cedar Mesa were unoccupied by Early Agricultural Period populations. Episodic use of open sites is also reported for the San Juan Basin (Vierra 1995). For large parts of the Colorado Plateau episodic occupations continue into later periods. Lipe and Matson (1971) refer to them as boom and bust cycles.

While Wills and Huckell (1994) may have focused on a pattern unique to the Colorado Plateaus, it is also possible that we are seeing an artifact of archaeology. Both Cedar Mesa and Black Mesa have been subject to intensive survey and excavation in the course of long-term contract projects. The project area of the Black Mesa work is probably one of the most completely documented places in the Southwest (Gumerman 1988; Powell 1988). Neither the Mogollon Highlands nor locations within the low basin and range deserts have been as intensively surveyed, excavated, tested, or dated. I might expect similar episodic use to be found in open sites in the general Mogollon Highland region. It is possible that there is more residential permanence of the low elevation cienegas and flood plains, primarily because water is far more localized and critical in the Sonoran Desert.

Another aspect of the episodic nature of the open site occupations of the Colorado Plateaus is troubling to Wills and Huckell (1994). Because they view the acquisition of agriculture as necessarily being beneficial to forager populations, in allowing these groups to be more effective hunters and gatherers, they see episodic use of a region as non-intensive and therefore not really optimal. However, this would seem to be a problem of scale. For the six to eight human generations of foragers who occupied Black Mesa or Cedar Mesa, the use of resources may well have been intensive. They may well have remained year-round within the piñon juniper zone, hunting deer and other large game, cultivating and storing crops, and taking advantage of windfall crops of rice grass or piñon nuts when these occurred.

Over many different time scales, however, Early Agricultural Period peoples in the Southwest were highly mobile. The evidence of the morphology of corn showing homogeneity suggests that local groups were not isolated from one another. Further, as Wills and Huckell (1994:46) note, "It is doubtful that any significant morphological differences exist between the Late Archaic pithouses or projectile points between the Tucson basin and Black Mesa." There is really nothing to suggest social differentiation of local populations. On the other hand, there is no reason to believe that all groups within the Southwest used domestic crops or that interactions among mobile groups were always peaceful.

Groups with stored foods—either agricultural crops or wild foods—not only had a safety net for lean periods of the year, they also had a resource that could be contested or stolen. Perhaps the use of rock shelters and cave sites for food storage and for burials was a way of demonstrating ownership of the stored resources on the Colorado Plateaus. The association of bell-shaped storage pits and burials in the sites in the Cienega Valley seems to be similar. Rather than indicating ownership or stewardship of territory, it may be that one's ancestors indicated ownership of the stores. The Late Archaic or Early Agricultural Period was also a time when some sites seem designed to withstand aggression and some burials also manifest evidence of having sustained deliberate violence. Archaic sites on the tops of land forms that are very difficult to access are reported from central Chihuahua (Roney 1996) and the Tucson Basin (Fish *et al.* 1993). It has also been noted that in the first good evidence of pithouse occupation in some regions, such as the Mogollon Mountains, sites are located on the tops of land forms that are difficult to access, and defensive layout is not unusual (LeBlanc 1989). Further, some Early Agricultural Period burials indicate unusual pre- and post-mortem wounds. A window of sorts into the Early Agricultural Period world is provided by examining White Dog Cave, a classic Basketmaker Cave site in northeastern Arizona. Cave sites offer preservation of otherwise perishable materials and the use of caves for burials, which became naturally desiccated mummies, also gives a unique view of the people themselves.

White Dog Cave, excavated in 1915 (Kidder and Guernsey 1915), derives its name from one of the excavated dog burials. A long-haired, white dog with brown spots, about the size of a small collie, was buried with an adult male human, possibly the dog's owner. The white dog represents one type or breed of ancient Pueblo dog. The other, also first known from White Dog Cave, is a small terrier-like dog with short hair, in this case white with black spots. The men and women buried in White Dog Cave were rather small in stature. Women were buried in White Dog Cave with necklaces of beads made of stone, snail shell, abalone shell, or seeds, but none of turquoise, a stone later very important in the region. Elsewhere on the Colorado Plateaus, some burials of the Early Agricultural Period were more richly adorned with turquoise ornaments, shell and stone beads, and more elaborate jewelry than later burials from the same places. This finding is surprising because luxury items and jewelry are more often associated with societies that are sedentary and dependent on agriculture rather than those with less dependence on crops.

Women's clothing included aprons of loose-hanging strings of soft fiber about 30 cm long bound to a waist cord of the same material. Men were buried without clothing. Both sexes however wore, and were buried with, woven, square-toed sandals. Frequently a new pair was interred with the body. These were made of yucca fiber or yucca and apocynum (Indian hemp). Both sexes also used robes for warmth. One kind of robe was made of tanned deerskin, sometimes with leather tie straps attached to hold it closed across the chest. The other type of robe was a light, warm covering made by wrapping strips of rabbit fur around yucca cords that were then tied together in close parallel rows. Babies had soft blankets made from the bellies of rabbit skins and diapers made from the soft interior bark of juniper. They had portable carrying cradles made of straight rods tied in a neat cross to a stick bent into an oval form.

In addition to the fabric made for clothing, the dry caves preserve various hand-woven items of daily use, all of which are a tribute to the skill of the people. Both human and dog hair was used in Basketmaker weaving but only women's hair was cut rather unevenly, presumably serving as a supply of fiber for woven fabrics. The men wore their hair long, tied in three bunches; one on each side of the head and one in the back. Some, but not all of the men, also had a queue made of hair taken from the crown of their heads. Slip noose snares made of fine string, usually human hair, could be used for taking small game and birds. Larger nets were made to stretch across the mouth of a gully or arroyo and block all game driven toward it by groups of people. One spectacular find from White Dog Cave is a net that is 240 m long and more than 1 m in width, with a 2 in. mesh of fine fiber string, composed of nearly 4 mi of cordage. Dark and lighter color fiber were woven into the net in a pattern such that trapped animals might see the dark areas as potential escape holes and go toward them, trapping themselves in the net, where they could be quickly killed.

Large, conical, burden baskets and tump lines were also hand-woven, as were trays used for winnowing and parching seeds. Smaller baskets were used for storage, and have been found filled with wild seeds, corn kernels, and weaving materials. Soft bags, sometimes split on one side, were shrouds for burials of flexed bodies. A large basket might also be inverted over the head. Bags and baskets were decorated with woven or painted designs in earthen colors: red from iron-oxide powder, yellow from limonite (yellow ochre), white from white clay, each mixed with water or grease. Brown, black, and blue pigments were obtained from plants and also mixed with water or grease. These colors were also used to paint figures on the rock walls of cliff faces near their caves, often human figures with broad shoulders, blocky bodies, and stick-like arms and legs. Hand prints are another common motif.

A glimpse into what may be the darker side of the people's spirituality is revealed in some of the burials. A fairly frequent pattern is the removal of heads and long bones from the grave after burial and attempts to protect the head through concealment. A young woman was buried in White Dog Cave with a trophy scalp made of human skin. In the caves the remains of fire are often found associated with burials and some human bones are burned. It is very difficult to understand the set of beliefs that formed the context for these strange treatments of human remains except by suggesting ideas associated with witchcraft or fear of sorcery.

DISCUSSION

A wealth of new data demonstrates that between 1500 and 1000 BC, maize was being used by hunting and gathering peoples in the low deserts, central mountains, and northern plateaus of the Southwest. There is no evidence of a route restricted by topography or elevation, nor is there evidence of a single secondary center of dispersal. Between 750 BC and AD 200, corn, squash, and beans were cultivated throughout the Southwest, but not all groups planted crops. Maize, beans, and squash became the cornerstone of horticultural Southwestern economies but other crops, some imported from tropical Mesoamerica and some indigenous to the Southwest, were incorporated as well.

The new data have stimulated rethinking the processes that would account for the acceptance of domestic crops in the Southwest. While there is scholarly debate about the causes, most agree that, initially, the crops must have had positive values and conferred advantages for those pursuing hunting and gathering ways of life. Except for those who argue that crops were brought to the Southwest by a migration of farming peoples, those who became the Southwest's first farmers were hunters and gatherers. Therefore the crops should have enabled them to be more effective at hunting and gathering. Table 5.2 provides a rough comparison of some of the nutritional aspects of domestic crops and wild plant foods used in the Southwest. Corn and beans compare quite favorably, in caloric content and protein, with many of the wild seeds and other foods. As discussed in Chapter 2, however, one of the characteristics of natural vegetation patterning in the Southwest is that large stands of a single plant type in one area are rare. This suggests that a great deal more energy was expended gathering wild seeds equal in caloric value to the corn that might be grown in a small field. If people normally move over large portions of the landscape as they gather and hunt, locating and collecting enough wild plant food does not constitute a problem. When movement is restricted, however, the advantage of having pure stands of an even moderately productive crop is obvious. Corn provides less food value than some foods, especially piñon nuts and walnut. Although piñon is widely distributed in the Southwest, piñon nut crops are extremely unreliable from year to year. Good yields occur in only 1 year out of 7 to 14 years in the same area. Yearly variability in production is true of other nuts as well (Wing and Brown 1979:147), including black walnut, which has a far more limited distribution in the Southwest than piñon.

The kinds of sites with evidence of agriculture also show evidence for the storage of surprisingly large quantities of food and the remains of dwellings. Storage pits and houses both indicate that groups with domestic crops were more sedentary than people had previously thought. One consequence of sedentism worldwide is an increase in population. Stored foods might have enabled groups to withstand annual or short-term lean periods that otherwise might have been lethal to some elements of their populations. On a very broad, regional basis, the numbers of people who depended to some extent on crops and those who did not, the numbers who were somewhat sedentary and those who were not, would increase at *different rates.* Initially, whether guarding food stores or access to territories, those who had crops seem to have been vulnerable to conflict and violence involving other groups. It is likely that raiders were among the non-agricultural occupants of the Southwest, or perhaps just those whose crops had failed during a season when others had been successful. Eventually, either through differential population growth directly or because higher numbers allowed some groups to expand into territories occupied by mobile hunters and gatherers, more and

TABLE 5.2 Nutritional Aspects of Cultivated Plants, Wild Plants, and Animal Foods of the Southwest

Class of food	Calories (per 100g)[a]	Protein (per 100g)[a]	Carbohydrates (per 100g)[b]
Crop			
Corn (*Zea mays*)[c]	348	8.9	72.2
Common Beans (*Phaseolus vulgaris*)[c]	340	22.5	61.9
Winter Squash (*Cucurbita pepo*)[c]	50	1.4	12.4
Pumpkin (*Cucurbita pepo*)[c]	26	1.0	6.5
Wild Plant			
Seeds			
Indian Ricegrass (*Oryzopsis hymenoides*)[d]	410	—	—
Lamb's Quarters (*Chenopodium* sp.)[c]	32	—	—
Pigweed (*Amaranthus* sp.)[d]	36	16.6	—
Saguaro (*Carnegiea gigantea*)[c]	609	16.3	54.0
Tansy Mustard (*Descurania pinnata*)[c]	554	23.4	71.0
Weed Seeds (*Chenopodium pallidicaule, C. quinoa, Zea mexicana*)[d]	340	12.0 (*C. quinoa* only)	—
Fruits			
Cholla (*Cylindropuntia* sp.)[c]	393	12.2	79.0
Prickly Pear (*Opuntia* sp.) - dry	218[d]	1.0[d]	62.0[c]
Saguaro (*Carnegiea gigantea*) - dry[c]	499	10.3	70.0
Yucca (*Yucca baccata*) - dry[d]	390	—	—
Nuts			
Black Walnuts (*Juglans* sp.)[c]	628	20.5	14.8
Piñon (*Pinus* edulis Englem)[c]	635	—	—
Other			
Cholla Stems (*Cylindropuntia* sp.)[c]	—	1.6	—
Mesquite Beans (*Prosopis juliflora*)[c]	419	14.9	73.0
Purslane (*Portulaca* sp.)[c]	20	—	—
Meat			
Deer (*Odocoileus hemionus*)[d]	126	—	—
Pronghorn (*Antilocapra americana*)[d]	146	—	—
Rabbits and Hares (*Sylvilagus audoboni, Lepus californicus*)[d]	135	—	—
Turkeys (*Meleagris gallopavo merriami*)[d]	170	—	—

[a]Edible portion only.
[b]Includes fiber.
[c]Adapted from Ford (1972).
[d]Adapted from Wetterstrom (1986).

more peoples would have become agricultural. The size of the regions that could be occupied exclusively by hunters and gatherers would become smaller and smaller, until no group could hunt and gather exclusive of any reliance on crops.

Once southwestern peoples became committed to agriculture because a return to hunting and gathering was no longer viable, a number of very sophisticated approaches to increasing crop yields were used. In some instances, technological devices were developed that permitted reliable yields in areas that do not support agriculture today. It is impossible to know many, if not most, of the agricultural practices used in the past in the Southwest, but some of the techniques documented among contemporary southwestern peoples certainly extended into ancient times. Among these, careful selection of field locations helps ensure sufficient water for corn. Fields may be placed in areas of deep soils with good moisture-retaining properties; on slopes that are exposed to the north or east, which receive less direct solar radiation and therefore hold moisture; within stream flood plains or the mouths of arroyos, which are naturally irrigated; or in sand dunes, which allow the penetration of moisture from the atmosphere and retard its evaporation. When corn is planted in locations where subsurface moisture is lacking, water from precipitation runoff or from streams or springs can be diverted during the critical periods of the growing season.

Sedentary ways of life with domestic architecture and storage facilities that include pottery are the hallmarks of ancient Southwestern cultures. Pottery particularly is at the core of the archaeological definitions of cultures that are described in the next chapter. Even with agriculture and the wonderfully ingenious methods of cultivation that were invented in the Southwest, no southwestern peoples could have been sustained without wild foods. Access to areas where game could be hunted and where wild plant foods could be collected was crucial for the survival of all human groups well into the twentieth century.

[1]Corn is known from Tornillo Shelter, dated to 1175 BC; the Archaic levels of Bat Cave, now dated to 1120 to 1340 BC; Fresnal Shelter, dated to 1540 BC. Swallow Cave, Chihuahua (Mangelsdorf and Lister 1956), Tularosa Cave and Cordova Cave also yielded numerous remains of corn (Kaplan 1963; Martin *et al.* 1954); radiocarbon dates indicate an age of about 300 BC for these cave deposits. In the Arroyo Cuervo area, Armijo and En Medio rock shelters contained evidence of maize (Ford 1981; Irwin-Williams and Tompkins 1968). In these shelters the evidence consists of maize pollen; although the findings from neither site have been published in detail, radiocarbon dates between 1500 and 550 BC are reported. Jemez Cave, in the Jemez Mountains (Alexander and Reiter 1935; Ford 1975, 1981), produced maize in an undated deposit beneath a level radiocarbon dated to 490 BC. Lo Daiska Rock Shelter, near Denver, contained corn in the earliest occupation levels (Irwin and Irwin 1959). A single radiocarbon date for the oldest occupation suggests a period from about 1150 to 2800 BC, but the stratigraphic association between the corn and the date is problematic (Ford 1981). O'Haco Rock Shelter, in the Chevelon Creek drainage of Arizona (Briuer 1975), yielded corn remains. Although dates of 3000 BC are reported for this occurrence, these have been questioned (Minnis 1980). O Block Cave, in the Pine Lawn Valley (Martin *et al.* 1954), produced maize that is dated to about 850–650 BC on the basis of radiocarbon dates. In addition to these sites, excavations at Ojala Cave (Traylor *et al.* 1977) near Bandelier National Monument, and at Fresnal Rock Shelter (Wimberly 1972), near Tularosa, New Mexico, have recovered maize in Archaic contexts, but the findings of neither project have been published in detail.

Maize pollen was recovered from the Cienega Creek site (Haury 1957; Martin and Schoenwetter 1960), but the reported radiocarbon dates obtained from two laboratories are so disparate (2250 BC and AD 250) that interpreting them is difficult. Redating of the Cienega Creek deposits produced dates averaging 500 BC

(Berry 1982). A single grain of maize pollen was recovered from the Double Adobe site (Martin 1963) and may date to about 1900 BC. Corn pollen was also recovered from the Matty Wash site near Tucson and may date to about 270 BC (Martin 1963).

Chapter-opening art: Maize plant (drawing by Charles M. Carrillo).

CHAPTER 6

Systematics of Southwest Culture History

All fields of knowledge develop special vocabularies that can be confusing for nonspecialists. This chapter and Chapter 7 provide a guide to the vocabulary used in southwestern archaeology and to classification by looking at the historical context within which they were developed. The vocabulary of southwestern archaeological systematics is based on classifications of architecture and pottery, material remains that together mark the end of the Archaic. This chapter, and Chapter 7, should be read quickly for a general overview and then referred to later as you use the text.

INTRODUCTION

The Southwest is a large land area, encompassing great environmental diversity, and inhabited by a variety of indigenous peoples. The history of the region extends back to at least 10,000 BC and is known primarily through archaeological research. I do not know the number of archaeological sites in the Southwest, but the number is much greater than the more than 500,000 sites recorded in various archaeological data banks and archives. To communicate about these sites, their contents, and distributions in space and over time, archaeologists use a variety of systems of classification. Some systems are very general, designed to encompass the region as a whole or major portions of it. Many more systems are used within localities but can be tied into the more general schemes. Because the vocabulary of these classifications is unfamiliar to the general public, southwestern archaeologists writing for the public and for students have sometimes presented novel, simplified schemes. It is my hope that this book can serve as a reference to the larger literature of the Southwest as well as describe variability in cultural remains from the area. Hence, I have chosen to provide the classificatory schemes that appear in the literature.

Knowledge about the history of any area develops in the context of research. The kinds of questions pursued in archaeology result from complex interactions among specific historical circumstances of investigations, the prevailing paradigms or theoretical orientations of the time, and available techniques of data recovery. In my view, providing the theoretical context for the various classifications makes them more easily understood. For that reason, the systems of classification are presented in their historical context in American archaeology and anthropology.

In only somewhat simplified terms, southwestern archaeology developed within three very general anthropological paradigms and perhaps the beginnings of a fourth. From the 1860s until about 1920, most field workers operated within the structure of unilineal evolution. From 1920 until 1965, historical particularism was the overarching structure, and from 1965 until the 1990s, southwestern archaeology depended primarily on versions of cultural ecology. Critiques of the ecological view are an important new phase but have not yet crystallized into a new paradigm. Rather, they suggest directions that may be pursued in the future. Each of these are briefly characterized in the next few pages. Keep in mind that each broad theoretical position has many variants with subtle distinctions that are very important to professionals. Also, at any one time, there are always some individuals behind and some ahead of the curve of whatever theory is popular. Noting the date when an article was published should help readers understand the perspective of the author. It will not guard against anachronisms of either the retrograde or the prescient sort. Finally, my theoretical periods follow historic contexts of archaeological research. Unilineal evolution corresponded with a period of general exploration of the Southwest. Historical particularism reigned during the dominance of professional, academic archaeology, including university and government-based research. Cultural ecological archaeology correlates with the continuation of academic research but is dominated by cultural resources management issues that arose in the context of the general national historic preservation movement. These include the National Historic Preservation Act of 1966, the National Environmental Policy Act (NEPA) of 1969, and the American Indian Religious Freedom Act (AIRFA) of 1978. The developing fourth theoretical position is occurring in a context that developed out of AIRFA and includes provisions of the Native American Graves Protection and Repatriation Act (NAGPRA) of 1994, that attempt to empower Native Americans in decisions regarding sacred and ancestral sites. On a more global basis, the emergent fourth context is one of post-modernism.

BEGINNINGS: THE 1860s TO 1920

Although the archaeological ruins in the Southwest (Figure 6.1) were known to indigenous Native Americans, Spanish explorers, and colonists, who predated American

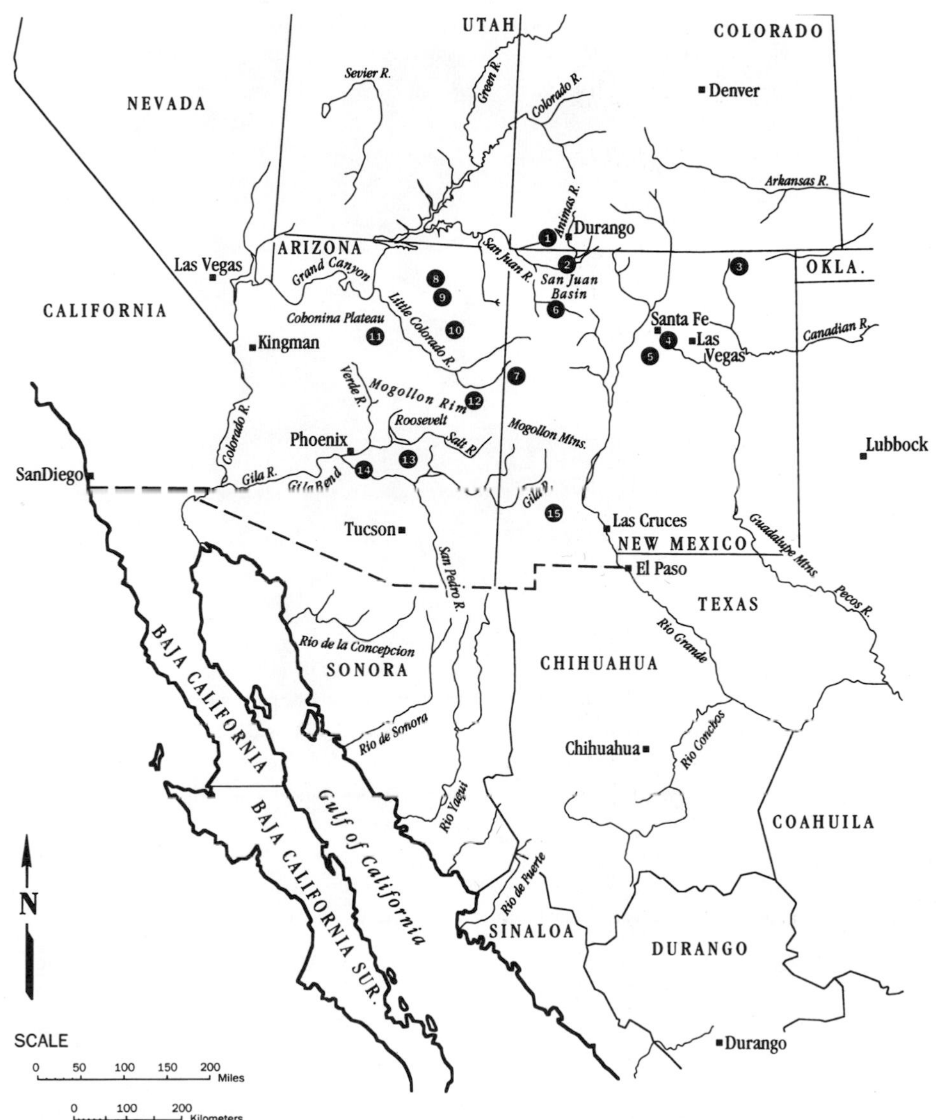

FIGURE 6.1 The sites on this map are important to the development of classification schemes in southwestern archaeology. Key: ❶ Mesa Verde (Cliff Palace); ❷ Aztec Ruin; ❸ Folsom; ❹ Pecos Pueblo; ❺ Galisteo Basin (San Cristobal Pueblo); ❻ Chaco Canyon (Pueblo Bonito); ❼ Zuni; ❽ Betatakin, Kiet Siel and Marsh Pass; ❾ Black Mesa; ❿ Hopi Mesas (Oraibi and Bacavi); ⓫ Wupatki (Sunset Crater); ⓬ Show Low (Whipple Ruin); ⓭ Globe-Miami District (Gila Pueblo, Harris Site, and Mogollon Village); ⓮ Snaketown; ⓯ Mimbres Valley Sites (Swartz Ruin, Cameron Creek Village, and NAN Ranch Ruin). (Map by David Underwood.)

FIGURE 6.2 Adolph F. Bandelier (photograph courtesy of the Museum of New Mexico; neg. no. 9155).

culture in the area, the development of southwestern archaeology took place within the broader framework of the history of the United States. The first recorders of southwestern antiquities, in the 1840s and 1850s, were not professional archaeologists because archaeology, as a discipline, did not exist. The recorders were associated with the U.S. Army reconnaissance of newly acquired Western territory. The earliest descriptions were by William H. Emory (1848) and J. H. Simpson (1850), as part of the army's topographical surveys.

Slightly later, a series of expeditions, both privately and publicly supported, provided the opportunity for a number of men, who are justifiably considered the fathers of southwestern archaeology, to enter the field. Among them were Adolph F. Bandelier,

FIGURE 6.3 Edgar L. Hewett (1865–1946) founded the School of American Archaeology and the Laboratory of Anthropology in Santa Fe (photograph by Jack Adams, courtesy of the Museum of New Mexico; neg. no. 7373).

Frank H. Cushing, Byron Cummings, Jesse W. Fewkes, Edgar L. Hewett, Walter H. Hough, Cosmo and Victor Mindeleff, John W. Powell, and James Stevenson (Figures 6.2 and 6.3). These men explored, often mapped, and sometimes excavated an enormous number of ruins throughout the Southwest. Many of their maps and notes are invaluable documents, not only in the historical sense, but in some instances because they have not been surpassed by more recent work. By traversing the Southwest on horseback and on foot and viewing hundreds of ruins, these men developed holistic perspectives on the Southwest that remains unmatched (Cordell 1989). Anyone undertaking archaeological research in the Southwest today should become familiar with the writings of Bandelier, Cushing, Cummings, Fewkes, Hewett, Hough, the Mindeleff brothers, and Powell. Many of their works have been reprinted, and there are biographies to serve as guides (e.g., Bandelier 1890, 1892; Chauvenet 1983; Cordell 1989b; Green 1990; Hensley 1983; Mindeleff 1891; Woodbury 1993).

Charged with collecting ethnographic and archaeological materials for Eastern museums, the early expedition leaders became familiar with the region's native peoples, often using information about them as keys to interpreting archaeological remains. There was no doubt among these men that ancestors of living native peoples had built and occupied the various sites that they saw in ruins. Interpretations of the uses of artifacts and architectural features and the meanings of design elements were taken directly from observing living peoples or recording the answers to their questions. The perspective of unilineal evolution emphasizes similarities among cultures, as these represent broad stages in human development. From this perspective, all Native Americans were thought to represent a single stage. As such, not much attention was given to trying to understand the history of specific cultural groups. In addition, the antiquity of human beings in the New World had not yet been demonstrated, so there was little appreciation for the potential age of some of the ruins. The lack of interest in developments over time was congruent with available archaeological methods. There were no techniques at hand to assign calendar dates to the ruins. Finally, the most visible remains throughout the Southwest were the ruins of large, compact villages that are very similar to the villages occupied by the modern Pueblos. In characterizing the entire Southwest as essentially homogeneous and as Pueblo, the early recorders of ruins were emphasizing the obvious (Cordell 1989b).

ESTABLISHING MEASURES OF TIME AND WRITING CULTURE HISTORIES: 1920 TO 1965

In the first two decades of the twentieth century, it became more common for those archaeologists working in the Southwest to have had academic training in anthropology and archaeology. University-trained scholars brought research problems and scientific methods that changed the field dramatically. Three men began the revolution in southwestern archaeology that would provide background to order remains with respect to the dimensions of time and space. Nels Nelson (1914, 1916) demonstrated the use of systematic stratigraphic excavation, A. L. Kroeber (1916) described the direct historical approach (working backward from the known) and frequency seriation of ceramics from surface collections, and Leslie Spier (1917) refined Nelson's and Kroeber's approaches and ordered sites in time using surface collections. All three focused on changes in pottery as their guide to changes over time.

Nelson's work in the Galisteo Basin, New Mexico, concerned demonstrating the chronological order of pottery styles area. He conducted test excavations at several sites. At San Cristobal Pueblo, which he knew had been abandoned in the early 1700s, Nelson excavated deep trash deposits in stratigraphic levels, enabling him to show the sequential order of pottery styles. He applied this general order to tests he had made at the other sites where the sequence was incomplete. Kroeber was working at Zuni, studying clan organization. In the evening, he would relax by walking over various abandoned sites in the vicinity of Zuni, first noting and later collecting potsherds. He observed that some kinds of ceramics, red ware, were common at Zuni Pueblo but occurred less frequently than white ware at other sites. Still other sites had only the white ware not found at Zuni. He suggested that, starting with the present, as represented by the sherds at still inhabited Zuni, one could order the sites in time through the decreasing frequency of red ware to white ware ceramics. It was Leslie Spier (1917) who applied, refined, and combined these approaches. Spier worked in the Zuni area conducting stratigraphic tests at some of Kroeber's sites to confirm Kroeber's sequence. He then examined the frequencies of the ceramic wares on the surface of sites that appeared to have had very brief occupations, enabling him to avoid problems of stratigraphic mixing. With these data, he was able to provide the temporal order of sites in the Zuni-White Mountain area from the sherds found on the surfaces of sites.

These three contributions marked a turning point in southwestern archaeology. They demonstrated that sites could be ordered relative to one another in time, that the principles of stratigraphy derived from geology could be applied to archaeology, and that ceramics are sensitive indicators of temporal change. In the years between these demonstrations and 1927, investigators applied the direct historical approach, stratigraphic excavation, and ceramic seriation to various areas of the Southwest, often to the sites that had been explored by Bandelier, Hough, Cushing, and others. The number and size of field projects undertaken in the Southwest in the 1920s is truly astonishing. In most cases, the expeditions were from large museums and universities on the East or West Coasts, with local institutions increasingly represented over time (Woodbury 1993). It is often a pleasure to read the field notebooks and reports of the time. Stratigraphic relationships are described in detail and in the best cases, there are wonderful, thoughtful discussions of puzzling features and unusual finds. I've been fortunate to learn a great deal from notes kept by Carl Guthe in 1917 (Cordell 1997), Kidder, and Earl Morris, and I recommend these notes, and others of the period, to all field archaeologists.

A key goal of these works was to define southwestern culture history. A major problem in developing an integrated chronological picture of southwestern cultures over time was the difficulty in correlating changes among areas. Most of the ruins in the Southwest had been abandoned prior to European contact, but few had been abandoned at the same time, so in most cases, it was not possible to use the direct historical approach. Also, the pottery-making traditions seemed to differ considerably from one locality to another. Hence, the sequence established for Zuni and the White Mountains would not necessarily be appropriate for the Galisteo Basin or the Pajarito Plateau. One of the most famous and ambitious projects ever launched in the Southwest was designed to firmly establish the major principles derived from the work of Kroeber, Nelson, and Spier in a complex archaeological situation, and to acquire materials that could also allow tying temporal developments in one area to other areas. This project was the expedition of the R. S. Peabody Foundation for Archaeology to Pecos Pueblo headed by A. V. Kidder (Figure 6.4).

Alfred Vincent Kidder was to become the acknowledged dean of southwestern archaeology and later continue distinguished work in Maya archaeology. Kidder was

FIGURE 6.4 Alfred V. Kidder, the acknowledged dean of southwestern archaeology, published the first synthesis of the ethnology and archaeology of the Southwest and convened the first Pecos Conference (photo by Merl Lavoy; courtesy of the American Museum of Natural History and the University of Colorado Museum).

brought to archaeology in 1907, when as an undergraduate premedical student at Harvard, he answered an advertisment in the *Harvard Crimson* for three men who might be accepted as summer "volunteers on an expedition to the cliff-dwelling country" under the auspices of the Archaeological Institute of America. Kidder, Sylvanus Morley (who would become a distinguished Maya archaeologist), and John Gould

Fletcher (who would become a poet and author) were the only three applicants, so all were accepted. The announcement had been placed by Edgar L. Hewett, who met the three easterners in Bluff, Utah, where he showed them a few ruins and turned them loose to survey and map archaeological sites for several weeks. Kidder returned to Harvard, where he continued in graduate school in anthropology, earning his Ph.D. in 1914 (Woodbury 1993).

Kidder began work at Pecos Pueblo in 1915 and continued, with interruptions, through 1929. Kidder (1931) was characteristically explicit in stating his reasons for selecting Pecos Pueblo for excavation. Pecos had the longest documented history of continuous occupation of any of the Rio Grande Pueblo ruins, having been a large town known to the Spanish explorers of 1540, and finally abandoned in 1838. The latter date allowed for the application of the direct historical approach. There were deep trash deposits that could be expected to yield material of considerable age. (The trash deposits were, in fact, deeper and more extensive than Kidder had initially anticipated, although they did not yield materials of great age.) Finally, Pecos was known to have been a major center of trade between the Pueblos and the Plains peoples. Therefore, Kidder suggested, "in its deposits are to be found bartered objects which permit accurate chronological correlation of other contemporary cultures, both Pueblo and Eastern" (Kidder 1931:589–590).

In 1924, based in part on the first six seasons of field work at Pecos and work that Kidder and others had already accomplished in the San Juan drainage (Kidder 1917) and elsewhere in the Southwest (especially Bandelier 1892; Cummings 1915; Fewkes 1911a, 1912; Hough 1914, 1920; Kidder and Guernsey 1919; Prudden 1903), Kidder (1924) published the first comprehensive synthesis of southwestern archaeology. The volume was a landmark and remains a classic. In it, Kidder summarized his work at Pecos, briefly described the modern Pueblo peoples of New Mexico and Arizona, and reviewed what was then known of southwestern archaeology. He organized the data available into the first historical reconstruction of the Southwest, identifying several areas in which more chronological information was needed (Kidder 1962:351).

The work at Pecos progressed at the same time that the astronomer A. E. Douglass developed tree-ring dating as a tool for archaeology. The basic principles involved in tree-ring dating were discussed in Chapter 2. Douglass's strategy was to obtain groups of timbers of different ages so that one group would overlap somewhat with another, allowing the chronology of rings to be extended. In 1919, this approach permitted Douglass to announce that Aztec Ruin, on the Animas, had been constructed some 40 years later than Pueblo Bonito in Chaco Canyon. The first Beam Expedition to obtain groups of timbers was organized in 1923 and sponsored by the National Geographic Society. After soliciting the aid of archaeologists and obtaining wood from various archaeological sites, Douglass developed another sequence of rings spanning 580 years, but this floating chronology was not tied to the sequence that began in 1280.

In 1928, the Second Beam Expedition was launched to extend the chronology back from occupied villages. Nearly 300 samples were obtained that brought the chronology back to 1300. There was one beam that seemed to go back as far as 1260, but there was still not a good tie to the floating chronology. So, the Third Beam Expedition was sent out in 1929, again with National Geographic support. This time, sites that probably dated to the key period were identified by surface ceramics and those that had charcoal on the surface, suggesting wood might be preserved, were targeted for testing. The expedition was led by Lyndon Hargrave, with the assistance of Emil Haury. One site they explored was the Whipple Ruin at Show Low, Arizona. There they excavated a beam that was given the field designation HH-39, the HH being the beginning initials of their surnames.

Haury (1962) retold this dramatic moment in southwestern archaeology. On Saturday, June 22, after several days of discouraging digging (not finding large beams), Haury (1962:58) reports his notes as saying, "Reed Whipple opened up Test 11, Room 4 this morning and shortly exposed a good-sized timber near the surface. Douglass and [Neil] Judd arrived from Flagstaff just in time to take pictures of it *in situ* and to help take it out."

Douglass then went to the wooden shed that served as their field laboratory to begin his field analysis. He continued analysis after a noon meal and into the evening, working while the young men stood talking quietly. Finally, Douglass announced that HH-39 had established the bridge (a very short one) between the historic and "floating" chronologies. With that one beam and his phenomenal memory of the samples he had obtained, Douglass proceeded, that evening, to provide calendar dates for most of the major Pueblo Ruins in the Southwest. Among the ruins that were immediately dated by this event were Pueblo Bonito, Aztec, Cliff Palace, Betatakin, Kiet Siel, and Wupatki (McGregor 1965; Wormington 1961). The benefits of tree-ring dating were, of course, immediately apparent to archaeologists, and during the 1930s, major institutions such as Gila Pueblo, the Museum of Northern Arizona, the University of Arizona, the Laboratory of Anthropology of the Museum of New Mexico, and the University of New Mexico established programs designed to secure wood specimens from archaeological sites. Many sites were dated.

Emil W. Haury (Figure 6.5) would also become a monumental figure in southwestern archaeology. He was brought into the field in 1925, when he worked in central Mexico with Byron Cummings, who was then dean at the University of Arizona. Haury transferred to Arizona, where he completed both his bachelor's and master's degrees and served as an instructor in archaeology. In 1930, he became assistant director of Gila Pueblo (see below), where he was assured of abundant field work and support for his further education. He completed his Ph.D. at Harvard in 1934. In 1937, he returned to the University of Arizona, where he became head of the Anthropology Department and a year later director of the just established Arizona State Museum. He continued in both positions until 1964 (Reid 1986).

By the 1920s, archaeologists working throughout North America had collected an abundance of exotic artifacts for museums and had a rough understanding of the kinds of remains in the country. The grand schemes of unilineal evolution, which had guided men like Bandelier and Powell (Cordell 1989b), fell into obsolescence in American anthropology. In the United States, unilineal evolution was replaced by a school of thought generally referred to as historical particularism and dominated by Franz Boas. Historical particularlism's primary concern is in defining the unique qualities and at-

FIGURE 6.5 Among the pioneers of Southwest archaeology are the members of the 1930 Gila Pueblo Foundation Grand Canyon Crew. Front row (left to right): Harold S. Gladwin, Nora Mac Curdy, Hilda Haury, Emil W. Haury, Pete Havens, and Russell Hastings. Back row: unidentified Gila Pueblo Staff (photo by P. Habler, courtesy of the Arizona State Museum).

tributes of specific cultures, rather than in comparing general trends of universal development. The specific characteristics and qualities of a particular culture or society might be understood in one of two ways in Boas's terms. The first way is to document its peculiar, unique history, to see how events came together in singular fashion to produce the specific culture. The second way is to understand the internal philosophy, the *geist* of the society, because each society was seen to modify contextual events to fit its internal spirit. Over the course of his career, Boas moved from the first method, documenting contextual histories, to the second, unraveling the internal cultural soul (Hatch 1973). Archaeology is fairly well-suited to the first Boasian strategy of tracing the events in specific past societies, though not to the second. The stratigraphic revolution in the Southwest was carried out by men who were trained in the Boasian tradition. With the use of stratigraphic principles and ceramic seriation, they could begin to put together the development of Native American cultures in different regions.

At the end of the summer season in August 1927, Kidder invited southwestern archaeologists and those in related disciplines to his field camp at Pecos to discuss fundamental problems of southwestern archaeology, develop a plan for resolving those problems, and "lay foundations for a unified system of nomenclature" (Kidder 1927: 489). The gathering at Pecos was the beginning of a tradition. Irregularly at first, but annually since the end of the Second World War, southwestern archaeologists reconvene the Pecos Conference at the end of the summer field season. The conference meets in various locations, but now returns to Pecos every five years. The major goal of the first Pecos Conference, that of developing a systematic nomenclature, was realized in the formulation of what is now termed the Pecos Classification. It provided the first conceptual framework for organizing the data of southwestern archaeology (Woodbury 1993).

THE PECOS CLASSIFICATION: THE FIRST FRAMEWORK

The participants at the first Pecos Conference wished to order developments in southwestern archaeology chronologically. At the time, chronological orderings could be based only on observations of stratigraphy supplemented by some historic records for the most recent end of the sequence. There were no techniques then available for assigning calendar dates to sites. Although tree-ring dating was being pursued, it was not until 1929 that the tree-ring sequence was firmly tied to the Christian calendar. The conference therefore defined culture stages characterized by diagnostic traits or elements. In theory, a stage could be defined by any of a number of traits. The conference participants selected those that showed variation over time or were indexes of "growth." Not surprisingly, architecture and ceramics were selected as key elements in the classification. The former was considered valuable in indicating cultural growth or refinement; the latter had been demonstrated to be temporally sensitive. For ceramics, it was decided that using changes in styles of cooking ware (rather than painted serving vessels) was the simplest for preliminary chronological considerations. The nomenclature adopted by the conference and the diagnostic traits for each culture stage are given here because they are still very much in use today.

Basketmaker I, or Early Basketmaker: This was a postulated pre-agricultural stage, and the one Pecos category that is no longer used. Rather, the developments envisioned are now considered Archaic (Chapter 5).

Basketmaker II, or Basketmaker: Pottery is not present; however, agriculture is known, and the atlatl (spear thrower) is used. As noted in Chapter 5, this may now be viewed as one regional manifestation of the Early Agricultural Period.

Basketmaker III, or Post-Basketmaker: Dwellings are pithouses or slab houses. Pottery is made. The cooking ware is plain, without plastic (scoring, incising, and appliqué) decoration. The people of this and the preceding Basketmaker stages do not practice cranial deformation.

Pueblo I, or Proto-Pueblo: This is the first period during which cranial deformation is practiced. Culinary vessels have unobliterated coils or bands at the neck (Figure 6.6), and villages are composed of above ground, contiguous rectangular rooms of true masonry.

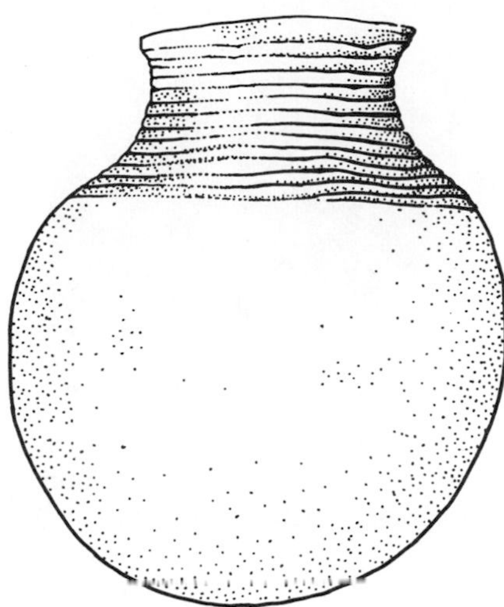

FIGURE 6.6 Unpainted culinary vessels with unobliterated neck coils are a hallmark of Pueblo I in the Pecos Classification (illustrated by Marjorie Leggitt, Leggitt Design).

Pueblo II: Corrugations extend over the exterior surfaces of cooking vessels (Figure 6.7). Small villages occur over a large geographic area.

Pueblo III, or Great Pueblo: This period is characterized by the appearance of very large communities and artistic elaboration and specialization in crafts.

Pueblo IV or Proto-Historic: Much of the Pueblo area is abandoned, particularly the San Juan region. Artistic elaboration declines and corrugated ware gradually disappears, giving way to plain ware.

Pueblo V or Historic: This period encompasses the time from AD 1600 to the present.

In addition to producing the Pecos Classification, the conference addressed other issues. There was general agreement that, although key elements in southwestern cultural developments, such as maize agriculture, were derived from Mexico, most of southwestern culture was the product of autochthonous growth. After discussion of the variety of shapes and internal features of kivas, the conference adopted a broad definition of the term: "A kiva is a chamber specially constructed for ceremonial purposes" (Kidder 1927:491). It was suggested that a binomial system of ware terminology be used in naming pottery types. The first name would refer to a place in which the type was well developed, and the second name or term was to be technologically descriptive. An example of this is Santa Fe Black-on-white. Finally, A. E. Douglass gave a report on his work with tree rings and appealed to those present to help gather specimens for his research. These subsidiary accomplishments of the Pecos Conference were all accepted by the participants.

FIGURE 6.7 During Pueblo II and Pueblo III of the Pecos Classification, plain and neck-banded pottery was replaced by vessels with overall corrugation (vessel from Tijeras Pueblo, in the Maxwell Museum of Anthropology; photo by Linda Cordell).

The Pecos Classification, as published, emphasized changes in skeletal characteristics (cranial deformation), architecture, and ceramics. At the time, the first were considered important because it was not known if the "long-headed" Basketmakers were of the same genetic stock as the "short-headed" Pueblo, who had posteriorly flattened skulls as the result of using hard cradle boards. The genetic continuity of Basketmaker and Pueblo populations is now generally accepted. Architecture and ceramics were used as diagnostic traits, in part, because these permitted comparison among areas. Kidder (1927) indicated that village types, sandals, pictographs, and other traits could also be interpreted as having undergone developmental change.

Several points should be made regarding the Pecos Classification itself. First, the scheme is developmental and not strictly chronological. Developments were not expected to be synchronous throughout the Southwest, nor were all developmental stages expected to be represented in every area (Roberts 1935b). The scheme carried no implications about the pace of change. There was no intent to presume a gradual transition from one culture stage to another, and some changes were expected to have been rather abrupt. Today, calendar dates derived from tree-ring studies are available for most of the Pueblo area.

The application of tree-ring dating to archaeological sites in the Southwest revealed that great antiquity (beyond a few centuries before the Christian era) for the Basketmakers could not be demonstrated. On the other hand, acceptance of the finds at Folsom indicated that humans had been in the Americas since the end of the Pleistocene. As Kidder (1936b:142) stated, "we immediately encounter a paradox, for while the upper end of our time scale is being distressingly compressed, its lower end is being vastly expanded by the recent unequivocal determination of the high antiquity of Folsom Man." The lower end of the chronology is now divided into Paleoindian and Archaic periods.

The most important modification of the Pecos Classification was restricting the geographic area to which it applied. It soon became obvious that the Basketmaker-Pueblo continuum was a phenomenon of the northern Southwest. In order to separate this area from other areas and other traditions in the Southwest, Kidder (1936a:590) suggested that the name *Anasazi* be applied to the Basketmaker-Pueblo sequence, which he stated, means "old people" in Navajo. (Actually, Anasazi means "enemy ancestors" in Navajo, but few archaeologists were aware of the precise translation.) In fact, Richard Wetherill, co-discoverer of the site we know as Cliff Palace at Mesa Verde, had used the term Anasazi at the Chicago World's Columbian Exposition in 1893 for those who had built the cliff dwellings at Mesa Verde (Cordell 1994). As Wetherill and others knew, the name Anasazi was widely used by the Navajo. In any case, the term Anasazi was quickly adopted in the literature of the Southwest.

At the Pecos Conference held in 1929, the general utility of the Pecos Classification was discussed. At that time, an entire group of archaeologists indicated that the classification did not seem to be useful for them. The members of this group were working in the Gila and Salt basins of central Arizona, where developments were dissimilar to those of the San Juan drainage. The distinctiveness of the Arizona deserts had been noted earlier (e.g., Mindeleff 1896) but had not been systematically explored. In 1931, researchers met at the headquarters of the Gila Pueblo Archaeological Foundation, near Globe, Arizona, and worked out a framework for classifying materials from the Arizona desert area. Later that year, the framework was reported at the Pecos Conference held at the Laboratory of Anthropology in Santa Fe (Woodbury 1993).

GLADWIN, HAURY, AND THE HOHOKAM: THE SECOND FRAMEWORK

Although field work in the Arizona desert had been initiated by Bandelier (1890, 1892), Cushing (1890), and others, the work that provided the basis for the Hohokam sequence was inspired by Kidder (Schiffer 1982:302). Most of the crucial research was carried out by Harold S. Gladwin and his associates at Gila Pueblo (Figure 6.8).

Gladwin had sold his seat on the New York stock exchange and was brought to archaeology by Kidder. According to Woodbury (1973:50), Gladwin wrote that his "archaeological career began at 10:30 a.m., August 24th [1924], on the road from Cameron to Oraibi, when Dr. Kidder pointed to a low mound and said, 'There's a ruin.' It looked like a prairie-dog's burrow, and I demanded to be shown. Sure enough, the mound was covered with sherds, and by the time we had made a collection, my future course was set."

It was Kidder who suggested that Gladwin work in the Lower Gila Valley, which was not as well known as other areas. Gladwin learned quickly. His approach to archaeological systematics eventually diverged from Kidder's, but he was dynamic, innovative, and insisted on meticulous field work. Gladwin applied the Piman name *Hohokam* to those whose remains he excavated. Although usually translated as "those who have gone" or "those who have vanished," Haury provides a more literal translation, referring to things that are "all used up":

> A characteristic of Piman languages is the manner of pluralizing the word by duplication of the first syllable. Thus, *hokam* is one thing all used up, and *hohokam* means more than one. . . . If a tire on one's automobile blows out it is hokam; if two go, hohokam (Haury 1976:5).

FIGURE 6.8 Group Photo from Gila Pueblo Foundation, Globe, Arizona. Harold S. Gladwin and Nora Gladwin are fifth and sixth from the left, respectively. Others are not identified (photograph taken about 1931–1933 and reproduced courtesy of the Arizona State Museum).

The major features distinguishing the Hohokam from the Anasazi are red-on-buff rather than black-on-white pottery; the use of the paddle-and-anvil technique to finish pottery, in contrast to the scrape-and-polish finishing done in the Pueblo area; rectangular, single-unit dwellings; cremations; and the use of extensive systems of irrigation (Roberts 1935b). The original Hohokam sequence was divided into six stages, although the first, the Pioneer period, was only inferred in 1931. As Harold Gladwin (Gladwin and Gladwin 1934:3) stated:

> Look as we would we could not find anything that we could point to as prior or introductory to a certain stage which appeared to be early, was uniform, and covered a wide area. . . . The horizon that was so uniform throughout the Gila Basin we called the Colonial Period, hoping that a day would come when we would be able to define a Pioneer Period.

Initially then, the Hohokam sequence included the Pioneer, Colonial, Sedentary, Classic, Recent, and Modern periods, with the Pioneer period being conjectural, as

Basketmaker I had been. The Pioneer was later confirmed in excavations at Snaketown, which were directed by Emil Haury, who was then assistant director of Gila Pueblo (Gladwin *et al.* 1938). Subsequently, a number of investigators have questioned whether the Pioneer remains are to be attributed to the Hohokam culture (DiPeso 1956; Schroeder 1953b). Other discussions (Gumerman and Haury 1979), have dropped the Recent and Modern periods, reflecting uncertainty in attributing continuity from the Hohokam to the modern Pima and Tohono O'Odham. In Gladwin's original scheme (Gladwin and Gladwin 1934), the diagnostic characteristics of each period are as follows:

Pioneer (conjectural): Subsequently defined in excavations at Snaketown and Roosevelt 9:6 and now accepted. Plain brown and red-slipped pottery; large, wattle and daub houses in shallow, excavated pits; cremation and inhumation.

Colonial: Pithouse villages, pit cremations, Santa Cruz Red-on-buff pottery, and Gila Plain ware, ball courts.

Sedentary: Contiguous room pueblos surrounded by compound walls, urn cremation, Sacaton Red-on-buff pottery, Gila Plain ware, and Santan Red ware.

Classic: Compounds continue, multistory adobe pueblos, platform mounds, Casa Grande Red-on-buff, Gila Red ware, and Gila Plain ware, followed by Tucson Red-on-buff and Gila Red ware, followed by Bachi Red-on-buff, Gila Red ware, Gila Polychrome, and San Carlos Red-on-brown.

Modern: Ranchería settlements, desert farmers or desert foragers with agriculture as subsidiary and modern wares (?). Currently, this period is not used, generally reflecting some doubt about the continuity from Hohokam to the modern O'Odham and Pima.

The Hohokam scheme is very similar to the Pecos Classification. Like the Anasazi stages, the Hohokam periods are defined on the basis of architecture and ceramics. Because cremation precludes noting physical differences in human head shape, the kind of burial treatment itself was used as a diagnostic. The scheme, proposed at the conference at Gila Pueblo in April 1931 and further ratified at the Pecos Conference in Santa Fe in September of the same year, established the Hohokam as a separate southwestern cultural tradition equal to that of the Anasazi. Not all southwesternists were convinced, of course. Woodbury (1993:123) reports that Emil Haury wrote to him of a conversation Haury had with Frank H. H. Roberts Jr. in which Haury had occasion to use the word Hohokam, and Roberts quietly said, "That's a lot of hokum."

HOHOKAM ORIGINS AND THE MOGOLLON: THE THIRD FRAMEWORK

In 1931, when the framework for the Hohokam was accepted, it was most important to emphasize the differences between Hohokam and Anasazi cultures. Also at that time, the origins of the Hohokam were not known because there were no known remains older than the Colonial period. Gila Pueblo organized a number of surveys to

FIGURE 6.9 Classic Mimbres Black-on-white bowl. At about AD 1000, the Mogollon of the Mimbres Valley, southcentral New Mexico, produced spectacular figurative and geometric designs on bowls, many of which were eventually placed in burial contexts (photo courtesy of the University of Colorado Museum, UMC 3140).

find the origins of the Hohokam. They found no ancestral Hohokam remains in northern Sonora or in the deserts west of the Hohokam heartland. North of the Hohokam area, along the Verde River valley, sites appeared to be Anasazi, not Hohokam. Expeditions surveying east to the upper San Francisco River area of New Mexico and then down along that river into southern New Mexico encountered sites and pottery that were distinct from both Anasazi and Hohokam developments (Gladwin and Gladwin 1934). Based on this information, the archaeologists who met at the Gila Pueblo Conference to formulate the Hohokam framework also recommended adopting another southwestern tradition on a par with the Anasazi and Hohokam. This was termed the *Mogollon*, after the Mogollon Mountains, which in turn, were named after Don Juan Ignacio Flores Mogollón, governor of the Province of New Mexico from 1712 to 1715. This proposal was also accepted by the Pecos Conference of 1931 (Woodbury 1993:123).

Long before 1931, investigators had explored the rugged Mogollon Mountain area of southeastern Arizona and southwestern New Mexico (e.g., Hough 1914, 1920). By then, the most detailed work had been carried out at sites in the Mimbres Valley, such as the Swartz Ruin (Cosgrove and Cosgrove 1932) and Cameron Creek Village (Bradfield 1931), which yielded the distinctive and spectacular Mimbres Black-on-white ceramics (Figure 6.9). These Classic Mimbres sites were single-story masonry pueblos with central plaza areas. Pithouses had also been found to underlie the pueblo structures. The presence of pithouses, pueblos, and black-on-white pottery logically led to the conclusion that the remains in the Mogollon area were a southern manifestation of the Basketmaker-Pueblo continuum, although the inspiration for the outstanding Mimbres Classic ceramics was problematic. In 1931 the Gila Pueblo surveys examined two sites in the Mogollon area, Mogollon Village and the Harris site, which yielded ceramics that seemed to reflect more Hohokam than Anasazi affiliation (Gladwin and Gladwin 1934; Haury 1936) and therefore warranted further investigation. These sites were excavated during 1933 and 1934 by Emil Haury. Comparing his data with both the Hohokam and Anasazi sequences, Haury found that there were enough differences among the three to support a separate designation for the Mogollon Mountain sites.

In many ways the Mogollon resemble the Anasazi; however, Haury noted important differences. First, red-on-brown and slipped-and-polished red ware pottery are not typically Anasazi. Second, the relatively deep Mogollon pithouses with ramp entryways are not like those in the Pueblo area. Mogollon pithouses also lacked certain floor features that were associated with pithouses in the San Juan region. On the basis of stratigraphy and some Pueblo trade ceramics, Haury was able to show that pithouses in the Mogollon region were in use until quite late and in fact were contemporaneous with Pueblo II surface structures in the San Juan region Anasazi. Third, Mimbres Classic above ground masonry pueblos were poorly constructed, which Haury interpreted as evidence that masonry construction techniques had been borrowed from the Anasazi. Fourth, Haury was impressed by the skeletal material from the Mogollon sites he excavated. These were characterized as a short-headed population, who, unlike the Pueblos, did not practice cranial deformation. In general, then, there seemed to be enough information to warrant a separate designation for the Mogollon. Finally, the Gila Pueblo surveys indicated that Mogollon ceramics, and presumably therefore Mogollon culture, were widely distributed geographically, extending from the Little Colorado River on the north to well into Chihuahua, Mexico, on the south, and from Globe, Arizona, on the west to the Rio Grande and El Paso, Texas, on the east.

There was no phase scheme or chronology for the Mogollon sequence when the designation was accepted in 1931. Haury (1936) named a number of phases for the Mimbres Valley. From earliest to latest, these are: Georgetown, San Francisco, Three Circle, Mangus, and Mimbres. Given the huge size of proposed Mogollon territory, there was variability from one area to another that researchers marked by developing different local phase sequences. In his study of the Mogollon, Wheat (1955) suggests a simplification by arranging various Mogollon developments into five general periods (termed simply Mogollon I-V). Valuable through Wheat's synthesis is, it was based on the relatively limited amount of chronological data available to him, and the more recent syntheses (Anyon *et al.* 1981; LeBlanc 1982; Rice 1980; Stuart and Gauthier 1981) do not use his categories. The awkward alternative is to point out broad similarities among the Mogollon branches but retain local phase designations. This is what is currently done. Also, as more is learned about Mogollon archaeology, there has been reduction in the geographical extent of Mogollon territory.

Roots, Stems, and Branches

In the 1930s, Gladwin and Gladwin (1934) introduced a classification scheme in the Southwest that was an attempt to unravel tribal histories. Gladwin emphasized that the indigenous peoples of the Southwest do not speak a single language. He therefore suggested recognizing different linguistic stocks: Shoshonean, Keresan, Tanoan, and Piman. In his forthright style, Harold Gladwin (Gladwin and Gladwin 1934:9) stated, "we have attempted to fit these stocks into the archaeological pattern of the Southwest." The use of spoken language to differentiate archaeological units assumes concrete relationships that have never been demonstrated. Gladwin's scheme involves a hierarchy of classificatory units. After linguistic stock, there are roots, stems, branches, and phases. The root is the most basic, inclusive category from which later peoples are believed to have developed, such as Basketmaker or Hohokam. Within roots, major geographic divisions are termed stems. Hence the Basketmaker root contains both a Little Colorado and a San Juan Stem. Stems, in turn, incorporate cultural branches. The San Juan stem is divided into Kayenta and Mesa Verde branches. Finally, branches are divided into phases, generally named after local geographic features, representing temporal and spatial variation. For example, within the Mesa Verde branch of the San Juan Anasazi, the La Plata phase is earlier than the Mancos phase. The scheme is very similar to those developed elsewhere in the United States at the time, such as the McKern (1939) or Midwest Taxonomic System.

In the Gladwin scheme, assemblages are organized on the basis of the number of traits they have in common. Sites with the most traits in common are grouped into the same phase. A practical problem arises at this point because some sites may have been occupied over a long enough period for considerable cultural change to have taken place, or sites may have been occupied at one time, abandoned, and then reoccupied later by peoples with a different cultural inventory. For these reasons, Harold S. Colton (1939) suggested that the component be added as an important conceptual device, a suggestion that was accepted by researchers. The component, which is the manifestation of a particular phase at an archaeological site, is the basic unit of classification. Similar components are grouped within the same phase. Colton (1939) also advised that the term focus be substituted for phase, because this modification would bring the southwestern scheme closer to the McKern system. Although this would have been a useful adjustment, it has been adopted only where Colton worked, in the region around Flagstaff. In practice, components within a relatively small geographic locale are first grouped together within the same phase on the basis of shared traits.

HAROLD S. COLTON, QUANTITATIVE METHODS: THE PATAYAN AND THE SINAGUA

Harold S. Colton was a professor of zoology at the University of Pennsylvania. His wife, Mary Russell Ferrell Colton, was a talented artist. Married in 1912, the two spent their honeymoon in Flagstaff, and when they returned four years later for a family vacation, became interested in the local archaeological sites (Downum 1990). Until 1925, when they were able to move to Flagstaff permanently, they spent summers pursuing a systematic program of survey and excavation of small sites, using the principles of stratigraphy and ceramic seriation developed by Nelson and Kroeber in New Mexico. Colton became director of the Museum of Northern Arizona when it was established in 1928. From that office, he continued his research program which also included detailed, technical studies of ceramics and the introduction of quantitative methods to study variability in artifact distributions.

In historic times the Colorado River area was inhabited by tribes speaking Yuman languages. The Gladwins designated the remains encountered along the Colorado River those of a separate Yuman root. While agreeing with the Gladwins that the Yuman-speaking tribes probably did have a long history of occupation along the Colorado River, Colton (1945) did not wish to assume that the archaeological materials encountered there were deposited by Yuman speakers. For that reason, he suggested that the term Patayan, meaning "old people" according to a Walapai interpreter, be applied instead of Yuman.

The oldest artifacts found in the Colorado River area were lithics (Rogers 1939). Colton (1939) used the kinds of pottery found in later assemblages as the basis for defining separate traditions and branches for the entire area. Along the lower Muddy and Virgin rivers of southern Nevada, the ceramic tradition was identified as Anasazi and termed the Virgin Branch. Ties of trade and possibly other interactions connected the Virgin Branch to the Kayenta Anasazi futher east. The archaeological ceramic-making tradition found in modern Walapai territory near Kingman, Arizona, was termed the Cerbat Branch of the Patayan (Colton 1939). Diagnostic Cerbat ceramics are Tizon Brown Ware of three sequential types: Cerbat, Sandy, and Aquarius Brown. The Cohonina from the area north and west of Flagstaff produced San Francisco Mountain Gray pottery. The final upland Patayan branch, the Prescott, also produced a gray ware, Prescott Gray (Stone 1987).

In the Patayan area, ceramic assemblages were unlike those of the Hohokam, Anasazi, or Mogollon. The Colorado ceramics were finished by paddle and anvil, but they were rarely painted and they varied in color from buff to reddish and gray (Figure 6.10). Most of the geographic area included within the definition of the Patayan was then known only from archaeological survey, so architectural forms and burial practices were largely conjectural (Colton 1939). Nevertheless, where data from excavation were available, architectural diversity was characteristic. Rectangular earth lodges with lateral entryways, masonry surface structures with small rectangular rooms, and deep pithouses lined with timber all were reported (Colton 1939).

The Patayan area was to include the upper and lower Colorado River, but Colton had little information about the lower Colorado River. Consequently, he relied on ethnographic descriptions of the Yuma, a practice which he admitted was dangerous. In an explicit and careful evaluation of the northern Colorado River materials, Colton compared the traits found with those known from the Anasazi, Mogollon, Hohokam, and Patayan as postulated from the ethnographic sources describing the Yuma. Table 7.5 reproduces this comparison for the Cohonina Plateau and for the Sinagua area around Flagstaff. Based on this comparison, Colton classified the Cohonina remains as Patayan and the Sinagua as Mogollon, based on the greatest percentage of shared traits in each case. Some investigators did not recognize the Patayan as a single cultural tradition because it appeared to be a mixture of ceramic and architectural traits from a number of areas.

At the Pecos Conference of 1956, held at the Museum of Northern Arizona in Flagstaff (Schroeder 1957), a number of archaeologists met to clarify the confusing Colorado River terminological situation. The group adopted the term Hakataya to refer to the culture of the upper and lower Colorado River and adjacent areas, based on the following characteristics: inundation (not irrigation) agriculture, hunting and gathering, stone-lined roasting pits for food preparation, ceramics finished by paddle-and-anvil technique but of varying colors resulting from uncontrolled firing, hermetically sealed vessels for food storage, mortars and pestles, percussion-flaked choppers rather than ground stone axes, temporary circular shelters, houses of variable form but generally not compact contiguous-room settlements, and predominance of cremation (although inhumation was practiced in some areas). Rock shrines and rock piles as trail markers were also considered important. It was suggested that Hakataya be applied to both the upper and lower portions of the Colorado River, with the name Patayan reserved for the upper portion and Laquish for the lower portion. The proposal was rejected by the 1957 Pecos Conference. The Pecos Conference agreed to retain the term Patayan for the entire area of western Arizona below the Grand Canyon.

In later syntheses, Schroeder (1960, 1979a) again introduced the term Hakataya but modified its referents. In this latter formulation, he argued that Hakataya should be used to refer to the basic brown ware tradition of most of Arizona, including the Patayan, the Sinagua, and the Pioneer period Hohokam remains that predate AD 500. In essence, this definition reflects Schroeder's view that the Hohokam, as an ethnic group, migrated into the Gila and Salt river valleys in about AD 500 and that the tremendous variation included within the rest of the Hakataya area can be ascribed to varying cultural influences. This broader definition of the Hakataya is difficult to accept because it incorporates diversity in virtually every aspect of material culture. For that reason, the usage in McGuire and Schiffer's (1982) summary of southwestern Arizona archaeology, and the precedent established by the 1957 Pecos Conference, the term Patayan is retained here.

Sinagua is the name Colton (1939, 1946) applied to archaeological remains found in the vicinity of Flagstaff. Some Sinagua traits, such as rock-tempered, predominantly paddle-and-anvil-finished, plain brown pottery, and masonry-lined pithouses, seem

FIGURE 6.10 Patayan Jar. Lower Colorado buffware jar with tapered, chimney neck rim and rounded "Colorado shoulder" (photograph courtesy of the Arizona State Museum).

distinctive from Anasazi, Hohokam, and Mogollon characteristics. On the other hand, there are significant similarities. Black-on-white painted ceramics are like those of the Anasazi. Hohokam ball courts occur in the area, and much of the pottery and architecture is within the range of the late Mogollon. The complex constellation of Sinagua traits has been variously interpreted. Colton (1939, 1946) considered the Sinagua a branch of the Mogollon. McGregor (1936, 1937) refers to the Sinagua as Patayan, and Schroeder (1979a) includes Sinagua within the Hakataya.

The Sinagua case is particularly interesting because rather than representing a new inventory of cultural traits or a new sequence of the appearance of features (as was true for the definition of the Hohokam and Mogollon), the Sinagua area reveals a complex blending of elements. At times, the area was distinctive. At other times, it incorporated elements of other defined cultural traditions. Initially, the assortment of external elements was interpreted as indicating migrations of various groups of people attracted by a local phenomenon—the deposition of volcanic ash.

Sinagua culture history was viewed in relation to the inferred effects of the eruption, beginning in AD 1064, that created Sunset Crater (Colton 1960; McGregor 1936, 1937; Pilles 1979). Three phases of the Sinagua tradition are recognized in material dated prior to 1064: Cinder Park, Sunset, and Rio de Flag, dating from about AD 500 to 700, 700 to 900, and 900 to 1064, respectively. Throughout this sequence, Sinagua culture seems to have uniform ceramics, architectural styles, settlement plans, and subsistence strategies. The characteristic ceramics are types of Alameda Brown ware, which is usually paddle-and-anvil finished ware. Trade ceramics from the Kayenta Anasazi and the Hohokam occur in the earlier phases.

During the Rio de Flag phase, Cohonina trade ceramics are common. House types show considerable variation and include circular or sub-square pithouses with lateral entries or antechambers, teepee-like structures, masonry-lined pithouses, and small masonry surface structures. Overly large circular pithouses may have been associated with intercommunity ceremonial activities. Pithouse villages are located along the edges of large basins or parks. Both rainfall and floodwater farming could have been practiced at the park locations. Stone field houses, check dams, and irrigation ditches are part of the farming technology used in areas away from the parks.

Colton (1939, 1946) and McGregor (1941) argued that the effect of the initial eruption creating Sunset Crater was the deposition of substantial amounts of volcanic ash, which acted as a mulch and also added nutrients to the soil. According to this interpretation, the ancient farmers recognized the benefits of this soil, and a number of culturally different groups then moved into the Flagstaff area to farm. Hence, the Hohokam, Mogollon, and Anasazi peoples joined the Sinagua, creating the contemporary (1070–1120) Padre, Angell, and Winona phases. Slightly later (1130–1200), these elements amalgamated in the Elden focus. This was succeeded by the Turkey Hill (1200–1300) and Clear Creek (1300–1400) foci, after which the volcanic ash was to have eroded away, causing the area to be abandoned for permanent occupation. While containing some lasting elements, this scenario has been reevaluated and modified.

Pilles (1979) notes that although major eruptions associated with Sunset Crater took place in the years 1064–1065 and 1066–1067, geological investigations in the 1970s indicate continued episodes of volcanic activity for a period of about 200 years after the initial eruption. Further, although volcanic ash does serve as an effective mulch, it does not increase the soil nutrients. Pilles (1979) finds no convincing evidence of either substantial population increase following the eruption or of substantial numbers of Hohokam, Mogollon, or Anasazi migrants. He argues that the Hohokam manifestation is limited to one or a few items at most sites, with the exception of a single pithouse and its adjacent trash mound at Winona Village (McGregor 1941). Pilles suggests that a Hohokam presence in the Flagstaff area may be better explained as part of the general expansion of the Hohokam out of the Gila-Salt river valleys, possibly to facilitate the acquisition and distribution of raw materials and other trade goods. With this interpretation, the single pithouse at Winona Village might represent a Hohokam trader engaged in a trading post-like situation rather than part of a transplanted Hohokam village (Pilles 1979:472).

Aside from the pithouse at Winona, the most substantial evidence of Hohokam intrusion is the presence of 13 ball courts in the Sinagua area. Pilles interprets these ball courts as an acceptance of Mesoamerican ceremonial complexes, without the Hohokam as agents in this introduction. The Hohokam evidence is the most substantial of all of the proposed migrant groups. The Kayenta Anasazi are credited with introducing masonry construction to the Sinagua, but Cartledge (1979) and Pilles (1979) both indicate that such construction was present prior to the eruption. The evidence

FIGURE 6.11 Archaeologists at Chaco Canyon in the 1930s (left to right): Karl Ruppert, Kirk Bryan (?), William Henry Jackson, Lynn Hammond, Neil Judd, F. H. H. Roberts, Jr., C. S. Scofield, and Monroe Amsden (photo courtesy of the U.S. Park Service).

for other colonies of migrants is far more tenuous. In this revised view, the later portions of Sinagua history are better understood in terms of local developments allied with general trends among the Western Anasazi.

Some Problems with Cultural Norms and Developmental Schemes

The Pecos Classification and the other developmental schemes used in the Southwest suggest that changes in architecture and ceramics occur synchronously within the same area. Although the phase schemes recognize that such change may not occur over very broad geographic regions (such as the entire Mogollon Mountains), it is generally assumed that at the branch level there should be little variation. The empirical data of archaeology have long shown that homogeneity within contemporary phases of the same branch does not always exist. A classic demonstration of this point is the recognition that within the Chaco branch (Figure 6.11) of the Anasazi culture, between about AD 950 and 1130, two entirely different architectural styles and site plans co-occur in the same very small geographic area. One style consists of large, multistoried, planned pueblos (such as Pueblo Bonito). The other style consists of single-story, small, unplanned pueblos (such as the village identified as Casa Rinconada). Ceramics from the large pueblos and small pueblos are virtually the same. Also within the Anasazi culture, the Chaco, Mesa Verde, and Kayenta branches are distinguished on the basis of architectural styles. Yet excavations have demonstrated that within the same site all three styles of construction may be present (Martin and Rinaldo 1960; Martin *et al.* 1961). Any scheme of classification that minimizes or ignores these kinds of variation will not be a faithful rendering of the diversity that can characterize the archaeological record.

From the foregoing it appears that one key result of the formulation of the Pecos Classification was the fragmentation of what had been regarded as a single basic southwestern culture into four ancient traditions (Anasazi, Hohokam, Mogollon, and Patayan), each characterized by slightly different constellations of material traits and developmental trends in burial practices, architecture, and ceramics. As southwestern archaeologists pursued their investigations, it became obvious that there are minor variations in trait complexes and in rates of change across geographic areas. Even within the Mogollon area, variations in house types or changes in technology were found from one river valley to another. Within the Anasazi area, the history of the upper Pecos Valley, as reflected at Pecos Pueblo and surrounding ruins, was found to be quite different from that already documented in the San Juan area.

In the 1920s and 1930s, virtually all variation in material culture was ascribed to cultural ("ethnic") differences among peoples. In Boasian anthropology, each culture, each living society, was described in terms of shared cultural norms. Culture itself was thought of as consisting of shared ideas, ideals, values, and beliefs. In archaeology, artifact types represented shared ideas about what the type should look like, be it a pot or a point. Variation was viewed as approximations of ideal types. In the Southwest, archaeologists equated differences in material remains to differences in cultures, in the sense of different peoples. In reality of course, archaeologists do not dig up societies, tribal boundaries, or languages without written records. Archaeological cultures are not ethnic groups. Among the key challenges of archaeology is to find ways of linking the material remains we work with to groups of people, understanding that quite often, those links are in no way direct or unambiguous.

There are other reasons why the normative framework may be inadequate for describing either contemporary or archaeological cultures; some variation may be functionally related to variations in activities. For example, sites of different sizes with different tool assemblages but sharing some tool types might represent seasonally differentiated activities among the same group of people (Goodyear 1975), rather than the settlements of culturally different groups of people who either traded some tools or who influenced each other in their ideas about a few classes of tools.

In addition to describing past lifeways, archaeology is concerned with describing the ways change occurs over time. The developmental schemes applied in the Southwest were prepared before methods of assigning calendar dates to archaeological sites were available. Consequently, either stratigraphic information or unverified notions involving trends in "refinement" were applied to facilitate the temporal ordering of remains. In these schemes, architecture is often considered an index of development and growth. It is assumed that there is a trend from simple, perhaps crude, forms such as pithouses to refined and perhaps complex forms, such as pueblos. For example, Haury (1936) interpreted the appearance of crudely built above ground pueblo structures in the Mimbres area as evidence that this architectural form had been borrowed from the Anasazi. Archaeological data available demonstrate that pithouses were in use in the Pueblo area in the Rio Grande Valley, the upper Little Colorado, and Black Mesa long after the Anasazi had "developed" the ability to build pueblos (Cordell and Plog 1979). Among the most recent pithouses built as dwellings were those constructed at the modern Hopi town of Bacavi in the twentieth century, many years after the Hopi and their ancestors had learned the technology of constructing above ground rooms. These examples suggest that pithouses and pueblos probably serve different functional purposes within the context of the entire culture. Either form may be used as a dwelling, depending on various behavioral and demographic factors. It is incumbent on archaeologists to define the circumstances under which each would be built, rather than to assume that one form is a more advanced elaboration of technology. When Kidder suggested that developmental patterns could be discerned in classes of archaeological material, such as rock art or basketry, the tools for chronological ordering were not available. The continued use of developmental schemes is not always warranted by current information.

In addition to describing lifeways and the course of change in cultures over time, archaeologists share with their anthropological colleagues the obligation to try to explain the patterned diversity in culture. Developmental schemes describe changes without providing any explanations for the particular change involved. In some cases, the change is viewed as a natural development, which, in view of the above discussion of the use of pithouses or above ground pueblos, cannot be accepted. Within the normative framework, as noted, material culture items are seen as reflections of ideas shared by members of a society. When a change appears in the archaeological record, a change involving material culture, it is frequently interpreted as being the result of the introduction of a new group of people with a different set of norms. For example, the appearance of multistoried great houses in the Hohokam area, along with polychrome pottery, was interpreted as evidence of an incursion of a new group of non-Hohokam people. Again, in view of the current paradigm, which emphasizes that variation in material items may reflect differences in function or social organization, such interpretations must be questioned.

As the studious reader of most southwestern archaeology books must notice, an enormous number of migrations have been postulated. Certainly some of the emphasis on migration is the result of the observation that most southwestern archaeological sites, and some entire regions, were abandoned after varying intervals of time (Cameron 1994). The inhabitants of these sites and regions must have gone somewhere, and migration into other areas is a logical supposition. Nevertheless, migration is not an easy phenomenon to demonstrate in the archaeological record (Morris 1938; Rouse 1958), especially if change in the material culture inventory can be ascribed to other factors. If archaeologists are to attempt to interpret change, then various explanations for particular changes, including migrations, must be evaluated against a set of independently derived data. Archaeology must follow the basic procedures of any science. When it does, we can have more confidence in proposed explanations for the variation we see.

CULTURAL ECOLOGICAL FRAMEWORKS: 1965 TO 2000

Boasian anthropology did not become outmoded in the same way unilineal evolution did through the development of a new professional, academic discipline. Rather, Boas's views were modified in the context of new questions posed among professional anthropologists in this country, in England, and in Europe. Where Boas increasingly found answers about cultural behavior in the nonrational, internal psychology of emotion and the human mind, others, particularly British anthropologists, began to focus on interactions among individuals, as mediated through kinship and other forms of social and political organization at the core of cultural behavior. In the United States, this focus was brought to the forefront when British social anthropologist A. R. Radcliffe-Brown accepted an invitation to teach at the University of Chicago (1931–1937), where his students included a generation of scholars who would revolutionize studies of Native American cultures (e.g., Fred Eggan, Robert Redfield, Sol Tax, etc.).

An interest in how cultural behavior was modified through interactions with the natural and cultural environment had always been part of early Boasian thought but was encouraged anew by similar interests in geography. A. L. Kroeber, who earned his Ph.D. at Columbia under Boas, founded the Department of Anthropology at the University of California, Berkeley, where among his many achievements, he continued research on the distribution of cultural elements (traits). His student Julian Steward, who also studied with the renowned geographer Carl Sauer, created a remarkably powerful synthesis of element distributions and cultural geography in what he termed the "concept and method of cultural ecology" (Steward 1955). Cultural ecology directs research attention at the interface between environment and cultural behavior. Rather than viewing the locus of culture change in a series of unconnected and equally valued norms (shared ideas, rules, beliefs), Steward proposed looking at those aspects of cultural behavior that could be demonstrated to most clearly articulate with the environment as sources and stimuli for cultural *evolution*. By reintroducing the environment, Steward, who had conducted archaeological research (Strong *et al.* 1930), was able to bring American archaeology back into a position of some importance to general anthropology.

Cultural evolution was embraced, and again brought to the forefront of anthropological research by Leslie A. White, who became the voice of anthropology at the University of Michigan, although White's approach was very different from Julian Steward's. White championed the development of anthropology as the *science* of culture, which could be studied as a system of behavioral components. As with any kind of system, a change in one component could be shown to cause changes in other components. In systems research sometimes very small changes in variables have disproportionately large, and generally unanticipated, consequences. The subsystems White focused on were technology (linked to the environment), sociology (social organization), and ideology. By virtue of an emphasis on technology and awareness of the environment, archaeology again becomes relevant. Further, White's insistence on a science of culture (White 1969) provided a method of investigation—the scientific method of hypothesis generation and testing that appealed to archaeologists, who of necessity depend as much on the natural and physical as on social science. White was very much within the general philosophical modernist tradition.

Steward and White had tremendous appeal to the growing number of anthropology students trained to be professionals immediately after World War II. These students, those who had studied social anthropology at the University of Chicago and all of their students combined, constituted a cohort that founded, chaired, and staffed the dozens of new anthropology programs that mushroomed on campuses throughout the United States during the 1960s. In general, the new programs were at state universities in the Midwest and West and at smaller state colleges and junior colleges that grew to accommodate the post-war baby boomers. Older, established, primarily East and West Coast institutions had established anthropology programs, and these were most often led by individuals trained "in-house" at these same institutions.

The singular post-World War II, modernist voice of archaeology who brought Leslie White's program along with some of Julian Steward's ideas, quantitative approaches advocated by Albert C. Spaulding, and his own thoughts to American archaeology was Lewis R. Binford. Binford's research program, referred to as new or processual archaeology, has been self-consciously scientific, anthropologically systemic, quantitative, and ecological. First at the University of Chicago; then at the University of California, Los Angeles for much of his teaching career; at the University of New Mexico; and now at Southern Methodist University, Binford has had enormous impact on archaeology worldwide and quite specifically, through students, on the U.S. Southwest. In the Southwest, his students have shared the arena with those who learned their anthropology at the older, established, traditional East Coast and West Coast universities. Binford himself has not done field work in the Southwest.

The catalyst for a southwestern focus for Binford's students was provided by Paul S. Martin and Chicago's Field Museum. Martin ran a graduate field school, sponsored by the National Science Foundation, at various locations in the Mogollon region. The virtually all-male field schools brought the nationally outstanding archaeological graduate students to the Mogollon Mountains, often providing data for the first doctoral dissertations in processual archaeology. Among those who attended Field Museum field schools were James N. Hill, William A. Longacre, Fred Plog, Ezra Zubrow, and Michael B. Schiffer.

The first two of Binford's students both are southwestern archaeologists: William A. Longacre and James N. Hill. Their studies of Carter Ranch (Longacre 1968) and Broken-K (Hill 1970) pueblos were milestone processual documents in two respects. First, they were self-consciously scientific in establishing propositions or hypotheses and devising various, often statistical, tests. Second, they were systems-oriented in proposing to examine post-marital residence rules and other features of social organization by examining artifactual data. One result of the scientific emphasis was that the Southwest increased its reputation for being a laboratory where innovative ideas could be tested. This in turn contributed to the view that archaeological sites are similar to experiments and that their primary value is scientific. Virtually all the public law developed in the 1960s that concerns archaeology considers the primary value of archaeological data to be scientific. While this puts archaeologists in the opposite corner from pot hunters, looters, and collectors, it also undervalues the aesthetic, spiritual, and ideological importance of archaeology, especially with regard to Native American values. This, in turn, has made it more difficult than it might otherwise be for archaeologists and Native Americans to work together as required by more recent U.S. federal legislation (see pp. 183 and 219).

The attempts to reconstruct past social organization were at first readily embraced by culture historical archaeologists, who viewed this novel approach as a way to truly reconstruct past lifeways, to see the Indians behind the artifacts, and to begin to do the kinds of studies social anthropologists would acknowledge as worthy (Woodbury 1993). Nevertheless, the pioneering studies of social organization were, correctly, criticized on both conceptual and methodological grounds (S. E. Plog 1980; Stanislawski 1969), and students soon moved away from narrow examination of post-marital residence rules. Nevertheless, the interest in organization, in the kind of groups and the functions of groups, in past societies remains an important area of inquiry today (Cordell and Plog 1979; Reid and Whittlesey 1990; Saitta 1994; Neitzel in press). Further, in focusing on organization, many found the works of Julian Steward increasingly valuable because cultural ecology set out to define the articulation between environmental features and kinds of sociocultural integration. This linkage is seen in models of the Archaic that depend on Steward's characterization of Great Basin band structure and discussions of the origin of Pueblo clans that consider Steward's study of room to kiva ratios among others (Adler 1994; Kintigh 1994; Vierra 1994b).

The processual archaeologists of the 1960s and early 1970s often found academic employment, though often at smaller, state schools than they themselves attended. By the 1980s, however, anthropology enrollments, like the college-age population in general, declined. Opportunities for work in archaeology were in government land management agencies and, increasingly, in small contract or consulting archaeology firms.

THE CONTEXT OF PUBLIC ARCHAEOLOGY FROM THE 1970s

Salvage archaeology, in conjunction with state highway projects, had begun in the 1950s (e.g., Wendorf 1956). Part of the more general conservation movement of the 1960s was passage by the U.S. government of the National Historic Preservation Act of 1966, the National Environmental Policy Act (NEPA) of 1969, and finally, in 1978, the American Indian Religious Freedom Act (AIRFA). Among the provisions of these acts are requirements to develop and maintain inventories of historic and cultural resource properties on federal lands, to manage those properties, and ensure that cultural resources are identified and located prior to any land-modifying activities that could threaten them.

The amount of federal land in the eastern United States might have made compliance with the 1966 act a matter of rearranging priorities. A map of federal lands in the Southwest suggests an enormous problem. The Southwest Region of the U.S. Forest Service along encompasses 20 million acres of land (Proper 1988). Federal lands in the states of Arizona and New Mexico only amount to slightly more than 59 million acres and the holdings of the National Park Service, Federal Indian Reservations, Bureau of Land Management, U.S. Fish and Wildlife, and Department of Energy. State lands, which are also public lands, of course, developed similar legal requirements.

Some agencies, such as the Park Service, have a history of archaeological research that dates to the Antiquities Act of 1906 and to the establishment of Mesa Verde National Park in 1907, as the first National Park to feature archaeological resources. Other agencies hired their first archaeologists in the 1970s and quickly implemented procedures to comply with the requirements of federal and state legislation. As a result, the 1970s and 1980s were decades during which most archaeological research in the Southwest came under the auspices of one or another cultural resources management program, and most archaeology students tried to prepare for careers with public agencies or private firms working on contracts.

The influence of large-scale contract programs on archaeology has been immeasurable; only a few effects are mentioned here. Most contract work is initiated by survey, and since an objective is to protect cultural resources, excavation is not the preferred option. A result is that far more recent information concerns survey rather than excavation. There has been consistent growth in knowledge about the distributions of sites with respect to features of the natural environment and other sites. There is a correlated literature on predictive modeling that concerns site locations. Most reports, unfortunately, appear only in the gray literature composed of small numbers of technical reports provided to firms, agencies, and a few specialized libraries. The legislation that accepted the scientific value of archaeology also required research designs. In order that research priorities be established, state agencies, monuments and parks, and the regional offices of federal agencies commissioned a series of overviews of geographical regions that were meant to provide baselines about what was known (e.g., Cordell 1979; Stuart and Gauthier 1981; etc.). These were to be updated on a regular schedule.

The first regional computer databases of archaeological sites were developed (Gumerman 1971; Euler and Gumerman 1978; Plog and Wait 1979), and continue to thrive. It became possible to look at site information for very large areas and to combine these data with increasingly sophisticated environmental and paleoenvironmental data. The first of the Southwest regional computerized data base projects was a voluntary association of archaeologists called the Southwestern Anthropological Research Group (SARG). Convened at Prescott College in 1971, SARG epitomized the ecological perspective of processual archaeology in the context of regional research. The SARG philosophy stated that "since the 1950's, archaeologists have turned increasingly from a concern with chronological frameworks and simple historical reconstructions to attempts at broad explanatory schemes, especially of culture change. Most of these projects have a theoretical approach based on some sort of ecological orientation" (Gumerman 1971:2). To overcome the problem of asking broad regional questions but being restricted to individual field projects, SARG adopted a research format that its members voluntarily agreed to pursue in addition to and in the course of their own research. Since all those involved were conducting survey projects at the time, the common research involved settlement archaeology, something that survey data might

FIGURE 6.12 The "Dynamics of Southwest Prehistory" symposium posed for their official portrait at the School of American Research, Santa Fe. Back row (left to right): Gregory Johnson (discussant), J. Jefferson Reid, Arthur Rohn, W. James Judge, Jeffrey S. Dean, Linda S. Cordell; front row (left to right): Paul Fish, Douglas W. Schwartz (chair), Steven A. LeBlanc, Fred Plog, George Gumerman (photo by Debra Flynn Post, courtesy of the School of American Research).

address. The question agreed upon by the group was "why are population aggregates located where they are?"

SARG provided a model of cooperative research, developed a computer database, held irregular conferences, and published results. As noted above, many federal agencies began hiring their first archaeologists in 1970. Young archaeologists took up posts on federal lands throughout the Southwest, often charged with developing research designs and mitigation plans for localities they had never before visited. Fortuitously, SARG provided direction in the form of a general research question that could be approached anywhere and a strategy to implement problem-oriented surveys. It is not surprising that the first 5 to 10 years of southwestern contract reports are dominated by questions about population aggregates and site locations.

SARG seems also to have been the ancestor of more recent conferences. As truly enormous amounts of data flooded in, the job of synthesis was left to smaller conferences organized by museums, federal agencies, or universities, and sometimes sponsored by research institutions such as the School of American Research, Santa Fe (Figure 6.12); the Amerind Foundation, Dragoon; Crow Canyon Archaeological Research Center, Cortez; Fort Burgwin Research Center, Taos; or the Santa Fe Institute, Santa Fe. There are now separate regular or irregular conferences on the Hohokam, Mogollon, and Anasazi and a currently biannual Southwestern Archaeological Conference that is thematically oriented (Minnis and Redman 1990; Wills and Leonard 1994).

Finally, a few truly enormous multiyear projects were undertaken and completed during these years. The first of these was the Glen Canyon Project (Jennings 1966), followed by, among others, the Black Mesa Project (Gumerman and Euler 1976; Gumerman 1988), the Dolores Project (Kohler *et al.* 1986), the Salt River Project (Keller 1986), the Central Arizona Project (Bayham 1983; Spoerl and Gumerman 1984), the Roosevelt Lake Project (Elsen and Clark 1995), and the Transwestern Pipeline Project (Amsden 1992; Winter 1991). These have generated literally tons of data and vast warehouses full of artifacts that it is probably nearly impossible to synthesize. In terms of systematics and vocabulary, most projects develop their own phase schemes in the course of work. Virtually no one but those who are doing the work or reading the reports is really familiar with more than two or three sequences. Consequently, there has been a return to using the broad schemes of classification for communication. Archaeologists really do talk about "Pueblo II," (or actually, P. II). They do refer to Classic Period Hohokam. Rather than being a small working conference during which problems of taxonomy are worked out, the Pecos Conference grew tremendously in size and became a venue to report contract projects recently undertaken or concluded.

Chapter-opening art: Drawing by Charles M. Carrillo

CHAPTER 7

New Frameworks, Elaboration, and Current Chronologies

This chapter continues the presentation given in Chapter 6. The sequences given the most attention here are not only well-studied but serve as bench marks for very broad patterns that characterize the Southwest during some time periods. Hence, they are frequently cited in the current literature. They include the key areas that seem to define the pace and character of changes in the ancient Southwest. New directions and themes of research are touched on at the end of this chapter. Again, this chapter can be skimmed and returned to as a reference later on.

INTRODUCTION

Since the 1930s, southwestern archaeologists have worked on the formulation of local and regional sequences and assigning calendar dates to them. There has been a continuing effort to link various remains to specific linguistic or ethnic groups. Not all of these efforts have been successful, and the literature reflects a considerable amount of controversy in interpretation. Chronological revisions make up a substantial portion of the literature of southwestern archaeology and will likely continue to do so. This chapter does not give the history of debates within various regions of the Southwest. Rather, a summary of regional frameworks and some assessment of recent chronological discussions and areas of disagreement are provided as background necessary to further treatment of the post-Archaic developments in the Southwest. A full discussion of regional development throughout the Southwest and issues surrounding the chronologies makes up much of the chapters of this book. This review is very brief and should serve only to provide a reference and mark areas in which further research is necessary. Most of this discussion involves regional traditions that have been introduced in preceding chapters. Others, such as the Fremont and the traditions of Sonora and Chihuahua, are discussed for the first time.

There have also been several attempts to synthesize information across regional traditions by focusing on larger patterns that occur in more than one area (e.g., Adler 1996; Gumerman 1994; Gumerman and Gell-Mann 1994). Such patterns include the formation of large settlements, periods of regional integration, and episodes of population dispersal and local abandonment of habitations. Discussion of the dynamics underlying these larger patterns make up most of the rest of this book. In this chapter, the patterns themselves and the various ways they have been interpreted are presented, followed by a brief discussion of some new directions being pursued in current research. The sequences discussed here are the ones most commonly featured in the professional and popular literature of southwestern archaeology.

THE ANASAZI

The Pecos Classification is still applied over much of the Anasazi area; however, it has been dropped for the Rio Grande Valley and supplemented by sequences of local phases in the Mesa Verde, Kayenta, Rio Puerco, Acoma, and other areas (Figure 7.1). Some of the commonly used local Anasazi phase sequences are given in Table 7.1. Because the most distinctive and most frequently compared Anasazi sequences are those of the Chaco Canyon, Mesa Verde, Kayenta, and Rio Grande branches, these are briefly discussed below.

Chaco Canyon

The abundant standing architectural ruins of Chaco Canyon have drawn archaeologists since the nineteenth century (Lister and Lister 1981). In part for that reason, the ancient developments in the canyon were seen as prototypically Anasazi. Intensive archaeological work begun in 1971 became the basis for understanding Chaco Canyon as the cornerstone for the development of a regional pattern that is unique in the Southwest, rather than typical, with some of its peculiarity relating to its great influence on surrounding regions (Crown and Judge 1991; Judge 1989; Lekson 1984; Vivian 1990). The scope of what is generally referred to as the Chaco Phenomenon or the Chacoan System is deferred to a later chapter. Paleoindian, Archaic, and Basketmaker II developments in the canyon are not of concern here. This section focuses on the Anasazi sequence in the Chaco area. Vivian (1990) provides the most comprehensive synthesis of Chaco archaeology available.

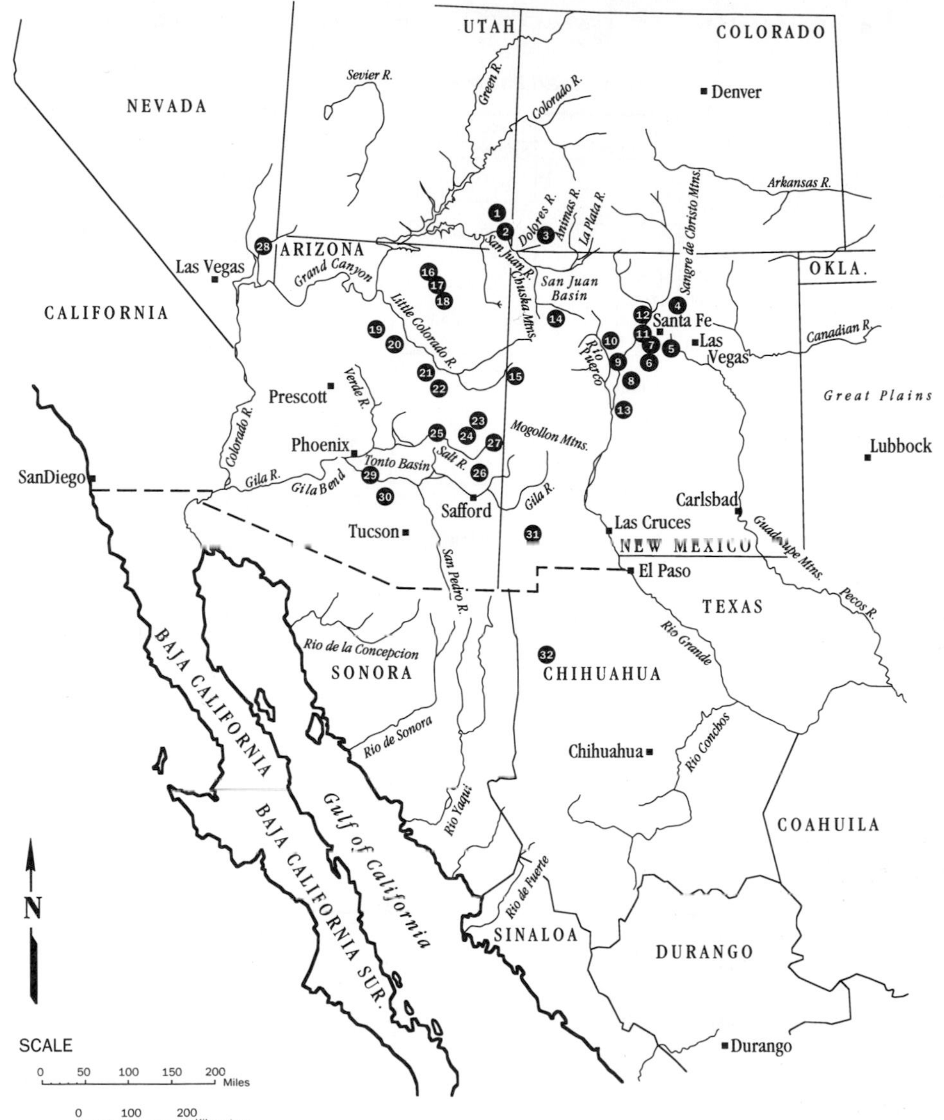

FIGURE 7.1 The sites discussed in Chapter 7 relate to current chronologies in the Southwest. Key: 1 Alkali Ridge; 2 Cedar Mesa; 3 Mesa Verde; 4 Taos District (Picuris); 5 Pecos Pueblo; 6 Galisteo Basin (San Cristobal Pueblo); 7 Arroyo Hondo; 8 Tijeras Canyon (and Paa-ko Pueblo); 9 Kuaua; 10 Jemez Pueblo, Unshagi and Giusewa; 11 Bandelier National Monument; 12 Otowi and Tsankawi; 13 Gran Quivira; 14 Chaco Canyon; 15 Zuni; 16 Tsegi Canyon (Scaffold House, Lolomaki, Batwoman House, and Twin Caves Pueblo); 17 Betatakin, Kiet Siel and Marsh Pass; 18 Black Mesa; 19 Waputki and Sunset Crater; 20 Winona Village; 21 Chavez Pass Pueblo; 22 Chevelon Drainage; 23 Hay Hollow Valley; 24 Forestdale Valley; 25 Grasshopper and Canyon Creek; 26 Point of Pines Region (Turkey Creek and Kinishba); 27 Reserve; 28 Virgin and Muddy Rivers; 29 Snaketown; 30 Casa Grande; 31 Mimbres Valley Sites (Swartz Ruin, Cameron Creek Village, NAN Ranch Ruin); 32 Casas Grandes. (Map by David Underwood.)

TABLE 7.1 Anasazi Phase Sequences

Date	Mesa Verde[a]	Chaco Canyon[b]	Kayenta[c]
1400			
1300		Mesa Verde	
1250			
1200	Mesa Verde	Late Bonito	
1150			
1100	McElmo		Toreva
1050	Mancos	Classic Bonito (Pueblo II)	Lamoki
1000			Wepo
950	Ackmen	Bonito (Early Pueblo II)	Dinnebito
900			
850			
800	Piedra	Pueblo I	Tallahogan
750			
700			
650		Basketmaker III	Dot Klish
600	Lino		
550			
500			

[a]Adapted from Varien *et al.* (1996:88).
[b]Adapted from Hayes *et al.* (1981:18) and Cordell and Gumerman (1989).
[c]Adapted from Plog and Powell (1984:6).

Basketmaker III sites date from about AD 400–500 to about AD 725 or 750. Sites generally consist of 1 to 12 subcircular, semi-subterranean pithouses with antechambers or large ventilator shafts and associated slab-lined cysts. Baketmaker III sites are often located on mesa tops bordering the canyon, but many undoubtedly lie buried by alluvium in the canyon floor. Locally produced ceramic types are Lino Gray and its decorated equivalent, La Plata Black-on-white. Initially, the designs painted on pottery of both traditions was much the same, with simple lines, which seem to have been derived from basketry patterns, on the interior of bowls (Figure 7.2).

With Pueblo I, dating from about AD 750 to 920, habitations changed to above-ground dwelling units with associated proto-kivas and later with kivas. Initially construction materials were jacal and adobe, and later were sandstone slabs and adobe or

FIGURE 7.2 Anasazi Basketmaker III pottery has simple designs, that seem to be derived from basketry patterns, painted on unslipped bowl interiors (illustrated by Marjorie Leggitt, Leggitt Design).

rough-coursed masonry. In addition to Lino Gray, neck-banded Kana-a Gray culinary vessels were produced. White Mound Black-on-white and Kiatuthlanna Black-on-white are the major painted types. There was an increase in the number of Pueblo I sites in the canyon, and these sites showed the beginning of a trend of movement off the mesa tops to canyon bottom locations. These developments parallel changes elsewhere in the San Juan Basin.

During early Pueblo II, AD 920–1020, there was a marked divergence in site types within Chaco Canyon. Although there was a slight decrease in the number of early Pueblo II sites, the number of habitation rooms per site increased, suggesting an increase in population. Most sites continued to be small, consisting of straight lines of a double tier of living and storage rooms, often built of coursed masonry, and a partially masonry-lined kiva. Diagnostic ceramics consist of the culinary type Tohatchi Banded, and the decorated type, Red Mesa Black-on-white. At the same time, construction at three sites, Una Vida, Pueblo Bonito, and Peñasco Blanco, departed from the typical pattern, in that each had rooms of more than one story, and wall construction at each was of a higher quality of craftsmanship than at other Chaco sites. (It should be noted that although each of these three eventually became large town sites, they were relatively small in the early Pueblo II period.) It has been suggested that these three sites may have served as local centers for the pooling and redistribution of agricultural resources (Judge 1989).

The period from AD 1020 to 1120 is referred to as Classic Bonito because it was during this time that construction at the major town sites was completed. These are the justly famous, multistoried planned sites of Peñasco Blanco, Pueblo Alto, Kin Kletso, Pueblo del Arroyo, Pueblo Bonito, Chetro Ketl, Hungo Pavi, Una Vida, and Kin Nahasbas within Chaco Canyon. Also at this time, soil and water control features were constructed in the canyon, and a system of roads linking Chaco with various outliers (multistoried pueblos in Chacoan style but well outside the canyon proper) were also built. In addition to these, most of the sites in Chaco Canyon and in the San Juan Basin continued to be relatively small, single-story sites. Ceramics at both village and town sites are of the same types: corrugated utility ware is initially Coolidge Corrugated and is later replaced by Chaco Corrugated. The major black-on-white types are Escavada and Gallup.

During the late Bonito phase (1120–1220), population in Chaco Canyon declined. There was some new construction at New Alto and Kin Kletso and a few small pueblos were built, but generally these were not made with the elaborate Chacoan masonry characteristic of the preceding period. Ceramics were dominated by imported types: culinary ware from the Chuska area, Sosi Black-on-white from the Tusayan (Hopi) area, and Mancos Black-on-white from the Mesa Verde area, or local imitations of the Mesa Verde type, McElmo Black-on-white. Finally, a Mesa Verde phase is distinguished within Chaco Canyon between AD 1220 and 1300. This period is characterized by occupational use of cave sites and the tops of buttes in addition to more traditional locations, a change in burial patterns, and the appearance of Mesa Verde Black-on-white and St. Johns Polychrome ceramics. Although once interpreted as evidence of a migration of Mesa Verde Anasazi into Chaco Canyon, other analyses (Toll *et al.* 1980) suggest that the change reflects increased economic interactions with the Mesa Verde Anasazi. By 1300, however, Chaco Canyon was no longer occupied.

The sequence presented above was derived from a series of tree-ring and archaeomagnetic dates. Chronological refinement is important, but the major issues in Chacoan archaeology do not involve chronology. Rather, the scale of developments in Chaco Canyon and coming out of Chaco Canyon is greater than that imagined earlier and is not known among the modern Pueblo peoples. Research issues involve finding ways to adequately describing the nature of the Chacoan system and attempting to explain how it developed from a Basketmaker III-Pueblo I base similar to that found in the rest of the Anasazi region.

Mesa Verde

Like Chaco, the Mesa Verde area was a center of early research. Subsequently, the Park Service conducted a multiyear, multidisciplinary study focused on Wetherill Mesa (Hayes 1964; Rohn 1989). More recently, the very large-scale Dolores Archaeological Project (Kohler *et al.* 1986; Lipe *et al.* 1988) involved intensive survey and excavations carried out in conjunction with damming the Dolores River. Currently, problem-focused survey and very limited excavation and testing are being carried out through Crow Canyon Archaeological Research Center (Varien *et al.* 1996). Adler (1996) is the best source of comprehensive summaries.

The Pecos Classification is applied to Mesa Verde (Table 7.1), supplemented by regional phases (O'Bryan 1950) and local phase schemes that differ between Wetherill Mesa (Hayes 1964) and the adjacent Chapin Mesa (Rohn 1977). The very local phase schemes are of most interest to researchers working within the Mesa Verde area. The Pecos Classification is used to characterize developments here because it is more general and it adequately fits the developments described (Rohn 1977:233; 1989).

Basketmaker II sites are known for the Durango and Animas areas (Morris and Burgh 1954) but not from the Mesa Verde proper. Basketmaker III dates from AD 575 or 590 to 750. Houses are shallow pithouses with antechambers oriented to the south. Banquettes, central clay-lined circular hearths, wing walls, four-post roof supports, and storage pits are typical house features. Sites are most often located on ridges on the mesa tops, although there are also indications that rock shelters were used. Stone implements include trough metates; fairly small, basal-notched projectile points (indicating the presence of the bow and arrow); and grooved stone mauls. The diagnostic ceramic type is the plain Chapin Gray. Painted Chapin Black-on-white also occurs.

Pueblo I dates from about AD 750 to 900. The distribution of sites is not uniform throughout the region. For example, Pueblo I sites are abundant in the Animas and La Plata drainages but are rare on western Cedar Mesa. Between AD 700 and 800, very large sites consisting of more than 100 contiguous surface rooms of jacal or adobe, in several parallel rows, associated with squarish pithouses are generally located on mesa tops. Recent excavations and reevaluation of older work have shown that most Pueblo I sites were occupied for only about 30 years or less, allowing archaeologists to make unusually precise population estimates (Wilshusen and Blinman 1992). These indicate larger populations than one might suppose. Conservative techniques indicate that some of these sites housed as many as 600 individuals in three separate, but closely spaced, settlement clusters. Even if they were only together for 30 years, this size suggests that social mechanisms were in place that were able to integrate individuals from several different households and to maintain that integration for more than a human generation. In the Dolores area, large Pueblo I sites were founded when rainfall conditions were particularly good for crops grown without irrigation (Kohler 1992). Chapin Gray and the neck-banded Moccasin Gray are the common utility types. Chapin Black-on-white, Piedra Black-on-white, Abajo Red-on-orange, and Bluff Black-on-red are the common painted types.

Pueblo II dates from AD 900 to 1100. Sites, generally smaller and more widely spaced than those of Pueblo I, occur on low ridges on mesa tops and on talus slopes (Hayes 1964; Rohn 1989). Early in the period, they consist of a few surface rooms, generally of jacal or unshaped stone set in abundant mud mortar, with associated circular kivas. Kiva features include low masonry pilasters, banquettes, ventilators, hearths, sipapus, and four-post roof supports. Later in Pueblo II, surface rooms are more generally of sandstone masonry and kivas are partially stone lined. Wall niches and six masonry pilasters are new documented kiva features. In addition to kivas, other ceremonial structures are tower kivas and very large kivas. Artificial reservoirs (for domestic water supplies), stone check dams, shrines, and field houses are also documented. Overall, there was probably population decline during this period. It is

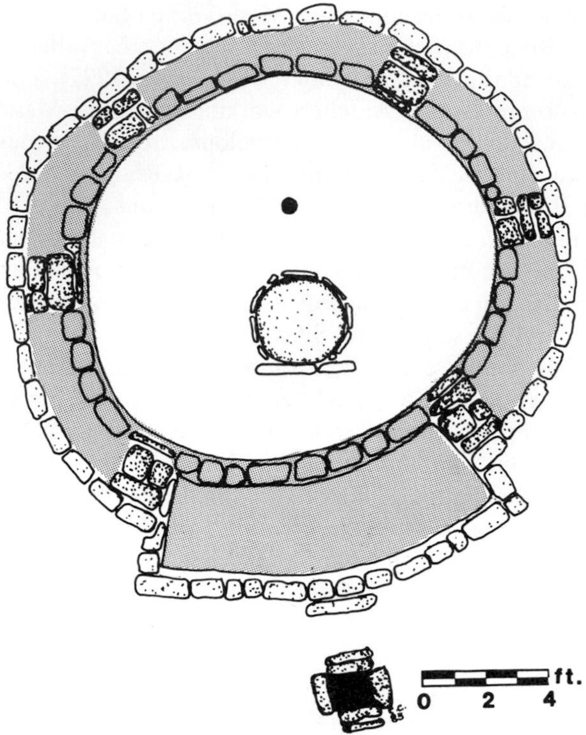

FIGURE 7.3 Typical Mesa Verde keyhole-shaped kiva (illustrated by Charles M. Carrillo).

suggested that population may have been lost to the Chaco area (Cordell 1981; Varien *et al.* 1996). Ceramic diagnostics of Pueblo II are the corrugated Mancos Gray, Mancos Corrugated, and Dolores Corrugated. The painted Cortez and Mancos Black-on-white are new types. Later in Pueblo II, red ware trade types (Puerco and Tusayan Black-on-red) were imported, as were Sosi, Dogoszhi, Gallup, and Escavada Black-on-white types.

Pueblo III dates from AD 1100 to 1300 (Rohn 1977, 1989). At the beginning of this period, population increases again in the region. Most sites are small and dispersed; however, there are also large, aggregated settlements. These are referred to as great houses. Some of the great houses meet the general criteria of Chacoan Outliers; others present less architectural standardization. Nevertheless, Mesa Verde great houses seem to have been founded within existing settlements of dispersed habitation sites and to have had some elements of public, integrative architecture (Varien *et al.* 1996). Early Pueblo III sites are located near canyon rims, in rock shelters on talus slopes, and in canyon bottoms. At most sites, kivas are wholly or partially enclosed by rooms and walls and display the Mesa Verde keyhole-shaped form (Figure 7.3). Habitations are often of two stories, and tower kivas are more common. Shrines, reservoirs, stone check dams, and field houses are present. Ceramics include corrugated utility types (two varieties of Mesa Verde Corrugated) and Mesa Verde Black-on-white. In addition to previously mentioned trade types, Wingate Black-on-red, Chaco Black-on-white, and Tusayan Polychrome have been identified.

By AD 1200 to 1300, nearly all habitation sites at Mesa Verde are located within rock shelters. Some sites are four stories high, but there is considerable variety in site form and size, in part resulting from the constraints of building in rock shelters. Outside Mesa Verde proper, there seems to be an increase in population density and an increase in site size. Isolated towers at the heads of canyons are prevalent to the west in McElmo drainage. Mesa top settlements decline in favor of locations at canyon heads and canyon rims, and some settlements have walls that would impede access to them. The last mentioned characteristics are interpreted as defensive, but not all sites of this time period have defensive characteristics (Varien *et al.* 1996). There is some, rather than pervasive, evidence of violence, and the consensus seems to be that raiding or threat of attack were more prevalent than actual combat. The typical Mesa Verde area, Pueblo III large site plan of multiple parallel roomblocks, each with its set of kiva and room units, gives way to more variety in layout over time, which is interpreted as a sign of experimentation with different kinds of organization (Varien *et al.* 1996: 99–100). Specialized agricultural features and shrines continue.

Mesa Verde Corrugated and Mesa Verde Black-on-white are present, and forms include canteens, mugs, dippers, and ollas, in addition to bowls and jars. A variety of perishable items have also been recovered, including leather moccasins, wooden fire drills, yucca-ring baskets, willow withe mats, rush mats, and prayer sticks. Most items, including pottery, were locally made. There is little that was imported into the region at this time. Recent studies (Lipe 1994) show that pueblo construction ended very quickly throughout the region, between the late 1260s and 1280, and shortly thereafter population declined. Most of the region was probably abandoned by the middle of the 1280s (Varien *et al.* 1996).

As was the case for Chaco Canyon, the Mesa Verde chronology is well developed. The Mesa Verde proper shows the gradual changes in architecture and ceramics that were expected to be characteristic of the Anasazi as a whole. This is not surprising because the Mesa Verde area was frequently used as a standard reference for all Anasazi development. Major research issues involve explaining the population shifts and movements throughout the region over time, the integration of great houses and small dispersed settlements, and the region's ultimate abandonment.

Kayenta

Syntheses of the Kayenta Anasazi (Figure 7.1 and Table 7.1) are the result of large-scale, long-term contract programs, for example, the Glen Canyon project (Jennings 1966) and the Black Mesa project (Gumerman and Euler 1976; Gumerman 1988), and surveys (Dean 1990, 1996b; Dean *et al.* 1978; Haas and Creamer 1993; Matson and Lipe 1978). Generally these have provided abundant high-quality information, including precise chronological and paleoenvironmental data.

In general, Basketmaker II and III materials, dating from around AD 200 to 750, are quite well represented. They include a variety of perishable items recovered from the classic Basketmaker Cave sites, including White Dog Cave in Marsh Pass (Guernsey and Kidder 1921). This early part of the Anasazi sequence is similar to that documented elsewhere. For example, there are circular pithouses; Lino Gray and Lino Black-on-white ceramics; one-hand manos; metates; and twined woven bags, basketry, nets, and sandals. Pueblo I (ca. 750–975) also parallels developments elsewhere in the Anasazi area with Kana-a Gray, Kana-a Black-on-white, and Black Mesa Black-on-white ceramics. Pithouses continue to be the most common habitations. Surface rooms, primarily for storage, are either in arcs or in L-shaped configurations and are jacal or jacal-and-masonry structures. As with the Mesa Verde district, some Pueblo I settlements are very large by any standard. A famous example is at Alkali Ridge, southeastern Utah (Brew 1946). Alkali Ridge Site 13 consisted of 130 surface rooms, 16 pithouses, and 2 kivas. While Site 13 is not unique for the Kayenta area, there are fewer large sites at this time than in the Mesa Verde region and elsewhere in the northern tier of Anasazi settlement.

Pueblo II (ca. 975–1150) witnessed a change to unit pueblos consisting of a tier of surface rooms facing a plaza with a kiva and trash mound. Rather than the large, Pueblo I sites, unit pueblos occur as dispersed "homesteads" throughout the region (Dean 1996b). It is also during this period that the Kayenta Anasazi population expanded to its greatest geographic extent. Ceramics include Tusayan Corrugated, Moenkopi Corrugated, and Kayenta Black-on-white. The amount of trade material (shell, ceramics, lithic materials) declines. The Kayenta area appears quite insular and isolated except that designs painted on some ceramics are in the widespread Dogoszhi style.

Although village aggregation occurred by AD 950 and 1050 in the Chaco Canyon and Mesa Verde areas, the same phenomenon did not occur until Pueblo III, perhaps as late as 1250, in the Kayenta area. Beginning about 1150, some areas (e.g., Black Mesa, the Virgin River) were apparently abandoned. Elsewhere (e.g., Tsegi Canyon) large pueblo sites were built. The term Tsegi phase refers to the last period of ancient occupation over much of the Kayenta region, dating from AD 1250 to 1300. Settlements with very different formal characteristics were constructed. Some consist of pithouses, others of unit pueblos, and others of rectangular, masonry, surface rooms arranged in a square on the perimeter of an open courtyard. Generally, villages were composed of room clusters, each consisting of living rooms, storerooms, and granaries. Kivas were generally circular and masonry-lined, keyhole-shaped kivas are also documented. The famous Tsegi Canyon sites of Kiet Siel, Betatakin, Scaffold House, Lolomaki, Batwoman House, and Twin Caves Pueblo were built and occupied between 1250 and 1300, when Tsegi Canyon was abandoned (Dean 1970). "Kayenta style" ceramics, consisting of negative-painted designs were produced from about 1150 to the 1300s. Although the Kayenta archaeological area was abandoned by 1300, Kayenta patterns continue in the middle Little Colorado drainage and other ancestral Hopi areas (Dean 1996b; Adams 1991).

In general, chronological problems have not assumed major proportions in the Kayenta area. As noted, most workers use local phase sequences, which are advantageous in terms of precision. A great deal of information has been brought together on past climate, paleoenvironment, and the distributions of settlements over time (Dean 1996; Gumerman 1988). Major research foci are on further elucidating the flexibility of Kayenta Anasazi settlement strategies and social organization and tying the final archaeological phases with ancestral Hopi communities.

Virgin Anasazi

The farthest west of the Anasazi branches is the Virgin, known from the Lower Virgin and Muddy rivers of southeastern Nevada. During the late Archaic before the differentiation of the Virgin Anasazi, split twig figurines occur in Virgin Anasazi territory as in Late Archaic sites of the Patayan tradition. The Pecos chronology of Basketmaker II through Early Pueblo III is used in the Virgin area with dates that are comparable to those of the Kayenta branch (Lyneis 1995). Pithouses were used during Basketmaker II, III, Pueblo I, and Early Pueblo II (to AD 1050). These were accompanied by cists that were arranged end to end in arcs by Pueblo I times. In Pueblo II, the storage cists are surface rooms, still arranged end to end. Although pithouses were in use throughout the sequence, Pueblo II and Pueblo III sites incorporated surface habitation rooms. Finally, habitation and storage rooms were loosely arranged around open courtyards. Site size is deceptive with respect to habitation. At the Pueblo III Mesa House site, only 3 to 5 of 30 rooms were used for habitation. The others were storage rooms. A variety of trade ceramics linked the Virgin Anasazi to their Anasazi neighbors further east (Lyneis 1995).

Rio Grande

The chronological framework used in the northern Rio Grande Valley was formulated by Wendorf and Reed (1955), supplemented by local phase schemes for various subareas (Table 7.2). Recent research involved multiyear research projects in Tijeras Canyon (Cordell 1980), the Pajarito Plateau (Hill and Trierweiler 1986), the Taos District (Crown 1991), Arroyo Hondo (Schwartz 1981), and Bandelier area (Kohler 1993). The Wendorf and Reed (1955) framework diverges significantly from the Pecos Classification. It includes a long preceramic period, lasting until about AD 600. The first ceramic period is termed the Rio Grande Developmental, dated from AD 600 to 1200. Sites dating to the beginning of this period are relatively rare. Sites dating to the later part of this period are more numerous. The earliest ceramic sites yield both Lino Gray and brown ware cooking pottery and San Marcial Black-on-white decorated ware. The slightly later sites (roughly contemporaneous with Pueblo I) yield neck-banded pottery of both the Kana-a Gray and Alma types. The pottery for these initial periods reflects both Anasazi and Mogollon traditions. Developmental period sites consist of rather simple circular pithouses, sometimes with associated above-ground jacal rooms. After AD 900, villages become larger and more numerous. Sites consisting of 10 to 20 surface structures and 1 to 4 kivas are reported. Ceramics

TABLE 7.2 Rio Grande Phase Sequences[a]

Dates	Taos	Chama	Gallina	Rio Grande
1400				
	Vadito	Biscuit A		
1350				Classic
1300				
	Talpa	Wiyo		
1250				Coalition
	Pot Creek		Llaves	
1200				
1150				
1100	Valdez			Developmental
			Capulin	
1050				
		Unoccupied no permanent villages		
1000				
950			Rosa	
900	Unoccupied ?			Archaic
850				
800				

[a]Adapted from Crown *et al.* (1996:190).

include Kwahe'e Black-on-white, considered a poorly made cognate of Chacoan types (Cordell 1979; Wendorf and Reed 1955).

The Coalition period (1200–1325) is characterized first by a shift from mineral-based black paint types to the carbon paint type, Santa Fe Black-on-white, in most of the northern Rio Grande and by the retention of subterranean round kivas. Rio Grande kivas are generally simple, adobe-lined, subterranean structures with four roof-support posts. At about 1300 there was a pronounced increase in population, increased regional differentiation, the appearance of above-ground kivas incorporated into roomblocks, and the production of Santa Fe and Galisteo Black-on-white ceramics. Pueblos were constructed of coursed adobe in some areas and of masonry in others (Cordell 1979).

The Rio Grande Classic (1325–1600) is characterized by production of red-slipped glaze-decorated ceramics in the central and northern Rio Grande region. The glaze ware was presumably made in imitation of the Zuni and Little Colorado area ceramics, where the use of glaze preceded its appearance in the Rio Grande. Not all sub-areas produced Rio Grande glaze ware. It was not locally made in the area of Taos or Jemez Pueblos. Pottery producing areas did trade glaze ware very widely, at times out onto the Great Plains (Shepard 1942). Population in the area reached its pre-Columbian maximum during the Classic. Large aggregated communities were present, and there was an elaboration of material culture. Some diagnostic traits are decorated pipes, elaborate axes, carved bone tools, stone effigies, mural paintings, and variety in vessel forms. Some of the well-known large Classic period sites are Paa-ko, Tijeras

Pueblo, Kuaua, Arroyo Hondo, San Marcos, San Cristobal, Giusewa, Unshagi, Otowi, Puye, Tsankawi, Tyounyi, and Pecos Pueblo. Many of the large Classic pueblos were occupied for only relatively brief periods or were occupied, abandoned, and reoccupied. The Historic period is dated from 1600 to the present. Excavations at Pecos Pueblo, Paa-ko, Unshagi and Picuris, and Gran Quivira provide most of the information for this period—in addition, of course, to ethnographic information from the modern Pueblo peoples and historic documents.

In the Wendorf and Reed formulation, the Rio Grande area is viewed as marginal to developments in the San Juan region. That is, stylistic developments are later than those in the San Juan, while kiva architecture and domestic crafts are viewed as simplified versions of those in the San Juan. Aggregation occurs only after the population increase following abandoment of the northern San Juan. Although these characteriziations are true, the Rio Grande Valley is relatively well-watered, with a natural environment that is not marginal compared with the San Juan Basin. Current research focuses on understanding the mix of subsistence strategies used to support large pueblo populations, the extent of intervillage and interregional trade, and transitions from the period prior to the Spanish entradas to the modern Pueblos.

THE HOHOKAM

The Hohokam sequence was established on the basis of excavations at the very large and complex site of Snaketown, where Pioneer period remains were found (Gladwin *et al.* 1938). In 1964 and 1965, Emil Haury (1976:97) returned to Snaketown in part to resolve conflicting interpretations of the chronology. The phase hallmarks of the Hohokam sequence are the ceramic types first described by Haury in 1938 (Gladwin *et al.* 1938), modified by the deletion of Santan Red ceramics and the Santan phase. Since the previous edition of this book (Cordell 1984), many of the difficult problems of Hohokam chronology have been largely resolved. Because Hohokam residential sites consist of pithouses with ephemeral superstructures, and because desert hardwoods are not amenable to tree-ring dating, there was no developed tree-ring chronology for the low desert region. Dean and others (1996) have recently begun a tree-ring chronology for the Tucson Basin, based on conifers, that extends to pre-Columbian times. Nevertheless, resolution of most of the Hohokam chronological problems has come about principally through large-scale application of archaeomagnetic and radiocarbon dating in the context of huge, multiphase contract projects. In 1980, there were fewer than 120 dates for the Hohokam region. By 1982, there were more than 800 (Crown 1990; Dean 1990; Eighmy and McGuire 1989). While investigators caution that not all chronological problems have been solved (Crown 1990; Dean 1990), current understanding of the Hohokam area over time is now not substantially different than that of the Anasazi and Mogollon traditions. As with these traditions, there is subregional variation within the Hohokam. The Gila-Salt basin near Phoenix, Arizona, constitutes the Hohokam core area where the phase sequence developed at Snaketown is applied. Outside this area, local phase schemes, reflecting

TABLE 7.3 Hohokam Phase Sequences

Date	Tucson Basin[a]	Pheonix Basin[a]	Santa Cruz[b]	Gila Basin[c]	Papagueria[c]
1450					
1400		Civano	Unknown Hohokam	Civano	
1350	Tucson				Sells
1300					
1250	Tanque Verde	Soho	Early Classic		
1200		?		Soho	
1150					Topawa
1100	Rincon	Sacaton	Sedentary		
1050					
1000	?	Santa Cruz			
950			Late Colonial	Sacaton	Vamori
900		Gila Butte			
850	Rillito		Early Colonial		
800		Snaketown		Santa Cruz	
750			Late Pioneer		
700					
650		Sweetwater			
600					
550		Estrella			?
500				Gila Butte	
450		Vahki		Snaketown	
400					
350					
300					

[a]Adapted from Dean (1994:91).
[b]Adapted from Downum (1993:23).
[c]Adapted from Dean and Greenleaf (1975:12).

different cultural trajectories, are used in the Tucson, Tonto, Safford, San Pedro, and Upper Santa Cruz basins, and the Papagueria south and west of Gila Bend (Table 7.3). This brief summary focuses on the Hohokam core area, following the discussion by Crown (1991).

The Pioneer period dates from AD 200 to 775. The earliest phase is characterized by plain brown pottery and small, squarish houses, corner-notched projectile points, flexed inhumations, and clay figurines (Crown 1991; Doyel 1990). By about AD 300, red-slipped ceramics are added, and by 500, red designs are painted on a gray, later in the Pioneer on a buff, background. Pioneer period houses were built in shallow, scooped out areas (houses in pits). They had jacal walls with a clay/mud exterior. House clusters consist of two to four houses facing each other across a courtyard. The house clusters appear to have been very stable social and economic units throughout the

Hohokam tradition. They are associated with distinct burial, trash mound, and work areas. Trash mounds were shaped, and later capped with caliche, clearly representing more than a place to dispose of debris. At Snaketown, three oversize structures in a central open area may have served special community functions. Hamlets made up of several courtyard groupings may have been occupied by about 100 individuals. Craft items include abundant clay figurines, carved stone bowls, censers, and palettes. Both inhumation and cremation were practiced. Throughout the Pioneer period, crops were most likely planted on river flood plains. By the end of the Pioneer period, irrigation canals were being constructed.

The Colonial period, AD 775–975, witnessed great expansion of the area occupied by the Hohokam. This is the period that was so well-represented in the Gila Pueblo surveys. Houses in pits continue, and true pithouses were also built. The first Hohokam ballcourts date to this period, with 34 known for the entire period from throughout the Hohokam area (Wilcox 1988). Hohokam ballcourts are oval, with floors sloping toward the center from an earth or rock berm. The courts vary in size, some as much as 80 m in length. While the way they were used is debated (Ferdon 1967), it is generally thought that they were derived from the Mesoamerican ballgame. Wilcox (1991) suggests that Hohokam ballcourts reflect basic elements in the Hohokam world view, that they were formally distinctive structures carrying the meaning that those using them shared a particular ideology as well as serving as an institution for social and economic interaction. Not all Hohokam sites of this period have ballcourts, suggesting social or functional differentiation among communities. Construction of irrigation canals increased greatly, and craft items such as shell jewelry, palettes, and figurines reached their most elaborate forms.

During the Sedentary period, AD 975–1150, the Hohokam tradition reached its maximum spatial extent and sites such as Snaketown their greatest size (Crown 1991). Most of the 206 ballcourts at 165 sites were in use around 750 to 1000 (Wilcox 1991). While craft items continued to be produced, they became less elaborate, suggesting to some that they were being produced by specialists (Crown 1983; Haury 1976). A few platform mounds were constructed at the end of the Sedentary, but the form became important in the following Classic period. By the end of the period, the size of the area settled by Hohokam began to shrink.

The Classic period, AD 1150–1400/1450, is generally divided into two phases, the Soho phase (ca. AD 1150 to 1300) and the Civano phase (ca. AD 1300 to 1400/1450). During the Classic, there was the first change in Hohokam domestic architecture and site layout. Houses in pits and post-reinforced caliche walled surface structures were built, as were adobe-walled houses. Adobe-walled rectangular compounds enclosed settlements of contiguous rooms of adobe houses and a plaza. At Casa Grande, Arizona, an adobe multistory great house was constructed. Ballcourts were not built after AD 1300; however, rectangular platform mounds were constructed at more than 40 sites in the core area (Crown 1991; Wilcox 1987). From the mid-1200s, houses were constructed on platform mounds and access to these houses was impeded by walls (Gregory 1991). Petrographic and chemical characterizations of pottery (Abbott 1996) suggest that when household clusters were walled off from one another by compound walls, the clusters interacted (exchanged less utilitarian pottery) somewhat less with each other than with other communities. Polychrome pottery replaces red-on-buff, and the elaborate palettes and projectile points were no longer made, but there may have been specialized production of utilitarian objects such as textiles, tabular knives, and ground stone axes (Neitzel 1991). Irrigation canals reached their maximum extent, and it was at this time that communities along a single canal would have had to cooperate in order to allocate water and maintain canals. There are at least 17 documented irrigation communities of this sort (Masse 1991; Wilcox 1991). Ceramic analyses (Abbott 1996) indicate that plain ware was exchanged within irrigation communities but red ware—perhaps used for more formal functions—was exchanged outside the irrigation community. Finally, sometime between AD 1350 and 1450, most sites in the Hohokam core area were abandoned, although end dates of the Hohokam tradition are not well established.

A great deal of field research continues to be done in the Hohokam area, much of it stimulated by modern housing and other development of the Arizona deserts. Among those topics being pursued are documenting and explaining variability in subsistence strategies over time in the various kinds of settings used by the Hohokam; understanding and explaining the ways core area Hohokam articulated with peoples throughout the expanded Hohokam territory; examining changes in production technology and exchange; and learning the ultimate fate of the Hohokam archaeological entity after 1450 (Adams 1996; Doyel 1989; McGuire and Villalpando 1989; Wilcox 1991).

THE MOGOLLON

Mogollon country, where brown ware pottery and pithouses occur together, extends from an eastern border near the Guadalupe Mountains, between Carlsbad and Las Cruces, New Mexico, west to the Verde River of central Arizona and from the Little Colorado River on the north to central Chihuahua and Sonora, Mexico, on the south. This truly enormous territory is more than twice the size of even the most generous estimates of the Colorado Plateau country occupied by the Anasazi, and much of this country is mountainous. The volcanic Mogollon Mountains rise to an elevation of 3365 m. Intermontaine basins drop well below 900 m. Patches of alpine meadow are found at the highest elevations. Cacti, sparse desert grasses, and shrubs dominate the lowest basins. At the elevations in between, ponderosa pine forest occurs above mixed piñon-juniper woodland and oak chaparral. Even today, the extremely dissected terrain makes east to west travel difficult.

Given the immense size of the area, its diverse and rugged landscapes, and the difficulty of transport, different cultural subtraditions seem to have developed at their own pace, in semi-isolation. This summary concentrates on a few specific sites and subregions where the bulk of archaeological surveys and excavations have been focused in order to highlight, as much as possible, the organizational features of Mogollon society (Table 7.4). These are the Mimbres, Reserve, and Pine Lawn areas of New

TABLE 7.4 Mogollon Phase Sequences

Date (AD)	Mimbres[ab]	Pine Lawn[a]	Point of Pines[a]	San Simon[c]
1500			Point of	
	Cliff		Pines	
1400				
1300	Black			
	Mountain			
1200	(Animas)		Pinedale	
		Tularosa	Tularosa	
1100	Classic			Encinas
	Mimbres			
	Mangus			
1000		Reserve		
	Three	Three	Reserve	
900	Circle	Circle		
				Nantack
800	San	San		
	Francisco	Francisco	Circle	
700			Prairie	Cerros
600	Georgetown	Georgetown		
		Pine Lawn		
500				
400		Archaic (Cochise)	Prepottery	Galiuro

[a]Adapted from Stafford and Rice (1980:15).
[b]Adapted from LeBlanc and Nelson (1986:2).
[c]Adapted from Greenleaf (1975:12).

Mexico and the Forestdale Valley, Grasshopper, and Q Ranch subregions of Arizona. Before proceeding, it should be noted that additional Mogollon branches are defined and include the Jornada (Lehmer 1948) and the Chihuahuan (Di Peso 1974). Recent work in northwest Mexico suggests that these are perhaps better viewed in their own terms, as discussed below.

The Mogollon tradition begins with the addition of pottery to the Early Agricultural period base. The earliest Mogollon phase has been termed the Cumbre phase in the Mimbres Valley, the Hilltop phase in the Forestdale Valley, and the Pine Lawn phase in the Reserve area. The earliest Mogollon pottery is undecorated brown or red/brown ware. The clays used to produce this pottery are generally of alluvial origin and did not require the addition of temper. Vessels were built up by coiling, then shaped and finished by scraping the coiled surfaces smooth. Vessel exteriors were then sometimes further polished, though not highly so. Some early pottery is decorated with a fugitive red wash or, later, a red slip. The most common vessel forms are jars, necked jars, small seed jars, and bowls.

The earliest Mogollon settlements known from the Pine Lawn, Forestdale, and Mimbres areas date from about AD 200 to 550. These contained from one to as many as 80 pithouses, although it is unlikely that many of the pithouses in the larger settlements were occupied at the same time. Early Mogollon houses were nearly round

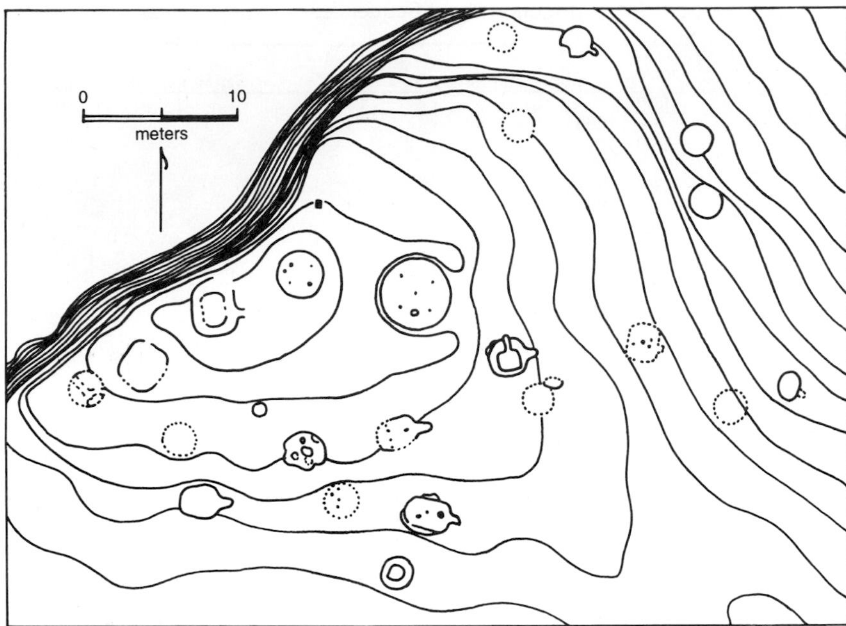

FIGURE 7.4 Topographic map with plan view of houses at the Bluff site, east-central Arizona. Early Mogollon sites are often located on ridge tops and other easily defended locations (illustrated by Marjorie Leggitt, Leggitt Design after Haury and Sayles, 1947).

pithouses, from about 3 m to about 5 m in diameter, excavated to depths ranging from 60 cm to 1.5 m. Roofs were either an umbrella type, with a central upright post serving as the main support, or they were domed, with the beams supported by marginal posts. The roofs themselves were made of thick logs covered by branches and layers of mud. An entry was on one side. Not all of the early pithouses have interior hearths. Some cooking was done out-of-doors, but the dwellings without hearths or ash-filled warming pits may not have been occupied in the coldest part of the year. Some families may have used rock shelters during the winter months. Household equipment and furnishings known from rock shelter sites include grass beds, rabbit fur or bird feather blankets, plant fiber scouring pads, fire drills, fire tongs, metates, and manos (Martin *et al.* 1954).

Initially, pithouse communities were located on prominent ridges, high bluffs, or isolated knolls, often with rock walls across the most accessible route to the settlement (Figure 7.4) (Haury 1940; Reid 1989). Below these hamlets, there is generally good agricultural land, often a river flood plain. The settings of early pithouses suggest an eye for defense.

It seems reasonable that residents of the early pithouse communities might have had to defend their food supply from raids—either from hunter-gatherers or other early farmers. The mountainous Mogollon region is favorable for hunting, and hunting continued to be an important aspect of Mogollon subsistence throughout the sequence. Early Mogollon hamlets were established within the same general areas as those supporting groups of people who continued a hunting and gathering way of life, since there is no reason to suppose that everyone in the Southwest or the Mogollon region adopted agriculture at the same time. Hence it is plausible that small communities with enough agricultural produce to store over a season felt threatened by potential raids from neighboring hunters and gatherers. Alternatively, it has been suggested that farming in the Mogollon Mountains would have been very risky because of short growing seasons and variable rainfall. Communities might wish to protect their stores from potentially aggressive agricultural neighbors whose crops had failed. Later, after about AD 550, pithouse settlements are moved to lower ground adjacent to streams or rivers and good arable land.

At about AD 550 there are changes warranting new phase designations (Georgetown Plainware period, Cottonwood). These are the production of San Francisco Red pottery—a highly polished, red-slipped type—construction of circular and D-shaped pithouses, and location of sites in various topographic settings. In the Mimbres Valley, sites are on the first terrace above the river. By about AD 650, red-on-brown pottery was being produced in the southern Mogollon area. This development has been termed the San Francisco phase (Haury 1936). Aside from the change in ceramics, the Mogollon cultural inventory remains as it had been before.

By about AD 600, the Mogollon built pithouses that were rectangular in shape with the side entryway including a ramp constructed to slope upward to the ground surface. Three or more sturdy upright posts supported the roof. Otherwise, construction and materials were as before. The early pithouses generally have one or more large interior subfloor storage pits. In later pithouses, these are less common, possibly because pottery vessels assumed a large part of the storage function. Central fire hearths are more consistently present during the later pithouse period.

Most early Mogollon settlements were tiny by any standard. Settlements with simultaneous occupation of four to six dwellings would have had a population of about 30 men, women, and children. This number is too small to reliably provide marriage partners or to offer access to diverse resources that might have been needed to offset poor crops or lack of success in hunting. A larger group must have interacted with one another on a fairly regular basis. A sense of just such a larger community is glimpsed in the construction of kivas used by groups of people from different households.

Three different community patterns developed (Reid 1989). At some of the moderate size to larger pithouse sites that have been excavated, there has been one or more oversized communal kiva structures. Sometimes these larger structures also have distinctive shapes and features, such as "lobes" constructed around the entryway. The arrangement of several pithouses and one community structure is apparent at the SU site near Reserve, New Mexico (Martin and Rinaldo 1947). SU (the name derives from a local cattle brand) contained at least 26 houses (Figure 8.8).

A second pattern (Reid 1989) is reflected in the many pithouse settlements that consist of only two or three spatially dispersed houses. Settlements of this type are common in the more mountainous central and western portions of the Mogollon region, such as Forestdale and Point of Pines. In these settlements all of the houses appear to have been used for normal residential functions, but there will generally be a large or great kiva. This kiva is physically set apart from the domestic structures but is also approximately central to the scattered dwellings.

A third pattern is noted in the Grasshopper region and perhaps elsewhere in the northern Mogollon subregions (Reid 1989). In this instance, small settlements are dispersed on the landscape but the larger of these will have a separate great kiva that may have functioned for the inhabitants of all the dispersed houses in the area. The term focal community has been used to indicate the social centrality of the settlements with great kivas. Typically, among Mogollon pithouse settlements of all varieties, there is no indication that houses are arranged in other than a haphazard or convenient fashion or in any particular relationship to one another. There appears to have been no settlement plan.

In general, the long period from about AD 550 to 950 witnessed great stability in the Mogollon area. Hunting and some gathering continued to be important even though agriculture was adopted everywhere. Early pithouses were large enough to shelter an extended family that may have been the unit of cooperative farming, hunting, and gathering. Many settlements seem to have consisted of only one or a very few families. Later pithouses are smaller but each settlement has more structures, perhaps indicating that the basic cooperating group was the nuclear family, several of which occupied the same hamlet. Pottery that initially had been only unpainted, rough, plain ware was decorated later in the sequence. A highly polished red slip was used on some vessels. Others were painted with red designs on a brown background. Once settlements in defensive settings were abandoned and pithouses were built close to arable land, Mogollon culture presents an almost static picture for nearly 400 years.

Sometime between AD 950 and 1150, three major changes occurred. Taken together, these are so striking investigators interpreted Mogollon settlements built after the changes as not Mogollon at all but as a regional variant of the Anasazi tradition. The most obvious change was in the kind of dwellings built. Mogollon residences changed from pithouses to above-ground pueblos with contiguous, rectangular rooms and open areas or plazas. Second, in some Mogollon areas, pottery that had long been brown or red ware was replaced by pottery that uses black paint on a white slip. In other areas, both red and white wares were produced. Third, although much more difficult to reconstruct, there was population growth and expansion into less productive agricultural areas.

The long tradition of Mogollon use of pithouses and the rough quality of Mogollon masonry were seen as an indication that building in stone was a skill newly introduced by the Anasazi, who had been building masonry pueblos for some 150 to 200 years before the Mogollon. The color scheme the Mogollon used on painted pottery had long been red paint applied to a brown background color. Use of black paint on a white background slip is also an Anasazi characteristic. The combination of the change in domestic architecture and pottery decoration led to the suggestion that the Mogollon had been taken over by the Anasazi. While not necessarily agreeing about an Anasazi "takeover," workers continue to argue about the nature of the Mogollon after

AD 1000, and the term Western Pueblo may be applied to the end of the Mogollon sequence in some areas that continued to be inhabited (Haury 1985, 1988).

This picture of cultural replacement can be challenged by examining the changes in pottery and architecture separately in different Mogollon localities. In the Grasshopper and Q Ranch area (Reid 1989) culinary brown ware was locally made. Very small amounts of both painted ware and some plain ware were imported from the Hohokam region early in the sequence, starting at about AD 600. By the end of the period at 1150, Hohokam ceramics no longer occur in the area but Anasazi trade ceramics are found. The transition from pithouse to pueblo occurs in the Grasshopper and Q Ranch regions between about AD 1000 and 1150. At first, small pueblos are thinly scattered on the landscape. During the 1200s, there are larger pueblos in the adjacent region of Point of Pines, but only small pueblos in the Q Ranch area. Reid (1989) suggests that most small settlements consisting of a few cobble masonry surface rooms may have been used only seasonally or, alternatively, continuously but for just a few years. After 1200, most masonry was of dressed stone similar to Anasazi building techniques. Both great kivas and smaller kivas in the same settlement suggest the continuation of a pattern of focal communities serving a highly dispersed population. The ceramics associated with these sites continue to be Mogollon brown ware. Locally made red slipped types were also used. Painted Cibola White Ware occurs in small numbers, probably as imports from the Silver Creek Valley to the north (Mills 1996). In contrast to the Mimbres Valley, discussed below, population numbers seem to have remained small and there was no development of a local black-on-white pottery tradition.

The period between AD 1150 and 1350 was one of dramatic changes throughout the Southwest that are discussed elsewhere in this book. Nevertheless, the excavated Chodistaas Pueblo provides information about the period for the Grasshopper Region. Chodistaas, an 18-room site, was constructed with walls of dressed masonry, in the Anasazi rather than Mogollon mode. A great variety of painted ceramic styles in black-on-white pottery are represented at Chodistaas (Crown 1981; Zedeño 1994). Much of this pottery was probably not manufactured locally. The suggestion made for Chodistaas is that the ceramic diversity reflects movement of people to the area and ethnic co-residence, rather than trade. Eventually, Chodistaas itself and two other excavated communities of approximately the same size in the region were burned, and the final aggregation of population in the subregion took place at Grasshopper Pueblo between 1275 and 1400. This seems to have involved a population increase deriving in large part from dislocations ultimately related to Anasazi populations abandoning the Plateau shortly before 1300.

In the Mimbres Valley of Mogollon country, dwelling form changed from pithouse to above-ground pueblos at about AD 1000 (Anyon *et al.* 1981; LeBlanc 1989). Slightly before this change, the Mimbres Mogollon modified the color scheme of their pottery first to red paint on a white round, then to black on white (Brody 1977). Technologically, Mimbres Classic pottery is not a gray paste pottery like those produced by the Anasazi. Rather, it is a brown ware like earlier Mogollon pottery. Only the slip is white or more often grayish or brownish. Before AD 1000, Three Circle Red-on-white, a similar pottery type, was made but it was painted with red paint on a white slip. Slightly later, also before AD 1000, pithouse dwellers were producing Mimbres Boldface Black-on-white, which was technologically identical to Mimbres Classic but differed from it in decorative style. The technology and stylistic changes that occurred in the late pithouse ceramics are viewed as evidence of an in-place development of Classic Mimbres pottery rather than change imposed by the Anasazi (Brody 1977; LeBlanc 1989).

Excavations of Mimbres sites, especially the NAN Ranch Ruin (Shafer and Taylor 1986), has demonstrated precedents for an in-place transition from Mogollon pithouse to pueblo architecture between AD 925 and 1070. Again, this leads to the view that the Mimbres Mogollon developed both stone pueblo architecture and black-on-white pottery in place with minimal influence from their neighbors (LeBlanc 1989).

Between AD 1100 and 1150, the long continuum of occupation of the Mimbres Valley breaks down. LeBlanc (1989) and Minnis (1985) attribute the demise of Mimbres culture, in part, to its success in that by AD 1100, Mimbres population had grown and settlement expanded throughout the valley. They suggest that firewood and game were depleted over time so that when several years of poor rainfall, beginning in AD 1150, caused crop failures, there were few backup resources left, and many Mimbres sites were abandoned. At about the same time, however, a new center of population was beginning to develop at Casas Grandes in what is today Chihuahua, Mexico. LeBlanc suggests that some Mimbres people may have migrated to Casas Grandes, while those who stayed in the Mimbres Valley were greatly influenced by their newly powerful southern neighbors. For example, cobble masonry was replaced by construction in adobe, the material used at Casas Grandes, and there was a change to polychrome ceramics and a new series of cooking ware. LeBlanc considers that the coherence and continuity we identify as Mimbres was gone by AD 1150. Later developments, the Black Mountain and Cliff phases, of the Mimbres area are related to external events. These are first, the growth of the site of Casas Grandes in Chihuahua, and second, the development of the "Salado" culture (Nelson and LeBlanc 1986). Both Casas Grandes and Salado are discussed briefly below and in greater detail in Chapters 11 and 12.

Overall, the differences between the Mogollon of the Mimbres Valley and those of the Grasshopper and Q Ranch regions are great. They are differences in size, numbers, and detail. The Mimbres Valley seems to have supported a larger and more sedentary occupation than the two more northerly regions. This, in turn, is attributed to the greater abundance of good farming land in the Mimbres area. With generally more people in the Mimbres Valley, the pace of change is accelerated. Some stylistic differences between the two areas may relate to their geographic distance from one another and their proximity to different neighboring traditions. The Mimbres people are seen as having been influenced more by their southern neighbors at Casas Grandes, whereas the residents of the Grasshopper Plateau are viewed as having greater interactions with the Anasazi whose territory adjoined theirs to the north.

Recent research in the Mogollon area focuses on understanding the beginnings of sedentism and the adoption and spread of agriculture, the transition from pithouses to pueblos as predominant residence forms, the degree to which various branches were isolated from outside groups, the stimulus for the representations on Classic Mimbres

TABLE 7.5 Sinagua Phase Sequences[a]

Date	Northern Sinagua	Southern Sinagua
1400	Clear Creek	Tuzigoot
1300		
	Turkey Hill	
1200	Elden	Honanki
	Padre	
1100		
	Angell-Winona	
		Camp Verde
1000	Rio de Flag	
900		
800	Sunset	Cloverleaf
700		
	Cinder Park	Hackberry
600		
500		
400		
		Squaw Peak
300		
200		?
100		
AD BC		Dry Creek

[a]Adapted from Pilles (1996:62).

bowls, and the ultimate reorganization of the Mogollon and Western Anasazi into the populations that were ancestral to the Western Pueblos. These issues are examined in subsequent chapters.

Many areas of the Southwest ceased to be inhabited on a permanent basis by agricultural peoples at about AD 1150. In those regions that continued to be inhabited, there were marked changes that began at about that time and continued, with accelerating pace in the late 1200s and 1300s, when very large areas of the northern Southwest experienced major population decline. These disruptions in occupation—and their consequences—are discussed in Chapters 11 and 12. Here it is worth pointing out that throughout most of the central Southwest—in a huge east-west band above the Mogollon Rim from Flagstaff, Arizona, to the Mimbres region of New Mexico—the period between about AD 1150 and 1450 is one of changing settlement patterns, local hiatuses, village aggregations, and population crashes (Mills and Crown 1995; Plog 1983a; Upham 1982). As noted, some of this area has been considered Sinagua (Table 7.5), some Western Pueblo.

In a review of the information from this area, F. Plog (1983a) suggests that during some periods, local areas developed strong patterns that influenced the ceramic assemblages and settlement configurations in other local areas. Further, the locations of strong patterns shifted over time. For example, between AD 1050 and 1100, Winona Village appears to have been an important center, although its influence was primarily within the Flagstaff area rather than regionwide. Between about AD 1125 and 1200, the Flagstaff area extended its influence as far east as the Chevelon drainage. The major large and distinctive sites near Flagstaff include Ridge Ruin, Juniper Terrace, and Three Courts Pueblo. Ceramics produced and traded throughout the area include late Alameda brown ware and Flagstaff and Walnut Black-on-white. After about 1270, the major center of population density and influence seems to have shifted south and east. Very large aggregated sites include Chavez Pass Pueblo, Kinnickinick, and Grapevine Pueblo. Plog (1983) envisioned the changes in influence as being primarily reflected in trade. However, for the Silver Creek area, Mills (1996) reports artifactual and architectural evidence of immigration and reorganization of communities beginning around AD 1275 and continuing to 1400. The artifactual data include evidence of local use of new, previously "foreign" ceramic technology rather than widespread trade as envisioned by Plog.

After AD 1200, in the area below the Mogollon Rim from Canyon Creek to Eagle Creek, very large, aggregated villages were founded at Turkey Creek in the Point of Pines region, at Kinishba, Tundastusa, in the Forestdale area, and at Grasshopper Pueblo. Graves and others (1982) interpret these large settlements as typical of Late Mogollon patterns. They argue that the organizational pattern was fundamentally different from that suggested by Plog and Upham for sites above the rim and not unlike that known among the Western Pueblos during historic times. Neither the kind of organization Plog (1989) and Upham (1982) envision over the area they discuss nor the complex interdigitation and reorganization documented by Mills (1996) is easily described within existing normative schemes. These views are described in greater detail in Chapters 11 and 12.

THE PATAYAN

Despite considerable research, the Patayan area remains poorly documented compared with other Southwestern regions. Particularly unfortunate is the lack of well-developed chronologies for the Patayan of the lower Colorado River. Nevertheless, Waters (1982) has suggested that Rogers' (1945) terms, Yuman I, II, and III, be replaced by Patayan I, II, and III but that his chronological scheme otherwise be unaltered. More archaeological information is available for the northern and upland Patayan area, but there continues to be disagreement regarding interpretations of the materials encountered.

Generally, three cultural manifestations are delimited in the upland Patayan region: Cohonina, Cerbat, and Prescott. The history of each of the three is expressed in terms of sequential foci, which are given distinct names. The Cohonina tradition was originally defined on the basis of ceramics—San Francisco Gray, a paddle-and-anvil finished ware generally fired in a reducing atmosphere. The tradition is found in the area west of Flagstaff and south of the Grand Canyon. The Cerbat, according to Euler (1977), were probably restricted to the desert and riverine areas bordering the Colorado River in the vicinity of the Mohave Valley from about AD 700 to about 1150. Their diagnostic ceramics are Tizon Brown Ware, an undecorated, oxidized, paddle-and-anvil finished pottery. The Prescott branch of the Patayan cultural tradition is an upland manifestation south of the Cohonina, in the vicinity of Prescott, Arizona. The diagnostic ceramics are several types of painted and undecorated Prescott Gray Ware that were fired in uncontrolled atmospheres, resulting in surface color variation from orange to brown to gray (Colton 1958; Euler and Dobyns 1962). Colton (1939) recognized two phases on the basis of intrusive Anasazi ceramics: the Prescott phase, dating from about AD 900 to 1100, and the Chino, dating from about 1025 to 1200.

A number of problems beset the formulation of a chronology for the remains of the ceramic period in the lower Patayan area (Waters 1982). These include a paucity of culturally independent dates (and no tree-ring or archaeomagnetic dates), very few vertically stratified sites, and considerable confusion regarding the definitions of various ceramic types. Both the lack of chronometric dates and the absence of vertically stratified sites relate to the geographic characteristics of the lower Colorado River Valley and the kind of cultural adaptation probably associated with this setting. Before the construction of modern dams, the Colorado River was characterized by very large annual floods that deposited massive amounts of silt along its lower courses (McGuire 1982:19). During the Historic period, the Yuma Indians of this area planted fields in the flood plain after the summer floods had subsided but moved to high ground, above the river, in the winter. The structures associated with the agricultural season were ephemeral and their locations changed from year to year, depending on shifts in the river channel and areas of silt deposition. Assuming that the prehistoric agriculturists of the lower Colorado River Valley practiced a similar farming strategy, the absence of stratified remains is expected, and the annual inundation and deposition of silt would obscure even the few cultural materials left behind.

The confusion surrounding the lower Patayan ceramic typology is the result of two different investigators using the same set of names for very different types. Thus, Rogers (1945) distinguished the lower Patayan types on the basis of differences in surface treatment, rim form, vessel form, and only secondarily on variations in temper. Schroeder (1952) relied on temper as the primary criterion for the various types, but used Rogers' (1945) type names. For the various reasons discussed by Waters (1982), the type definitions applied by Rogers and as presented by Waters are accepted here. Although no adequately refined Patayan chronology exists, Waters' discussion is considered most useful in providing a baseline for the future construction of such a sequence.

As discussed by Waters, the Patayan chronology is divided into three developmental periods, with chronological implications. These are simply labeled Patayan I, II, and III. Patayan I includes five ceramic types (Colorado Beige, Colorado Red-on-beige,

Colorado Red, Black Mesa Buff, and Black Mesa Red-on-buff), all of which display direct chimney-neck rims on jars, the Colorado shoulder on jars (Figure 6.10), red clay slip, burnishing, rim notching, punctate and incised decorations, lug-and-loop handles, and the manufacturing process of hemispherical casting and basket molding. The chronological position of this assemblage of types is based on its association with intrusive Hohokam sherds at two stratified sites, five radiocarbon dates, and its absence at Patayan II and Patayan III sites. The intrusive Hohokam sherds are Santa Cruz Red-on-brown of the Colonial period. The five radiocarbon dates, which were obtained from charcoal, range in age from AD 825 ± 80 to 1050 ± 65. Although Waters suggests dates of about AD 700 to 1050 for Patayan I, on the basis of the "old wood" problem and associated difficulties with the Hohokam chronology, a beginning date closer to AD 875 or even 900 is probably more reasonable.

The ceramic types considered diagnostic of Patayan II are Tumco Buff, Parker Buff, Palomas Buff, Salton Buff, and their painted red-on-buff equivalents (e.g., Tumco Red-on-buff). Attributes of ceramics that are new in the Patayan II assemblages include recurved rims, stucco finish, new vessel forms, and an increase in fine-lined geometric designs. The chronological placement of Patayan II depends on geological interpretations and the dating of Lake Cahuilla, some intrusive sherds, radiocarbon dates, similarities in design between the Hohokam-type Casa Grande Red-on-buff and the Patayan Tumco Red-on-buff, and the absence of the diagnostic types from Patayan I and Patayan III sites. Although Waters comments on the wider geographic distribution of Patayan II than Patayan I ceramics, the chronology of this period is far from precise. Waters suggests dates of between AD 1000 and 1500. Some ceramics of Patayan III—Palomas Buff, Parker Buff, and their painted equivalents—continue from the previous period. Colorado Buff and Colorado Red-on-buff are new types. Waters notes that the differences between Patayan II and Patayan III ceramics are subtle. Three radiocarbon dates and the association of the Patayan III ceramic types with metal and glass items at some sites support the placement of these types within the Historic period, from AD 1600 to the late 1800s and early 1900s. One of the changes associated with the Patayan III period is the desiccation of Lake Cahuilla and the subsequent redistribution of the Patayan population.

A final comment on the paucity of information regarding the Patayan ceramic period chronology is warranted. Although Patayan sites have been identified as trails, rock shrines, and habitation sites, no sites with architectural features have been excavated. Most remains appear to be of ephemeral limited-activity camps. McGuire (1982: 220) cites Rogers' description of a Patayan jacal structure, uncovered from 2.5 m of Colorado River silt near Andrade, Baja California, as a clear indication of the difficulties encountered in defining the kinds of settlements associated with this group.

THE FREMONT

The Fremont tradition, considered by some to be southwestern, lies north of the Anasazi and Patayan areas in Utah and westernmost Nevada (Figure 7.1). First defined

TABLE 7.6 Fremont Geographic Variants and Phase Dates[a]

Great Sale Lake
Levee phase, AD 1000–1350+
Bear River phase, AD 400–1000
Uinta
Whiterocks phase, AD 800–950
Cub Creek phase, pre-AD 800
San Rafael
(No phases recognized) AD 700–1200
Sevier
(No phases recognized) AD 780–1260
Parawan
Paragonah phase, AD 1050–1300
Summit phase, AD 900–1050

[a]Adapted from Jennings (1978).

by Morris (1931) on the basis of work in the Fruita area of central Utah and initially viewed as a peripheral variant of the Anasazi, subsequent investigations warrant its interpretation as a separate culture tradition with five regional variants: Great Salt Lake, Uinta, San Rafael, Sevier, and Parawan (Table 7.6).

Among the traits considered useful in characterizing the Fremont in general is the production of unpainted gray wares using the coil-and-scrape technique. Some ceramic types have plastic decoration, and some late Fremont types are decorated with black paint. The Fremont tradition is also characterized by the use of moccasins (as opposed to the sandals of the Anasazi area) of a distinctive type, composed of three pieces of hide, with a single untanned piece with the dew claws retained, made from the hind leg of a large animal, serving as the sole. Another Fremont diagnostic is the one-rod-and-bundle basket. Fremont sites generally consist of a few pithouses with associated storerooms or granaries. The latter are either masonry or adobe. Kivas are not documented for Fremont sites. Agriculture apparently depended on the distinctive type of corn, Fremont dent, that may have been well adapted to short growing seasons. An abundance of faunal remains and wild plant foods may indicate that the Fremont were less dependent on agriculture than were the Anasazi. The abundant rock art in the Fremont area is stylistically different from that of adjacent areas (Figure 7.5). Two other Fremont traits have been seen as linked to the Mogollon area: the "Utah" type metate with a shelf in addition to the grinding surface, which is known from early Mogollon sites, and the frequent use of a fugitive red pigment on pottery, which may have been an attempt to copy Mogollon red wares. Finally, some Fremont sites and localities are known for elaborate, unfired clay figurines, which are unique among Southwestern figurines (Jennings 1978:155–234).

FIGURE 7.5 Visually striking Fremont petroglyphs differ stylistically from those of surrounding areas (illustrated by Charles M. Carrillo).

There is considerable controversy in the literature regarding Fremont origins, ethnic affiliation, and the eventual fate of Fremont peoples (e.g., Aikens 1966; Gunnerson 1969; Jennings 1978; Lipe 1978; Madsen and Berry 1975). Nevertheless, the five variants of Fremont culture have been defined and dated, and some have been divided into sequential phases (Table 7.6). The views regarding Fremont origins may be summarized as follows. Earlier investigators tended to regard the Fremont as derivative of the Anasazi, perhaps a regional development stemming from the expansion of Anasazi communities after about AD 950. This view has not fared well, largely because Fremont sites have been dated antecedent to the Anasazi expansion of this time.

Another interpretation characterized the Fremont as Plains-related, emphasizing the importance of bison hunting reflected in some Fremont sites and the use of moccasins, teepees, shields, and shield pictographs. This view has also been largely abandoned, even by those who initially proposed it (Aikens 1966, 1978). Jennings considers the Fremont to be a development from a local Desert Archaic base in response to the same early Mogollon or Hohokam "pulsations from southwestern New Mexico and northern Mexico that triggered the Anasazi developments" (1978:155–156). These pulsations are to have reached the Fremont area by about AD 500. This interpretation of Fremont origins is probably the most widely accepted, although Madsen and Berry

(1975) have argued that there is an apparent hiatus between Late Archaic and Fremont assemblages that may span a period of as much as 2000 years. Further dating of early Fremont sites should eventually resolve this issue.

The question of Fremont ethnic affiliation is, of course, not separate from that of Fremont origins. Thus, if the Fremont are seen as regional variants of the Anasazi, their ethnic affiliation is viewed as being Pueblo (Gunnerson 1969). In this regard, both Virgin branch Anasazi and Kayenta branch Anasazi have been associated with the Fremont. Ethnic affiliation with the northwest Plains peoples, particularly the Athapaskans, has also been suggested. Neither of these two views is currently in favor, and as noted, the Fremont are generally considered to be a separate, distinct southwestern culture with internal regional variation. The eventual fate of the Fremont is, at present, equally poorly understood. As Table 7.6 indicates, not all areas were abandoned at the same time, and it is possible that there was considerable population redistribution within the Fremont area after AD 1150 or 1200 (Lipe 1978). Attempts to link the Fremont with the northern Paiute, Shoshone, Comanche, and southern Paiute (Gunnerson 1969) have been effectively criticized (Euler 1964; Lipe 1978), as has the attempt to link the Fremont with Athapaskan speakers of the northwest Plains. Lipe (1978:388) suggests that "the Fremont drifted south during the 1200s and 1300s, much as the Anasazi did, perhaps in response to similar pressures," although he notes that evidence of the incorporation of Fremont groups into Pueblo cultures is notably lacking.

THE INTERNATIONAL FOUR CORNERS AND NORTHWEST MEXICO

Kelley and Villalpando (1996) point out that Northwest Mexico has been an area of interest to archaeologists working from both Mexico and United States since the 1920s. Nevertheless, far less work has been done in the region than north of the international border. Archaeologists trained in Mexico viewed the region as rather impoverished from a Mesoamerican context. Those workers who were trained in the U.S. ventured into the region because they were interested in Mesoamerican–Southwest connections. Largely, because such connections are not very obvious, many subsequently lost interest. Nevertheless, enough work has been done and recently synthesized (Doyel 1993; Foster and Weigand 1985; Kelley and Villalpando 1996; Phillips 1989) to allow division of the vast region into smaller, archaeologically more homogenous areas and to begin to provide chronologies for these. The areas generally distinguished are: Casas Grandes of northern Chihuahua; Jornada of northeastern Chihuahua and southeastern New Mexico; the Rio Sonora; the Trincheras culture area of northern Sonora and southern Arizona; the Loma San Gabriel culture area of southern Chihuahua and northern Durango; and the Huatabampo culture area of southern coastal Sonora and north coastal Sinaloa. Archaic cultures were widespread throughout these areas, and hunting and gathering peoples continued to inhabit the rugged mountains of the Sierra Madre Occidental and some interstitial desert regions. Elsewhere, particularly along the well-watered valleys such as the Casas Grandes and Rio Sonora, various agricultural societies developed.

Unfortunately, chronological sequences are not as well developed for these as they are for those north of the international border. It is therefore difficult to describe developments over time in these sub-areas with much clarity. For example, Loma San Gabriel sites are mostly small hamlets of surface dwellings. Pottery consists of simple bowls and jars of plain red, white, and red-on-brown design. The culture as a whole is considered possibly ancestral to modern Tepehuan; however, sites have not been chronologically differentiated within a 1200 to 1600 year sequence (Phillips 1989:380).

By far the most influential treatment of Northwest Mexico was the perspective Charles Di Peso presented based on the Joint Casas Grandes Project, which he directed from 1958 to 1961 (Di Peso 1974; Di Peso *et al.* 1974). Di Peso developed an elaborate chronology that has not stood the test of time. He had divided the Casas Grandes sequences into three periods. From oldest to most recent, these are the Viejo, Medio, and Tardio, each with a series of purportedly sequential phases that were to extend from about AD 700 to the mid-1600s. While recent work has permitted placing the Medio period, when most of the impressive sites of what Di Peso termed the city of Paquimé was built (see Chapter 12), in the fourteenth century (Dean and Ravesloot 1993), neither the period or phase sequence can be verified. The existence of the Tardio period has been questioned (Kelley and Villalpando 1996). Recent survey and excavations south of Casas Grandes in the Babicora and Santa Maria basins (Kelley and Stewart 1992) are beginning to provide dated contexts for materials that predate the 1300s, and hence promise to extend the sequence back before AD 1000.

Obviously, problems of chronology will continue to require attention in Northwest Mexico. Other issues also require the attention they are getting. Among these are establishing the scale and social complexity of sites along the Rio Sonora, in the Casas Grandes area, and in the Trincheras area (Kelley and Villalpando 1996). In each of these sub-areas, regionally organized, possibly state-level societies have been postulated and their degree of complexity debated. Rather than trying to organize these into traditional pigeon-hole categories (i.e., petty chiefdom, state, statelet), current work focuses on describing the distribution of items from these sites, whether site hierarchies exist, and other proxy measures of social scale. There are also many very large areas over which ancient hamlets are scattered, like the Loma San Gabriel area, that need to be differentiated and better understood. Also, camps of hunters and gatherers and of fishing peoples indicate the simultaneous presence of different modes of subsistence throughout the region. Understanding these and their relationships to agricultural groups is another area of ongoing concern.

ATHAPASKAN SPEAKERS: NAVAJOS

The Navajos and the Apaches are the only Athpaskan-speaking peoples in the Southwest, and today Navajo population growth is among the fastest among Native American peoples in the United States. Navajos occupy lands, particularly in the four-corners of Arizona, Utah, Colorado, and New Mexico, that were at one time inhabited by ancestral Pueblos. A tremendous amount of archaeology has been conducted on

Navajo land. Yet, most of that research has concerned ancestral Pueblos rather than Navajos, and there is no consensus about when Athapaskan-speaking peoples entered the Southwest, which route they likely traveled, or what their traditional material culture looked like prior to their interactions with Pueblo peoples and Europeans in the Southwest.

Major research on Navajo archaeology occurred during the context of the Navajo Reservoir Project (Eddy 1966) in northern New Mexico. As part of this research, Dittert (1958a, 1958b) proposed a cultural chronology that began with a Dinétah phase that was proposed to extend from pre-European times to the Pueblo Revolt of 1680. A later Gobernador phase, dated from 1700 to 1775, refers to a time of intense interaction between Pueblo and Navajo people as both fled the repercussions of the Spanish Reconquest of New Mexico, and as Navajos expanded from their traditional homeland. Succeeding periods of Navajo history are marked by the removal, by the U.S. Army, of the Navajos and some Apaches, to the Bosque Redondo in eastern New Mexico, in the Long Walk of 1863–1867. The Navajos were kept at Fort Sumner, in misery and poverty, until the negotiation of their final treaty in 1868, when they were allowed to return to their land (Brugge 1994).

The existence and character of the Dinétah phase has been debated for years; however, there has been a great amount of new archaeological, ethnohistoric, and historic work relating specifically to the Navajos that has helped clarify early Navajo history. Some of this work occurred as part of Navajo Land Claims cases and some as contract archaeology at places such as Black Mesa, Arizona; the Abiquiu Reservoir Project in New Mexico; Blanco Canyon, New Mexico; the Chuska Mountain area of the Arizona-New Mexico border; Canyon de Chelly; and the Grand Canyon (see Towner and Dean 1996). Although there is still no agreement about the "earliest Navajos" in the Southwest, there are likely Navajo sites now radiocarbon dated to the 1500s (Hancock 1992; Hogan 1989). Further, it appears that the Gobernador phase Navajo sites were indeed defensive, but there is little indication that vast numbers of Pueblo refugees lived among the Navajo in the Navajo homeland. Rather, there was a variety of interactions, including trade, among Athapaskan-speakers and Pueblos that may have extended back to the 1500s (Towner and Dean 1996). There are separate phase schemes used to refer to local developments of Navajo culture. The key issues of date of arrival and route of entry continue to be debated. However, much Navajo archaeology has turned toward documenting changes in subsistence practices, land use, and settlement strategies, and identifying mechanisms of Navajo culture change (Towner and Dean 1996:15–16). There is also an annual Navajo Studies Conference that has been bringing together traditional Navajo leaders and educators, historians, ethnologists, and archaeologists.

SOUTHWESTERN ARCHAEOLOGY FOR THE TWENTY-FIRST CENTURY

As you would suspect, there already have been conferences on the course of archaeology in the next century (Wandsnider 1992), and of course it is impossible to know how accurately they characterize the future. There are consistent themes that can be mentioned. During the 1970s and continuing into the 1980s, processual archaeology underwent internal evaluation as well as external criticism. Binford's archaeological proscriptions and prescriptions had focused on elaborating a systemic view of culture—one in which archaeologists could address issues of a social or ideological nature and refine methods by which models and propositions could be evaluated and hypotheses tested. Neither of these general perspectives prevented archaeologists from making potentially ambiguous or untestable assumptions about the past (Binford 1983; 1989:16–19).

The outcome of this particular difficulty for processual archaeology resolved itself for Binford in his call for what he termed "middle range theory" (Binford 1983). Middle range theory is required to link the statics of the contemporary archaeological record with the dynamics of behavior that archaeologists want to study. In contrast to general anthropological theory that relates to behavior, change, evolution, etc. and that might be borrowed from other disciplines, middle range theory is to be constructed to serve archaeology and to be strictly archaeological theory. Further, the only way that such theory could be built is from observations archaeologists make in the world of their experiences. These could include experiments, ethnoarchaeology, and the use of historic documents (see Binford 1989).

Many archaeologists have not accepted the challenge of developing middle range theory, in Binford's (1989) terms. On the theoretical level, there is a general retreat from processual archaeology and a move toward a variety of post-modern approaches, reflecting academic scholarship worldwide. The heterogeneity and divergence in theoretical direction appear as a lack of consensus about central questions worthy of focused research and few agreed upon frameworks for research. Archaeologists now espouse a number of intellectual affiliations and characterize themselves with diverse labels such as a-historical, behavioral, cognitive, critical, ecological, empirical, evolutionary, feminist, functional, historical, Marxist, processual, post-processual, and structuralist (Cordell 1994). Despite the lack of a single, coherent focus, archaeologists are combining innovative research methods with questions generated by their various perspectives that are providing rewarding information. For example, focusing on gender issues has given us a better understanding of technology and organization of craft production (Crown and Wills 1995; Mills and Crown 1995), burial treatment and social organization, differences in diet (Simon and Ravesloot 1995; Speilmann 1995), and other issues. Similarly, petrographic study of ceramics combined with chemical analysis of clays and studies of ceramic design are allowing exciting views of ancient craft specialization, local and regional exchange, and probable cases of migration and intermarriage (e.g., Mills and Crown 1995). Some archaeologists are assembling large numbers of ethnographic and ethnohistoric cases that provide richer insights into issues such as migration (Cameron and Tomca 1995) and aggregation and land-tenure (Adler 1996). A tremendous amount of work continues to be done within the purview of contract archaeology. These studies are generating volumes of carefully collected data that are beginning to be mined to provide solutions to long-standing questions about chronology, cultural identity, organization, and change over time.

There is concern about the lack of funding for archaeological research. At the same time, land managing agencies have integrated avocationalists into their programs. It is interesting to watch a decline in contract reports and an increase in avocationalist attendance and reports at Pecos Conferences since the late 1980s. Most archaeologists express willingness to work with Native American groups, although few know how to begin doing so (Goldstein 1992). There are some archaeologists who, rightly or wrongly, believe NAGPRA and other initiatives will make it impossible to do archaeological research at all in the Southwest. These are, perhaps, balanced by hopes that GIS systems and data access on the Internet will generate novel research strategies, involving all kinds of participants in open communication (McManamon 1992). Where negotiations with Native Americans are taking place, most archaeologists have found the exchange of views stimulating and highly rewarding. Archaeologists are very aware that what they do is often viewed as obscure. Yet, they continue to believe that there are lessons from the past and that archaeology is worthwhile for public investment. Being able to communicate the results of archaeological research as well as archaeological methods has risen to the top of many archaeological agendas (Shott 1992).

SUMMARY AND CONCLUSIONS

The literature of southwestern archaeology is written in a vocabulary that is tied to developmental and normative views of culture, whether or not contemporary archaeologists find these views appropriate for describing the patterning of similarities and differences in material culture. Three very broad and general chronological periods are distinguished. These are the Paleoindian, the Archaic, and the "later" periods. Within the third category archaeologists distinguish four major cultural traditions: Anasazi, Hohokam, Mogollon, and Patayan. Within each of these four cultural traditions, various branches and phases have been defined, although those of the Patayan are the least well documented. This chapter has provided keys to the technical vocabulary of southwestern archaeology so that interested readers can access the vast literature of the field.

Although archaeologists view local phase schemes as a convenient shorthand for characterizing the assemblages of particular areas at particular times, such schemes obscure certain characteristics of the archaeological record. There have been times and places within the Southwest when local diversity in ceramic and architectural styles is more characteristic than homogeneity. Diversity may also characterize the rates at which various attributes change. There have been other times when very similar ceramics and architecture occur over very broad regions, cross-cutting branches and the larger cultural traditions. It is difficult to describe and explain local heterogeneity in architecture and ceramics as well as instances of homogeneity in these classes of material culture by reference to shared cultural norms. Southwestern archaeologists continue to use the normative vocabulary of historical particularism to describe the material remains they encounter. Nevertheless, they have also moved toward developing explanations of patterning found in the material record of archaeology by turning to systemic and ecological views of culture that relate observed patterning to factors of the natural environment, technology, social organization, and ideology. These are explored in the chapters to follow.

Chapter-opening art: Pinedale pot (drawing by Charles M. Carrillo).

CHAPTER 8

Southwestern Communities to AD 800: Settling Down and Settling In

The widespread appearance of houses and ceramics marks a change from high residential mobility to a more sedentary way of life. The change involved the use of new kinds of tools and facilities. The functional and technological aspects of these tools and facilities are discussed in this chapter. The chapter also looks at inferences archaeologists have made about the specific uses of these tools, human social organization, mobility patterns, and belief systems based on characteristics of domestic architecture and settlement layout. The chapter concludes with discussion about the general transition from semi-subterranean houses to above ground, often contiguous-walled dwellings.

INTRODUCTION

Throughout the Southwest, the end of the Archaic coincides with the use of pottery and the construction of houses, generally pithouses. While there are examples of Late Archaic houses (see Chapter 4), there is little evidence of even seasonally sedentary settlements in the Southwest before about AD 200. Between about AD 200 and 800, settlements were established from the Grand Canyon to central New Mexico and from Cedar Mesa in southern Utah and the Dolores River area of Colorado to Sonora and Chihuahua, Mexico (Figure 8.1).

The earliest settlements vary in size and the length of time over which they were occupied. They are composed of separate, noncontiguous, semi-subterranean houses

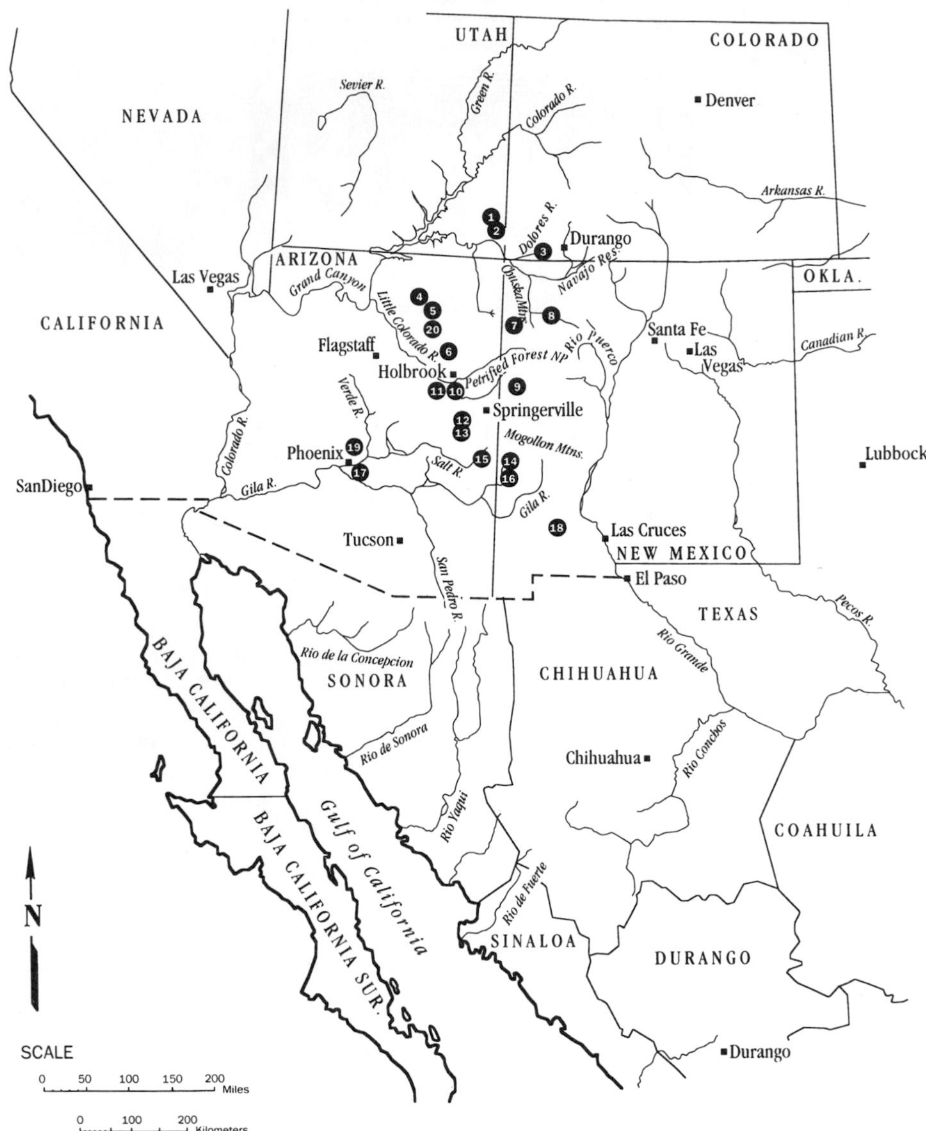

FIGURE 8.1 The sites discussed in Chapter 8 are important to the discussion of the shift to sedentism in the Southwest. Key: ❶ Elk Ridge; ❷ Cedar Mesa; ❸ Mesa Verde; ❹ Long House Valley; ❺ Black Mesa; ❻ Hopi Buttes; ❼ Tohatchi Flats; ❽ Chaco Canyon (Shabik'eschee); ❾ Zuni (Cibola); ❿ Flattop Site; ⓫ Chevelon; ⓬ Hay Hollow; ⓭ Forestdale Valley (Bluff Ruin); ⓮ Pine Lawn Valley; ⓯ Black River Drainage; ⓰ Reserve (SU Site); ⓱ Snaketown; ⓲ Mimbres Valley (NAN Ranch Ruin, Galaz Site); ⓳ Agua Fria/New River Drainage; ⓴ Bacavi. (Map by David Underwood.)

that are generally oval to circular in shape. Many settlements have special community structures. The inventory of material culture items associated with the early settlements includes grinding stones, projectile points, scrapers, knives, baskets, nets, and other items that were also part of Archaic assemblages. Ceramics were an important early addition to the basic material culture inventory. By about AD 500, bows and arrows replaced spears and darts.

The term Formative stage is used in the Southwest as it is throughout the Americas, for the appearance of settled life (Flannery 1968; Martin and Rinaldo 1951; Willey and Phillips 1958). When archaeologists use the term Formative for the co-occurrence of houses and ceramics, they sometimes suggest that there was also dependence on agriculture and occupation of year-round villages (e.g., LeBlanc 1982; Woodbury and Zubrow 1979). Use of the term Formative in the Southwest, however, may not be appropriate. By definition, the stage requires a secure resource base and social mechanisms that can integrate and sustain settled communities. In certain resource-rich settings it is possible to support sedentary communities without agriculture (Willey and Phillips 1958:144–46). In the relatively food-poor and marginal environments of the Southwest, however, the production of crops is essential for the survival of even seasonally sedentary communities. In the Southwest before about AD 850, there was great variability in the degree of dependence on crops, continued seasonal movement in most areas, and settlements that were far too small at any point in time to have constituted a demographically and socially viable village (Diehl 1996; Fish *et al.* 1990; Gilman 1987; Braun and Plog 1982).

A result in part of the variable environments of the Southwest and the possibilities these offer for various techniques of reliable agricultural production, as well as of the kinds and abundance of important wild resources, the character of settlements greatly varies. In some areas and at some times, settlements were truly tiny, consisting of only one or two houses. Elsewhere, small dispersed hamlets are the predominant settlement type. In a few areas, fairly large communities replace the hamlets early in the period, whereas some locations did not permit sustained occupation by horticulturalists at all and were soon abandoned.

In many parts of the world, the Formative stage is a brief episode that gives way to complex, socially stratified societies. In the Near East and in Mesoamerica, towns, large ceremonial centers, craft specialization, and cities succeed the first settlements relatively rapidly. Raish (1992) provides a comparison of the length of time during which this transition occurred in those areas where it did. In those parts of the world, it is often difficult to study the early settlements archaeologically because they are generally located under later, much larger settlements. In contrast to this development pattern, small settlements and villages remained characteristic forms throughout the ancient Southwest. Frequent abandonment and lack of substantial reoccupation at many sites in the Southwest allows relatively easy archaeological access to them. An examination of Southwestern habitation sites therefore permits considerable insight into a form of settlement that is often obscured elsewhere. But it must be remembered that Southwestern settlement types are not appropriate models for early village life in those areas where complex societies developed. The temporal stability of the village model in the Southwest suggests that the opportunities and pressures that led to urbanization in other settings did not exist, and the Southwestern settlements must reflect a different set of social and economic constructs.

In the Southwest, the importance of agriculture, during this period, is inferred from macrobotanical remains, the tools and facilities used in food preparation and storage, and though not without debate, studies of bone chemistry (Gilman 1987; Hegmon 1989; Matson and Chisholm 1991). Considerations of economic and social organization rely on analyses of the formal characteristics of settlements and their spatial distributions, generally compared with ethnographic information (Hegmon 1989, 1994). This chapter first examines the formal characteristics of early Southwestern settlements; the features and artifacts of the archaeological record. As noted above, the early settlement period witnessed the construction of houses and the use of ceramics. In Chapter 6, differences in methods of house construction and in ceramic manufacture and design were seen to be basic to the culture historical reconstructions prevalent in Southwestern archaeology. In this chapter a more general and functional view of these objects is offered. The distribution of settlements and interpretations of settlement social organization are also discussed.

SETTLEMENTS, TOOLS, AND SUBSISTENCE

Archaeologists have interpreted the subsistence economies of the early settlements from botanical and faunal remains and from the kinds of tools and containers found. Corn, beans, and squash were cultivated throughout the Southwest. Cotton was an addition in the lower Sonoran Desert and in those areas of the Plateaus where the growing season was sufficiently long for the crop. No further discussion of these crops is necessary here but two general observations are in order. First, nowhere in the Southwest were settlements sustained entirely on agricultural produce. Second, the particular wild resources that continued to be significant varied from one region to another.

Stone and Fiber Tools

Manos and metates were used throughout the Southwest to grind plant seeds. Initially the basin metate and the small one-hand mano are most common, but slab and trough metates and larger two-hand manos increase in frequency through time (Figure 8.2). The changes in grinding tools are generally thought to indicate an increasing reliance on corn at the expense of wild plant seeds and increasingly more efficient grinding (Diehl 1996; Hard 1990; Martin 1950; Mauldin 1993). However, as Adams (1993) notes, the changes in shape relate to efficiency that is only indirectly linked to more dependence on crops. The generally fairly large and corner-notched projectile points associated with the earliest settlements are similar to those of the Late Archaic. They were most likely used with spears and spear throwers or atlatls. Other flaked stone tools include large choppers, knives, scrapers, and drills. Later in the

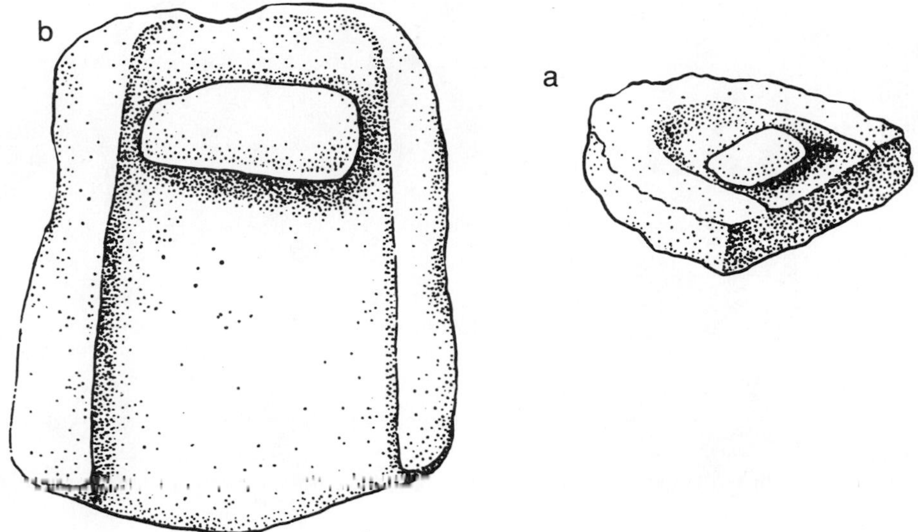

FIGURE 8.2 Manos and metates were used to grind seeds into flour throughout the Southwest. Deep basin metates and small one-hand manos (a) were replaced over time by large trough metates and two-hand manos (b), a change argued to reflect a shift from wild seeds to corn (illustrated by Marjorie Leggitt, Leggitt Design).

Archaic, small side-notched or stemmed points replace the larger forms, and this is generally interpreted as indicative of a change to the use of the bow and arrow (Amsden 1949; Glassow 1972).

Glassow (1972) suggests that the change from dart points and spears to bows and arrows may be related to the increasing importance of agriculture and an associated restructuring of other subsistence activities. He proposes that as people invest more time in agriculture, hunting, which would still be necessary to supply high-quality protein, should become more efficient. He suggests that the bow and arrow would have provided this efficiency by allowing ambush hunting in more thickly wooded locations and perhaps by increasing the variety of smaller animals that could be effectively hunted (Glassow 1972:298–299). Similarly, Gilman (1995), following Goodyear (1989) and Nelson (1981), suggests that a decrease in the percentage of tools made from very fine, unflawed, cryptocrystalline stone compared with tools made from less workable but more durable stone, regardless of availablility of source material, may reflect a need for more easily maintained tools and flakes used for repetitive tasks related to agriculture rather than tools needed for hunting.

Perishable items are known from the excavations of caves and rock shelters in the northern and mountainous portions of the Southwest and show continuity from the Late Archaic (Guernsey and Kidder 1921; Martin *et al.* 1952; Morris and Burgh 1954). From these locations, a variety of baskets has been recovered, as were blankets of

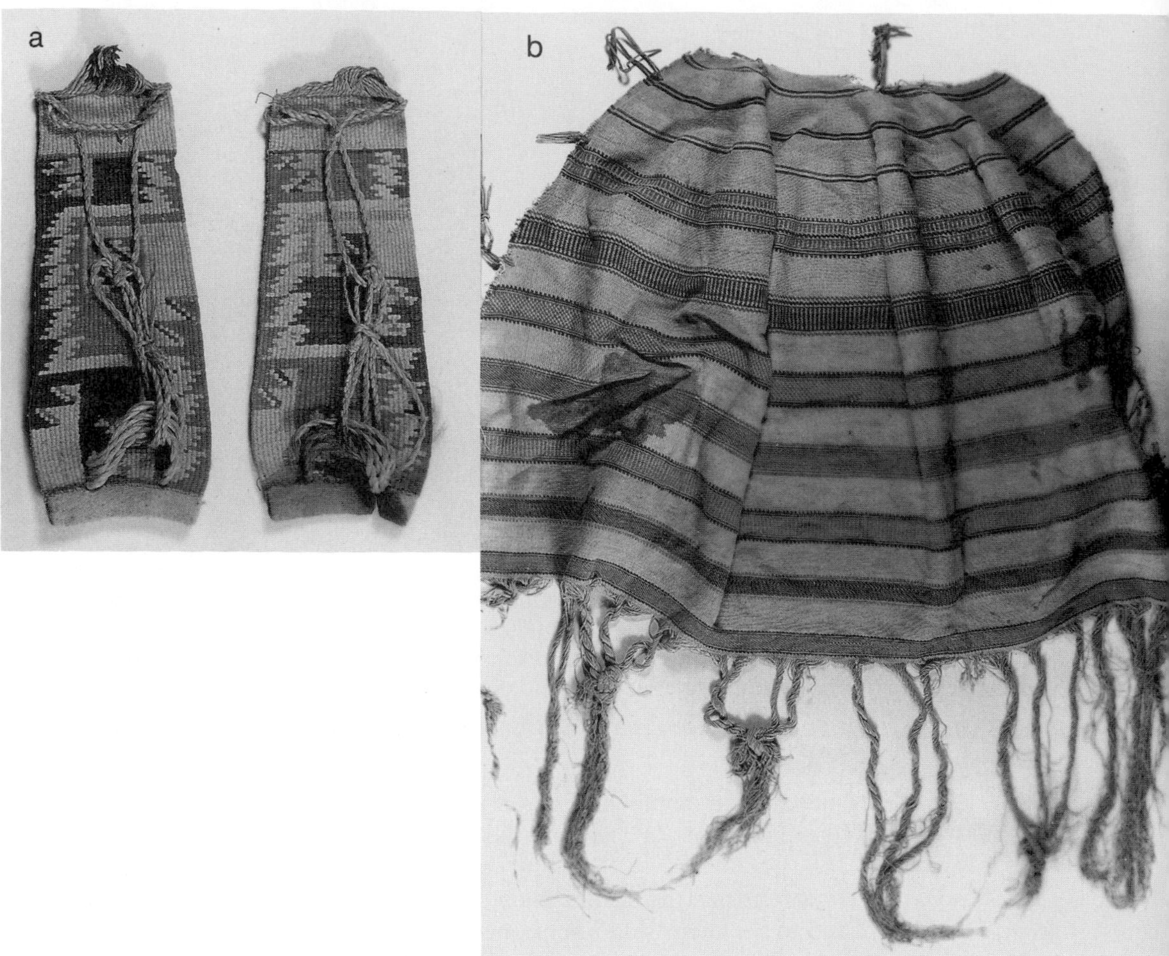

FIGURE 8.3 As their name implies, the Basketmakers are known for basketry and textiles finely crafted from wild plant fibers and hair and preserved in dry rock shelter sites. Among these items are (a) patterned sandals (UCM 2462); (b) bags (UCM 2343); (c) cradles with rigid, twig frames, and (d and e) square-toe sandals of different types (photos a and b courtesy of the University of Colorado Museum; c, d, and e illustrated by Marjorie Leggitt, Leggitt Design after Kidder and Guernsey (c) [1919] and (d and e) after Guernsey and Kidder [1921]).

cordage wrapped with fur and feathers, cradle boards, and sandals made of yucca, tulle, and other plant fibers. Other perishable materials consist of plain-weave cotton cloth, braided sashes, string aprons, cordage, and knotted netting (Figure 8.3). Bone awls and needles, used to make baskets and textile materials, are commonly found in early habitation sites.

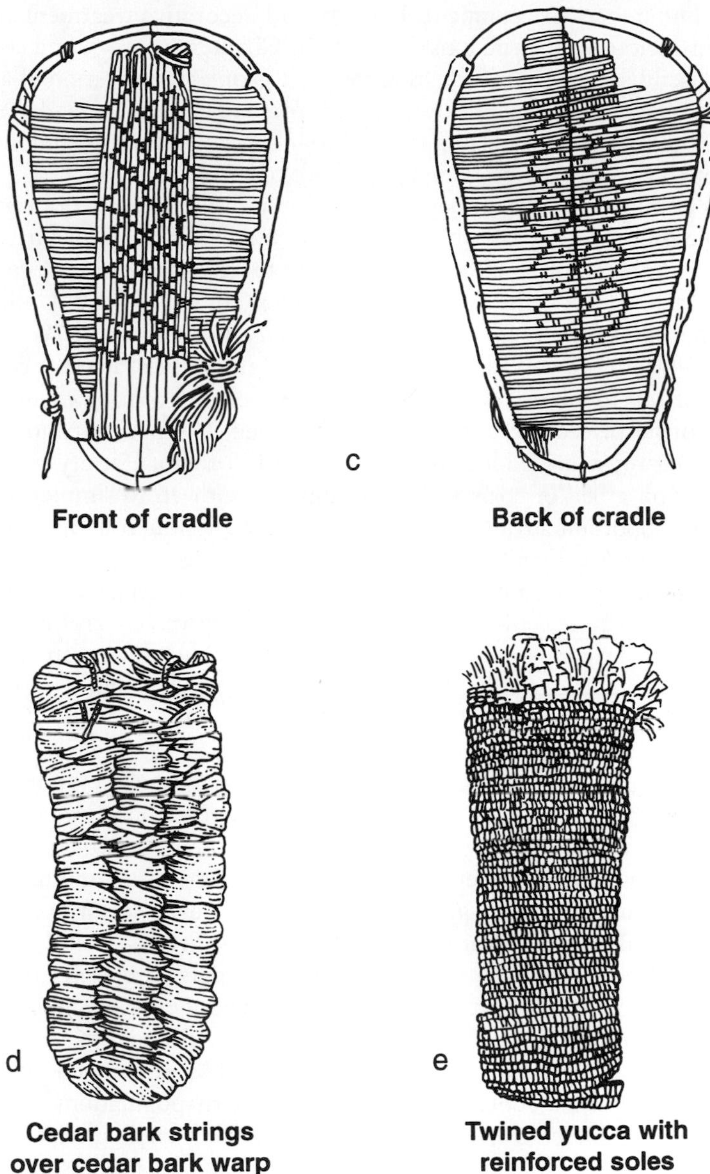

FIGURE 8.3—*Continued*

Pottery

The earliest ceramics in the Southwest date to about AD 200 (cf. Berry 1982; LeBlanc 1982; Schroeder 1982; Whittlesley 1995). By AD 500, the use of ceramics was widespread. Differences in ceramic technology and decorative treatment are basic to the culture historical reconstructions discussed in Chapters 6 and 7, and ceramics are indeed very useful sources of information for discussion and resolution of a variety of archaeological issues. Essentially, however, ceramics are containers, and their appearance in the Southwest can be related directly to increased sedentism and indirectly to increased population and the growing importance of agriculture.

Ceramic containers, because they are both heavy and fragile, are not very useful to highly mobile groups, especially those lacking pack animals, rafts, or boats. Ceramic vessels can be used for storing either liquids or dry foods. They can keep contents safe from insects and rodents if they are sealed with stone or clay covers. Unlike baskets, they do not become more fragile with age (Woodbury and Zubrow 1979:59). Ceramic containers are also more versatile for cooking than are baskets. Baskets can be made watertight, but this involves a fairly complicated process of coating them with pitch. Baskets cannot be placed directly on fires, and when it is necessary to warm their contents, heated rocks are added to the liquid within them. Pottery vessels can be placed directly on a bed of coals and their contents allowed to simmer unattended. This can be an important advantage among peoples with numerous activities to complete in order to survive. Further, pottery is well-suited to cooking gruel—food that is reconstituted by the addition of liquid. Hence pottery is particularly useful to people who are using a great deal of dry, stored foods. Pottery vessels are made relatively quickly, especially in comparison to baskets, and a single potter can make several vessels and fire them at one time. On the other hand, baskets and bags have longer use-lives than pottery (Arnold 1985; Brown 1989; Crown and Wills 1995; Gilman 1995; Glassow 1972).

Despite these advantages of pottery, it is not necessarily true that pottery production requires a negligible increase in labor or was easily accommodated into the activities of the women who most likely produced and used pottery containeres. Crown and Wills (1995) suggest that in societies practicing some agriculture and mixed hunting and gathering, women do plant gathering and horticulture. Pottery production requires collecting additional quantities of raw materials, firewood, and water. It also requires learning how to make and then making the pots. Preparing dry foods for boiling requires an additional investment of time and energy; for example, hours spent grinding corn. They maintain that if pottery production and use fit easily within women's schedules, then pottery would have been used as early as the first cultigens appear. Crown and Wills contend that as southwestern populations became more sedentary they could increase the size of their fields, or they could intensify cultivation of existing fields, or they could alter their food storage and processing techniques. While they may have done all three, it is the last that is visible archaeologically in the form of pottery. Pottery and its associated cooking technology, they suggest, increases the amount of nutrient-rich food available; it does not decrease the amount of labor invested in food preparation.

The differences among the kinds of ceramics made and used in the Southwest relate to variations in production techniques. All ceramics are composed primarily of clay. The mineral constituents of naturally occurring clays vary with the source material from which the clays are derived. Some clays have more ferrous components than others and these will generally take on brownish to reddish color on firing. However, the color of fired clay also depends on the amount of air permitted to circulate in firing. Within certain limits, the basic color of ceramic vessels can be determined by the potter despite differences in locally available clays. Recent technological studies (Wilson and Blinman 1995) distinguish gray, white, and red ware pottery. Gray ware was generally unpainted and unslipped and was fired in a neutral atmosphere. Most gray ware vessels were used for cooking and storage. Decoration, when present, is in the form of surface texturing such as corrugation. White ware pottery is often painted with designs, generally a dark color paint on a light gray or white background. Although color contrast can be achieved with most clays, Wilson and Blinman (1995:6) state that for clays with moderate or high iron content, the potter must exercise precise control so that firing removes just enough oxidation to remove organic material from the clay but not so much that iron compounds are changed from ferrous gray to ferric red. The required "neutral" atmosphere is very difficult to maintain, so most ancient potters selected low-iron clays to produce white or gray ware. The low-iron clays are found throughout the Southwest but are less common than moderate- to high-iron clays. Further, the potters that produced painted white ware had to match clays with the paint type because some clays do not retain organic pigment. Red wares, like white wares, were used for serving and storage. They were produced by selecting iron-rich clays and strong oxidation firing. Since some red wares have gray streaks or cores, the same clays could be used for both white and red wares, but oxidation had to have taken place during at least the final stages of firing to produce the red color (Wilson and Blinman 1995). Iron-rich clays are available throughout the Southwest.

Pottery cannot be made from very pure clay because pure clay will shrink and crack when it is dried and fired. Consequently, potters generally add nonplastic materials to clays. These materials, collectively referred to as temper in the archaeological literature, also strengthen vessel walls. In the Southwest, sand, crushed or ground rock, and crushed potsherds were commonly used as temper. Temper particles can be seen, and often identified, under magnification. They provide valuable clues about the locations in which the pottery was likely produced. For example, certain kinds of temper, such as fragments of igneous rock, have a limited geographic distribution. If ceramics are found to contain temper that is unavailable in local geological formations, either the vessels, or the temper, are likely to have been imported. Similarly, extreme geological heterogeneity in temper may indicate a variety of production locations.

Technically, vessel walls are made of a combination of clay and temper, a combination referred to as the *paste*. If the pot is to be painted, it is desirable to have a smooth surface on which to apply the design. Sometimes this surface is achieved by covering the exterior of the vessel with a thin coat of pure clay, the *slip*. Clays used for the slips were selected because of the color they assume when fired. For example, some clays are nearly pure kaolin and will fire to a clean white color. Other clays will fire red or yellow or buff. The background color of most painted Southwestern ceramics is the color of the slip. The paste color may be quite different and can be seen only by exposing a fresh surface in cross-section. The clays in the slips and in the paste must

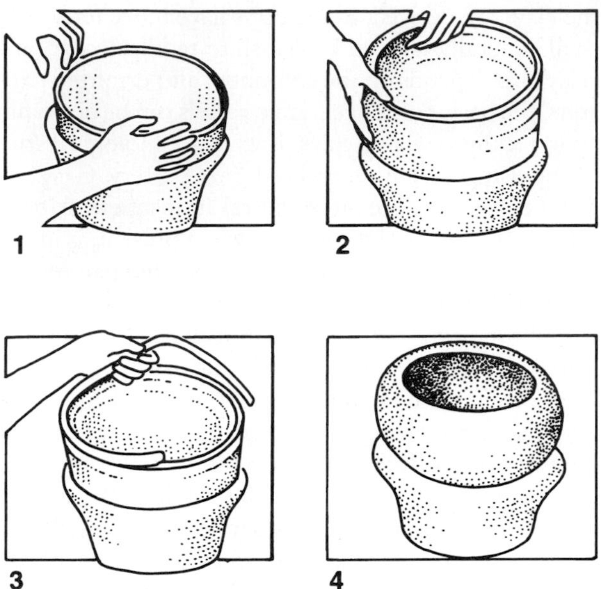

FIGURE 8.4 Southwestern pottery was built up by adding coils of clay one to another. Further shaping was done either by scraping with a sherd or piece of gourd or by paddling holding an anvil stone inside the vessel (illustrated by Marjorie Leggitt, Leggitt Design).

also be compatible so that the slip is not lost in firing. Iron-rich slips were not applied over low-iron clays, for example (Shepard 1939, 1942, 1954).

Throughout the Southwest (and in fact the Americas) pottery was handmade without use of the potter's wheel (Figure 8.4). In the eastern and northern parts of the Southwest, the Mogollon and Anasazi areas, pottery vessels were usually built up by coiling and finished by scraping with a gourd or similar item (Figure 8.5). In the lower Sonoran Desert (the Hohokam and most of the Patayan area), pottery vessels were also made by coiling, but the vessel walls were then thinned and smoothed by using a paddle and anvil, leaving the surface with a dimpled texture. In the Mogollon region, brown plain ware pottery predominated, but polished, slipped red and brown wares with red painted designs were also made. In the Anasazi area, ceramics were generally gray plain wares, or else the ceramics had a gray or white surface color and were decorated with black painted designs. In the Hohokam area, buff to brown plain pottery was most common. Hohokam painted pottery was buff colored with designs executed in red paint. In the Patayan area, ceramics were gray, buff, or brown. Upland Patayan painted pottery is generally black on gray. Along the lower Colorado River Valley, ceramics were rarely painted, but when paint was used it was a reddish color.

The paints used to produce pigments for designs were derived from a variety of materials. These are generally grouped in two broad categories—carbon and mineral. Carbon (organic) paints were made by boiling selected plants, such as the Rocky

FIGURE 8.5 This Pueblo woman demonstrated the steps in making pottery for photographer Merl Lavoy in 1930. (a) She rolls a coil of paste beside bowls that have been partly and fully shaped. (b) She paints a jar with a grinding stone for pigment and small bowls, one of which contains slip clay, at her side (photo courtesy of the University of Colorado Museum).

FIGURE 8.6 Rocky Mountain bee plant was boiled and commonly used as a source of black pigment for paint used to decorate pottery (illustrated by Marjorie Leggitt, Leggitt Design).

Mountain bee plant (Figure 8.6). Pigment in carbon-based paint is soluble and is applied in solution. Hence, they can seep into the slip, producing lines with faintly blurred edges. Mineral paints were produced by grinding a variety of pigment ores, such as hematite or iron oxide, and adding them to an organic flux, where they remain in suspension. The mineral particles do not seep or bleed into the slip, and so they produce lines with distinct edges. The use of mineral-based paints centered in northwestern New Mexico, especially in the San Juan Basin, and extended east to the Rio Grande and south to the Mogollon country. West of this, in the Kayenta area and farther west, a carbon-based black pigment was used. The two traditions coexisted until potters in the central Anasazi area, the San Juan Basin, Mesa Verde, and Chuska drainage switched to carbon pigments. This occurred gradually between about AD 1050 and 1200. South of these areas, from the Rio Puerco east to the edge of the Great Plains, mineral paints were retained until nearly AD 1600.

Late in the culture history of the Southwest (after AD 1300), a particular kind of mineral paint was used very widely. This was a lead- or copper-based paint referred to as *glaze* because it vitrifies on firing. The glaze was used only for decoration and never to completely cover and seal the vessel surface. Most painted vessels, and some unpainted ones, were polished before they were fired. Polishing was done with smooth, hard pebbles and produced a shiny surface. Studies of southwestern ceramics are so numerous that they can fill entire small libraries. Archaeologists, in particular, have approached the classification of ceramics in a variety of ways. Studies of southwestern ceramic technology were done in the early years of Southwestern archaeology, but the most systematic and detailed approach was pursued by Anna O. Shepard (Kidder and

Shepard 1936; Shepard 1939, 1942, 1954), whose work provides the foundation for the kinds of analytic studies that are crucial to contemporary archaeological questions regarding ceramic production, distribution, and trade.

The earliest ceramics throughout the southwest are predominantly plain wares, without texturing or paint. Recent discoveries and detailed analyses of these early southwestern ceramics show that initially the ceramic industries of the entire region were undifferentiated. The earliest southwestern pottery has been termed the Plain Ware horizon (Whittlesey 1995), with sites distributed from the Northern San Juan to southern Arizona and from the Petrified Forest to central and southern New Mexico. Plain Ware horizon ceramics are a friable, plain brown ware, produced by coiling thin ropes of clay and smoothed by a variety of techniques including scraping the interior and exterior surfaces smooth with a gourd or other similar object, polishing, or in some areas paddle and anvil finishing. Brown ware has long been thought to be a hallmark of Mogollon culture (see Chapter 6), which is a major reason that the Mogollon tradition is viewed as extending from Flagstaff, Arizona, to El Paso, Texas, and south into southern Chihuahua and Sinaloa. It has long been believed that the difference between Mogollon brown ware and Anasazi gray ware was technological, reflecting a cultural choice: Brown wares were thought to be fired in an oxidizing atmosphere, where air is allowed to circulate openly during firing, whereas gray wares were fired in a reducing atmosphere, from which air is blocked.

Technological studies (Wilson and Blinman 1995) demonstrate a more interesting and complicated picture. The early Plain Ware horizon pottery is made from iron-rich alluvial clays found in alluvial bottom lands. These clays are "self-tempered" with sand inclusions so that there is no need to add additional nonplastic material. Wilson and Blinman (1992) suggest that this kind of clay was used when people were farming alluvial bottom lands, possibly when neither their social networks nor the annual patterns of movement included areas where there were better-quality geological clays. Whittlesey (1995) finds that Plain Ware horizon sites show a broad range of similarities in material culture, despite the diverse environments in which they are found. With respect to the ceramics, she notes that neckless jars (seed jars) and bowls are the predominant forms and that the diverse forms that typify later Hohokam ceramics do not occur. It is not until between about AD 400 and 500 that technological differentiation among ceramic traditions occur, and this is perhaps best understood in the context of organizational changes that accompanied increased sedentism (Hegmon 1994).

Houses

Throughout the Southwest, the earliest post-Archaic houses were pithouses, structures in which some portions of the house walls are actually the earth sides of an excavated pit (Crown 1990; Gilman 1987; Whittlesey 1995). The pithouses are generally round to oval or bean shaped, and about 4.5–5.0 m in diameter. Their floors were usually dug to a depth of about 0.5 m below the surface of the ground. There is variation in house floors. Some are discernible only as sterile earth compacted through use. Some are of bedrock, and others are of finished mud or clay. Unless the pithouse burned, remains of walls and roofs are rarely preserved, so it is difficult to describe the variation in these architectural features. In the Durango, Colorado, area, Morris and Burgh (1954) excavated pithouses with superstructures of cribbed logs laid horizontally in abundant mud mortar. Cribbed-log superstructures are also known from pithouses excavated in the Navajo Reservoir area of northwestern New Mexico (Eddy 1966). More commonly, the portions of pithouse walls that extend above the surface of the ground consisted of a framework of poles set vertically around the edge of the pit, interlaced with small twigs, and then completely covered with mud on the exterior. In many pithouses, the interior earthen walls were lined with upright slabs.

In cases where the pithouse interior was relatively small, the vertical poles may have been bent to form part or all of the pithouse roof. Some reconstructions indicate gabled pithouse roofs supported by a crossbeam set on posts aligned along one axis of the house. A common technique that seems to have become more widespread through time was to support the roof on four post supports arranged in a quadrilateral pattern (Bullard 1962). Although a simple opening in a wall may have served as an entryway into some small pithouses, parallel-sided, lateral, inclined entryways are common features in the early pithouses (e.g., Haury and Sayles 1947; Lipe and Matson 1971).

Within the earliest pithouses, floor features vary. In the Durango area (Morris and Burgh 1954); at the Flattop site in the Petrified Forest, Arizona (Wendorf 1953b); at the early Navajo Reservoir District sites (Eddy 1966); and at the Bluff Ruin in the Forestdale Valley, Arizona (Haury and Sayles 1947), firepits with ash and charcoal but without other evidence of burning, such as oxidized walls, occur in some—not all—houses. Some pithouses lack hearths entirely (e.g., Ciolek-Torrello 1995). Pithouses that lack interior firepits are frequently interpreted as having been occupied only seasonally. Some archaeologists have suggested that the ephemeral hearths may have been used for occasional cooking. Other investigators have interpreted these features as heating pits that were used to hold rocks that had been heated at outside hearths. A variety of subfloor storage pits is commonly found in the early pithouses. These might be circular, jug shaped, basin shaped, flat bottomed or bell shaped, and undercut (Ciolek-Torrello 1995; Haury and Sayles 1947).

Through time, pithouse form underwent change and in most areas became standardized, with the regularly occurring styles and shapes varying in different regions. For example, in the Mogollon region, pithouse shape ranged from generally round or oval to rectangular with rounded corners to rectangular. After their initial appearance in the same area, pithouses also generally decreased in size. Firepits, often slab or cobble lined, became standard floor features and were set into the floor at the center axis of the room in front of the entryway.

In much of the Anasazi area, pithouses were built with adobe wing walls separating the house into two main areas (Figure 8.7). Metates have been found set into the floor in the smaller vestibule area, suggesting that this part of the house served as a kitchen and food preparation area. In both Mogollon and Anasazi areas, a sipapu (small hole in the floor considered to represent the shipap or place through which people emerged from the lower world in Pueblo belief) are sometimes located toward the back of the house. Other features commonly found in Anasazi pithouses include ventilator

FIGURE 8.7 (a) Photograph of excavated Anasazi Basketmaker III pithouses and (b) artist's reconstruction of a similar structure. Note antechamber and wing walls, upright slabs lining walls, and dividing interior space. Photography is of 5MT1, Yellow Jacket, Colorado (courtesy of the University of Colorado Museum; the drawing is by Marjorie Leggitt, Leggitt Design).

openings, slab or adobe deflectors, and benches or raised platforms around most or all of the room perimeter. The deflectors were located between the central hearth and ventilator shaft and presumably served to guide incoming air away from the open fires. As Anasazi pithouses became more standard in form and features, they often were equipped with hatch entries through the roof, and the impressions of ladder posts are frequently found beneath these on the opposite side of the hearth from the deflector and ventilator.

The earliest post-Archaic houses in the Hohokam region continue the Archaic pattern of ephemeral oval houses, between 3 and 5 m square, with bell-shaped subfloor storage pits, but lacking hearths and formal entryways. Slightly later houses are larger (6 to 25 m^2) but of varied shape—from oval and square to subrectangular. These have formal, plaster-lined hearths positioned centrally and in front of a defined entry. These entries were flanked by bulging walls that were thickly plastered (Ciolek-Torrello 1995; Huckell 1993).

It is only later that Hohokam houses were houses built in pits, and for a while, both true pithouses and houses in pits were built (Whittlesey 1995). In houses in pits, although house floors were excavated some 10–20 cm below the surface of the surrounding ground, the house walls were nearly always made entirely of a framework of poles covered with reeds, grass, and dirt. A four-post roof-support pattern was usual in square houses, and a two central-post pattern, with auxiliary posts along house edges, was used in rectangular houses. Small adobe-lined hearths were located in front of the entryway about halfway between the entry and the centerline of the house (Haury 1976:72). Haury indicates that most hearths do not seem to have been used for large fires but perhaps held embers brought in from outside fires. Finally, although pits and cists are features of Hohokam settlements, these are outside houses rather than both outside and inside.

Within the last decade, archaeologists working in the Mogollon, Anasazi, and Hohokam areas have recognized a Plain Ware horizon that appears to be remarkably uniform throughout the Southwest. It is characterized by plain, brown, self-tempered pottery and residential pit structures with similar internal features. Other similarities include the ground and chipped stone assemblages. Evidence of this horizon has come to light through salvage excavations into very deeply buried deposits that were obscured by overburden or later constructions. Remains dating to the Early Plain Ware are virtually invisible from the surface.

A CONSIDERATION OF PITHOUSES

Pithouses were constructed up until modern times in some parts of the Southwest, but in general, this form of house gave way to multiroom surface pueblos on the Colorado Plateaus and the mountainous northern Southwest and to separate houses in pits in the Hohokam area. Several archaeologists have attempted to explore general processual factors involved in the transition from pithouse to pueblo (e.g., Gilman

1983, 1987; Lipe and Breternitz 1980; Plog 1974; Wills 1991), and a few scholars have specifically examined the functional aspects of pithouses.

Farwell (1981) considered the thermal properties of pithouses and found them to be more efficient in conserving heat than are pueblos. Citing studies indicating that heat is lost more slowly in underground structures without any additional insulation than in above-ground structures with the best modern forms of insulation, she calculated the thermal efficiencies of a pithouse and of a four-room surface pueblo excavated at locations at similar elevations. The calculations for the surface structure were made using two rooms with southern exposures and adobe walls that were 25 cm thick. Her work considered heat lost through wall openings and heat transmitted through wall surfaces. Her results indicated that while the pithouse would lose 19,614 BTUs per day over the winter months, the surface pueblo would lose 50,540 BTUs each day. As Farwell (1981:46) noted, "occupants of the pueblo room would have to provide 30,836 more BTUs per day (the equivalent of 30,836 kitchen matches) in auxiliary heat than the pithouse residents to achieve the desired 60 degrees F temperature on an average winter day."

Farwell (1981) considers other aspects of the thermal efficiency of pithouses, such as the lack of effect of the wind-chill factor on ground temperature and the effect of the ground as a heat sink. She suggests that although no single factor such as thermal advantage is likely to have been the most important reason for building pithouses, she concludes that the pithouse would require less energy to heat either in fuel or manpower to collect fuel than the surface structure. In a study that provides a partial test of Farwell's (1981) conclusion, Stuart and Farwell (1983) consider the influence of thermal factors by examining the correlation between pithouse depth and altitude (elevation). In general, because winter temperatures decrease with increasing elevation and because the temperature of the ground gradually increases with increased depth until a certain level is reached, one would expect that deeper pithouses would be found at higher elevations. In fact, they found a high positive correlation between elevation and pithouse depth; the cooler the winter, the deeper the pithouse.

In another study, Gilman (1987) examined a variety of factors, including thermal efficiency, in the use of pithouses. Using ethnographic examples from a worldwide sample, she found that the distribution of pithouses correlates with areas in which cold winters can be expected. She also found that pithouses are used by groups whose settlements are of relatively small size and who are either nonagricultural or practice agriculture on a limited scale. In the ethnographic sample, groups using pithouses were semi-sedentary, living in pithouses only during cold months. It is possible that many of the pithouse settlements in the northern and in mountainous areas of the Southwest were used only during the winter.

The discussion of pithouse thermal efficiency suggests one plausible reason for the distribution of pithouses in the Southwest, particularly the later absence of pithouses in the warm lower Sonoran Desert. The discussion also indicates that other factors such as settlement size, subsistence, and degree of residential permanence are also important. Before examining these further, some of the other formal characteristics of early southwestern settlements need to be discussed.

The shape of pithouses, in contrast to above-ground pueblos, is also a subject of inquiry. Most pithouses are circular to oval, while above-ground pueblos consist of contiguous, rectangular rooms. In a study of ethnographic examples worldwide, Kent Flannery (1972) found that circular dwellings occur in settlements, which he terms "compounds," where the architectural shape reflects the organization of production. In societies with compounds, stored food is generally communally owned and kept in public areas. Houses are owned and used by individuals rather than by families.

Compound settlements are more common among bands of hunters and gatherers than among agriculturalists. There is marked sexual division of labor in compound settlements, and while these settlements are small, periodic population aggregation occurs in times of resource abundance. In communities with rectangular housing, which Flannery (1972) calls villages, houses are owned and used by families, storage areas are private, although there may be some special structures where community sharing takes place, and the family as a whole is the unit of production and consumption. Flannery (1972) suggested that sedentism, characterized either by compounds or contiguous rectangular rooms, is a function of the effort to control resources by establishing permanent communities in places where there is resource abundance. The resources in question need not be agricultural. Often, they are not.

Gilman (1987) and Hunter-Anderson (1986) also find correlations between the organization of labor and the shape of dwellings. In rectangular houses, especially those with multiple rooms, tasks that occupy a great deal of time and/or special equipment can be segregated from general activity space. Milling rooms are a good example. All different kinds of activities take place in round dwellings, but these are usually of short duration and if special equipment is required, it can be moved in and out of position quickly. Stored food easily can be segregated in settlements with rectangular rooms, and access to storerooms can be guarded if these are entered through other rooms. As Gilman (1987) states, it is difficult to add many separate semi-subterranean round structures together without walls collapsing.

SETTLEMENT SIZE, SETTINGS, LAYOUT, AND NONRESIDENTIAL STRUCTURES

The number of pithouses in the early settlements varies considerably. For example, on northern Black Mesa, Arizona, average site size is about three to four pithouses (Gilman 1983). Survey data from Cedar Mesa and Elk Ridge, Utah; the Agua Fria, Chevelon, and middle New River drainages; Long House Valley; the Grand Canyon, Arizona; and the Cibola (Zuni) area of New Mexico, suggest an average of two pithouses per early settlement (Plog *et al.* 1978). On the other hand, sites consisting of 25 to 35 pithouses are documented from the Forestdale Valley, Hay Hollow Valley, and Petrified Forest, Arizona; and the Pine Lawn Valley and the Navajo Reservoir District, New Mexico; and elsewhere (Eddy 1966; Lightfoot and Feinman 1982; Plog 1974). Much larger sites are also recorded. One site in the Black River drainage, Arizona (Wheat 1954), is estimated to contain more than 100 pithouses. This variation in size has been interpreted in a variety of ways, including reflecting social differentiation, differences in length of occupation, and number of episodes of reoccupation (see below). Although some settlements were undoubtedly larger than others, it is difficult to determine how many houses in a particular settlement were inhabited at the same time.

The problem of estimating settlement size is even more difficult for Hohokam settlements. Many Hohokam settlements were occupied for long periods of time because required proximity to water sources, and later to irrigation canals, limited their distributions. Even though settlements were relatively permanent, individual houses had very short lifespans. Because house walls were made of twigs, reeds, and mud, they deteriorated quickly after abandonment. Usually the only house remains left for the archaeologist are hard-packed floors. If the pit structure did not burn, there is no evidence of it on the surface. Particularly when a settlement consists of houses scattered over more than a square kilometer, determining the number of houses at each site and how many were occupied at one time is exceptionally difficult. Wilcox and others did estimate that there were about 173 houses at Snaketown during the early Pioneer period (see Haury 1976:75–76 for a discussion of the problem, and Wilcox *et al.* 1981).

In addition to houses, the early settlements contain a number of extra mural features. These are most commonly pits and cists of various kinds that served as storage areas, and outdoor hearths and roasting ovens for cooking. In the absence of the excavation of complete site areas, it is not possible to determine how many outside firepits and storage pits or cists were commonly associated with each settlement. On northern Black Mesa, early settlements had an average of six outside pits, of various shapes, per structure (Gilman 1983:248). Plog (1974:137) reports a range from 0.14 m^3 to 4.25 m^3 of storage space per dwelling unit in the Hay Hollow area. Wherever excavation has encompassed surfaces outside houses, both storage pits and hearths have been located.

By AD 550 to 650, the typical house on the Colorado Plateau was a shallow pithouse that was round, or square with rounded corners, with an antechamber and fairly consistent floor features. These include a central hearth, ash pits, often mud dividers or wing walls that separate activity space inside the dwelling, and some interior storage cists. Within this general pattern, there are a variety of regional variations. In the Kayenta area, and the San Juan Basin, pithouse walls are often lined with upright slabs. In the Kayenta region, storage pits are consistently located behind the pit houses. In the Mesa Verde region (Rohn 1989), one excavated site, the excavated Gilliland Site, consisted of four pithouses and numerous outside work areas with ramadas (shade structures), all completely encircled by a stockade. In the Mesa Verde region, pithouse entryways are oriented to the south. In Chaco, the entryways are to the southeast, and there are many other minor differences as well.

In the early settlements consisting of only two or three houses, there is no indication that the structures were used for other than residential functions. At virtually all the larger early settlements that have been excavated, however, one or more community or special-function structures have been identified. Where pithouse settlements occur, these special structures are similar to pithouses but are distinguished, usually, because they are larger, have unusual architectural features, and lack evidence of domestic activities. For example, LeBlanc (1983:67) describes Pithouse 8 at the Galaz site in the Mimbres Valley as an early great kiva. This structure was round, with a diameter of about 7 m and a floor area of about 37 m^2 (about two-and-one-half times the size of the average domestic pithouses at the site). In addition, Pithouse 8 had stylized adobe pillars adjacent to the projected rampway. These features are similar to those found in later Mogollon great kivas. Finally, although the pithouse had burned, there were no domestic artifacts (bowls, metates, etc.) on the floor. Rather, the floor contained a series of large, flat stones, which LeBlanc suggests served as seats or the bases of seats for the spectators of ceremonies.

A nearly identical structure was excavated in the Hohokam area at the Houghton Road site, near Tucson. There, among smaller pit structures, was a larger, more deeply excavated, bean-shaped pit structure with a plastered floor and plastered walls and two large plastered pillars flanking the entryway. According to Ciolek-Torrello, had its entryway not been partially destroyed by a modern waterline trench, the structure "would be morphologically identical to the most common type of Mogollon communal house" (Ciolek-Torrello 1995:557). Oversize pit structures from sites in the Phoenix basin and from Snaketown may also have served communal functions (Gladwin 1948; but see also Haury 1976:68). Later, near the end of the Pioneer period in the Hohokam area (ca. AD 600 or 700), the principal evidence cited for community-wide cooperation is the irrigation canals.

In the Anasazi area, oversized structures with nondomestic features occur at many sites. Shabik'eschee Village, at Chaco Canyon, dating to AD 450 to 550, is a good example. The site consists of 18 pithouses, more than 50 exterior storage pits, and a circular structure, usually called a great kiva. This feature had a low encircling interior bench, a central fire pit, and slab-reinforced walls enclosing approximately 94.5 m^2 of floor area (Roberts 1929; Wills 1991).

The Early Plain Ware horizon sites in the Hohokam area lack well-developed middens. Structures at these sites are not oriented with respect to each other or in a consistent direction. On the basis of these observations and the presence at these sites of bell-shaped storage pits that generally suggest long-term caching of food, excavators have concluded that these sites were not occupied by fully sedentary populations (Ciolek-Torrello 1995). This is supported by the presence of upland resources, indicating that maize agriculture was not the basis of subsistence. It is slightly later in the Hohokam sequence, by the Vahki phase (ca. AD 300), that Hohokam houses are built in clusters of two to four that face each other across a courtyard area (Crown 1991; Doyel 1987; Wilcox *et al.* 1981). This formal, courtyard group remains a consistent, stable feature of Hohokam communities throughout the Hohokam sequence. They are associated with distinct middens, burial areas, and work areas.

Within the Southwest in general, aridity, unpredictable rainfall, and short growing seasons in the northern and mountainous areas create situations of high risk for horticulturalists. It is not surprising that many small settlements failed to sustain themselves. Further within the Southwest those groups living at high northern elevations would face the most risk of crop failure. It might be expected that there would be a higher rate of settlement abandonment in these settings than in the lower Sonoran Desert. These factors may account for the fact that Hohokam settlements appear to have been inhabited continuously for longer periods of time than Anasazi or Mogollon settlements. The differences in subsistence security may also have been important to defensive considerations and the topographic settings selected for the early settlements.

Unfortunately, there are two few Pioneer period Hohokam sites known to generalize about their topographic settings beyond accessible water and arable land (Haury 1976; Masse 1981). However, Haury (1976:9) commented specifically on the lack of defensive considerations in the positioning of Snaketown: "The flatlands location of Snaketown and the eventual dispersal of residence units over nearly a square kilometer of landscape together with the absence of close by natural refuges, suggest that the choice of location was not influenced in the slightest by fear of hostile people."

This lack of defensive positioning contrasts with early Mogollon settlements that are commonly situated on high bluffs or ridges, to which access is difficult, and some investigators (Anyon *et al.* 1981) have used the hilltop setting as one of the hallmarks of the early pithouse period. The specific topographic settings of early Anasazi settlements seem to be more diverse than those of the Mogollon, although again the tops of benches and bluffs were commonly selected and possibly for the same reasons. Although a variety of explanations for this strategy, including aesthetic considerations and the need for resources available at higher elevations, have been offered, the need for defense is likely. Early Mogollon settlements were established within areas that contained groups of people who continued a hunting and gathering way of life. It is unlikely that everyone in the Southwest adopted sedentary horticulture at precisely the same time. It is plausible to suggest that small communities with enough agricultural produce to store over the winter felt or were threatened by potential raids from neighboring hunters and gatherers. It may also be suggested that given the higher risks to agriculture in mountainous southwestern settings, settlements would want to protect what foods were being stored from potentially hostile agriculturalists whose own crops had failed.

In both the Anasazi and Mogollon areas after about AD 500, pithouse settlements are more consistently located away from high eminences and instead are on alluvial terraces or the first bench above rivers. This shift in settlement location has been interpreted as indicating greater reliance on agriculture (Glassow 1972). It is also possible that the change involved the development of social mechanisms that served to integrate settlements in effective opposition to remaining hunter-gatherer populations and to each other for effective sharing to even out local food shortages.

SOCIAL ORGANIZATION

In the earliest settlements across the Southwest there is a lack of a formal arrangement of houses and formal midden areas. This and the use of outdoor storage pits and cooking hearths are all characteristics of societies with low population densities. Some observations anthropologists have made of small-scale societies are of interest because they are far from experiences we face in our lives today. In such societies the space in which daily domestic activities, such as tool preparation and eating, takes place is public in full view of all settlement residents. Anthropologists who live for extended periods among people in small settlements have to adjust to a lack of both privacy and regard for personal property that is foreign to their usual experience. As summed up by Forde and Douglas:

> Social relations are of the personal face-to-face kind. Everyone has known everyone else from childhood, everyone is related to everyone else. The sick and unfortunate are able to depend on the kindliness of immediate neighbors. The sharing of tools and supplies to meet individual shortages are matters of moral obligation between kinsfolk and neighbors (1956:16).

Some amount of surplus that can be stored, if only over the winter season, is required for the degree of residential permanence implied by the existence of the early southwestern settlements. Yet in times of food shortages, small settlements are highly vulnerable. An individual's or family's rights to stored food may be respected at most times, but if times are bad, people will be expected to share what they have; and because what one has is in full view of the community, it is not possible to hoard. A number of scholars (e.g., Colson 1979; Scudder 1971; Turnbull 1978) note a regular sequence of behaviors that takes place among small-scale societies facing food shortages. At first people consume less desirable, less nutritious famine foods. If the problem persists, food preparation and eating are done in private to avoid sharing. Finally the settlements disintegrate and families move away to forage or try to join kinsmen in areas that are not experiencing deprivation. Archaeologist Paul Minnis (1996) has developed a general model that includes and expands on this approach, differentiating what he terms catastrophic and impinging shortages. Both types of shortages result in culture change but for impinging shortages, change is often incremental.

Archaeologists must rely to some extent on ethnographic observations of such small-scale societies to develop inferences about past social organization. Yet neither one-to-one analogies nor untested assumptions are appropriate to the kinds of situations faced by archaeologists. One useful approach was pioneered by Martin (1950) regarding the social organization of the Mogollon of the Pine Lawn Valley, New Mexico. Martin synthesized general trends in the archaeological data and made some assumptions about the meaning that might be attached to these trends. He then offered some interpretations based on Murdock's (1949) classic ethnographic cross-cultural study of social structure. Martin's study was a landmark. In recent years, observations that are similar to his have been used to infer corporate groups, social hierarchies, alliances, and differences in mobility patterns. Studies of each of these are discussed below.

Although Martin (1950) began with the Archaic Chiricahua Cochise, from whom he saw direct continuity to the Pine Lawn Mogollon, this summary concerns his observations and interpretations of the Mogollon settlements from about AD 500 to 1000. The trends Martin addressed in the archaeological data are as follows: House size became smaller; the number of houses in each settlement and the number of settlements increased; the number of metates per house and the number of tools in general per house decreased; finally there was a decrease in the proportions of basin metates and mortars to slab and trough metates.

Martin suggested that the change in house size reflected a shift from houses that were occupied by extended families to nuclear family households. The decline in the number of metates and other tools in each house was viewed as strengthening this interpretation. At the same time, the increase in the number of houses and settlements suggested an overall population increase. Martin suggested that mortars and basin metates might be correlated with the processing of wild plant seeds, whereas slab and trough metates indicate corn processing. He therefore proposed that the change in metate shape showed an increasing reliance on agriculture that was important to the increase in population. Murdock's study suggested that matrilocal residence, matrilineal descent, matrilineal inheritance, politically independent settlements, and probably monogamy are also reasonably inferred from the subsistence and settlement interpretations.

Ten years after Martin's work appeared, Bluhm (1960) published an analysis of settlement patterns in the Pine Lawn Valley that modified one of Martin's interpretations. Bluhm noted that whereas the larger settlements had one or more ceremonial structures, such structures were lacking in the small pithouse settlements. Rather than presuming complete settlement autonomy, then, she concluded that the ceremonial rooms may have served both the large settlements and a number of small settlements, so there may have been multisettlement communities in the valley at an early time (Bluhm 1960:542).

In 1982, Lightfoot and Feinman reevaluated social organization in Mogollon pithouse settlements from a different perspective, and proposed that variability in houses in larger settlements reflected hierarchical social differentiation. They assumed that there is a continuum from household-based political systems to village-level organizations where managerial decisions are vested in one or several village leaders. They cited a number of theoretical statements suggesting that with increased sedentism, population growth, agricultural intensification, and increased volume of long-distance trade, supra-household decision-making positions are required. Village leaders may function full- or part-time, but they constitute an administrative level separate from the rest of the local population.

Lightfoot and Feinman (1982) assumed that village leaders would occupy larger than average pithouses. Using site reports, they examined large pithouses in excavated settlements. They found these houses to be associated with greater than expected storage space and nonlocal goods, and that the settlements in which they were located were near rivers, which they suggest were ancient trade routes. They concluded that control over interregional exchange may have been an important factor in the development of decision-making structures. They found that in a comparison of the group of large pithouses with other pithouses, the former are statistically significantly associated with more storage space, evidence of agriculture (macrobotanical remains of corn), and more nonlocal goods (marine shell, turquoise, or Hohokam ceramics). The larger pithouses were also found to be generally closer to great kivas than other houses in the settlement. A key problem in this study, one that was acknowledged by the authors, is that the pithouses within the settlements may not have been occupied at the same time. Another assumption is that settlement leaders occupy houses that are, in fact, larger than others. Much finer control over the basic chronological positions of the settlements and their component structures is essential before inferences about supra-household decision-making is possible. It is important to know if larger settlements were occupied longer than smaller settlements or if larger settlements were reoccupied more frequently than smaller settlements.

Wills and Windes (1989) examined some of these issues in their study of Shabik'eschee Village (mentioned above). This site is one of the settlements Lightfoot and Feinman thought reflected supra-household decision-making. They conclude that there is no evidence for hierarchical social differentiation; rather, most of the houses appear to have been used only occasionally over a very long period of time. The Wills and Windes (1989) study included information from both Roberts' (1929) excavations and more recent work. Using information about debris in room fill; amount of ancient remodeling and reuse of structures, and studies of tree-ring dated pithouse settlements, they argue that there is evidence for recycling of house structures, rather than distinct occupations, over a period of time between the mid-500s and early 700s. Thus, the size of the settlement at any one brief period of time is not well known. Further, the free-standing, semi-subterranean storage structures are in publicly accessible space not clearly associated with specific dwellings. Not all storage areas were free-standing. There are also at least five pithouses that had antechambers that provided additional storage space. Wills and Windes (1989:358) conclude that the data from Shabik'eschee are consistent with the highly mobile ("compound" settlements) of bands of hunters and gatherers, lacking persons who permanently or for the long-term were supra-household decision-makers. Rather, they believe that there was a small, core group of year-round residents at the site represented by those houses with interior storage space and a larger group that assembled periodically when local environmental conditions permitted. While discounting the idea that hierarchical social differentiation was present, Wills and Windes (1989:359) "point out that the apparent mix of public and private storage at Shabik'eschee suggests an important shift away from communal sharing considered characteristic of mobile hunter-gatherers."

The amount of exterior storage space at Shabik'eschee and other Basketmaker III sites can be substantial. For example, a site labeled L.A. 4169 on the Upper San Juan River, reported by Hammack (1992), yielded two compact clusters of pits that had been excavated into a clay ridge and then burned in place. They became what Hammack calls in-place terra cotta storage jars. Samples from five of the pits yielded archaeomagnetic dates that were not only close to AD 600 but indicated that the pits had been fired at the same time. The pits yielded a volume estimate of 5.0 cubic meters each. Given the admittedly extreme assumption that all of the pits had been in use at the same time, Hammack estimated a total of 110.5 m^3 of stored food. Using commonly applied figures based on maize, she finds that the storage capacity of the site would have fed at least 138 persons, or 27 families, for a period of one year! This site and Shabik'eschee Village suggest that there would have been times when there was a great abundance of some food resource, allowing large population aggregates, at least temporarily. How frequently these local abundances occurred is not known. It is generally believed that these occasions were unusual. Still, the estimated storage capacity at L.A. 4169 gives one pause when thinking that the early Anasazi were leading difficult and economically impoverished lives.

A different approach to social organization was suggested by Fred Plog (1983b), who was concerned with the differential spatial and temporal distributions of strongly normative patterns in architecture and ceramics in the Pueblo Southwest from about AD 400 to the time of the Spanish Conquest. He argued that before the 1960s, southwestern archaeologists generally excavated sites that promised to have abundant material culture remains (see Chapter 6). Sites selected for excavation were usually large, with surface indications of substantial architecture and quantities of identifiable ceramic types. The ceramic types were viewed as the most reliable indicators of the temporal placement of the site and its cultural affiliation. The majority of excavated sites, then, were those that were large and had diagnostic material culture inventories. The data from these sites form the frameworks on which southwestern culture history has been written. The sites themselves, however, are not necessarily representative.

With major salvage and cultural resource management archaeology projects, archaeologists recorded, tested, and excavated thousands of sites that were not typical but appeared to be representative. Subsequent work has largely confirmed the observation that over much of the northern Southwest, from the beginning of known settlements, most sites are small and seem to have been inhabited for rather short periods. Many of these sites yield ceramic inventories that are not clearly diagnostic. For example, site survey information from the San Juan Basin of New Mexico, which includes the large, distinctive sites of Chaco Canyon, lists 6759 Anasazi sites that could be assigned to a general temporal framework. Another 1440 sites, however, are listed simply as unknown Anasazi (Cordell 1982). Similar observations have been made for most of the Colorado Plateaus (see papers in Adler 1996).

Plog (1983b) argued that for all time periods, those sites showing strong normative patterns differ organizationally from contemporary, nondiagnostic sites. He thought that sites with strong patterns reflected *alliances* characterized by some evidence of specialized production, widespread trade and exchange, and sometimes evidence of social ranking or stratification. Plog used the term *weak pattern* to refer to the assemblages at nondiagnostic sites. The earliest alliances Plog defined he called the Adamana and White Mound patterns. Both refer to pithouse settlements. Adamana pattern sites date to within the period between about AD 400 and 700 and occur in the Little Colorado area of Arizona from the vicinity of Holbrook south to Springerville. Adamana sites consist of shallow pithouses bounded by stone cobbles. Typically situated on high bluffs or mesas, several sites contain large, communal structures. The diagnostic ceramics are Adamana brown ware, a paddle-and-anvil-finished, rough-surfaced, sand-tempered pottery. Sites dating to the same period, but outside the Adamana area, exemplify what Plog referred to as a *weak pattern*, in that they are small and heterogeneous, contain limited quantities of trade items or evidence of agricultural intensification, and are socially egalitarian. White Mound sites, named after White Mound

Village in eastern Arizona (Roberts 1939), are more recent, dating to between AD 750 and 850. They generally consist of a row of jacal surface-storage rooms, a pithouse/kiva, and a trash mound. The ceramics associated with White Mound sites are a group of stylistically very similar types—Kana-a, Kiatutlanna, and White Mound Black-on-white. Compared with the distribution of Adamana settlements, the White Mound pattern is much more widespread, extending from the Rio Grande Valley to Flagstaff and north to south throughout the Anasazi area. Nowhere over that enormous area, however, are White Mound sites particularly numerous. In some drainages, they occur among smaller, more heterogeneous, apparently contemporary sites.

There are serious problems with Plog's (1983b) view that I discuss briefly here, but the observation that interactions among some sets of sites and over very great distances have operated since early times in the Southwest is an important one. In the immediate context of a discussion of the social organization of the earliest settlements, Plog's (1983b) treatment is somewhat vague or misleading. Both Adamana and White Mound patterns relate to pithouse settlements. The patterns differ in scale and in the distinctiveness of their ceramic assemblages. Yet, on the basis of Plog's discussion of alliances, they should be organizationally similar. Inasmuch as he characterizes all strong normative patterns as examples of alliances, there is no discussion of how different alliances were structured. Some of the proposed alliances were very extensive geographically—others involved agricultural intensification. It is highly unlikely that all alliances were organized in the same way over time. For the earliest alliance, there is no evidence of social hierarchy. Some early sites may appear large simply because they were occupied more often than others. It is important that we understand what kinds of interactions underlie the similarities we observe. Some insight into the organizational structures that might have underlain differences in early pithouse settlements can be gained by comparing two such settlements in different environmental contexts. This is what Wills (1991) has done.

Wills (1991) contrasts Shabik'eschee Village (discussed above), at Chaco Canyon, and the SU site in the rugged Mogollon Mountains, near Reserve, New Mexico. (The name SU derives from a local cattle brand.) Both sites date between AD 450 and 550. Shabik'eschee Village may have contained a maximum of about 70 pithouse-size structures, the SU site about 35 such structures. Both sites are on ridgetops and represent the first pithouse and ceramic producing stages in their respective areas. Shabik'eschee Village is a Basketmaker III, Anasazi site, the SU site is a Pine Lawn Phase, Mogollon site (Figure 8.8). At Shabik'eschee Village, the pithouses exhibit wing walls that segregate internal space, whereas such spatial separations are not present at the SU site. The single, large, circular kiva at Shabik'eschee has no counterpart at the SU site. There, a single communal structure is close to the size of some of the houses, which were simply domestic structures.

In contrast to the very small domestic Shabik'eschee structures, those at the SU site are large, variable, and contain numerous interior storage pits. Wills (1991:169) suggests that pithouses at Shabik'eschee Village are small enough to have been built by one individual, but such could not have been the case at the SU site. Very few burials were excavated at Shabik'eschee Village, and only one from a house, whereas 53 individuals,

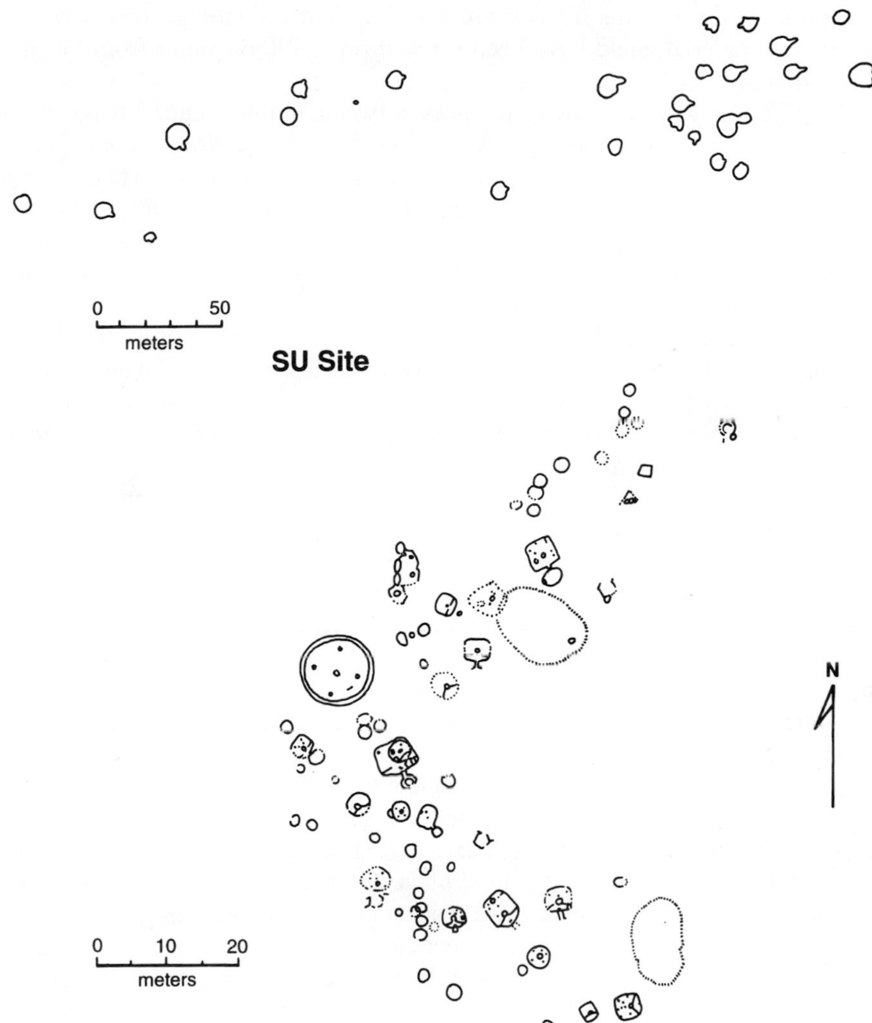

FIGURE 8.8 Site plans of the SU site (top), a Pinelawn phase Mogollon pithouse site and Shabik'eschee Village (bottom), an Anasazi Basketmaker III pithouse site. Wills (1991) argues that the larger houses at the SU site sheltered entire families that reoccupied the site, probably seasonally, for many years. Shabik'eschee, on the other hand, was probably occupied only episodically with single families using several of the small structures (illustrated by Marjorie Leggitt, Leggitt Design, after Wills [1991]).

37 from houses, were excavated at the SU site. As discussed above, exterior storage features were abundant at Shabik'eschee Village, but houses had little or no inside storage space. At the SU site, interior pits are abundant and storage area in the large houses, where material could have been stacked on the floor, hung from beams, or both, was great.

Willis (1991) argues that the differences between Shabik'eschee Village and the SU site are not related to "ethnicity" (Anasazi vs. Mogollon). Nor do the differences reflect the presence at either site of a hierarchy of social status or participation in a regional alliance network. Rather, Wills suggests that the sites reflect different mobility patterns based on different economic emphases related to more and less abundant natural settings. Shabik'eschee Village seems not to have been occupied by one group over a long period. Rather, it was used periodically, when resources were abundant. At those times, the large co-resident group required a community structure (the kiva) for social integration. The houses at the SU site could well have sheltered entire families and the site itself seems to have been occupied, probably seasonally, by the same group of people over a long period of time. If the single community structure did integrate the settlement, it did not integrate as large a group as did the kiva at Shabik'eschee Village. Wills argues that the greater temporal stability of the community at the SU site is a function of its location in the mountainous area of abundant wild resources that would have supplemented corn. Wills is particularly impressed by the potential abundance of piñon nuts. He contrasts this with the relatively impoverished environment of the San Juan Basin setting of Shabik'eschee Village.

While I agree with Wills that Shabik'eschee Village and the SU site differ organizationally and that the difference reflects unlike mobility patterns, I am not convinced that he has identified the key resources involved. In my view, the rather sparse environmental setting of Shabik'eschee Village and the countless additional Basketmaker III villages in the northern San Juan Basin correlate with dune areas that irregularly produce two or sometimes three crops of Indian ricegrass a year, depending on available moisture. This wild crop is available in late spring and summer when people might well have been planting corn on the flood plain of Chaco Wash or other small drainages. Ricegrass seeds can be stored. I also suspect that wild game—particularly deer—and wood resources may have been as important to the stability of the SU site as were piñon nuts. Both Shabik'eschee Village and the SU site were excavated before archaeobotanical materials were routinely collected. The opportunity to evaluate our different views lies among the many sites that display similar contrastive characteristics.

In sum, archaeological interpretations of social organization in the early pithouse settlements have developed considerably from Martin's (1950) original statements. There has been recognition of the likelihood that the settlements were not all politically, socially, and economically independent. Bluhm's (1960) initial observations were critical in this regard. Further work has demonstrated marked heterogeneity in the forms, sizes, and assemblage inventories of these settlements. The culture historical explanations of the past are not adequate to represent the variation in and the similarities *among* regions that the newer frameworks address. The contrasts among settlements have been interpreted as indicating differences in social organization, including the degree of group mobility and the size of population aggregates. Whether or not these interpretations are substantiated by subsequent research, they are an important contribution.

EVIDENCE OF ANCIENT BELIEFS

The period between about AD 400 and 600 (Basketmaker III, Early Pithouse period) seems to have been a time when much of what we see as ancestral to Pueblo peoples crystallized over the Plateaus and in the Mogollon region. This pattern includes the full range of cultivated crops of corn, beans, and squash and pottery production. In the Anasazi area of the Colorado Plateaus, it also included iconography in the form of rock art. There is a Pueblo style, first seen in Basketmaker III (Schaafsma 1980), consisting of strongly pecked elements that include depiction of a flute player (Figure 8.9) in a variety of forms including a humpback. In traditional Hopi legend, there is a humpback flute player, named Kokopelli. Other elements in this style appear to be masked figures, and masking is a significant element in Pueblo rituals. There is also an example of distinctive iconography in ceramic decoration. Three bowls from each of three Basketmaker III sites from Durango, Colorado; Tohatchi Flats, New Mexico; and the Hopi Buttes region of Arizona have the same design of figures dancing in a circle. Alternate figures have the same Hopi maiden butterfly hair style (Figure 8.10), and the figures in the dance are recognized by Hopis today.

These combinations of economic, organizational, and ideological elements that are so obviously essentially Pueblo led scholars to view Basketmaker III as an emergent

FIGURE 8.9 Pictograph of a flute player. The stick figure style is typical Basketmaker III. This may be an early representation of the legendary Hopi personage Kokopelli (illustrated by Marjorie Leggitt, Leggitt Design).

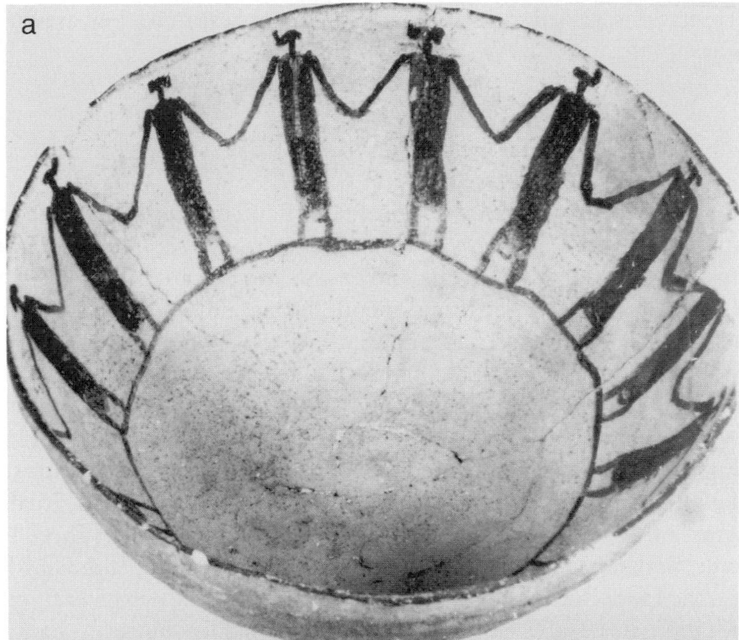

FIGURE 8.10 These are two of three Basketmaker III bowls painted with the same dancing figures: (a) from Durango, Colorado and (b) from Tohatchi, New Mexico. Alternate figures have traditional Hopi maiden hair styles (a, UCM 9509; b, UCM 9578; both courtesy of the University of Colorado Museum.

Pueblo culture. It is also worth contemplating the truth that we do not know what these symbols meant in Basketmaker society or whether or not the elements that we see as interrelated were so in Basketmaker behavior or beliefs. In part because it appears that many Basketmaker III pithouse settlements were occupied only seasonally, the mobility that was part of the Basketmaker III economic strategy implies a set of community and regional relationships that were quite different from those of later sedentary Pueblos.

The issues of great mobility, particularly in the context of the kinds of large, periodic aggregations of people suggested by Shabik'eschee Village and the terra-cotta storage pits at site L.A. 4169, on the San Juan, suggests that some of the more easily recognizable iconography may have signaled alliances among peoples who otherwise might be considered distinct populations. Whittlesey (1995) mentions several examples of what she suggests may be cases of ethnic co-residence. These includes Anasazi "traits" in Mogollon and Hohokam sites, possibly pure Mogollon sites in Hohokam territory, and both Hohokam and Mogollon house types occurring in the same settlement. Although Whittlesey may be correct in inferring ethnic co-residence, I suspect that we may be seeing various kinds of affiliations that functioned to integrate peoples, in different ways, and for different periods of time, over broad regions that were not isolated from one another. In such fluid social context, ethnicity as it is understood in today's society seems unlikely.

THE PITHOUSE-TO-PUEBLO TRANSITION

Throughout the northern and mountainous parts of the Southwest, between about AD 700 and 1000, there was a change from settlements composed of pithouses to settlements consisting of multiroom surface structures with adobe or masonry walls. In some areas, such as the Mesa Verde, the change was apparently gradual, with a row of jacal surface rooms being built behind a pithouse and used for storage while the pithouse continued to be used for habitation. Later, people moved into the surface rooms, and the pithouses, with modifications in architecture, were used as ceremonial rooms or kivas. In other areas, such as the Mogollon region, the change from pithouses to pueblos appears to have been more abrupt. Whether gradual or rapid, the change in the nature of settlements has been a subject of archaeological inquiry since the 1920s.

In the Hohokam region, there is a change from pithouses to first, houses in pits, and later, houses enclosed by compound walls. Since Hohokam houses in pits do not have contiguous walls, the specific arguments made to explain the change in house styles on the plateaus and in the mountains are not generally considered relevant. Nevertheless, some of the more general statements about more specialized organization of space do relate to Hohokam house clusters. House clusters consist of two or more Hohokam dwellings arranged facing one another on opposite sides of a courtyard. This formal arrangement persists throughout much of the Hohokam sequence.

Before discussing explanations for the change, two qualifications are in order. First, on the plateaus and in the mountains, although pithouse settlements are typical prior to AD 1000 and pueblos after that date, pithouses continued to be constructed and used into more recent times. In New Mexico, for example, Stuart and Farwell (1983) note that some 60 pithouse sites dating to the post-AD 1000 period have been excavated, and many more are known from site survey. As mentioned previously, pithouses were built in the early twentieth century at the Hopi settlement of Bacavi (Whiteley 1982). Second, in some parts of the northern Southwest, pithouses were in use up to the time the area was abandoned in ancient times and no transition to pueblo architecture was made. With these primarily temporal qualifications in mind, it is clear that no single event or exogenous variable (such as a widespread climatic change or diffusion of the idea of above-ground housing) can logically be invoked to explain the transition where it occurred.

Three approaches toward an explanation of the change from pithouse to pueblo are discussed here: Plog (1974, 1979) explored the change as one example of a general model of growth; Gilman (1983, 1987) examined the change from the perspective of the architectural forms themselves; and Shafer (1993) addressed accompanying changes in symbolism and cosmology. Although distinct, the approaches are in fact complementary.

Plog (1974) focused on the Basketmaker-to-Pueblo transition as an instance of more general processes of technological change derived from a general model of growth in developing nations of the modern world. The model was of interest to him because it provided precise statements about the processes of change. The relevant dimensions of the growth model are *population*, *differentiation*, *integration*, and *energy*, each of these with a number of variables. For example, *population* refers to the number of individuals within an area, the age structure of the aggregate of these individuals at a given time, and the density of individuals at a specific time in a defined area. The literature of developing countries indicated that seven variables were plausibly related to growth. These provided a set of hypotheses for examining the Basketmaker-to-Pueblo transition.

To examine hypotheses derived from the model, Plog (1974) developed test implications that could be used with archaeological data. For instance, he used the number of dwelling units that are inhabited at a given time as an archaeological measure of population. The model specifies that a change in population should be associated with the technological transition. If the model is correct, Plog argued, the number of dwelling units should increase rapidly during the Basketmaker-to-Pueblo transition; the rate of increase should be as great or greater than at any other time in the culture history of the region being considered and should result in a population maximum for the region. If the model is accurate there should also be changes in the density of population, which is measured by the number of sites per unit area, the mean distance between sites, and the nearest neighbor distribution of sites.

Although all the details of Plog's (1974) study cannot be elaborated here, it is important to explain how the seemingly rather abstract concepts of *differentiation*, *integration*, and *energy* were examined archaeologically. *Differentiation* refers to a diversity in activities; it might be measured archaeologically by examining changes in the number of different kinds of limited activity sites or in the diversity in the location of sites. Within sites, differentiation would be reflected in changes in the room-to-room variability in artifacts and in artifact distributions in extramural areas of sites. *Integration* involves the more complex or more effective coordination of activities. Plog considered three variables relevant to integration: (1) changes in the kinds of family groups within and between sites; (2) changes in social roles, which might be examined by observing changes in the differential treatment of individuals within burial populations; and (3) the appearance of new integrative structures reflected in distinct architectural units. Although there are a number of ways in which *energy* might have been measured, Plog (1974) decided not to include it as a dimension in his study. The decision reflects a paucity of data for the area in which his study was conducted as well as a need to make more assumptions than he felt were warranted.

Using survey and excavation data from the upper Little Colorado River Valley, supplemented by information derived from the archaeological literature, Plog found that in the upper Little Colorado area the transition from Basketmaker to Pueblo was accompanied by a population increase and an increasing differentiation of activities. New integrative structures also appeared during the transition, specifically kivas. Plog suggested that kivas may have been the centers of a redistribution system that would have been a new strategy of integration. Plog also cited burial data that indicate little evidence of social differentiation during the Basketmaker III period but good evidence for status differentiation at Pueblo sites.

Although the data confirmed that the Basketmaker-to-Pueblo transition was associated with changes in the dimensions predicted by the general model of growth, drawing causal inferences about the relations among the dimensions of the model required a different analytical approach. Plog used multivariate statistical analyses. These indicated that the technological changes associated with the transition are a result of differentiation, which in turn is caused by population increase. Changes in integration associated with the transition appear to be more a result of attempts to manage increasing numbers of individuals than attempts to manage increasingly differentiated activities (Plog 1974:156). Moreover, the statistical analyses indicated that the relations among the dimensions of the model were more unlike during the transition than they were before or after it occurred. This, in turn, suggested that the processes of change are not gradual or broadly cumulative, but that the transition was set in motion by underlying events or "kickers" that disrupted conditions of equilibrium.

Plog's (1974) data from the upper Little Colorado showed that by about AD 500, pithouse settlements had become quite large, and they were gradually abandoned as population dispersed into smaller settlements. The dispersal does not coincide with climate change, and Plog suggested that it was the result of a failure to develop appropriate social mechanisms of integration. The dispersal would have had detrimental effects on the economy of the local group because established networks of hunting, gathering, and sharing would have broken down, necessitating, Plog (1974) argued, a resource base that would be more productive with fewer individuals. He proposed that it was within this context that a commitment to agriculture was made. The new subsistence strategy was apparently successful and led to a period of population increase, which further seems to have initiated the period of growth marked by the Basketmaker-to-Pueblo transition. During the transition, of course, new mechanisms of integration were developed. Subsequently, others have suggested that the appearance of new varieties of maize may have been a key stimulator of change (i.e., Lightfoot 1984), but this is not well-supported by archaeobotanical data. An argument for increased intensity of maize processing, and possibly a new variety of maize, may fit Plog's model but again adequate archaeobotanical data are lacking (Diehl 1996).

Plog's (1974) discussion of the Basketmaker-to-Pueblo transition raises a number of important issues. One of his goals was to examine the change in terms of a more general model of growth. The success of the model indicates that the change is an example of broader, underlying processes rather than something to be understood only in particularist, culture historical terms. The study also demonstrates some of the difficulties involved in developing test implications that are appropriate for archaeological data, and some of the variables Plog included in his study are ambiguous indexes of the behaviors of interest. For example, he used studies of social integration at two Hay Hollow Valley sites in which the number of social groups had been inferred from the nonrandom distributions of ceramic design elements within roomblocks at the sites. A number of subsequent studies have questioned these inferences on empirical and theoretical grounds. Similarly, he assumed that an increase in the number of small pithouse settlements indicates an increase in population. Although not an unreasonable assumption, the same observation can also indicate an increase in residential mobility if the pithouses were not occupied year-round.

Plog later (1979) reworked some of the results of his study in light of general discussions of the complexity of episodes of change, and he found some problems with his initial interpretations. The restudy suggested that population growth and the organization of work, or intensification, were more closely linked than indicated in the original analysis. One of Plog's original (1974) conclusions was that although the model was useful in explicating the processes involved in the Basketmaker-to-Pueblo transition, it did not fully explain the change. Certainly, archaeology is very far from being able to fully explain any complex cultural transition, and Plog is not to be faulted for his admission.

Gilman's (1983, 1987) view also considers the change from pithouse to pueblo to relate to population growth, and to increased agricultural activities and greater sedentism. She accepts the basic contention that population growth entailed increased dependence on agriculture, and in turn, changed information networks among groups of people and the timing and character of food preparation and storage activities. When people depend on wild food resources and limited agriculture, food may be stored at various times during the year or as it becomes available. Stores are used only when wild foods are not available. In the northern Southwest this may be over a period of just a few weeks during the winter. Since wild foods must be gathered over very large areas in the generally resource-poor Southwest, high mobility and extensive information networks are necessary. With increased dependence upon crops, food that is to be stored becomes available over only the few weeks of the autumn harvest, but larger quantities of food must be prepared for storage in the interval. The labor requirements of agriculture necessitate increased sedentism and there must be larger quantities of stored food to last over a greater part of the year. The storage requirements of agriculturalists also include seed for the following season and, given the unpredictability of crops in many parts of the Southwest, enough corn for emergencies that can last for a year or more. Group mobility and extensive information networks become less important, but the time spent processing food for storage (grinding corn and cooking) greatly increases.

Gilman's (1983, 1987) analysis focused on the differences between pithouse and pueblo architectural forms as they relate to different ways in which space is used. She did not attempt to examine all possible alternative methods of house construction or storage techniques. Rather, she developed some reasonable expectations based on her ideas of the use of space and then examined a worldwide sample of societies to see if her expectations were supported. She then considered the southwestern situation as a particular example of more general patterns. Although her discussion involves much greater detail than can be addressed here, some of her major points follow.

Gilman (1983, 1987) suggests that as the lengths of time for food preparation and cooking increase they will occupy special locations within a structure in order not to interfere with other activities. Because these tasks must be conducted throughout the year and at times of inclement weather, she argues that they will be done indoors. They might of course be done indoors in below-ground structures, but as the use of space becomes more specialized it would become necessary to build contiguous below-ground rooms. Gilman cites a number of modern ethnographic examples in which precisely this type of dwelling is built in areas where winters are cold and the thermal efficiency of below-ground dwellings is important. They are also instances in which the special conditions of the soil and climate allow contiguous below-ground rooms to be built without the danger of walls collapsing. These conditions do not exist in the Southwest. The courtyard group of Hohokam settlements also reflects more specialized use of space if the courtyard itself is considered part of the domestic work space. With the generally mild and dry desert climate, it is not necessary that everyday tasks be moved indoors.

Gilman supposes that the reasons for moving stored foods from pits and cists to above-ground structures are not the same as those involved in deciding to live above the ground level. She suggests that the increased length of time over which food is stored among agricultralists is the key factor. Where food is stored for a year or more it must be protected from rain seepage and burrowing rodents. Above-ground storerooms become a logical solution and one that predominates in the ethnographic record of agricultural societies depending on grain crops.

The specialized above-ground storage and living spaces need not of course be contiguous and settlements need not be composed of massed blocks of storage rooms and living rooms. Gilman suggests that although the thermal properties of pithouses are superior to those of above-ground structures, when the latter are necessary for other reasons (such as the ones she describes) the arrangement of the surface rooms in the pueblo style is more thermally efficient than other plans. She notes that pueblo-like arrangements are distributed throughout the world among agricultural groups in areas where winters are cold and the soils and climate do not permit contiguous underground rooms. One might note here that the separate Hohokam dwelling structures may relate to the mild winters in the Lower Sonoran Desert.

There are likely to be important factors that Gilman did not consider. For example, despite the probable thermal efficiency of massed roomblocks there were many parts of the northern Southwest in which one- and two-room masonry or jacal structures were the standard post-pithouse structural form and a rancheria pattern of dispersed homesteads prevailed. A number of reasons might be suggested to explain the differential occurrence of aggregated pueblos and dispersed homesteads, such as differences in agricultural technologies and field systems, in regional population densities, or in the local availability of wood for winter fuel. In each case, however, it would be appropriate to specify the conditions thought to be causal and to examine these on a global basis.

In Plog's (1974, 1979) and Gilman's (1983, 1987) studies, change is explored as part of more general phenomena. Whether viewed from the perspective of architectural change or as an example of general growth, the transition is portrayed as complicated, involving the restructuring of activities and new methods of integrating communities. Shafer (1993) agrees that many of the changes involved in the transition from pithouse to pueblo are explicable in technological, functional, and economic terms, but he also suggests that some of the specific features of the change may be related to cosmological symbolism and belief. He notes that in folk culture around the world, house form can incorporate symbols important to a people's world view. Shafer's study focuses on NAN Ranch Ruin, a Mimbres Mogollon site in southwestern New Mexico. The pithouse-to-pueblo transition at NAN Ranch Ruin occurred between AD 925 and 1070. Although slightly later in time than the Anasazi examples, the uniquely well-preserved Mimbres architecture at the site allowed Shafer to describe the transition in detail.

Shafer (1993) described the transition between pithouse and above-ground pueblo architecture at NAN ranch in terms of four stages. In the first stage, the pithouses are rectangular with ramp entryways. Circular, clay-lined hearths with deflector stones are located between the center of the room and the ramp. Toward the end of this stage, modified pithouses were built with walls lined with river cobbles. A cobble and adobe wall was built across the ramp entryway, closing it off, and at the same time, a hatch entry was opened in the roof. A rectangular shape was used for hearths and these were completely or partially framed by stone slabs. Slightly later, rooms with sunken floors were constructed. Burials now were interred consistently in flexed position in pits under the room floor in those areas of the room away from the central activity areas of the hatchway and the rectangular hearth. Finally, all of these aspects of room configuration and building materials were retained in the surface pueblo rooms. In fact, sometimes sunken floor rooms were retained as part of the surface pueblo (Figure 8.11).

Unlike the pithouses before them, surface rooms are differentiated with respect to function. Living rooms have a central, rectangular, slab-lined hearth, air vents, well-prepared floors, and several roof support posts. These rooms are also larger than rooms

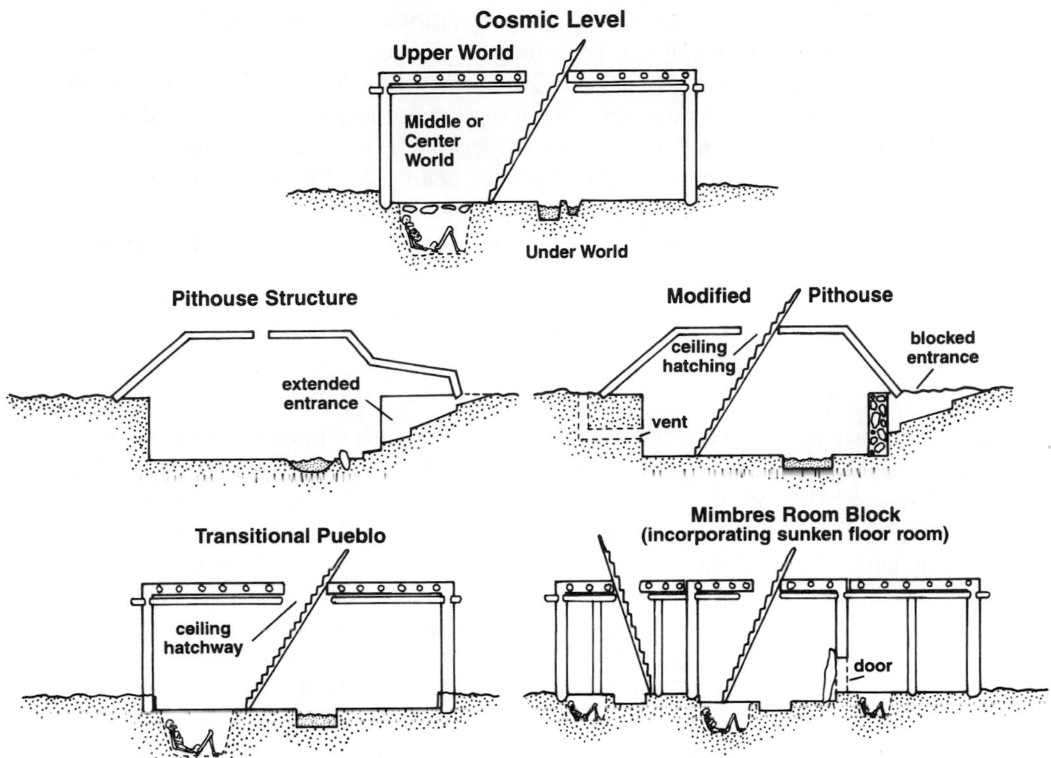

FIGURE 8.11 Suggested architectural development of Mimbres Mogollon surface pueblo rooms from Mimbres pithouses, after Shafer (1993) (illustrated by Marjorie Leggitt, Leggitt Design).

that are thought to have been storerooms because they lack hearths and other features. At the NAN Ranch Ruin it was possible to determine the sequence in which rooms were built by using the uniquely well-preserved architectural stratigraphy and tree-ring, radiocarbon, archaeomagnetic, and obsidian hydration dates. Shafer defined households as those rooms that were built during the same construction episode and that were joined by interior doorways. Doorways did not consistently occur between all rooms that were constructed at the same time, and none of the doorways led to outside space. Entry to the household was through hatchways in the roof. The typical household clusters at NAN Ranch Ruin consist of one large living room and most often one but occasionally two connecting storage rooms.

The arrangement of community space in the surface pueblos suggests continuity with the late pithouse villages. There are clusters of contiguous rooms and open courtyard and plaza areas but no particular arrangement of these in the settlement. Placement of roomblocks is described as haphazard. There does seem to have been change in community organization reflected in the ceremonial or communal architecture. Great kivas were used during the beginning of the period but seem to have been abandoned before the end of the period. There is evidence that some small rooms were used for ritual activities. Some of these were semi-subterranean and equipped with air shafts to the surface. This form of room is rather like kivas of the Anasazi area. Other particularly large surface rooms also may have been used for ceremonial activities. Shafer (1993) notes that courtyard space may have been locations for some aspects of ceremonies that are appropriate for all community members to see, as is the case in the modern Pueblo villages.

SUMMARY

In the early centuries of the Christian era, people throughout the Southwest constructed houses and made pottery, activities that made them more visible in the archaeological record than more mobile people before them. The appearance of houses, storage facilities, and ceramic containers was made possible by an increased dependence on agriculture. Within the generally risky environments of the Southwest, agriculture was neither productive nor certain enough to provide subsistence security, and a number of cultural behaviors were used to mitigate subsistence problems.

In the northern and mountainous parts of the Southwest, the success of horticulture is more uncertain than in the Lower Sonoran Desert. In the more risky settings, early settlements seem to have been positioned defensively, perhaps in an effort to ensure that the stores were protected from hostile incursions by neighboring groups of people. In these areas too, the multiplication of storage structures and the eventual adoption of above-ground storerooms may be in response to requirements for storing food for longer periods of time and for more frequent lean periods. The early use of pithouses throughout the Southwest may be in part due to the thermal efficiency of these types of dwellings and to relatively low population densities. Pithouses seem to reflect continued mobility, on a seasonal basis or longer. Within pithouse settlements, differences in the sizes of structures and the locations (interior or exterior) of storage pits also relate to differences in mobility patterns and probably to the sizes and compositions of basic economic units. In the southern deserts, crop production was probably more secure, settlements were not located in defensive situations, and specialized storerooms were not built. Following the earliest appearance of houses, the lack of true pithouses in the Hohokam area may be related to warmer winter temperatures. Continuity of house clusters and courtyard units in the Hohokam area suggests that time-consuming and specialized activities, such as grinding corn, may have been done out-of-doors in the courtyard area.

Initially, there was great homogeneity in the architecture, settlement layouts, stone tools, and ceramics throughout the Southwest. This suggests continuity with the Archaic and a lack of cultural (or ethnic) differentiation. Somewhat later, there is heterogeneity in architectural forms, settlement layout, and ceramic assemblages that does not pattern spatially or temporally in ways that are compatible with normative culture historical interpretations. The transition to more sedentary settlements implies that new organizational principles were adopted by southwestern peoples. These involved more specialized use of space; the construction of special community or ceremonial buildings, perhaps associated with redistribution of goods; and the development of exchange systems among some settlements. These do not seem to be associated with marked differences in social roles or social hierarchies.

By AD 800, small groups of people cultivating crops for at least part of their livelihood had spread throughout most of the Southwest. The very presence of groups of people limited the mobility of others. As a consequence, investment in crops increased, a variety of ingenious agricultural strategies developed, as did social mechanisms that included some and excluded others from pooling or sharing food. By AD 800, different kinds of settlements appear within regions and although there is less homogeneity than archaeologists traditionally expect, local areas do differentiate one from another. This differentiation, in agricultural strategies and in material culture, is the subject of the next chapter. Throughout the Southwest, and interdigitated among settlements showing regional patterning, are numerous small settlements with heterogeneous architectural patterns and apparently less indication of trade. The possible relations among these different kinds of settlements have only begun to be explored. However, heterogeneity becomes more marked in succeeding centuries, and some of the strong normative patterns seem to indicate short-lived attempts at regional integration. These manifestations are examined in later chapters.

Chapter-opening art: Pithouse and antechamber (drawing by Marjorie Leggitt, Leggitt Design).

CHAPTER 9

Expansion (AD 800 to 1000)

From AD 800 to 1000, agricultural occupation of the Southwest reached its maximum geographic extent. At the same time, the major geographic sub-area traditions differentiated from each other. This chapter explores the kinds of communities that may have developed in different regions of the Southwest, and draws inferences about the way they were socially organized and the kinds of agricultural technologies that supported them.

INTRODUCTION

On the Colorado Plateaus, the expansion period encompasses Pueblo I and early Pueblo II of the Pecos Classification. The corresponding periods are the Colonial and early Sedentary for the Hohokam of the Sonoran Desert (Figure 9.1), and the Late Pithouse period for the Mogollon. The major regions are differentiated by ceramics, house types and village layouts, community structures, ritual objects, and trade goods. At this time it is possible, for example, to talk about a Hohokam pattern. At the same time, at a smaller scale, differences are apparent within each major tradition. The differences among Kayenta, Virgin, Mesa Verde, and Chaco branches of the Anasazi tradition are examples.

The geographic expansion of settlement throughout the Southwest bespeaks great success of the ancient inhabitants. Given the harsh and uncertain natural environment,

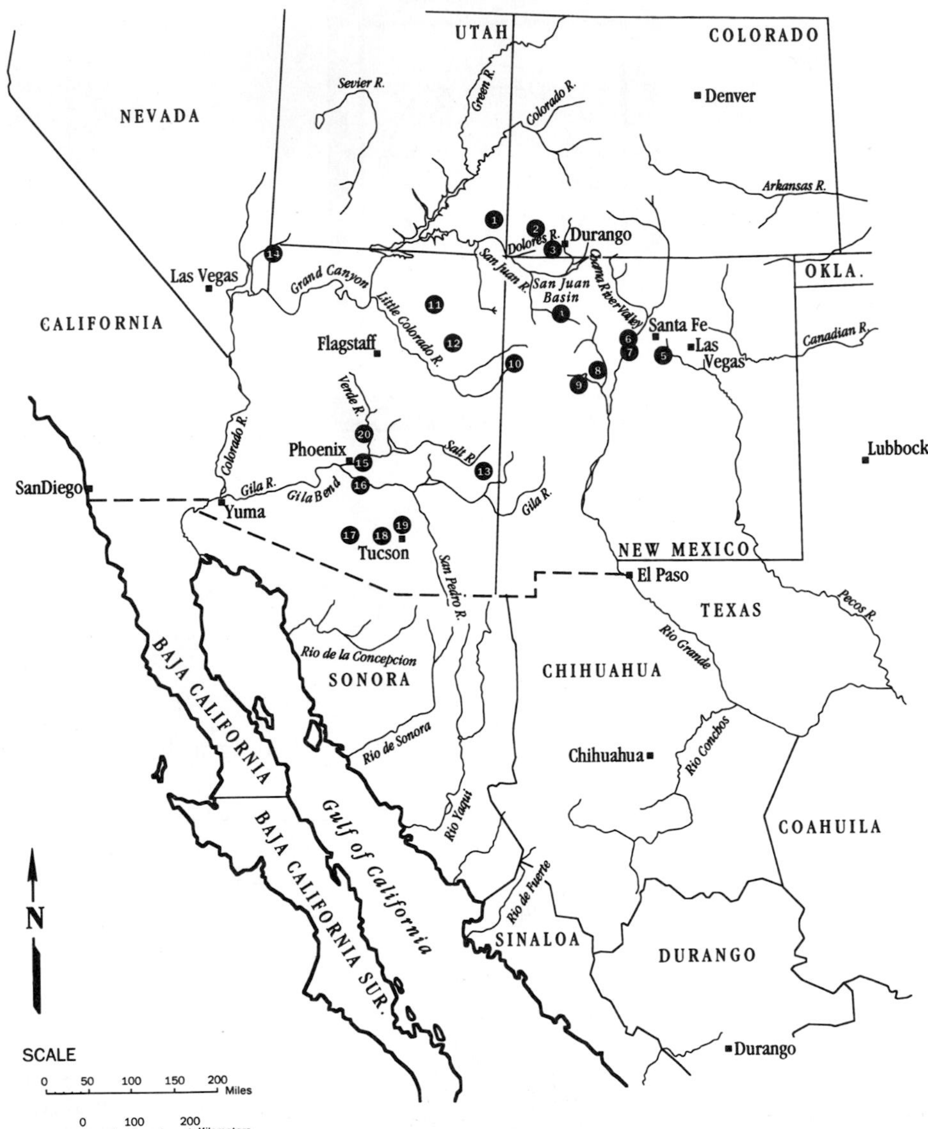

FIGURE 9.1 These sites, villages, and localities are important to discussions of the expansion of agricultural communities in the Southest. Key: ❶ Alkali Ridge; ❷ Dolores Area (Duckfoot Site, McPhee Reservoir); ❸ Mesa Verde; ❹ Chaco Canyon; ❺Galisteo Basin; ❻ Cochiti Pueblo; ❼ Santo Domingo Pueblo; ❽ Laguna Pueblo; ❾ Acoma Pueblo; ❿ Zuni Pueblo; ⓫ Black Mesa; ⓬ Hopi; ⓭ Point of Pines; ⓮ Virgin River; ⓯ La Cuidad; ⓰ Snaketown and Gila Butte; ⓱ Ventana Cave; ⓲ Gu Achi; ⓳ Picacho Basin and Tucson Basin Sites (Marana Community and Dairy Site); ⓴New River Area. (Map by David Underwood.)

the success must be traced through two dimensions: social and technological. Once southwestern peoples became committed to agriculture because a return to hunting and gathering was no longer viable, very sophisticated approaches to increasing crop yields were developed. In several instances technological devices were developed that permitted reliable yields in areas that do not support agriculture today. Sedentism and dependence on stored foods, generally cultivated crops in the Southwest, are mutually reinforcing. As people depend more on crops and invest more labor to ensure their success, it becomes necessary to integrate more people into the activities of farming. Means of organizing communities to share labor and food are required. It is also likely that means of excluding some people from sharing must also be developed.

Archaeologists do not excavate groups that participated in sharing or cooperated in agricultural labor. Rather, inferences about social organization are made on the basis of the material remains of houses and settlement features. This chapter first examines the archaeological remains of the Hohokam, Anasazi, and Mogollon of this period, along with inferences made about these regarding the organization of communities of people. This is followed, in each case, by examples of agricultural strategies in the low deserts, the plateaus, and the mountains, as these are also inferred from archaeological data.

The kinds and combinations of agricultural features associated with ancient southwestern agriculture are diverse, and several archaeologists have proposed typologies to describe them (e.g., Doolittle 1991; Hayes 1964; Plog and Garrett 1972; Woodbury 1961). Here the discussion largely follows Vivian (1974). Generally the term agricultural feature is applied to modifications to the landscape that function to control water or soil erosion or both. Agricultural systems are combinations of discrete features. Field houses, which are usually small structures built near fields and occupied during some or all of the agriculture season, also may be part of agricultural systems, although they did not serve to conserve soil or moisture. Field houses are generally not considered agricultural features per se but their use may be significant in regard to issues of land tenure (Kohler 1992). It is not always easy to distinguish between features constructed to conserve soil and those built to conserve water because most of the known types of features do both. To confuse the matter even more, some soil and water control features, constructed to prevent damage to houses or villages, are not associated with fields or with agriculture.

Some features are used in dry land farming, that is, farming without irrigation. Among the most common are bordered gardens, seed beds, check dams, contour terraces, and rock piles. Bordered gardens are generally rectangular pits enclosed by low earth or stone borders. Some bordered gardens are covered with a mulch of gravel (see below). Bordered gardens often occur in contiguous grids, covering very large areas. Seed beds, used for the germination of seeds, are narrow enclosures (generally less than 1 m wide) with rock or masonry walls. The soil inside seed beds extends to the top of the rock border and is usually fine with a high content of organic material (Doolittle 1992). Check dams consist of one or several low stone walls constructed across arroyos. Soil builds up and is held behind each dam, creating small field areas. The dams also slow the flow of water in the arroyos, allowing it to soak into the ground, hence prevention erosion. Contour terraces are lines of stones, either one or two courses high, built along the contours of slopes. As their name suggests, rock piles are low, rounded heaps of cobbles, often capping smaller mounds of earth, that enhance moisture retention (Fish *et al.* 1992, and see below).

Canals, ditches, headgates, and diversion dams are features that function to move water from one place to another. They are part of irrigation systems, as the term is generally used. Canals are wide, deep channels cut into the ground that serve to carry water. Ditches, narrower and shallower than canals, function the same way canals do and are often associated with them. Headgates are features of stone or earth that are used to control the flow of water from a canal or ditch into a sluice. Diversion dams of either earth or stone temporarily impound water, restricting its flow into a canal or ditch. Finally, reservoirs that either are entirely manmade or incorporate natural depressions are found in many parts of the Southwest. The reservoirs, however, seem to have been used to store water for domestic uses rather than for agriculture.

Agricultural features are exceptionally difficult to date, and the proximity of the features to sites that are dated is used as a rough indication of the ages of the agricultural features. As imprecise as such age determinations are, there is very little evidence for the construction of agricultural features in the mountains and on the plateaus of the Southwest before about AD 900. The Hohokam heartland is so dry that some irrigation, perhaps from hand-dug wells, may have been necessary to produce any crop at all where floodwater farming was not possible (see below). Over most of the Southwest before AD 900, population densities were apparently low enough that subsistence security was ensured through a combination of hunting, gathering, and agriculture. Movement to new areas was a possible alternative to investing in agricultural features. Reduced mobility seems to have been a key to the development of elaborate agricultural systems, especially outside the low deserts. With the spatially spotty and locally unpredictable nature of summer precipitation in plateau and mountain settings, investment in nonportable features is not as appropriate as moving.

Available information shows that the distribution of water and soil conservation features in the Southwest crosscuts both cultural and natural areas. Irrigation canals, for example, are not limited to the Hohokam area or to the Lower Sonoran Desert. However, the scale of Hohokam canals greatly exceeds those on the plateaus. Systems combining various devices are found throughout the Southwest. Some of the diversity in agricultural systems encountered, their appropriateness with respect to the habitats in which they are found, and some insights about the degree of organization of labor and technological skills required to build and maintain them are illustrated by the studies discussed below. Some of the studies are not restricted to a single period, culture area, or environmental zone. Rather, they illustrate the effects of local environmental conditions, prevailing climate, and population density on the subsistence system represented.

The course of agriculture in the Southwest from about AD 500 to recent times reflects a pattern of geographic expansion and contraction, population dispersal and aggregation. Some areas were colonized successfully and in them agricultural communities were quite stable. In other areas there were initial attempts to support agricultural communities but these were finally abandoned. In some areas agricultural production was increased substantially through the use of various technological innovations such as water-control features. In these situations quite large communities developed with elaborate mechanisms of social integration. Not all of these were ultimately successful and despite considerable efforts to ensure a successful crop and distribution of food to consumers, relocation, abandonment, and reorganization were all necessary at various times.

THE LOW DESERTS: COLONIAL AND SEDENTARY HOHOKAM ORGANIZATION

As described in Chapter 6, before the first excavations at Snaketown, there was no information about Hohokam origins because all visible sites seemed to represent a similar widespread and well-developed pattern. That pattern was established and spread between about AD 800 and 1150 during the Colonial and Sedentary periods. On the broadest level, the pattern is characterized by the development of irrigation systems, large villages, elaborate arts and crafts, public architecture such as ballcourts, formal mortuary ritual, and geographic expansion (Doyel 1987). Specifically, with community subsistence tied to irrigation agriculture, residential mobility was greatly reduced. Houses became larger, reflecting a need for additional, differentiated storage space. Irrigation opened new lands for farming on terraces above the river flood plains. Cremation became the most common burial treatment, with elaborate stone palettes, stone censers, and clay figurines as components of mortuary ritual (Doyel 1991). Trade with Mesoamerica is reflected by the presence of iron-pyrite mosaic mirrors. Intrusive ceramics indicate exchange with the Anasazi and Mogollon (Crown 1991). Hohokam sites of the Colonial and Sedentary periods were not stamped out cookie-cutter fashion; there were certainly differences among sites in various subregions, such as the Phoenix and Tucson basins and the New River areas. Also, within each subregion, there were sites reflecting population aggregates (usually termed villages) and scattered dwellings (referred to as rancherías). Nevertheless, the basic components of Hohokam *village* sites and patterns of integration are broadly similar.

At the lowest level, within village sites, individual house structures are grouped around an open courtyard or plaza that had continuity over time as houses were added or abandoned (Howard 1985; Wilcox *et al.* 1981). The entryways of individual houses open to the courtyard/plaza. If houses have interior features, these are aligned with the entry (Doelle *et al.* 1987). Most houses were used for both storage and domestic activities, although in some large courtyard groups, the smallest house may have been used only for storage.

Some courtyard groups had communal cooking ovens (*hornos*), trash mounds, and burial areas. It is thought that between about 16 and 20 individuals may have occupied each courtyard group. At a more inclusive level, clusters of courtyard groups arranged around outside activity areas sometimes also with hornos, trash mounds, and cemeteries are referred to as village segments. They are distinguished by being spatially

FIGURE 9.2 Hohokam ballcourt. The excavated west half of ballcourt number 1, Snaketown, 1935. View is to the east (photograph by Emil W. Haury, courtesy of the Arizona State Museum).

separated from other such units (Doyel 1991; Howard 1982). At large villages, the village segments are loosely arranged around a great central plaza, with trash mounds and later one or more ballcourts. In the succeeding Classic period, platform mounds are the public architectural features. In the Hohokam area, the term ballcourt is applied to oval, bowl-shaped features flanked by earthen embankments because they are thought to be analogous to ballcourts in Mesoamerica and to have been used in the ritual ball game played throughout Mesoamerica, Central America, and parts of the Caribbean (Scarborough and Wilcox 1991) (Figure 9.2). This interpretation is discussed below. Hohokam ballcourts fall within distinct size classes. With crest to crest dimensions of as much as 20 m in length and 10 m in width to more than 70 m in length and 30 m in width and depths of about 1 m (Wilcox 1991) these were clearly public architectural features requiring a substantial labor force to build. Several hundred people may have occupied a Hohokam village simultaneously. Very large villages, such as Snaketown, may have had as many as 2000 inhabitants, although a number closer to 1000 is probably a better estimate (Doyel 1991; Fish and Fish 1991).

Most Hohokam villages are not as large as Snaketown. Most would have had populations numbering in the hundreds rather than thousands. Fish and Fish (1991) point out that organization that functioned at the supravillage level would have been required for mating, risk management, labor procurement, craft production, and so forth. Also, wherever comprehensive surveys have been carried out remains of populations living dispersed in between villages have been found. Hohokam communities integrated these dispersed populations into "bounded units centered on pivotal sites" (Fish and Fish 1991:162). Pivotal sites are defined on the basis of the presence of ballcourts and population size for this time period. Later, during the Classic period, platform mounds are defining characteristics.

Plotting the distributions and examining the spacing between public architecture components allows estimating the size of the areas integrated in each supravillage unit. In the Phoenix basin the average linear distance between ballcourt sites is 5.5 km (Wilcox and Sternberg 1983). Interestingly, this linear distance is maintained during the Classic period between platform mound sites, although there is little overlap in the two sets of sites. The regularity in spacing, and continuity in this regularity, along canals and canal segments, "may define an optimal distance over which agricultural travel and day-to-day communications concerning canal function could be carried out within a single community or between adjacent communities" (Fish and Fish 1991: 163). While there are far less data available for site distributions in nonriverine settings, Fish and Fish (1991) have documented settlement clusters around separate ballcourt communities in the Tucson and Picacho basins. The locations of settlements correspond to sources of water for agriculture and domestic use that would have been available year-round.

The hierarchical levels of Hohokam organization just described, courtyard group, village segment, village, and community, have been interpreted in terms of social organization. While the interpretations are reasonable and are discussed here, it is worth recalling that they depend on assumptions that may not be entirely justified. At the most basic level, the courtyard group (Figure 9.3) is most often viewed as the residential locus of single extended families, with separate house structures for each nuclear family. The courtyard group is then seen as being held together by kinship, and probably a single form of post-marital residence (such as matrilocality). The size and long-term continuity of courtyard groups is interpreted as indicating the ability of a prominent household head to maintain cohesion among families. These interpretations, as Fish and Fish (1991) indicate, depend upon a clearly established functional equivalence of houses, suggesting that all were used for domestic activities and storage by a nuclear family, and their simultaneous occupation. Neither of these is easy to demonstrate given less than intact assemblages in house abandonment contexts and imprecision in available dating techniques.

Not all sites have supra-household village segments. Rather, they tend to be associated with the larger sites. They have been interpreted as representing corporate groups or lineages that would have pooled labor and shared or provided access to well-watered or irrigated agricultural land. Among the criteria defining these units, the one that would fit the lineage model is the shared cemetery area. However, this feature is not consistently associated with village segments. In some villages, cemetery areas are further localized within the courtyard group. Nevertheless, viewing village segments as corporate groups is widely accepted (Fish and Fish 1991).

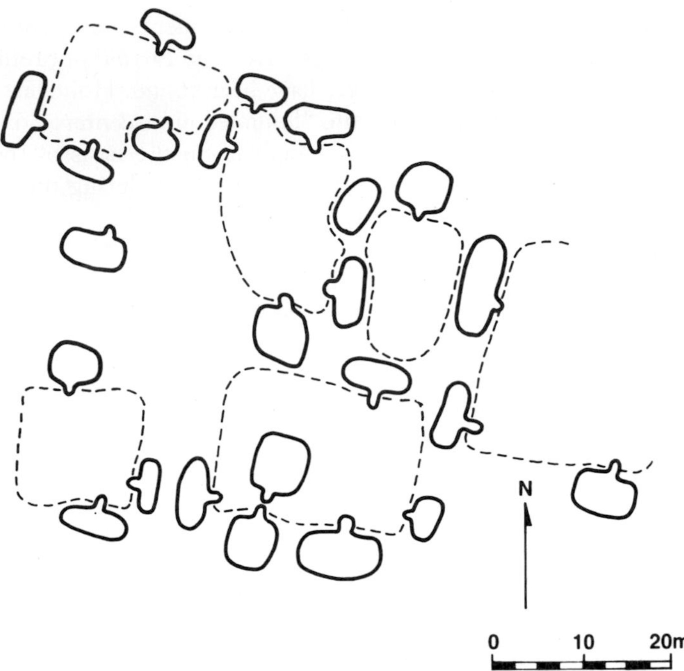

FIGURE 9.3 Before AD 1150 at many Hohokam sites, houses faced central courtyards. The stability of the courtyard group suggests that these were occupied by extended families over time (adapted from Sires and Doyel [1987] by Marjorie Leggitt, Leggitt Design).

At the larger village sites, the arrangement of village segments around an open plaza area with ballcourts at the edges of the plazas indicates that the settlement as a whole operated as a unit at times. It is likely that where ranchería settlements occur outside such villages, their inhabitants may also have participated in ritual activity within the large village. Key issues here are understanding the relationships that might have pertained among the various segments making up the village as a whole and the function(s) of the ballcourts themselves. With respect to relationships among village segments in Colonial and Sedentary sites, there is no evidence of differentiation among those within the same village with respect to either their placement or contents (Fish and Fish 1991). Differences in the abundance of exotic items and quality of craft items have been noted among cemeteries within the same village (Nelson 1981). These observations suggest that there may have been higher-status individuals within each village but they were likely recruited from any or all of the village segments. The village segments themselves do not appear to have been of unequal status or importance.

There is no conclusive evidence that Hohokam ballcourts were either derived from central Mexico or used for the performance of a ritual ball game. In fact, Ferdon

(1967) argued that they may have been used as dance grounds for a ceremony similar to one performed by the Akimel O'Odham. Two rubber balls have been found at Hohokam sites, but neither was in association with a ballcourt (Haury 1937). Further, variations of the ritual ball game were played throughout Nuclear America, frequently without a court. Nevertheless, as Wilcox (1991) points out, a version of the ball game could have been played in the Hohokam ballcourts. In Wilcox's view, a very old idea of a ceremonial ball game could have been part of the most ancient Hohokam traditions of knowledge, perhaps having been derived from Mesoamerica, along with corn, during the Archaic. In the Colonial period, the Hohokam "independently invented" the ballcourt/ball game in a context that served a necessary integrative role. With irrigation that developed at the end of the Pioneer period, the Hohokam found themselves with population increasing differentially—the greater rate of increase associated with irrigated lands. Older exchange neetworks among settlements would have been disrupted, and "formalization of the ballgame, then may have been a social mechanism to adjust to the new realities of exchange flows in southern Arizona, following the success of irrigation" (Wilcox 1991:123).

Wilcox goes on to point out that ceremonial exchange systems are a way of mobilizing a great many people to transport goods (presumably primarily food) to be exchanged at a specific place and time. In this view, the ballcourt network "marks the presence of a ceremonial exchange system that choreographed and regulated regional exchange flows among a set of contiguous local populations" that shared in the Hohokam cultural identity that included, among other things, cremation, pyrite mirrors, copper bells, and of course ballcourts (Wilcox 1991:124–125). In this view, some of the expansion of the Hohokam system is seen as the result of local populations participating in this Hohokam cultural identity, and likely benefiting from the success of macroregional exchange mediated through ballcourt ritual. In my view, the thrust of Wilcox's argument that shifts discussion away from viewing the Hohokam as an ethnic group and elaborating the functional aspects of ritual provides valuable insight into the probable kinds of social constructs archaeologists may be able to define in their data. Wilcox (1991) sees his model as plausible yet untested. This in turn suggests that developing the means of testing his model is a worthwhile effort to make.

Masters of the Desert: Hohokam Canal Irrigation

The Hohokam heartland, along the lower Salt and middle Gila rivers of central Arizona, provides an excellent example of intensive agriculture on a major scale. Early Spanish explorers, military observers, and Anglo-American settlers were impressed by the remains of extensive systems of irrigation canals. At one time or another at least 579 km of ancient canals have been mapped in the Phoenix area alone (Nicholas 1981). Early archaeological tests indicated that some canals had been dug to a depth of more than 2 m and were 3 m wide (Haury 1937; Hodge 1983; Woodbury 1961).

Most archaeologists have been pessimistic about obtaining details of Hohokam agricultural practices and subsistence because modern agriculture and more recently urban growth have obliterated Hohokam living sites and canals. As early as 1903,

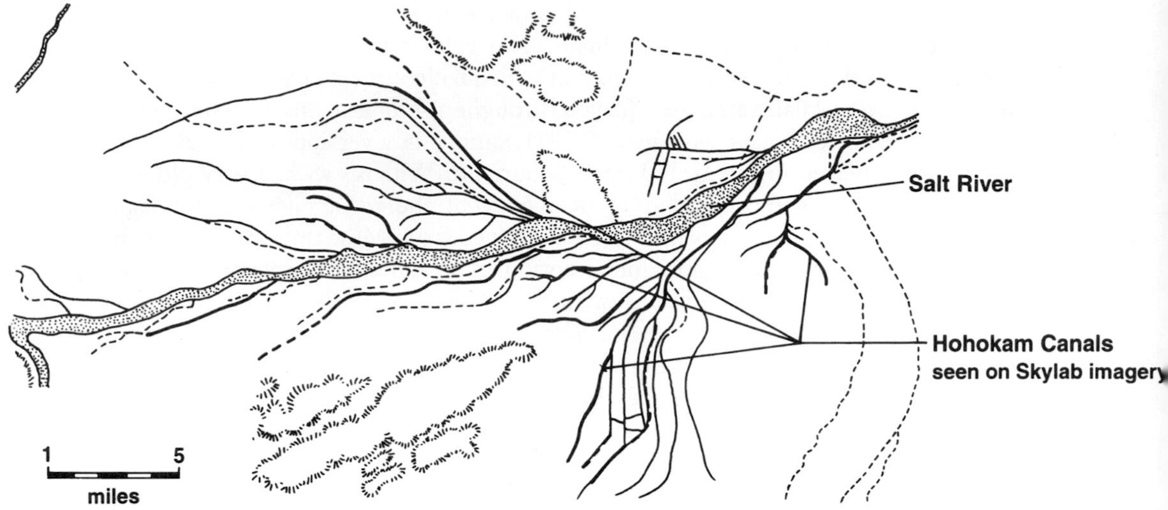

FIGURE 9.4 Hohokam canals in the vicinity of Phoenix mapped from the ground by Turney in 1929 and from Skylab imagery in 1980 (adapted from Ebert and Lyons [1980] by Marjorie Leggitt, Leggitt Design).

H. R. Patrick lamented the loss of most Hohokam canals in the vicinity of Phoenix. Although it is true that much information is forever lost, archaeologists have learned a great deal about Hohokam irrigation and subsistence, and the application of new techniques of data recovery may permit the acquisition of additional information in the future.

One of the major goals of Haury's 1964–1965 excavations at Snaketown was to obtain a clearer understanding of the history of Hohokam irrigation agriculture. Toward that end, intensive and extensive excavations of canals at Snaketown were undertaken (Haury 1976:39). Archaeological testing and excavation in conjunction with urban development projects have also greatly augmented our knowledge of Hohokam irrigation strategies, farming, and additional subsistence techniques (e.g., Breternitz 1991; Doolittle 1991; Gasser and Kwiatkowski 1991; Graybill *et al.* 1984; Masse 1981; Nicholas and Neitzel 1984). Figure 9.4 shows a detailed study of aerial photographs that enabled Nicholas (1981) to map the growth of Hohokam canals in the vicinity of Phoenix, and a study of Skylab and Landsat satellite imagery suggested that some traces of Hohokam canals are still detectable within urban areas (Ebert and Lyons 1980). The research conducted at Snaketown, augmented by the work of Nicholas and Neitzel (1984), Ackerly and others (1987), with Doolittle's (1991) comments, and Gasser and Kwiatkowski's (1991) detailed discussion of botanical remains from Hohokam sites, forms the basis of the discussion below.

In the Hohokam heartland, water is the limiting factor for agricultural success. The growing-season length of about 260 days is adequate for all crops grown in the Southwest and it permitted the Akimel O'Odham to obtain two crops a year of selected domesticates. Rainfall however is only between about 19 and 25 cm annually. About half of this falls in high-intensity summer thunderstorms, the rest in milder winter rains. Corn is the most common plant species recovered from riverine Hohokam sites. Cultivars of the Hohokam included five different species of beans, squash, bottle gourds, and cotton. Five plants found in Hohokam sites have undergone morphogenic changes that indicate domestication. These are little barley grass (*Hordeum pussilium*), Mexican crucilo, tobacco, amaranth, and wild potato. An additional crop complex of plants cultivated or tolerated in Hohokam fields include *chenopodium*, tansy mustard, milk vetch, and maygrass (Bohrer 1991). Despite the impressive array of crops, the Hohokam depended greatly on wild plant foods. Mesquite is abundant at Hohokam sites and may have been a staple food. Macrobotanical and pollen remains indicate that saguaro seeds and fruit, carpetweed seeds, various grass seeds, hedgehog cactus seeds and fruit, wild lily roots, desert four o'clock roots, cholla buds, and cattail roots and catkins were also eaten.

Hohokam irrigation engineering is impressive by any standard. Haury (1976) suggested that the Pioneer period canal at Snaketown headed at Gila Butte, some 5 km east of the site. From there water could have been diverted to the upper terrace above the Gila River flood plain and to Snaketown, which is on that terrace. If enough water was available it could then have been used for fields on both the upper and lower terraces and on the flood plain. The remains of a Pioneer period canal were located on the edge of the upper terrace on the southwestern side of the site. This canal, in contrast to later ones at Snaketown, was relatively broad, shallow, and unlined. Later canals at Snaketown were U or V shaped in cross section and lined with mixtures of clay and loam.

The initial excavation of the canals was only the beginning of the labor investment for the Hohokam. Silt and apparently refuse clogged the waterways, necessitating periodic cleaning. As Haury noted, piles of silt removed from the canals may have substantially modified local topography. In addition, canal walls were breached as water sought the quickest path to the river. Haury's excavations revealed several areas in which breaches had been repaired during the period in which the canals were in use.

As Doolittle (1991) points out, most of the excavated and studied Hohokam canals are the largest canals and canal segments in the system, and those with the greatest archaeological visibility. Along with these canals, the Hohokam irrigation systems included vast networks of smaller canals, lateral ditches, and headgates. At Snaketown, excavations of diversion areas revealed lines of post holes indicating headgate structures made of a series of posts that probably served as upright frames for horizontally laid branches and brush. Diversion dams of this type were recently constructed by the Akimel O'Odham. They do not last more than about a year, and were regularly rebuilt. In addition to headgates, water had to be slowed and kept in the fields. Doolittle notes that this requires the construction of various kinds of water spreading devices and earthen bunds within each field. These too would have had to have been maintained on a regular basis.

Archaeologists confront several interpretative problems in their discussions of Hohokam irrigation and subsistence. First, the data available are clear in showing highly developed technological skill in the construction and maintenance of irrigation systems, but the data also indicate that a great diversity of wild plants were used for food. If the Hohokam were sophisticated hydrological engineers, then why did they rely heavily on wild foods? Second, did the construction and maintenance of the irrigation systems entail elaborate mechanisms of social control or might the canal systems have developed incrementally over time? These issues, although not entirely resolved, have received considerable attention. Recent research suggests several answers and provides directions for future inquiry. Consideration of the hydrological regimes of the Gila and Salt rivers and examination of the ways in which irrigated fields modify the landscape are important toward clarifying the first question. Research by Nicholas and Neitzel (1984), Ackerly and others (1987), and Doolittle (1991) suggests directions that might be pursued to answer the second.

The Gila and Salt rivers originate in the mountains of east-central Arizona, and both are fed by winter precipitation and summer thunderstorms. Water levels are therefore high twice during the year, in late spring and again in late summer. The biannual floods enabled the Akimel O'Odham to obtain two crops a year in recent times (Bohrer 1970; Castetter and Bell 1942). Variability however is characteristic of the precipitation pattern and in any given year, one or both periods of high water might fail to occur. In a discussion of the Akimel O'Odham ecosystem, Bohrer (1970) showed that there were no conflicts between the schedules of activities involved in agriculture and in wild plant gathering. The Gila River Akimel O'Odham could harvest their first crop in late June, but if that crop failed, they could harvest saguaro seeds in July. A second crop could be planted at the end of July and the beginning of August. If there was a lack of summer rains and the second crop failed, mesquite pods could be gathered in September. In any one year then, subsistence activities could have involved both agriculture and gathering.

Castetter and Bell (1942) note in the twentieth century, the water let out of the Gila was highly unreliable from year to year, and there were crop failures as often as 2 years out of 5. The Akimel O'Odham compensated by gathering wild plant food. Castetter and Bell estimated that perhaps 60 percent of their diet was based on wild plant gathering. The variety of wild plant remains in Hohokam sites could reflect years in which agricultural production failed completely. In addition, Hohokam fields created a well-watered habitat for plants and animals in addition to corn. Some plants, such as chenopodia, amaranth, and agave, were encouraged within garden areas and used as food. In addition, small game, such as jackrabbits, were attracted to Hohokam fields, and "garden hunting" probably supplied important protein to Hohokam settlements (Szuter 1991). Riverine Hohokam in different areas used slightly different mixes of wild and domestic plant foods. Some of these probably reflect local topography. Others may indicate a form of product specialization for trade.

Accounts of modern and historic Akimel O'Odham agriculture are probably best viewed as being suggestive rather than as direct analogs for the Hohokam, at least because indigenous populations were much reduced as a result of European contact. We do not know exactly how many Hohokam settlements were contemporary, how many canals were in use at the same time, or whether ancient population densities were such that competition for irrigation water or for wild plant resources were additional problems requiring social solutions.

The difficulty in precisely dating the construction of Hohokam canals and determining the sizes of the settlements they served also inhibits interpretations of the degree of social coordination required to construct and maintain them. In most instances quite small segments of canals have been exposed in excavations and these are dated on the basis of the ceramic assemblages recovered from them. If canals have been dug through trash deposits that predate them they will contain ceramics reflecting an age earlier than that of their use. If canals are dated simply on the basis of their proximity to sites, precise age determinations are not possible. Based on his work at Snaketown, Haury (1976) interpreted the development of Hohokam irrigation as a rather gradual process in which irrigation systems were slowly expanded and elaborated. His view was that construction of the Pioneer period canal at Snaketown did not require a large, coordinated labor force and the work could have been accomplished by the informal cooperation of as few as 50 men.

Work by Nicholas (1981) and Nicholas and Neitzel (1984) supports Haury's interpretation of the modest scale of Pioneer period canals though not of a gradual expansion of the system. Nicholas was concerned with interpreting the extent of Hohokam irrigation systems along the Salt River south of Phoenix, and as noted, she relied on examination of a series of aerial photographs. Recognizing all the problems inherent in dating agricultural features by their proximity to dated sites, she cautiously used the method to infer the relative scale of Hohokam irrigation during the major Hohokam developmental periods. Like Haury, she found that the Pioneer period canals were relatively simple and suggests that their construction did not require highly structured coordination of a vast labor force. Her discussion indicates a persistence of this condition until the Hohokam Classic. At that time however she finds that the canal systems south of Phoenix had numerous branches. And it is important that the three canal systems in her area were interconnected in Classic times. She tentatively suggests that this major expansion in the irrigation systems depended on the prior development of complex sociopolitical institutions.

Nicholas and Neitzel (1984) applied the method of dating canal segments by their proximity to dated sites in the region south of the Salt River in order to develop a sequence of expansion of the canal system. Recognizing difficulties with the method, and attempting to control for them, they suggested that the canals had not been built all at once but had been lengthened and increased in number over time, as more land was brought under irrigation, presumably as a response to population increase. Based on excavations at the site of La Ciudad in Phoenix, Ackerly and others (1987) revealed that known large canal segments actually overlie numerous buried, earlier canals that had been in use for only short periods of time (Figure 9.5). They argued that this demonstrated that canals were modified and reworked so that it becomes necessary to rebuild a canal rather than to continue to modify the old one. Doolittle (1991) points out that these views are not entirely incompatible, but he notes an error in the Nicholas and Neitzel study. Because irrigation canals are hydraulic systems they must involve coordination of stream velocity and gradient to get water into fields. Velocity and

FIGURE 9.5 (a) Hohokam irrigation canal on Salt River near Scottsdale, Arizona. The vehicle emphasizes the size of the burm and the scale of the canal itself (photography by Helga Teiwes, courtesy of the Arizona State Museum). (b) Cross section of a Hohokam irrigation canal, with B. Bruce Masse, at the site of Pueblo Grande, Arizona (photograph by Helga Teiwes, courtesy of the Arizona State Museum).

gradient are influenced by a number of factors, including the shape of the canal, its depth, whether it is straight or sinuous, etc. If velocity and gradient are appropriate for water delivery to a set of fields, they will no longer be adequate if additional fields are to be irrigated. Hence, canals cannot be added onto when the amount of irrigated land is increased. Rather, the entire canal system must be reengineered and rebuilt. It is also true that keeping a canal functioning when the amount of land it serves does not change requires nearly constant maintenance and small modifications. "For the most part, once canal systems are in place and operating, they can be expanded only by rebuilding the entire network at one time" (Doolittle 1991:147).

Further, Doolittle (1991) argues that the amount of labor expended and organization involved in increasing the size of an irrigation system increases at some exponential rate. Whereas small systems can be rebuilt quickly, perhaps between growing seasons and with small amounts of unskilled labor, when populations become large and dense, this is impossible.

> Perhaps as early as the Colonial period, the demand for food in the Salt and Gila valleys had not only reached a critical point, but it was so great that, by themselves, farmers probably could not make the necessary modifications to their field systems during the off season.... Not only could farmers not afford to make such reallocations of their time and energy, but the necessary enlargements were of such a magnitude that they could not be carried out using trial-and-error construction techniques. A staff of learned professional civil engineers and a large organized labor force was needed (Doolittle 1991:149).

Agriculture in the Deserts

Outside the Hohokam core area of the middle Gila and Salt drainages, agricultural technology developed that allowed cultivation in a variety of desert settings. Some of these included using smaller rivers, such as the Santa Cruz, in addition to uplands. Others used only ephemeral streams and concentrated the small amount of summer precipitation. Haury (1950) had defined a Desert branch of the Hohokam to refer to sites outside the Phoenix Basin core. In his formulation, the Desert branch practiced only a minimal amount of agriculture and achieved a lower level of cultural development than the River branch Hohokam, who could produce agricultural surpluses. More recent archaeological data confirm that farming in these desert settings was at least as old as farming in the core area and that farming involved many crops in addition to maize. Further, these settings eventually developed specialized agricultural systems that became important parts of very large exchange networks. Even from the Colonial period, however, ties of exchange in craft ire united the core and peripheral Hohokam. This section builds on the diversity in Hohokam farming technology that was discussed above, using Gu Achi (Masse 1980), a predominant Colonial period site near Santa Rosa, Arizona, supplemented with information from the Dairy site in the northern Tucson basin (Fish *et al.* 1992).

The excavation of Gu Achi was undertaken as a salvage project by archaeologists from the Western Archaeological Center of the National Park Service for the Bureau of Indian Affairs. The analysis of the Gu Achi data was conducted by Masse (1980) several years after the excavation had been completed. Gu Achi provides an example of an extreme situation because despite the fact that the site was large, covering an area of 150,000 m^2, and was continuously occupied between about AD 500 and 1150, with the most concentrated period of settlement between AD 850 and 1000, it is in an area with no perennial water. The Dairy site is located on an alluvial fan above the Santa Cruz River Valley, north of Tucson Basin. Because the area is one of the few near Tucson that had not been subject to extreme modern development, it was selected for a long-term survey and testing project directed by Paul Fish, Suzanne Fish, and John Madsen for the Arizona State Museum. The major focus of the Northern Tucson Basin survey eventually became the Marana Community, an enormous Classic period multi-site, integrated community. Only a small part of the Dairy site extends beyond the early agricultural period and into the Colonial period; however, the site provides excavated information on the Preclassic occupation of the area.

According to Masse, the resources of the desert near Santa Rosa include a diversity of lithic source material. Two vegetative communities, an upland community dominated by paloverde and saguaro and a community characterized by creosote and bursage found primarily on the alluvial valley floors, offer abundant edible plants. In addition, the ephemeral streams of the desert support riparian species such as mesquite and other useful plants. Fauna resources are also diverse and include bighorn sheep, deer, antelope, jackrabbits, cottontails, and other smaller animals. Although all of these resources are potentially useful, water is the limiting factor for human settlement. There are no permanent streams, and springs are few. The closest permanent spring to the site of Gu Achi is at Ventana Cave, more than 20 km away.

The amount of precipitation received in the southern Arizona desert follows a diminishing gradient from east to west. At the eastern edge, near Sells, rainfall is between about 23 and 30 cm. In the far western area, near Yuma, it is only 7.6 cm a year. In the vicinity of Gu Achi and the Dairy site, rainfall averages about 25 cm a year. More than half of this moisture occurs during the summer growing season. This amount of moisture alone is not sufficient for agriculture unless local topographic features concentrate the rainfall and runoff water from a network of washes, permitting agriculture on outwash slopes. According to Hackenberg (1964), a minimum of 17.8 cm of rainfall is necessary to sustain the kind of floodwater farming pursued by the Tohono O'Odham today. There must also be sufficient fertile alluvial soils on outwash slopes to form an apron of top soil and plant material at arroyo mouths. These aprons, or fans, are referred to as *akchin* in the Papago language and are often the sites of fields. Both Gu Achi and the Dairy site are located on outwash fans. The most important topographic feature for the Colonial period settlement at Gu Achi is Gu Achi Wash, a broad wash containing about a meter of silty alluvial fill that borders the site.

The year-round occupation at Gu Achi required water for drinking as well as for crops, but there is no permanent water at the site. Masse suggests that the first occupants may have excavated shallow wells in the bottom of Gu Achi Wash, a Tohono O'Odham method of obtaining water known to have been used at least since the Archaic. During the later, more intensive stages of occupation, however, a reservoir with an interior diameter of 30 m was constructed at the site. A mud turtle, a reptile that requires permanent water, was among the faunal remains recovered, indicating that the reservoir held water throughout the year.

Information about the subsistence base at Gu Achi and the Dairy site was derived from macrobotanical and pollen analyses, faunal studies, and a consideration of site survey information from their surrounding areas. While rabbits are the most abundant faunal resources at Hohokam sites, the fauna recovered from both Gu Achi and the Dairy site are diverse. Faunal remains from Gu Achi are scant. Of the mammals, jackrabbits are the most abundant, followed by bighorn sheep and mule deer. Other mammals identified include cottontail rabbit, squirrel, badger, and bobcat. Despite this variety the minimum number of individual animals (MNI) is only 22. Rabbits are also the most numerous remains from the Dairy site but taxonomic richness is similar to Gu Achi, with 14 different taxa identified. In contrast to Gu Achi, the remains of artiodactyls (deer or sheep) are relatively abundant, making up 13 percent of the identifiable fauna.

A lack of fauna is common at Hohokam sites, although Tohono O'Odham villages obtained between 12 and 15 deer annually, in addition to numerous rabbits and smaller animals. Masse discusses several possible explanations for the limited amount of archaeological animal bone, including scavenging by dogs and coyotes, poor preservation, and the possibility that hunters butchered animals in the field and returned little bone to the village. These may be important, but none can be conclusively demonstrated. The degree to which the residents of Gu Achi depended on hunting remains unknown.

Wild or semi-cultivated plant remains (pollen and macrobotanical samples) from Gu Achi indicate the collection and use of mesquite pods and paloverde beans, agave, and prickly pear. Mesquite and paloverde were available within the flood plain in the immediate vicinity of Gu Achi. The agave and prickly pear had to be obtained from the foothills and mountain flanks considerably north of the village. The remains from the Dairy site were similar, with especially high recovery of mesquite, saguaro, and other wild plants suggesting that they were important components of the diet.

The evidence for agriculture at Gu Achi consists of hundreds of charred corn kernels, corn pollen, cotton pollen, and cotton seed. A morphological study of the corn suggests that it may have been grown under conditions of moisture stress. At the Dairy site, corn, cotton, squash, and agave occurred from the earliest levels, with bottle gourd and beans added later on. As at Gu Achi, corn pollen was ubiquitous. Pollen of chenopodia and/or amaranth occurred in high frequency at the Dairy site, although these plants are not common to the area today. Since both occur in disturbed ground and may have been encouraged or tolerated in fields, Fish and others suggest that they indicate ancient modification of the ground surface, probably for fields.

Masse considered the possibilities of two farming strategies at Gu Achi: dry farming, dependent on rainfall, and *akchin* farming, dependent on rainfall and runoff. Irrigation from a permanent water source would have been impossible at Gu Achi. Masse notes that dry farming was practiced widely by the Hohokam; however, because of inadequacies in rainfall, dry farming relied on the use of a variety of water-conserving

FIGURE 9.6 Cross section of an excavated rock pile feature at a site in the northern Tucson Basin. These features, located in fields, conserved moisture for plants planted in them (photo by Paul Fish, courtesy of the Arizona State Museum).

devices. These included check dams, contour terraces, and some bordered gardens. In two Hohokam areas, these features are absent. Hohokam settlements near Gila Bend have no indication of dry farming or water-conservation features. This is to be expected because the area is extremely arid, with an annual mean of only about 15 cm of rainfall. The remains of water-conserving devices are also absent in the eastern desert, despite the fact that it receives about as much rainfall as those areas in which Hohokam water-conserving devices occur. However, Masse noted that piles of rock, about 1.5 m in diameter and 20.3 cm high, do occur in the eastern desert. The suggestion that these features may have augmented runoff to fields located downslope from them was evaluated by Fish and others because these features are also common in the northern Tucson basin (Figure 9.6). Some of the rock piles in the Tucson basin were excavated and many more were studied. They are not located in areas where they might have served to divert runoff water to adjacent fields; rather, they are in settings that were fields. It was found that the rock piles do conserve moisture for plants planted in them. They also protect plants from rodent damage at the roots. Fish and others develop a convincing argument for the use of rockpile fields for agave cultivation in the northern Tucson basin, where during the Classic period, the crop became an economic specialty. Perhaps the less extensive nature of the rock pile fields at Gu Achi indicate less agave production in the Colonial period.

The topographic setting at Gu Achi is appropriate for *akchin* farming. Brush diversion dams and ditches, low brush dikes, embankments, and small ditches may all be used to divert runoff from Gu Achi Wash to *akchin* fields. The technical components of *akchin* farming are similar, therefore, to those used by Hohokam practicing riverine irrigation. The difference is that in *akchin* farming, the water source is not permanent. Yields from *akchin* farms can be substantial—up to 25–30 bushels of corn per ha. Masse suggests that *akchin* farming was the predominant form of subsistence production at Gu Achi and that it was productive enough to sustain a permanent residence at the site for more than a century.

Archaeological material from Gu Achi includes abundant evidence of the manufacturing of marine shell items. Finished marine shell objects, such as bracelets, are abundant in the Hohokam sites of the Gila and Salt drainages. Hence, close ties between sites such as Gu Achi and those of the core Hohokam area are indicated. The technological similarities between the devices used in *akchin* farming and those used in canal irrigation, as well as the evidence of shell manufacture, indicate that cultural similarities between Hohokam living in both areas are closer than separate cultural branch status may imply. This contention is further supported by the relatively early dates for the major settlement at Gu Achi (AD 850–1000), indicating that the level of cultural development was similar to that achieved in the riverine area at the same time. It is important that despite an unfavorable natural environment, the desert Hohokam were able to establish large settlements and to specialize in production of marine shell items.

House-Lot Gardens

House-lot gardens are generally small plots adjacent to dwellings in which a variety of plants are cultivated. They are important among agricultural people worldwide, although from a botanical perspective they have most often been studied in tropical settings. William Doolittle (1992) examined modern house-lot gardens in the Valley of Sonora, Mexico, as well as ethnographic descriptions of these features from throughout arid Chihuahua, Sonora, and Sinaloa. These provided a set of archaeologically visible characteristics that enabled him to suggest locations of ancient house-lot gardens in the Valley of Sonora. This discussion derives from Doolittle's study; however, Fish and others (1984) also suggest that the Cerro de Trincheras sites of the Tucson Basin may also have served as house and house-lot gardens. The potential importance of house-lot gardens to the Hohokam of southern Arizona has also been demonstrated by Szuter (1991). Szuter found that the abundance of small animal remains in Hohokam sites reflected a pattern of garden hunting that provided critical dietary protein.

Concentrating on features that would be visible to the archaeologist, Doolittle (1992) finds that house-lot gardens in northern Mexico are typically bounded by low stone walls, which deter pedestrian traffic and assist in preventing mulch from being washed away. House-lot gardens are also typically situated on the south side of dwellings and slightly downslope from the house. Doolittle suggests that this setting is selected to provide maximum sunshine for plants and helps prevent houses from being flooded in summer thunderstorms as well as facilitating washing away of household refuse and watering of crops.

In his survey of ancient house-lot gardens in the Valley of Sonora, Doolittle (1992) identified 10 rings of rock, each about 1 m in diameter, associated with six residence sites. He suggests these may have been enclosures for growing ornamental plants as is current practice by the Rarámuri and other groups. Thirteen low rock enclosures at several sites are most similar to the modern and ethnographic house-lot gardens. These are rectangular, measure 4–5 m on a side, and are consistently downslope from confirmed house sites.

Doolittle's study suggests that archaeologists would benefit by looking more closely for similar features and examining other "enigmatic" features for possible horticultural functions. Doolittle's study would benefit as well from chemical and pollen tests from the features he identified in Sonora.

THE COLORADO PLATEAUS: ANASAZI COMMUNITY ORGANIZATION

The period between AD 800 and 1000 (Pueblo I and early Pueblo II of the Pecos Classification) witnessed great geographic expansion of settlement on the plateaus. By the end of the period, the Anasazi reached their greatest territorial extent. In the western Anasazi region, peoples of the Kayenta Anasazi tradition expanded north of the San Juan and west to the Grand Canyon and the Virgin River area of southern Nevada. As Gumerman and Dean (1989) noted for the Kayenta area, Pueblo II habitation sites occupied "virtually every conceivable spot," avoiding only flood plains during times when they were being buried by streams depositing quantities of sediment on them. The expansion occurred during a time when the tree-ring and hydrologic records indicate depressed water tables, erosion, and low and unpredictable precipitation from year to year. These conditions, in addition to the diversity in environmental settings settled, suggest that the period may have been one of experimentation for agriculturalists trying to find reliably productive locations despite poor and variable climate (Cordell and Gumerman 1989:9).

Anasazi settlements in Pueblo I and Pueblo II were quite standardized. Typically, Pueblo villages consist of long, double arced rows of contiguous surface rooms with a deep squarish pit structure placed to the south, or in front of the surface rooms (Figure 9.7). The surface rooms are generally of jacal construction, rather than masonry, but they served both for storage and as residences. Back rooms that lack floor features, especially hearths, most likely were used for storage. Interior doorways connect these to front rooms with hearths. These, in turn, may open on a portico or outside work area, often also with hearths. Within any one site, there is variation in the sizes and internal features of the structures. This suggests variation in both the sizes of groups using the structures and the range of activities for which they were used. Suites of Pueblo I roomblocks and associated pit structures were apparently built as a unit (Lightfoot 1992).

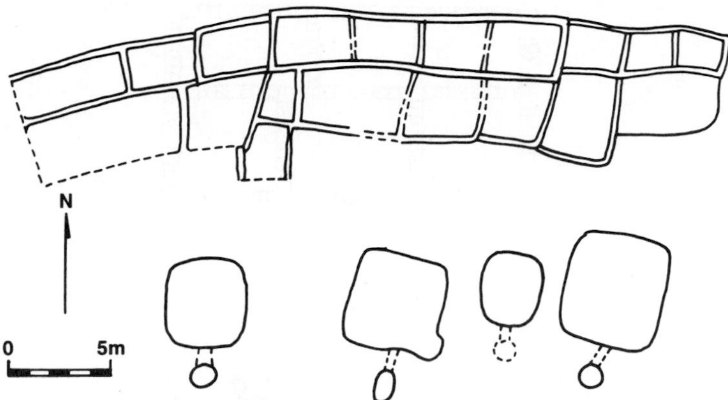

FIGURE 9.7 Plan of the Duckfoot site, a relatively small Pueblo I site that nevertheless preserves the common pattern of rows of rooms behind a pitstructure (adapted from Lightfoot [1992] by Marjorie Leggitt, Leggitt Design).

In some places dating as early as the Pueblo I villages, but usually to Pueblo II times, are *unit pueblos*, first described by T. Mitchell Prudden (1903, 1914, 1918) and today generally called Prudden unit pueblos (Figure 9.8). Prudden unit pueblos consist of masonry surface structures—arranged in a line, arc, or L—a kiva, and a refuse midden. Again, these components are generally oriented north to south. The pit structure in the unit pueblo is fairly formal, generally masonry lined. Hence it is called a kiva, assuming its functional equivalence to ceremonial structures in modern Pueblo villages. In fact, it is not until sometime around AD 1000 that there are highly specific local traditions in kiva architecture. For example, Mesa Verde kivas are known for stone pilasters and, eventually, assuming a keyhole shape (Figure 7.3). In the San Juan Basin, kivas are generally round with an interior encircling bench. Common kiva floor features include a hearth or firebox, a deflector, and a ventilator. A small hole in the floor is referred to as a *sipapu* by archaeologists because this is the term used for it in modern pueblos where similar features symbolize the *shipap*, the place where humans emerged from the underworld. Until at least this degree of specialization is apparent, pit structures are quite variable in feature and assemblage characteristics. Prior to that, it is unlikely that pit structures were used exclusively for ritual or communal functions and should probably not be called kivas.

Discussions of social organization during Pueblo I ultimately depend on archaeological evaluations of momentary site size or how many segments of surface rooms and associated pit structures were occupied simultaneously. Some Pueblo I sites are very large. For example, the quintessential, though not the largest, Pueblo I site was excavated in 1939 at Alkali Ridge, in southern Utah (Brew 1946). Alkali Ridge Site 13 consisted of 130 surface rooms, 16 pithouses, and 2 kivas. Site 13 is not unique. Sites that are similar in size have been recorded in several locations in southwestern Colorado

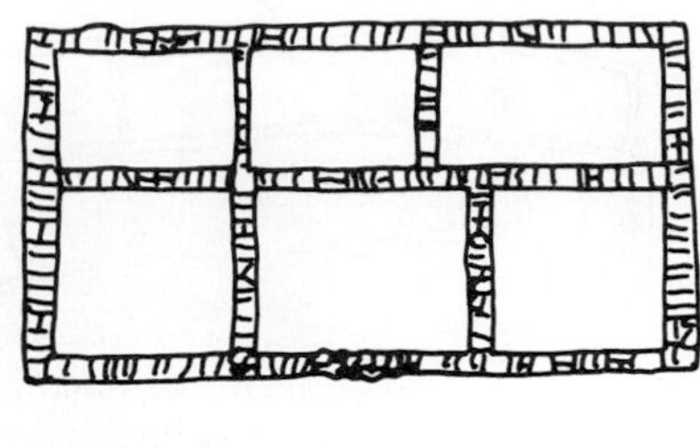

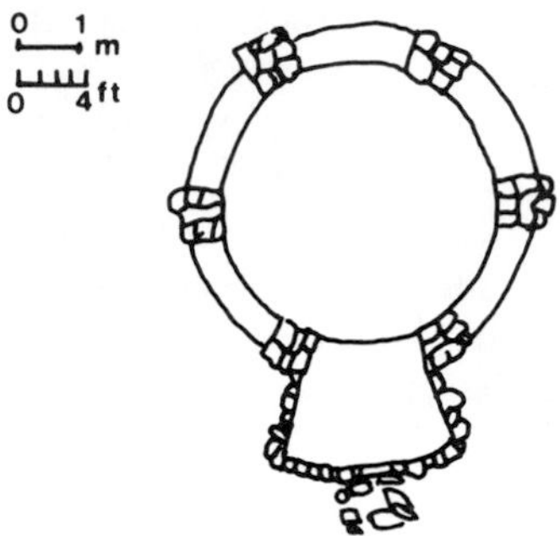

FIGURE 9.8 Typical Prudden Unit Pueblo. Unit pueblos consist of a series of masonry surface rooms, a kiva, and a trash mound oriented along a north–south axis (adapted from Prudden [1918] by Charles M. Carrillo).

and southeastern Utah. Recent excavations and reevaluation of older work have shown that most Pueblo I sites were occupied for only about 30 years or less (Lightfoot 1992; Wilshusen and Blinman 1992). The brief duration of these settlements should make it easier for archaeologists to estimate their size at any one point in time. On this basis, Wilshusen and Blinman (1992), using ceramic microseriation and conservative techniques of estimating population, argue that some Pueblo I sites housed up to 600 individuals at one time in separate, but closely spaced, settlement clusters. Wilshusen and Blinman are correctly cautious in their estimates; however, their idea that room/pit structure clusters at Pueblo I sites were occupied simultaneously was based on excavation data in which Pueblo I village structures were sampled, rather than excavated completely.

The Duckfoot site in southwestern Colorado is a smaller Pueblo I site that was excavated completely (Lightfoot 1992). The site consisted of 19 single-story surface rooms and four pit structures (Figure 9.7). Three hundred and seventy-five tree-ring dates allowed reconstructing the building sequence in great detail. Lightfoot was able to show that the site consists of three architectural suites that were built in 3 to 5 years, with no significant interval separating their construction. The fourth pit structure, however, was built about 15 years later. Lightfoot's entirely justifiable conclusion is that the Duckfoot site did not grow by accretion. Rather, it was established by a single immigrant group.

The Duckfoot site, in size, might represent one cluster in a large Pueblo I site, such as Alkali Ridge. While I accept Lightfoot's inference that a single group of people built the Duckfoot site, there is enough slight variation in the dates of construction to make me cautious about accepting Wilshusen and Blinman's contention that all clusters of large Pueblo I sites were occupied at the same time. If Wilshusen and Blinman are correct, social mechanisms were in place that could reduce potential conflicts among 600 individuals at least for periods of about 30 years. Within localities such as Mesa Verde, some archaeologists argue that the clusters of Pueblo I villages represent the largest population reached by the Anasazi (Hayes 1964). Others suggest that although Pueblo I villages do tend to occur in clusters, not all clusters of villages are occupied at the same time.

Pueblo I seems to represent one aspect of a longer term Anasazi pattern. Simply stated, there were times when larger populations were supported but they did not last very long. There was an oscillation between aggregation and dispersal that becomes an oscillation between occupation and abandonment at a different scale. If dispersed populations aggregate in one place, then most of the land they once occupied is abandoned unless there is immigration from outside. From the perspective of one area, the cycles become what Lipe and Matson (1971) refer to as Boom and Bust. The lack of stability of aggregated populations derives from one of two factors: the inability of the southwestern environment to support aggregates over any really long period of time and/or the failure of mechanisms of social integration to keep people together.

Kohler (1992) observed that large Pueblo I sites near Dolores, Colorado, were founded when rainfall conditions were particularly good for crops grown without irrigation. At the same time, areas to the west and at lower elevations, in general, were not experiencing moisture regimes favorable for dry farming. Some of those areas of low elevation saw local abandonments at this time, as people moved to higher settings. In the more arid western portion of the Colorado Plateau, settlements remained small.

Questions about why and how populations aggregate are central ones in archaeology, as they are in anthropology, geography, and certain fields of biology. Kohler (1992; Kohler and Van West 1996) argues that the centralization of population into large settlements creates difficulties for farmers. Some, if not most, fields will be further away from living areas, requiring farmers to spend time walking to and from fields and carrying harvests greater distances than if households were dispersed next to their fields. There must then have been some perceived advantage in forming large settlements. Kohler suggests that one advantage of Pueblo I aggregation was that it facilitated sharing agricultural food among community members. At the same time, because only members of the same community were tightly integrated socially, limits could be placed on the extent of the network for sharing. In those low elevation subregions where dry farming was more tenuous at the time, individual households may have been able to move to new locations in the face of failure of agricultural crops. Hegmon (1996) demonstrates, by a computer simulation, that restricting the pool of households among whom sharing is conducted is a better strategy than either hoarding or unrestricted sharing.

Beyond the local level, there were general features and symbols that seem to have integrated much of the Anasazi area during Pueblo I. Black-on-white ceramics share a design style, called Kana-a or Red Mesa, that is very similar throughout the region, although the pottery was made locally and might differ in technological details, such as type of pigment. Items of trade included marine shells, shell artifacts, and pottery. The trade pottery is generally San Juan red ware. This include types made in southern Utah and traded out to the Mesa Verde, Chaco, and Kayenta areas. This red ware does not make up substantial percentages of decorated ceramics in the regions into which it was traded but demonstrates information flow throughout very large parts of Pueblo territory.

Partially contemporary with the large Pueblo I sites are the Prudden unit pueblos, which continue and are the numerically dominant settlement type through Pueblo II in much of the Anasazi area. In an analysis of the literature, Gorman and Childs (1981) found that the term unit pueblo is used very consistently by archaeologists, but that there is more than one type of unit pueblo. The different types of unit pueblo do not cluster geographically or temporally. This observation indicates that the variation is not the result of culture historical factors. One subtype consists of a single site that is different simply in that it has the smallest number of surface rooms. Gorman and Childs suggest that this reflects attenuated settlement growth, for the site was apparently abandoned shortly after it was occupied. Another subtype consists of three sites that apparently grew to larger sizes than other unit pueblos, perhaps indicating greater site longevity. Two remaining subtypes are similar in size and plan. However, one has surface rooms that are divided into more spatially discrete blocks than is common among the unit pueblos in general. Gorman and Childs suggest that these two subtypes of unit sites represent social variants of the same settlement class, with the group showing spatially discrete blocks having been formed by the amalgamation of two or more previously distinct social groups. The authors admit that this interpretation requires testing.

Other archaeologists, considering the uniformity of unit pueblos, have emphasized either the directional spatial arrangement of the components or the sizes of the settlements. Reed, for example, considered the orientation of components highly significant, noting that "it surely must reflect something basic in personality structure, outlook, national character—something comparable to the difference between the Spanish inward-facing patio-type house on the edge of the street and our front-facing dwellings with the lawn on the outside" (1956:13). Those who have addressed settlement size and the number of surface rooms and kivas have proposed social interpretations, generally referring to the unit pueblos as clan, family, or lineage houses, and Prudden (1918) himself referred to them as clan houses. Discussions of the origins of Pueblo clans have figured prominently in both the ethnology and archaeology of the Southwest. On this subject, most recent scholars are indebted to the thoughts of Julian Steward, who addressed the issue from the perspective of cultural ecology.

Steward (1955) was interested in the origins of matrilineal Western Pueblo multiclan settlements. He argues that the origins of Pueblo clan organization could be understood in terms of economic and ecological factors. Steward did not see any *organizational* differences between late Basketmaker settlements and the early Pueblo ones. He proposed that later in Pueblo II when there is evidence of the development of more aggregated Pueblo settlements, small groups were amalgamated but did not lose their social and ceremonial integrity (Steward 1955:163). Citing a fairly consistent ratio of five or six rooms to each kiva as evidence, Steward argued that the initial social unit in the late Basketmaker settlements was a local lineage because each cluster of houses consisted of more than one family and he could imagine no other motive than kin relationships for families living together. The later amalgamation of local groups, in which the room-to-kiva ratio was maintained, suggested a system of exogamous nonlocalized clans. Steward's linking of nonlocalized clans to aggregated communities makes sense for the site clusters of Pueblo I. Most recent archaeological data suggest that unit pueblos are far too small to have been communities in any sense. Gumerman and Dean (1989) note that unit pueblos rarely contain more than 12 rooms. Such sites could hardly have accommodated more than a moderately large extended family. Nevertheless, they appear quite self-contained and economically independent. On the other hand, Rohn (1989) comments that for the Mesa Verde and Northern San Juan in general such unit pueblos could not have been functioning communities in any sense. Although they are treated as separate sites by archaeologists, they do cluster spatially on the landscape. The larger spatial clusters are more likely communities of day to day interaction.

For the western Anasazi area, Gumerman and Dean (1989) also observe that although the early years of Pueblo II saw considerable exchange in raw materials for stone tools and finished products, there is increasing use of local resources that becomes dominant by AD 1000. By that date there are highly specific local traditions in ceramics and architectural forms. At the same time that much of the Anasazi area was looking inward and becoming provincial in terms of decreased exchange and interaction, those in Chaco Canyon and the San Juan Basin were expanding and becoming a major regionally organized system. As is discussed in Chapter 10, the Chaco system developed during a period when rainfall was adequate for corn, and farmers should have prospered. Perhaps it was the relatively benign climate, as a background, that enabled the rest of the Pueblo II world to remain self-contained and self-sufficient. If so, this background was so forgiving as to allow virtually any settlement and economic strategies to work. In success, there may well have been the seed of eventual decline. As Anasazi farmers extended their houses and fields to increasingly peripheral areas, they depleted game, firewood, and probably some wild plant foods. Many of the peripheral areas were also marginal for corn with respect to soils and growing conditions. When conditions reverted to their difficult "normal," or to the drought of 1130, the communities on the edge of both the spatial extent of the Anasazi realm and the conditions appropriate for the Anasazi way of life were the first to be abandoned and left in ruins.

Diverting Runoff at Chaco Canyon

Chaco Canyon, in the San Juan Basin of northwestern New Mexico, contains some of the most spectacular Anasazi sites anywhere in the Southwest. During the eleventh century, Chaco Canyon was the center of a large, regionally organized system of ancient roads and related communities. A discussion of that system is deferred until the next chapter. This is a summary of the agricultural technology, based largely on the work of R. Gwinn Vivian (1970, 1974, 1990, 1995), whose 1990 book is, to date, the most comprehensive summary of Chacoan archaeology. His work is supplemented by research conducted in the course of the 15-year, multidisciplinary effort by the Chaco Center of the National Park Service and the University of New Mexico (Betancourt and Van Devender 1981; Hall 1977; Robinson 1979; Schelberg 1992; Toll *et al.* 1980) and subsequent analyses that rely on data from those projects (Sebastian 1992).

The San Juan Basin as a whole is arid and barren. Precipitation in the basin is about 20 cm annually compared with 40 to 50 cm at the higher basin margins. Basin soils vary considerably, with those in the canyon itself considered among the poorest. Above the canyon, there are large areas of exposed sandstone and shale, and soils are lacking. Today, Chaco Wash is an entrenched ephemeral stream, but there are indications that it was not entrenched during the entire period of prehistoric occupation of the canyon (Bryan 1954; Hall 1977). Diurnal temperature variation in the canyon is high, especially in spring. There is a 45 percent chance that the growing season will be less than 110 days, and therefore inadequate compared with the 115 to 130 days needed by traditional Hopi corn.

Within the basin, Chaco Canyon is relatively well watered but the moisture does not derive directly from precipitation. Rather, the source of the moisture is from runoff. Vivian (1995) terms the Chacoan solution a *complex* of strategies involving runoff irrigation. The idea of a complex of strategies seems apt. It is likely that the variety of techniques were developed, adapted, and modified over time. By the eleventh century, the system would have been composed of elements that had been added and incrementally improved (Doolittle 1990).

There are detailed, though not entirely consistent, paleoenvironmental reconstructions for Chaco Canyon. These indicate that overall, the climate during the Anasazi occupation was similar to that of the present. Tree-ring reconstructions of precipitation (Robinson 1979) show somewhat low and variable precipitation in the ninth and tenth centuries, with a more reliable increase in precipitation in the eleventh century (Sebastian 1992; Vivian 1989).

There are no living streams in Chaco Canyon. The Chacoan agricultural system, then, provides an interesting comparison to Gu Achi, where the basic technology also involved the use of runoff. In Chaco Canyon at least three methods of floodwater farming were practiced: terracing along the cliff edges, *akchin* farming as at Gu Achi, and canal irrigation using runoff on the north side of the canyon. The elaboration at Chaco reflects the influences of different topographic features and probably a larger labor pool.

Catchment areas for runoff lie within the canyon branch but are narrow so that water reaches the canyon by way of many short, generally small, quite evenly spaced, side canyons (Figure 10.3). This distributes water quite evenly throughout the canyon, reducing its velocity. Landforms on the north side of the canyon produce more runoff because there is a larger intercliff zone of impermeable soils on that side. The most prevalent, distinctive, ancient water control systems in Chaco Canyon consist of a

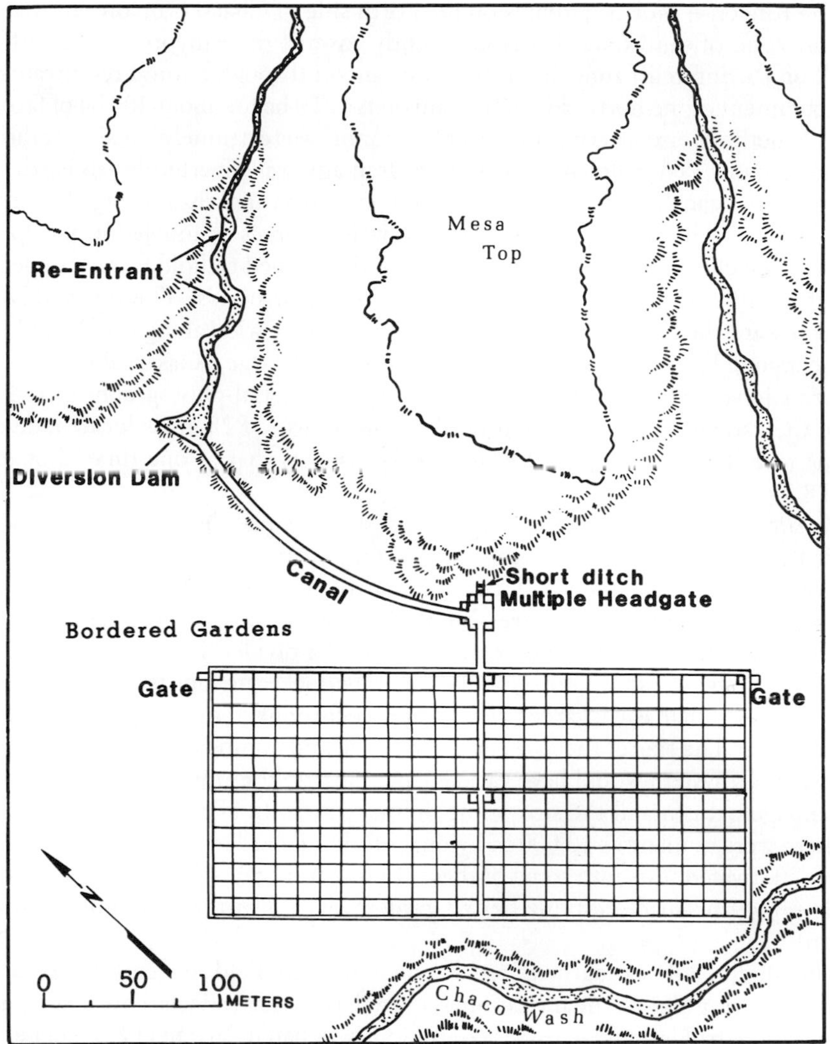

FIGURE 9.9 Rincon-4 North field system at Chaco Canyon. Runoff from the Mesa top drains into the canyon through natural reentrants. The dam and the canal funnel the water into a multiple headgate from which a short canal brings the water to the bordered garden. Excess water could be drained into Chaco Wash (adapted from Vivian [1974] by Charles M. Carrillo).

combination of dams, canals, ditches, headgates, and earth-bordered gardens (Vivian 1974). These systems captured runoff water from the intercliff zone above the canyon to divert it to fields and bordered gardens on the canyon floor. One of these systems, the Rincon-4 North system, is illustrated in Figure 9.9.

The Rincon-4 North system is on the north side of Chaco Canyon. Above it is an intercliff zone of sandstone that slopes gently toward the canyon rim. Runoff from rainfall on the intercliff zone drains into the canyon through natural re-entrants. The total catchment of the north side of the canyon is 4250 ha for about 400 ha of farmland.

The method for collecting and diverting runoff was extremely consistent throughout the canyon. Water flowing down each drainage was diverted by an earthen and masonry dam near the mouth of the side canyon into a canal that averaged 4.5 m wide and 2 m deep. The stone-lined or masonry-walled canals channeled water up-grade alongside the cliff edge to a masonry headgate that served to hold water momentarily while it was distributed into small ditches or overflow ponds. The intercliff zone is narrow toward the head of the canyon but it is relatively wide along the lower 14.5 km of the canyon. The diversion systems, and most of the large, Anasazi sites, are located along this lower portion of the canyon. Vivian used aerial photographs of the north side of the canyon to locate re-entrant drainage areas. Of 28 areas located, diversion systems were found in 17, and Vivian (1995) suspects that at one time, they existed in all 28.

Vivian (1995) notes that ensuring a more nearly equal distribution of floodwater to irrigated fields was made possible by dividing farming areas into major bordered plots that were further subdivided into many small gridded gardens of standard shapes and sizes. Aerial photographs were also used to locate the bordered gardens. One of these near the site of Chetro Ketl consists of 4.8 ha divided into two canal-bordered plots. Each of the plots contains a number of individual earth-bordered gardens. Vivian (1974) suggests that each garden was irrigated through temporary openings in the earth borders. The size of the gardens and the size and number of plots associated with each diversion system would have varied depending on the amount of land available in the drainage pattern and the size of the drainage area. In all, Vivian (1974) estimates that there were as many as 10,000 individual bordered gardens on the north side of the canyon. Excavated tests into some of these (Loose and Lyons 1976) revealed extensive land-leveling; the surface of one buried garden varied less than 2 cm over a distance of 23 m.

The degree of standardization in the Chacoan field systems is remarkable. Whether or not that standardization required or even reflects any sort of supra-settlement control is an issue that is continuously debated. Vivian (1995) suggests that it did not. He does point out that distribution of crops throughout the settlements in the canyon during the tenth century might have had to involve supra-settlement organization.

Risk and Agricultural Expansion on the Colorado Plateaus

The two examples discussed here provide new insight into Anasazi use of the Colorado Plateaus. Both studies build on data from long-term contract archaeological projects and both use novel research approaches and methods of analysis. The first example is from Black Mesa, Arizona, a large landform that includes the modern Hopi towns on its southern margin. The second example is from the Dolores River of southwestern Colorado, just north of Mesa Verde. The Black Mesa Archaeological Project was conducted by the Center for Anthropological Investigations at Southern Illinois University, on land leased to the Peabody Coal Company by the Navajo and Hopi tribes over a 17 year period beginning in 1967 (Gumerman 1988). As part of this project, Powell (1983) examined the settlement strategies of the Black Mesa Anasazi and was able to show that despite considerable investment in architecture, most of the sites in her area were not occupied year-round. Her study made innovative use of ethnoarchaeological and archaeological data. Her results have implications for reevaluating the settlement histories of other Southwestern areas.

Northern Black Mesa was occupied from about 600 BC to AD 1150. Previous research had suggested that throughout this time there had been population growth and an increasing dependence on agriculture. Agriculture could not have been very reliable, however, because annual rainfall varies from 25 cm on the southern edge of the mesa to 50 cm on the northern edge, with marked variability in rainfall patterning from year to year. There are no permanent sources of water within the lease area. The length of the growing season is also highly variable and ranges from about 120 to 150 days. There are detailed paleoclimatic studies of sediments, pollen, and tree rings that suggest oscillating conditions of drought and more mesic intervals in the past (Gumerman 1988). There was no overall trend toward lower water tables, surface erosion, or deforestation.

The structure of the environment at Black Mesa indicates that reliance on agriculture would have been very risky. Laboratory analyses of plant remains from excavated sites did not indicate any evidence of increasing dependence on corn over time. Also, compared with many parts of the Southwest, the habitation sites on Black Mesa are quite small—their modal size is about 16 m^2. These observations, combined with ethnographic information about Native American peoples practicing some horticulture in similarly risky environments, led Powell to consider the possibility that the habitation sites on Black Mesa were not occupied year-round.

To examine the possibility of seasonal use of the Black Mesa Anasazi sites, Powell analyzed the material culture correlates of 34 recently abandoned, seasonally occupied Navajo camps. She emphasized variables that would be most useful in determining the season of use, rather than variables that relate to cultural differences between Anasazi and Navajos. Her concern was also with isolating variables that could be measured in the archaeological record. The first variable she considered was the proportion of interior space to total site space, because it is likely that more activities are carried out indoors in winter than in summer so that there would need to be a larger area of protected indoor space in winter habitations than in summer houses. Statistical analyses of the Navajo data supported this proposition. Powell also found that Navajo summer field house structures were smaller than structures at fall piñon camps and that the amount of outside activity area was greater at the field houses than at the piñon camps. Powell compared the total site size for summer and winter sites and found a statistically significant difference in size, with summer sites being larger.

Powell looked at differences in the distributions of hearths and artifacts at Navajo field houses and piñon camps, finding that the winter piñon camps had interior hearths necessary for warmth and lacked outside hearths; summer field houses had both outside and inside hearths. Finally, artifact densities were higher at piñon camps, following from the observed differences in overall site size.

Applying these results to Black Mesa Anasazi sites, Powell found that she could divide the Anasazi sites into two groups based on the amount of interior space. Small sites had fewer than 14.8 m^2 of inside space; large sites had 17.2 m^2 of inside space or more. In accord with her expectations about possible summer use of the small sites, she found that these had proportionately more outside than inside hearths. Artifact density was not appreciably different on small and large sites. As she expected, she found that the large sites had more interior hearths, suggesting that these were occupied in winter. Contrary to her expectations, small sites had less exterior area than large sites.

Powell divided the Anasazi sites into time periods. She examined small sites dating before AD 1050, small sites occupied after 1050, large sites occupied before 1050, and late large sites dated post-1050. She found that small sites were similar in the variables measured for the duration of the occupation of Black Mesa. There were differences between large early sites and large late sites. Over time there was an increase in total site size within the large site category. Large late sites had fewer outside hearths than large early sites, and only within the category of large late sites did more than one inside hearth per habitation unit occur. In some respects, then, the large early sites were similar to the small sites.

To further evaluate the possible seasonal use of the Black Mesa sites, Powell attempted to use independent data derived from analyses of faunal and macrobotanical remains. Although these data were less than satisfactory, she found that the large late sites had some animals that were obtained in the spring as well as the most diverse fauna of all sites. These sites also had more diverse floral remains. She found that the floral diversity at all small sites and early large sites was virtually identical. Powell acknowledges that some of the variation could be due to differences in the length of time that sites were used and the number of people using the sites. However, after reviewing all her analytic results, she concludes that:

> Small sites were occupied during the summer, and large late sites were occupied year-round. Large early sites are a problem; however, I am swayed by the structure sizes and the low floral diversity, as well as by the midden and storage patterns, to suggest that this group of sites, too, was seasonally occupied, but during winter (Powell 1983:128).

The implications of Powell's research for interpretations of northern Black Mesa are great. She was unable to confirm either an increasing dependence on agriculture or a trend in continuous population growth. Her research suggests that the area was used only seasonally until AD 1050, when there is evidence of year-round occupation. During the early portion of Black Mesa occupation, the summer residences of the population would be outside the study area. Given the shift to year-round use of the region, resource depletion could have occurred rather rapidly, nearly ensuring its abandonment within 100 years.

Very similar situations may have occurred in other areas of the northern Southwest. As long as regional population densities remained low, seasonal movement may have been an option for many people. The effects of reduced mobility, possibly resulting in resource depletion and aggregation, were also a focus of research for the Dolores Archaeological Project (Kohler and Matthews 1988) and later work that expands from it (Kohler and Van West 1995; Van West 1996).

The Dolores Archaeological Project (DAP) was begun in 1978, when the Bureau of Reclamation contracted with the University of Colorado to recover data from the area to be affected by the construction of McPhee Reservoir in southwestern Colorado. The project concluded in 1985 (Breternitz *et al.* 1980; Lipe and Kohler 1988). Subsequent research on Anasazi settlement of the surrounding region (MAP) was carried out through research at Crow Canyon Archaeological Center (Lipe 1992) and additional doctoral dissertations (e.g., Adler 1990; Van West 1996).

Anasazi occupation of the DAP area began in the AD 600s, increased through immigration in the 700s and again in the mid-800s, and declined drastically in the late 800s or early 900s, after which it did not recover (Kohler 1992). For the larger, surrounding study area, Anasazi settlement began about AD 500 and ended in 1300 with general regional abandonment (see Chapter 11). The focus here is on the ninth century DAP, with supplemental research on the period between about AD 900 and 1100/1150. The DAP reveals a common pattern in Anasazi expansion in that local population growth stops with aggregation. Kohler (1992) examined this as an ecosystem process.

In Kohler's (1992) model, initial Anasazi colonization of the DAP area relied on use of fields watered by flood water in canyon bottom settings. These fields are naturally restored annually and can be farmed continuously. With increased immigration, farming expanded to the mesa tops, where soils are often thin and there is no natural nutrient replenishment, and where the piñon-juniper vegetation can be fairly easily removed by fire. Kohler suggests that the Anasazi practiced shifting agriculture, burning the piñon-juniper, which would provide a few years of water-conserving, nutrient enriched mulch, and then moving. He notes "If burning killed the trees and shrubs then more water would be available for crops, especially if planting near the base of dead trees where crops could benefit from tree stream flow" (Kohler 1992:621). The incompletely burned trees would also provide a small supply of firewood. But this mesa top farming strategy is not sustainable because of the very slow regeneration rates of the woodland.

The mesa tops opened up large areas of farmland, but it was high risk, depending on the variable rainfall, and it was nonsustainable. At some point, the strategy depletes wood needed for fuel, wild plant and game resources, and agricultural land. Kohler argues that high residential mobility continued until nearly the end of occupation, when population aggregated into a few, large settlements. At that time, field houses first appeared as well. Kohler suggests that the field houses were likely more important "markers" that would limit or preclude access to land to newcomers, rather than a result of trying to limit the cost of maintaining fields at sore, distance from residences. In either case, however, the underlying reason for field houses is the increase in population that curtails residential mobility. In the Dolores case, the Anasazi became locked into a system that is not sustainable, further immigration was checked, and with continued climatic fluctuation, the only option left was emigration, resulting in local abandonment.

The pattern of residential mobility (or short-term sedentism) is also noted in the Mimbres Mogollon area during the fourteenth century (Nelson and LeBlanc 1986). The crucial importance of this residential mobility was demonstrated by a computer simulation experiment designed by Van West (1996) for the larger area of which the DAP is a part. Van West's simulation assumed that the success of dry land farming is predominantly a function of precipitation and the water-retention properties of soils. She divided her study area into 45,4000 units of 4 ha each and, using a GIS system, recorded the distribution of 98 soil types, subsequently reduced to 11 soil classes, particularly relevant to water retention within the area. She then calculated an index (the Palmer Drought Severity Index, PDSI) of soil moisture that is temporally sensitive and climatically integrative for each soil class based on precipitation and temperature records from five modern weather stations in the region. The index reflects the previous month's water deficit surplus and temperatures. In essence, Van West produced a map of crop potential at a resolution of 4 ha units.

To reconstruct the crop potential for the period of Anasazi occupation, Van West used the tree-ring reconstruction of retrodicted monthly precipitation based on the model of Rose and others (1981). This model provides estimated precipitation by month from AD 900 to 1970, and from it, Van West (1996:218) derived "55 long-term reconstructions of PDSI, one for each combination of elevational stratum and soil moisture group." She then used these along with long-term records of crop yields by soft classification, to retrodict the productivity of the study region, by year, from AD 900 to 1300.

Van West's GIS model is complicated and difficult to visualize. She has produced an animated version on video that enables one to see estimated crop yields as color variation across the map of her study area as these change over simulated years. For our purposes here, the most important result of her reconstruction is that even with quite high population estimates for the ancient occupation of the region, there would always have been enough productive land to support that population in the study area as a whole. However, accessing the land over time would have required population mobility. Hence, as long as people could move, they could farm and have enough land. If mobility was restricted—within the study area as a whole—agricultural groups could not survive over time.

Agriculture in the Northern Rio Grande Valley

The Rio Grande Valley of New Mexico today is the home of most of the modern Pueblo Indians. Compared with the environment occupied by the modern Western Pueblo (the Hopi towns, Zuni, Acoma, and Laguna), the Rio Grande area is generally characterized as more favorable for agriculture. Precipitation in the northern Rio Grande is greater than it is to the west. Surface water is more abundant, and the waters of the Rio Grande are available for irrigation. Furthermore, because today the Rio Grande Pueblo villages irrigate their fields with water from the Rio Grande and its tributaries, most ethnographic studies of the Pueblos (e.g., Dozier 1970; Eggan 1950; Wittfogel and Goldfrank 1943) emphasize the importance of irrigation and its presumed consequences for Eastern Pueblo social organization. In a passage that is often cited, Dozier presents this view succinctly:

> This concentration of populations appears to be correlated with the development of irrigated farming on the Rio Grande and suggests as well a developing social and political organization commensurate with the demands of the incipient waterworks society. The Rio Grande Pueblos were well on the road toward economic surpluses and the development of a complex society (Dozier 1970:30).

Hence, the importance of moieties, permanent or life-long officers, and curing and war societies of the Rio Grande Pueblos is seen as deriving largely from the requirements of large-scale irrigation and only limited use of dry farming. There are two problems with this view. First, it is unlikely that irrigation using the Rio Grande was central to Pueblo occupation of the valley. Second, survey and excavation data reveal very large areas of agricultural features associated with ancient rainfall-fed field systems that are not used today but have not been entirely forgotten by the Pueblos.

Ancient dependence on the Rio Grande flood plain for agriculture and irrigation using Rio Grande water is unlikely because of four factors. First, as Ford (1972) noted, there have been devastating floods. The classic example is the destruction in 1886 of not only the fields but much of the Pueblo village of Santo Domingo. The importance of flooding, prior to European settlement and overgrazing, is not known; however, Archaic sites along the Rio Puerco of the East, a major tributary of the Rio Grande, were found under 1 to 3 m of alluvium (Wimberly and Eidenbach 1980:7), suggesting that it could have been a problem. A second problem is related to flooding and irrigation. Irrigation waters provide nutrients that replenish soils and are beneficial for agriculture. Conditions of poor drainage and high evaporation, however, can lead to deposits of salts and other minerals that are inimical to crops. A study in the vicinity of Cochiti Pueblo (Fosberg 1979; Fosberg and Hussler 1979) found that during the fourteenth and fifteenth centuries, as agriculture expanded to poor-quality soils, at least some of these developed heavy concentrations of salt. These studies suggest that agricultural land was removed from the system on a short-term basis through floods, or for much longer periods of time through salinization. Third, studies of Spanish Colonial documents (Simmons 1969; Swadesh 1974) cite difficulty in clearing bench lands of dense stands of vegetation. The studies suggest that land along the river that could be cleared without iron tools was severely limited by the eighteenth century. Finally, when crops are planted along the river and irrigated, both fields and individual plants are quite close together, increasing the risk of crop loss through crop disease and insect pests (Ford 1972). In sum, despite the abundance of water from the river, the Rio Grande Valley is not without risk for agriculturalists. The problems encountered by agriculturalists—flooding, salinization, dense vegetation, insect pests, and crop disease—are not ameliorated by the labor intensification or technological solutions that were available to the Anasazi. Rather, solutions include expanding agriculture to settings where rainfall agriculture could be practiced and buffering agricultural shortfalls through gathering and hunting.

The expansion of agriculture to areas dependent on rainfall faces the same risks as it does elsewhere in the Southwest. Modern climatological data spanning the past

FIGURE 9.10 (a) Part of a cobble-bordered, gravel-mulched plot in the Rio del Oso Valley, New Mexico. The north arrow at the bottom of the picture is in an ancient ditch. The gravel-mulched plot with stone borders diverted run-off to simple stone terraced fields (photo courtesy of Kurt Anschuetz).

50 years show that rainfall is insufficient for successful corn cultivation in several portions of the Rio Grande drainage. Elsewhere, especially in the northern Rio Grande Valley and in the adjacent mountains, the growing season is often too short for corn and other crops. Although the presence of a large river and areas of relatively high precipitation might indicate that little labor investment would be made in technological features appropriate for conserving moisture, archaeological surveys document water-conservation systems over very extensive areas of land. The kinds of systems recorded include contour terrace bordered gardens, series of check dams, and bordered gardens with gravel mulch. The gravel-mulch gardens are limited in extent but because they are not used by Pueblo peoples today, the way that they functioned has been a subject of considerable interest and research. This discussion is based on the work of Anschuetz (1995; Anschuetz *et al.* 1985; Maxwell and Anscheutz 1992); Ware (Ware and Mensel 1992), and Lightfoot (1993).

Gravel mulch is a covering of pea- or fist-sized rock within a bordered field area (Figure 9.10). Gravel-mulch gardens are most common along the Chama, a Rio Grande tributary, and in a few locations in the Galisteo Basin. In both areas they probably date between the twelfth and sixteenth centuries. Precipitation in the Chama Valley is generally adequate for corn, but potential annual evapotranspiration is three

FIGURE 9.10—*Continued* (b) Ancient agricultural fields are often better documented in aerial photographs than on the ground. Here, the photograph is of an extensive system of bordered fields between Zia and Jemez Pueblos (photo by Tom Baker, Aerial Archaeology).

times the quantity of average realized annual rain and snow values. Of note, May and June, the months during which Pueblo crops germinate, are the driest in both Chama and Galisteo Basin. The Chama flows through a high elevation narrow valley, surrounded by high mountains. Elevation and cold air flow patterns create great risk of local late spring and early fall frost. The problem of a short growing season also occurs in the Galisteo Basin but is less severe than a lack of moisture, especially before the summer monsoon.

In the Chama, gravel-mulch plots, with and without cobble borders, are located on low mesas and terraces. They depend on direct precipitation for their moisture. They are generally located on a surface where an impermeable caliche layer underlies sand, and their massive construction makes them impervious to runoff. Excavation of some Chama gardens revealed a heterogeneous mixture of stone and alluvial sand that had been piled on the natural ground surface, resulting in a modified root zone some 20 to 40 cm thick. In the Galisteo Basin, gravel-mulch garden plots were on relatively flat sites with southern exposures and in association with a single soil type, one in which a well drained soil overlies a soft of mixed pebbles, gravel, and sand. In the Galisteo Basin, the soil type provided the "raw material" for the lithic mulch.

In both Chama and Galisteo Basin settings, gravel mulch increases the amount of water available to plants (as will any mulch) by increasing infiltration and hindering evaporation. In addition, gravel mulch stabilizes soil temperature. It reduces air movement near the ground and affects the temperature of the upper few centimeters of soil, and because gravel is a good conductor of solar radiation, it will increase soil and ground temperature, which can extend the length of the growing season. Interestingly, pollen studies from the gravel-mulch gardens from the Chama and one of its tributaries have yielded both maize and cotton pollen. The effectiveness of the gravel mulch in extending the growing season must have been considerable. As yet, gravel-mulch gardens in the Galisteo Basin have yielded only maize pollen. It is likely that the properties of gravel mulch were used for different ends by the ancient Pueblo farmers, perhaps primarily to extend the growing season in one case and the soil moisture in the other.

AGRICULTURE IN THE MOUNTAINS

In the Mogollon region, the time period AD 800 to 1000 corresponds to the Late Pithouse period, characterized by a change from round to rectangular pithouses, the development of communal structures or great kivas, and an increase in interregional exchange. The large sites had about 125 pit structures, but since the period is 450 years long, it is unlikely that more than a small fraction of these were inhabited at one time (Cordell *et al.* 1994). Many settlements consist of only two or three spatially dispersed houses, especially in the central and western portions of Mogollon country. If there is a great kiva it is physically separated from domestic structures but may be approximately central to the scattered dwellings. In the northern Mogollon area, near modern Cibique, Arizona, small settlements are dispersed throughout the area but the largest of these have a separate great kiva that may have served the inhabitants of the entire area. No matter what the variety of settlement, there appears to be no plan in the placement of dwellings. There is not a great deal of evidence of exchange with other regions, but what evidence there is indicates relationships with those who were geographically closest. Hence, in the southern Mogollon region, Hohokam trade ceramics are found, whereas in the north, exotic sherds likely come from the Anasazi area.

In terms of subsistence patterns, Mogollon settlements are often viewed as less dependent on agriculture than their contemporary Hohokam or Anasazi neighbors. Faunal remains are generally more abundant in Mogollon sites, when they are preserved. On the other hand, the Mogollon did invest in a great variety of agricultural features, although perhaps not until AD 1000 or later. The still classic description of Mogollon agriculture is provided by Woodbury's (1961) study of Point of Pines. A resume of that work is given here. It should be noted that recent studies by Creel and Adams (1985), Ellis (1995), and Sandor and others (1991) have further documented canals and terrace systems in the Mimbres Mogollon area.

The research at Point of Pines, near the San Carlos Indian Reservation, Arizona, was conducted in the context of the University of Arizona's Arid Land Program, which was designed as an interdisciplinary effort to conduct basic research about long-term use of arid lands. The Point of Pines area had been the location of the university's field school since 1946, and field school projects provided an immediate context for Woodbury's work.

Woodbury's study concerns farming practices that probably date to the period between about AD 1000 and 1450, when the population of the area achieved its maximum size. From about AD 1000, people at Point of Pines were living in masonry pueblos, most quite small but a few quite large. The largest of these covered an area of about 10 ha and consisted of about 800 ground-floor rooms. Following this peak, the population declined until the area was abandoned.

The ancient villages and farms described by Woodbury occur within a zone of low ridges separated by small valleys with intermittent streams. Much of the area is grassland interspersed with ponderosa pine and smaller stands of piñon and juniper. The nearby Nantanes Mountains would have provided a hunting area for deer, peccary, turkey, bear, and smaller game that were important food resources for the ancient inhabitants.

From the perspective of agriculturalists, conditions at Point of Pines are relatively more favorable than they are in many areas of the Southwest. The frost-free period is estimated to be about 165–170 days and the mean annual precipitation about 46–48 cm. About one-third of the precipitation occurs as winter snow that penetrates the ground and is important for the germination of seeds in the spring. The spring season, from April through June, receives the least amount of precipitation during the year. Precipitation during July and August is characterized by high-intensity thunderstorms, sometimes accompanied by hail, which can damage crops. There is high variation in precipitation from year to year, and early frosts would also have adversely affected crops.

Woodbury suggests that the occurrence of two distinct geological deposits in the area may have been important to village location and agriculture. Some of the ridges at Point of Pines are composed of conglomerate and tuff. These have been rounded to nearly flat summits that were used as village and farm sites. Other ridges are capped with basalt, weathered into rugged badland surfaces that offer no topsoil for farming. Agricultural land may be available below the low scarps at the edges of these formations. Another relevant observation is that soils in the area are shallow and easily eroded when the natural cover of vegetation is removed. Not surprisingly, many of the agricultural features observed at Point of Pines served to conserve soil. Agricultural fields at Point of Pines depended entirely on rainfall. Ancient wells and reservoirs are located in the area but seem to have been used only for domestic purposes. The agricultural features at Point of Pines are bordered gardens, check dams, and contour terraces.

The most common type of field pattern at Point of Pines consists of series of terraces that follow the contours of slopes. Most occur on slopes with gradients of about 5 percent. These features would have slowed runoff from heavy rainstorms and retarded soil erosion. The rocks and boulders of these features occur throughout the area, so construction of the linear borders would have resulted in the clearing of long strips of land for cultivation. Bordered gardens occur as contiguous grids, generally on gentle slopes and on nearly level areas. Check dams across arroyos at Point of Pines occur on slopes ranging from 5 to 21 percent in groups of from 10 to 50. Woodbury suggests that the primary function of the terraces was to hold soil behind them, forming a series of small fields. Additionally, they would have slowed runoff, allowing it to penetrate the field, and retarded gullying. All three of these features occur at W:9:30, the Clover Park site (Figure 9.11), where they surround a village of about six rooms.

The field systems described occur throughout the Point of Pines area in a diversity of settings. Woodbury suggests that the overall strategy of farming was similar to that practiced at the modern Hopi villages, in that planting a diversity of field locations would have lessened the risk of crop failure in any one caused by either an abundance or a deficiency of rainfall. Of course, specific field types found at Hopi do not occur at Point of Pines because of differences in local topography.

DISCUSSION

The focus of this chapter has been on the agricultural technologies that permitted regional expansion of communities throughout the Southwest by AD 1000. The reduced mobility entailed in agricultural intensification also requires social mechanisms of resolving disputes, recruiting agricultural labor, and sharing harvests. Archaeologists cannot excavate corporate groups or ancient labor parties. The best we can do is note regularities in household, settlement, and community layouts and by reference to ethnographic cross-cultural studies try to infer and evaluate our inferences about the nature of the groups that composed them. With this in mind, it appears that the Hohokam pattern involved ways of integrating households, villages, and supra-village organizations over several generations. The evidence for this among the Pueblo I Anasazi communities in the northern San Juan is moot. Rather, it appears that the

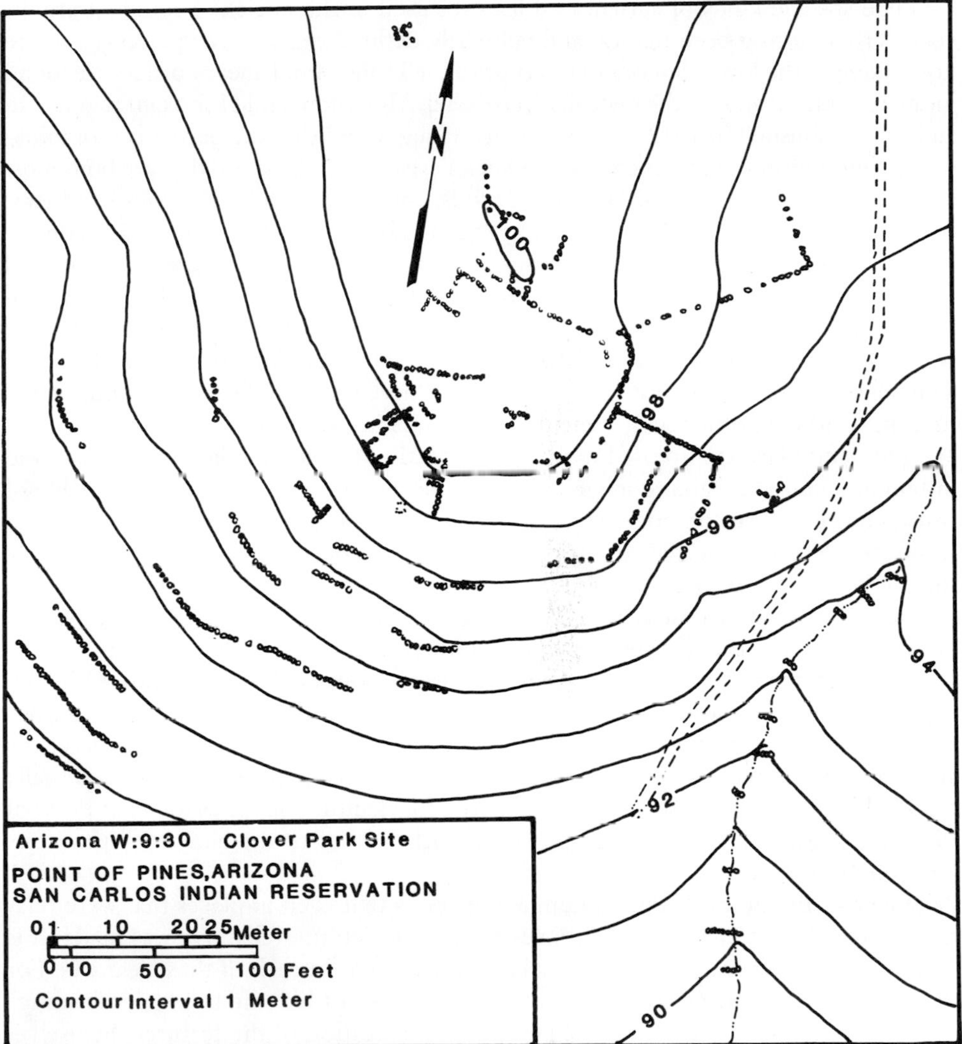

FIGURE 9.11 Agricultural features at the Clover Park Site, Point of Pines Arizona. Terraces follow the contours of the slopes. Bordered gardens appear as partial grids. A series of check dams was constructed along the arroyo (adapted from Woodbury [1961:17] by Charles M. Carrillo).

Pueblo II unit pueblos were appropriate for short-term sedentism and fluid social networks. Only in Chaco Canyon do larger aggregates remain. However, even among the core area Hohokam and the Chacoan Anasazi, prior to AD 1000, there does not appear to be hierarchical ranking of individuals within settlements.

The specific kinds of agricultural features used in the ancient Southwest are diverse, cross-cutting both natural and culturally defined regions. Irrigation canals are not unique to the lower Sonoran Desert or to the Hohokam. Linear borders are found in the mountains and on the plateaus, in Anasazi, Mogollon, and Hohokam regions. In an article published in 1972, Plog and Garrett suggested that the particular combinations of agricultural features constructed in an area should be those that are both most appropriate to the particular land forms, soils, and water conditions found and least costly in labor to build and maintain. They used information from modern soil conservation and agricultural studies to evaluate the effectiveness of different agricultural features on land of increasingly steep slope. Although there is some overlap, they found that the effectiveness of irrigation gives way to gridding with single courses of stone and finally to terracing as the slope increases. The particular kind of analysis they used would also be appropriate for evaluating the effectiveness of different agricultural features in relation to other environmental characteristics, such as soil type.

Plog and Garrett also used modern information to estimate labor costs involved in building and maintaining irrigation canals, bordered gardens, or terraces made of two or more courses of stone, and contour terraces or grids made of one course of stone. As would be expected, grids and terraces of one course of stone are far less costly than irrigation canals; bordered gardens or terraces of two or more courses of stone fall between in labor cost. Using Woodbury's analysis of Point of Pines, Plog and Garrett compared the distribution of agricultural features with their expected distribution based on the actual areas of land of different slopes at Point of Pines. Although a complete analysis would have included other aspects of the Point of Pines environment as well as estimated labor costs for the agricultural features found there, the analysis indicated a close agreement between the expected pattern and the one actually found. Their study suggests that the diversity of agricultural features found at Point of Pines is, in part, due to the attempt to suit each feature to the characteristics of its location in the landscape.

Overall, the Point of Pines example illustrates that even in places that were relatively favorable for agriculture, an investment in agricultural features was made. It is also important to recall that there is a labor investment in each of these features. For this reason Anscheutz (1995) comments that he does not like the term "dry farming" because it suggests a passivity belied by the sophistication of the features themselves and their success. Anscheutz's comment is an important reminder that today Euro-Americans cannot grow cotton at the high elevations of the northern Rio Grande and Chama Valley nor have modern experiments at growing corn in Chaco Canyon been successful enough to have provided enough corn for a single meal.

Agricultural features occur relatively late in the occupation of the area, when they are present. This suggests that alternative options, particularly moving to another location, were no longer feasible. In fact, movement—either seasonally as at Black Mesa or periodically as in the Dolores project area—was probably a very commonly selected option, occurring at different temporal and spatial scales until curtailed by eventual European colonization of the Southwest.

The data suggest that a level of regional population density or restricted mobility must be reached before an investment in agricultural features is made. The particular features selected reflect local topography and rainfall conditions primarily and demonstrate the abundant technological skill of all ancient southwestern farmers.

The amount of labor invested in the construction of agricultural features was quite variable with Black Mesa, the Dolores area, and Point of Pines at the lower end; the Rio Grande Valley, Gu Achi, and the Tucson Basin perhaps representing a middle range; and Chaco Canyon and the Hohokam heartland the upper end of the scale. The examples suggest that construction of features is not undertaken until local population densities are high enough to require it and only some kinds of systems are effective for agricultural intensification. The amount of water in Gu Achi Wash would not increase no matter what labor investment was made. The floods and short growing seasons of the Rio Grande Valley could only be controlled to a limited extent. Where intensification could benefit the people dramatically, it seems to have sustained further growth, which seems to have been the case in Chaco Canyon and in the Hohokam heartland. The data are far from conclusive but in these two areas it appears that certain mechanisms of social control and a degree of sociopolitical complexity were required for the further expansion of the agricultural systems. When this level of social development was achieved, the growth of both systems was again great. In the Chacoan San Juan Basin and the Classic period Hohokam, regional systems developed. These are the subject of the next chapter.

Chapter-opening art: Prudden unit pueblo (drawing by Charles M. Carillo).

CHAPTER 10

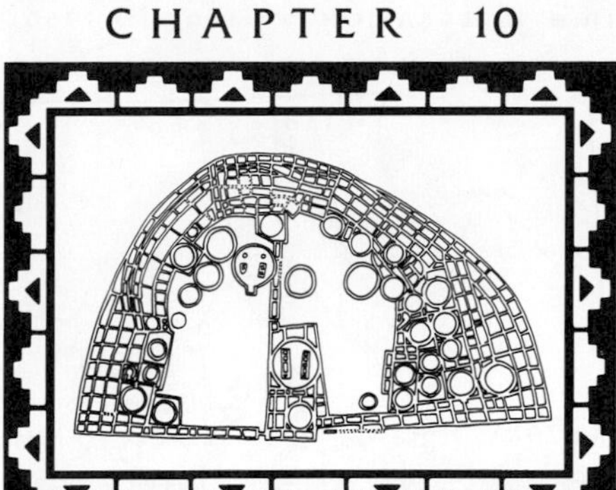

Integration (AD 1000 to 1250)

By the eleventh century, agricultural communities had been established in all parts of the Southwest where farming was possible. As population continued to grow, agriculture was intensified in locally appropriate ways such as stream-fed and runoff irrigation, terracing, and *akchin* farming. Different means of community organization were also established. Three different patterns of social integration developed and spread over wide areas. These are termed regionally integrated, aggregated, and dispersed. Each of these is described and exemplified in this chapter.

INTRODUCTION

By AD 1000, communities of farmers were established throughout the Southwest—nearly from Las Vegas, Nevada, to Las Vegas, New Mexico, and Durango, Mexico, to Durango, Colorado (Figure 10.1). Where possible, agricultural production was intensified if it had not been so previously. Gravity-fed canal irrigation from rivers and streams occurred in the Hohokam and Mimbres Mogollon regions. Rainfall-fed runoff irrigation was used in those parts of the Anasazi areas that lacked streams appropriate for use in irrigation. In regions where relatively high population densities could be supported, social means of integrating populations developed that may be discerned through patterned features in the archaeological record.

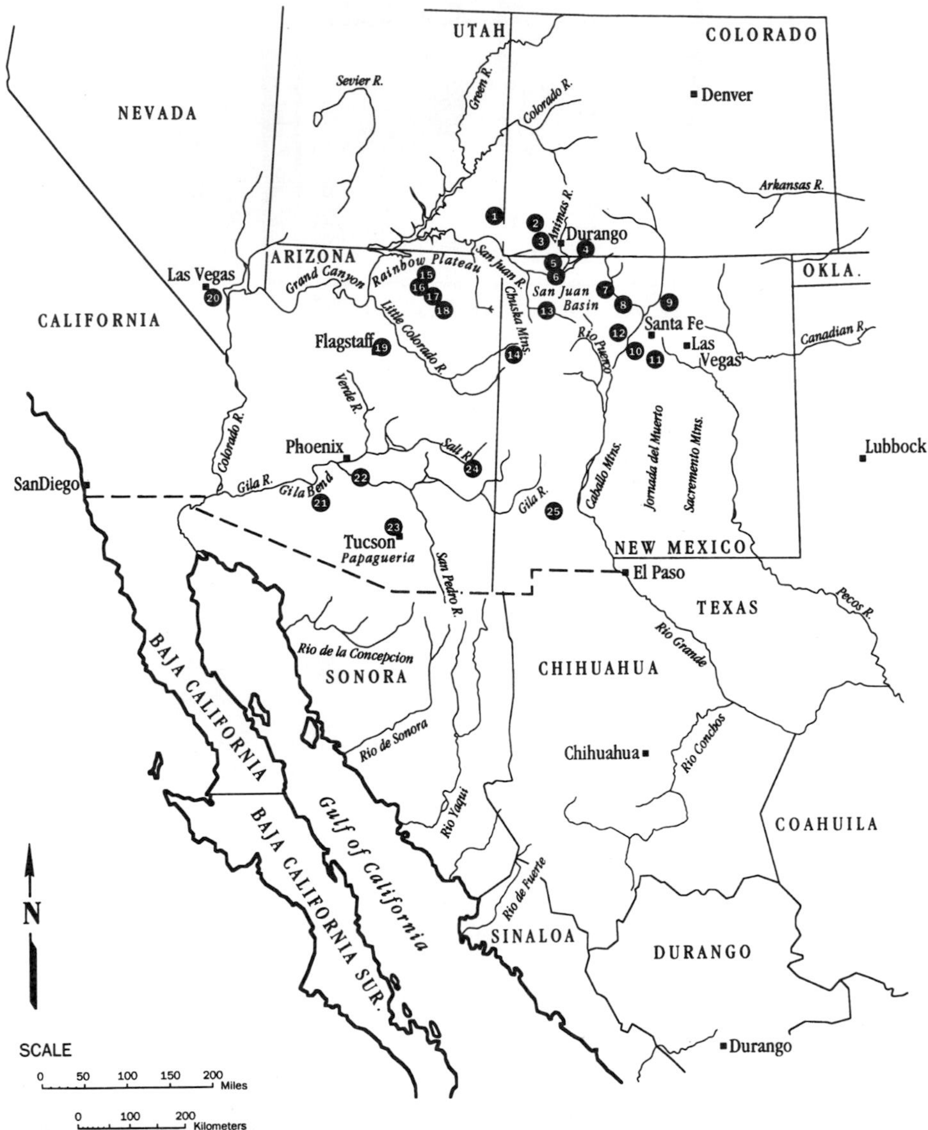

FIGURE 10.1 The sites located on this map are key to the discussion of integration in the Southwest. Key: 1 Alkali Ridge; 2 Dolores Area (Grass Mesa Village); 3 Mesa Verde (Mummy Lake, Mug House, Adobe Cave, Fire Temple, Sun Temple, Fewkes Canyon, and Chapin Mesa); 4 Chimney Rock Pueblo; 5 Aztec Ruin; 6 Salmon Ruin; 7 Gallina District; 8 Chama District; 9 Taos District; 10 Santa Fe District; 11 Galisteo Basin (Cerrillos Hills); 12 Jemez Mountains; 13 Chaco Canyon Sites; 14 Manuelito Canyon; 15 Tsegi Canyon; 16 Betatakin and Kiet Siel; 17 Long House Valley; 18 Black Mesa; 19 Winona Village and Ridge Ruin; 20 Main Ridge (Lost City and Mecca Sites); 21 Gatlin Site; 22 Snaketown; 23 Marana Community; 24 Point of Pines; 25 Mimbres Area (Mattocks Ruin, Cameron Creek Ruin, Swarts Ruin, Galaz Site, and NAN Ranch Ruin). (Map by David Underwood.)

Paralleling distinctions Irwin-Williams (1980a) drew between nucleated, aggregated, and dispersed social systems, I distinguish regionally integrated, aggregated, and dispersed categories to describe the social landscapes of the time. Briefly, regionally integrated systems have two defining characteristics. They have hierarchies of year-round settlements, and they integrate very large amounts of territory through quite formally marked systems used to produce and exchange materials, pool labor, and perhaps redistribute produce or population. The marking, in public architecture, monuments, and symbols, reflects shared ideological traditions. Regionally integrated systems are here exemplified by the Chaco Anasazi and the Classic period Hohokam. Aggregated social systems refer to those places where people resided in relatively large, year-round dwellings, generally called pueblos, with architectural features, such as kivas or special ceremonial rooms, that served to integrate large numbers of people. Aggregated systems of the eleventh and twelfth centuries are exemplified here by the Mesa Verde Anasazi, the Mimbres Mogollon, and the Kayenta Anasazi. Dispersed systems are those in which small to medium size settlements characterized the area. They occur in areas in which regional population density is lower than elsewhere at the same period. Settlements were occupied year-round but often for relatively short periods of time—a pattern sometimes called short-term sedentism, following Nelson and LeBlanc (1986). Dispersed systems of the eleventh and twelfth centuries are exemplified by the Rio Grande Valley, the Jornada Mogollon, and the Muddy and Virgin Anasazi. Within their own areas, each of these three types of systems provided subsistence and social security for generations of people, and some characteristics of these systems persisted into later periods of time while others did not.

REGIONALLY INTEGRATED SYSTEMS

During the second half of the eleventh century, a large part of the northern Southwest was involved in a regional system of interaction centered at Chaco Canyon, New Mexico. Neither the nature of this system, the way it was organized, nor the way it functioned is well understood. Yet it is the subject of a great deal of recent archaeological research and intense interest. Another large and complicated social network developed among the Classic period Hohokam at about the same time. Interpretations of both these systems and the data upon which they are based are discussed in this chapter. In the midst of and surrounding these large, regional systems, people lived in more simply organized communities—reflecting a considerable amount of adaptive diversity. Examples of these other groups are also discussed here. In the long run, those outside the Chaco and Hohokam systems may have contributed the most to the societies that came after them.

The Chaco Phenomenon

In the tenth century, a distinctive organization developed within Chaco Canyon, New Mexico. Localized at first, the system eventually incorporated an area of about

65,000 km^2 of the San Juan Basin and adjacent uplands. The term Chaco Phenomenon was first used by Cynthia Irwin-Williams (1972) to refer to this regional system. The attributes that define the Chacoan system are the presence of two different kinds of settlements, called great houses and small house sites, that were built and in use at the same time in Chaco Canyon itself; Chacoan outlier communities throughout the San Juan Basin; ancient roadways apparently linking outliers and canyon settlements; evidence of agricultural intensification in the canyon; objects that indicate widespread exchange; interaction; and perhaps some specialized production of craft items. Chacoan outliers are sites that are outside Chaco Canyon yet exhibit Chacoan style building and ceramics and are often connected to the canyon by means of a roadway or visual communication system (Judge 1979:901) (Figure 10.2). Some Chacoan outliers have associated small house communities, others do not. The nature and form of the system changed over time between AD 1000 and 1300.

Chaco Canyon itself, because of its spectacular standing masonry walls, was the subject of some of the earliest archaeological exploration in the Southwest (Jackson 1878; Simpson 1850), and some of the earliest large-scale scientific expeditions and excavations (Judd 1924, 1927; Pepper 1920; also see Lister and Lister 1981; Vivian 1990). More recent research derives primarily from a 15-year, multidisciplinary study by the Chaco Center of the National Park Service (Judge *et al.* 1981; Judge and Schelberg 1984; Lekson 1986), and sustained excavation and survey at the Chacoan outliers of Salmon Ruin (Irwin-Williams 1972, 1980b), Bis sa' ani (Breternitz *et al.* 1982), Chimney Rock Pueblo (Eddy 1977; Malville and Matlock 1993), Guadalupe Ruin (Pippin 1987), Aztec (Morris 1928; Stein and McKenna 1988; Stein and Fowler 1996), and Navajo Springs (Warburton and Graves 1992). A tremendous amount of research on the extent of the Chacoan system, its roads and outliers, resulted from surveys and excavations conducted by archaeologists in the context of cultural resources management studies (e.g., Fowler *et al.* 1987; Fowler and Stein 1992; Kinkaid 1983; Marshall *et al.* 1979, 1982; Stein and Fowler 1996). Our understanding of the changing role of Chacoan outliers has been immeasurably enhanced by the architectural studies of Fowler and Stein (1992; Stein and Fowler 1996). A comprehensive single volume synthesis of Chacoan archaeology was published by R. Gwinn Vivian (1990), along with book-length studies of aspects of Chacoan developments (e.g., Lekson 1986; Sebastian 1992). There is also an edited volume (Crown and Judge 1991) that specifically compares Chaco and the Hohokam and one (Adler 1996) that examines the aftermath of Chaco in terms of the "areas in between." This discussion makes extensive use of these resources and others cited in the text.

The View Inside Chaco Canyon The core area of Chaco Canyon is only a 16.1 km stretch along Chaco Wash, near the center of the San Juan Basin, New Mexico. The basin itself is a huge, low, dry landform with few trees. Yet despite the bleakness of the landscape and the aridity, the Anasazi built 14 magnificent pueblo great houses in Chaco Canyon between about AD 900 and 1150 (Figure 10.3). Abundant wood used in ancient construction provides an unusually precise tree-ring chronology and paleoclimatological reconstruction for Chaco Canyon (Dean and Warren 1983; Judge 1991).

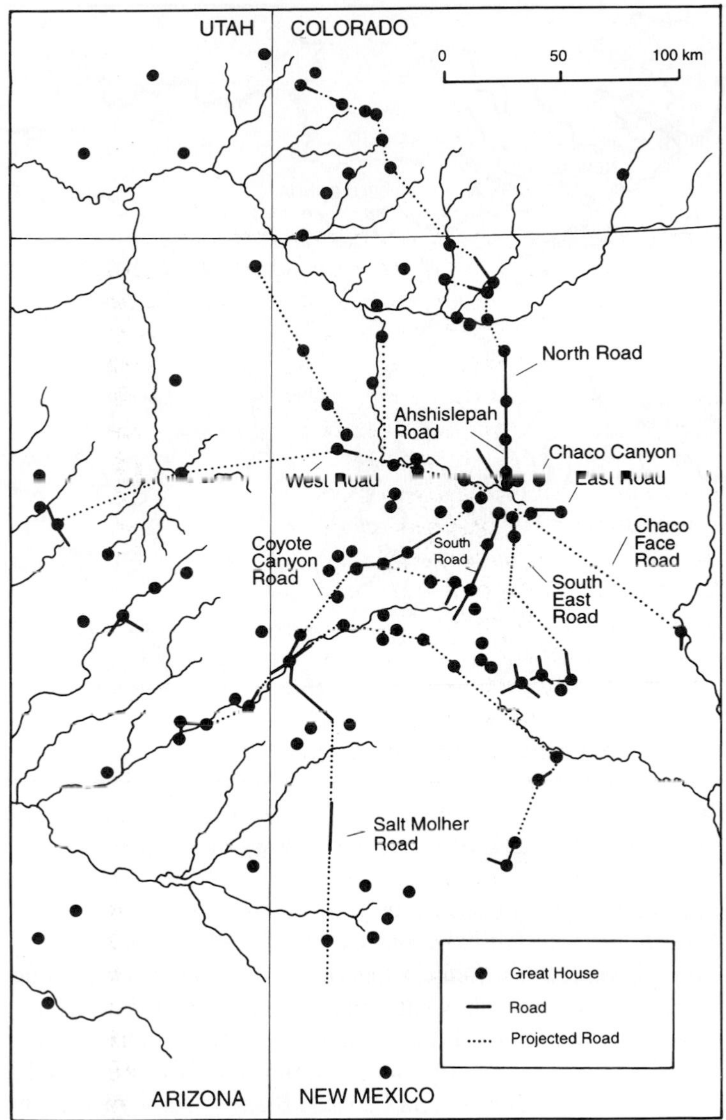

FIGURE 10.2 Chacoan outliers (closed circles) are built in Chacoan masonry style and have a Great Kiva, tower kiva, or both. They are generally linked to Chaco Canyon by an ancient roadway. Those road segments shown as solid lines have been verified on the ground. Those shown by dashed lines are documented from aerial photographs (adapted from Lekson *et al.* [1988] by Marjorie Leggitt, Leggitt Design.)

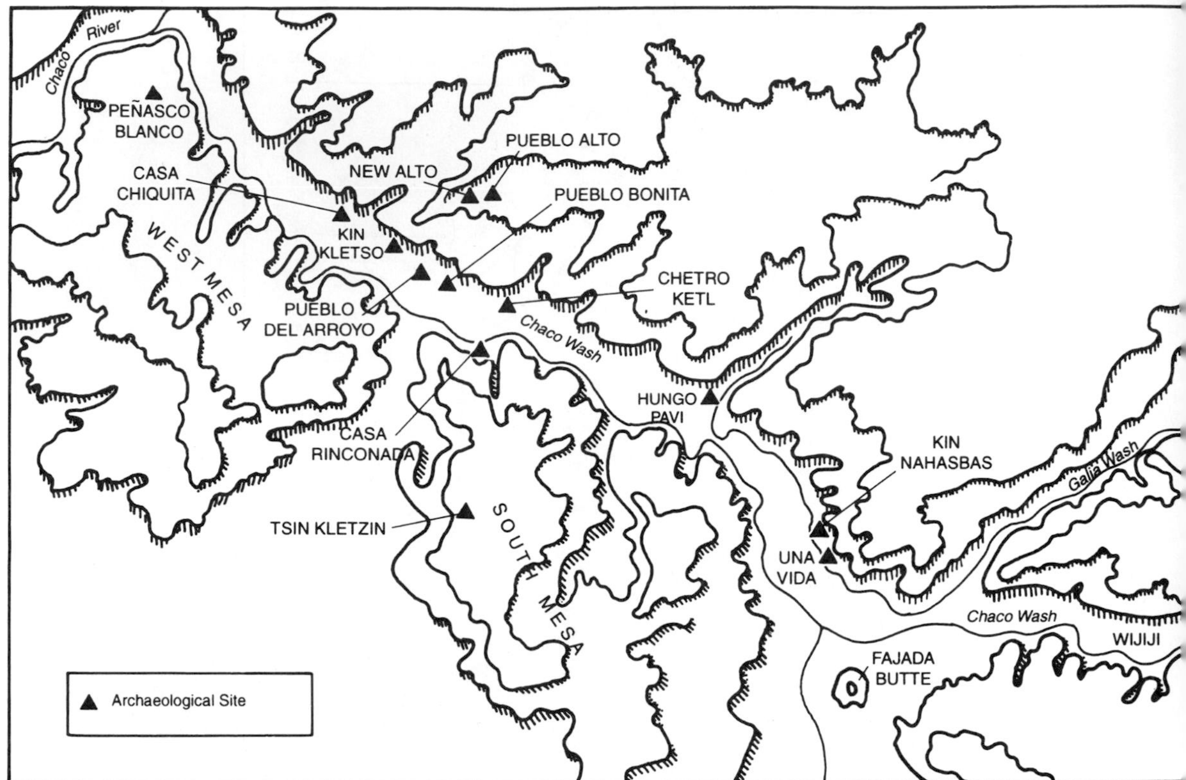

FIGURE 10.3 The 14 Great House Sites of Chaco Canyon are the nucleus of the Chacoan Regional System (adapted from Lekson *et al.* [1988] by Marjorie Leggitt, Leggitt Design.)

The chronological framework used for Chaco Canyon divides the sequence during which most construction took place into phases named for the canyon's largest and best known site, Pueblo Bonito (Figure 10.4). The Early Bonito phase dates from about AD 850 to 1000. During this period, construction of the first multistory great houses—Una Vida, Pueblo Bonito, and Peñasco Blanco—took place. This period of building is associated with Red Mesa Black-on-white, a pottery type, decorated, with black mineral paint.

The second, or Classic Bonito phase, began in about AD 1000 and lasted until about AD 1100. It was a period during which older structures were enlarged and new great houses were built. Pueblo Bonito and Chetro Ketl are the best known. Great houses are highly formal, multistory, masonry structures, often associated with an earthen berm. The masonry is of a distinctive form, called core-veneer, in which a stable inner wall of interlocked slabs is faced on either side with thin sandstone veneer. There was also a major effort devoted to the construction of great kivas, 18 of these

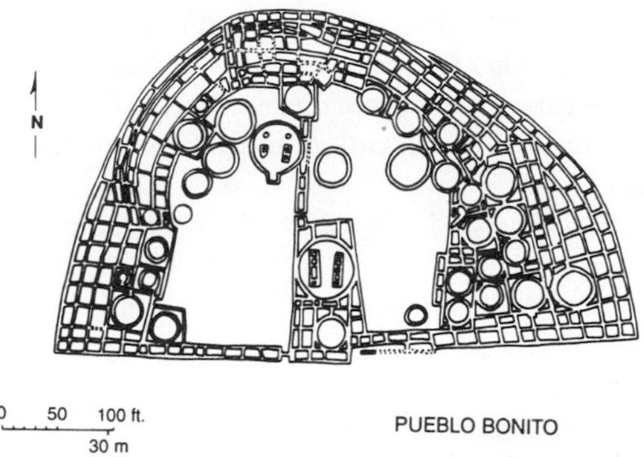

FIGURE 10.4 Pueblo Bonito (a) and Chetro Ketl (b) are the largest Great Houses in Chaco Culture National Historic Park. The side canyon next to Chetro Ketl would have received runoff from the mesa top that was then diverted to fields (drawing and photo courtesy of the U.S. National Park Service).

enormous features having been built during this time. Red Mesa Black-on-white pottery continued as before, but Gallup Black-on-white was added.

The Late Bonito or McElmo phase, between AD 1100 and 1150, witnessed changes in both building style and ceramic types. McElmo great houses are more compact than their predecessors and the masonry style that characterizes them resembles stonework of the northern San Juan–Mesa Verde area. Although there are many McElmo phase sites in Chaco Canyon (e.g., Kin Kletso, Casa Chiquita, New Alto, and

T'sin Kletsin), the center of the Chacoan world had moved north to outliers, primarily on the San Juan. This was also the time when most Chacoan roads were built. The pottery, like the architecture, shows a northern affinity. The diagnostic type is carbon black painted Chaco-McElmo Black-on-white that resembles pottery being made in the northern San Juan.

Stein and Fowler (1996) also distinguish a Post-Chaco phase dated from AD 1150 to 1250 and a Big House period of AD 1250 to 1300. The Post-Chaco phase may be represented by Pueblo del Arroyo in Chaco Canyon, but is best characterized by sites in Mañuelito Canyon, southwest of Chaco, and by one structure at Aztec on the San Juan. There was continued construction of roads and masonry walls replacing the earthen berms that had enclosed Chacoan great houses. Architecture of the Big House period consists of an elevated platform with a central sunken court (or courts), a great kiva, and a perimeter wall. It too is well-represented outside Chaco Canyon itself, although there are sites in the canyon that belong to this period. Between about AD 1200 and 1300, the few Anasazi who remained in Chaco Canyon were most closely affiliated with the northern San Juan. By 1300, Chaco Canyon and most of the northern Anasazi Southwest was no longer inhabited.

Within Chaco Canyon, the great house and small house sites are so dissimilar that it was generally believed that small house sites predated the great houses or that the two were manifestations of different cultural groups (Gladwin 1945). The term Hosta Butte phase was used to refer to the small house sites and Bonito phase to the great houses. That the two are essentially contemporary was first demonstrated by Florence Hawley Ellis (1934a, 1937a) on the basis of tree-ring dates. That the two types of sites reflect the same basic culture is shown by their similar material inventories. Because the two are contemporary, *phase* is not an appropriate designation. In his influential publications, Gwinn Vivian (1970) used the terms town and village to reflect the formal planning of great houses versus the amorphous character of the small sites, a distinction that I followed in the first edition of this book (Cordell 1984). Here, following Vivian's (1990) more recent work, I use great house and small house because most of the small house sites are too small to have been sustained multigenerational communities, while the term "town" is ambiguous with respect to organizational features.

The small house sites are not homogeneous with respect to room configuration, size, or method of wall-construction (McKenna 1984; Truell 1986; Vivian 1990); however, many are similar to the earlier Pueblo II sites throughout the Anasazi region. Small house sites are far more numerous than the great houses. Small houses are typically single-story structures, with an average of about 16 rooms. They appear to have grown accretionally, rooms having been added as needed. The small house sites are generally oriented southeast. Their walls are of somewhat irregular, simple compound masonry (Figure 10.5). Rooms are typically small (6 m^2) with low ceilings. Plazas are open, rather than being enclosed by walls or roomblocks. Kivas are also small, with vertical post or pilaster roof supports. The shapes of small kivas are diverse, with both a keyhole shape that is most common in the Mesa Verde region, and a style with a wide bench common in Chaco Canyon. Small house sites do not have great kivas (discussed below); however, a single great kiva (such as the one at the cluster of

FIGURE 10.5 BC-53 is one of the small house sites in Chaco Canyon. In contrast to the Great Houses, these are single-story structures with kivas incorporated into the roomblocks (photograph by Frank H. H. Roberts, Jr., courtesy of the U.S. National Park Service).

small sites referred to as Casa Rinconada) may have served several small house sites (Figure 10.6). Burials occur in refuse or in subfloor locations. Small house sites are distributed on both the north and south sides of Chaco Canyon and throughout much of the San Juan Basin. They are apparently more numerous in the vicinity of great houses and Chacoan outliers. The room-to-kiva ratio is approximately 6.5 to 1 (Hayes 1981a:59; Vivian 1970, 1990). Small house sites also lack tower kivas and imported luxury items.

The most striking aspect of the Chaco great houses is that they are planned structures. This does not mean that they were first constructed in their ultimate form. Tree-ring samples taken from Chacoan great houses reveal that some early great house sites in the canyon, such as Pueblo Bonito, Una Vida, Peñasco Blanco, and among the outliers, have older core sections that date to the late 800s. The site plans for these early structures are similar to large Pueblo I sites, such as Site 13 on Alkali Ridge, Utah, and Grass Mesa Village of the Dolores area, southern Colorado. However, these early portions of great houses are characterized by suites of big rooms that are not thought to have been habitation rooms because they lack features such as ash pits and hearths. The floor areas for rooms in these suites, ranging between 25 and 54 m^2, are two-thirds larger than those of typical Chacoan small houses of the same time period.

FIGURE 10.6 The Great Kiva at Casa Rinconada, Chaco Canyon served several small house sites (photographed by Steve Lekson, courtesy of the U.S. National Park Service).

The lack of habitation features argues against the sites having been simply scaled up versions of domestic sites. Hence, Windes and Ford (1992) suggest that they were used for storage. Other Chacoan great houses, such as the outlier Salmon Ruin, were built initially according to their final Chacoan form. In either case, construction episodes resulted in formal buildings reflecting a single design. In plan view, great houses are C-, D-, or E-shaped (Lekson 1984; Lekson *et al.* 1988).

Compared with small house sites, great house sites in Chaco Canyon are large, averaging 216 rooms, and multistoried, with as many as four floors (Figure 10.4). Room size is also large and ceilings are high. Great house sites were constructed of cored, veneered masonry in which the load-bearing wall core was composed of rough flat stones set in ample mortar, with each stone oriented to only one face of the wall and overlapping or abutting the stone on the reverse face, creating a structurally sound wall. The wall core was then covered on both sides with sandstone ashlar, often in alternating bands of thick and thin stones, forming various patterns. The strikingly decorative veneers (Figure 10.7) were then covered with adobe plaster or matting.

FIGURE 10.7 Decorative sandstone veneers are characteristic of Chacoan Great Houses. (a–c) From Pueblo Bonito in Chaco Canyon; (d) from Aztec, the largest of the Chacoan outliers. a, b, and c are different in style, which occurred over time (photographs of a–c courtesy of the U.S. National Park Service; photograph of d courtesy of the University of Colorado Museum).

a
b
c
d

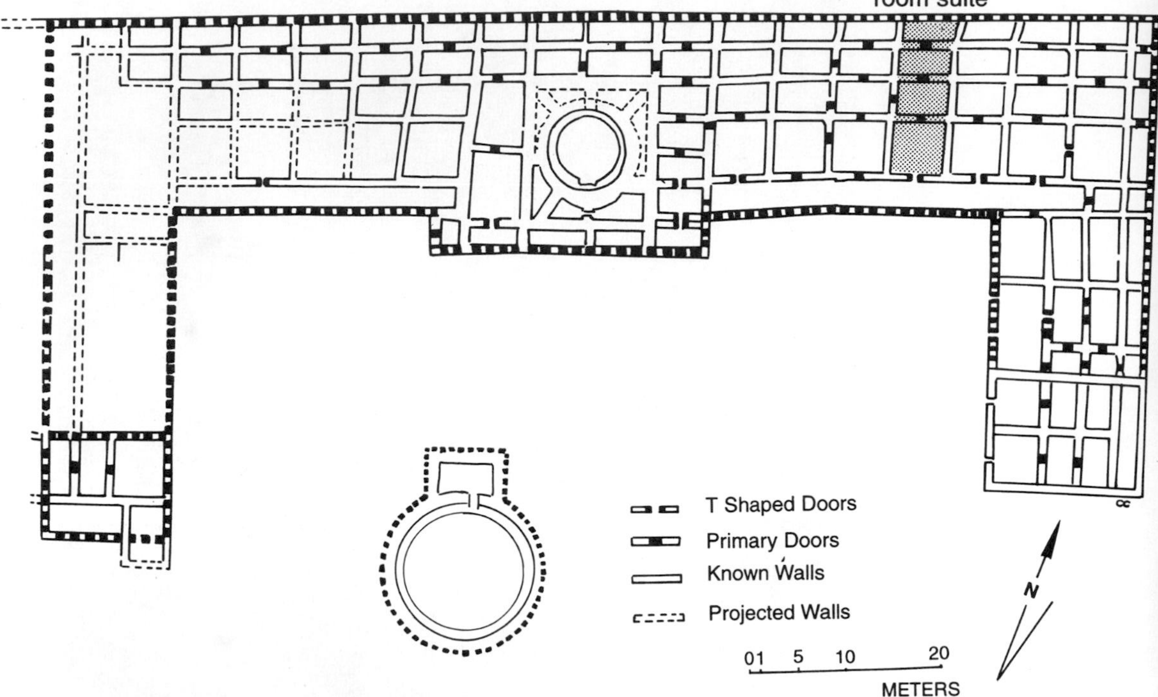

FIGURE 10.8 Plan of Salmon Ruin, Bloomfield, New Mexico. Plan shows the Chacoan construction phase III (AD 1100 to 1107) at the site. A standard room suite is shaded. (Adapted from Irwin-Williams [1980] by Charles M. Carrillo)

Great house sites are oriented to the south with plaza areas almost always enclosed by a roomblock or a high wall. A very common arrangement of interior space is the room suite, a series of rooms in a direct line from front to back linked by doorways. In such room suites, the front rooms are larger than back rooms that are thought to have served a storage function (Figure 10.8). Common architectural details include T-shaped doorways (Figure 10.9) and stone lintels (Figure 10.10).

Small kivas within the towns occur in a ratio of 1 to every 29 rooms. Some of the great house small kivas were roofed with wooden poles as though woven into a large inverted basket. In contrast to the small house site kivas, at least some of the great house small kivas had cribbed roofs supported by horizontal logs apparently placed at regular intervals along low benches. One cribbed roof was found to contain as many as 350 dressed pine timbers (Figure 10.11), many of which must have been imported from considerable distances (Lekson 1984:32; Lister and Lister 1981:79). A recent estimate indicates that at least 250,000 pine timbers were used in construction in Chaco Canyon. In the wood-poor setting of Chaco Canyon, the use of cribbed-log roofs and other structural timbers may be considered a "constructional extravagance"

FIGURE 10.9 T-shaped doorways and formal, aligned doorways with timber lintels are seen inside Pueblo Bonito, Chaco Culture National Historic Park (photo courtesy of the U.S. National Park Service).

that must have had tremendous symbolic and likely ritual meaning (Marshall and Doyel 1981:61).

Each of the nine great houses in Chaco Canyon proper has at least one great kiva in the plaza area. Isolated great kivas, great kivas associated with a group of small house sites, and great kivas at some Chacoan outliers are also documented. Chacoan great kivas are unusual, both in terms of their size and their distinctive floor features. The great kiva at Casa Rinconada is about 19.2 m in diameter; a great kiva at Chetro Ketl (Figure 10.12) is 16.8 m in diameter. Antechambers are commonly associated with great kivas, with the entry to the kiva either through recessed masonry stairways or by ladder. Floor features are oriented north-south and include square, raised fireboxes, paired masonry "vaults," and roof supports consisting either of four masonry columns

FIGURE 10.10 Massive masonry walls at Pueblo Bonito. Lintels support doorways in both upper and lower floor rooms (photo courtesy of the U.S. National Park Service).

FIGURE 10.11 Cribbed log roof of a small kiva in Pueblo Bonito. Huge numbers of logs were used to roof these structures. The logs were transported into Chaco Canyon from as far away as 60 km. An estimated 250,000 logs were used in construction in Chaco Canyon alone (photograph courtesy of the University of Colorado Museum).

FIGURE 10.12 The Great Kiva at Chetro Ketl is 16.7 meters in diameter. The standard Great Kiva features include the wall niches and encircling bench, central square raised firebox, paired rectangular masonry "vaults," and stair entryway. The antechamber beyond the stairs is also a common feature (photograph courtesy of the U.S. National Park Service).

or four massive timbers. The function of the "vaults" is not known. Suggestions range from their having been covered with boards and used as foot drums to their having been filled with earth and used as planting boxes for beans that are forced to germinate early in kivas among the Pueblos today. Huge, shaped sandstone disks were used as seatings for the roof-support timbers (Figure 10.13). Wall niches or crypts are commonly recorded for great kivas; those at Chetro Ketl II were sealed with masonry and contained strings of stone and shell beads and pendants (Vivian and Reiter 1965). Although it is difficult to estimate the depth of great kivas because the original wall height is not always known, Judd (1922:115–116) estimated that a great kiva at Pueblo Bonito had a wall height of 3.35 m. Considering the size of these structures and the

FIGURE 10.13 Great Kiva at Chetro Ketl during excavation in 1936. The massive sandstone disks were supports for the equally huge roof-support timbers (photograph courtesy of the U.S. National Park Service).

fact that they were largely subterranean, the amount of labor necessary to construct them was enormous. Fourteen tower kivas (Figure 10.14) are documented at Chacoan great houses. These are circular kivas of two or more stories. Although some are free standing, they are most often incorporated within a roomblock and enclosed by rectangular walls with rubble filling the intervening spaces.

As virtually all investigators have discussed, to their chagrin, burials are scarce at Chacoan great houses. Hayes (1981a:62) notes that only between 50 and 60 individuals can be associated with the Classic Bonito construction at Pueblo Bonito, with an estimated 695 rooms that were occupied over a period of 150 years and, according to Judd, should have experienced between 4700 and 5400 deaths. Luxury goods associated with Classic Bonito great houses include cylindrical vases, copper bells, macaw skeletons, human effigy vessels, pottery incense burners, *Strombus* or *Murex* shell trumpets,

FIGURE 10.14 Salmon Ruin, Bloomfield, New Mexico is a large Chacoan outlier. Note the similarity in ground plan to Classic Bonito style in Chaco Canyon. The arrow points to the tower kiva. The Great Kiva can be seen in the plaza (photograph courtesy of the U.S. National Park Service).

painted tablets, effigies of wood, and inlay of inlay of selenite, mica, or turquoise on shell, wood, or basketry. Many of these were found exclusively with a series of burials in the old core section of Pueblo Bonito (Aikens 1986).

Within Chaco Canyon, Classic Bonito great house sites are located only on the north side of the canyon. This directional association breaks down when the outliers are included. Hayes noted that the north-side placement of the great houses would have given them southern exposures providing greater solar radiation, making winter temperatures milder and winters slightly shorter. He also suggested that the north-side placement within the canyon proper allows for easier direct visual communication to the signaling stations that are also part of the Chacoan system. Probably most important, however, is that the north side of the canyon has access to the runoff from the intercliff zone above that was the source of irrigation water for the fields in the canyon.

The headgates, dams, and ditches of the water-control systems are on the north side of the canyon (Vivian 1974, 1990; also see Chapter 9).

That ancient roadways occured in Chaco Canyon had been known for decades to its Navajo residents and to the early archaeologists who worked there. Parts of the roads were first described in print by Holsinger (1901), and Gladwin (1945) reported that Navajos living in Chaco Canyon thought the Anasazi had used the roads to move timbers into the canyon. Judd (1927) referred to the same roads as ceremonial highways. The revelation of the 1970s was that the roadways extend far beyond the canyon confines. Subsequently, there has been a systematic attempt to define them and trace their extent (Kincaid 1983; Kincaid *et al.* 1983; Lyons and Hitchcock 1977; Obenauf 1980; Robertson 1983; Vivian 1989).

Among the most consistent attributes of the Chacoan roads is their straight course. They are not contoured to topographic relief. Changes in direction are accomplished with a sharp angular turn rather than a curve. When roads approach a major topographic obstacle, such as a cliff or ledge, they are associated with stairways or ramps. The stairways vary in form from shallowly pecked finger- and toe-holds, to masonry steps of two or three stones piled in front of a rock ledge, to well-constructed flights of wide steps with treads and risers cut out of the bedrock (Figure 10.15). Ramps are either stone or earth-filled masonry structures.

The roads vary in their form and preparation. In some instances they were cut into bedrock or through aeolian soil to a depth of about 1.5 m. Other roads were simply created by the removal of vegetation, loose soil, and debris. Some road segments were lined with masonry borders; others are visible only as slight swales on the landscape. The widths of the roadways are also distinctive. Major roadways are about 9 m wide and secondary roads are about 4.5 m wide (Vivian 1972). The degree of formality and the width of the roads are greatest in the immediate vicinity of Chaco Canyon itself or the distant outlier. The extent of the roads has been defined through the use of aerial photography, with some ground-checking and more limited excavation, but the entire road system is not completely documented (see below).

Signaling stations are arc-shaped stone structures, associated with roads, and located on high points with direct line-of-sight visibility to the Classic Bonito towns. The efficacy of the stations was demonstrated experimentally when archaeologists working in Chaco Canyon equipped themselves with railroad flares and stationed themselves at these features. At 9:00 P.M. the flares were lit and visual communication was established between each signaling station and its two neighboring stations. The only locations at which the flares could not be seen were in the vicinity of the modern town of Crownpoint, where electric lights interfered. Although some may object that the use of railroad flares does not constitute a true test, the experiment lends some credence to the interpretation of the otherwise rather enigmatic features.

The roads present two technical difficulties for archaeologists. They are difficult to date and to ground check. Because the roads are associated with Classic Bonito phase sites in Chaco Canyon, they have been tied to the major developments of the Chaco Phenomenon. For example, some of the roads lead from Chaco Canyon toward outliers such as Salmon Ruin, Aztec, and Kin Bineola. Other roads appear to lead to

FIGURE 10.15 Jackson Staircase, Chaco Canyon. Well-constructed steps cut into the bedrock are components of the Chacoan road system (photograph courtesy of the U.S. National Park Service).

specific areas where resources that were brought into Chaco Canyon were acquired, such as the Chuska Mountains, where pottery was likely produced and building timber obtained. In other instances, particularly outside the San Juan Basin, there is less evidence that roadways that are physically associated with Chacoan outliers are connected to other roads or lead to Chaco Canyon. Many of these outliers date after AD 1150, hence after the Classic Bonito phase. Stein and Fowler (1996), among others, suggest that in these situations, the road segments may represent an ideological affiliation ("earthern umbilicals") with the canyon rather than an economic or political connection to the larger system.

Various estimates of the extent of the roads have been published. At one extreme is the figure of 2400 km of ancient roadways. This large number includes all segments mapped from photographs whether or not they have been checked on the ground (Figure 10.2). The most conservative estimate, based only on segments known through "ground truth" is far less but still more than 208 km in length. As the Listers (1981: 147) state, "No other aboriginal land communication system of such magnitude and purpose has been recognized north of Mexico. Certainly it was a product of group organization, controls, and a lot of human energy." It is also, as Lekson (1991) states, the system of roads that gives coherence to what the Chacoan system of outlier great houses and communities was and to the probability that there was a system at all.

Roads Lead Outside Chaco Canyon: The Outliers Until the late 1970s, archaeologists viewed the sites in Chaco Canyon as a relatively isolated Anasazi development. The extent of the road system was first identified in aerial photographs, and later partially ground-checked. Natural erosion and modern development precelude complete ground-checking of all suspected road segments. The initial outlier surveys (Marshall *et al.* 1979; Powers *et al.* 1983) had different motives and used different criteria to identify outliers. Marshall and others (1979) were concerned with the development of the Chacoan system over time. Hence, they defined outliers that were earlier and later than the Classic Bonito construction in Chaco Canyon itself. Powers and others (1983) were more interested in connectivity and the road segments themselves became more important criteria. In both instances, there was a tendency to be more inclusive than exclusive because there was great concern that modern land development might destroy the evidence of the system before it had been well defined. Largely for these reasons, Chacoan outliers are heterogeneous in their formal characteristics, and they are defined differently by different investigators (Lekson 1991).

Judge (1991) articulated seven criteria useful for identifying outliers in addition to their being located outside Chaco Canyon proper. (1) There is a central masonry structure that is larger than the average surrounding sites in the area. (2) The central structure has large rooms, and (3) a large kiva or kivas. (4) The large structure and kiva(s) have a planned appearance. (5) There is a great kiva. (6) There is generally an ancient road and/or signaling system associated with the community of small sites at the large structure. (7) Ceramics include Chacoan types, especially Gallup Black-on-white. Using these criteria or slight modifications of them, between 70 and 110 outliers are currently listed. These vary in distance from Chaco Canyon itself and in their form. Most important, they include sites that were not built or in use simultaneously. If one were to map all the postulated Chacoan outliers, the Chacoan system would be synonymous with most of the Eastern Anasazi (Wheat 1983), the Western Anasazi, and include sites in the Mogollon area as well.

Clearly, a better understanding of the outliers and their changing relationship to Chaco Canyon and each other depends on being able to precisely date the outliers, to understand their development within their local as well as regional context, and to establish the kind of connectivity they had with Chaco Canyon. As yet, this has not been accomplished, although beginnings have been made for a handful of outliers that have been subject to excavation and recent study. These include Aztec (Morris 1915; Stein and Fowler 1996), Salmon Ruin (Irwin-Williams 1980a, 1980b), Bis sa' ani (Doyel 1992; Marshall and Doyel 1981), Chimney Rock (Eddy 1993), Guadalupe Ruin (Pippin 1987), and Navajo Springs (Warburton and Graves 1992).

Even among these sites, there is great diversity. For example, Bis sa' ani and Guadalupe Ruin are great house sites with associated communities of small houses. Bis sa' ani, a 20-room outlier on a ridgetop above Escavada Wash, just north of Chaco Canyon, was established at about AD 1130, making it contemporary with New Alto, Casa Chiquita, and Kin Kletso, among others, in Chaco Canyon, and with other outliers, especially those north of Chaco. Guadalupe is a 50-room outlier on Guadalupe Mesa, above the Rio Puerca on the far eastern edge of the San Juan Basin southeast of Chaco Canyon. It dates initially to the period AD 920 to 1050. The site was modified between 1050 and 1130 but was probably not abandoned until 1250 or 1300.

The oldest structure at Bi sa' ani is a 20-room pueblo built of puddled coursed adobe, a form of construction so far unique to Chacoan contexts in the San Juan Basin. (The use of adobe "turtle backs" and jacal occurs in the basin, but coursed adobe construction had not been documented previously.) The exterior of the structure was apparently decorated with a bright band of red plaster at the base and white plaster above it. All of the construction material used at Bi sa' ani, an estimated 1250 m^3 of rock and earth, was carried up to the ridgetop from below, and most of the rock was obtained from a source about 1 km away. Although most of the artifacts found within the structure are typical early twelfth century Bonito style, some of the ceramics are Socorro and San Marcial Black-on-white, types prevalent in the central and southern San Juan Basin and the Rio Grande Valley. The three other structures on the eastern side of the ridge consist of massive Chacoan masonry buildings, including four kivas. The ruin on the western portion of the ridge is a single enclosed masonry kiva backed by an elevated block of 10 masonry rooms. Among the artifacts from the Bi sa' ani assemblage are a cache of cult objects found in the adobe structure, five shell beads, a copper bell, and a few stone ornaments including a turquoise pendant and a highly polished jet ring. Exotic forms of ceramics (effigies, cylinder vases) were not encountered.

The artifact assemblage from Bi sa' ani does not indicate that food storage or craft-related activities (manufacture of stone tools, ceramics, etc.) were important activities at the site. Utility vessels occur in relatively high frequency, and nearly two-thirds of these exhibit carbonization, indicating that they were used for cooking rather than for storage. Corn and squash remains were recovered from the site, as were various wild plant taxa. The latter did not contain species maturing in spring or early summer, suggesting that Bi sa' ani was only fully occupied in the late summer and fall. Marshall and Doyel (1981:51–52) note that food processing and preparation do not necessarily mean that these areas had strictly domestic functions but are often associated with public functions as well. The 37 small house sites below the Bis sa' ani Great House are contemporary with it, and appear to have been established by an immigrant group. They show a high percentage of Socorro and San Marcial Black-on-white and Mogollon brown ware ceramics. Some are of puddled coursed adobe construction (Doyel 1983).

In contrast, Guadalupe Ruin, like most Chacoan outliers, is built of core veneer masonry. Pippen (1987:174) comments that while the ground plan of the site is like many similarly dated sites in the San Juan Basin, the masonry style and orientation of doorways is most like the original, core structure at Pueblo Bonito. The most abundant painted pottery associated with the Chacoan occupation, as well as on the small house sites in the vicinity, is Gallup Black-on-white. Several small fetishes and pieces of inlay were recovered, but there was, on the whole, little exotic material found at Guadalupe Ruin. Although Guadalupe Ruin is small, not connected to Chaco Canyon by a defined roadway, and the farthest east of the outliers, it exhibits characteristics, and changes over time, that are much more like the contemporary developments in Chaco Canyon than at Bis sa' ani, which is geographically closer to the canyon but was built slightly later. Only exceptionally precise dating can begin to sort out similar sequences and questions of contemporaneity among the 70 to 110 proposed Chacoan outliers. This has not been accomplished. Nevertheless, documenting changes over time will be critical to understanding the "Chaco Phenomenon."

The Chaco Phenomenon Redux Until the 1970s, archaeologists discussing relationships between Chaco Canyon and the greater Southwest often invoked traders from Mesoamerican civilizations as instigators of the developments at Chaco (DiPeso 1974; Hayes 1981a; Kelley and Kelley 1975). The *pochteca* were a class of long-distance traders, middlemen, and sometimes spies who occupied special status within Aztec society. The Aztec period in Mesoamerica occurred several hundred years after the Chaco Phenomenon; however, the model was used as an analogy suggesting that a group of similar long-distance traders operated out of earlier states in Mesoamerica and in their activities, created the Chaco Phenomenon. Even the most ardent devotees of indigenous development of the Chaco Phenomenon do not deny that there was trade with areas far to the south. The presence of macaw skeletons indicates trade, as do copper bells and possibly shell inlay. Documenting trade from north to south is far more difficult. At present, it seems most reasonable to consider the few items of Mesoamerican origin in Chaco as evidence of some long-distance trade, principally in luxury goods. Yet, there are enough specific differences between the other items mentioned and their supposed Mesoamerican counterparts to question that derivation (e.g., Obenauf 1980; Weaver 1981), and some of the traits themselves seem to be logical developments within the Anasazi system (e.g., irrigation devices).

Irwin-Williams began the discussion of the Chaco Phenomenon in the context of her excavations at Salmon Ruin, a huge Chacoan outlier of about 290 rooms, a great kiva, and a tower kiva built in three planned building episodes between 1088 and 1106 (Figure 10.14). Excavations indicate that foundations for the entire town were laid out prior to construction. Productive specialization at Salmon was inferred from milling rooms and a room that contained metates in all stages of manufacture, maintenance, and repair. The milling rooms each contained an average of six to eight milling stones

FIGURE 10.16 Chacoan pitcher. Unusual forms such as this are found at Chacoan Great House sites but not at the small house sites. At Salmon Ruin, the forms are more frequently associated with the Great Kiva than other parts of the site (photograph courtesy of the Museum of New Mexico, neg. no. 21840).

set in place, but there were only four such milling rooms among the rooms dating to the Chacoan occupation of the site.

The large front rooms at Salmon Ruin contained high frequencies of jars of all kinds, indicating a primary storage function. Ceremonial features, such as the great kiva, had high frequencies of bowls and unusual forms such as canteens and pitchers (Figure 10.16), suggesting food consumption and ceremonial use but not food preparation or storage. The wares represented at Salmon include both locally produced San Juan types and intrusive Cibola ceramics. Irwin-Williams (1980a) used the distributions of these to examine possible origins of the founders of the pueblo, which assumes that the ceramics were excavated from areas in which they were used rather than just discarded. She found that locally produced San Juan pottery dominates the room suites, suggesting that the potters belonged to the local population. However, she rejected the idea that the founding population was purely local and borrowed ideas and traded ceramics from the Chaco. She states this is unlikely because

> what is present in these large outliers is not simply a group of "traits," objects, or architectural characteristics. Rather, it involves an integrated cultural phenomenon reflecting a high degree of

> technical knowledge and specialization and a centralized authority structure, tight social control and membership in a complex network economically and physically linked to the Chaco (Irwin-Williams 1980a:163).

The distribution of ceramic wares imported from the Cibola area was, in fact, neither random throughout the pueblo nor patterned in a way that would indicate general accessibility to imported goods. Rather, the Cibolan ceramics were concentrated in the residences on the west side of the pueblo and at specialized activity areas such as the milling rooms, the milling-stone production and repair room, and the tower kiva and its associated rooms. This distribution suggests that the founding population was composed of both a local San Juan group and a group of Chacoan origins, and that the specialized ceremonial and production and processing activities were controlled by the Chacoan elements. The distribution of Narbona Pass chert, an imported, high-quality lithic material, essentially follows that of the imported Cibolan ceramics and lends additional support to the idea that specific activities involved personnel with access to the Chacoan system.

The research at Salmon also concerned itself with the question of social or economic ranking. Non-Cibolan imported ceramics, which might be considered status items, were found not to distribute with the Chaco-related group. Although differential mortuary treatment is a good indicator of social ranking, in the Salmon case, as with other Chacoan sites, the lack of burials precluded this kind of inquiry. In fact, only three burials could be related to the Chacoan occupation at Salmon. Finally, the standardization in both size and arrangement of the room suite units indicated no evidence of internal social or economic ranking with regard to differential use or control of space within the site.

There are two, not necessarily conflicting, models of the nature of the Chacoan system that are imbedded in Irwin-Williams' discussion and most of those that followed her. One model is primarily economic. It views the system in the context of production of good crops and craft items. The roads are interpreted as means of transporting goods from outliers to the central canyon, perhaps for redistribution. The second model views the system as primarily ideological. The roads become symbolic connections between communities and interactions are in the form of pilgrimages at which food, which may be imported, is incidentally consumed. In most models of Chacoan development, their authors argue that the emphasis of the system—more or less ideological or less economic—changed over time.

Another regional interpretation of the Chaco Phenomenon emphasizes the potentially integrative nature of Chacoan astronomical observations. Agricultural peoples throughout the world are concerned with calendrical observations. Modern Pueblo peoples make such observations for the timing of ritual and secular activities. A number of investigators have examined alignments of architectural features and rock art for their relevance to astronomical observation. None of these studies is conclusive, but some results are suggestive. For example, two third-story, exterior, corner windows at Pueblo Bonito may have been used to record the sunrise at the winter solstice (Reyman 1976). In a widely cited case, Sofaer and others (1979) describe a solar marking construct consisting of boulders and a spiral petroglyph at Fajada Butte. Others (Reyman 1980)

FIGURE 10.17 Solstice window at Pueblo Bonito. The window may have been positioned to permit the observance of the sunrise at winter solstice (photograph courtesy of the U.S. National Park Service).

are not convinced that it is associated with the Anasazi occupation at Chaco. Wall niches in the great kiva at Casa Rinconada have been related to observations of the sunrise at solstices and equinoxes (Figure 10.17) (Morgan 1977; Williamson *et al.* 1977), but this case is ambiguous because the observations would not be possible if the great kiva were roofed.

W. James Judge (1989) notes that the three earliest great houses in Chaco Canyon, Pueblo Bonito, Una Vida, and Peñasco Blanco, are each located at the confluence of major drainages with Chaco Wash. He suggests they may have controlled the agricultural land associated with these drainages and may therefore have accumulated significant amounts of surplus because of the relatively benign rainfall regime of the time. Judge suggests that in addition to surplus agricultural production, the sites in Chaco Canyon began to play a central role in the processing of turquoise. Turquoise does not naturally occur within Chaco Canyon, or the San Juan Basin. The closest source area is the Cerrillos Hills in the Galisteo Basin south of Santa Fe, New Mexico. Nevertheless, turquoise was processed at tenth-century sites in Chaco Canyon, and Judge suggests that in obtaining turquoise and turning it into finished items important in ritual, the residents of Chaco may have been developing a commodity that could be exchanged for food when conditions worsened. There are no Chacoan outliers in the vicinity of the Cerrillos Hills; however, it is important to Judge's model that the earliest outliers, such as Guadalupe Ruin, do lie to the south of Chaco Canyon.

During the eleventh and beginning of the twelfth centuries, the paleoclimatic data indicate variable conditions for agricultural production followed by a period during which rainfall was relatively abundant for sustained intervals. This was also a time when there was a great deal of new construction in Chaco Canyon and when the older sites were enlarged. Judge (1989) notes that among the new great houses, such as Pueblo Alto, there is no longer a direct connection with the confluence of drainages. Other considerations seem more important to site locations. Judge maintains that Chaco's becoming a major center was tied to the nonmaterial, primarily ritual, aspects of society. He states that in the AD 1000s, periodic visits to the canyon to obtain turquoise became increasingly formal under some kind of ritual metaphor. Concurrently, alliances with the outlying communities would become more formalized as a way of integrating communities through exchange of nonritual material goods. Finally, according to Judge (1989:239–240), "as the system became formalized—that is, as it began to develop into a true system—administration of the exchange networks would have become necessary and could easily have fallen to those residents of Chaco Canyon, particularly if turquoise was the primary material symbol of the ritual and was controlled by the residents of Chaco."

During the period of favorable moisture conditions, between AD 1045 and 1080, construction at great houses in the canyon increased tremendously but most of the building was of storage rooms. Judge suggests that the number of people resident in the canyon at this time was not very great. Because there were facilities in the canyon for many more people than probably lived there permanently, Judge argues that the canyon had become a locus for periodic pilgrimages during which food and other goods were distributed through centers under religious sanctions.

The McElmo phase in the canyon, and the basin, began with a series of changes that indicate a reorganization of the Chacoan system. McElmo phase buildings are compact, generally lacking open plaza areas, and more closely resembling structures in the northern San Juan area (Figure 10.18). Rooms and passageways in older buildings at Chaco were subdivided into smaller spaces. There was a renewed intensity of construction of village sites. Judge suggests that these changes, in addition to the abundance of Chaco-McElmo Black-on-white pottery, indicate that Chaco was no longer central to the organization of the region. Rather, Chaco seems to have become, once again and after a long period of time, primarily residential. The focus of a different kind of regional organization that emerged at this time, Judge proposes, may have been at Aztec or Salmon, one of the two huge northern outliers. Judge emphasizes the observation that activity in Chaco Canyon did not decline at this time. In fact, it may

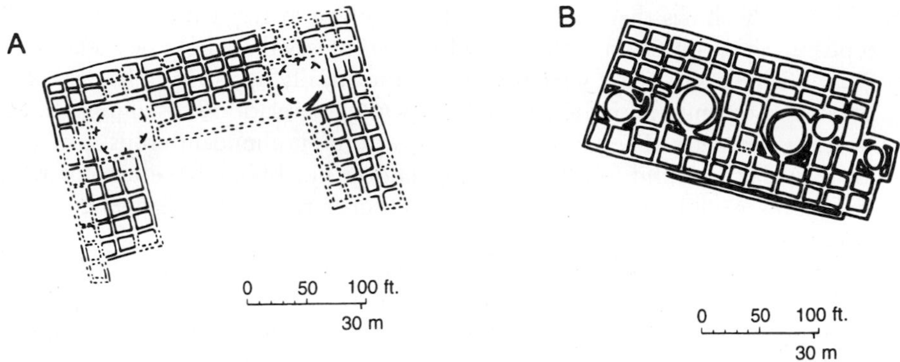

FIGURE 10.18 (A) Wijiji and (B) Kin Kletso are McElmo-style buildings, showing compact site plans (courtesy of the U.S. National Park Service).

have increased with a larger fully resident population. However, Chaco was no longer the ideological or physical center of the region.

Finally, a major drought that began in 1130 and lasted until 1180 coincided with decline and change in the Chacoan regional system. The evidence for these changes is a lack of new construction after 1130 in the canyon and at some outliers. There is also a hiatus in trash deposition at some sites, such as Pueblo Alto. Judge remarks that the "end" of the Chacoan system does not appear to coincide with evidence of violence in the canyon itself. The abandonment of structures seems to have been orderly, with most useful items being taken, presumably by those who were departing. Judge suggests that the end of the system was triggered by environmental factors and perhaps further encouraged by prior "supersaturation" of the canyon. He maintains that the success of the Chacoan system may have brought many more people into the canyon than it could support, even periodically, if there were a decrease in resources. The Chaco decline is, in part, attributed to its success.

In sum, Judge's (1989) model for Chaco emphasizes the variable climatic conditions of the basin and the ability some residents of Chaco would have to buffer some of that variability by virtue of their location at the confluence of two drainage systems. Later on, they buffered crop deficits by producing turquoise objects needed for ritual. The fluorescence of Chaco is attributed to its role in bringing food into the canyon and redistributing it out through periodic pilgrimage fairs. Judge's scenario, like some others, characterizes the entire basin and Chaco as marginal for agriculture. Hedging against local shortages in production is accomplished largely through the mechanism of redistributing food. Redistribution is a general form of exchange, described in the ethnographic literature. It requires that food be amassed in one place and then given out according to the social rules in the particular society in the course of fulfilling social and ritual obligations.

Lynne Sebastian (1992) offers a different view. She used retrodicted precipitation information from tree-ring analyses to develop a computer simulation of annual crop yields. Her study shows that severe crop deficits were infrequent during the Early Bonito phase. She proposes that the agricultural surpluses that could be accumulated during the Early Bonito phase were used opportunistically by the local leaders of the early great house communities to establish dependency relationships among villages that were less fortunate. The Chacoan leaders, with their abundant crops, could "afford" to provide feasts and festivals for their poorer neighbors, in return for which these neighbors would owe them their loyalty. Furthermore, the leaders competed among themselves for followers by being generous.

During the eleventh century, Sebastian (1992) argues that power in Chaco was related to religious knowledge, but that followers were drawn to particular leaders because of their success in competitive displays of power and wealth that are primarily visible today in architecture. She maintains that eventually, the great houses became hulks of featureless rooms, many built and sited so as to emphasize their mass rather than serve specific functions. In the same way, she states, the roads, the elaborate veneer walls, the wooden floors, the wooden roofs in a treeless desert all seem to be constructed for the sake of ostentation.

Sebastian argues that the outlying communities may reflect one of two situations. Some may have been the client communities of particular Chacoan leaders, owing periodic labor and continuing loyalty. Others, she suggests, may have organized themselves in order to mimic the successful postures of the Chacoan leaders, a behavior documented in the anthropological literature of various parts of the world (Flannery 1972). In contrast to Judge, Sebastian considers Chaco Canyon itself somewhat of an oasis in a poor and unpredictable area. She suggests that leaders use whatever they can to consolidate and further expand their leadership power, and that if leaders are successful, others outside the system may use the trappings of that success to their own advantage. Yet a different perspective is offered by Gwinn Vivian.

R. Gwinn Vivian (1989, 1990) considers the differences between the great house communities and the small house sites in Chaco, at least initially, to be a result of two different ethnic populations from different geographic derivations. One group originated south of Chaco in the Red Mesa area, the other north of Chaco in the San Juan River country. Vivian's view depends upon an analogy he makes between the presence of irrigation features in association with the great houses of Chaco and the kind of organization present among the Rio Grande Pueblos, where irrigation agriculture has long been practiced. He finds an economic explanation for the roads largely untenable because there are several instances in which roads run parallel to one another for miles for no apparent reason. Unlike some who see the great houses as largely empty ceremonial constructs, Vivian views both great houses and small house sites as primarily residential. The great house populations are differentiated because they managed, as well as profited from, the runoff irrigation systems he discovered.

Vivian's explanation for regional aspects of the Chacoan system, the roads and outlier communities, is that they were established by groups from Chaco Canyon who were seeking improved farmland on the more productive edges of the San Juan Basin. The outliers were often established within existing small house communities but were linked to Chaco Canyon by roads that had both functional and symbolic purposes.

FIGURE 10.19 Sedentary-period Hohokam jars. Sacaton Red-on-buff jars with pronounced vessel shoulders (courtesy of the Arizona State Museum).

Their symbolic function was to link certain outliers with their parent villages or, more generally, their Chacoan homeland.

In all of the scenarios discussed, the failure of Chaco and the regional system is linked to the major drought that began in 1130. If prior to this time, almost any agricultural strategy was seen to work, by 1140 or 1150 the drought was so severe that virtually nothing did. However the system functioned, it did manage to produce agricultural surpluses in some years, and these fed workers at least while they built and plastered walls, carried timbers, and ground turquoise beads. Surplus production was not possible anywhere in the 1130s and 1140s or, if some small surplus could be produced, perhaps no one wanted to use it to pay for the trappings of the failed management. In the end, although the Chaco system no longer functioned, Chacoan symbols, such as aspects of Chacoan architecture, road segments, tower kivas, and berms, continued for two centuries and perhaps longer (Stein and Fowler 1996). For a time, Aztec was a northern center of the post-Chaco era. Eventually perhaps Chaco was simply a memory used and reflected among people whose worlds were very different from those ever experienced by the eleventh-century residents of Chaco Canyon.

The Late Sedentary and Classic Period Hohokam

The period between AD 1000 and 1250 cross-cuts two divisions of the Hohokam chronology, the Sedentary and the Classic, during which there were major changes in the ways Hohokam society was organized. Nevertheless, during the late Sedentary and Early Classic, the Hohokam were organized into multisite communities, and Hohokam settlement extended over a very large area. The Gila and Salt River basins, in the vicinity of modern Phoenix, are considered the Hohokam core area because there are more large sites with elaborate features such as ball courts and platform mounds, more decorated pottery (Figure 10.19), and the most extensive irrigation systems in this location. Outside the core area, evidence of Hohokam settlement extended over an enormous region—from Flagstaff to Gila Bend and Point of Pines to south of Tucson. Evidence of interaction among communities throughout the region allows us to describe a regional system that changed over time. This section makes use of data from recent excavations, surveys, and syntheses that cover the Hohokam "core" of the Gila and Salt basins, the region north of Phoenix, the Tucson Basin, and the lower Gila (Doelle and Wallace 1991; Doyel 1980, 1991; Fish and Fish 1991; Fish *et al.* 1980; Fish *et al.* 1992; Netizel 1991; Wilcox 1980, 1991; Wilcox and Sternberg 1983; Wood and McAllister 1980).

The basic organizational units of Hohokam sites, courtyard groups, village segments, villages, and communities, that were established in the larger sites of the Colonial period (see Chapter 9), continue into the Sedentary. Villages with ballcourts appear to have been focal or central to a community that consisted of both smaller villages and scattered rancherías. In the largest village sites, houses in the inner habitation zone tend to be more formal in arrangement of the courtyard groups than those outside the inner zone. While there is no evidence that there were status differences among these households, there appears to have been differential treatment of the dead. Doyel (1980) found that some cremations are associated with quantities of mortuary offerings, such as figurines, finely serrated projectile points, and copper bells. Other cremations have only a few sherds or lack grave goods entirely. Ritual objects dominate Sedentary period crafts and are the most elaborate produced at any time by the Hohokam. Neitzel (1991) suggests that they were produced by part-time specialists. Craft items include serrated projectile points, figurines, shell beads, heavy shell bracelets, carved shell and stone ornaments, Strombus trumpets, and etched and painted shell ornaments. These and imported items, such as copper bells, again, occur at the larger sites. At Snaketown, a very large site, an unusually high 40 percent of the Sedentary ceramics are painted, and very large storage jars, some holding up to 30 gallons, are also found in Sedentary period contexts (Figure 10.20).

A complex set of relationships seems to have pertained with respect to Hohokam shell procurement, manufacture, and exchange. The Gulf of California and the Pacific are the ultimate sources of the shell, but shell ornaments were apparently manufactured in only some locations and differentially distributed to others. In a study that remains suggestive rather than conclusive because of differences in sample size, McGuire and Schiffer (1982:245–259) showed that sites with the most unfinished shell items, indicating manufacture, and the lowest number of finished shell items, occur in the western Papagueria. Sites in the eastern Papagueria, on the other hand, have significantly less shell, but most of this shell is in the form of finished items. Sites in the Gila Bend and the Salt drainage are similar to each other, but different from either group of Papagueria sites in that they have an intermediate amount of shell and an intermediate amount of unfinished shell. McGuire and Schiffer (1982:249) propose that the western Papagueria served as a specialized center for the procurement and manufacture of shell for exchange to the Gila Bend and Gila-Salt core. Within this network, the relative roles of the western and eastern Papagueria were socially defined because the eastern Papagueria is closer to the Gulf of California than either Gila Bend

FIGURE 10.20 Sedentary-period Hohokam ceramics (collections of the Arizona State Museum; photograph courtesy of the Arizona State Museum).

or the Gila and Salt basins, yet little shell manufacturing occurred there. Masse (1980) has suggested that the western Papagueria may have been trading shell to the Gila Bend and Gila and Salt core area for agricultural produce, an idea that merits further investigation.

Although the Hohokam core centers near Phoenix, the desert near modern Gila Bend must have had an especially close relationship with the core. Among the most elaborate Sedentary Hohokam sites recorded is the Gatlin site near Gila Bend (Wasley 1960; Wasley and Johnson 1965). The site consisted of a platform mound that was modified and repaired through six stages of construction, each time being capped with caliche plaster. Eventually the platform mound consisted of a flat-topped rectangular structure, 3.7 m high, with sloping sides measuring about 29 m in length, 21 m in width. In addition to the platform mound, the Gatlin site contained 22 trash mounds, two oval ballcourts, two crematoria, and an irrigation canal. The site yielded evidence of the manufacture of shell jewelry, finished shell objects, copper bells, and a macaw skeleton. Despite extensive testing throughout the site, only two pithouses were located, indicating that the Gatlin site was a highly specialized ceremonial site. Data

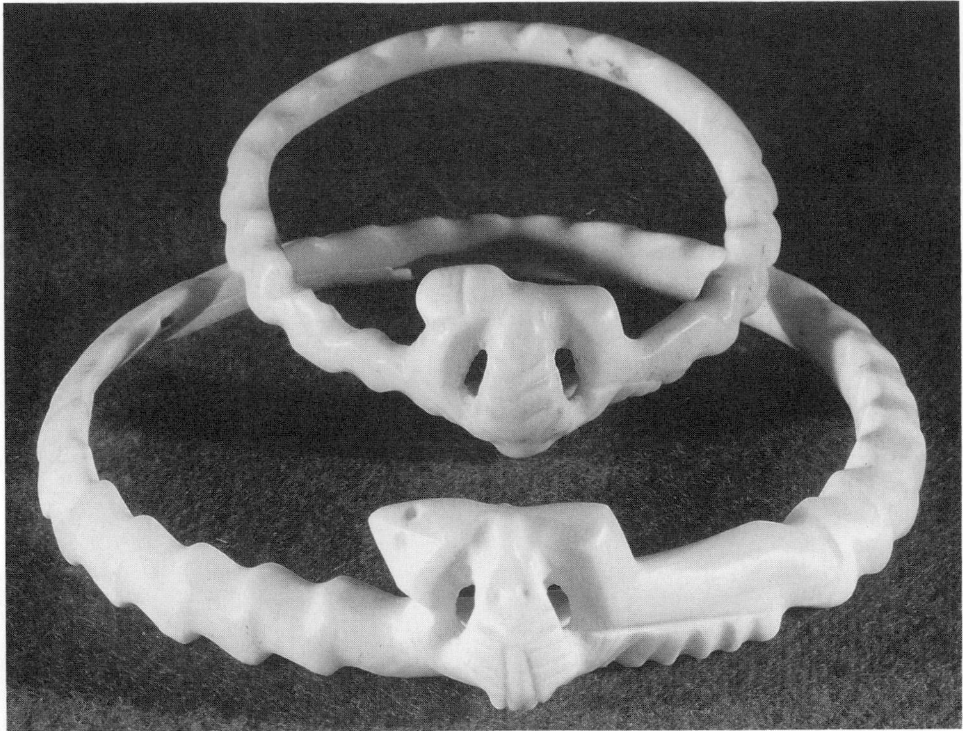

FIGURE 10.21 Hohokam shell bracelets. These are glycymeres shell carved with birds and snake motifs. Shell items may have been produced in the western Papagueria and widely traded (photograph by Helga Teiwes, courtesy of the Arizona State Museum).

from site survey and excavation indicate that the population of the Gila Bend area reached its greatest density during the Sedentary period.

Another complex set of relations existed between the Hohokam core and areas to the north, particularly the Verde Valley and Flagstaff region (Fish *et al.* 1980). The Verde Valley sites, perhaps in part because they are closer to the Gila and Salt basins, exhibit more Hohokam items than do the Flagstaff-area sites. Some specific items, such as copper bells, are lacking in the Verde Valley sites, however, but are present near Flagstaff. Although full-scale migrations of Hohokam colonists have been postulated to account for Hohokam items in the Verde and Flagsaff regions, this is not supported by finding a complete complex of mundane Hohokam domestic items. From the Pioneer and early Colonial period, a scattering of core area Hohokam ceramic sherds occurs on sites in the Verde Valley and around Flagstaff. In the Sedentary period, when Verde Valley sites consist of both very large villages and dispersed, ranchería settlements, ballcourts and mounds occur at the larger sites. At one Verde Valley site, both local and Hohokam style pithouses were found in addition to unfinished argillite items in Hohokam styles, and large numbers of shell bracelets (Figure 10.21). After AD 1000, the settlement pattern in the Verde changed, and large villages no longer occurred in the upper valley, but were present in the middle Verde and continued to feature public architecture, including adobe-capped mounds.

The distributions of Hohokam traits north of Phoenix have been interpreted as representing changing patterns of interregional trade. Fish and others (1980) suggest that before the Sedentary period, trade was down-the-line or village-to-village trade, which can produce geographically broad chain-like networks that explain the presence of Pioneer and early Colonial Hohokam sherds on Flagstaff-area sites. The Hohokam may have provided the Flagstaff area with a few items of Mexican origin, such as copper bells, macaws, and onyx ornaments. From AD 700 to 1000, Verde Valley sites, like Sedentary period sites in the Hohokam core area, consist of both very large villages and ranchería settlements. As in the core area, ballcourts and mounds occur only at the larger sites. Fish and others (1980) suggest that this may be evidence of a more intensive trade mechanism, which they term expeditionary trade, in which one party travels to the source of the desired goods. Traders may develop relations with local people who procure resources for exchange, or they may extract the resources themselves. They (Fish *et al.* 1980) observe that the establishment of expeditionary trade may depend on the nature and status of the resident population.

With increased and more intensive trade relations, formalized trade routes are expected to develop. Two of these are tentatively identified between the Verde and Flagstaff regions (Fish *et al.* 1980). The authors further suggest that trade fairs or periodic markets would occur during periods of most active trade, and that these activities might be associated with ceremonial activities and formalized trading centers. It is possible that, with regular predictable trade, professional full- or part-time traders may be present in the resource area. Pilles (1979) suggests that this situation may account for the presence of a "typical" Sacaton phase pithouse at Winona Village. It is also possible that the famous "magician" burial from Ridge Ruin (McGregor 1943), near Winona Village, was of an individual involved in the interregional trade.

Most investigators interpret the large geographic extent of the Sedentary Hohokam as evidence of a shared ideology that also served as an institution for economic and social interaction. As noted, Wilcox (1991) suggested that ballcourts reflect basic elements in the Hohokam world view in that they were distinctive structures carrying the meaning that those using them shared elements of a common belief system, but the distribution of ballcourts is so great that it is likely that local groups participated differentially in the Hohokam system of beliefs and exchange. During the Sedentary, the system extended far beyond the Hohokam area, incorporating locations at which resources such as red argillite, serpentine, turquoise, obsidian, and jet were obtained.

If Hohokam ballcourts are considered simply indications of a certain level of social integration, the trade network extended from Gila Bend on the west to the Point of Pines area on the east, and from Tucson to Flagstaff. Given the enormousness of this area, it is not surprising that considerable variability would characterize the "Hohokam" presence. It would appear from the data presented that some of the variability can be related to the character of local populations involved in Hohokam interactions and the nature and degree of intensity of the Hohokam presence. The data do not

FIGURE 10.22 Hohokam copper tinkler bell. Copper bells appear in the Sedentary period and were widely traded to some but not all sites (illustrated by Charles M. Carrillo).

indicate the establishment of pure Hohokam colonies in most areas; however, whether Hohokam traders stimulated the development of local social complexity or simply operated within a sphere of already highly organized groups is not known. The excavation of sites of different periods and of different sizes within those periods is necessary to clarify this issue.

Some aspects of and questions about the Hohokam system, during the Sedentary period, are similar to those discussed for the eleventh century Chaco system. In both cases, structures with great ideological significance (ballcourts vs. great houses and great kivas) were established in areas where irrigation allowed expansion of agricultural production and during a time of relatively abundant rainfall throughout the Southwest. The system expanded outside these core areas, as evidenced by the distribution of ball courts and mounds in one case and Chacoan outliers in the other. The specific structures suggest the importance of the ideological component as the context for development of a regional system. In each case there is less indication of actual colonists than of local populations accepting the ideology, perhaps along with a few individuals, and participating in the exchange networks differentially. In both cases, sets of distinctive esoteric artifacts occur regionally only on some sites (Chacoan cylindrical vessels, turquoise, inlay, pyrite mirrors, copper bells, and parrots; Hohokam serrated projectile points, large quantities of elaborately made shell items, carved stone, copper bells, and parrots) (Figure 10.22). In neither case is there extensive evidence of social ranking or stratification. Some burials have many more craft items than others but households appear to be equal. Largely because of the shell in the Hohokam area, the actual evidence of manufacture and exchange of items throughout the system is much better documented in that case than for Chaco.

By the end of the Sedentary, at about AD 1150, the nature of Hohokam settlement changed. This is remarkably synchronous with the end of the Classic Bonito phase construction in Chaco Canyon itself and the change there to more domestic use of space. During the succeeding Classic period in the Hohokam core area, irrigation canals reached their maximum extent, and it was at this time that communities along a single canal would have had to cooperate in order to allocate water and maintain the canals. Settlements interacting in these ways have been termed "irrigation communities," at least 17 of which have been documented (Masse 1991; Wilcox 1991).

Most of the 206 ballcourts at 165 sites (Figure 10.23), were in use at 750–1000, but after about 1250, no new ball courts were built (Wilcox 1991). Large, rectangular mounds were built at more than 40 sites between 1150 and 1300. Villages consisted of clusters of houses and mounds, often surrounded by rectangular-shaped walled enclosures made of adobe and referred to as compounds. Pithouses and surface structures built with adobe, wood, and stone were constructed within the compound wall. Doyel (1991) states that although there is variation, the number of houses within a compound is similar to the number of earlier pithouses in the earlier courtyard pattern, which suggests organizational continuity. In the mid-1200s, wall construction became more massive and some multistoried buildings were constructed. The four-story structure at Casa Grande is an example of the culmination of this kind of massive building. Wilcox (1987) has suggested that Casa Grande served as an elite residence that permitted astronomical observations to be made.

Between 1250 and 1325, the function of the mounds changed in that houses were constructed on them and access to these houses was impeded by walls (Gregory 1991). The remaining population was housed in off-mound compounds and in outlying units. Doyel (1991:255), noting that most Hohokam did not live on platform mounds or even in compounds, suggests that the residential use of platform mounds represents a "consolidation of power on the part of local elites."

As the increased irrigation canals suggest, Hohokam agriculture expanded during this period. New types of spindle whorls, which allowed spinning of very fine threads, indicate that cotton textiles may have been a commodity produced by specialists. Neitzel (1991) states that while the specialist-produced ritual craft items of the Sedentary period were no longer made, specialized production of utilitarian objects (textiles, tabular knives, ground stone axes) and status symbols (shell and stone jewelry) occur at sites with platform mounds.

Evidence of productive specialization at the village level is provided by the Classic period Marana community in the Santa Cruz drainage, northern Tucson Basin (Fish *et al.* 1992; also see Chapter 9). During the Sedentary period, there were two ballcourt communities of about equal size, one on the Santa Cruz River, the other on the pediment of the Tortolita Mountains (Figure 10.24). Population in the Classic seems to have trebled from previous levels, suggesting immigration as well as in situ growth (Fish and Fish 1972:103). In the early Classic the ballcourt communities coalesced, spanning the basin from river to mountains. A platform mound site, supplied by a canal, was built on a poorly watered and previously unused portion of the upper bajada slope (Fish and Fish 1991:164).

The kinds of settlements making up the Marana community include the central platform mound site with compounds; smaller compound sites; habitation sites without compounds; *trincheras* sites with residential and agricultural features; large communal fields devoted to agave production; and large, nonresidential sites that were devoted to exploiting saguaro cactus. Paleobotanical data (Fish *et al.* 1992) indicate that some sites seem to have specialized in producing corn, others in agave, while still others in saguaro and cholla. Tabular knives are distinctive artifacts associated with agave processing and, as noted, may have been produced by specialists. Within the community, there

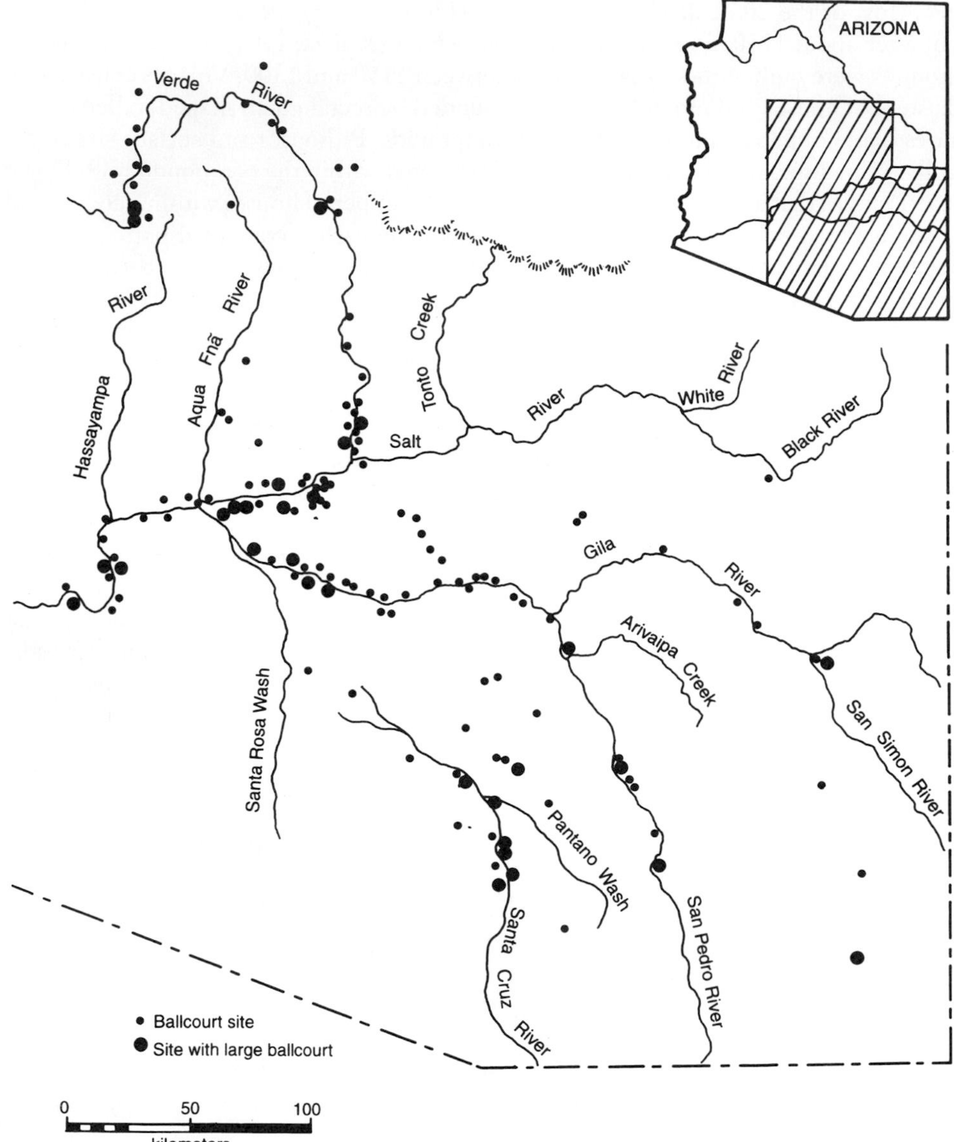

FIGURE 10.23 The 206 ball courts at 165 Hohokam sites were in use mostly between 750 and 1000; however, after 1250 no new ballcourts were built. The concentration of ballcourts is in the Phoenix and Tucson basins (adapted from Wilcox [1991] by Marjorie Leggitt, Leggitt Design).

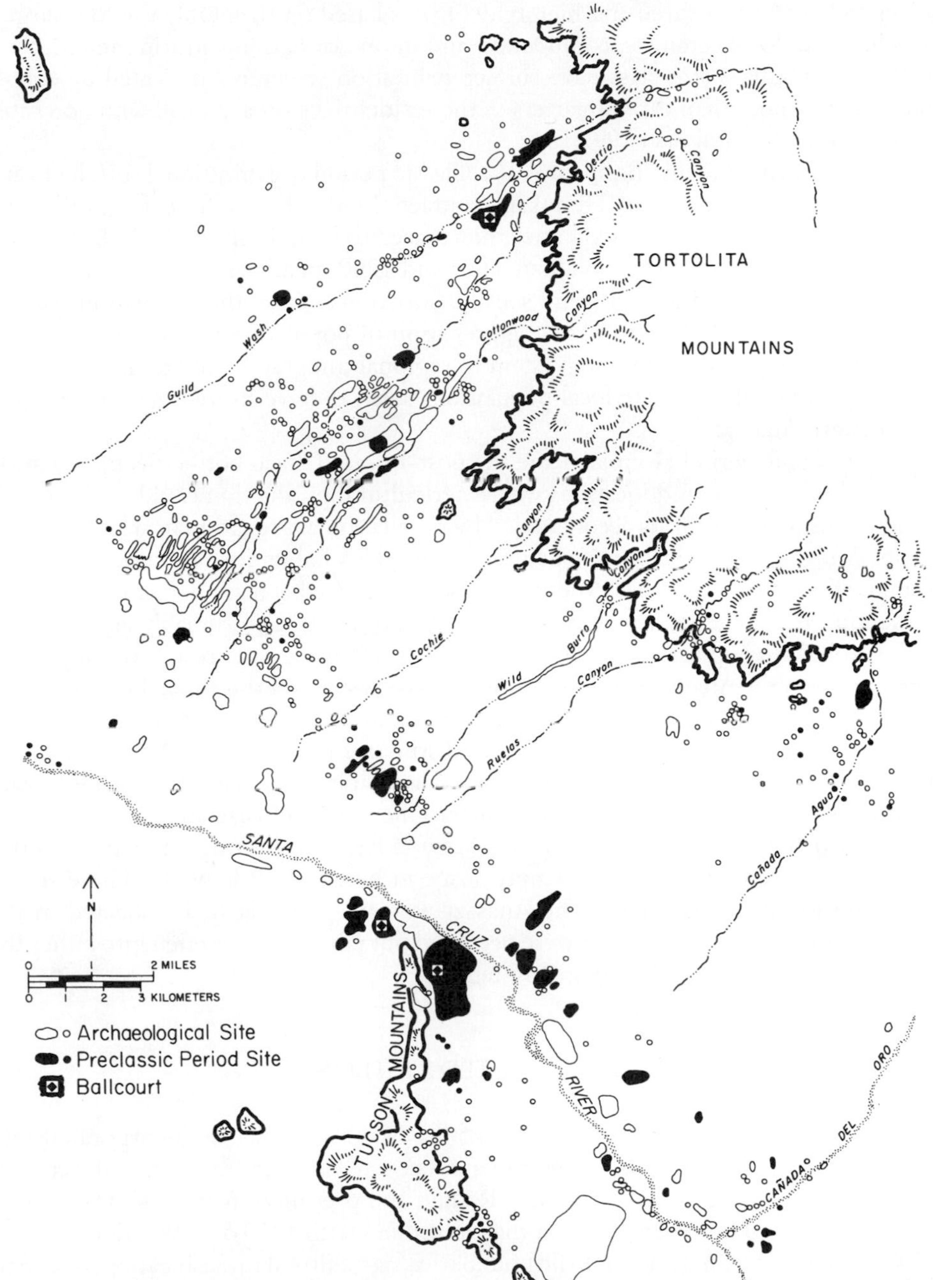

FIGURE 10.24 Sedentary period ballcourts at the Marana community in the Tucson Basin (courtesy of Paul and Suzanne Fish).

seems to have been a three-tier hierarchy of sites based on size. Only the four largest sites have nonlocal ceramics, compounds, and in one case, the platform mound. Sites in the intermediate size class have surface habitation structures indicated by cobble outlines. Yet more than three-quarters of the residential sites are small with no visible architecture (Fish and Fish 1991:164).

North of the Phoenix Basin core, the Classic period organizational shift had variable effects on the areas of Hohokam contact. In the Flagstaff region, ballcourts continued to be constructed long after they ceased to be built in the Hohokam heartland (Fish *et al.* 1980). Between about 1130 and 1200, many large sites are known in the Flagstaff area, and diversity and social distinctions within the population are evident. After about 1200 there was an aggregation of population into fewer but larger sites and participation in another system of regional integration and exchange. In the Verde area after about 1150, local populations seem to have shifted their alliances to the Western Anasazi.

The Classic period Hohokam and the post-Bonito Chaco both reflect population increase in core areas and locations where agricultural production could be increased. In both culture areas this is accompanied by population aggregation into larger settlements. More space in Chacoan structures was used for habitation as opposed to either storage or ritual, and the platform mounds seem to have been secularized in that they now supported domestic structures. However, only a small, presumably elite, portion of the Hohokam population lived on the mounds. In my view, there are striking differences between the Anasazi and Hohokam regional systems at this time. The Hohokam continued to manifest productive specialization and interregional exchange, although the items involved are unlike the previous distinctive ritual objects. Anasazi sites, on the other hand, seem to be dominated by local assemblages of artifacts. The Hohokam continued to support and elaborate site hierarchies based on size and distinctive artifactual distributions, but as Anasazi sites became larger, reflecting population aggregation, there were great areas of empty space in between settlements. These spaces constitute local abandonment. The Anasazi pattern, particularly, is reflected in the many parts of the Southwest that were occupied but not well-integrated into either the Chaco or Classic Hohokam regional systems.

AGGREGATED SYSTEMS

Between about 900 and 1150, most of the Southwest was *not* incorporated into either of the ongoing regional systems in a direct way, nor were most areas the centers of their own regionally based systems. Rather, the prevailing pattern seems to have been of continued local development that continued until 1250 or 1300. This is not to say that cultural elaboration, stylistic boundaries, agricultural intensification, or extensive trade were lacking outside the regional systems. On the contrary, population density increased in many areas; stream fed irrigation and soil- and water-control features were constructed; communities became quite large; structures reflecting village-level organization were built; and recognizable traditions of ceramic styles developed and continued. The differences between the regional systems and aggregated systems are in the presence of regionally based exchange and settlement hierarchies in the regional systems and in the absence of regionally based hierarchies elsewhere. The contrasts are here elaborated by examining examples of areas that supported large, aggregated populations. These are the Mesa Verde and the Mimbres, geographically north and south of the Chaco system respectively.

Mesa Verde

The Mesa Verde area provides a good contrast to Chaco Canyon for several reason. The two are representative of the San Juan Anasazi tradition and therefore share a number of general cultural features. They are in close proximity to each other and interacted in a variety of ways over time. Finally, the Mesa Verde type of organization survived that of Chaco, and came to influence the Chaco region.

The Mesa Verde area covers a broad region north and northwest of the San Juan Basin. Compared with Chaco Canyon, the environment of the Mesa Verde is relatively lush. Because of its altitude and latitude, it is not as dry as other parts of the Southwest. The climax vegetation consists of piñon and Utah juniper, with fairly dense understory shrubs. Although the water sources are neither very numerous nor completely reliable, there are many seeps and springs. Hayes (1964) surveyed Wetherill Mesa, a portion of Mesa Verde National Park, as part of the Wetherill Mesa Archeological Project. Hayes (1981a) also surveyed Chaco Canyon for the National Park Service. Results of the two surveys are interesting "because they were as nearly comparable as two surveys could be. They were conducted by the same man—using the same techniques, recording the same kinds of data, and applying the same prejudices" (Hayes 1981a:20).

Hayes found that site density in Chaco Canyon was about half that on Wetherill Mesa. Chaco Canyon had a greater number of Navajo sites than the Navajo, Ute, or Euro-American sites at Mesa Verde. If only the Anasazi sites are considered, site density at Chaco Canyon is 49/km^2 and at Wetherill Mesa 129/km^2. The difference is even more outstanding when the dense vegetation of Mesa Verde is considered because small and unobtrusive sites are more likely to have been missed in that setting. Hayes emphasizes that, because sites were more likely to have been missed because of the topographic and vegetative conditions at Mesa Verde, the magnitude of the difference in Anasazi settlement between Chaco Canyon and Mesa Verde is impressive.

The full sequence of Anasazi development from Basketmaker through Pueblo III is present in the Mesa Verde region, with Anasazi occupation ending at about AD 1300. The demographic trajectory from 600 to 1300 is one of population growth. There was an initial period of population aggregation in Pueblo I times (the 800s and see Chapter 9), but this was spotty geographically so that locally population appears to have declined. By the 1200s, there was a dramatic increase in site size and number (Varien *et al.* 1996), followed by abandonment for habitation.

While there are many similarities between the Mesa Verde and Chaco, especially compared with other Anasazi branches, Gordon Vivian (1959) outlines differences between them from about AD 950 as follows: (1) the presence in Chacoan kivas of low, wide benches and subfloor vents, and the general absence of these features, but the use of pilasters, above-floor vents, and masonry deflectors in Mesa Verde kivas; (2) the general absence of burials in Chacoan sites and their more frequent occurrence at Mesa Verde sites; (3) the use of mineral-based pigments in pottery decoration in Chaco but the use of organic-based paints in the Mesa Verde region; and not specifically mentioned by Vivian, but of importance, are (4) differences in masonry construction with the use of core-veneer masonry at Chaco and the use of single- or double-coursed masonry at Mesa Verde. Most important from the perspective of regional development, however, are the differences between village and community organization at Mesa Verde sites and at Chaco (previously discussed). These should be understood within the context of the San Juan Anasazi region as a whole where, as Reed (1946) observed, Chacoan influence was stronger until about 1150, and Mesa Verde influence predominated thereafter.

Rohn (1977) made an important contribution in distinguishing between sites (each notable building, in some cases each distinguishable artifact locus, such as a ceramic scatter) and communities (local groups) "determined not by kinship but by spatial proximity that brings its individual members into face-to-face contact" (Rohn 1977: 266). This distinction is one that is commonly made by ethnologists, and it is used by archaeologists working in the Mesa Verde area (Varien *et al.* 1996). Varien and others (1996) suggest that an important function of communities thus defined is regulation of access to resources, particularly arable land. They point out that by the early AD 1000s communities consisting of small, dispersed habitation sites were located on productive arable land throughout the Mesa Verde region. Each habitation site might have been occupied by only one or two households. Such household units, however, continued, eventually serving as the "building blocks" of later, larger communities. By the late 1000s, great house public architecture appeared and served to integrate the dispersed communities. The great houses are at the essence of what Reed (1946) viewed as Chacoan, and there is still debate about whether these structures represent an intrusion of Chacoans or their political system or an attempt by local people to emulate Chacoan structures. An example may help clarify the question.

On Chapin Mesa, on the Mesa Verde proper, the Mummy Lake II settlement dates to AD 950 to 1000. It consisted of some 36 separate habitation sites with an estimated population of about 200–400 people. The size of the Mummy Lake settlement is attributable to the construction of the artificial water supply at Mummy Lake, an impressively engineered reservoir with associated features, indicating great technological skill and labor organization. One of these sites (Pipe Shrine House, Site 809) was excavated by Fewkes (1923). The floor plan of the site is shown in Figure 10.25. According to Rohn (1977), rooms numbered 1–9, consisting of single-coursed masonry with chipped-edge stones, were constructed first. Later, the occupants added the east, south, and west wings in pecked-face masonry, some single- and some double-coursed walls. The kiva also showed remodeling, finally having the narrow bench, six pilasters, and a subfloor ventilator typical of the kivas in Chaco Canyon. The additions and remodeling, in different masonry styles, suggest a local population incorporating some features of a Chacoan great house. They are completely different from the

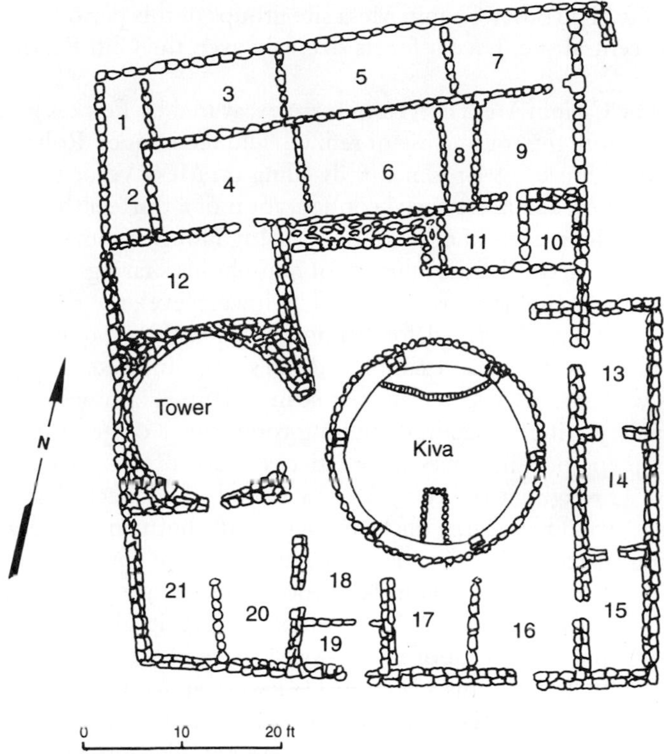

FIGURE 10.25 Pipe Shrine House, Mesa Verde National Park. The north room block (rooms 1–9) was constructed first. Later, the east, south, and west roomblocks were added and the kiva was remodeled (adapted from Rohn [1977] by Charles M. Carrillo).

planned Bonito-style structures of the Chacoan system. Varien and others (1996) refer to these communities as multiple-household clusters, which they suggest are analogous to roomblock groups of later, much larger, aggregated Pueblo III sites.

After AD 1200, populations throughout the Mesa Verde area moved off the mesa tops and therefore away from the best agricultural land. This change is noted both for small as well as large sites (Varien *et al.* 1996). Between 1200 and 1300, the population focus on Chapin Mesa shifted from the area around Mummy Lake to Cliff and Fewkes canyons. The late Pueblo III settlement in the latter area consisted of 33 habitation sites with an estimated total of between 530 and 545 rooms, 60 kivas, and possibly between 600 and 800 people. Site size within this group ranges from a one-room site to Cliff Palace, the largest ruin on Chapin Mesa, with an estimated 220 rooms and 23 kivas. Rohn (1977) suggests that about half of the thirteenth-century population of Chapin Mesa inhabited this site group. Despite the dense concentration of population, there is very little in the Fewkes Canyon group that indicates any form site or social hierarchy. It does appear as though the largest settlement, Cliff Palace, was central to the community. The other Chapin Mesa site groups of this period also have one large, more or less central site. Except for its size, however, the Cliff Palace structure is not unusual.

The major Chapin Mesa cliff ruins were excavated by Fewkes in the early part of this century, before the routine use of refined field techniques. Rohn (1971), however, excavated Mug House, a 94-room cliff dwelling on Mesa Verde that provides a great deal of information about the social configuration of a thirteenth-century settlement. Rohn identified four levels of organization at Mug House: room suites (corresponding to households), courtyard units (clusters of households sharing a common courtyard), moieties, and the community as a whole. The lowest level, the room suites, should be compared with those described for Salmon and for the "modular units" at Chaco Canyon. Unlike the Chacoan examples, Rohn's work indicates that the Mug House room suites were not constructed all at once in a planned fashion.

The primary criteria used in delimiting room suites center around mutual accessibility of their component spaces and relative isolation of these same spaces from other room suites. Throughout the ruin, doorways tend to connect clusters of rooms and outdoor areas around one large nuclear space. Wall abutments generally indicate separate building stages between suites as well as sequential construction within a single unit (Rohn 1977:31). Three examples of room clusters are given in Figure 10.26. In describing Suite 12/1, Rohn (1977:33) comments that it consists of two storerooms, two dwelling rooms, and most of the enclosed space in the back of the cave in which Mug House is located. Rooms 12/1 and 11/1 were apparently constructed first, with Rooms 57 and 14 added later to increase the amount of storage space. The courtyard units (of which Figure 10.27 is an example) also show additions and modifications over time. The earliest courtyard units at Mug House resemble earlier habitation units found on the mesa top, generally consisting of a series of contiguous rooms with an associated kiva and a refuse heap. The units are referred to as courtyard units because the kiva roof served as a ground-level courtyard for the adjoining house clusters. Rohn's reconstruction of the courtyard units at Mug House indicates that initially there was but one courtyard unit. Later there were four units, two within Mug House Cave itself, one in nearby Adobe Cave, and one at a site in the immediate vicinity. During the latest period, these four merged into one pueblo.

The suggested dual division is less convincing. Rohn infers that it came into being only during the latest period of occupation and was marked by a six-room suite with entryways from three of the rooms to the north and three to the south but no direct access between north and south portions of the pueblo (Figure 10.27). In addition, the five kivas in the northern sector are architecturally very similar to each other, whereas the three kivas in the southern sector do not resemble each other. Finally, studies of wall abutments indicate that construction in the southern segment did not begin until the northern segment had attained a large size. The community level distinguished by Rohn consists of the inhabitants of Mug House and the residents of several smaller contemporary sites in the immediate vicinity. As Rohn points out, in social terms the community would have included those people who are frequently in day-to-day interaction, and the sites involved are all in very close proximity and apparently contemporary.

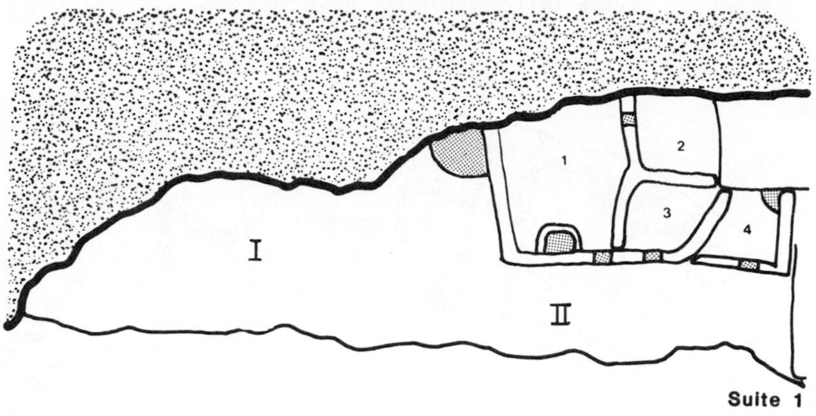

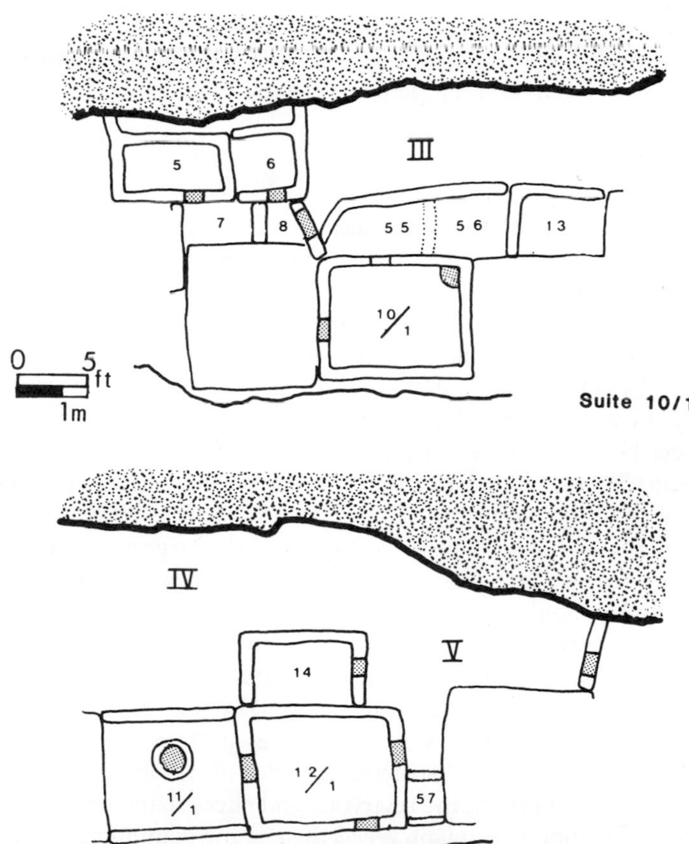

FIGURE 10.26 Domestic room suites at Mug House, Mesa Verde National Park. Rooms within each suite are accessible to each other but are not easily entered from other room suites. In suite 12/1, rooms 11/1 and 12/1 were built first and rooms 14 and 57 were added later (adapted from Rohn [1971:32–33] by Charles M. Carrillo).

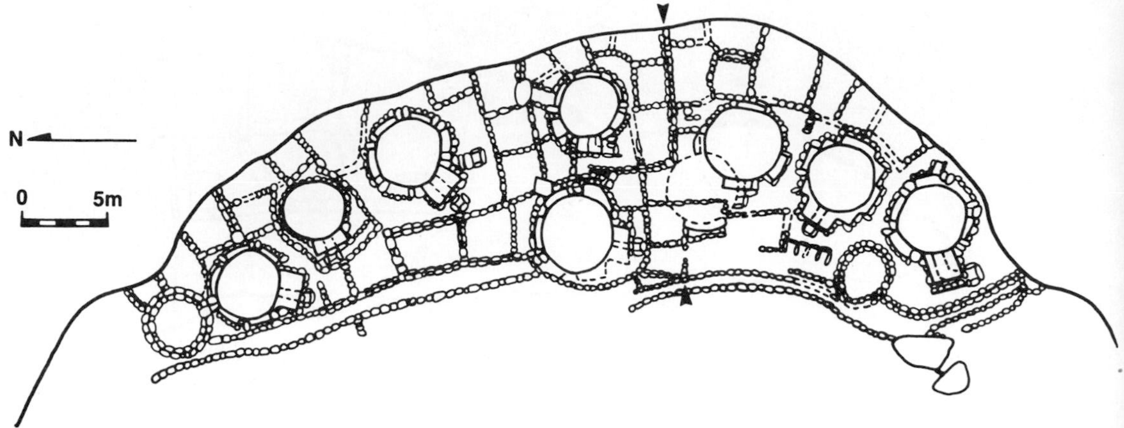

FIGURE 10.27 Plan view of Mug House, Mesa Verde National Park. Arrows indicate suggested dual division of the site. Courtyard units are formed by the rooms associated with each kiva (adapted from Rohn [1971] by Marjorie Leggitt, Leggitt Design).

After AD 1150, when great house construction ceased in Chaco Canyon and the pace of aggregation at Mesa Verde increased, the organizational role of great houses changed. Public architecture became quite variable in form and possibly in function. This is indicated by the differences between Fire Temple and Sun Temple, associated with the Fewkes Canyon group. Fire Temple, well described as a modified great kiva (Cassidy 1965), is a rectangular structure with adjoining rooms on each side that may have served as antechambers. Wall construction is of double-coursed block masonry with a narrow interior core. Except for its shape, the ruin has features that are similar to the great kivas of Chaco Canyon (Figure 10.28): paired vaults, bench, and raised firebox. Sun Temple (Figure 10.29) is a D-shaped structure with two massive (1.22 m thick) stone walls enclosing two kiva-like features. The kivas had Chacoan subfloor ventilators. The two ceremonial structures and the large scale of construction at the cliff dwellings in Fewkes Canyon certainly indicate village integration and ceremonial organization. Yet, neither these nor other structures on Chapin Mesa are suggestive of hierarchies of community settlement. The only other class of functionally different habitation sites found appears to be that of field houses.

In essence, despite the constraints imposed by the shapes of caves and rock overhangs in which they were built, the communities at Mesa Verde did get very large. The multiple kivas and specialized structures, such as Fire Temple, indicate considerable ceremonial activity. Further, the reservoirs and check dams suggest technological skill and cooperative labor investment. Nevertheless, the planning and stylization of building so evident in the Bonito structures are not apparent at Mesa Verde, and there is little indication that the communities were centralized or nucleated as opposed to aggregated. Even large structures such as Mug House show a development from a smaller community, with additions and modifications of structures being common.

FIGURE 10.28 Fire Temple, Mesa Verde National Park. The floor features of this site are similar to those of the Great Kivas of Chaco Canyon (see Figure 10.12) including paired vaults, bench, and raised firebox (photograph courtesy of the U.S. National Park Service).

FIGURE 10.29 Sun Temple, Mesa Verde National Park. Two massive stone walls enclose two kiva-like features that had Chacoan subfloor ventilators (illustrated by Charles M. Carrillo).

The question remains, however, why a long-term, presumably successful dispersed settlement pattern at Mesa Verde gave way to an aggregated one when it did. Varien and others (1996) suggest a model of regional population packing, resource depletion, intensification of resource use, and higher potential for conflict. They state that over time, increasing population in dispersed communities associated with prime agricultural land would limit overall mobility options and deplete some resources. The decrease in mobility options is reflected in a dramatic increase in field houses, check dams, contour terraces, and reservoirs that would have had the further affect of tethering local populations to these investments. As they state:

> In the case of the Mesa Verde region, the longer the region was occupied, the more of its own history of occupation and land use constrained the mobility options of its people and communities. The cultural landscape was a mosaic of socially negotiated spaces filled with potential symbols of ownership, including abandoned structures, burials in abandoned sites, and agricultural features. This history of land use probably served to restrict the area that was open to new settlement (Varien *et al.* 1996:103).

Mimbres

The Mimbres area during the Mimbres Classic (AD 1000 to 1130) also supported large, aggregated sites. It is a good contrast to both Chaco and Mesa Verde. The Mimbres Classic is virtually contemporary with the Bonito phase at Chaco, and people in both areas must surely have been aware of each other. The Mimbres, unlike the Mesa Verde Anasazi but like their neighbors the Hohokam, had stream-fed irrigation. Mimbres is different from Chaco and the Hohokam in lacking hierarchies of habitation sites and regional integration.

The Mimbres area is where Haury (1936) first defined the Mogollon tradition, but it was known earlier for pueblo sites that yielded fine black-on-white pottery (Kidder 1924). The Mimbres Classic is best known for its aesthetically appealing, finely painted pictorial (Figure 10.30) and geometric (Figure 10.31) ceramic bowls. Over the years, Mimbres archaeology has been a tense battleground between dedicated researchers (e.g., Cosgrove and Cosgrove 1932; LeBlanc 1983; Nesbitt 1931; Shafer 1991, 1995) and looters. Whole Classic Mimbres bowls are most often recovered in burial contexts, individuals having been interred with one or more Classic bowls inverted over or near their heads. Mimbres pottery appeals to our aesthetic. The quality of the design execution, the association of pottery with burials, and the fact that the Mimbres buried their dead under room floors provided the context for tragic loss of information about Mimbres way of life.

Mimbres pottery has attracted art collectors for nearly a century. It was in the late 1960s and early 1970s, however, that Classic Mimbres bowls began to bring considerable sums in the international art market. Commercial looters, using heavy equipment to dig through ancient houses to get to the subfloor burials, could and did completely obliterate archaeological sites in a matter of hours. We do not know how many Classic Mimbres bowls were ever made. Knowledgeable sources estimate that there may be as many as 10,000 in public and private collections around the world. This astounding

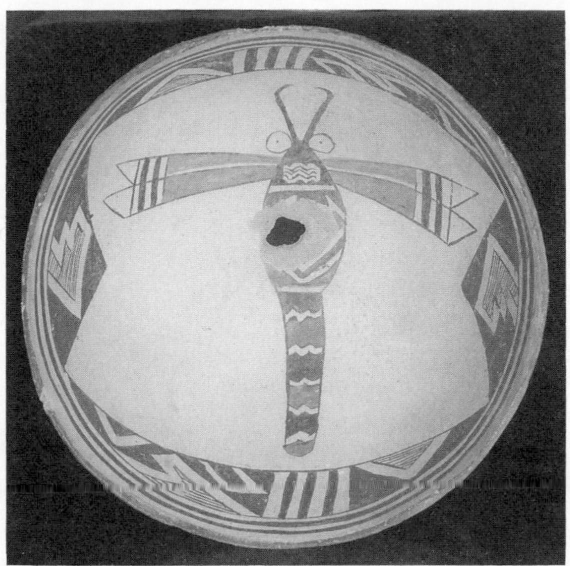

FIGURE 10.30 Classic Mimbres bowl with pictorial dragonfly design. Classic bowls are often recovered in burial contexts. The small hole was punched in the center of the bowl before it was placed in the grave site (photograph courtesy of the University of Colorado Museum, UCM 3138).

FIGURE 10.31 Classic Mimbres bowl with geometric design (photograph courtesy of the University of Colorado Museum, UCM 3188).

FIGURE 10.32 This is the site of a 50-room Classic period Mimbres village that was completely destroyed in the mid-1970s by looters using the bulldozer in the upper left of the remains of the site (photograph courtesy of Steven LeBlanc and the Mimbres Foundation).

figure is testimony to the devastation of archaeological sites in the Mimbres Valley of New Mexico and to much of the information these sites might have provided about the daily lives of the Mimbres people (Figure 10.32). Thanks largely to the efforts of archaeologist Steven A. LeBlanc, who established the Mimbres Foundation for Archaeological Research, the use of power equipment by collectors is no longer legal. Nevertheless, most Classic Mimbres sites were devastated by recreational or commercial looters. Since the 1970s, archaeologists have invested in reexcavating those sites that had been looted with hand tools, and finding that a great deal of information can be salvaged.

Among the best-known Classic Mimbres sites are the Mattocks, Cameron Creek, and the Swarts ruins. Work at two others, the Galaz site and the NAN Ranch pueblo

(Anyon *et al.* 1981; Shafer 1982, 1991, 1995; Shafer *et al.* 1986), is emphasized here. Both of these sites do, in fact, conform to the Classic Mimbres type. Classic Mimbres pueblos were built over late pithouse villages. The arrangement of community space in the surface pueblos suggests continuity with the late pithouse occupation. In both late pithouse village and later pueblo, there are clusters of rooms around open courtyards and plazas. In Mimbres pueblos, room clusters are often on either side of a plaza. Recent surveys and testing programs document extensive Classic Mimbres age irrigation canals on tributaries in the Mimbres drainage. Irrigated fields would have provided food for the population that was increasing rapidly in the Late Pithouse period as well as required the attention of an on-site labor force.

The construction materials of Mimbres pueblos is far from impressive. A common building form in the Classic was a series of contiguous, single-story, rectangular rooms with walls made of unshaped river cobbles set in abundant adobe or mud mortar. In other instances, unshaped slab masonry was used. Roofs were supported by the walls and from one to three or four roof-support posts. Most studies of the composition of Mimbres sites are hampered by the generally poor state of preservation of structures and by the overt destruction of many Mimbres sites by treasure hunters. Information from the NAN Ranch site and the Galaz site shows that Classic Mimbres pueblos grew accretionally. At both sites, there were a few spatially separated clusters of core surface rooms to which other room clusters were added. At the NAN Ranch site, Shafer (1982) examined wall junctures to determine the horizontal sequence of room construction. He defined rooms that were linked by common doorways and built during a single construction episode. His data therefore are comparable to those obtained by Rohn at Mug House and by Irwin-Williams at Salmon. The room clusters at NAN Ranch pueblo are more comparable to those at Mug House than to the formal room suites characteristic of the Bonito construction at Salmon. Entry to each room cluster appears to have been through a roof hatchway. The number of rooms in each room cluster varies somewhat, room clusters were added to, and rooms within them were sometimes divided. Shafer suggests that the number of rooms in cluster was probably a function of the space needs of the residential groups. Rooms that can be interpreted as primarily habitation rooms were somewhat larger than other rooms in the cluster and generally had interior features such as hearths. Smaller rooms at both the NAN Ranch pueblo and the Galaz site generally had well-prepared floors but lacked interior features, often had only unpainted ceramics, and seem to be reasonably interpreted as storage rooms. Shafer interprets some rooms as household shrines. These rooms are distinguished by a special hearth complex consisting of a slab-lined hearth and adjacent bin, by adjacent storage rooms, and by the observation that most of the burials are found under the floors of these rooms. Since not all room clusters have these special rooms, Shafer proposes that those that did housed core lineages who maintained rights (through their ancestors) to irrigated lands. The room clusters with household shrines would then have been the social core of the community. Those occupying room clusters without household shrines may have been incorporated into the community from outside, not had claim to irrigated land, and have been expected to be the first to leave if there were inadequate harvests.

There is also community architecture at Classic Mimbres sites. Early in the Classic, communal structures were very large, rectangular, semi-subterranean kivas, showing considerable continuity to Mogollon kivas of preceding periods. The floor area of one such structure at the Galaz site was 146.8 m^2. This structure and others had rampways oriented to the east. Ceremonial offerings or caches were sometimes located below the floor. For example, in this large structure objects found below the floor included a carved shell effigy, a painted tuff frog, beads, crystals, a *glycymeris* shell bracelet, and turquoise, shell, and stone beads and pendants. During the Mimbres Classic, these large kivas were no longer used, and the plaza area may have become the focus of public, community ceremonies. Some ceremonial rooms located in Classic Mimbres pueblos were too small to have served the village as a whole and may have been used by village segments (sodalities of one kind or another—i.e., either kin or non-kin based). These rooms lacked quadrilateral roof-supports, were entered through the roof, and had ventilators.

Mimbres Classic pottery also serves as a key source of information about Mimbres social organization, and perhaps ideology. Despite the common association of Mimbres Black-on-white bowls with burials, researchers have not been able to discern differential mortuary offerings that might indicate social hierarchies. Compositional studies do not support craft specialization above the household or settlement level. There are several manufacturing places in the Mimbres area. It has been suggested (Brody 1977; Hegmon and Trevathan 1996) that the pottery was painted by men rather than women because "male activities" are frequently represented and birth scenes are portrayed inaccurately. The evidence for gender specialization is provocative but hardly conclusive. Whoever made the pottery, it was not made specifically for mortuary rituals. Mimbres bowls are found in habitation contexts as well as with burials. In cases where they have been found with burials, the bowls' interiors show wear marks that would have resulted from using a gourd dipper on the inside of the bowl. Hence, the bowls seem to have been used for general serving functions before they were interred as burial offerings. Mimbres bowls were traded to the Jornada Mogollon area (see below), and the few intrusive ceramics in Classic Mimbres sites derive from that area as well. Shafer suggests that this trade was in the context of Jornada visitors attending ceremonial feasts at Mimbres villages and returning home with gifts of Mimbres pottery.

Shafer (1991) notes that in folk culture around the world, house form can incorporate symbols important to a people's world view. Some of the ideological factors, in turn, can be linked to characteristics of designs on Classic Mimbres pottery. Specifically, Shafer suggests that the Mimbres people shared a belief system that included a multilayered universe, the emergence of humans from an underworld, and aspects of ancestor worship (cf. Moulard 1981). The architectural reflection of the multilayered universe is found in the ceiling hatchway and the placement of the dead under room floors. Passage up a ladder and through the hatchway then reenacts and symbolically represents the emergence from an underworld. Interment of the dead with a pot, with a small hole punched in it, inverted over the individual's head may symbolize allowing the spirit of the individual to pass from the nether world into the upper world as a

FIGURE 10.33 Classic Mimbres bowl with single central bird figure (photograph courtesy of the University of Colorado Museum, UCM 3127).

Mimbres ancestor. Shafer notes that the Mimbres Classic style that occurs with these burials has a bordering or framing line as a consistent feature and agrees with interpretations that view the framing lines as symbolic representations of the division between worlds in the multilayered universe.

Other attributes of Mimbres painted pottery can only be guessed at. In his study, Brody (1977) found that geometric designs occur on bowls and the other forms, such as jars and ladles, and about half the known Mimbres painted bowls carry geometric paintings. Representational paintings occur only on bowls. On more than half these, there is only a single figure. The figure may be animal, human, or a mythic being combining attributes of both (Figure 10.33). Some bowls have two, or far more rarely, three or more painted figures (Figure 10.34). On only about 15 percent of known bowls with representational paintings are the paintings narrative. In the narrative scenes, figures have some relationship to events, to narrative content, to each other, and to an imaginary environment (Figure 10.35).

In his tabulation of subject matter on 733 figurative vessels, Brody (1977) comments that compared with the wealth and variety of species in the Mimbres environment, the number of creatures depicted is remarkably limited. Yet, neither the pattern of the selection of creatures or its meaning is clear. Further, there are few hints about

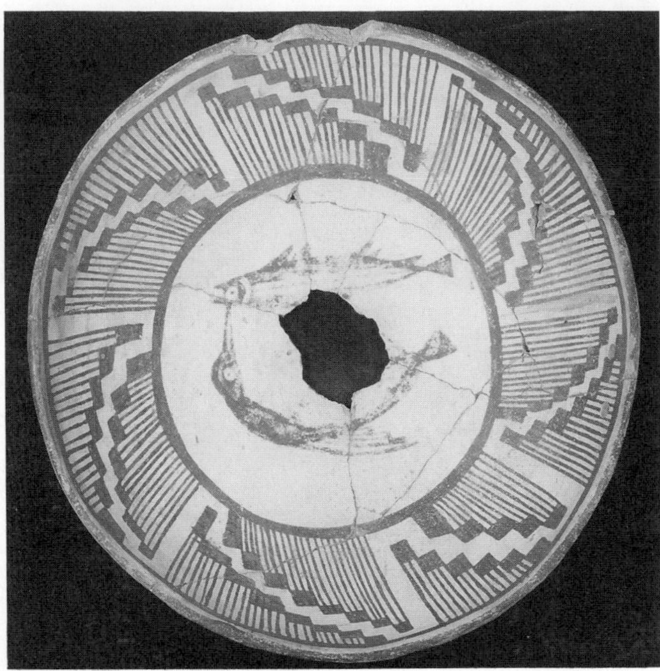

FIGURE 10.34 Classic Mimbres bowl depicting two animal figures: a bird and a fish (photograph courtesy of the University of Colorado Museum, UCM 3200).

either topic in the oral literature of living southwestern people. Certainly some animals that are important in Pueblo oral literature are depicted, but others, just as important, are not. Finally, Brody remarks that neither economic importance, rarity, ubiquity, character, or potential decorative value seems to have been a factor for selecting the figures portrayed. Myth, history, and literature are certainly the factors that were used but may never be known.

Between AD 1100 and 1150, the long continuum of occupation of the Mimbres Valley breaks down. LeBlanc (1989) and Minnis (1982) attribute the demise of Mimbres culture, in part, to its success. As Mimbres population grew and settlement expanded throughout the valley, communities eventually were established on land that is marginal for agriculture. Firewood and game were depleted over time so that when several years of poor rainfall, beginning in AD 1150, caused crop failures, there were few backup resources left, and many Mimbres sites were abandoned. Shafer (1996) supports linking the abandonment of the Mimbres area to failures in the prime, irrigated, agricultural land, perhaps through a drop in river flow that made irrigation impossible.

The number of trade items and the distances over which trade items were transported in the Classic Mimbres vary, but the items do not seem to reflect large quantities

FIGURE 10.35 Classic Mimbres bowl with narrative scene. Note the kill hole in the center of the vessel (photograph courtesy of the University of Colorado Museum, UCM 3158).

of exotic goods. Shell is present, mostly in finished items, as it is in the preceding Mogollon phases. Turquoise does appear in jewelry, but it probably originated locally in the copper-bearing deposits near the Mimbres Valley. Mimbres Classic ceramics had limited distributions outside the Mimbres area proper. In fact, the only area in which they appear in quantity is the Jornada Mogollon region. And conversely, Jornada Mogollon jars occur in Mimbres contexts. Hence, it appears that there were special relationships between the Mimbres and Jornada areas. These can be compared with similar patterns that existed between the Mesa Verde and the Rio Grande Valley (see Chapter 11).

Kayenta Anasazi

The Kayenta branch of the Anasazi occupied the area west of the Mesa Verde branch to Navajo Canyon and extending south to interior Black Mesa and north to the Rainbow Plateau. This is a huge area and one of particular interest here in that it manifests little to no contact with or influence from the Chacoan or Hohokam systems. Yet its final trajectory was similar to other Anasazi areas. In addition, an aggregated community pattern developed very quickly and can be seen in detail.

Beginning about AD 1000, Prudden unit pueblos, consisting of a block of masonry or jacal surface living and storage rooms facing a kiva and a trash midden, were built throughout the region. Most of these are very small. The largest have about 30 rooms (Dean 1996b). At this time, the Kayenta branch reached its maximum spatial extent. There is no evidence of site hierarchies or locally integrated communities.

At about AD 1150 until 1250, the Kayenta settlement pattern and distribution changed dramatically (Dean 1996b). Throughout this time there was local abandonment of all the peripheral areas, probably as a result of the same episode of drought that seems to have triggered the cessation of building within Chaco Canyon itself. Population migrated to areas with well-watered arable land in the center of the Kayenta region, creating empty areas between population centers (Dean 1996b:34). Two new types of sites were occupied at this time: plaza sites and pithouse villages. Plaza sites, which may represent a coalescence of two or more unit pueblos, consist of one or more masonry roomblocks facing a central plaza with a central kiva. These sites are not large. None exceed 50 rooms. Pithouse sites are not well documented but seem to consist of scattered pithouses, surface storage structures, semi-subterranean storage structures, and kivas. The Tsegi phase of AD 1250 to 1300 witnessed further abandonment of peripheral areas and population aggregation in Tsegi Canyon, Long House Valley, and Kayenta Valley. Dean (1996b:36) indicates that, based on abundant tree-ring dates, between AD 1250 and 1286, nearly 700 people moved into the previously sparsely inhabited Tsegi Canyon, establishing 20 villages that range in size from one or two households (perhaps 5 to 15 persons) to more than 100 individuals. By 1300, Tsegi Canyon, as with the rest of the Kayenta area, was abandoned by the Anasazi.

Tsegi phase communities are composed of room clusters that are functionally differentiated rooms (generally one or two living rooms, one to 12 storage rooms, and a grinding room) grouped around an unroofed courtyard. At some sites, groups of room clusters and kivas form discrete units within larger sites. Plaza sites that have been excavated consist of room clusters. Courtyard pueblos consist of room clusters around single or multiple courtyards, oriented along linear open areas that resemble "streets." Tree-ring dates and analyses of the structural elements from which they came allowed Dean (1969) to show how the very large cliff dwellings of Betatakin and Kiet Siel (Figure 10.36) were built and organized.

Betatakin was founded in 1267, although the cave in which it is located was first occupied in 1250 (Figure 10.37). Three room clusters were built in 1267, and a fourth was added in 1268. In 1269 and 1272, a number of trees were felled, cut into appropriate lengths for use as primary and secondary beams, and stockpiled. These beams were used to build more than 10 rooms and at least one kiva in 1275. After 1275, rooms were added at a slower pace, until a population peak of about 125 persons was attained in the mid 1280s. Dean's analysis strongly suggests that the immigration to these sites in 1275 was anticipated and planned for, and that the subsequent growth was probably the result of internal population expansion. Kiet Siel is larger than Betatakin, consisting of 155 rooms and six kivas. Its architectural history is divided into five periods, beginning in the late 1240s or early 1250s. From 1272 through 1275 the site experienced major immigration, followed by two periods of modification and remodeling. In

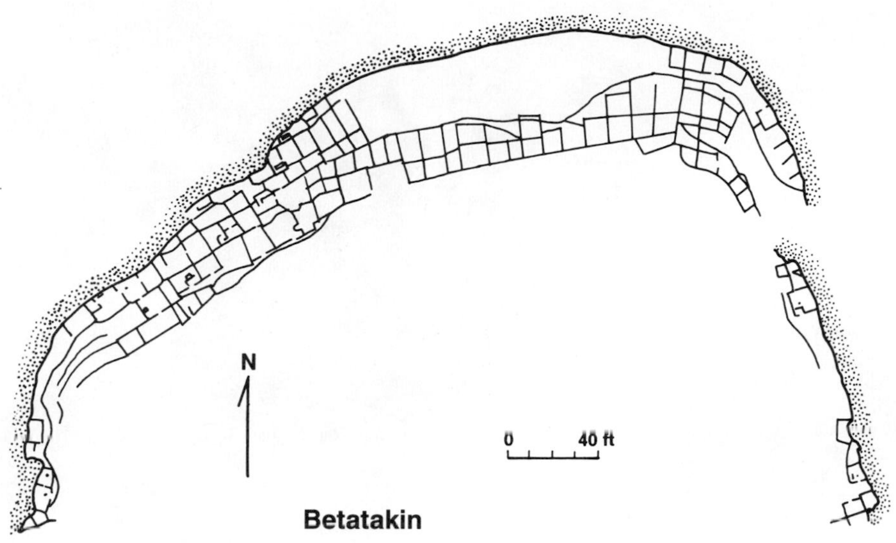

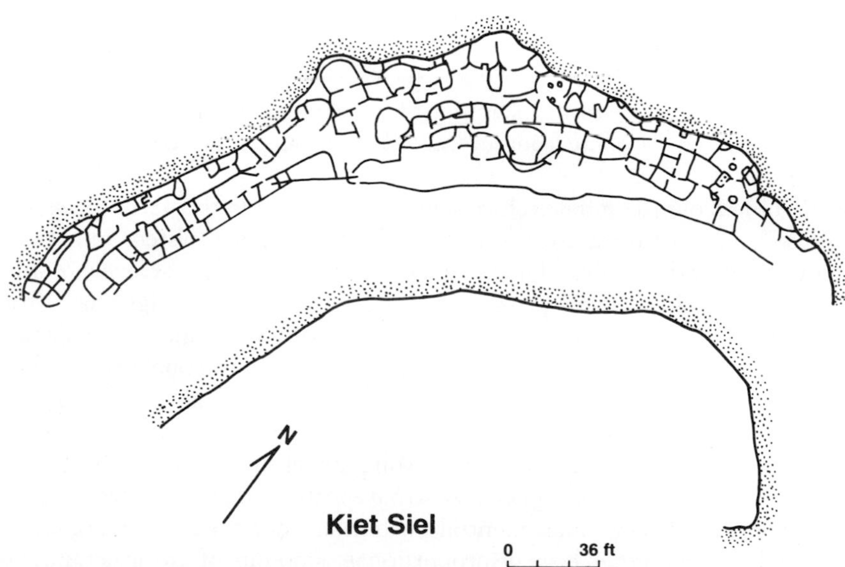

FIGURE 10.36 Despite similar size and layout of Betatakin (top) and Kiet Siel (bottom), large cliff dwellings in Tsegi Canyon, Arizona, tree-ring studies of their fabrication by Jeffrey Dean (1969) revealed completely different histories of construction and occupation (adapted from Dean [1969] by Marjorie Leggitt, Leggitt Design).

FIGURE 10.37 Betatakin Ruin, Navajo National Monument, is the largest cliff dwelling in Arizona (photo by H. F. Robinson, courtesy of the Museum of New Mexico, neg. no. 37394).

contrast to Betatakin, there was no planning or preparation for immigrant groups. Rather, settlers seem to have come from several different sources. It too was abandoned by 1300 at the latest.

Dean (1996b) recognizes a hierarchical settlement system in the Tsegi phase sites of Long House Valley, but these are not integrated into a regional system and at each level residential, rather than public, functions are primary. At the lowest level are small to medium habitation sites located proximate to arable land. These might have from 1 to 10 room clusters, and all were occupied year-round with a full range of secular and ceremonial activities represented. The next certain level are "central pueblos" that have all the attributes of residential sites and are set apart by nearly always being plaza pueblos, having central "spinal" roomblocks constructed of double-faced masonry that is absent from residential sites, and having reservoirs for capture and containment of a domestic water supply. Most central pueblos also have features that restrict access, such as ramps, corridors, and cross-walls. Central pueblos are not necessarily larger than residential pueblos, nor do they have disproportionate amounts of exotic ceramics or other potential status items. They are variously interpreted as having served as a ritual core and defensive center for surrounding residential pueblos (Haas and Creamer 1993). The defensive character of aggregated settlements is discussed further in Chapter 11 in the context of regional abandonment.

The examples of aggregated systems discussed, such as that of the Mesa Verde, Kayenta, and Mimbres areas, are of interest, in part, because the size of some of the settlements might lead to the conclusion that they functioned within regionally integrated systems. They are also of interest because they are recognizable stylistically; that is, they manifest particular forms of architecture and ceramics that are quite homogeneous throughout their local areas. Between about AD 900 and 1300, in many parts of the Southwest, far more dispersed systems of community organization seems to have prevailed. To give a better understanding of the range of community types, a brief description of examples of dispersed systems is given.

DISPERSED SYSTEMS

The Rio Grande Valley

The central and northern Rio Grande Valley, from about Albuquerque north, is of interest in part because it became a major center of Pueblo population after AD 1300 and continues to be so today. Yet, it was only sparsely inhabited from AD 900 to 1300, a period that encompasses part of the Rio Grande Developmental and Coalition periods, as described by Wendorf and Reed (1955; also see Chapter 7).

Excavated habitation sites that date before 1150 most often consist of pithouses, some with associated jacal structures and outside work areas. For the most part, pithouse architecture is relatively simple in that these houses are either round or rectangular with an interior hearth and roof-support posts being the most consistent internal features. Wing walls, benches, pilasters, and other features known from pithouse architecture in the San Juan drainage are lacking. The simplicity of Rio Grande pithouses is not a reflection of a lack of labor investment in housing. In mountainous areas, pithouses were excavated to a considerable depth, involving great expenditures of energy. In the Taos area, for example, pithouses in excess of 3 m in depth and 5 m in diameter are reported (Woosley 1980). Pithouses at lower elevations and latitudes, such as those on the Rio Grande terraces in the vicinity of Albuquerque, are generally considerably shallower. Quantitative data allowing an assessment of the degree of agricultural dependence reflected at these small pithouse communities are lacking, and it is not known if the sites were occupied on a year-round basis. Some investigators (Blevins and Joiner 1977) suggest that many sites were used only seasonally. Settlements in the middle and northern Rio Grande area were relatively small, perhaps consisting of two to four pithouses, sometimes with associated jacal structures. The sparse population indicated does not appear to have interacted frequently or with great intensity with the people of the San Juan area, which would have been the closest regionally organized system. No known Chacoan outliers exist in the Rio Grande Valley. As noted above, the resources of the Rio Grande Valley might have been attractive to the Chacoans, especially the turquoise of the Cerrillos Hills and perhaps the obsidian and cherts of the Jemez Mountains. Nevertheless, direct evidence of exploitation of these resources is lacking for this period.

Most ceramics from the Rio Grande area at this time were probably locally produced, although this has not been substantiated by compositional studies. Of interest, however, is that many of the local ceramic types are considered *cognates* or local imitations of types that were produced in the San Juan area. For example, in the Taos, Santa Fe, and Albuquerque areas, mineral-painted types such as a local variety of Red Mesa Black-on-white, Taos Black-on-white, and Kwahe'e Black-on-white are viewed as copies of Chacoan types. The various cognate ceramics produced certainly indicate general knowledge of the San Juan Basin area and, perhaps, some cognitive attempt to affiliate with this larger system. Still, the overall view is one of a dispersed population living in relative isolation. In the immediate vicinity of Albuquerque and somewhat south, ceramic assemblages are more diverse and include various Mogollon types or imitations thereof, such as Corrales Red (Frisbie 1967) and types, such as San Marcial Black-on-white, that are common in the Rio Grande area south of Albuquerque.

Between AD 1150 and 1250, population increased in some parts of the northern Rio Grande. On the Pajarito Plateau, small surface pueblos of about 10 rooms were constructed, and in the Santa Fe district, at least one pueblo of 120 surface rooms, eight small kivas, and one great kiva (Stubbs and Stallings 1953) has been excavated. Nevertheless, throughout most of the region, population density increased during the period but remained low. Crown and others (1996) note some interesting patterns for the northern Rio Grande as a whole. Between AD 1270 and 1300, population peaked on Pajarito Plateau after the neighboring Gallina district was abandoned. The Chama district, which is closer than the others to the Mesa Verde-San Juan, and might be expected to have been the first to receive population from that source, did not receive major population influx until after 1350. Population aggregation occurs throughout the region between 1250 and 1300 regardless of preceding population size or growth rate. Hence, even those locations where population declined, such as the Pajarito, experienced aggregation. Crown and others conclude with the observation that by 1300, the majority of sites in all districts of the region are large (more than 50 rooms) and reflect population aggregation. The patterns of aggregation are described fully in Chapter 12, as examples of community organization that followed the abandonment of the San Juan and Mesa Verde regions.

The Jornada Mogollon

Perhaps an even more dramatic case of a dispersed settlement system is that of the southern Jornada Mogollon on the southeastern edge of the Southwest. The southern Jornada Mogollon tradition extends from the northern end of the Caballo Mountains to the junction of the Rio Grande and Conchos rivers on the south, and from the Sacramento Mountains to the El Paso area. Hence, the southern Jornada area is in close proximity to both the Casas Grandes and Mimbres areas as well as adjacent to the southern Plains. The low basins are dry. They were probably occupied only intermittently by people using any agriculture. Perhaps more often, groups were mobile, depending on wild resources. Less than 5 percent of the recorded Jornada Mogollon sites are classified as habitation sites. Rather, the sites are typically sherd and lithic scatters, which indicates a highly mobile population. The option of mobile hunting of bison on the southern Plains is one that was taken when bison were present.

As described by Lehmer (1948), the period between AD 900 and 1100, referred to as the Mesilla phase, is characterized by the use of pithouses, some reliance on agriculture, and social and economic ties with the Mimbres Valley represented by the occurrence of Mimbres Boldface and Classic Mimbres Black-on-white. Stuart and Gauthier (1981) also point out that the ceramic assemblage also includes types, such as Red Mesa Black-on-white, that extend the region of interaction even further to the northwest to the southern edge of the San Juan Basin. By 1150, even this evidence of some dependence on agriculture ended. There are a few sites of 20 to 30 rooms at higher elevations that date to about 1200. By sometime after 1300, both the basins and mountain sites seem to have been abandoned, and the suggestion is that the former inhabitants of these areas may have moved out on the Plains to hunt.

The Lowland Muddy and Virgin Anasazi

Anasazi occupation of the southwestern portion of the Lower Sonoran Desert of Nevada was limited to the interval between AD 1000 and 1150 (Lyneis 1996). The region receives only 10 cm of precipitation a year, only about a third of which falls during the summer. With that limitation, Anasazi settlement depended on irrigation. There is general agreement that Kayenta Anasazi moved into the area during the general population expansion and dispersal of Pueblo II. The basic residential unit, established by that time, did not change throughout the occupation period.

The residential unit consisted of at least one habitation room and associated, contiguous storage rooms arranged in a loose C-shape. Structures were likely made of jacal with upright slabs or boulders as basal support. Lyneis (1996) reports that some sites are very large. For example, the Main Ridge (also known as Lost City) (Figure 10.38), excavated by Harrington in the early 1920s, consists of a cluster of 44 "houses" that included more than 203 rooms. Recent surface collections show that the 14 remaining multiroom households, with 106 storage rooms and 18 habitation rooms, were at least roughly contemporaneous. As Lyneis states, despite their size, there is no evidence of any form of community facilities. Each household was separate. Another site, the Mecca site, is also quite large, but many sites consist only of one or two households. Lyneis comments that the large C-shaped pueblos might have been seasonal residences—presumably used in winter—of families that dispersed to fields during the agricultural season. Alternatively, they might be year-round. Interestingly, at some late sites, there is physical separation of storage from habitation rooms, suggesting "loosening ties between individual families and their stored produce" (Lyneis 1996:18).

At about 1150, Anasazi occupation of this far western area ceases. How connected this abandonment was to the geographic shrinking of the area occuped by the Kayenta Anasazi is debated. Lyneis (1996) does not find enough data to support a gradual movement from west to east that would suggest that the Lower Muddy and Virgin Anasazi migrated toward the Kayenta core. Another possibility is that they moved

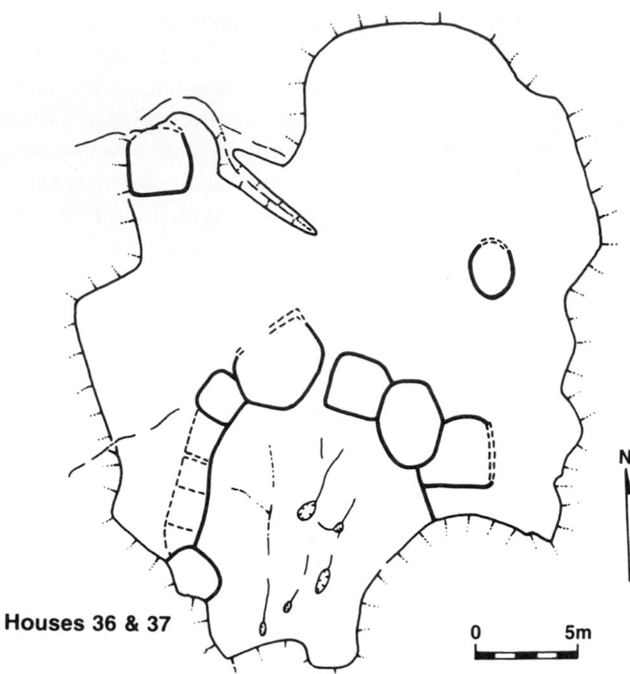

FIGURE 10.38 Domestic unit from the Main Ridge (also called "Lost City,") site, Nevada. Despite the alternative name and relatively large size, there is no evidence of any kind of community facilities at the site; each household was separate. Illustration by Marjorie Leggitt, Leggitt Design, after Lyneis (1996).

north to join agricultural Fremont populations in central Utah. Lyneis (1996) also finds the drought of the mid-1100s an unconvincing reason for Anasazi abandonment because agriculture would have been based on irrigation, and the river systems are not likely to have been adversely affected by this particular decline in rainfall. She notes that while salinization of irrigated fields may have been a problem, as it has been for modern farmers in the area, it is as likely that the geographic retraction of the Kayenta Anasazi in their core area might have left this most western occupation in undesirable isolation.

DISCUSSION

Between about AD 900 and 1150, village life had spread throughout much of the Southwest. In the past, archaeologists emphasized the differences among the remains in each of the major culture areas (Anasazi, Mogollon, and Hohokam) and within each of these areas by reference to distinct cultural or ethnic traditions (Chapter 6). More recently, archaeological interpretation has been concentrated on the organizational heterogeneity within each of the culture areas. From this perspective, the similarities in organization among the Chaco Anasazi and the Sedentary and Classic period Hohokam are highlighted. Each of these systems shows evidence of standardization in architectural construction, public architecture, craft specialization, settlement hierarchies, multicommunity organization, and substantial trade networks.

As yet, there is little agreement about the exact ways these systems were organized, the impetus for their development, or the way they functioned. The integration of ceremonial systems seems to have been important in each case, but it is not clear how trade was organized, labor groups recruited, or even part-time craft specialists supported. It is likely that each of the major systems was organized slightly differently. Characterizing their differences and similarities are important issues for future archaeological research. In any case, in both the Anasazi and Hohokam regions, there was great organizational change in about AD 1100.

Despite the fact that each of the major regional systems seems to have incorporated a large area, most of the people living in the Southwest at the time of these systems seem to have been participating in more simply organized systems, which continued until about AD 1300. Two patterns of systems that lack hierarchical development were presented. An aggregated system was exemplified in the discussions of the Mesa Verde, Mimbres, and Kayenta areas; a dispersed pattern by the Rio Grande, Jornada areas, and Lower Muddy and Virgin Anasazi. Aggregated systems contain very large sites, but the sites are predominantly residential and appear to be aggregates of formerly dispersed local communities. There were undoubtedly social mechanisms serving to integrate these villages, but relatively egalitarian relationships among household residential groups are reflected in the architecture of these settlements. This architectural observation suggests that the aggregated communities were organized in ways more nearly approximating modern Southwestern peoples than were the regionally integrated systems. Future research needs to address this issue.

In the Rio Grande, Muddy, and Virgin Anasazi areas; the Jornada Mogollon region; and probably much of the Patayan area as well, populations seem to have remained relatively more mobile throughout the period. It is likely that villages, when they existed, were small and perhaps somewhat temporary. They may have housed only a few related families and been sustained as much by gathering and hunting as by agriculture. After about AD 1150, the nucleated systems seem to have failed in the northern Southwest (see Chapter 11). When these systems collapsed, however, the organizational strategies reflected in both the aggregated and dispersed systems continued. This situation indicates the regional importance of organizational heterogeneity and adaptive flexibility. The presence of aggregated and dispersed systems might provide models of successful forms of integration.

Chapter-opening art: Figure of Pueblo Bonito (courtesy of the U.S. National Park Service).

CHAPTER 11

Abandonment: A Complex Social Phenomenon

Starting at about AD 1130, and increasing markedly in pace in the late 1200s, sites over very large areas of the Southwest were no longer inhabited by those who had occupied them, providing archaeologists and laymen with an enduring puzzle. The term abandonment is generally used by archaeologists to refer to this occurrence. Some Native Americans object that the word abandonment may imply that the people lacked interest in former residences or no longer visited or used a former homeland. In fact, while I can think of no better term, the word abandonment has been used to refer to several different kinds of complicated social change and population movement that should be kept conceptually distinct. When used here, the word abandonment does not preclude revisiting areas for a variety of reasons other than full-time occupation. New chronological studies, new paleoenvironmental data, analyses, and syntheses allow a better understanding of the complex nature of abandonment phenomena. In addition to exploring reasons that people may have left permanent dwellings in some areas, archaeologists have turned their attention to looking at what drew people to the new areas in which they settled. This chapter looks at processes influencing abandonment at different scales, from single sites, to small geographic areas and large regions.

INTRODUCTION

At the time of their discovery by Euro-Americans, the more spectacular ruins of the Colorado Plateaus—the cliff dwellings of the Mesa Verde, the multistoried stone ruins of Chaco—had long been deserted by their builders. The general similarities in architecture and other material culture remains between these ruins and modern Pueblo villages left little doubt as to the ultimate fate of the people who had occupied the now ruined dwellings, but explaining the abandonment of the northern portion of the Pueblo heartland became the subject of popular speculation and scientific interest. As Varien and others (1996:104) comment, the topic "has generated hundreds if not thousands of term papers and countless media evocations of a sublime and impenetrable mystery." In fact, most notions that were initially advanced to explain the plateau abandonment have been neither confirmed nor entirely discarded, and each continues to have its advocates.

The term abandonment has been applied to a variety of phenomena—at different scales—that are more productively viewed, potentially, as different kinds of events. For example, abandonment has been applied to situations of depopulation and to instances of a cessation of major building without depopulation. Abandonment has also been used to refer to instances in which large regions were depopulated and to cases in which local areas or even single sites were deserted. Treating this diversity as though it is the end result of the same causal factors or processes leads to considerable confusion. A reexamination of the data in light of conceptually more precise statements of the kind of behavior reflected in the archaeological record is therefore here presented first, followed by a review of both push and pull factors implicated by various scholars and the currently available data that either tend to support or contradict them.

VARIETY OF ABANDONMENT PROCESSES

The numerous ruins of the Southwest attest to abandonment of single sites as a common phenomenon, at least among ancestral Pueblo peoples. Parsons (1939:14) characterized the Pueblo people as semi-nomadic, and Kidder (1962:149) commented that the Pueblos were "ready to abandon their dwellings on what seems to us as the slightest pretext." Outside of the Anasazi and Mogollon regions, Hohokam settlements were occupied over longer periods of time, but the complicated overlapping patterns of house-floors indicates that individual Hohokam houses were also short-lived. Hantman (1983:158–163) demonstrated that the mean length of occupation for all dated sites on the Colorado Plateaus is 80 years. This mean is biased by the inclusion of many very large pueblos. If only small sites (10 rooms or less) are examined, the mean occupation is 34 years. The use-life of Hohokam pithouses has been estimated to be about 15 years. The pattern of relatively frequent movement contrasts markedly with occupation patterns among Old World Near Eastern agriculturalists, where *tells* representing the accumulated settlement debris of millennia are salient features of the landscape. At one level of analysis, then, southwestern archaeologists must determine factors that underlie residential mobility.

In addition to the abandonment of single sites, many local areas were inhabited for only brief periods or were inhabited intermittently over longer periods by people who were sedentary enough to have constructed durable dwellings rather than temporary shelters. For example, the Gallina area of New Mexico (Figure 11.1) was occupied

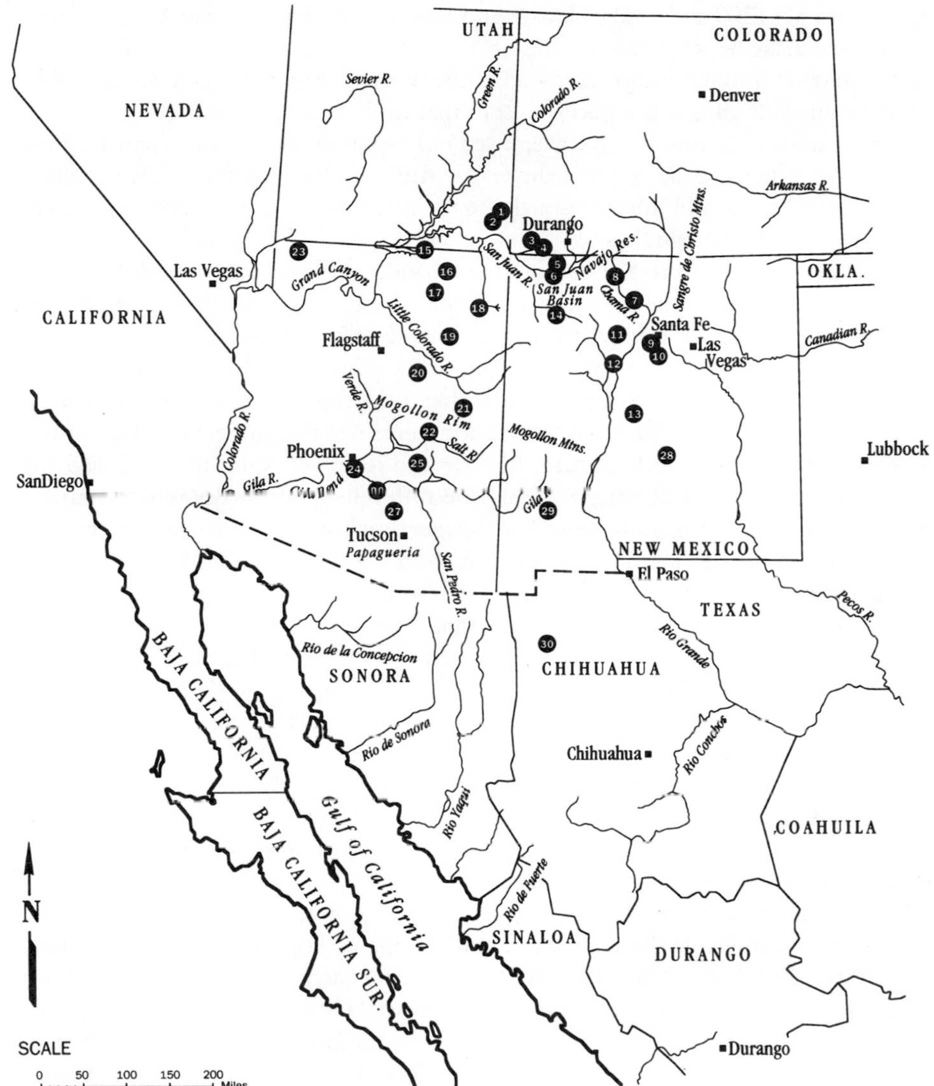

FIGURE 11.1 The sites located on this map feature in the discussion of abandonments. Key: 1 Comb Wash and Milk Ranch Point; 2 Cedar Mesa; 3 Sand Canyon Pueblo and Castle Rock Pueblo; 4 Mesa Verde; 5 Aztec Ruin; 6 Salmon Ruin; 7 Chama District; 8 Gallina; 9 Arroyo Hondo; 10 Galisteo Basin; 11 Jemez Mountains; 12 Cochiti (White Rock Canyon); 13 Salinas Pueblo District; 14 Chaco Canyon; 15 Navajo Mountain; 16 Betatakin and Kiet Siel Ruins; 17 Black Mesa; 18 Canyon de Chelly; 19 Hopi; 20 Anderson Mesa; 21 Hay Hollow; 22 Grasshopper Area; 23 Virgin Valley; 24 Mesa Grande, Los Muertos, La Ciudad; 25 Gila Area; 26 Casa Grande; 27 Marana Community; 28 Sierra Blanca/Capitan Highlands; 29 Mimbres Area; 30 Casas Grandes. (Map by David Underwood.)

between about AD 1200 and 1300. Matson and Lipe (1978) describe the Anasazi occupation of the Cedar Mesa, Utah, as one of boom and bust, with Anasazi occupation dating from AD 200 to 400 followed by a hiatus, reoccupation briefly in the late 600s followed by another gap, and a period of occupation between about 1100 and 1270. The Grand Canyon appears to have been used only sporadically by a variety of different groups. It would be expected that the explanations offered for short-term or periodic use of localities would not necessarily be the same as those given for short-term use of single structures or single sites.

Very large regions of the Southwest were abandoned by villagers before contact with European culture. In the far west, the Virgin Anasazi area was abandoned before 1200. The Kayenta Anasazi region, the Mesa Verde, San Juan Basin, and large areas of the Mogollon Mountains were abandoned by 1300. The upper Little Colorado and White Mountains, the Tucson Basin, and other outlying Hohokam districts were abandoned by 1450. These large-scale abandonments are the subject of most of the abandonment models in the literature. Clearly the level of explanation offered for synchronous regional abandonments should be different from those used for either site or local abandonments. Following Euro-American contact, sometime in the late sixteenth through the seventeenth century, much of the southern Rio Grande Valley, the Jornada Mogollon region, the Salinas Pueblo district, and the core area of the Hohokam were abandoned. Currently, these late abandonments are viewed as similar to the pattern of the large-scale regional abandonment in the thirteenth century because the size of the affected area is great. In my view, however, the abandonment that occurred between 1130 and 1200 is similar to that in the sixteenth and seventeenth centuries, and both differ from the abandonment between the late 1200s and 1450. As described in more detail below, the abandonment at the early and late end of the continuum reflects population pulling in and using less territory more intensively. On the other hand, the period between the late 1200s and 1450 witnessed massive dislocations of population.

Mention has also been made of distinguishing abandonment from the cessation of major building episodes or the disruption and change of highly distinctive archaeological patterns. For example, an abundance of tree-ring dates indicates that the Classic Bonito sites in Chaco Canyon were constructed between AD 950 and 1150, and it had long been thought that the canyon was abandoned by the Bonito population in the late twelfth century to be replaced sometime later by migrants from the Mesa Verde. However, Toll and others (1980) have demonstrated that, although Bonito style construction did cease, neither abandonment nor the complete disruption of the Classic Bonito trade network ensued. Rather, Chacoan structures were modified, rooms were subdivided, and the resident population of the canyon may actually have increased for a time—though it was less visible archaeologically. A change in pattern of building, rather than abandonment and subsequent reoccupation, is also the major feature of the transition from the Sedentary to the Classic Hohokam. A similar change in pattern occurred in the Mimbres area following the Mimbres Classic.

In much of the older southwestern literature, changes in pattern were interpreted as evidence of migration and replacement of one cultural group by another. An incursion of migrants from the Mesa Verde was to have occurred in Chaco Canyon and at some outliers, such as Salmon and Aztec. As will be discussed below and in more detail in the next chapter, a migration of Salado people was postulated for the Mimbres and the Hohokam areas. These interpretations have been questioned and found to be too simple. Rather than indicating abandonment and later immigration, some changes in pattern may involve a change in the intensity of use of a particular area. For example, areas that supported agricultural production might be left as buffer zones where gathering and hunting are pursued, or in the Chaco case, public architecture might have been subdivided and used for ordinary domiciles. Even if the change in activities involved the same group of people, the nature of the archaeological record will be one in which there is an apparent discontinuity—one that might be interpreted as abandonment and reoccupation. An examination of changes in pattern, particularly involving large geographic areas, must distinguish periods during which there was a lack of major construction from periods during which there were changes in the use of land or structures. Explanations for each of these will differ considerably from explanations that are appropriate for abandonments of single sites or small local areas. Each of these diverse phenomena, which have sometimes been grouped together as examples of abandonment, are examined separately here.

Abandonment of Single Sites

Explanations for the abandonment of single sites must reflect the nature of the occupation represented by the site; some sites were temporary field houses that show little labor investment, whereas other sites not only provided year-round shelter for groups of people but contained ceremonial facilities (such as kivas) that were important to community integration. Field houses and similar temporary structures might have been abandoned for any number of reasons, including their structural decay during seasons when they were not maintained or the disuse of the field with which they were associated. Fields themselves might be abandoned for reasons that include a decline in soil fertility, mineralization, changes in weather patterns, or soil erosion. For example, Hack's (1942) data from the modern Hopi villages documents an upstream movement of fields with progressive arroyo cutting. In a study of ancient fields and field houses in the White Rock Canyon-Cochiti area of New Mexico, Fosberg (1979) and Fosberg and Husler (1979) noted an expansion of field houses to locations of poor quality soils during the fourteenth and fifteenth centuries and documented heavy salt concentrations in the soils at a field house locality. This work suggests that the field houses were abandoned because of irreversible mineralization damage to the soils. Work by Nials and others (1989) documents instances of flooding in the Salt River Valley that would have destroyed existing Hohokam canals and fields.

More permanent sites, including fairly large settlements, may also have had brief periods of occupation despite considerable labor investment in their construction. Some studies indicate that as long as there was sufficient land for cultivation, settlements moved—possibly in response to the local effects of minor climatic changes or to the depletion of resources. For example, in a study of changes in settlement location on Mesa Verde, I (Cordell 1975, 1981) quite accurately predicted the abandonment of some sites and the continued occupation of others from the tree-ring record of rainfall fluctuations and the effect these would have had on arable land. The study correctly predicted that during very dry intervals, sites that were near agricultural land that did not retain moisture and were distant from water sources such as springs and arroyos would be abandoned, while sites that were in settings that conserved moisture would continue to be occupied. The study also correctly identified locations that would be abandoned when there was greatly increased rainfall. These were sites located at high elevations, those with northern exposures and those in immediate proximity to water sources that could inflict flood damage.

Single sites might also have been abandoned because local resources were depleted. In another study that considered data from Mesa Verde, Stiger (1979) hypothesized that continual cutting of trees in the course of swidden (slash and burn) agriculture reduced the forest and resulted in eventual mineral depletion of the then overused soils. Using data from the Dolores Project, near Mesa Verde, Kohler and Matthews (1988) found changes in the kinds of wood used for fuel over time as well as in plant and animal foods that also suggest deforestation. In their view, the diminished wood resources could have resulted in site abandonment even if soil fertility did not decline. Firewood is another crucial resource that is often depleted around dwellings, and the need for fuel for cooking and heating may result in households relocating. Eventually, people would have had to go too far to obtain wood for building, heating, and cooking. As long as there were lands elsewhere, relocation was an appropriate option.

In a study that considered southwestern data from a global perspective, Raish (1991) found that the period of time during which people occupied villages was shorter in North America than in Europe or Asia. She attributes the difference to the absence of domestic food animals in North America, arguing that villages would be abandoned as local game supplies were depleted.

Local Abandonments

A commonly occurring southwestern pattern was the abandonment of limited geographic areas, such as a single small drainage, valley, or adjacent uplands. Several different behaviors seem to underlie this pattern. One of these was examined in Chapter 10. From about AD 1000 to 1130, agricultural communities reached their greatest geographic extent. In some cases, such as the Muddy and Virgin valleys, ancient farmers settled where agriculture is largely impossible today. In other cases, such as over much of the upland Kayenta area, agriculture was established at about the limits possible for dry farming. With even minor decreases in rainfall, these experiments became untenable and the localities involved were abandoned. Although occasionally there is some mystery about where the population relocated (e.g., Lyneis 1996), in other instances, population increase in adjacent areas reveals the likely destination (Dean 1996a; Varien *et al.* 1996).

In some cases, small areas were inhabited and abandoned repeatedly with little mystery regarding the probable relocation of the groups involved because continuities in material culture have been found in adjacent areas that could have absorbed a population increase. Cedar Mesa, Utah, mentioned above, provides a classic case of this sort. Matson and Lipe (1978) found an apparent hiatus in occupation between Basketmaker II, locally dated from about AD 200 to 400, and late Basketmaker III, dated to the late AD 600s. They view the transition between Basketmaker II and Basketmaker III as an expansion of the agricultural component of the subsistence base that was permitted by acceptance of improved cultigens or improved techniques of farming dependent on rainfall. When this change occurred, there was also an apparent local abandonment of Cedar Mesa, suggesting that the economic shift occurred in areas that were better suited to rainfall farming. These areas would have been at somewhat higher and better watered locations to the northeast and east. Survey data from Comb Wash east of Cedar Mesa and from Milk Ranch Point northeast of Cedar Mesa both manifest little Basketmaker II occupation, but considerable Basketmaker III habitation, suggesting that the Cedar Mesa population could have moved to either Comb Wash or Milk Ranch Point or to comparable nearby locations.

Similarly, in their overview of ancient New Mexico, Stuart and Gauthier (1981) comment on several areas in which there are apparently alternating highland and lowland occupations. Basketmaker sites dating to about AD 350–600 tend to be in upland settings between about 1220 m and 1520 m. Late Basketmaker and early Pueblo I sites, dating to about AD 600–700, are located at lower elevations. There is an upland shift in site location at about AD 750. Their data suggest that between AD 850 and 1140 there is a general pattern of both upstream and downhill site movement followed by a change to downhill locations between 1200 and 1300. The period from AD 1300 on is one in which the bulk of the population seems to have been located along rivers, hence primarily at low elevations. They find this pattern between the Jornada Mogollon lowlands and the Sierra Blanca/Capitan highlands of southeastern New Mexico, the Galisteo Basin and the Sangre de Cristo Mountains, and the Pajarito Plateau and the middle Rio Grande Valley. Stuart and Gauthier's (1981) observation was confirmed in a detailed example of analyses of population changes in the Pajarito Plateau/Santa Fe vicinity (Orcutt 1991). In fact, as Crown and others (1996) found for the period after 1300, after the Four Corners region was abandoned, it was possible to trace a population "bulge" from the Chama and northern Rio Grande to the south and southeast *if movement between lowlands and highlands was also taken into consideration.* The elevation changes, discussed above, were determined by examining survey information derived for all of New Mexico by a variety of institutions, and the consistency of the documented patterns is quite striking.

Very similar observations were made by Euler and others (1979) from a compilation of interdisciplinary data for the Colorado Plateau that were acquired as part of the long-term Black Mesa Archaeological Project (Gumerman 1988). The study by Euler and his colleagues (1979) indicates generally moist conditions from about AD 450 to 850, dry conditions from about 850 to 950, and a long, relatively wet period from 950 to 1425, within which are short intervals of drought at about 1150 and 1300. Finally, there appears to have been a trend to generally increasing moisture after 1500. The authors argue that "major population trends are both parallel and reciprocal to the long-term hydrologic fluctuations" (Euler *et al.* 1979:1098). They view population as expanding within the drier areas of the Colorado Plateaus (Hay Hollow Valley, Grand Canyon, Hopi Buttes, Cedar Mesa, Black Mesa, and Canyon de Chelly) during wet intervals and as either abandoning these areas or decreasing occupation of them during dry periods. Reciprocally, the Mesa Verde and Navajo Reservoir districts, which are generally wetter and higher, are seen to support population growth during periods of decreased moisture and to lose population during wet intervals. In this view, local abandonments are at least partially correlated with population growth and expansion into other areas.

Matson and Lipe (1978) explained the Cedar Mesa population movements primarily in the context of dryland farming. The moves to higher elevations where precipitation is expected to be greater than at lower altitudes is seen as a predictable response to conditions of drought as long as uplands remain uninhabited and open to newcomers. Stuart and Gauthier (1981) also suggested that the shifts they documented may reflect adaptations to regional changes in precipitation patterns, in their case, particularly the seasonal distribution of rainfall. Yet, the very broad geographic scope of these movements and the fairly slow pace at which they seem to occur may suggest that the underlying mechanisms might have been changes in ground water levels that would have been obvious to ancient farmers as arroyos were down cut or aggraded (Crown *et al.* 1996; Karlstrom 1988). Reconstruction of a hydrologic curve for the Colorado Plateaus (Karlstrom 1988) supports this broader generalization (Dean 1996a; Dean *et al.* 1985; Euler *et al.* 1979; Gumerman 1988).

Changes in settlement form, especially a shift from dispersed hamlets to aggregated settlements, will cause abandonment of single sites and can cause abandonment of localities. A consistent pattern in the Southwest after about 1200 is the aggregation of population in fewer large settlements. Population aggregation would, of course, entail abandonments of numerous small sites. In a study of sites in the Hay Hollow Valley, Arizona, Zubrow (1972, 1974) attempts to elucidate the aggregation process by reference to both a change in the relative abundance of resources and the necessities of maintaining community activities. Zubrow argues that population growth is a function of the carrying capacity of the environment and that a population will first fill optimal areas and then expand into less productive zones. If there is no change in the abundance of resources, it is expected that populations will fill the optimal zones first, the next most optimal zones next, and so on. If there is a change in carrying capacity involving a decrease in resources, the expectation is that less optimal zones will be depopulated first. Zubrow examined this model using data from the Hay Hollow Valley and found that up to AD 1150 the population of marginal zones increased after the best zones were full. After 1150, however, there was a drop in the population curves, and the less optimal zones were abandoned. The change was interpreted as reflecting a shift in the seasonality of rainfall, inferred from palynological studies (from summer to winter dominant), which would have adversely affected agriculture. Zubrow considers the abandonment of less optimal zones to have occurred for social reasons. Even the less optimal zones could have supported some people, but the numbers that might have continued to live there were probably too low to permit the continued functioning of a community. To sustain community activities such as marriages, ceremonies, and reciprocal exchanges of labor or food, the inhabitants of the marginal zones would have joined ongoing communities in the optimal zones.

A link among community land-use, aggregation, and abandonment is explored by Adler and others (1996). Using data from the Mesa Verde region, these authors examine a model in which aggregation occurred in the context of regional population packing. They suggest that prior to the thirteenth century, individual households within a community could have repositioned themselves to access specific farmlands or resource areas. They point out that when single dwellings are abandoned, but the community is intact in the area, people generally retain rights for some period of time to land and resources they are not currently using. Landscapes become crowded—not only with people, but with their rights of access to resources. With increased regional population growth and aggregation, it becomes increasingly difficult if not impossible for individual households to relocate within a community without infringing on another's rights of access. Without the option to reposition on the landscape, aggregated communities have no flexibility if the land they occupy cannot be farmed more intensively or reliably. Such aggregated communities were vulnerable to any perturbation, such as the droughts and other climatic uncertainties of the late thirteenth century (see below), and large-scale movement resulting in local abandonment may follow.

A different view of aggregation and local abandonment was presented by Hunter-Anderson (1979) in a study of land-use patterns in the Cochiti area of New Mexico. The Rio Grande in general, and the Cochiti area in particular, saw an increase in population after 1300. Hunter-Anderson interprets population aggregation as a result of demographic influx and competition for the home range. A clustering of the population should occur at the expense of dispersed upland settlements, which are abandoned to leave buffer areas between population aggregates. The abandoned uplands are then used for hunting, gathering, and limited farming. Evidence of these activities would be an ephemeral and essentially nondiagnostic archaeological record that would have the appearance of abandonment.

In general, the abandonments of local areas recurred frequently in the Southwest. Explanations for these occurrences invoke changes in subsistence practices and movement to areas where new or different subsistence strategies are more appropriate, changes in the amounts and seasonal timing of rainfall and population movements to well-watered areas, the adjustment of populations to changes in cutting and filling of arroyos, and abandonment of marginal or wooded buffer areas as a concomitant of processes of population aggregation. These explanatory frameworks are amenable to testing with the techniques available to archaeology today, although tests involve a great investment in paleoclimatic and paleoenvironmental reconstruction, in addition to detailed and comparative analyses of excavation and survey data. For example, if abandonment of upland areas left buffer zones among aggregated settlements, then there should be no decrease in game or wild plant foods at aggregated communities. In some cases, such as the studies at Black Mesa (Gumerman 1988), detailed paleoenvironmental data have been amassed, analyzed, and generally found to support the interpretations made above.

In the Black Mesa case, and others from the Colorado Plateaus (e.g., Van West 1996), movement from one locality to another—either up or down stream or up and down in elevation—depends on the landscape being relatively empty of other people. Once agricultural communities were established throughout the various settings of the Southwest, and areas that were marginal for agriculture were apparently used for hunting or foraging, the mobility option became less possible. Regional population densities required more drastic solutions. For those of us who live in urban settings, it is hard to imagine a landscape that is considered full when it is occupied only by people living in small, widely dispersed settlements. Our urban areas are supported by worldwide markets and transportation systems. In the arid, resource poor Southwest, without the ability to transport food over appreciable distances on a regular (daily or weekly) basis, large urban populations cannot be supported. If movement locally within a region is precluded by settlements of other people or their traditional use-areas, abandonment of the region in question may become the only viable strategy.

Regional Abandonment

As Fish and others (1994) state, the term region lacks precise definition in southwestern archaeology. They suggest that it corresponds approximately to major topographic or ceramic subdivisions such as the Anasazi branches or the Tucson Basin Hohokam or the Mountain Mogollon (see Chapters 6 and 7). Looking at abandonment at the regional scale allows looking at pan-southwestern patterns and relationships. Fish and others (1994) comment that conditions particular to each region that was abandoned may have been critical to the specific timing and nature of that instance; they are not likely to be sufficient to explain the very widespread and essentially synchronous nature of the events throughout the Southwest. These occurred across the entire Southwest from about AD 1250 through 1450, although within specific regions abandonment was much more rapid. In the Mesa Verde region, for example, abandonment seems to have occurred between 1280 and 1300 (Varien *et al.* 1996). A notion of the numbers of settlements that were involved in the abandonment can be gained by comparing the maps in Figures 11.2 and 11.3. In human terms, for the Mesa Verde region, Varien and others (1996) estimate that between 5,000 and 10,000 people left the region within 20 years. They state that, "the demographic and chronological data indicate a rate of depopulation that cannot be accounted for by a gradual decline resulting from a slight excess of death over birth rates. Consequently, either catastrophic decline or emigration seems the more likely for this final phase" (Varien *et al.* 1996:104).

One can divide the proposed explanations for abandonment in a variety of ways: catastrophic or processual, cultural or environmental, or single or multiple cause, for example. None of these is entirely satisfactory, for there are always some explanations that have aspects pertaining to more than one mode. Within the past five or six years, archaeologists have turned to looking at abandonment in terms of push factors and pull factors. This focus is important because it fully addresses continuity in southwestern populations past the abandonment into later times, which also highlights the complex social factors involved in population relocation. This discussion considers push

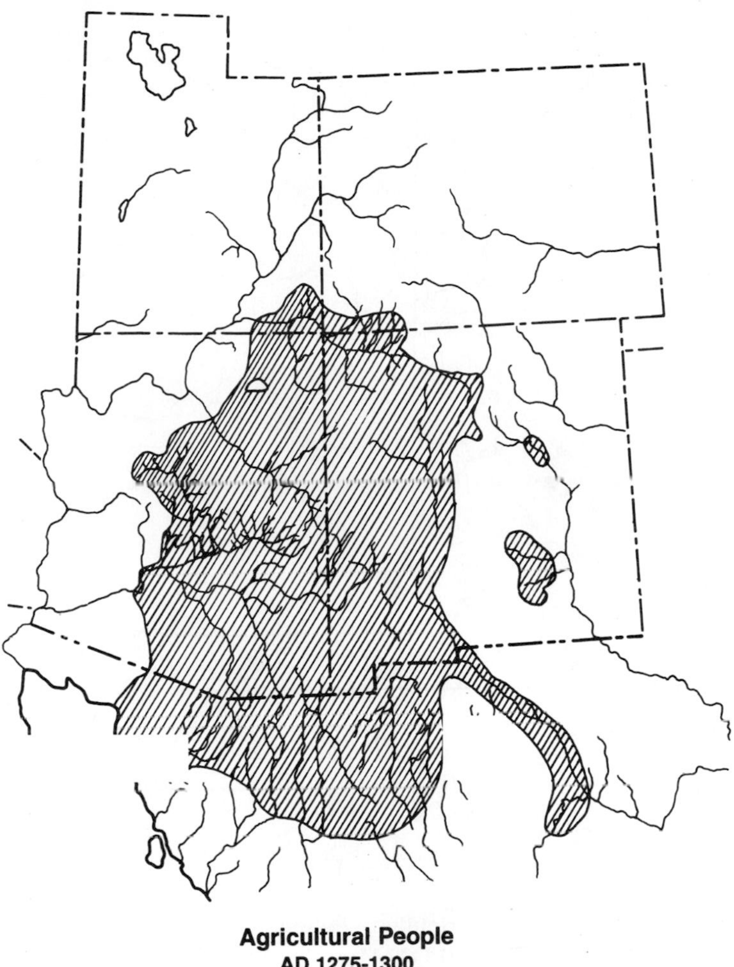

FIGURE 11.2 This map shows the geographic extent of agricultural people in the Southwest between AD 1275 and 1300 (adapted from Fish *et al.* 1994 by Marjorie Leggitt, Leggitt Design).

and pull factors. Some of these, especially the push factors, were developed in the traditional archaeological literature of the Southwest. They are described here updated with the most current evidence available.

CULTURAL PUSH FACTORS

Warfare models have long been proposed for the abandonment of the Anasazi Southwest. They are usually differentiated into those that invoke fighting with

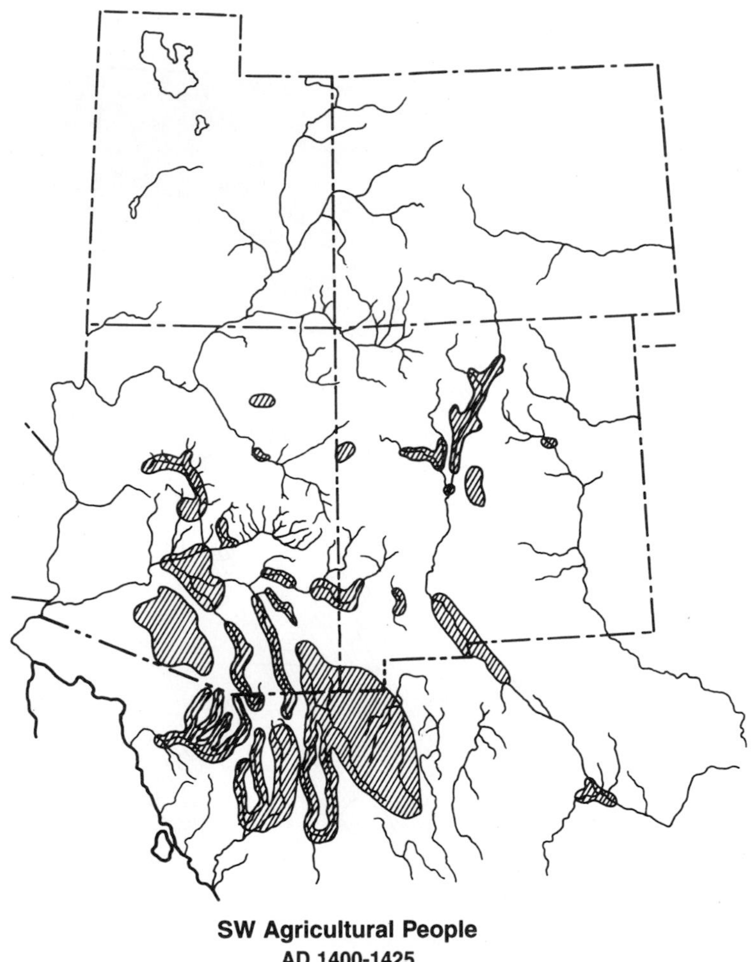

FIGURE 11.3 This map shows the geographic extent of agricultural people in the Southwest between AD 1400 and 1425 (adapted from Fish *et al.* 1994 by Marjorie Leggitt, Leggitt Design).

non-Pueblo, particularly Ute or Athapaskan peoples, and those that cite internecine warfare among Pueblo peoples themselves. Harold Gladwin was an articulate proponent of the idea that the Pueblo were driven from their homes by hostile nomads. He wrote, "in every village in the Southwest at AD 1200, the same questions are being asked: Where to go? What to do? to obtain relief from the ceaseless persecution of the marauding Athabascans [sic]." (Gladwin 1957:269).

The notion of warfare with nomads, either Athapaskan or Ute, is plausible because in the post-Spanish period there have been times of considerable hostility between Pueblo and non-Pueblo groups. Pueblo legends and stories describe the Navajo as traditional enemies, and folk-sayings caution that Navajo and Apache could be fearful adversaries. There are also Navajo and Ute traditional stories of interactions with ancient Anasazi in locations such as the Grand Canyon and Mesa Verde (i.e., Begay and Roberts 1996). Despite this, there are two oft-stated objections to invoking the Ute or "Athapaskan menace" as a reason for abandonment. First, as Linton (1944) pointed out, the Utes and Athapaskans were strong enemies of the Pueblos only after they had acquired horses from the Europeans. Far less numerous than the Pueblos, and lacking the ability to carry out swift surprise attacks that the horse made possible, nomads would have been at a tactical disadvantage. Second, relating specifically to Athapaskan-speakers is the fact that despite years of research there is no convincing evidence that they were in the Southwest much before the arrival of the Spaniards. There has long been an interest in documenting proto-Navajo or proto-Athapaskan-speakers in the Southwest. The interest has been rekindled in the context of historic preservation and cultural resources management studies, some undertaken by the Navajo Nation Historic Preservation Department. Although the known geographic extent of early (pre-Fort Sumner) Navajo occupation of the Southwest has been greatly expanded by this work, as yet the oldest documented Navajo remains date to about AD 1500, and one possibly proto-Navajo site to between AD 1350 and 1500 (Brown 1996). Since these dates are after the Anasazi abandonment of the northern San Juan region, recent advocates of nomads as instrumental in the abandonment favor the Ute as possibilities (Haas and Creamer 1996).

Another problem with the notion of warfare with the Athapaskans as a reason for the abandonment is that, in historically and ethnographically documented situations, Pueblos and Athapaskans were often involved in close and rather friendly interactions. This is true especially during the time of the great external threat posed by the Europeans, between the Pueblo Revolt of 1680 and de Vargas's reconquest of 1692–1696, but at other times as well, Pueblos and Navajos lived together (Brugge 1996). The refugee communities in the Largo-Gobernador area and in the Jemez Mountains were among locations used by both peoples (Brugge 1983). After the reconquest (1696), the Pueblos again revolted against the Spaniards and some fled from their villages; for example, the Picuris fled and remained for about 10 years with Apache groups on the Plains (Brown 1979). In times of peace, there was considerable trade between Pueblos and Athapaskan peoples. For example, Brown (1979) notes that relations between the Picuris and the Apaches were generally friendly, and Jicarilla families visited the pueblo and participated in feast days during the summer.

The apparent paradox of the Historic period Pueblo-Athapaskan relations is that, although the Athapaskan are viewed as traditional enemies, much of the interaction among these groups involved friendly social relations and trade. Using historic interactions between La Junta villagers of northern Mexico/southwest Texas and bands of Apaches as a model, Kelley (1952) demonstrated how periods of peaceful trading alternated with times of hostile raids, depending on environmental conditions. Kelley suggested that under normal conditions villagers had sufficient agricultural produce to trade with the Apaches, and the Apaches had surpluses of meat to offer in exchange. During times of drought, neither group had enough surplus to trade. Village women would have to forage more widely, at the same time that Apaches were most likely to have been turned away from the villages without food and would most likely be expected to have ill feelings toward the village. Kelley's argument considers a condition of the natural environment as a key variable underlying the character of Pueblo-Apache interactions.

Given the lack of evidence for the presence of Athapaskan groups in the Southwest, hostility from Athapaskan speakers specifically is not supported. Linton's (1944) arguments against small groups of nomads successfully attacking populous pueblos still seems appropriate. However, given climatic deterioration and disruption of social networks and usual trade relationships among Pueblo peoples, semi-nomadic groups might well have successfully harassed villages.

Today, after some years of neglect, inter-Pueblo warfare is again a popular topic (Haas and Creamer 1993, 1996; Wilcox and Haas 1994) implicated in regional abandonment. Davis (1965) and Ellis (1951) pointed out that the characterization of Pueblo groups as essentially peaceful is inaccurate and that, prior to subjugation by Europeans, internecine conflict and warfare may have been prevalent. The evidence for this position consists of the ethnographically documented importance of warrior sodalities (and scalp societies) among the Pueblos, the military success of the Pueblo Revolt of 1680, and historically recorded inter-Pueblo combat at the time of the reconquest. Although it is undeniable that no group of people is "inherently" peaceful, and fighting probably was of considerable importance among the Pueblos, whether such warfare accounts for the abandonment of large areas is debated.

Wilcox and Haas (1994), who espouse the importance of warfare in general in the ancient Southwest, note that evidence of conflict appears episodically in the archaeological record. The most convincing case study cited by Wilcox and Haas is from the Gallina area in the Jemez Mountains of New Mexico. Evidence of warfare includes mass burials with arrows imbedded in skeletons, 34 percent of the documented habitation sites having been burned, 69 percent of habitations being in defensible locations, and 42 percent of Gallina skeletons having been found unburied on floors of burned house structures. The entire Gallina occupation dates between AD 1200 and 1300; however, the Jemez Mountains were not abandoned in 1300 and many, though not all, archaeologists accept Reiter's (1938) position that the Gallina were ancestral to modern Jemez Pueblo. The problem becomes one of linking warfare to regional abandonment.

Another good example of warfare comes from the Grasshopper Plateau of the Mountain Mogollon region (Fish *et al.* 1994; Reid 1989; Reid *et al.* 1996). There three excavated sites that date to the period beginning in about 1280—Chodistaas, Grasshopper Spring, and a site known as AZ P:14:197—show evidence of having been burned. However, as with the Gallina area, the Grasshopper Plateau was not then abandoned. Rather, population moved to a larger site, Grasshopper Pueblo. Reid and others (1996) suggest that further aggregation may well have been a response to a need for defense.

In an extensive survey and testing program designed to locate evidence of warfare in the Kayenta Anasazi region, Haas and Creamer (1993, 1996) "consistently found sites located in extraordinarily defensive positions in the late Pueblo III period"

FIGURE 11.4 Long House, Mesa Verde National Park, in 1908. Whether Mesa Verde cliff dwellings such as this were built primarily or particularly for defense has been debated for years (photograph by Jesse Nusbaum courtesy of the Museum of New Mexico, No. 60564).

(Haas and Creamer 1996:208). The Trincheras sites of southern Arizona (see Chapter 6) are considered primarily defensive by some authors (Wilcox 1979a; Wilcox and Haas 1994) though not by others (Fish and Fish 1989). A similar debate has been ongoing in regard to the defensive nature of Mesa Verde cliff dwellings (Fiure 11.4) (Cordell and Halpern 1975; Rohn 1977, 1989). An examination of the admittedly limited information on Pueblo warfare, combined with cross-cultural data, do not support this interpretation for cliff dwellings. At Mesa Verde, most of the crops and many of the storage structures are located on the mesa tops in places that cannot successfully be guarded from caves located some 6–12 m below. Cliff dwellings offer virtually no defense against ambush attacks. In daily tasks of going to and from fields and to and from water sources, the cliff dweller is in complete view on narrow paths and on toe holds or stairways cut into the rock. An ambush party need only lie in wait. The defensive nature of the cliff dwellings is probably most convincing if one considers an attack directed toward the destruction of an entire village. It is difficult to imagine large numbers of enemy warriors sneaking up the talus slopes or jumping silently down

FIGURE 11.5 Watch Tower, Mesa Verde National Park. Isolated towers at Mesa Verde and elsewhere in the northern San Juan may have served as lookouts for defense. Some towers, however, are not situated to afford a view and some are connected to kivas by tunnels, suggesting additional functions (photograph by Fay Cooper Cole, courtesy of Lewis R. Binford).

6.5-m cliffs to sack a village. On the other hand, if the few reports of attacks on entire villages are credible, Pueblo warriors had developed methods to gain access to villages primarily through intrigue (Figure 11.5). Ellis reports of the Jemez:

> In what seems to have been a favorite method of retaliation, members of an aggrieved group posed as guests or watched until all the men of an offending village had left on a hunting trip. Then little packets containing pine tar and fragments of pine needles or dried juniper leaves were tucked around kiva- and house-beams where they would not be noticed. Later, a light touched to one packet caused it to burst into flame, much as if the material had been soaked in gasoline. The fire spread quickly from packet to packet through the kiva rafters so quickly that the men inside the kiva suffocated before they could escape (Ellis 1951:187).

Certainly, if such tactics were employed by the Mesa Verde Anasazi, the least desirable location for a village would be inside a rock shelter limited both in space and escape routes. Alternative motives for living in cave or rock shelter sites include expansion of agricultural activities and the concomitant removal of villages from potentially cultivable land, or the extra protection from the elements afforded by natural shelters.

The latter might become important if groups invested more time in subsistence pursuits than in village construction and repair.

In the Northern San Juan and Mesa Verde area, skeletal evidence indicative of warfare was recovered from Castle Rock and Sand Canyon Pueblos, from the "Charnel House Tower," and from the West Pueblo at Aztec (Martin 1929; Morris 1924; Wilcox and Haas 1994; Varien *et al.* 1996). However, in other large sites such as Mug House and Long House on Mesa Verde, there are no human remains associated with abandonment or terminal occupation (Rohn 1971; Varien *et al.* 1996). Further, Turner (1983, 1989; Turner and Turner 1990) has documented multiple instances of disarticulated, fragmented, and partially burned human remains that indicate dismemberment and possible cannibalism. The cases discussed by Turner are from the entire Anasazi sequence, suggesting that the ritual involved (Turner suggests association with witchcraft) was part of the Anasazi pattern rather than isolated behavior restricted to the late 1200s.

These data taken together suggest that warfare and interpersonal violence were part of the way of life of all southwestern peoples. However, whether they were primary causes of abandonment is debated. Generally, the results of warfare are that victorious groups may either subjugate their enemies and extract tribute or labor from them or drive them away and occupy their land and villages. If there are casualties, there is regional reduction in population; however, demographic studies indicate that the population recovery following such catastrophes is generally quite rapid. These observations suggest that warfare and violence may have been a symptom of problems relating to abandonment rather than its cause. Nevertheless, the recently revitalized interest in ancient southwestern warfare has encouraged thinking about the role of warfare in similar societies throughout the world and in cultural development in general.

Another frequently cited cultural cause of abandonment is factionalism and internal strife within villages. The ethnographic case most frequently cited is the twentieth century example of the Hopi village of Old Oraibi (Bradfield 1971; Levy 1992; Titiev 1944; Whiteley 1988). The net result of the long-term factional dispute at Old Oraibi was the almost complete abandonment of that village and the founding of several others (New Oraibi, Bacavi, and Hotevilla). Critics of factionalism as an explanation for abandonment have argued that the conflict at Old Oraibi was largely the result of U.S. Government intervention in the Hopi way of life; it therefore is not an appropriate example of abandonment in the pre-Euro-American period. However, the possibly inappropriate use of this example as an analog may not be the key issue. Factional disputes are unfortunately common in villages throughout the world; they could indeed account for the depopulation of a village, as well as for the founding of new ones. They do not account for regional depopulation.

Colton (1960) was among the first to discuss systematically relating abandonments to the effects of epidemic diseases. He emphasized that prior to the major depopulation of the Colorado Plateau, Anasazi were living in quite large, aggregated settlements. Within these settlements, trash was sometimes deposited in unoccupied rooms, and burials were placed in abandoned rooms and in mounds in the immediate vicinity of living areas. Colton suggested that crowded conditions, the proximity of trash to living areas, and possibly contaminated water supplies would have been ideal for the spread of potentially devastating epidemic diseases. More recently, the abundant tree-ring dates from regions such as Mesa Verde confirm the rapidity with which abandonment took place. This, combined with lack of evidence of reoccupation, again raises questions about episodes of massive population loss through mortality.

Providing conclusive evidence of ancient epidemics of pan-regional scope is a very difficult task. Biological anthropologists are wary of diagnosing specific diseases from skeletal evidence. Archaeologically recovered populations may not be representative of the actual burial population of a community. There are vagaries of preservation, dating, analysis, and interpretation. Nevertheless, in recent efforts Martin (1994), Nelson and others (1994), and Swedlund (1994) examined the general health and demographic characteristics of skeletal series from good contexts from Black Mesa, Chaco Canyon, Mesa Verde prior to abandonment, and Arroyo Hondo and Casas Grandes (Chihuahua) that postdate the abandonment in the late AD 1200s. The Black Mesa population, which represented people living in small dispersed communities, showed the least evidence of disease and nutritional stress. The Mesa Verde sample was large enough to allow comparison of remains from the early occupation to those from the period just prior to abandonment. Interestingly, the later group showed increased evidence of nutritional stress and a decline in the mean age at death, but there was no evidence of epidemic. The population that was most stressed and showed the greatest biological disruption was Arroyo Hondo, a large aggregated community but one that postdates the abandonment. The general health situation of the pre-abandonment population examined shows problems with inadequate protein, disease associated with weaning, and a continuing low level of infectious disease. It is not indicative of a pandemic. Swedlund (1994:54) imagines an Anasazi historian of the abandonment period writing, "our numbers continue to grow, but we do not feel very well."

In the older literature of southwestern archaeology, influences from Mesoamerican civilization were seen as having inspired the regional systems that developed in Chaco Canyon and among the Classic period Hohokam (see Chapter 9). Today, because of a lack of data to the contrary, those systems are viewed as indigenous developments. In the older models, systemic collapse (especially of Chaco) and the later abandonment were attributed to disruption of the Mesoamerican connections (Di Peso 1974: Vol. 4). In current writing, there is a continued interest in the overall, long-term effects of the collapse of the regional systems on abandonment (Adler 1996; Cordell 1996; Judge 1989; LeBlanc 1989a; Wilcox 1996).

In general, the regional systems are described in terms of ecological functionalism (McGuire *et al.* 1994), which views them as elaborate devices for maintaining homeostatic relationships between human populations and their environment (Nelson *et al.* 1994:121). While such an approach can often remain vague, three specific implications that can be derived from descriptions of the regional systems are relevant here. These are: (1) exchange, (2) pooling labor, and (3) maintaining peace. If any of the three were in place and then disrupted, abandonment is a possible consequence. In regard to exchange, if exchange of foodstuffs was a key feature of the regional systems, then system collapse would have threatened people's lives quite directly. Toll (1991), however, describes the lack of evidence of trade in food for the Chaco system and similar observations have been made for the Hohokam (Doyel 1991). The evidence for exchange of food may be invisible archaeologically if the context of exchange was intercommunity ritual. The current very widespread view of both Classic Bonito and the Sedentary Hohokam systems is one in which a preeminent role is given to regulating ritual that would have involved public ceremonies, pilgrimages, feasting, and food sharing (see Chapter 10 and Crown and Judge 1991), times at which food is widely distributed among celebrants. The debate about the importance of pooling labor involves questions about how much labor and central control of that labor was needed to maintain and distribute water in the Hohokam irrigation systems and for the Classic Bonito runoff systems in Chaco Canyon (Masse 1991; Vivian 1990). Further, most of the San Juan Anasazi did not depend on fields irrigated by large integrated systems (Varien *et al.* 1996). Nevertheless, the post-abandonment distribution of population in the Southwest (Figure 11.3) is a strong argument for the development of intensive irrigation agriculture *as a consequence* of abandonment. This is discussed below under "pull" factors. Finally, regarding maintaining peace, there is less evidence of warfare and violence in the Southwest at the eleventh century height of Chaco and Sedentary Hohokam systems (Haas and Wilcox 1994), but the role of warfare in the subsequent abandonments is debated.

In sum, the cultural reasons cited to explain the late thirteenth-century abandonments of the Colorado Plateaus account for some of the features observed archaeologically. Although there is no evidence of an Athapaskan intrusion at the time, warfare among Pueblo groups may have caused local population decline and the abandonment of some villages. Factionalism also would be expected to have affected only single villages at a time and should have been accompanied by evidence of the founding of new communities rather than regional depopulation. Although evidence of epidemic diseases is lacking, pre-abandonment populations were suffering a continuing level of nutritional stress. Overall systemic stress as a result of the failure of regional systems to continue to integrate peoples throughout the Southwest is an ongoing area of research related to abandonment. Questions that are being addressed in this regard are (1) how and to what degree did the regional systems function to sustain population growth throughout the Southwest, (2) were there exogenous factors that triggered their collapse, and (3) why was there a lag in time between the system failures (or at least drastic changes) of 1150 and the abandonment of some regions in the late 1200s.

ENVIRONMENTAL PUSH FACTORS

The potentially devastating effects of drought were among the earliest suggested reasons given for abandonments (i.e., Hewett *et al.* 1913). It was not until 1929 as a result of Douglass's work in dendroclimatology and dendrochronology that a specific incident of drought was linked to depopulation of the Plateaus. Douglass (1929) calculated that there had been a great drought in the northern San Juan area between

1276 and 1299, and he argued that the people, being heavily dependent on agriculture, could not survive this episode and so abandoned their homes. The great drought of 1276 to 1299 does correspond strikingly well with the final depopulation of the central Mesa Verde region (Varien *et al.* 1996). However, as the tree-ring chronology that Douglass himself made available showed, some sites, such as Betatakin and Kiet Siel, had been built in the 1270s and 1280s, when they should have been abandoned if the great drought were of regional importance. It is also true that the modern Hopi towns that are located in an area that is drier than the Mesa Verde were founded before the drought and continued to be inhabited through it. The great drought notion is best applied to the Mesa Verde, but tree-ring data from that location show that there were a series of severe droughts prior to the one between 1276 and 1299, and in spite of these, the Mesa Verde was not then abandoned.

Van West (1994, 1996) developed a tree-ring based model of effective moisture and crop production for a large area in the Mesa Verde region. Her results indicate that throughout the occupation and through the abandonment, enough food could have been grown to support the population. Van West's study is particularly enlightening because she showed that variability in crop yield within her study area would have required that the inhabitants move or otherwise have access to land in different locations. Yields were adequate to feed the population as long as mobility was possible. By the 1200s, population density was such that mobility was no longer possible. An important lesson from this study is that drought in combination with social and demographic factors would have put the population at risk. It is unlikely that a great drought on the Colorado Plateaus would have been relevant for the abandonment of Classic period sites in the Hohokam region. As mentioned, flooding has been viewed as a continuing problem in that area (Nials *et al.* 1989).

Among the modern Western Pueblo, supplemental water is usually obtained by diverting flood water from arroyos. Both Hack (1942) and Bryan (1929, 1941) proposed that during periods of deficient rainfall (though not necessarily times of severe drought) water tables would be lowered and arroyos would cut deeper channels and erode headward. Entrenchment and the headward cutting of arroyos can greatly reduce the amount of field area over which flood water could be diverted. The progression of these events would cause fields to be abandoned and would lead eventually to the population movement from the Colorado Plateau. Bradfield (1971) was able to show that headward cutting of arroyos greatly decreased the amount of land the modern Hopi of Oraibi could cultivate in the vicinity of their village. The tension engendered by the land shortage was an important element in the factional dispute that eventually split the village. Although lowering water tables and arroyo cutting are severe problems for southwestern agriculture and should not be underestimated, there are difficulties in attributing some aspects of regional abandonments to these factors. Some of the objections to the "great drought" notion can also be applied to the arroyo-cutting hypothesis. A lowering of the water table regionally would probably have more severe effects on the Hopi mesas, which were not abandoned, than on the Mesa Verde, which was. There are also cultural practices that encourage arroyo cutting. Probably the most significant ones for the Anasazi were clearing land for agricultural fields and cutting firewood (Betancourt and Van Devender 1981; Lister 1966). Anasazi technology also included the use of check dams and terraces that served to conserve soil and prevent arroyo cutting. The Mesa Verde area in particular has numerous ancient terraces and check dams that are still conserving soil today.

Major efforts in paleoenvironmental reconstruction were part of the long-term Black Mesa Archaeological Project (Gumerman 1988) and the Chaco Canyon project (Judge 1989). In addition, the Laboratory of Tree-ring Research undertook substantial regional research along with these projects and independently (Dean 1996a; Dean and Robinson 1978; Robinson and Cameron 1991; Rose *et al.* 1981). The results of these efforts provide new data and exciting new insights into regional paleoclimatic events.

As described in Chapter 2 (pp. 56–61), tree-ring indices measure the frequency and amplitude of deviation from the mean in precipitation. A network of 27 climate-sensitive archaeological tree-ring chronologies has been developed that covers the Southwest north of the Gila River (Dean 1996a and Figure 11.7). These data were used to develop reconstructed annual variation in precipitation for the northern Southwest and stream flow for the Salt and Verde rivers (Dean 1996a; Dean and Robinson 1977; Graybill 1989). Figure 11.6 shows dendroclimatic variability over time for the Colorado Plateau. Hatched intervals are those in which there was high temporal variability when transitions from high to low values were rapid. Figure 11.6 shows variability across space indicating whether climatic conditions differed among areas (high variability) or were similar from one place to another (low variability).

Also as discussed in Chapter 2, there have been essentially two different precipitation patterns in the Southwest over the past century. A bimodal pattern occurs north and west of a line from the Gila to Moenkopi Wash, and a unimodal pattern with summer dominant rainfall occurs east and south of that line (Figure 2.2). A principal component analysis of the 27 tree-ring chronologies (from 27 stations) for the period AD 966 to 1988 segregated the stations into two principal components, each of which loaded heavily for one or the other rainfall pattern. As Dean (1996a:40) states, "the resemblance is strong enough to suggest that the spatial distribution of the two dominant principal components represent the persistence of the unimodal vs. bimodal precipitation pattern for at least the last millennium."

When successive hundred year intervals, overlapped by 50 years, were examined by principal component analysis, nearly all intervals patterned the same way (Figure 11.7), except for the period between AD 1250 and 1450 "when the long-term pattern broke down into chaotic distributions of three or four principal components that exhibit no logical geographic patterning" (Dean 1996a:43). As Dean notes and examinations of Figure 11.8 indicates, there is little change in the southeastern component, suggesting that the unimodal pattern was little changed. The major changes were in the northwest, precisely those areas that were finally abandoned between the late 1200s and 1450.

Neither the exact climatic meaning of the chaotic pattern nor specific implications for human behavior have as yet been worked out. However, a pattern that had been in place for at least 550 years provides the kind of long-term stability that establishes human carrying capacity. Generally we would not expect a behavioral response to have

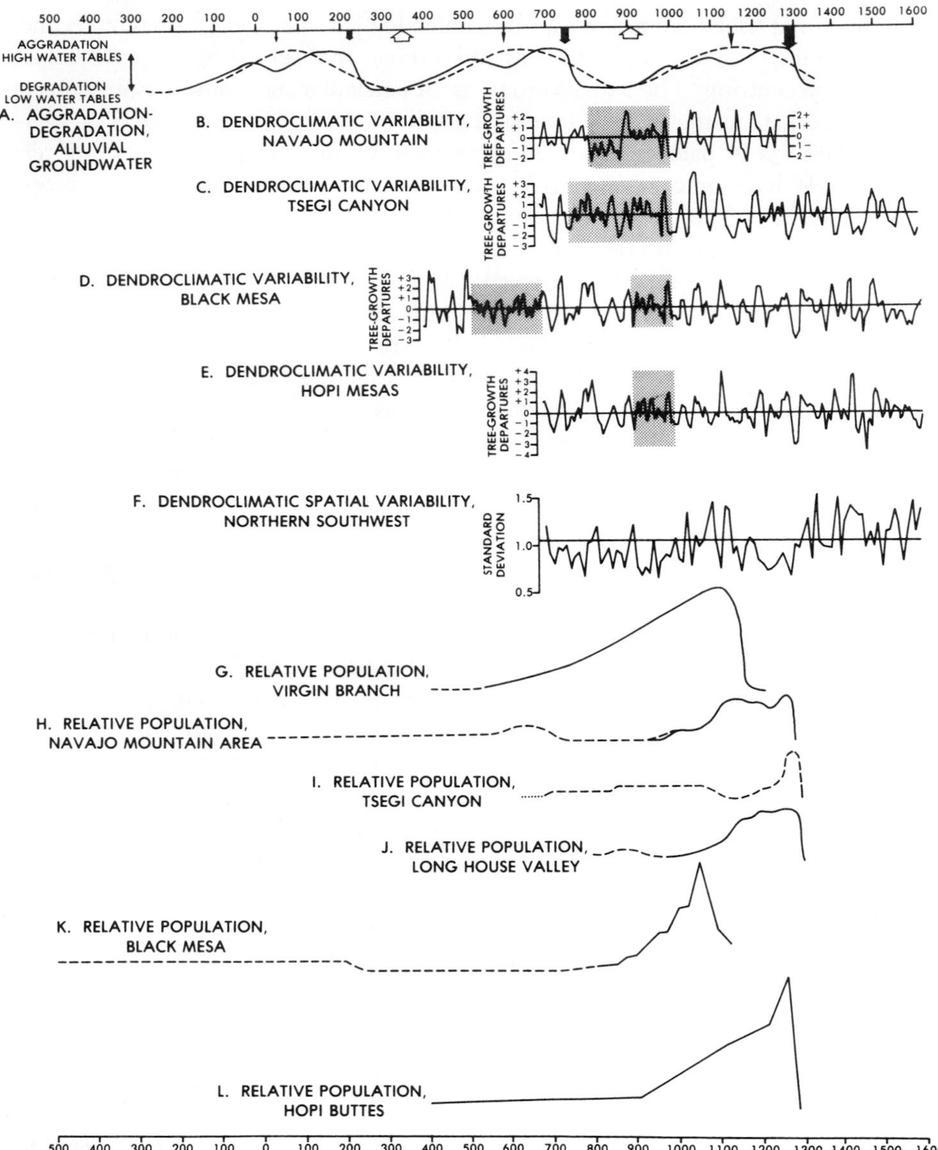

FIGURE 11.6 This chart shows variability in environmental factors (water tables, precipitation) and population levels across the Colorado Plateaus. Rainfall variability is shown both in time (B, C, D, E) and over space (F) (from Gumerman [1988] courtesy of George J. Gumerman).

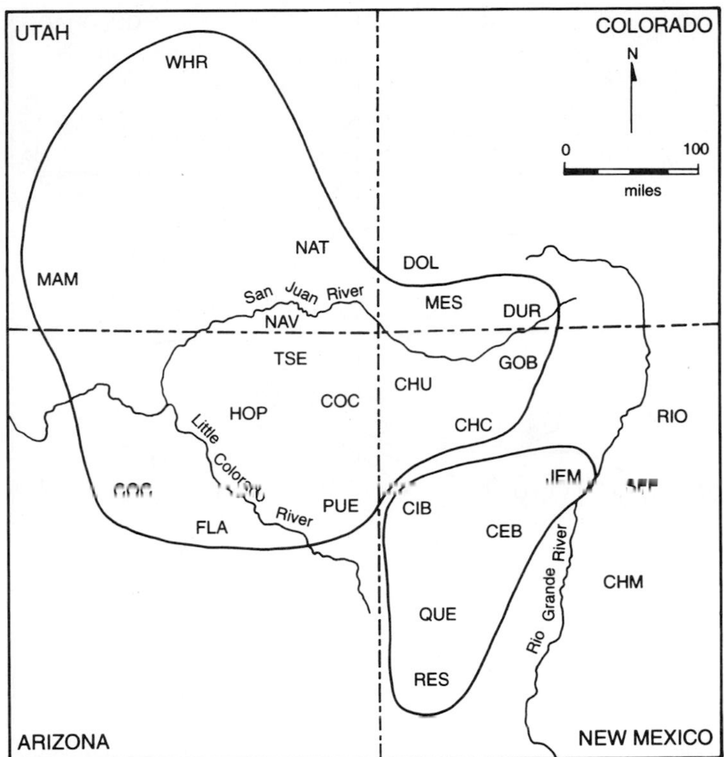

FIGURE 11.7 Principal component analysis of retrodicted average precipitation for 27 climate stations across the Southwest for the years AD 739–838 yielded the two clusters outlined on the map. The two clusters closely match the unimodal vs bimodal rainfall pattern recorded in modern times and observed today (compare to Figure 2.2 in Chapter 2) (adapted from Dean [1996a] by Marjorie Leggitt, Leggitt Design).

developed to meet disruption of such very long term patterns. People would not know what to do to buffer unexpected—and chaotic—rainfall patterns. It is quite likely that nothing people could do would have succeeded long enough to ensure long-term survival. Placing the event in context may help explicate its consequences.

By AD 1000, human population had expanded throughout the Colorado Plateau. By 1200, the landscape was full enough so that mobility had long been precluded as an option for small groups experiencing local shortfalls. It is probable that structured arrangements of exchange had existed for long periods. It is not necessary or likely that these were used every year. Rather, there must have been relationships that could be counted on in highly stressed circumstances. Given the long-term stability of the two different rainfall patterns, it is possible that some or many of these relationships were

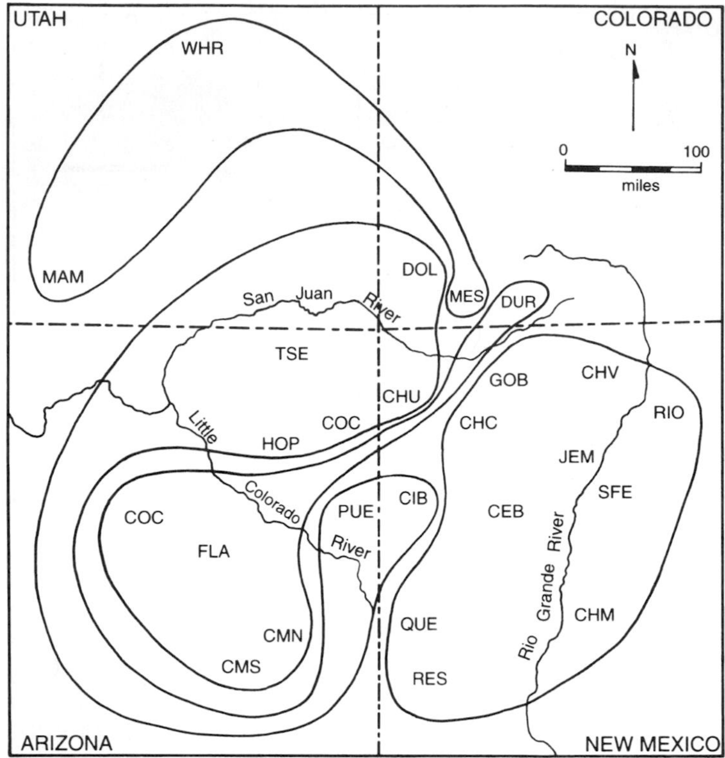

FIGURE 11.8 Principal component analysis of retrodicted average precipitation for 27 climate stations across the Southwest for the years AD 1339–1438 shows no clear pattern; the long-term pattern seen in Figure 11.7 broke down (adapted from Dean [1996a] by Marjorie Leggitt, Leggitt Design).

between groups normally experiencing different patterns. We can imagine such relationships as perhaps similar to those discussed above in the context of Kelley's (1952) analysis of warfare between villagers and Plains dwellers. Under normal conditions, cordial relationships existed between groups. These were disrupted when neither group had expected surplus. The 200-year chaotic rainfall distributions of the Colorado Plateau may have been a time when no group experienced "normal" conditions and when no one could predict who might have a surplus.

A suggestion that such relationships may have existed is provided by a study Rautman (1993, 1996) conducted for a very different area and time period. Rautman used data from modern climate records and focused on the extreme eastern edge of Anasazi territory, but she developed a model of social networks relevant to our interest here.

She demonstrated, through an examination of ceramic trade ware, that reciprocal exchange patterns were established between locations that were close to one another but also manifest opposing or complementary climate regimes. In essence, relationships were not with the closest neighbors but the closest neighbors that could be expected to be experiencing weather patterns different from yours.

In a study of broad-scale ceramic distribution patterns (Figure 11.9), Roney (1995) demonstrated a continuous distribution of thirteenth century ceramic styles from the northern San Juan south-southeast to the Rio Grande Valley near Socorro. If this distribution integrated large areas that were experiencing complementary climatic regimes, it would support an application of Rautman's findings to the San Juan. To evaluate fully whether reciprocal relationships, as described by Rautman, were operating in the northwestern region of the ancient Pueblo world, it would be necessary to document specific localities of reciprocal exchange prior to abandonment and to examine how they were affected during the 200 year interval of chaotic rainfall distributions. This is an exciting possibility.

PULL FACTORS

Maps comparing the distribution of population prior to and after AD 1400 indicate that there was a shift to the south and to irrigable land. The match with movement to land that could be irrigated by gravity-fed systems (Figure 11.10) is striking, although not all such land was occupied. Varien and others (1996) regard the movement to regions that had reliable summer precipitation patterns as significant. In this case, people would have been drawn to locations where farming was less risky than those that they left behind. An additional observation can be made in view of Dean's (1996a) recently reported findings. Those areas to which people moved, predominantly in the south and southeastern portions of the Southwest, are precisely those areas that did not experience the chaotic precipitation patterns of AD 1200 to 1400. Precipitation may have been highly variable, and often poor, in these settings but if there were social relationships in place that buffered agricultural shortfalls, they are likely to have continued to have been successful throughout the 200-year period when similar systems would not have worked in the more northern areas. This is particularly important because a major regional center at Casas Grandes, in Chihuahua, was developing in the 1200s, outside the region experiencing chaotic rainfall patterning.

As we will examine in more detail in Chapter 12, the post-abandonment era witnessed a remarkable flourishing of novel religious forms, specifically katcina iconography, trade networks, and new interaction spheres. Many of these are currently understood to have developed through processes involving integration of new population, hence, as responses to abandonment rather than as pull factors. However, Varien and others (1996) suggest that in learning more about the beginnings of these phenomena we might find in their early stages factors that might have attracted migrants.

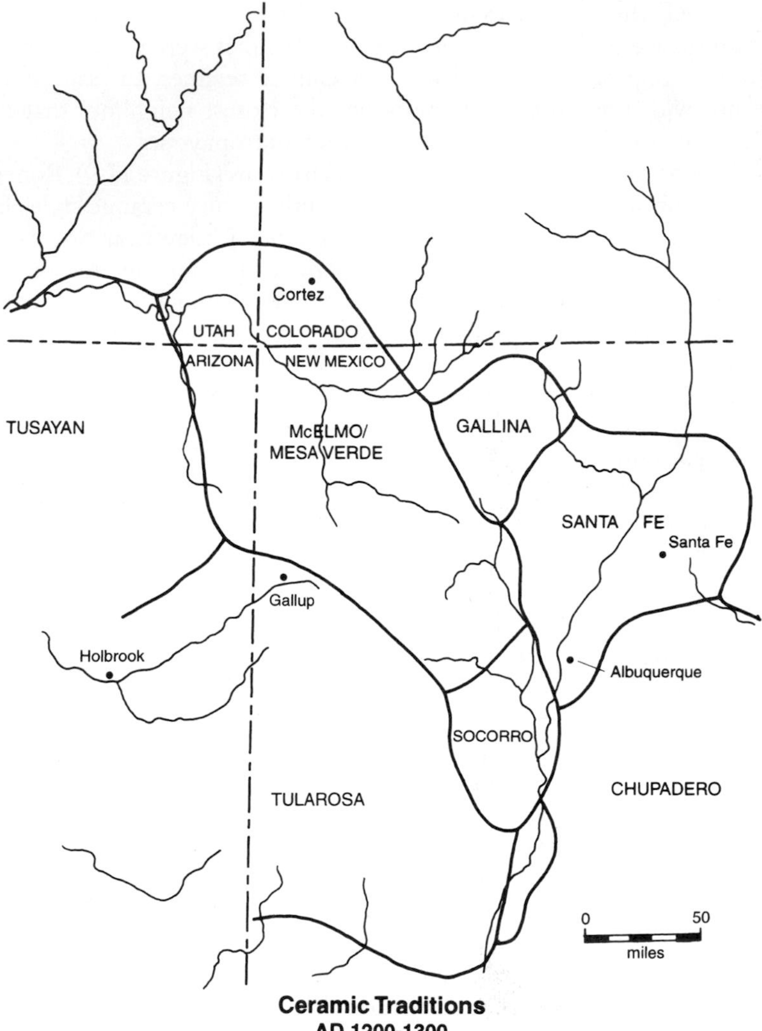

FIGURE 11.9 Map of the distribution of major ceramic traditions in the northern Southwest between AD 1200 and 1300 (adapted from Roney [1995] by Marjorie Leggitt, Leggitt Design).

Commenting on Mesa Verde material culture that did not survive the move to new locations, Varien and others (1996) specifically mention aspects of religious architecture such as small, circular, "household" kivas, front-oriented settlement plans, and civic architectural features such as free-standing towers and multistory D-shaped structures. They remark that as groups moved further south they would certainly have accepted new cultural forms but "perhaps these communities had religious ideologies

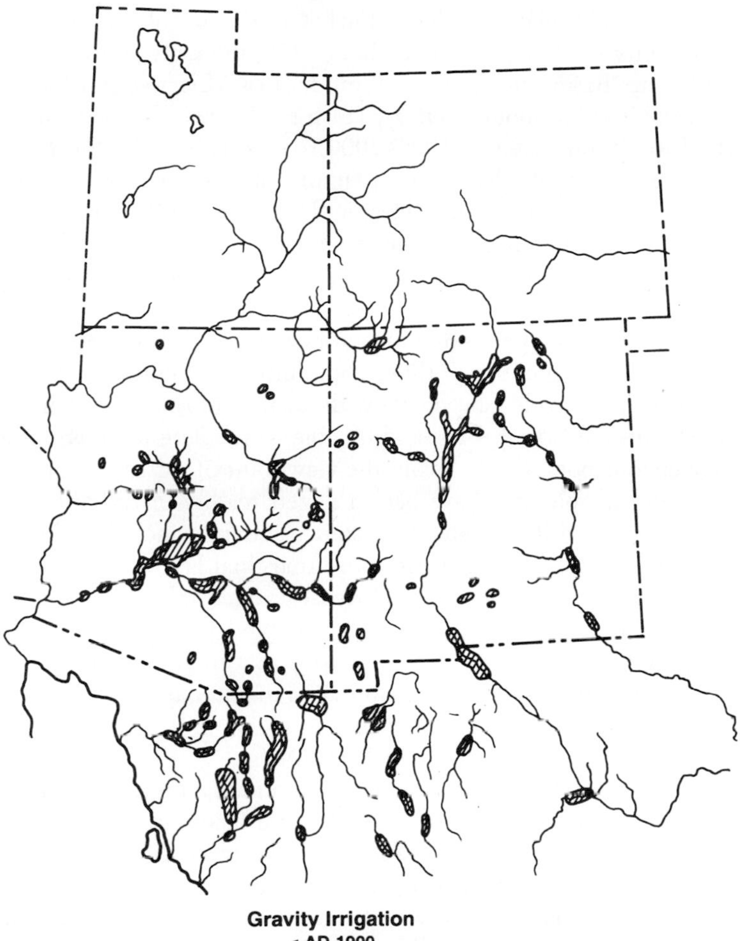

FIGURE 11.10 Map of the distribution of land irrigated by gravity fed systems (adapted from Fish *et al.* 1994 by Marjorie Leggitt, Leggitt Design).

and practices that were part of the attraction for the immigrants from the north" (Varien *et al.* 1996:105). Considering the social stress involved in abandonment as well as the likelihood that the people they joined shared some ideological relationships with the migrants, the Mesa Verde population may have seen joining groups further south as an opportunity for spiritual revitalization (Varien *et al.* 1996).

Wherever dwellings were constructed after 1300, there is a substantial increase in site size, suggesting new thresholds of population aggregation. These are discussed in Chapter 12, but as an example, on the Grasshopper Plateau of the Mountain Mogollon region, the distribution of pueblo size suggests a ceiling of about 120–140 rooms per pueblo prior to the founding of Grasshopper Pueblo, with three roomblocks of more than 100 rooms each. Similarly, while the Early Classic Hohokam sites making up the Marana Community were abandoned at about 1350, the truly enormous Late Classic sites of the Phoenix Basin, such as Mesa Grande, Los Muertos, and La Ciudad, continued to be inhabited for about a century (Fish *et al.* 1995). In the Chama district of the northern Rio Grande, sites of 1000–2000 rooms date to the fourteenth century. Those who favor warfare models as push factors suggest that very large population aggregates were attractive for defense (Haas and Creamer 1996). Others point out that larger aggregates also potentially provided more labor for agricultural intensification. Such efforts might have provided attractive subsistence security although the labor costs were high.

No matter what the congeries of pull factors were, as Fish and others (1995) point out, the organizational structures of those communities accepting migrants had to be sufficiently flexible to provide newcomers with means of production (land and water), assign them appropriate social roles, and be able to mediate interactions among enlarged heterogeneous populations. From the viewpoint of existing community aggregates, immigrating people may have been utilized readily in riverine irrigation and other labor intensive or differentiated subsistence activities including farming, extractive specialties, or farming adjacent and more marginal lands. Again, in this regard, Roney's (1995) demonstration of the broad stylistic zones linking the regions that were abandoned with the areas that at least later accepted immigrants is relevant. This observation suggests that very broad mechanisms that might encourage immigration were in place and perhaps groups were encouraged to join ongoing communities where they had established networks of social relationships, stemming from the kinds of local reciprocal ties suggested by Rautman (1993, 1996).

In sum, none of the entirely cultural or environmental push factors or the cultural or environmental pull models available provides a sufficient explanation for the abandonment phenomenon. Most writers would probably agree that the causes were complex, entailing push and pull factors with environmental and cultural aspects. As stated at the beginning of this chapter, however, abandonment itself is a rather more complex process than is sometimes imagined. If explanatory models are to be developed and evaluated, they must apply to accurate descriptions of the events to be explained.

DISCUSSION

Abandonment of southwestern villages has long been considered a great mystery by laypeople and archaeologists alike. The traditional literature suggests many reasons for abandonment, none of which is entirely acceptable or entirely refutable. In this chapter it has been argued that one impediment to understanding abandonment derives from conceptual problems in not distinguishing different scales of abandonment or changes in behavior that falsely give the appearance of abandonment. Another problem is not fully describing the context (historical and environmental) in which abandonment at large scales took place.

First, single sites throughout the Southwest were rarely occupied for more than one or two human generations. Discussions of abandonment must consider that this level of residential mobility was the rule and not an exception. Second, relatively small areas, such as single stream valleys, were frequently abandoned, with the population moving only short distances. These local abandonments are often attributable to changes in agricultural practices or adjustments to minor climate change. The very broad regularity with which some of these adjustments took place suggests that there may have been an underlying factor such as adjustment to long-term processes in regional hydrology. In these instances movements over short distances was only an option as long as population density was low enough throughout the Southwest to accommodate them. It is also expectable that local movement was preferable to warfare or major technological investments that would have involved high risk, such as building elaborate water conservation features that would still depend on variable precipitation.

Another process that causes relatively small areas to be deserted is population aggregation. Population aggregation was examined in Chapter 9 and is considered again in Chapter 12. Here we can note that most discussions of population aggregation focus on what fairly large communities do. They can amass and coordinate labor for agricultural intensification, such as irrigation, or provide large, intimidating forces and structures for defense. However, the fact that aggregated communities can do these things does not mean that is why people came together in the first place. It is possible that as small dispersed communities failed because of a diminution in resources, such as firewood, game, or productive agricultural land, people were forced to join ongoing settlements that were favorably situated in that with additional labor, more individuals could be supported. Those migrating to such communities may have done so to maintain social or ritual obligations. It also seems true that there is often a secondary aggregation that occurs in any region once one community aggregates for any reason. That is, the large community—no matter why it came into being—can bring together large groups of people for a variety of activities that will give them a competitive advantage compared with dispersed settlements in their vicinity. People in the vicinity of a large settlement may have chosen to aggregate if that were economically possible. Once aggregation occurs in any region, it appears to be complete.

In my view, the abandonments of peripheral areas that occurred between 1100 and 1200 were versions of these local abandonments. There is usually not much disagreement about where the local population went or that there was a drought in 1130 that made it impossible to farm many areas that had been occupied and farmed until that time. In order to evaluate the nature of these abandonments, it would be useful to compare the *pace* and *mode* of abandonment among areas that were deserted at this time. If abandonment was relatively gradual or "leisurely," as it appears to have been in the Virgin and Muddy Valleys, for example, it could imply lack of a perceived external crisis. The mode of abandonment can also suggest the distance people migrated, and that the migration was local. For example, the fact that very few whole, still usable metates have been recovered from sites on northern Black Mesa suggests that people moved to nearby locations. This contrasts to a site near Navajo Mountain (Lindsay *et al.* 1968), in which metates were leaned against walls and deliberately broken (Fish *et al.* 1995). Detailed excavation data are required to make these comparisons before drawing general conclusions.

In broader terms, it seems as though during the years of relatively abundant summer rainfall between about AD 1000 and 1130, small agricultural villages spread throughout the Southwest. It is possible that the existence of a regionally organized system centered in Chaco Canyon and one centered among the Sedentary Hohokam communities of the Phoenix Basin provided an interim of peace and security. With the very real drought of 1130, many areas that today do not support agricultural communities were abandoned. As people moved inward, a change in pattern occurred in Chaco Canyon itself, and a different pattern change took place throughout the Hohokam region. In Chaco, and at some outliers, the shift in pattern involved subdividing domestic or household space, and turning large centralized storage and ceremonial areas into domestic space. Similar pattern changes have been noted in the Classic period of the Hohokam. The Hohokam Classic is divided into two phases: the Soho, dating from about 1150 to 1350, and the Civano, dating from about 1350 to 1425. During the Soho phase, there was a pulling in of the population. The Soho phase witnessed the abandonment of sites in the Gila Bend and lower Verde Valley; however, it has been suggested that population density in the Salt Basin may have *increased*, as it did in the Papagueria. During the Soho phase, irrigation systems seem to have been consolidated. Neither the highly organized systems of the Chacoan San Juan nor the Sedentary Hohokam were able to maintain themselves structurally or energetically past 1150. Initially, there was the *appearance* of population decline, but the situation may have been one of decentralization, reduced coordination of labor, and changes in village layout, as agriculturally marginal lands were abandoned and large-scale construction of public architectural features (great houses, great kivas, ball courts) ceased and in some cases, former public space was turned into housing.

There is little doubt about where population was distributed in the early 1200s (Figure 11.2). As discussed in Chapter 10, elements of the old Chacoan ideological system seem to have lingered and been remolded in the Cibola area and at Mesa Verde. Very large settlements were built in the canyons of the Kayenta area, along the Little Colorado River area, Anderson Mesa, the Flagstaff region, the Phoenix Basin, and in northern Chihuahua. The large-scale regional abandonments of the mid- to late-AD 1200s and 1300s seem to me to be more complex than those of the preceding period. I believe they reflect the nature of the social network that preceded them in the face of a largely external crisis that in turn occurred in the context of extremely limited mobility (see Adler *et al.* 1996). In contrast to the rather frequent movements in and out of limited areas, regional abandonment of this scale was uncommon in the Southwest. Warfare, inter-pueblo violence, witchcraft, disease, the collapse of social integration, resource depletion, droughts, arroyo cutting, and a 200-year period of unpredictable spatial distributions of rainfall all seem to have been involved to some extent. Those locations of reliable summer rainfall which also had allowed gravity-fed irrigation may have been attractive locations for relocation. These, plus attractive religious ideologies and large groups of people who could provide security from potential raids, seem also to have been sought.

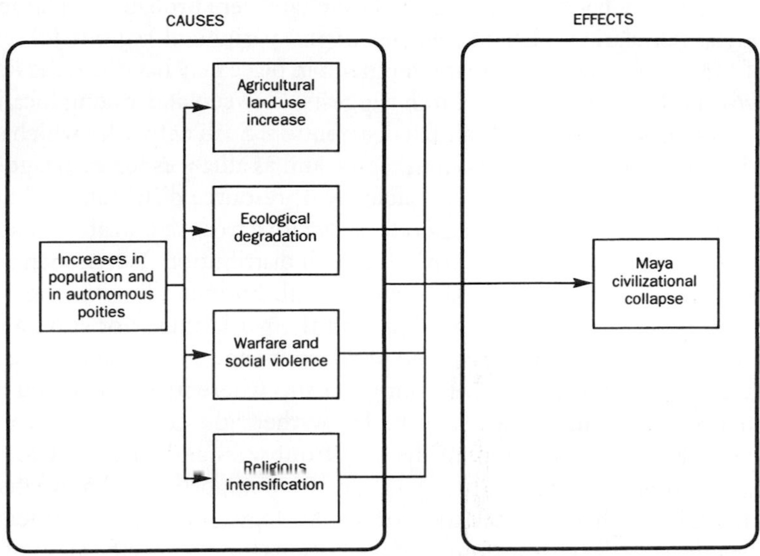

FIGURE 11.11 Representation of traditional models describing the "collapse" of Mayan civilization show that most reputed causes are quite similar to those advanced for Anasazi regional abandonment of the northern Southwest. (From Claudio Cioffi-Revilla, *Evolution of Maya Politics in the Ancient Mesoamerican System*, Long-Range Analysis of War (LORANOW) Project, University of Colorado, Boulder, Colorado 1997).

Momentarily stepping far outside a southwestern perspective, I would note that the "reasons" listed above for regional abandonment in the Southwest are nearly identical to those normally advanced for the "collapse" of Classic Maya Civilization in Mesoamerica (Figure 11.11). As in the case for the Southwest and its Native peoples, the modern Maya are the best evidence for the fact that Mayan culture did not disappear. My observation of similarity is not grounded in any thought that the same event caused disruptions in both regions—chronologically the phenomena are many centuries apart. Rather, it is striking to me that archaeologists can come up with virtually the same list of causal factors when they are dealing with regionally organized societies in a desert and state-level societies in a tropical rain forest. The observation of similarity encourages me to suggest that reliance on and subsequent destabilization of regional social networks, without the ability to either increase food production or develop a larger, more integrated political system, were factors important to abandonment or collapse in both regions.

In the Southwest, the areas in which production can be increased are limited to those where gravity-fed irrigation is possible. These were almost the only areas that remained occupied and in which population increase followed abandonment. The regional networks at Chaco and among the Hohokam were probably not large enough to support the populations that moved out of the peripheral regions following the drought of 1130. Those networks that did remain in place may have been, as Rautman's (1992, 1996) and Roney's (1994) research suggests, between and among localities that experienced reciprocal patterns of rainfall distribution. Such networks, which probably functioned through periodic ceremonies, feasts, and as alliances for marriage partners or other social roles, simply increased efficiency of resource distribution. They could not increase production. They were therefore sensitive to destabilization that came in the form of 200 years of chaotic patterns of rainfall distribution. When such a network fails, the gods have failed. Ritual and ceremony fail. Former allies may become enemies. Trusted leaders may become witches, and the world must not seem a very safe place. On the other hand, those who lived in the south and east—outside the realm of unpredictability—and those who lived along streams where irrigation could be developed or increased may have been seen to know the right ceremonies, worship the appropriate gods in correct ways, and be safe from wars and witches. Clearly, I am being overly creative in scenario writing. But, it is not important to know what people may have thought. Rather, with the tools of archaeology and paleoclimatology we can evaluate the effects of the chaotic rainfall distributions for our specific areas of interest. We can examine pre- and post-abandonment local level exchange patterns and look for complementarity in climatic variation, and we can examine the modes and pace of abandonment in those areas that were abandoned as well as the pace and character of growth in those areas that remained inhabited.

Clearly too, my scenario would have to be slightly modified for the Hohokam, unless the unusual rainfall pattern on the Colorado Plateau was a causal factor in the floods that have been implicated in the demise of many Hohokam canal systems (Nials *et al.* 1989). Surveys in the Papagueria (Goodyear 1975) indicate increased use of the eroded slopes and uplands during the Sells phase, which is contemporary with the Classic. Many of the upland sites seem to have been loci of wild plant procurement and processing. The changes from the Soho to the Civano phase have received somewhat less attention. In the Tucson Basin, the presence of some Salado polychromes indicate that the area was being used to some extent by people affiliated with one of the regional developments of the fifteenth century. Salado polychromes first appear in the central Hohokam area during the Civano, as do surface structures with solid adobe walls, multistoried great houses (such as the famous great house at Casa Grande) and walled compounds—all signs of affiliation with groups to the south and east.

At nearly the same time that the northern San Juan, northwestern tier of Anasazi, and Mogollon settlement was abandoned, new organizations were developed in the south and southeast. These are described in the next chapter. A final note that takes us a step ahead in time is that while abandonments continued into the post-European period, by and large those that occurred after 1500 were similar in character to the local abandonments of the twelfth century, although the causes were quite different. The root cause of course was the disruption and havoc of the European exploration, conquest, and colonization. The similarities are that the abandonments were often local rather than regional in scope. They were often associated with population aggregation—that was legislated by colonial policy and colonial need for defense—and they were most often relocations within relatively short distances.

Chapter-opening art: Drawing by Charles M. Carrillo.

CHAPTER 12

Reorganization

The period following the regional abandonment of the late thirteenth century and lasting until AD 1700 witnessed tremendous and nearly continuous change throughout the Southwest. There was change in the geographic extent of human occupation, change in settlement size to very large settlements, change brought about by the development of new religious beliefs and forms of community organization. These are reflected in distinctive pan-regional art styles in ceramic decoration, kival murals, and rock art. There were then the drastic changes that occurred as reactions and adjustments to foreign invasions. This chapter describes these changes and explores contrasting interpretations and perspectives on the fabric of the social landscape of the newly reorganized Southwest.

INTRODUCTION

Following the disintegration of the first systems of regional integration and the end of major residential use of large areas of the Southwest, several new patterns emerged (between about AD 1275 and sustained colonization by Europeans in 1700). The new features included the redistribution of aggregated populations in parts of the Southwest that formerly were thinly populated, the formation of very large communities in some areas, and the production and wide distribution of new and colorful types of ceramics. The archaeological recovery of highly distinctive representational art from this period affords a rich view of aspects of southwestern culture archaeologists rarely see.

Those abandoning vast areas of the Southwest were leaving their homes, fields, and traditional hunting and gathering territories, all those known places from which they had derived their livelihood for centuries, and moving to areas where they would have known some people but where landscapes could not have been known in detail. In this kind of world, beset with novel fears, new institutions that could integrate people of heterogeneous backgrounds would be highly advantageous. Several archaeologists infer the existence of such integrative institutions from the symbolically rich and vividly colored painted pottery of this period, from the equally spectacular, but rare, scenes painted on the walls of kivas, and from specific widespread and stylistically complex rock art. The processes and new institutions envisioned by archaeologists do not present a unified view. Some differences are a result of focusing on different media or on different regions. For example, an interpretation based on rock art may not agree with one based on pottery. Or, the distribution of ceramic types in the southern Pueblo area may suggest institutions different from those indicated by the distribution of other ceramic types in the eastern Pueblo region.

If there is one pattern that all who work on this period of adjustment recognize, it may be summed up in the word *crystallization.* That is, many of the specific forms, designs, symbols, or motifs can be traced to much earlier periods, but in the fourteenth century, they came together in new ways, forming new patterns. Similarly, architectural elements that had wide spatial distributions and served diverse functions became part of a new spatial vocabulary at this time. There is little that is completely novel to this period. Rather, the organization of elements and their crystallization into new patterns constitute the innovation.

Many of the very large sites (Figure 12.1) of this period were intensively tested or excavated during the first half of the 1900s. The work was accomplished with two goals in mind. First, using the direct historical approach, these sites could provide a relative chronology back from known times of abandonment. Second, large sites would yield the most abundant and diverse artifacts, providing what was thought to be a more complete picture of ancient culture. Early, chronologically oriented studies were conducted in New Mexico at San Cristobal, Pueblo Largo, Pueblo Blanco, and San Lazaro

---

FIGURE 12.1 The sites located on this map are important to the discussion of reorganization in the Southwest after 1300. Key: ❶ Mesa Verde; ❷ Salmon Ruin; ❸ Gallina Area; ❹ Chama Area (Tsiping, Te'ewi, Pajarito Plateau, Howiri, Tsama, Sapawe); ❺ San Juan Pueblo; ❻ Santa Clara Pueblo (San Gabriel del Yunque Area) and (Tsankawi, Tshirige, Puye, Otowi); ❼ Nambe; ❽ Taos Area (Pot Creek Pueblo, Old Picuris, "Cornfield Taos"); ❾ Jemez Area (Unshagi, Giusewa); ❿ Zia Pueblo; ⓫ Arroyo Hondo and Pindi Pueblo; ⓬ Pecos Pueblo area (Rowe Ruin, Arrowhead, Dicks Ruin); ⓭ Galisteo Basin (San Cristobal, Pueblo Largo, Pueblo Blanco, San Lazaro); ⓮ Albuquerque Area (Kuaua, Alameda); ⓯ Tijeras Area (Pao-ko, San Antonio); ⓰ San Marcos; ⓱ Sandia Mountains, Bernalillo; ⓲ Acoma; ⓳ Pottery Mound; ⓴ Salinas Pueblo area (Quarai, Gran Quivera, and Abo); ㉑ Capitan Area; ㉒Manuelito Plateau; ㉓ Zuni

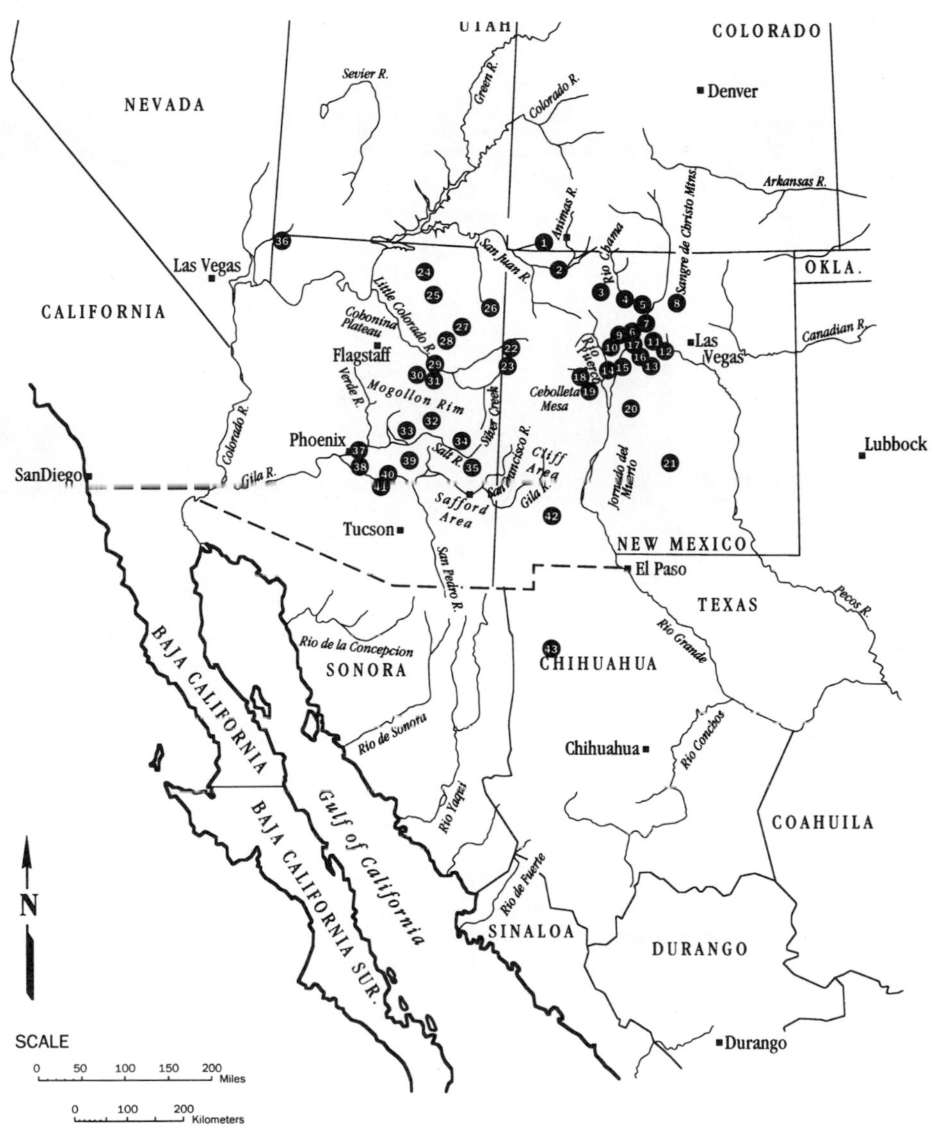

FIGURE 12.1—*Continued* (Mats'a'kya, Kwa'kin'a, Hawikuh); 24 Tsegi Canyon (Betatakin, Kiet Siel); 25 Black Mesa; 26 Canyon de Chelly; 27 Antelope Mesa (Awatovi, Kawaika-a); 28 Hopi (Walpi, Polacca Wash); 29 Winslow, Homolovi Ruins; 30 Anderson Mesa (Little Colorado, Chavez Pass Pueblo); 31 Chevelon; 32 Grasshopper Ruin, Canyon Creek; 33 Sierra Ancha Sites; 34 Kinishba; 35 Point of Pines; 36 Virgin River; 37 Phoenix Area (Pueblo Grande, Superstition Mountains); 38 Los Muertos; 39 Globe-Miami District (Gila Pueblo, Togetzoge, Besh-ba-gowah); 40 Escalante Ruin; 41 Casa Grande; 42 Mimbres Valley; 43 Casas Grandes. (Map by David Underwood.)

FIGURE 12.2 Pecos Pueblo, Pecos National Historical Park, New Mexico. The view is to the south toward the church and Park Service Buildings. The kiva in foreground was reconstructed for visitors. Pecos was one of the largest of the historic pueblos. By 1836, the population had declined to only 27 individuals who traveled to Jemez Pueblo where their descendants continue to reside. A. V. Kidder excavated Pecos in the first half of the twentieth century (photograph by Fred Mang, courtesy of the U.S. National Park Service).

in the Galisteo Basin (Nelson 1914); at Pecos Pueblo (Figure 12.2) (Kidder 1924, 1958); at Tyounyi, Otowi, Tsirege and other sites on the Pajarito Plateau (Hewett 1906, 1909; Mathien 1990); at the ancestral Zuni sites of Hawikuh (Hodge 1937; Smith *et al.* 1966), Halona:wa, and Heshọtauthala (Kintigh 1985); and at the ancestral Jemez Pueblo sites of Unshagi and Giusewa (Reiter 1938).

In Arizona, similar kinds of investigations were carried out at large sites in the vicinity of Hopi, such as Kawaika-a and Awatovi on Antelope Mesa (Montgomery *et al.* 1949; Smith 1952, 1971), at Chavez Pass Pueblo, and at Chevelon and the Homolovi Ruins near Winslow (Adams and Hays 1991; Fewkes 1896, 1904). In addition to chronology, these investigations and others continuing into more recent times have been concerned with the origins of specific Pueblo and non-Pueblo linguistic groups or "tribes" (Cordell 1995; Ellis 1967; Ford *et al.* 1972; Hall 1944).

More recent work on sites of this time period has been directed toward elucidating the nature and degree of social integration reflected within the large aggregated communities and among these sites and their sustaining areas (e.g., Clark 1969; Crown and Kohler 1994; Crown and Wills 1995; Kintigh 1994; Longacre *et al.* 1982; Spielmann 1991a; Upham 1982). Some investigators argue for the presence of social ranking within communities and economic interaction among individuals occupying elite status. Many more find the evidence for social ranking unconvincing, but are nevertheless interested in describing the means by which novel forms of integrating large numbers of people was achieved.

Because so much of Native southwestern culture remains intact today, many investigators focus on finding the origins of specific institutions in this period. Katcina ceremonialism among Pueblo peoples is the classic example (Adams 1991; Crown 1994; Hayes 1994/5?; Schaafsma 1994; Schaafsma and Schaafsma 1974). Finally, because the period under consideration terminates with the presence of European colonists in the Southwest and the first written accounts of southwestern peoples by outsiders, there is great interest in understanding the many facets and results of this terrible disruption of Native peoples (e.g., Cordell 1989, 1994; Doyel 1989; McGuire and Villalpando 1989; Merbs 1989; Spielmann 1989; Upham 1982; Upham and Reed 1989; Wilcox and Masse 1981).

This chapter first examines the distribution of settlements that were founded in the very late 1200s and early 1300s. The more common site plans of these communities are also discussed. The chapter then explores the potential role of the site of Casas Grandes (or Paquimé) in Chihuahua as a focus of a new pan-regional system. From there, the chapter describes the characteristics and distributions of the ceramic diagnostics of the period, particularly those that seem to reflect widespread networks of social interaction and trade. The form, content, and interpretations of the art styles of this period are discussed, specifically in regard to how they provide information about subsequent Pueblo systems of ritual and beliefs. The continuing debate about the origins of these rituals is reviewed.

The chapter revisits issues about the nature of some southwestern societies at the time of contact through an update on research projects in the Western Pueblo area. This chapter then briefly describes the European perspective of the period of Spanish conquest and colonization. Finally, some of the issues relating to Athapaskan and Spanish invasion, disruption of the native traditions, and continuing accommodations are explored.

DISTRIBUTIONS AND PATTERNS OF SETTLEMENTS

Most of the Rio Grande Valley and immediately adjacent portions of eastern New Mexico were not densely inhabited by sedentary peoples before 1300. There were quite large villages of pithouses and associated surface structures in the mountains near Taos and in the Gallina country northwest of Santa Fe (Cordell 1979; Crown and Kohler 1994; Green 1976; Hibben 1948; Woosley 1980) and numerous small pueblos of contiguous above-ground rooms scattered throughout the valleys of the Rio Grande and its tributaries. While a few of these pueblos were quite large, they do not compare in number or size with the later sites in the area (Cordell 1979, 1996; Cordell *et al.* 1994; Dickson 1979; Spielmann 1991a; Wendorf and Reed 1955).

Some of the better known, very large sites of the Chama River valley, the Pajarito Plateau, and the Taos area include the 600 room Te'ewi (Wendorf 1953b), Tsiping, Howiri, Tsama, the Sapawe (a vast adobe ruin that has multiple roomblock and plaza areas covering an estimated 29 ha), Tsankawi, Tshirege, Puye (the ancestral Santa Clara pueblo), Otowi, Tyounyi (Figure 12.1), Pot Creek Pueblo, Old Picuris, and "Cornfield Taos" (the ancestral Taos village) (Cordell 1979; Dick 1965b; Ellis and Brody 1964; Hewitt 1906; Steen 1977; Wetherington 1964). Further south, near Santa Fe, large, late prehistoric pueblos include Arroyo Hondo (Creamer 1993; Habicht-Mauche 1993; Schwartz and Lang 1972), Cieneguilla Pueblo, Pindi Pueblo (Stubbs and Stallings 1953), and the Galisteo Basin pueblos—Pueblo Largo, San Cristobal, San Marcos, Las Madres, and Pueblo Lumbre (Creamer and Renken 1994; Dutton 1963; Lang 1977a; Lightfoot 1993; Lightfoot and Eddy 1995). There is a series of large sites of this period along the upper Pecos, for example, the early portions of Pecos Pueblo, Rowe Ruin, Arrowhead, and Dick's Ruin (Cordell 1979, 1996; Holden 1955; Kidder 1958). Continuing south along the east side of the Sangre de Cristo and Sandia Mountains, the Salinas Pueblos include Quarai, Gran Quivira, Abo, Pueblo Pardo, and Tenabo (Hayes *et al.* 1981; Spielmann 1991, 1994). Near Albuquerque, aggregated pueblos include Kuaua, Alameda, Paa-ko, Tijeras, and San Antonio (Cordell 1979; Lambert 1954; Tichy 1938). South of Albuquerque, the large and unusual site of Pottery Mound (Hibben 1975) dates to this period, as do the Piro pueblos described by the early Spanish explorers (Cordell and Earls 1982b; Earls 1987; Marshall 1991; Marshall and Walt 1984). On the southeastern edge of the Southwest, the Lincoln phase sites of the Capitan and Jornada del Muerto areas (Kelley 1966) are manifestations of the eastward expansion of Southwestern peoples. Many, though not all, of the sites listed here have components that were occupied during and after the Spanish Conquest. Some, such as Pecos, Abo, Quarai, Gran Quivira, and some of the Piro villages, became the sites of seventeenth-century Spanish missions.

An interest in site layout and the presence or absence of kivas and their specific features relates to two issues of concern to archaeologists. One question is whether similarities in architectural features allow tracing migrations of people from the San Juan into the Rio Grande drainage. Another matter is whether site layout and kiva features permit identification of new integrative social features—such as katcina ceremony. In fact, sites of the Rio Grande area and eastern New Mexico exhibit considerable variation in construction materials and techniques. Some, like Sapawe, Kuaua, Arroyo Hondo, Pot Creek Pueblo, Tijeras Pueblo, Pottery Mound, and the Lincoln phase sites, were built of coursed adobe. The larger sites had multiple plaza areas surrounded by roomblocks, one very large kiva or great kiva, and frequently smaller kivas as well. Other large sites, such as Tsiping, Tsankawi, Pecos (Figure 12.2), and Rowe Pueblo, are multistory, multiplaza masonry pueblos. The Piro pueblos are somewhat smaller than those farther north. One excavated example was constructed of coursed adobe with an interior core of unshaped river cobbles. Again, small round kivas and sometimes a very large kiva are typical, but kivas are neither uniformly present nor always round. For example, at Tijeras Pueblo there were sequentially, a very large round kiva (20 m in diameter) and rectangular kivas that were incorporated within roomblocks (Cordell 1979). In none of the excavated examples of kivas, however, were the elaborate floor features known from Chacoan great kivas (benches, niches, paired vaults, etc.) present. The lack of these features has been problematic for some archaeologists, who would view the major, aggregated Rio Grande pueblos as the result of population influx from the San Juan Basin. It should be recalled however, that the Chacoan system failed about 200 years prior to the construction of these Rio Grande sites. If the Chacoan great kivas were emblematic of their cultural contexts, that context had long been gone. The later, post-Chaco great kivas of the Zuni region were probably built before those in the Rio Grande Valley, and they also lack floor features (Kintigh 1994).

The Mesa Verde is also viewed as a population source for the Rio Grande pueblos. Hence archaeologists have also been concerned by the absence of small kivas and other architectural features that seem to have dropped out of the Anasazi inventory when Mesa Verde was abandoned (Varien *et al.* 1996). At the same time, some types of Rio Grande ceramics, particularly Galisteo Black-on-white, resemble and are considered a local cognate of Mesa Verde types (Cordell 1994, 1996; Ford *et al.* 1972; Roney 1995). The major issue is that whereas the large, aggregated sites of the Rio Grande area suggest a population influx, and the archaeological record of the then deserted San Juan Basin and Mesa Verde indicate that they are likely sources for this population, there are no known sites that are so closely similar to those of the source areas that they can be considered evidence of a migrant community (Roney 1995).

The kind of migration pattern that might produce a "site unit intrusion" (Rouse 1958:64) is relatively rare archaeologically and ethnographically. The best case for such an intrusion in the Southwest was described by Haury (1934:6) at Point of Pines, and I (Cordell 1995) suggested that Morris (1938) made a similarly good case in Mummy Cave, Canyon de Chelly. Roney (1995) states that Prieta Vista on the Rio Puerco reflects this kind of immigration from Mesa Verde in the early 1200s (also see Bice and Sundt 1972), and that Gallina Springs and three sites on the Palomas drainage represent post-1300 site unit intrusions from the Mesa Verde area into areas already occupied by local people. Interestingly, Gallina Springs and the Palomas drainage sites, in the Tularosa Basin and southern Rio Grande respectively, are very far south of both the San Juan Basin and the Mesa Verde. There does not appear to be any sites of similar age and configuration in between.

A common pattern of migration in the ethnographic literature is for family groups to follow separate migration paths, integrating themselves into ongoing communities where they have ties of kinship or friendship (e.g., Colson 1979; Scudder 1962). Archaeologically, this form of migration would be visible primarily as a regional increase in population. Interestingly, as Roney (1995) pointed out and as mentioned in Chapter 11, there are links of ceramic styles between donor and recipient areas that predate abandonment and migration. The change from relatively small, dispersed settlements to large, aggregated villages is a different, but related, aspect of the problem. Because very large villages are important in other parts of the Southwest, aggregation is treated separately in more detail below.

Changes in population distribution and population increase also occurred in the Acoma and Zuni areas (Anyon and Ferguson 1983; Kintigh 1985, 1994, 1996; Ruppé 1966). On the western flanks of Cebolleta Mesa, west of Acoma Pueblo, the period between 1200 and 1400 witnessed a change in settlement distribution and site plans. The southwestern portion of Cebolleta Mesa was abandoned, but very large, planned, defensive sites were built farther to the north. Among these are sites consisting of between 200 and 367 rooms, one of which is associated with a sandstone masonry defensive wall that still stood to a height of more than 3 m in the twentieth century. Ruppé (1966:330) notes that the population of the areas around Acoma that he surveyed was greater than it had been previously, suggesting migration into the area. Although he anticipated that supporting evidence of migration would be found in the recovery of greater amounts of "foreign" ceramics, this was not the case. The amounts of imported ceramics appear to have remained about the same as they had been.

In the Zuni area, there were also marked changes in settlements. Between 1175 and 1275, there was an increase in site size from previous periods, and also closer spacing of sites. Most sites at this time were located at fairly high elevations in settings where runoff from large watersheds could be tapped for agriculture. Between 1275 and 1400, the high valley sites were completely abandoned and population aggregated within fewer exceptionally large (more than 1000 rooms), multistoried pueblos with roomblocks arranged around internal plazas and walls encircling the sites (Kintigh 1985, 1994, 1996). These very large sites seem not to have been occupied for long periods, and there was a relocation of sites toward downstream settings at this time. Between 1400 and 1700, the Zuni district continued to be dominated by large sites. Six of these (Hawikku, Mats'a:kya, Kyaki:ma, Kwa'kin'a, Kechiba:wa, and Halona:wa) were inhabited into the seventeenth century. In contrast to the previous period, the later sites seem to have had longer periods of uninterrupted occupation (Smith *et al.* 1966), and it was not until about 1700 that the population of Zuni was restricted to a single permanently occupied village at Halona:wa, or present-day Zuni Pueblo (Ferguson 1983; Kintigh 1985). A long period of residential stability also characterizes Acoma Pueblo, which may have been continuously inhabited from about 1200.

The distribution of settlements in the Anasazi area west of Zuni parallels that to the east. Prior to 1200, the inhabitants withdrew from the northern portions of Black Mesa, the Virgin River area, the Cohonina Plateau west of Flagstaff, and much of the Kayenta region, with the exception of the Tsegi Canyon area (Dean 1970, 1996b). Large aggregated pueblos, consisting of from 50 to several hundred rooms, were located at Anderson Mesa, the middle Little Colorado, Silver Creek, Hopi Buttes, and Tsegi Canyon. Dean's (1970) analysis of tree-ring dates from the Tsegi Canyon sites, including Betatakin and Kiet Siel, indicates that the Tsegi phase, which consisted of large cliff dwellings, lasted only 50 years, from 1250 to 1300. Other sites, such as Chavez Pass Pueblo, Awatovi, and Kawika-a, were occupied for much longer periods. Sites on the Hopi mesas that were apparently small villages in the 1100s grew to 200 or more rooms by the 1300s and 1400s (Adams 1983).

Typically, the large Western Pueblo sites are of multistory masonry construction, with plazas surrounded by roomblocks. Kivas are of both circular and rectangular form. Large aggregated sites and apparently some population influx are also noted for the mountainous portions of eastern Arizona near the Mogollon Rim, and within the Gila, Salt, and San Pedro drainages. Some of the better known of these sites are Kinishba (Cummings 1937, 1940), Canyon Creek, and other sites in the Sierra Ancha (Haury 1934), Point of Pines (Haury 1958; also see Chapters 6 and 7), Four Mile (Fewkes 1904), Turkey Creek (Lowell 1991), Table Rock (Martin and Rinaldo 1960), Hooper Ranch (Martin *et al.* 1962), Bailey Ruin (Mills and Crown 1995), Casa Malpais (Hohmann 1990), and Grasshopper Ruin (Graves and Longacre 1982). Specifically within the Tonto Basin and Globe-Miami areas of central Arizona, the aggregated villages of the fourteenth century include Gila Pueblo (Gladwin 1957), Togetzoge (Schmidt 1928), Besh-ba-gowah (Vickery 1939), and Tonto Ruin (Steen *et al.* 1962). The Tonto Basin sites have been termed Salado (Gladwin and Gladwin 1930) because they reflect a constellation of traits that the Gladwins thought originated within the Salado branch of the Mogollon and intruded into the Tonto area. These traits include compound pueblos with multistory contiguous rooms; post-reinforced adobe walls; extended inhumations; and Pinto, Tonto, and Gila polychrome ceramics (Figure 12.3). There is considerable debate about the utility of defining the Salado as a cultural entity and viewing the appearance of these traits as evidence of an invasion of foreign elements (Doyel and Haury 1976; Lange and Germick 1992). The issue is discussed in greater detail below. Nevertheless, there is an apparent population increase and the restructuring of settlements in the Tonto Basin, the San Pedro Valley, the Safford area of Arizona, and the Cliff region of New Mexico.

Between 1350 and 1425, the Hohokam heartland also witnessed settlement restructuring, and possibly initially, population increase, as is indicated by "Salado" features at sites such as Los Muertos, Casa Grande, and the Escalante Ruin group (Doyel 1975, 1976b, 1989; Weaver 1972). The population aggregates of the Arizona desert and mountain regions were not as stable as those of northern New Mexico in that the very large villages apparently were not inhabited into the sixteenth century. The core Hohokam area is one in which there was population loss between 1450 and the time of the Spanish entradas into that territory in the late seventeenth century. Estimates of the indigenous population in 1450 vary widely—figures of 60,000 and 30,000 have been suggested (Doyel 1989:144), but a widely cited reference gives 3,000 for the villages occupied in 1700 (Ezell 1983). Whether the loss occurred as a result of indigenous factors or was a result of the entradas and conquest is not resolved. There is also little agreement among archaeologists about the manifestations that can be regarded as ancestral to the modern O'Odham and Pima, and whether there is continuity from the Hohokam to these groups (Doyel 1989). Nevertheless, there is no indication that the "Salado" compounds were inhabited much later than about 1450.

FIGURE 12.3 Jars of (A) Tonto Polychrome and (B) Gila Polychrome are both diagnostic Salado polychrome types. One interpretation of the appearance of these types in the Hohokam area is that they were introduced by non-Hohokam migrants (photographs courtesy of the Museum of New Mexico; neg. nos. 17980 and 17973).

The effects of abandonments and population redistribution around 1300 rippled throughout the still inhabited Southwest. As peoples migrated into already occupied areas, new forms of social integration and ways of interacting among villages were devised. Four developments that archaeologists have discerned as new integrative institutions that came together between 1300 and 1600 are described here. These are a mercantile system, alliance systems, a "Southwestern Regional Cult," and katcina belief systems and ritual. The existence of a mercantile system was proposed to explain the development and operation of the imposing multistory adobe compounds of Casas Grandes (Paquimé) in Chihuahua. These were occupied and expanded throughout the fourteenth and fifteenth centuries. The regional influence of Casas Grandes as a center of population and craft specialization is discussed below.

PAQUIMÉ

Some archaeologists who are exploring "pull factors" in the regional abandonment of the northern Southwest are interested in the possible role of Casas Grandes as center of a new regional system (Lekson 1996). Casas Grandes, in northern Chihuahua, Mexico, was extensively excavated by Charles Di Peso (Di Peso *et al.* 1974), who headed the multiyear Joint Casas Grandes Project, a combined effort of the Amerind Foundation of the United States and the Instituto Nacional de Antropologia y Historia of Mexico. The importance of Casas Grandes had not been underestimated, but the site was not placed in appropriate chronological context until 1993, when a revised tree-ring chronology for the site was published (Dean and Ravesloot 1993).

The Casas Grandes area lies in the relatively high Basin and Range country of northern Chihuahua. Throughout most of its history, the Casas Grandes region generally resembled other southwestern culture areas in terms of artifact inventory and settlement form. Specific items most closely resemble those of the Mogollon. The Casas Grandes Valley itself is wide, fertile, and relatively well watered, and the indigenous, Mogollon-like population experienced a general population growth. During a period termed the Medio by Di Peso (1974), a number of radical changes occurred in the Casas Grandes area that he attributed to the influence of *pochteca-like mercenaries* from unspecified states in central Mexico. Abundant wood was used in construction at Casas Grandes, but most timbers had been squared and therefore were missing outer rings so that very few cutting dates were obtained. Based on extremely limited radiocarbon dates, Di Peso (1974:2) interpreted these changes as beginning in 1060, hence contemporary with Chaco Canyon. Restudy of the tree-ring material from the site of application of a method of estimating cutting dates based on the ratio of rings of heartwood to rings of sapwood provided a much revised chronology. The current dating of the Medio period phases are: Buena Fé AD 1253–1306 to AD 1359–1413, and Paquimé AD 1218–1271 to AD 1390–1444 (Dean and Ravesloot 1993:96). As described below, the change in dating significantly affects interpretation of a potential regional role for Casas Grandes.

During the first part of the Buena Fé phase of the Medio period, the population was organized into what Di Peso (1974: Vol. 2) refers to as the City of Paquimé. At this time, Casas Grandes apparently consisted of a series of 20 independent but associated house clusters, each with an open plaza area surrounded by an enclosing wall. The houses were single-story adobe structures, and the configuration of settlement is described as resembling that of the Late Classic period, Phoenix Basin Hohokam site of Los Muertos, with which it is contemporary according to the current dating. Although the house compounds were separate, a single water system served the entire site. Architectural features included massive cast "mud concrete" bearing walls, T-shaped doorways, raised fire hearths, square-column fronted galleries, and stairways. Among the ceramic containers, some of the Buena Fé phase storage jars had a capacity of nearly 18 gallons. A variety of painted ceramic types were produced locally, including Ramos Polychrome. Within the excavated Buena Fé compound, referred to as the House of the Serpent, rows of rectangular macaw breeding boxes were found. Palynological data provided evidence of the original nesting material, and eggshell fragments, skeletons, and holes for wooden perches made it possible to interpret the use of these features. If, as is suggested, the macaws were traded, Casas Grandes would be the likely source of these birds found among the Anasazi.

At the succeeding Paquimé phase (now AD 1218–1271 to AD 1390–1444), the entire city of Paquimé was reorganized and rebuilt. Di Peso (1974:2), thinking Paquimé was occupied at the same time as Chaco Canyon, compared the two. At its height, the Casas Grandes system was much larger than that of Chaco. It encompassed an area of about 87,000 km^2, and Paquimé itself is estimated to have housed about 2240 people. After remodeling, multistoried adobe complexes were built, and a great deal of space, estimated at about one-half the site, was allocated for public and ceremonial use. Unlike the Chacoan area, the domestic units formed the central core of the "city," and the public and ceremonial areas were distributed outside of this core. Among the public and ceremonial features were double T-shaped ballcourts; a small T-shaped ballcourt with subfloor burial groups that included some individuals who were dismembered, probably ceremonially; stone-faced platform and effigy mounds; an elaborate subterranean walk-in well; a reservoir; a system of stone slab-covered drains; and an open area Di Peso considered a market. The domestic space was provided by massive multistoried dwellings, the walls of which are well described by Bandelier as "not of adobe but a kind of marly concrete, mixed with pebbles and small stones" (quoted in Di Peso 1974:5:440). The ends of the vigas (roof beams) generally had been squared (accounting in part for the missing outer tree-rings). A little over half the domestic rooms at Paquimé had evidence of bed platforms raised about a meter off the floor.

Di Peso interpreted Paquimé as a Mesoamerican mercantile *pochteca* frontier outpost that incorporated the local population. Largely because of the chronological error of placing the site in the eleventh century, he also suggests a number of similarities or parallels with the Chacoan system (Di Peso *et al.* 1974:208–211). These are particularly interesting in light of the revised dating of Paquimé because they indicate, as do the persistence of trade-networks and architectural features (see Chapter 10 and Stein and Fowler 1996), modification and spread of Chacoan "emblems" after that system had ceased to function. According to Di Peso (Di Peso *et al.* 1974:208–211), Paquimé's similarities with Chaco are that both were regional systems based on a capital (or core area) and satellite communities; however, the Paquimé system was much larger than that of Chaco. Another difference is that Paquimé is a single, very large site, whereas the Chacoan core area consists of several separate communities within Chaco Canyon. The Paquimé system, like Chaco, was linked through a system of roads and signaling stations, but the roads at Paquimé are not as wide or as consistently engineered as those of Chaco. Both systems had elaborate water-control features. Those at Casas Grandes included stone check dams, terraces, ditches, and the reservoirs mentioned above. Certain details of architectural structure are also similar, including aligned T-shaped doorways, shaped sandstone disks used as timber seatings, square columns, and stairways in buildings. In addition, the two masonry-enclosed refuse mounds at Pueblo Bonito may be similar to some of the stone-faced mounds at Paquimé. Another similarity of interest is that the Medio period at Paquimé shares with the Bonito sites an extreme underrepresentation of burials. Finally, and obviously, both Paquimé and Bonito structures indicate a considerable amount of planning and organization of labor. The specific features shared by Paquimé and Chaco may represent ideological legitimization of Paquimé as the "heir" of Chacoan regional influence (Lekson 1996).

In terms of the way in which Paquimé may have functioned, there is similarity with Chaco as well. Both seem to have been less involved in specialist craft production than previously thought (Figure 12.4). Di Peso (1974:2) had concluded that Casas Grandes was a city, involved in the production of goods for regional and long distance distribution. The materials he cited as part of the distribution system are Ramos Polychrome pottery, turquoise, copper, shell, and scarlet macaws. Ramos Polychrome is a distinctive pottery type once thought to have been produced only at Casas Grandes and widely traded. Compositional studies (Woosley and Olinger 1993) indicate that the Ramos Polychrome produced at Casas Grandes was distributed to communities within a radius of about 75 km of that site. Outside of that limit, sites with Ramos either made the type themselves or received it from a variety of possible sources where it was produced but not from Casas Grandes.

Turquoise is not as abundant at Casas Grandes as were other minerals. Still 2.2 kg of turquoise were recovered, mostly from rooms that Di Peso considered warehouses (Minnis 1984, 1988). Turquoise assumes somewhat greater importance in Di Peso's writings than its relative abundance might indicate because this stone is thought to have been much valued by Mesoamerican states far to the south in central Mexico. Di Peso (1974:2) suggested that Paquimé had been established as a mercantile outpost of one of these central Mexican states. In his later writing, Di Peso (1984) viewed Paquimé as the center of a large regional system, but one somewhat more independent of central Mexican origins.

Copper was produced in several areas of West Mexico, but Casas Grandes is the northernmost of these, yielding 14.6 kg of copper, including 688 artifacts. These were made by a variety of techniques, including cold hammering and lost wax casting. Copper ore was found in two rooms that may have been warehouses or work rooms. The artifacts were found in a number of contexts. Minnis (1984, 1988), who has collated

FIGURE 12.4 Casas Grandes polychrome effigy jar (photograph courtesy of the Museum of New Mexico, artifact no. 20679/11).

and summarized the information from Casas Grandes, suggests that like turquoise, copper may have been made for use at Casas Grandes itself rather than primarily for export. Indeed, in study and restudy of the 622 copper bells excavated from 93 sites in the U.S. Southwest and northwest Mexico, Vargas (1995) is persuasive in demonstrating that on technological and stylistic grounds, these originated in West Mexico and not at Casas Grandes.

Nearly 4,000,000 shell artifacts (1324.5 kg) were excavated at Casas Grandes. Most came from two rooms, one of which also had a large cache of copper artifacts. Di Peso (1974:2) inferred that the room served as a warehouse, whereas Minnis (1983) suggests that it might represent hoarding by a high status group or individual. The amount of finished shell items is impressive, and in my mind is rather more than a single individual or group would hoard. Second in quantity only to shell at Casas Grandes is Redrock ricolite (or serpentine) from the Upper Gila River in New Mexico. Ricolite appears in great quantity at Casas Grandes in raw form, as production debris and as finished artifacts (Lekson 1992). More than 300 scarlet macaw skeletons were recovered at Casas Grandes from parts of the site that contained pens with eggshell, perches, and grain, suggesting that macaws were bred there. It is quite likely that most of the 144 scarlet macaw skeletons recovered from sites in the U.S. Southwest came from Casas Grandes, but given the relative abundance of macaws at Casas, Minnis (1988) again suggests that the birds were used primarily by residents of Casas Grandes itself, perhaps for their feathers.

Archaeologists will surely debate the mercantile nature of Casas Grandes for years. We will certainly learn more about the ways resources were procured at Casas and distributed out from the site. In the present context, it is of interest that Casas Grandes developed as an enormous and significant center with influence that is seen as deriving from its economic and political status. It has not been described as having been the locus of origin for one or more of the religious movements that are thought to have been integrating forces among refugees from recently abandoned districts to the north. Yet, I suspect that in emphasizing the manufacturing and trade aspects of Casas Grandes, we are failing to appreciate how these institutions are imbedded in religious and ceremonial systems in most nonindustrial societies worldwide. I suspect that we are distorting the "glue" that held the Casas Grandes system together.

The Diablo phase, now dated from AD 1400/1450 to about 1500, followed the Paquimé phase and is described (Di Peso 1974:2:319) as a time when two and one-half generations sat idly by and watched the magnificent city of Paquimé fall into disrepair. The artisan-citizens continued to produce an abundance of marketable goods, but civil construction and public maintenance all but ceased. As had been the case at Chaco and some of its outliers, various public and ceremonial areas were modified into living areas. During the Diablo phase, the population within Paquimé apparently increased. Domestic living space was increased by subdividing some rooms and particularly by altering and subdividing open public space. The square-columned galleries were walled off and subdivided into rooms in a way that is very similar to that described for the Chacoan outlier Salmon Ruin. Burials of the Diablo phase were sometimes placed in the former plaza drains, and the wells were no longer used. As with the McElmo occupation of Chaco, Salmon, and other outliers, the population of Paquimé remained in residence long after public construction had ceased, and abandonment finally occurred near 1500.

The parallels I have cited regarding the Chacoan system are important in understanding the process through which certain major settlements seem to have lost their public character. The redating of Casas Grandes makes it abundantly clear that when it was at its height, the Chacoan system had been gone for 200 years. Similarly, Casas Grandes could not have been the inspiration for either the Mimbres Classic phase or the Sedentary Hohokam, as Di Peso (1974:4:208–211) had suggested, because these too were long gone. Rather, the revised chronology places the height of Casas Grandes within the same time period as the Salado manifestation, the Civano and Tucson phases of the Hohokam, the Animas and Cliff phases in the Mimbres Valley, Pueblo IV of the Anasazi, and the El Paso phase of south-central New Mexico and southwestern Texas (Dean and Ravesloot 1993:102).

SALADO

A brief recapitulation of the controversy surrounding the Salado is given here because it exemplifies a larger problem in the archaeological interpretation of cultural identity. As noted above, the Gladwins (e.g., 1934, 1935) suggested the name Salado be applied to a "people who colonized the upper Salt River drainage" from the Tonto-Globe area. The evidence for a Salado intrusion into the Hohokam heartland was the apparently abrupt appearance of Salado polychrome pottery, coursed adobe multistory great houses (at Casa Grande, especially), and extended inhumations under room floors. Within the Hohokam heartland and in fact at Casa Grande and Los Muertos, paddle-and-anvil finished Hohokam buffware ceramics, cremations, and single-story adobe compounds continued as part of the archaeological record of the Hohokam Classic period. Further, the Hohokam canal system was maintained, if not expanded, during the Classic; Hohokam platform mounds continued but became secular and probably related to a status class. The existence of two ceramic traditions, architectural styles, and burial modes at the same sites led many investigators to the conclusion that "Salado people" had peacefully colonized the Hohokam area, and that "the two societies, with their distinctive brands of southwestern culture, lived side by side in apparent peace for more than a century" (Willey 1966:228).

There is a long history of debate about the Salado focused on who they were and from where they came. The Salado have been viewed as Mogollon, as Anasazi, as a "blend" of Mogollon and Anasazi, and as a "blend" of Anasazi and Hohokam. They have been described as originating within the Tonto Basin and Globe-Miami area (Gladwin and Gladwin 1930; Hawley 1932), the Flagstaff area (Schroeder 1953a), the upper Little Colorado (Steen *et al.* 1962), and the Casas Grandes area of Chihuahua (Di Peso 1976; and for reviews, see Doyel 1976b; Hohmann 1992; Lekson 1992; Lindsay and Jennings 1968; Whittlesley and Reid 1982; papers in Lange and Germick 1992).

Continuing discussion on the Salado (e.g., Doyel and Haury 1976; Lange and Germick 1992) has concentrated primarily on describing local and regional manifestations that have been termed Salado and on examining the locations at which the Salado traits are demonstrably early. While no consensual view has prevailed, recent data and syntheses suggest why there has been a move away from trying to understand the Salado in terms of a "people" or cultural group. The defining criteria of "the Salado" are three types of polychrome pottery: Pinto, Gila, and Tonto polychrome (Figure 12.3). These are distinctive red-slipped vessels with black and white painted designs (Colton and Hargrave 1937; Crown 1994). Of these, Pinto Polychrome is both the earliest (dating from about AD 1270/1280 to 1300) and the most narrow in both temporal and spatial range and in formal character. It is found on sites in a narrow corridor from east-central to southeastern Arizona and occurs almost exclusively in bowl form (Crown 1994:17–18). Gila and Tonto polychromes occur in both bowl and jar forms. The dating of Tonto Polychrome is less secure than Gila Polychrome; nevertheless, they seem to be sequential types dating to the fourteenth century. Gila Polychrome dates to after 1300, is most abundant in the mid-fourteenth century, but continues into the 1400s. Tonto Polychrome seems to have been produced from about 1350 to 1450. As Crown (1994:20) cogently states in reference to the Salado concept, "no suite of material traits is consistently associated with Salado polychromes in southwestern sites." Hence, no criteria of domestic or public architecture or mode of burial co-occur constantly with the diagnostic pottery of "Salado culture."

Essentially, the same conclusion is reached on the basis of new excavation and chronometric data in various regions postulated as the geographic locus of origin of the Salado. Casas Grandes is one of the sites at which Gila Polychrome occurs. When it appeared to Di Peso that the site dated to the eleventh century, he suggested that Gila Polychrome had originated there. With revised dating, that conclusion is no longer viable. Further, Casas produced its own widely imitated ceramics, Ramos and other Chihuahuan polychromes. Architecturally, except for being made of adobe-like material rather than stone, Paquimé does not resemble sites in the Salado heartland of the Tonto, Globe-Miami area. There are some large adobe sites that have architectural features that resemble Casas Grandes, notably Joyce Well in New Mexico near the Mexican border, but many more adobe sites have Chihuahuan polychrome pottery types yet lack the diagnostic architectural features typical of Casas Grandes (T- or I-shaped ball courts, raised firepits, etc.) (Lekson 1992).

In the Hohokam heartland, Salado ceramics occur at a small percentage of Classic period sites and, in fact, make up a very small percentage of the ceramics at most sites where they do occur (Weaver 1976). Traits that had been considered evidence of a Salado intrusion, such as inhumation, and adobe-walled compounds have antecedents in the area. Inhumations occur in pre-Classic Hohokam contexts and in Classic Hohokam sites associated with non-Salado ceramics. Adobe-walled compounds in the Hohokam area are not exclusively associated with Salado ceramics (Pailes 1963). Multistory adobe great houses are exceptionally rare in the Hohokam area. In other words, the notion that large Classic Hohokam settlements were composed of ethnically distinct co-resident populations, as described by Willey (1966, see above), does not agree with current information from the Phoenix Basin, Hohokam core area.

Recent work in the Tonto Basin, Globe-Miami area, the presumed Salado homeland, has provided a continuous series of both radiocarbon and archaeomagnetic dates that show no gap between pre-Classic Hohokam use of this area and Salado sites. Hence the original model of either Mogollon "Salado" or Anasazi "Salado" migrating into an empty Hohokam periphery and subsequently moving into the Hohokam core area does not work. Further, in the Tonto Basin, large masonry pueblos and sites with adobe compounds are contemporary, not sequential, again suggesting that the architecture and ceramics are not providing the same information about social entities (Hohmann 1992).

In a thoughtful discussion of the Salado issue, based on data from the Tonto Basin, Whittlesey and Reid (1982) argue that insufficient attention has been given to describing assemblage variability among contemporary sites in the Hohokam core area and its peripheries. For example, their analyses indicate that the method of vessel thinning (paddle and anvil vs. coil and scrape), which has been used as a cultural or ethnic marker for distinguishing Hohokam from Salado ceramics, varies with vessel form. They suggest that the Tonto Basin was used over time by a diversity of groups, some more closely allied to the Hohokam and some to the Mogollon. By AD 1200, after the Hohokam system contracted spatially, the Tonto Basin became more similar to the Mountain Mogollon. Whittlesey and Reid, however, eschew cultural labels. They state that "it is abundantly clear that traditional conceptions of monothetic cultural types (Hohokam, Mogollon, Anasazi) and their cultural varieties (Salado, Sinagua, and others) cannot cope with the polythetic phenomena that we see throughout the Southwest after AD 1150" (Whittlesey and Reid 1982:80).

Given the difficulties in locating a Salado homeland and in consistently defining the Salado manifestation, it is preferable to relinquish the notion that the Salado were a people with a cultural identity. It appears more productive to relate the changes in the Hohokam area to a structural reorganization of Hohokam society and Hohokam participation within a pan-southwestern system of interaction (Doyel 1976b; Gumerman and Weed 1976; Weaver 1976). There are two major areas of inquiry that should be pursued once this research direction is selected. First, there seems to have been more than one pan-southwestern system of interaction operating after 1350. A larger issue is trying to sort out how each of these systems were organized and how they might have related to each other. Second, it is important to try to specify the kinds of structural reorganization or economic interactions that led to recognition of the diverse Salado patterns (Adams 1991; Crown 1994; Lekson 1992; Upham 1982). These are not easy questions to answer. While some directions being taken toward answers are considered here, be warned that there are as yet no agreed upon solutions.

Salado Ceramics and Regional Organization

Lekson (1992) specifies three patterns *in ceramics* that are demonstrable in the post-1300 Southwest. These are the Salado ceramics of Tonto and Gila polychromes, the Casas Grandes pattern of El Paso and Chihuahuan polychromes, and the Rio Grande pattern of glazewares. The distribution of these pottery types from the areas in which they were produced is clinal. Hence, in locations closer to Casas Grandes there will generally be more Chihuahuan pottery than at sites farther away. Lekson (1992) remarks that at Bloom Mound, a site about equidistant from the Tonto Basin and Casas Grandes, there is one each Gila Polychrome and Ramos Polychrome pot (Kelley 1984). One key factor that was clearly stated in 1986 by Nelson and LeBlanc and is verified by a variety of new data is that pottery says one thing and architecture another or several others in that architecture does not behave in a similarly clinal fashion from one or more sources. Later, in the fourteenth and fifteenth centuries, sometime perhaps between 1375 or 1425 and 1500, the Tonto, Gila, and Chihuahuan polychromes drop out. The Rio Grande glazes continue to be produced in a variety of styles in the central Rio Grande Valley, and new series of types, the Jeddito yellow wares from the Hopi area, Sikyatki polychromes from Zuni, and Biscuit ware pottery in the northern Rio Grande, seem also to distribute clinally over very, very large areas. Again, the pottery distributions are not consistently tied to specific architectural styles or types.

Crown (1994) has studied extant collections of the Salado polychromes in terms of four models of their production and distribution. The first is that Salado pottery served as a symbol of authority or in exchange relationships among elites in the manipulation of prestige within a regional system. The second proposes that the Salado polychromes symbols an economic interaction but one not regulated by elites. In this view, the pottery and other items would have been widely traded or exchanged among participants of the system but should not occur on sites outside the economic sphere of influence. The third model is that the pottery symbolized the introduction and spread of a new religious ideology. Finally, the fourth, already discounted on the basis of questions discussed above, was that the pottery distribution was the product of a distinct migrating ethnic group. Crown (1994) developed a series of test implications for each of the proposed models. Her analysis was based on 119 whole Salado vessels from 77 archaeological sites. The test implications involved examining vessel form, the context from which they were recovered, design analyses, and limited neutron activation analysis, among others. On the basis of these tests, Crown ruled out all but the model that the Salado polychromes symbolized a new religious ideology that she termed the "Southwest Regional Cult."

The earliest of the Salado polychromes is decorated in a distinctive style called Pinedale that contains a series of distinctive images and symbols that Crown suggests make up an iconic system. She refers to the system as an outward reflection of her Southwest Regional Cult. The images include parrots, snakes, horned serpents, eyes, the sun, and stars. As a system, these icons occur on pottery and other media, such as rock art (Figure 12.5), and have meanings Crown relates to water control and fertility. Both the icons and the meanings are quite general, occurring in ancient and modern Mesoamerican and Pueblo religions. In the Southwest, icons of the Southwest Regional Cult were painted on pottery as early as Classic Mimbres, dating to the 1000s. While all the icons may be found on Mimbres pottery, the reverse is not true. Many symbols and other unusual paintings occur only on Mimbres pottery. In addition, the contexts in which Mimbres and later pottery occur are very different from those of the "Southwest Regional Cult." When Mimbres bowls occur in burials, they are part of standard burial patterns that suggest a single burial ritual. The later pottery occurs in a variety of burial modes. The earlier Mimbres pottery is associated with long-lived settlements and in fact is found with the in-place development of above-ground pueblos from pithouse communities. The later pottery is found at many newly founded villages. Crown states that an argument could be made for the Mimbres representations being part of an ancestor cult. This is not true of the later Southwestern Regional Cult. She maintains that the imagery of the Mimbres area was used for many centuries in the Southwest and that it crystallized in the Southwestern Regional Cult in the late thirteenth century.

Crown (1994) describes her Southwestern Regional Cult as comparable to similar belief systems known for Africa and elsewhere. Regional cults are neither the ancestor cults nor other kin-based religions common in tribes, nor are they "universal" world religions, such as Catholicism or Buddhism. Regional cults emphasize shared values and concern with the earth and fertility. They tend to develop during times of social disruption. They can unify people of diverse backgrounds. The cult could have coexisted with several different, perhaps local, ideologies. As described, the Southwestern Regional Cult includes aspects of the katcina iconography but also aspects of other

FIGURE 12.5 (a) Following Crown (1994), this Salado polychrome bowl in the Pinedale style has an image of a horned serpent thought to relate to water control and fertility. (b) The Tonto polychrome bowl design may represent a serpent, sidewinder, or feathered serpent, according to Crown (1994). The image is similar to one (c) in a petroglyph in Chaco Canyon (adapted from Crown [1994] by Marjorie Leggitt, Leggitt Design).

religious systems in Mexico and the U.S. Southwest. According to Crown (1994), a cult of this sort might well have been highly advantageous among the ethnically heterogeneous villagers of the post-abandonment Southwest.

Crown's study is important in demonstrating a consistent set of symbols that occur on pottery that was produced over a very broad area in the early fourteenth century. She has also shown that these symbols occur on vessels that vary greatly in design layout and style, in technology of manufacture, in vessel form (small and large bowls, and jars), and context of recovery (inhumation, cremation, room, and trash deposits), etc. The tests she generated for the models she evaluated are convincing. It seems highly unlikely to me that Salado polychromes were the product of a single culture or people, nor were they distributed only among a restricted group of elites. On the other hand, I think use of the term cult suggests an unfortunate reification. In the anthropological if not the popular literature, cults are groups of people that share aspects of belief and generally ritual. Without knowing how membership is recruited, what rituals are involved, or what else cult members do, the term is about as useful as "organization." It carries little content. By specifying a "regional cult" that lies on a continuum between ancestor worship and universal religion, I do not think much has been clarified or that all possibilities have been exhausted. I would suggest, as with broadening our notion of "mercantile" in discussions of Casas Grandes, that we must begin to model the ways the iconic repertory that Crown has identified functioned within the larger cultural systems of which it was a part.

Carlson (1970) defined six temporally significant though partially overlapping design styles for the time span during which the White Mountain red wares were produced. These are distinguished primarily on the basis of the treatment of motifs and layout or focus rather than on design content. Each of the design styles is similar or related to those produced on black-on-white ceramic types. One type of White Mountain red ware—St. Johns Polychrome—and one design style—Pinedale—are of particular interest in the context of the present discussion. St. Johns Polychrome was made between about AD 1175 and 1300. St. Johns Black-on-red was among the most widely distributed and technologically variable types known in the Southwest. The spatial distribution of St. Johns extends from Mesa Verde on the north to Casas Grandes on the south. It has been found as far east as Pecos, New Mexico, and as far west as the Chino Valley in Arizona. Carlson notes that the type is most frequent to the south and west of the center of this enormous area. He suggests that the types were made in the Cibola area, perhaps in more than one locality. The temporal and spatial distribution of St. Johns Polychrome is interesting. It was produced very late in the Chacoan period and continued to be made and traded through the collapse of the Chacoan system. Although the kinds of petrographic analyses that would help determine the specific loci at which it was made have not been done, the abundance of the type at sites near Zuni, at Manuelito Canyon, and along the Tularosa and San Francisco rivers suggests that these areas began to become population centers before the final dispersal of populations out of the Mesa Verde and San Juan Basin areas. The Pinedale style appears on some late St. Johns vessels but becomes common between about AD 1300 and 1375. The style is similar to the preceding Tularosa style but is bolder in execution, contains more squiggled line fillers and less repetition of motifs, and focuses decoration on the entire field of bowl interior. In addition to the Salado polychromes, types with Pinedale style are considered ancestral to Chihuahuan polychromes, Hopi Yellow Ware ceramics (e.g., Kintiel and Klagetoh Polychrome), and some are ancestral to Zuni pottery (Heshotauthla Polychrome). The Hopi and Zuni types, in turn, inspired the Rio Grande glazes produced by the Pueblo of the Rio Grande Valley. The Rio Grande glazes were produced between about AD 1300 and 1700, initially probably in imitation of the St. Johns and Heshotauthla polychromes of the Zuni area that had been traded into the Rio Grande Valley. The use of glaze black paint for decoration occurred in some White Mountain and Zuni ceramics until the mid-1400s; however, after that time the use of this kind of paint was continued only in the Rio Grande Valley area. The glaze itself was achieved by using copper and manganese or copper and galena (lead ore) as pigments.

Petrographic work by Warren (1977) suggests that the earliest Rio Grande glazes were made at a number of different centers in the vicinity of Albuquerque and were widely traded not only in the Rio Grande area itself but also to the adjacent plains. After about 1450, sites in the Galisteo Basin became production locations for glazes with cream-yellow colored interior slips. Although glazes originating in the Galisteo Basin were traded to other localities within the Rio Grande Valley, especially to sites on the Pajarito Plateau and the Santa Fe Plain, they seem not to have been distributed as widely south of Albuquerque or east of the Sandia Mountains.

Finally, during the 1600s, glaze pottery was produced at only a few locations: the Salinas area, the Galisteo Basin, and at Pecos Pueblo and Zia Pueblo (Snow 1982). During the early Spanish Colonial period, some glaze pottery was made that incorporated European forms such as soup plates and pitchers, and Pueblo pottery was widely used by the Spanish colonists. Following the Pueblo Revolt of 1680 and the Spanish Reconquest of 1692, both Pueblo and Spanish colonial economies underwent considerable reorganization. By the mid-1700s, Spanish land grants and mineral claims precluded Indian access to their previous sources of lead, and the native production of glaze-painted ceramics ended (Snow 1982).

In sum, a tradition of polychrome ceramic manufacturing began in the Zuni area in the twelfth century with the White Mountain red wares. The color schemes and design layouts of ceramics produced from the late twelfth century into the 1700s show a considerable homogeneity throughout much of the Southwest. In some places, local production by some groups continued pre-twelfth-century traditions. For example, in the Jemez, Taos, and Chama country of the northern Rio Grande Valley, a black-on-white and black-on-gray tradition continued despite the neighboring contemporary manufacture of glaze polychromes.

Crown (1994) makes a most important point when she notes that the Salado polychromes are one of an array of southwestern ceramics that incorporated a single style (termed Pinedale by Carlson 1982) on at least some of their ceramic vessels. The Pinedale style in this sense follows the standard archaeological definition of a horizon style. Further, the Pinedale style later differentiated into regional variants. As Crown (1994:179) indicates, this pan-southwestern process needs to be understood (Figure 12.6).

In commenting on the need for a broader view of the initial post 1300 distributions, Lekson (1992) points out that there were three relatively unpopulated, prime upland regions for hunting and gathering until about 1050 to 1200. These are the Rio Grande Valley, the Mogollon Highlands, and the northern Sierra Madre in Mexico. These may have been hinterlands preserved as resource areas by the older regional systems represented by Chaco and the Sedentary Hohokam. In the 1200s, without

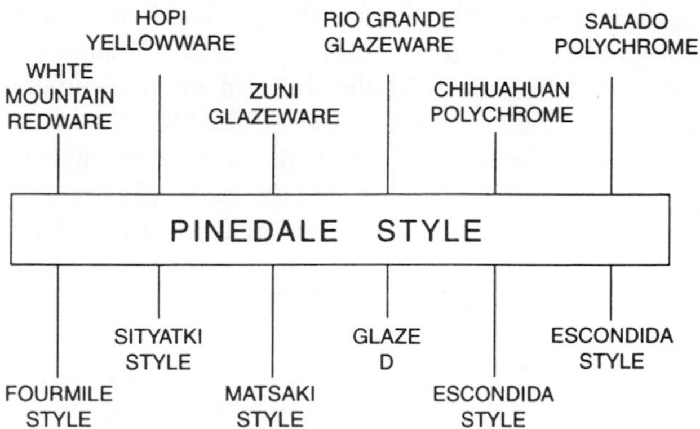

FIGURE 12.6 Crown (1994) suggests that the Pinedale style, consisting of distinctive images and symbols, is best seen as a horizon marker that cross-cuts a series of Southwestern pottery traditions and in turn gives rise to a variety of ceramic types (after Crown [1994]).

some kind of protection, populations began to encroach on these areas. Lekson suggests that the mix of subsistence strategies used by the groups moving into the Mogollon Mountains and the Sierra Madre did not last, and could not be intensified, so that by 1450 or so they were abandoned. The Rio Grande was different because as the abundance of wild resources diminished, irrigation could provide increased agricultural yields. Lekson acknowledges that a similar scenario would have been possible in the Phoenix Basin but it did not take place. He offers the suggestion that availability of bison from the Great Plains may have made the difference in the Rio Grande. I find his suggestion interesting but believe it is unlikely because there is very little evidence that bison were available to Rio Grande populations before about the middle of the sixteenth century (Cordell 1996). Lekson has made important points by focusing attention on the clinal distributions of pottery styles and movement of people into previously nearly empty upland resource regions. He has not described the ways these local populations interacted with each other or the center at Casas Grandes. If Casas Grandes, during the Medio period, functioned as a regional trade center, we must have a better understanding of how that trade was organized and pursued. Grebinger (1971, 1976) suggests that participation in a vast trading network was organized through the activities of families of long-distance traders and regularized interaction among communities in adjacent valleys. This notion is intriguing but requires that details be elaborated, specified, and evaluated.

HIERARCHIES, ELITES, OR JUST BIG SITES?

In the 1980s, a major debate among archaeologists involved opinions about whether the large Western Pueblo communities of the fourteenth century were politically similar to modern Pueblo villages. Those who argued that they were similar in being basically egalitarian and tribal had focused their discussion on Grasshopper Pueblo, a very large site below the Mogollon Rim on an old channel of the Salt River Draw (Graves *et al.* 1982; Longacre and Reid 1974; Reid and Whittlesey 1990). Others saw the large sites as having been organized through social hierarchies and supra-village alliances coordinated by individuals of elite status. Those who favored hierarchies and elites framed their argument in terms of Chavez Pass Pueblo, an ancestral Hopi village on Anderson Mesa about 96 km distant from Grasshopper Pueblo (Upham 1982, 1987; Upham *et al.* 1989; Upham and Plog 1986). In the previous edition of this book (Cordell 1984), the two perspectives were presented as alternative case studies. The amount of ink spilled over the course of this debate is extraordinary and no attempt at a complete bibliography is offered here. As is sometimes the case, there was some productive discussion about differences in underlying assumptions, frames of reference, and analytic methods. The debate was never resolved on the basis of these two sites and continues to exist to some extent in the context of these and other sites and other time periods (Neitzel in press; Cordell, in Neitzel in press; Saitta 1994; Spielmann 1994), including the rather different perspectives on the mercantile nature of Casas Grandes described above.

Two empirical issues have been clarified. Based on analysis of the stratigraphic position of ceramic types, Upham (1982) assumed that Chavez Pass Pueblo existed within a cluster of small contemporary communities. This seems not to have been the case. The data support the conclusion that the small communities predated Chavez Pass and that as with the Grasshopper region and others, when aggregation occurred, it was complete (Dean *et al.* 1994; Upham and Reed 1989). Further, as discussed above in the context of both Ramos and the Salado polychromes, without appropriate analysis of clays and tempers, it is virtually impossible to learn which vessels of a single type have been imported into an area or locally made. Without such information, inferences about trade networks are potentially unreliable.

One of the issues that remains unresolved is how to go about finding appropriate analogs from which to draw inferences about past social organization and how to proceed to test those inferences which we do make. This question is an important one for archaeology, clearly transcending the Southwest. These questions were raised many years ago by Aberle (1970), commenting about reconstructions of ancient Pueblo social organization. They have been raised more recently by Wolf (1982) in the context of ethnology as a whole. In fairly concrete terms, we may note that in historic times, no Pueblo community has amassed the amount of diverse craft items that were apparently stored at Casas Grandes. In modern times, no peoples of the Southwest built ball courts of any shape or constructed huge platform mounds with domestic structures on their summits. Yet, it is also clear that these things were done by the ancestors of modern native Southwesterners.

Given the warnings of both Aberle (1970) and Wolf (1982), it seems most reasonable not to attempt to find the perfect analog for past social organization among the modern societies of the ethnographically documented world. What does seem appropriate is to describe as accurately as possible how things appear to have worked from the archaeological record. For example, what was really traded, over what distance, over what period of time? How widespread were systems of iconographic symbols, on what media, and over what period of time? We may then approach the ethnographic literature for a set of correlated behaviors that may be examined archaeologically. For example, we may examine the ethnographic record for distances over which different kinds of goods produced by part-time craft specialists and then by full-time specialists are normally distributed in the absence of motor, animal, or water transport. If there are strong patterns of correlation, these can be compared with our archaeological data. We will assuredly not find single whole societies that "match" our archaeological cases. We may also have to learn to differentiate dimensions along which to measure our data and different levels of abstraction in framing our queries. In my opinion, however, it will be worth the effort (Cordell, in Neitzel in press; see also Adler 1993). We may also begin to explore patterning in data from the modern world in contexts that we believe we understand and see how those changed as we work backward in time. This last approach has been taken by Adams (1991) in his exploration of the development of katcina belief systems among the Pueblos.

KATCINA CEREMONY

Adams (1991) argues that the katcina ceremonies, specifically, developed as an institution of social integration among Mogollon and Anasazi villages in the upper Little Colorado region in the fifteenth century. Hence, he views the origin of the katcinas as being slightly later and occurring northeast of Crown's (1994) suggested origin of her postulated Southwest Regional Cult. For centuries, the Upper Little Colorado area was at a cultural boundary between Mogollon and Anasazi traditions. It seems also to have been a major area of refuge for people moving south out of the Four Corners region.

Among the modern Pueblos, katcinas serve as mediators between the people and the gods, bringing the people's needs for rain and the fertility of crops to the attention of the gods. They are also generalized ancestral beings in that the dead can and do become katcinas. Katcina ceremonies are nearly universal in the Pueblo villages but are most apparent today among the western villages of the Hopi, Zuni, and Acoma. Among the modern Rio Grande Pueblos, the public aspects of katcina ritual became private and secret in response to Spanish repression of Native religion. Among the Western Pueblos, katcina dances are performed in the central plaza before a spectator audience. During the ceremonies, the katcina spirits are impersonated by initiated men who become katcinas themselves by dancing with objects that they call *friends* and Western Europeans call masks. The katcina rituals involve elaborate costumes and dancing that reflect long periods of planning and preparation (Figure 12.7). The public katcina performances involve cooperation among the various elements (clans or kiva groups) of the Pueblo villages. Adams (1991) views these aspects of katcina ceremony as requiring cooperation that cross-cuts households and clans.

FIGURE 12.7 Among the Western Pueblos today, katcina figures appear in elaborate costumes of which the *friend* or mask is diagnostic of a specific personage or character. Here the figure represented by this doll, or *tihu*, is a hummingbird (illustrated by Marjorie Leggitt, Leggitt Design).

In Western Pueblo society, male clan elders are the village leaders. There are also two classes of katcinas, chief katcinas and dancing katcinas; the distinction mirrors that between clan elders and other initiated males in Western Pueblo society. In this way, katcina performances serve to institutionalize aspects of Western Pueblo social and political organization. In Adams' (1991) view, the qualities of cooperation among residence and kin groups as well as the reflection of the Western Pueblo organizational features were well-suited to integrating villages formed by the heterogeneous elements brought together in the wake of the abandonments of the late thirteenth century.

Recognition of katcina ceremony in archaeological materials requires identification of material correlates of katcina beliefs. The correlates Adams (1991) describes are symbols such as the masks themselves, the group performance and its setting in a plaza, the kiva where dances are planned and practiced, private rest areas used between specific performances, and preparation and distribution of specific kinds of food, especially the wafer-thin corn bread called *piki* that is made by the Hopi.

The masks that are the key features of the dances today are unlikely to become part of the archaeological record or to be preserved archaeologically. It is no surprise that no katcina masks have been found in archaeological context. Some katcina symbols such as lightning or snake designs and the terraced cloud motif (Figure 12.8) are very

FIGURE 12.8 The terraced cloud motif is an ancient Pueblo symbol that is geographically widespread. It is one of the symbols incorporated into modern katcina iconography (illustrated by Marjorie Leggitt, Leggitt Design).

ancient Pueblo symbols and are older and more widespread geographically than the katcina ritual itself. Other elements, such as rectangular kivas, are not functionally specific to katcina beliefs but serve a variety of uses. Nevertheless, Adams (1991) maintains that the principal features of katcina beliefs that may be found archaeologically are village plans with enclosed plazas, rectangular kivas, and griddle stones for making piki bread. He argues that these came together in the 1300s in the upper Little Colorado River area.

Adams' view has been challenged (Crotty 1995; Crown 1994:219–221; Schaafsma 1980, 1994a), as is discussed below; however, he argues that the spread of the katcinas can be identified archaeologically by the symbols on ceramics, kiva wall murals (Figure 12.9), and in the Rio Grande area, in rock art. Adams suggests that katcina beliefs may have started out as a version of ancestor worship, but an important aspect in the development and spread of katcina beliefs was for villages to publicly indicate that they participated in the rituals. In the upper Little Colorado and the Hopi areas, the signal involved pictorial representations of masks, masked figures, and other katcina symbols painted on pottery and in murals on the walls of rectangular kivas. These forms of representation also spread to the east and are found at Pottery Mound and Kuaua, large villages in the Rio Grande area, and Las Humanas (Gran Quivira) on the edge of the Plains (Figure 12.1). The pottery style that is most closely associated with katcina depiction, in Adams' view, is the Fourmile style of White Mountain red ware, one of the "decendant" styles of the Pinedale style (Figure 12.6).

Crown's (1994) primary objection to Adams' interpretation is that his criteria for recognizing the origin of katcina beliefs focus on when those beliefs apparently became public, not when they began. She sees the origin of katcina ideology as much older, deriving from symbolic elements expressed on Mimbres pottery, in rock art, and in the icons painted on the Salado polychrome pots. Some perspective on aspects of the debate may provide clarification. As indicated in the introduction of this chapter, few completely new forms characterize the post-1300 Southwest. Rather, there is a crystallization of older elements in new ways. Emphasizing the symbols associated with katcina belief will lead to finding very early and widespread evidence of aspects of what became elaborate katcina ritual. Focusing on the context in which katcina ritual is

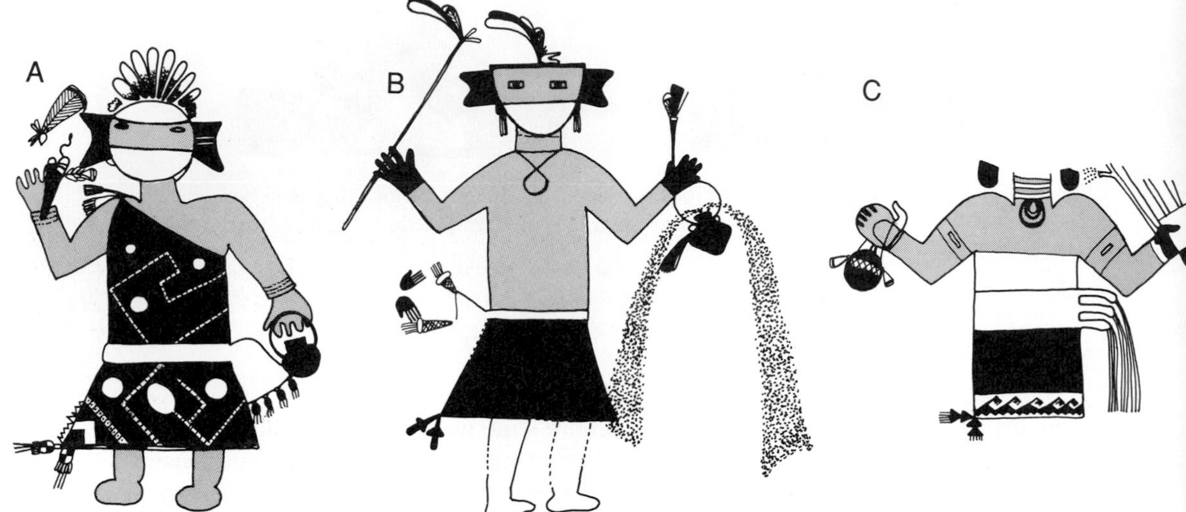

FIGURE 12.9 Kiva mural figures from the widely separated sites of (A) Pottery Mound, south of Albuquerque; (B) Kuaua near Bernalillo, north of Albuquerque, and (C) Awatovi, an ancestral Hopi site on Antelope Mesa, Arizona are different in minor details but are similar in execution. Kiva murals are invaluable sources of information. Many of the symbols and rituals are recognizable to modern Pueblo peoples (all illustrated by Charles M. Carrillo, (A) with permission from the Maxwell Museum; (B) from Dutton [1963:Figure113], and (C) from Smith [1952] with permission of the Peabody Museum of Archaeology and Ethnology, Harvard University).

performed today and its potential role in integrating people of diverse backgrounds shifts attention to the public—and democratic—aspects of the ritual. The performance itself is seen as having crystallized out of older elements sometime after 1300. There is consensus between Adams (1991) and Crown (1994) regarding the development of katcina beliefs and rituals in the Southwest, rather than seeing them as having been introduced from central Mexico. The same conclusion has been reached by study of the fourteenth and fifteenth century kiva mural depictions.

Kiva Murals, Rock Art, and Katcinas

The practice of painting on kiva walls is documented as early as Pueblo II among the Anasazi (Brew 1946; Smith 1952). Prior to the fourteenth century, however, paintings were either simple lines and dots or small, stylized figures, not shown interacting with each other. It is not until the late fourteenth and fifteenth centuries that such paintings depict elaborate, colorful, composed figurative and geometric scenes. Five archaeological sites provide the most abundant and best preserved evidence of this strong tradition of Pueblo religious art. The sites are widely separated geographically: Two sites, and the first to be excavated, are Kawaika-a and Awatovi, ancestral Hopi sites on Antelope Mesa in the Jeddito area of Arizona (Montgomery *et al.* 1949; Smith 1952). Two other sites are Kuaua, on the banks of the Rio Grande just north of Albuquerque (Dutton 1963), and Pottery Mound, located on the Rio Puerco of the East, south of Albuquerque (Hibben 1975). The last site, Las Humanas, at Gran Quivira, is in central New Mexico on the edge of the Great Plains (Hayes *et al.* 1981).

These sites are not precisely contemporary, and details of the paintings differ among them; however, the murals share many similarities, including technical methods of execution, plan, and symbols. For example, the murals depict single figures, altars, and scenes that include masked dancers (Figure 12.9). Figures are commonly shown wearing flaring kilts with sashes and holding similar ritual objects such as staffs, gourd water containers, and quivers. Some of the kiva paintings are of geometric designs that are very similar to those painted on the contemporary Hopi Sikyatki polychrome ceramics (an elaborated descendant of the Pinedale style and late White Mountain red wares). Other designs, however, are naturalistic. The naturalistic designs in the kiva murals show a variety of costumed figures, masked figures, emblems, plants, insects, mythical creatures, feathers, birds, and other animals. Although several of the figures are done as isolated elements, some of the paintings show figures interacting in scenes along one or more walls. The murals incorporate symbolic elements that are recognizable among Pueblo people today and many of which are still used in ritual context, such as lightning motifs, terraced clouds, and moisture representations. The detail in costumed figures provides an extraordinary view of textiles, headdresses, and other adornment that is rarely preserved archaeologically (Figure 12.7). In each case, the ritual nature of the paintings is reflected not only in their subject matter but also by the practice of deliberately plastering over the painting, presumably once its purpose had been fulfilled. One wall at Kuaua had 85 layers of plaster of which 17 were painted. At each of the sites except Las Humanas, the murals were executed on the walls of rectangular or square kivas. At Las Humanas, murals occurred on the walls of three circular kivas and six rectangular rooms.

Controversial aspects of the kiva murals involve their particular origin, mode of introduction into the Southwest, the degree to which their content represents a pan-Pueblo symbolic structure, and whether the murals and their symbolic content derive from Mesoamerican sources (e.g., Brody 1979; Di Peso *et al.* 1974:301–308; Hibben 1975; Kelley and Kelley 1975; McGuire 1980). Helen Crotty (1995) has produced the first complete analysis and synthesis of data on all known examples of painted kivas that clarifies and resolves most of these questions. She explains that the idea that the mural art derived from the Valley of Mexico was first proposed by Beals in 1943, when he suggested that the religious cult centered on the Aztec rain god Tlaloc had been transformed into the Pueblo katcina beliefs. This diffusionist claim was championed and expanded by Frank Hibben (1966, 1967, 1975) when he argued that a flat-topped "pyramid" that he excavated under pueblo roomblocks at Pottery Mound was certain evidence of Mexican influence.

Crotty (1995) notes that much of the argument and its subsequent elaborations derived from faulty chronology that resulted from a lack of tree-ring dates from the appropriate sites. Like Adams (1991) and Crown (1994), Crotty (1995) examines other contexts of the specific mural depictions and style, especially on pottery. She finds evidence of contacts and trade relationships between the Western and Rio Grande Pueblos that had received little attention. Excavations that I supervised at Pottery Mound in 1979 yielded a cremation with well over 100 olivella shell beads (Cordell 1980). Because Pottery Mound is a large adobe pueblo, and the "pyramid" at Pottery Mound fits the definition of a Classic period Hohokam platform mound, in my opinion, Pottery Mound comes as close as anything in Arizona to a Late Classic Hohokam "Salado" platform mound site.

I further concur with Crotty (1995) as she concludes that

> examination of the style and content of the murals and related arts reveals no evidence of a sudden change after AD 1300 that can be traced to a Mexican source. Instead, life forms were increasingly depicted in Anasazi arts beginning in the late 1200s and eventually found their fullest expression in mural art after 1400. . . . The fluorescence of mural art, which followed innovations in ceramics technology and decoration, seems to have resulted from the meeting and blending of various Puebloan cultural traditions in the relocations of the thirteenth and fourteenth centuries. No single dominant influence, either native or foreign, can be identified (Crotty 1995:xix).

Crotty (1995) also notes that the mural portrayals contain only a small percentage of masked figures, few of which can be identified with historic katcinas. Hence, a direct association with modern katcina ritual appears unlikely.

In an analysis of rock art, Schaafsma and Schaafsma (1974:539) define a "Rio Grande Style" that in many ways parallels the fourteenth century kiva art. The Rio Grande style of rock art, especially as represented in the Galisteo Basin south of Santa Fe, incorporates masks and masked figures. The Schaafsmas suggest that the "Rio Grande Style" derives from the Jornada Mogollon area and represents the introduction of katcina ceremonialism in the Southwest. They argue that the katcina rituals entered the Pueblo world between 1325 and 1350 and spread from the Rio Grande Valley west to Zuni and Hopi within the fourteenth century. Although it is very difficult to interpret rock art and date it with any accuracy, the Schaafsmas' discussion emphasizes the pan-Pueblo nature of the art forms described. However, Crotty (1995) notes that the mask forms in Jornada rock art are completely different in style from those on pottery and kiva murals. She suggests that this argues for much greater antiquity of the use of masks than is normally credited, and she agrees with Adams (1991) that those representing the presence of katcina ceremonies derive from the west.

As with Crown's (1994) Southwestern Regional Cult, the katcina rituals seem to have crystallized out of diverse and very ancient elements in Pueblo culture. The ceremonies and beliefs were very successful in integrating Pueblo peoples of different languages and histories. They were particularly successful at times of population movement and concomitant social stress. The late sixteenth and early seventeenth centuries were also a time of movement and distress as Athapaskan-speaking peoples moved into the Southwest. These newcomers were never integrated into the Pueblo social world, but there are intriguing suggestions that, were historical circumstances different, they might have been.

EUROPEANS, APACHEANS, AND CHANGE

In 1528, Alvar Nuñez Cabaza de Vaca and three companions, survivors of the ill-fated Navarez expedition to Florida, were shipwrecked on the Texas coast south of present El Paso. They traveled west across the Sierra Madre Occidental and, in 1536, made contact with their fellow countrymen, possibly as far north as the lower Yaqui Valley (Riley 1987:17). The party reported learning of wealthy agricultural towns far north on the Rio Grande. Their story was instrumental in leading to the entradas, first of Fray Marcos de Niza to the Zuni region in 1539, and then to the large, well-organized Coronado expedition of 1540–1542 (Cordell 1989).

The Spaniards expanded into the Southwest from two directions, each at a different time. Initially, there was rapid exploration and colonization from New Spain, northeast into the Pueblo country. The secular impetus for this thrust was greed for mineral wealth; the religious involved in this colonial effort were Franciscans. Nearly a century later, Spaniards moved into Arizona through Northwest Mexico, after having incorporated Native peoples along the way. This move was also motivated by the desire for mineral wealth and for Indian labor for the mines and haciendas, but its pace was slower, defense against hostile nomadic tribes was important from the beginning, and during most of the period, missionary effort was controlled by the Jesuits (Cordell 1989a).

In the year 1540 the Francisco Vasquez de Coronado expedition made its way from Compostela to the Zuni Pueblo of Hawikuh. Members of Coronado's forces explored as far west as the Grand Canyon. Pedro de Tovar's group encountered the Hopi villages and Hernando de Alvarado visited Acoma and the Rio Grande Pueblos from modern Bernalillo to Taos and journeyed east to Pecos and the Great Plains. The Coronado expedition wintered in Bernalillo, and in the spring of 1541 returned to Pecos. Some members of the expedition were sent to Taos to obtain supplies. Others were led far onto the Plains, where they became mistrustful of their Indian guide, killed him, and returned to the central Rio Grande Valley. As the general situation deteriorated and the troops threatened mutiny, Coronado retreated to Mexico in the spring of 1542. Juan de Padilla, a Franciscan, and two lay brothers who had been left behind were killed by the Native people. Not until 1581 did another European expedition enter the Southwest, that of Fray Agustin Rodriguez and Captain Francisco Chumascado. From 1581 on, expeditions of soldiers and friars, and soon colonists, forever changed the relations of groups to each other and to the land.

European documents provide the first written eyewitness accounts of Southwestern peoples. The wealth of descriptive materials constitute an invaluable resource, but one that must be used with care. The Southwest was explored, conquered, and colonized under the Spanish Empire. The cultural values and historic forces affecting the Spanish explorers and colonists are generally poorly understood by people of the Anglo-American tradition. Sixteenth-century Spain had been united only recently (1492) under a single strong monarchy, which had expelled its Moorish overlords from Spanish territory. The important arena for Spanish accomplishment was in Europe, where the strongest competition for power lay with the newly developed mercantile states of the north (principally Holland and England). Spanish exploration and conquest was fueled by a strong nationalism in which Catholicism was a major component. Colonies were sought in order to provide mineral wealth for the monarchy and human souls for the Church. In the Americas, Spain had been remarkably successful in these endeavors. The Aztec Empire had been conquered in 1521 and the Inca Empire in 1535. The rich Mexican mining areas were supplying quantities of silver for the Spanish crown. When Coronado's expedition reached New Mexico in 1540, lured by tales of the wondrous Seven Cities of Cibola, the disappointment must have been acute. Not only was there a lack of obvious mineral wealth, but the scale of the local societies was far smaller than either the Aztec Empire or the Spanish monarchy. It is often difficult to interpret Pueblo social, economic, and political organization from the first-hand accounts of the Spanish chroniclers because their frame of reference is one Anglo-Americans are poorly equipped to understand.

In addition to our problems in interpreting Spanish documents, we must remember that the effects of European diseases and Spanish administrative policies drastically changed the social and settlement landscape of the Southwest. Native southwestern peoples had no immunities to European diseases. Hence they suffered very high mortality levels. For example, as late as 1853, a severe smallpox epidemic struck the Hopi First Mesa villages. The First Mesa population of 1200 persons was reduced to 650 by 1862 (Adams 1981:327). Using various lines of evidence, Upham (1982:39) estimates that within 100 years of their first contact with Europeans, the Western Pueblos of Hopi, Zuni, and Acoma lost 75–80 percent of their populations. In his review of various archival records, Schroeder (1979b:239) lists 61 pueblos known to have been abandoned since 1540. Although reasons other than epidemic disease are given for some of these abandonments, disease is an all-too-common factor in most cases. Heavy population losses must have had profound effects on Pueblo economy and political organization. For example, some villages may not have been able to perform traditional ceremonies because there were not enough people to carry out important roles, or the leadership positions of various societies could not be filled. It is also possible that there were not enough able-bodied people to plant, tend, and harvest crops. Villages that could not continue to survive socially may have joined other villages, such as the inhabitants of Pecos did when they went to Jemez in the nineteenth century.

Southwestern societies, particularly the Pueblos, were greatly influenced by Spanish Colonial policies. Conversion of the Indians to Roman Catholicism, supported by a complex body of law and procedures, was a primary aim of the colonial effort. Before the codification of the Law of the Indies in 1680, it was legal to pursue Indian conversions by force if necessary. Not only were Indian religious practices prohibited and religious paraphernalia confiscated and burned, but Indian religious leaders were tortured and killed. One effect of the Spanish policy was that "the native priesthood became implacable foes of the Spaniards" and native religious practices were continued in secret (Simmons 1979:181). Before 1680, Indians were required to pay tribute and labor to Spanish colonists under the *encomienda* and *repartimiento* systems. The encomienda was a grant of tribute from either a particular pueblo or a group of Indians to the person holding the grant (the *encomendero*). The repartimiento was a system of conscripting Indian labor for Spanish farms, haciendas, or mines. Although the Indians were supposed to be paid a wage for their labor, abuses were common (Simmons 1979: 182). As a logical outcome of the injustices of the Spanish system, the Pueblos united in revolt against the Spaniards on August 10, 1680. The revolt led to the withdrawal of the Spaniards from New Mexico for 12 years. The revolt dislocated some Pueblo populations and influenced the structure of subsequent inter-Pueblo interactions (Kessell 1989). After the 1680 revolt and the extended reconquest begun by Diego de Vargas in 1691–1692, some Pueblo villages were never reoccupied, Pueblos were built in inaccessible locations, and some Pueblo people established communities with other more distant Pueblos and with Athapaskan-speakers.

According to Spanish law, land that was tilled by the Indians could not be confiscated by colonists. The law also required colonists to establish their communities on land not already occupied by the Indians. These regulations provided for physical separation of Indian and Hispanic communities. Although it is probably true that the absence of Spanish colonists within Indian villages enabled the Indians to preserve many of their cultural traditions, the rules would have served to disrupt aspects of the Native system. For example, Spanish settlements were established around and among Pueblo villages. European domestic livestock grazed on land that had provided wild plant and animal foods for the Pueblos. It is difficult to know precisely how much daily or seasonal interaction characterized the relations among Pueblo villages in the fifteenth century, but the presence of the Spanish Colonial settlements probably disrupted and diminished these interactions.

The seventeenth century documents provide the first written observations of the Southwest, yet the accounts were written by men whose roots were in a political and intellectual tradition that was completely alien to the societies they encountered. The experiences of the Spanish explorers and colonists were also markedly different from those of the British settlers of the eastern United States, whose traditions are at the core of American society; therefore, the Spanish accounts are sometimes difficult for modern Americans to appreciate. The native peoples of the Southwest were vassals of the Spanish Empire until 1821, when Mexico achieved independence from Spain. To understand the impact of nearly 300 years of Spanish Colonial rule on the native peoples of the Southwest, it is necessary to be familiar with the cultural traditions of Colonial Spain as well as those of the Indians of the Southwest. Despite these problems, Historic period archaeology in the Southwest can be of inestimable value. The use of documents in addition to archaeological and Native history and ethnographic information provide an exceptionally rich view that is rarely available from one of these sources alone. Brief examples are provided here.

HISTORY, LEGEND, AND ARCHAEOLOGY AT AWATOVI AND WALPI

An unusually productive view of the Spanish conquest comes from the Hopi villages. Although the Spanish impact was less intensive among the Hopi and Zuni than among the other Pueblo villages, the historic record of this period at Hopi is supplemented by archaeological information that is lacking elsewhere. When Coronado stopped at Zuni in 1540, he dispatched some of his party to Hopi. They were led by a general, Pedro de Tovar, and a Franciscan friar, Juan de Padilla. It was not until 1629, however, that missions were established at the Hopi villages. Eventually, seventeenth century mission churches were built at Awatovi, at that time, the easternmost Hopi village on Antelope Mesa; at Shongopavi, on Second Mesa; and at Oraibi, on Third Mesa. The largest of these was San Bernardo at Awatovi.

In the seventeenth century, the village of Awatovi, on Antelope Mesa, was the easternmost Hopi village and the site of the Franciscan mission of San Bernardo de Aguatubi. Between 1630 and 1680, there were normally only between three and five priests resident among the Hopi. At Awatovi, the Spaniards directed that the mission church be built directly over the principal kiva and that all Native religious objects be surrendered and destroyed. The villagers at Awatovi seem to have complied, not unwillingly, with most of the Spaniards' requests. The Spanish missionization at Awatovi was their most successful among the Hopi. According to the Spanish documentary record, a miraculous cure of a blind Hopi boy by the Franciscan friar Francisco Porras in 1629 was behind this success. Whether or not such an event actually occurred, the missionary achievements can be attributed, in part, to the character of Porras himself, who was an outstanding churchman of his times. He was responsible for building the magnificent mission church of San Bernardo and baptizing many Awatovi. He is also credited with having learned to speak the Hopi language. Nevertheless, during the Pueblo Revolt of 1680, the mission church of San Bernardo de Awatovi was destroyed. The mission has been excavated by the Peabody Museum of Harvard University (Montgomery *et al.* 1949). Following the reconquest of 1693, missions were again established among the Pueblo except among the Hopi, who successfully resisted. As there were no European survivors of the revolt at Hopi and documents were burned, there are no contemporary written accounts of the actual events. The archaeological excavations demonstrate that San Bernardo was indeed burned. Subsequently, the Awatovi remodeled the friary and occupied it as part of the pueblo.

At Hopi the events of 1680 marked the end of the Spaniards' church and the Christian God. It was victory for the katcinas in all the villages and remained so because the Hopi were never again successfully admininstered as a part of the Spanish Empire. Yet, for their own reasons, the Awatovi continued to bury Christian Hopi at the burned mission, and in contrast to all the rest of Hopi were prepared to invite the Spaniards back in 1700. This they were not permitted to do by other Hopi.

According to an account written in 1732 (cited in Montgomery *et al.* 1949:222), in 1700 two Franciscan friars traveled to the Hopi, and at Awatovi they successfully converted the Indians and baptized many of them. During their stay they were threatened by Indians from the other Hopi villages, whom they tried, unsuccessfully, to convert. Intending to return with soldiers to protect the Christian Indians of Awatovi and the mission, the friars left. Upon their departure, Hopi warriors from several other villages raided Awatovi. According to the historic accounts, archaeology, and Hopi legend, Awatovi was burned, many of its men were killed, and captives, primarily women and children, were taken to the other villages. According to a Hopi legend recorded by Fewkes (1893), on the way back to the other villages, several of the captives were killed, dismembered, and cruelly mutilated. Excavations at Awatovi provided data that make the Hopi destruction of Awatovi comprehensible, and subsequent archaeological work and osteological research lends support to the Hopi legendary account.

The friars who came to Awatovi in 1700 were apparently not content with obtaining only the reconversion of the residents of Awatovi. Rather, they planned to use Awatovi as a staging area for the reconversion of the other Hopi villages to the west. That the Awatovi complied with the request was shown archaeologically when the foundations of the barracks were excavated in the 1930s. The return of the Spaniards to Awatovi was therefore a very real threat to the rest of the Hopi. The destruction of Awatovi may be viewed as a reaction to this threat by all the Hopi. The mutilation of some of the Awatovi captives was verified through osteological analysis of human skeletal remains excavated in 1964 at a site on Polacca Wash (Olson 1966). At least 30 individuals, of both sexes and all age groups, were found in a mass burial about 6.5 km from the Hopi villages. Analysis of the bones (Turner and Morris 1970) revealed the individuals to be of Western Pueblo physical type, and "all had been intentionally and violently mutilated at the grave site. Skulls, jaws, and long bones were broken with multiple crushing, splintering, and fracturing blows while the bone was still vital" (Turner and Morris 1970:330). The osteologists also note that some of the bones indicate cannibalism. A radiocarbon date of 1580 ± 95 years places the mass grave within the Historic period, and Turner and Morris (1970) conclude that the evidence best fits the Hopi account of the incident as related to Fewkes.

Walpi (Figure 12.10), a First Mesa Hopi village, was established shortly after 1690 and continues to be inhabited today. Archaeological work was undertaken between 1975 and 1977 in conjunction with a program of village restoration (Adams 1981, 1983). During the project, archaeologists partially excavated 97 rooms and mapped 103 rooms. A great deal of information about room function, room ownership, and chronology was obtained from the current residents of Walpi. Chronological information, especially important to the findings discussed here, was obtained from the Hopi and from tree rings. While Spanish friars, institutions of government, and religion were all rejected by the Hopi, they did assimilate what they considered useful: metal plows and hoes for farming; melons, apples, peaches, and apricots; mutton and chicken; methods of weaving with wool; new ways of working wood; and skill in crafting metal tools. Hopi pottery dating to the mission period includes European forms such as shallow, flare-rimmed stew bowls and bowls with a single coil affixed to the base, replicating the ring-base of European wheel-made pottery. In addition, the Pueblos used various European motifs in painted designs on these and more traditional forms made between 1630 and 1680.

Walpi was founded in 1690, 10 years after the successful Pueblo Revolt. Between that date and the 1730s, the population of all the Hopi villages, including Walpi, swelled as refugees from the Rio Grande villages tried to remove themselves as far as possible from the threat of Spanish reprisals for the revolt. The excavations at Walpi provide data that reflect the very strong anti-Spanish feelings. All European vessel

FIGURE 12.10 Walpi, a First Mesa Hopi village, was established about 1690 and is inhabited today. In the 1970s, the village participated in a restoration project that included archaeology (photograph taken in 1931, courtesy of the University of Colorado Museum).

forms and Spanish design motifs disappear from the Hopi pottery. The forms of bowls and jars and the designs used are similar to the Rio Grande pottery of the period, a fact that seems to reflect the refugee elements in the Hopi communities and the close ties the Hopi established with these people.

Droughts at Hopi during the 1730s were the impetus for many Rio Grande Pueblo refugees to begin returning home. Tano from the Galisteo Basin stayed, however, and founded Hano, the First Mesa village that is still occupied by their descendants today. After 1750, anti-Spanish feeling abated somewhat. According to Adams, Spanish elements once again appear on Hopi pottery, but their form, overall organization, and motifs are a mixture of Spanish, Hopi, and Rio Grande design. Tragedy struck again, when a major drought affecting Hopi occurred between 1777 and 1780, followed by a smallpox epidemic that swept through the Hopi villages in 1781. In response to these events, a number of Hopi families temporarily moved to Zuni, Acoma, Zia, and other pueblos where they had friends or relatives. When the drought ended and the Hopi returned to their villages, the pottery they subsequently produced was much changed. The unslipped light yellow, tan, or orange pottery that had been made previously was replaced by pottery with white slips that resembled Zuni and Acoma pottery. Spanish forms, such as stew bowls, and Spanish design elements again became popular. Adams (1981) indicates that these were assimilated indirectly by the Hopi through their acculturated friends at other villages. This kind of pottery continued to be made into the American period until it was replaced by Hopi revival pottery, which was inspired by Jeddito Yellow ware from archaeological sites.

The Walpi study demonstrates that material culture, especially ceramic form and design, can be a remarkably sensitive indicator of cultural events. It also shows the ways in which knowing the "facts of history" can help elucidate changes in the material culture record. In the absence of historic documentation, it would be difficult to ascertain whether the reintroduction of Spanish influence in ceramics had been a result of direct or of indirect contact with the Europeans.

ARCHAEOLOGY AND TRADITIONAL HISTORY OF THE O'ODHAM AND HOPI

Examining the late precontact history of the Arizona deserts from Spanish missionary accounts is frustrating because by the time Jesuit chroniclers entered the region, the Hohokam great house and platform mound sites had long been deserted. A lack of continuity in material culture and continuous occupation of settlements between the modern O'Odham residents of the region and the Hohokam have made the "disappearance" of the Hohokam a topic of debate (Doyel 1989). Lynne Teague (1993) offers information derived from both oral traditions and ceremonial practices of both the O'Odham and Hopi people that relate to a series of events prior to European contact. The events themselves and the oral descriptions of them contain elements that have been verified archaeologically. Teague's study remind us of some of the difficulties of moving from archaeologically defined cultures to traditional histories of peoples and language groups that are marked by different criteria and do not coincide with the archaeological boundaries.

In O'Odham traditional history, there are accounts of warfare on the Gila and Salt rivers that are quite consistent from one group to another. In these accounts, Elder Brother, a culture hero of the O'Odham, and the Hohokam leader/priests became angry with one another so that war between them occurred. Both Elder Brother and the Hohokam spoke the same language and were of the same culture. In the story, they are distinguished by wearing different kinds of clothing. Elder Brother recruited his supporters from O'Odham living in far southern Arizona and northern Mexico. In the accounts, Elder Brother and his warriors attack very specific places, the houses of the Hohokam leader/priests and not those of the ordinary Hohokam. The sites that are named as having been attacked are an archaeological inventory of Late Classic period platform mound sites along the Gila River. As Teague (1993) states, it is of interest that large sites with mounds but that date earlier than the Late Classic are not mentioned despite the fact that they are often just as visible on today's landscape. Additional confirmation comes from a chant that is described as having been sung by the warriors.

The chant mentions an ocatillo stockade. Recent archaeological investigations have located stockade structures made of perishable materials surrounding platform mounds. The accounts tell of attacking Pueblo Grande on the Salt River but then differ as to other Salt River sites. The traditional histories also tell of a catastrophic flood that followed a drought during the time of the warfare. Streamflow studies (Graybill 1989) have verified a drought and approximately contemporary flood in 1358.

Finally, at the conclusion of the war, the traditional history states that some of the O'Odham went north to the pueblos. Others went south where the Pima and Akimel O'Odham now live. Those who left the region were from the Salt River villages west of Pueblo Grande. They were fleeing both the social disruption and the floods. Those who went south intermarried with newcomers and became the modern Akimel O'Odham.

If such a battle and movement of O'Odham to the Pueblos occurred, logically, Pueblo peoples should have similar accounts. As Teague (1993) relates, they do. One traditional Hopi history specifies that a series of related clans, including the Water Clan, originated in the south at Palatkwapi. Although one version identifies Palatkwapi with a Sinagua site on the Verde River, another states that it is near Phoenix, beyond the Superstition Mountain. A segment of that history related by Teague includes a description of prosperous Hopi with fields irrigated by canals from the river and "taxation by means of doing some donation work on the canals and ditches at certain times of year" (Nequatewa 1936, quoted in Teague 1993). The description is significant, of course, since riverine irrigation is not possible at Hopi. Finally, specific incidents of the battle are included in both O'Odham and Hopi versions of the history.

It should not be surprising that traditional histories are historically accurate, as both these and the history of Awatovi demonstrate. An additional aspect of these histories that corroborates our enhanced understanding of the period just prior to European contact is the facility, and apparent frequency, with which different peoples were incorporated into other societies. Perhaps it was the existence and continuation of social institutions that had served to incorporate the heterogenous populations that came together after the Four Corners region was abandoned that permitted some O'Odham to become Hopi. It is possible too, that some Athapaskan speakers were nearly incorporated as well.

SOUTHERN ATHAPASKANS: APACHE AND NAVAJO

Today, the closest neighbors of many of the traditional peoples of the Southwest are Athapaskan-speaking Indians whose original homelands are in interior Alaska and Canada. One Athapaskan-speaking tribe, the Navajo, has the fastest rate of population growth of any North American Indian tribe. Despite their prominence in the twentieth century, there is little agreement among scholars regarding when these peoples entered the Southwest or by which routes they came (see Chapter 11). Unfortunately, most archaeological data are ambiguous on these issues; there are problems interpreting the early historic documents and linguistic data as well.

FIGURE 12.11 A Navajo woman spins wool at the entrance to her *ramada* (shade structure). Traditional Navajo economy depends upon shepherding, an activity introduced with European livestock. Today wage labor is increasingly important (photo by Merl Lavoy 1930, courtesy of the University of Colorado Museum).

Since the introduction of European livestock, most southern Athapaskan groups have pursued a way of life that includes limited agriculture and stock raising. The "typical" residence pattern is generally dispersed, and most groups moved several times each year to obtain grazing land for their livestock. Agricultural techniques are identical to those of other Southwestern peoples. Much of the material culture that is recognizable as southern Athapaskan relates to their adaptations as stockmen (Figure 12.11), for example, single-family shelters (either wickiups or hogans), corrals, sheep pens, and saddles. Because livestock was introduced into the Southwest by the Spaniards, the herding adaptation and associated material culture are not useful in identifying southern Athapaskan remains that date prior to the sixteenth or seventeenth centuries.

It is also well known that the southern Athapaskans have displayed considerable adaptive flexibility over time, a fact reflected in the settlement patterns and items of material culture available for archaeological study. For example, during the Refugee period following the Pueblo Revolt and de Vargas's reconquest, Navajo and Pueblo refugees lived together in the Largo-Gobernador area. The refugee sites consist of stone masonry pueblitos, which are defensively located and impressive in their extent (Brugge 1983). Navajos produced a polychrome pottery that was similar to contemporary

Pueblo styles. Reed and Reed (1992b) suggest that the pottery, Gobernador Polychrome, which is distinctively Navajo, is also within the Hopi Yellow ware tradition. Their view is that at least some groups of Navajos were participating with Hopis in a broadly structured system of alliance and interaction. On the eastern edge of the Southwest, some archaeologists (Gunnerson 1969; Gunnerson and Gunnerson 1971) regard a particular type of micaceous pottery as Apachean, while others (Schaasfma 1976) find it difficult to distinguish between similar types produced at Taos, Picuris, and Nambé pueblos in the seventeenth and eighteenth centuries. If so, perhaps the easternmost Navajos and Apaches were also allied to their Pueblo neighbors.

The early Spanish documents are also ambiguous regarding the identification of Southern Athapaskans. The Spaniards at first used the term Querecho to refer to any nomadic group of people they encountered. Some scholars (e.g., Forbes 1960; Gunnerson and Gunnerson 1971; Schroeder 1979b) routinely translate Querecho as "Apache" and suggest that the Spanish descriptions might be valuable clues to the distribution of these people in the sixteenth century. Opler, however, argues that Querecho was a generic term, noting specifically that "whenever the traits described are more specific, they do not seem to be particularly Apachean" (1983:383). Upham (1982:47–51), in fact, suggests that some of the peoples that the early accounts refer to as Querecho may have been indigenous Pueblo peoples who were not living within compact villages, but pursuing a more mobile way of life, perhaps living in rancherías. The concern here, however, is that none of the usual sorts of information—material culture, historical linguistics, or Spanish documents—is an unambiguous guide to the identification of early historic or protohistoric southern Athapaskan remains.

SPANIARDS, PUEBLOS, AND BUFFALO HUNTERS

A less detailed and generally quite different scenario of the effects of Spanish and Pueblo interaction is available from Pecos (Kessell 1979; Kidder 1958; Spielmann 1983, 1991a) and Las Humanas (Gran Quivira) (Hayes *et al.* 1981; Spielmann 1989, 1990, 1991) on the extreme eastern edge of the Pueblo world. Here, the groups involved included nomadic Apache and the Comanche from the Plains in addition to Pueblos and Spaniards. The official Spanish Colonial documents and the letters of colonists are supplemented by archaeological work of Kidder (1958) at Pecos; Vivian (1964), Hayes (Hayes *et al.* 1981), and Spielmann (1991a) at Las Humanas; and Speth (1990, 1991) at sites on the extreme western edge of the southern Great Plains. In addition, Habicht-Mauche (1991) contributes an important study of some of the material culture of the protohistoric southern Plains groups. The rich documentary history of Pecos has been synthesized by historian John Kessell (1979). Only the most cursory sketch of this work can be given here.

In the fourteenth and fifteenth centuries, a convergence of processes affecting the Rio Grande area and the southern Plains brought about well-developed interactions among groups of both areas. Pueblo farmers experienced increasing climatic deterioration at the same time that their population was swelled by refugees from the Four

Corners. Concurrently, the Plains margins that for centuries had been occupied by generalized hunter-gatherers came to be inhabited by new groups who, while still nomadic, were more specialized bison hunters.

Whenever they could, the Pueblos of Pecos and Las Humanas planted enough corn to ensure a surplus, aiming at being able to store two years' worth of corn and seed corn. Spielmann (1991a) notes that an economy based on mutually beneficial exchange developed between Pueblos and Plains groups in the mid-fifteenth and sixteenth centuries. Pecos and Las Humanas, the eastern border pueblos, became centers of articulation between Pueblos and Plains. They took in both Pueblo and Plains products and transferred goods between the two areas. Bison hides and meat moved west from Pecos and Las Humanas. Corn, pottery, obsidian, and turquoise moved east (see also Baugh 1991; Levine 1991). The historic record documents annual trade fairs that took place at Pecos when semi-nomadic Plains hunters camped at the pueblo for weeks while engaged in exchange. Kidder's excavations at Pecos yielded Plains-manufactured items such as knives made of Alibates flint from Texas and Apache ceramics.

The trade, however, was more than a reciprocal exchange of material goods. Habicht-Mauche (1987, 1991) shows that between 1500 and 1700, southern Plains groups not only accepted Rio Grande Pueblo-made glaze decorated pottery but were producing their own version of Pueblo unpainted cooking and storage ware. Finding such vessels on sites far to the east of the Pecos River, in camping places used by semi-nomadic hunters, reflects the existence of intensive relations between Pueblo and Plains peoples. Habicht-Mauche maintains that the cooking pottery demonstrates that a tradition of food-preparation and the technology associated with it were disseminated. For this to have happened, interactions must have been very close, possibly involving intermarriage.

The first Spanish capital established in 1598 at San Gabriel del Yunque at the confluence of the Rio Chama and the Rio Grande at San Juan Pueblo (Figure 12.1) and the second capital, built in 1610 at Santa Fe, were much closer to the Rio Grande Pueblos than were any Spanish administrative centers to Hopi. Further, Hispanic colonists established themselves in the Rio Grande Valley, whereas there were no Spanish Colonial villages in the vicinity of the Hopi. The proximity of the Spaniards and Pueblos allowed the Spaniards to directly tax the Rio Grande Pueblos for labor and tribute. At the same time, the more nomadic Plains tribes came to demand European products such as horses, guns, and iron tools.

The pre-Revolt Spanish tax on Pueblo labor and the demand of the Spanish Empire for tribute in corn, hides, and tallow disrupted the ongoing exchange between Pueblos and Plains peoples. Pueblos could not produce enough to feed themselves, pay tribute to the Spaniards, and maintain their obligations to trade with their neighbors on the Plains. Further, the Spaniards themselves entered into trade with the Plains groups. One of the changes that seems to have occurred in this case was the development among the Pueblos of factionalized communities and an incipient class system composed of high status leaders versus everyone else. The leaders acted as middlemen for the Spaniards both in collecting tribute and coordinating the trade of Pueblo goods for products from the Plains. As long as tribute was paid and trade maintained, they were able to enrich themselves to some degree at the expense of their own communities and the Spaniards. When there were agricultural shortfalls and the Pueblos could not meet their trade obligations, the situation deteriorated into armed conflict between Pueblo and Plains groups, especially the Comanche. After the reconquest, this raiding and warfare contributed significantly to eventual abandonment of Pecos, Las Humanas, and other eastern margin villages.

The Spanish documents report that Colonial Governors dealt only with specific leaders or headmen among the Pueblos. Sometimes, these individuals were provided with goods to exchange with the Plains peoples. At the time of the Revolt, the leaders at Pecos and the Galisteo Basin Pueblos were not interested in taking part in the Revolt although the populace of these pueblos did. At least some of the disorder and internal fighting that characterized the period between 1680 and the beginning of reconquest in 1692 stems from this insidious factionalism.

The changes European conquest wrought on the Pueblos cannot be overestimated. At the most basic level, European diseases, such as smallpox, that were accidentally transmitted to the Pueblos drastically reduced their numbers. The death toll was also increased by over-taxing Pueblo labor and taking food from the villages by force, and through the internecine fighting and hostilities among Pueblos, Apache, and Comanche. While the Europeans did introduce new crops and domestic animals that supplemented the dogs and turkeys the Pueblos already had, European livestock changed the character of the native vegetation. Familiar gathered foods that might have made the difference between survival and starvation when maize crops were poor, no longer grew in abundance in the altered habitat.

DISCUSSION

Following the abandonment of large areas of the Southwest in the late thirteenth and early fourteenth centuries, large aggregated communities were founded in previously sparsely inhabited areas. Some of these sites are recognized as ancestral villages by modern Pueblo people. At some of these sites, too, rock art and kiva mural representations depict figures that are recognizably aspects of katcina ritual, which is an important component of modern Pueblo religion.

Other aspects of the archaeological record of the fourteenth century depart from modern Pueblo culture. For example, the stylistic homogeneity in ceramic design, an abundance of traded ceramics at some sites, and the detailed similarities among the kiva mural depictions from widely separated areas suggest a higher level of intervillage interaction than is characteristic of the modern period. The nature of relations among aggregated villages is the subject of research and scholarly disagreement.

The year 1540 marks the end of the pre-Columbian period in the Southwest. The imposition of Spanish Colonial policies and the introduction of European diseases, new crops, and domestic animals forever disrupted traditional patterns of adaptation. The written accounts of the Spanish chroniclers, however, provide the first views of Southwestern societies from a European perspective. The documentary data are a rich source of information that can greatly elucidate the archaeological record. There are, of course, ambiguities in the documentary history, but comparisons of the Native American and Spanish histories and archaeological records, as demonstrated by the work at Awatovi and Walpi, are leading to a clearer understanding of the ways events are reflected in the archaeological record. It is hoped that innovative use of these materials will eventually provide a better basis for understanding both the prehispanic period and the historic integration of traditional Southwestern cultures and their southern Athapaskan neighbors.

CONCLUSION

The Southwest provides an extraordinary record of human behavior over a period of 11,000 years. The archaeological remains have been of interest to scholars for more than 100 years. Archaeology in the Southwest, as elsewhere, has become increasingly specialized and technical, and it is probably impossible to present a synthesis of the ancient Southwest that adequately represents all the complexities of the "current state of the art." Nevertheless, my intent has been to provide the interested student with a means of access to the vast literature of southwestern archaeology and a sense of both the current understanding of the past and the areas of disagreement requiring new and innovative research. One of my hopes is that some interested students will be inspired to conduct the research that needs to be done and that others will develop an enhanced appreciation for the record of human accomplishments in the Southwest.

The Southwest is of interest for many reasons that have been examined in the preceding chapters. From my perspective, one of the most intriguing is the record it provides of flexible and heterogeneous responses to environmental diversity and extremes. The arid Southwestern climate, with cold winters and hot summers, establishes a difficult baseline for human societies. The long archaeological record indicates that successful adaptation was accomplished, in part, by maintaining a diversity of subsistence and organizational options. At any one time, the people of the Southwest engaged in a mosaic of behavioral strategies, ensuring the success of at least some of them.

Chapter-opening art: Historic photo of the Hopi village of Mishognovi (photograph courtesy of the University of Colorado Museum).

REFERENCES

Abbott, David R. 1996. Ceramic Exchange and Strategy for Reconstructing Organizational Developments among the Hohokam. *In* "Interpreting Southwestern Diversity: Underlying Principles and Overarching Patterns," edited by Paul R. Fish and J. Jefferson Reid, Anthropological Research Papers No. 48, pp. 147–158. Arizona State University, Tempe.

Aberle, David F. 1970. Comments. *In* "Reconstructing Prehistoric Pueblo Societies," edited by William A. Longacre, pp. 214–224. University of New Mexico Press, Albuquerque, and School of American Research, Santa Fe.

Ackerly, Neal W., Jerry B. Howard, and Randall H. McGuire 1987. "La Ciudad Canals: A Study of Hohokam Irrigation Systems at the Community Level," Anthropological Field Studies No. 17. Arizona State University, Tempe.

Acklen, John C. 1982. Ceramic Analysis. *In* "Anasazi and Navajo Land Use in the McKinley Mine Area near Gallup, New Mexico," edited by Christina G. Allen and Ben A. Nelson, Vol. I, Part II, pp. 578–596. Office of Contract Archeology, University of New Mexico, Albuquerque.

Adams, E. Charles 1981. The View from the Hopi Mesas. *In* "The Protohistoric Period in the North American Southwest, AD 1450–1700," edited by David R. Wilcox and W. Bruce Masse, Anthropological Research Papers 24, pp. 321–335. Arizona State University, Tempe.

Adams, E. Charles 1983. The Architectural Analogue to Hopi Social Organization and Room Use, and Implications for Prehistoric Southwestern Culture. *American Antiquity* **48**:44–61.

Adams, E. Charles 1991. "The Origin and Development of the Pueblo Katsina Cult." University of Arizona Press, Tucson.

Adams, E. Charles, and Kelley Ann Hays (editors) 1991. "Homol'ovi II: Archaeology of an Ancestral Hopi Village, Arizona," Anthropological Papers No. 55. University of Arizona Press, Tucson.

Adams, E. Charles 1996. The Pueblo II–Pueblo IV Transition in the Hopi Area, Arizona. *In* "The Prehistoric Pueblo World, AD 1150–1350," edited by Michael A. Adler, pp. 48–58. University of Arizona Press, Tucson.

Adams, J. L. 1993. Technological Development of Manos and Metates on the Hopi Mesas. *The Kiva* **58**:331–344.

Adams, Karen R. 1994. A Regional Synthesis of *Zea mays* in the Prehistoric American Southwest. *In* "Corn and Culture in the Prehistoric New World," edited by Sissel Johannessen and Christine A. Hastorf, pp. 273–302. Westview Press, Boulder.

Adler, Michael A. 1990. Communities of Soil and Stone: An Archaeological Investigation of Population Aggregation Among the Mesa Verde Region Anasazi, AD 900–1300. Ph.D. dissertation, Department of Anthropology, University of Michigan. University Microfilms, Ann Arbor.

Adler, Michael A. 1996. Fathoming the Scale of Anasazi Communities. *In* "Interpreting Southwestern Diversity: Underlying Principles and Overarching Patterns," edited by Paul R. Fish and J. Jefferson Reid, Anthropological Research Papers No. 48, pp. 97–106. Arizona State University, Tempe.

Adler, Michael A. 1996. "The Great Period": The Pueblo World during the Pueblo III Period. *In* "The Prehistoric Pueblo World, AD 1150–1350," edited by Michael A. Adler, pp. 1–10. University of Arizona Press, Tucson.

Adler, M. A., T. Van Pool, and R. D. Leonard 1996. Ancestral Pueblo Population Aggregation and Abandonment in the North American Southwest. *Journal of World Prehistory* **10**(3): 375–438.

Adovasio, James M. 1993. The Ones that Will Not Go Away: A Biased View of Pre-Clovis Populations in the New World. *In* "Kostenki to Clovis: Upper Paleolithic-Paleo-Indian Adaptations," edited by Olga Soffer and N. D. Praslov, pp. 199–218. Plenum Press, New York.

Adovasio, James M., J. Donahue, and R. Stuckenrath 1990. The Meadowcroft Rockshelter Radiocarbon Chronology 1975–1990. *American Antiquity* **55**:348–354.

Adovasio, James M., J. D. Gunn, J. Donahue, and R. Stuckenrath 1978. Meadowcroft Rockshelter, 1977: An Overview. *American Antiquity* **43**:632–651.

Agenbroad, L. D. 1980. Quaternary Mastodon, Mammoth and Men in the New World. *Canadian Journal of Anthropology* **1**(1):99–101.

Agogino, George A., and James J. Hester 1953. The Santa Ana Pre-ceramic sites. *El Palacio* **60**(4):131–140.

Aikens, C. Melvin 1966. "Virgin-Kayenta Cultural Relationships," Anthropological Papers 79, Glen Canyon Series 29. University of Utah, Salt Lake City.

Aikens, C. Melvin 1976. Cultural Hiatus in the Eastern Great Basin? *American Antiquity* **41**: 543–550.

Aikens, C. Melvin 1978. The Far West. *In* "Ancient Native Americans," edited by J. D. Jennings, pp. 131–182. Freeman, San Francisco.

Akins, Nancy J. 1986. "A Biocultural Approach to Human Burials from Chaco Canyon, New Mexico," Reports of the Chaco Center No. 9. Branch of Cultural Research, National Park Service, Santa Fe.

Alexander, H. C., and P. Reiter 1935. "The Excavation of Jemez Cave, New Mexico," Monograph 4. School of American Research, Santa Fe.

Allan, William C., A. Osborn, W. J. Chasko, and David E. Stuart 1975. An Archeological Survey: Road Construction Right-of-Ways, Block II, Navajo Indian Irrigation Project. *In* "Archeological Reports, Cultural Resource Management Projects," edited by F. J. Broilo and D. E. Stuart, Working Draft Series 1, pp. 91–143. Office of Contract Archeology, University of New Mexico, Albuquerque.

Amsden, Charles Avery 1949. "Prehistoric Southwesterners from Basketmaker to Pueblo." Southwest Museum, Los Angeles.

Amsden, Charles W. 1992. Archaeological Survey of the San Juan Lateral, Chaco Mea Route. *In* "Across the Colorado Plateau: Anthropological Studies for the Transwestern Pipeline Expansion Project," Vol. 111. Office of Contract Archaeology, University of New Mexico, Albuquerque.

Anderson, Edgar, and Hugh C. Cutler 1942. Races of *Zea mays:* Their Recognition and Classification. *Annals of the Missouri Botanical Garden* **29.**

Anschuetz, Kurt F. 1995. Two Sides of a Coin: Early Pueblo Indian Farming Practices in the Rio Arriba and the Rio Abajo of the Northern Rio Grande Region. Paper presented at the 60th Annual Meeting of the Society for American Archaeology, Minneapolis.

Anschuetz, K. F., T. D. Maxwell, and J. A. Ware 1985. "Testing Report and Research Design for the Medanales North Project, Rio Arriba County, New Mexico," Laboratory of Anthropology Note 347. Museum of New Mexico, Santa Fe.

Antevs, E. 1948. Climatic Changes and Pre-white Man. *University of Utah Bulletin* **38**(20): 167–191.

Antevs, E. 1955. Geologic-Climatic Dating in the West. *American Antiquity* **20**:317–335.

Antevs, E. 1959. Geologic Age of the Lehner Mammoth Site. *American Antiquity* **25**:31–34.

Antevs, E. 1962. Late Quaternary Climates in Arizona. *American Antiquity* **28**:193–198.

Anwalt, Patricia R. 1981. "Indian Clothing Before Cortes: Mesoamerican Costumes from the Codices." University of Oklahoma Press, Norman.

Anyon, Roger, and T. J. Ferguson 1983. Settlement Patterns and Changing Adaptations in the Zuni Area after AD 1000. Paper presented for the Anasazi Symposium, San Juan Archaeological Research Center and Library, Bloomfield.

Anyon, Roger, and Steven A. LeBlanc 1980. The Architectural Evolution of Mogollon-Mimbres Ceremonial Structures. *The Kiva* **45**:253–277.

Anyon, Roger, Patricia A. Gilman, and Steven A. LeBlanc 1981. A Re-evaluation of the Mimbres-Mogollon Sequence. *The Kiva* **46**:209–225.

Arnold, D. E. 1985. "Ceramic Theory and Cultural Process." Cambridge University Press, Cambridge.

Axlerod, D. I. 1967. Quaternary Extinctions of Large Mammals. *University of California, Berkeley, Publications in Geological Science* **4**:1–25.

Bachuber, Frederick W. 1971. Paleoclimatology of Lake Estancia, New Mexico. Unpublished Ph.D. dissertation, University of New Mexico, Albuquerque.

Bailey, R. G. (compiler) 1980. Description of the Ecoregions of the United States. *U.S. Department of Agriculture, Forest Service Miscellaneous Publication* **1391.**

Baker, Craig, and Joseph C. Winter (editors) 1981. "High Altitude Adaptations along Redondo Creek: The Baca Geothermal Project." Office of Contract Archeology, University of New Mexico, Albuquerque.

Baker, Ruth L. 1996. Strategies on the Frontier: Archaeobotanical Perspectives from the Edge. Paper presented at the 61st Annual Meeting of the Society for American Archaeology, New Orleans.

Bamforth, Douglas B. 1985. The Technological Organization of Paleoindian Small-Group Bison Hunting on the Llano Estacado. *Plains Anthropologist* **30**:243–258.

Bamforth, Douglas B. 1991. Flintknapping Skill, Communal Hunting, and Paleoindian Projectile Point Typology. *Plains Anthropologist* **36**(137):309–323.

Bandelier, Adolph F. 1890. Final Report of Investigations among the Indians of the Southwestern United States (Part 1). *Papers of the Archaeological Institute of America, American Series* **3.**

Bandelier, Adolph F. 1892. Final Report of Investigations among the Indians of the Southwestern United States (Part 2). *Papers of the Archaeological Institute of America, American Series* **4.**

Baugh, Timothy G. 1991. Ecology and Exchange: The Dynamics of Plains-Pueblo Interaction. *In* "Farmers, Hunters, and Colonists: Interaction between the Southwest and the Southern Plains," edited by Katherine A. Spielmann, pp. 107–127. University of Arizona Press, Tucson.

Bayham, Frank E. 1982. A Diachronic Analysis of Prehistoric Animal Exploitation at Ventana Cave. Ph.D. dissertation, Department of Anthropology, Arizona State University, Tempe.

Bayham, Frank (editor) 1983. "The Picacho Reservoir Archaic Complex: A Research Design." Office of Cultural Resource Management, Department of Anthropology, Arizona State University, Tempe.

Beadle, G. W. 1981. Origin of Corn: Pollen Evidence. *Science* **213**:890–892.

Beals, Ralph L. 1943. Relations Between Mesoamerica and the Southwest. *In* "El Norte de Mexico y el Sur de los Estados Unidos," pp. 245–252. Sociedad Mexicana de Antropologia, Mexico City.

Beckett, Patrick H. 1980. "The Ake Site: Collection and Excavation of LA 13423, Catron County, New Mexico." Cultural Resources Management Division, Department of Sociology and Anthropology, New Mexico State University, Las Cruces.

Beckett, Patrick H., and Richard S. MacNeish 1994. The Archaic Chihuahua Tradition of South-Central New Mexico and Chihuahua, Mexico. *In* "Archaic Hunter-Gatherer Archaeology in the American Southwest," edited by Bradley J. Vierra, Contributions in Anthropology 13(1), pp. 335–371. Eastern New Mexico University, Portales.

Begay, Richard M., and Alexandra Roberts 1996. The Early Navajo Occupation of the Grand Region. *In* "The Archaeology of Navajo Origins," edited by Ronald H. Towner, pp. 197–212. University of Utah Press, Salt Lake City.

Bennett, C. L. 1979. Radiocarbon Dating with Accelerators. *American Scientist* **67**:450–457.

Benz, Bruce F., and Hugh H. Iltis 1990. A New Synthesis of Middle Paleolithic Variability Studies in Archaeological Maize I: The Wild Maize from San Marcos Cave Reexamined. *American Antiquity* **55**:500–512.

Berman, M. J. 1979. "Cultural Resources Overview of Socorro, New Mexico." U.S. Government Printing Office, Washington, DC.

Berry, Michael S. 1982. "Time, Space and Transition in Anasazi Prehistory." University of Utah Press, Salt Lake City.

Berry, Michael S., and Claudia Berry 1986. Chronological and Conceptual Models of the Southwestern Archaic. *In* "Anthropology of the Desert West: Essays in Honor of Jesse D. Jennings," edited by Carol J. Condie and Don D. Fowler, Anthropological Papers 110, pp. 253–327. University of Utah, Salt Lake City.

Betancourt, Julio L., and Thomas R. Van Devender 1981. Holocene Vegetation in Chaco Canyon, New Mexico. *Science* **214**:656–658.

Betancourt, J. L., T. R. Van Devender, and P. S. Martin 1990. "Packrat Middens: The Last 40,000 Years of Biotic Change." University of Arizona Press, Tucson.

Bice, Richard A., and William M. Sundt 1972. "Prieta Vista, a Small Pueblo III Ruin in North Central New Mexico." Albuquerque Archaeological Society, Albuquerque.

Binford, Lewis R. 1968. Post-Pleistocene Adaptations. *In* "New Perspectives in Archaeology," edited by S. R. Binford and L. R. Binford, pp. 313–342. Aldine, Chicago.

Binford, Lewis R. 1977. Forty-seven Trips. *In* "Stone Tools as Cultural Markers," edited by R. Wright, pp. 24–36. Australian Institute for Aboriginal Studies, Canberra.

Binford, Lewis R. 1979. Organization and Formation Processes: Looking at Curated Technologies. *Journal of Anthropological Research* **35**:255–273.

Binford, Lewis R. 1980. Willow Smoke and Dogs' Tails: Hunter-Gatherer Settlement Systems and Archaeological Site Formation. *American Antiquity* **45**:4–20.

Binford, Lewis R. 1981. Behavioral Archaeology and the "Pompeii Premise." *Journal of Anthropological Research* **37**:195–208.

Binford, Lewis R. 1982. The Archaeology of Place. *Journal of Anthropological Archaeology* **1**:5–31.

Binford, Lewis R. 1983. "Working at Archaeology. Studies in Archaeology." Academic Press, New York.

Binford, Lewis R. 1989. "Debating Archaeology. Studies in Archaeology." Academic Press, New York.

Binford, Lewis R. 1994. System Integration of "Fragmentary Oddments": The Challenge of Settlement Pattern Approaches. *In* "Archaic Hunter-Gatherer Archaeology in the American Southwest," edited by Bradley J. Vierra, Contributions in Anthropology 13(1), pp. 527–565. Eastern New Mexico University, Portales.

Binford, L. R., and W. J. Chasko, Jr. 1976. Nunamiut Demographic History: A Provocative Case. *In* "Demographic Anthropology: Quantitative Approaches," edited by E. B. W. Zubrow, pp. 63–144. University of New Mexico Press, Albuquerque.

Blanton, R. E. 1978. "Monte Alban: Patterns at the Ancient Zapotec Capital." Academic Press, New York.

Blevins, Byron B., and Carol Joiner 1977. The Archeological Survey of Tijeras Canyon. *In* "The 1975 Excavation of Tijeras Pueblo, Cibola National Forest, New Mexico," edited by W. James Judge, Archeological Report 18, pp. 126–152. USDA Forest Service, Southwest Regional Office, Albuquerque.

Bluhm, Elaine A. 1960. Mogollon Settlement Patterns in Pine Lawn Valley, New Mexico. *American Antiquity* **25**:538–546.

Bohrer, Vorsila L. 1962. Ethnobotanical Materials from Tonto National Monument, Arizona. *In* "Archeological Studies at Tonto National Monument, Arizona," by Charlie R. Steen, Floyd M. Pierson, Vorsila L. Bohrer, and Kate Peck Kent, edited by Louis R. Caywood, Technical Series 2, pp. 75–114. Southwestern Monuments Association, Globe.

Bohrer, Vorsila L. 1970. Ethnobotanical Aspects of Snaketown, a Hohokam Village in Southern Arizona. *American Antiquity* **35**:413–430.

Bohrer, Vorsila 1981. Methods of Recognizing Cultural Activity from Pollen in Archaeological Sites. *The Kiva* **46**:135–142.

Bohrer, Vorsila L. 1991. Recently Recognized Cultivated and Encouraged Plants Among the Hohokam. *The Kiva* **56**(3):227–237.

Bolton, Herbert E. (editor) 1930. "Spanish Explorations in the Southwest, 1542–1706." Scribner's Sons, New York.

Boserup, Ester 1965. "The Conditions of Agricultural Growth." Aldine, Chicago.

Boyer, J. 1982. An Economic Model for Navajo Habitation Site Locations. *In* "The San Juan Tomorrow: Planning for the Conservation of Cultural Resources in the San Juan Basin," edited by Fred Plog and Walter Wait, pp. 107–126. National Park Service, Southwest Region, and School of American Research, Santa Fe.

Bradfield, Maitland 1971. Changing Patterns of Hopi Agriculture. *Journal of the Royal Anthropological Institute* **30.**

Bradfield, Wesley 1931. "Cameron Creek Village: A Site in the Mimbres Area in Grant County, New Mexico," Monograph 1. School of American Research, Santa Fe.

Bradley, Bruce A. 1993. Paleo-Indian Flaked Stone Technology in the North American High Plains. *In* "Kostenki to Clovis: Upper Paleolithic-Paleo-Indian Adaptations," edited by Olga Soffer and N. D. Praslov, pp. 251–262. Plenum Press, New York.

Bradley, B. A., and G. C. Frison 1987. Projectile Points and Specialized Bifaces from the Horner Site. *In* "The Horner Site: The Type Site of the Cody Cultural Complex," edited by G. C. Frison and L. C. Todd. Academic Press, Orlando.

Bradley, B. A., and D. Stanford 1987. The Claypool Study. *In* "The Horner Site: The Type Site of the Cody Cultural Complex," edited by G. C. Frison and L. C. Todd, pp. 405–434. Academic Press, Orlando.

Bradley, Norman A. 1991. Flaked Stone Technology in the Northern High Plains. *In* "Prehistoric Hunters of the High Plains," edited by George C. Frison, pp. 369–397. Academic Press, San Diego.

Braun, David P., and Stephen Plog 1982. Evolution of "Tribal" Social Networks: Theory and Prehistoric North American Evidence. *American Antiquity* **47**:504–525.

Breternitz, Cory Dale (editor) 1991. Reprinted from: "Prehistoric Irrigation in Arizona: Symposium 1988," Publications in Archaeology No. 17, pp. 139–154. Soil Systems, Phoenix.

Breternitz, Cory D., David E. Doyel, and Michael P. Marshall (editors) 1982. "Bis sa'ani: A Late Bonito Phase Community on Escavada Wash, Northwest New Mexico," Papers in Anthropology No. 14. Navajo Nation, Window Rock.

Breternitz, Cory Dale, and David E. Doyel 1983. Methodological Issues for the Identification of Chacoan Community Structure: Lessons from the Bis sa 'ani Community Study. Paper presented at the 48th Annual Meeting of the Society for American Archaeology, Pittsburgh.

Breternitz, David A. 1966. An Appraisal of Tree-Ring Dated Pottery in the Southwest. *Anthropological Papers of the University of Arizona* **10.**

Breternitz, David A., Robert A. Bye, Steven E. James, Allen E. Kane, and Ruthann Knudson 1980. Research Design and Operations Management, Dolores Project. *Contract Abstracts and CRM Archeology* **1**(2):17–21.

Brew, John O. 1943. On the Pueblo IV and on the Katchina-Tlaloc Relations. *In* "El Norte de Mexico y el sur de Estados Unidos: Tercera reunion de mesa redonda sobre problemas antropologicos de Mexico y Centro America," pp. 241–245. Sociedad Mexicana de Anthropologia, Mexico, D.F.

Brew, John O. 1946. Archaeology of Alkali Ridge, Southeastern Utah. *Papers of the Peabody Museum of American Archaeology and Ethnology* **21.**

Briuer, F. L. 1975. Cultural and Noncultural Deposition Processes in Chevelon Canyon. Unpublished Ph.D. dissertation, University of California at Los Angeles.

Brody, J. J. 1977. "Mimbres Painted Pottery." University of New Mexico Press, Albuquerque.

Brody, J. J. 1979. Pueblo Fine Arts. *In* "Southwest," edited by Alfonso Ortiz, Handbook of North American Indians, Vol. 9, pp. 603–608. Smithsonian Institution, Washington, DC.

Broilo, Frank J. 1971. An Investigation of Surface-Collected Clovis, Folsom, and Midland Projectile Points from Blackwater Draw and Adjacent Localities. Unpublished M.A. thesis, Eastern New Mexico University, Portales.

Brown, Donald N. 1979. Picuris Pueblo. *In* "Southwest," edited by Alfonso Ortiz, Handbook of North American Indians, Vol. 9, pp. 268–277. Smithsonian Institution, Washington, DC.

Brown, Gary M. 1996. The Protohistoric Transition in the Northern San Juan Region. *In* "The Archaeology of Navajo Origins," edited by Ronald H. Towner, pp. 47–70. University of Utah Press, Salt Lake City.

Brown, Gary M., and Patricia M. Hancock 1992. The Dinetah Phase in the La Plata Valley. *In* "Cultural Diversity and Adaptation: The Archaic, Anasazi, and Navajo Occupation of the Upper San Juan Basin," edited by Lori Stephens Reed and Paul F. Reed, Cultural Resources Series No. 9, pp. 69–89. Bureau of Land Management, New Mexico.

Brown, J. A. 1989. The Beginnings of Pottery as an Economic Process. *In* "What's New? A Closer Look at the Process of Innovation," edited by S. E. van der Leeuw and R. Torrence, pp. 203–224. Unwin Hyman, London.

Brugge, David M. 1963. "Navajo Pottery and Ethnohistory," Navajoland Publications Series 2. Navajo Tribal Museum, Window Rock.

Brugge, David M. 1983. Navajo Prehistory and History to 1850. *In* "Southwest," edited by Alfonso Ortiz, Handbook of North American Indians, Vol. 10, pp. 489–501. Smithsonian Institution, Washington, DC.

Brugge, David M. 1994. "The Navajo-Hopi Land Dispute: An American Tragedy." University of New Mexico Press, Albuquerque.

Brugge, David M. 1996. Navajo Archaeology: A Promising Past. *In* "The Archaeology of Navajo Origins," edited by Ronald H. Towner, pp. 255–272. University of Utah Press, Salt Lake City.

Bryan, Alan L. 1965. Paleo-American Prehistory. *Occasional Papers of the Idaho State University Museum* **16.**

Bryan Kirk 1925. Date of Channel Trenching (Arroyo Cutting) in the Arid Southwest. *Science* **62**:338–344.

Bryan, Kirk 1929. Flood-water Farming. *Geographical Review* **19**:444–456.

Bryan, Kirk 1941. Precolumbian Agriculture in the Southwest as Conditioned by Periods of Alluviation. *Annals of the American Association of Geography* **31**(4):219–242.

Bryan, Kirk 1954. The Geology of Chaco Canyon, New Mexico, in Relation to the Life and Remains of the Prehistoric Peoples of Pueblo Bonito. *Smithsonian Miscellaneous Collections* **122**(7).

Bryan, K., and J. H. Toulouse, Jr. 1943. The San Jose Non-Ceramic Culture and its Relation to Puebloan Culture in New Mexico. *American Antiquity* **8**:269–290.

Bryson, R. A., D. A. Baerreis, and W. M. Wendland 1970. The Character of Late-Glacial and Post-Glacial Climatic Change. *In* "Pleistocene and Recent Environments of the Central Great Plains," edited by W. Dort, Jr. and J. K. Jones, Special Publication 3, pp. 53–74. Department of Geology, University of Kansas, Lawrence.

Bullard, William R., Jr. 1962. The Cerro Colorado Site and Pithouse Architecture in the Southwestern United States prior to AD 900. *Papers of the Peabody Museum of American Archaeology and Ethnology* **44**(2).

Buskirk, Winfred 1986. "The Western Apache, Living with the Land Before 1950." University of Oklahoma Press, Norman.

Butzer, Karl W. 1991. An Old World Perspective on Potential Mid-Wisconsinan Settlement of the Americas. *In* "The First Americans: Search and Research," edited by Tom D. Dillehay and David J. Meltzer, pp. 137–156. CRC Press, Boca Raton.

Cameron, Catherine M. 1994. Migration and the Movement of Southwestern Peoples. *Journal of Anthropological Archaeology* **14**(2):104–124.

Cameron, Catherine M., and Steve A. Tomka (editors) 1993. "Abandonment of Settlements and Regions: Ethnoarchaeological and Archaeological Approaches." Cambridge University Press, Cambridge.

Campbell, John Martin, and Florence Hawley Ellis 1952. The Atrisco Sites: Cochise Manifestations in the Middle Rio Grande Valley. *American Antiquity* 17:211–221.

Carlson, Roy L. 1965. Eighteenth Century Navaho Fortresses of the Gobernador District. *University of Colorado Studies, Series in Anthropology* **10** (Earl Morris Papers 2), Boulder.

Carlson, Roy L. 1970. White Mountain Redware. *Anthropological Papers of the University of Arizona* **19.**

Carlson, Roy L. 1982. The Polychrome Complexes. *In* "Southwestern Ceramics: A Comparative Review," edited by Albert H. Schroeder, No. 15, pp. 201–234. American Archaeologist, Phoenix.

Carpenter, John Philip 1996. El Ombligo en la Labor. Differentiation, Interaction and Integration in Prehispanic Sinaloa, Mexico. Unpublished Ph.D. dissertation, Department of Anthropology, University of Arizona, Tucson.

Carpenter, John P., and Guadalupe Sanchez 1997. "Prehistory of the Borderlands, Recent Research in the Archaeology of Northern Mexico and the Southern Southwest," Arizona State Museum Archeological Series No. 186. Arizona State Museum, Tucson.

Cartledge, Thomas R. 1979. Cohonina Adaptation to the Coconino Plateau: A Re-evaluation. *The Kiva* **44**:297–317.

Cassidy, Francis 1965. Fire Temple, Mesa Verde National Park. *In* "The Great Kivas of Chaco Canyon and Their Relationships," by Gordon Vivian and Paul Reiter, Monograph 22, pp. 73–81. School of American Research, Santa Fe.

Castetter, Edward F. 1935. Uncultivated Native Plants Used as Sources of Food. Ethnobiological Studies in the American Southwest 1. *University of New Mexico Bulletin, Biological Series* **4**(1), Albuquerque.

Castetter, Edward F., and Willis M. Bell 1942. "Pima and Papago Indian Agriculture." University of New Mexico Press, Albuquerque.

Chapman, Richard C. 1985. Architecture and Use of Site Space. *In* "Class II Cultural Resource Survey, Upper Gila Water Supply Study, Central Arizona Project," edited by R. C. Chapman, C. W. Gossett, and W. M. Gossett, pp. 347–358. Deuel and Associates, Inc., Albuquerque.

Chauvenet, Beatrice 1983. "Hewett and Friends." Museum of New Mexico Press, Santa Fe.

Christaller, W. 1966. "Central Places in Southern Germany" (translated by C. W. Baskin). Prentice-Hall, Englewood Cliffs.

Christman, Donald, Richard S. MacNeish, Jamshed Mavalwala, and Howard Savage 1996. Late Pleistocene Human Friction Skin Prints from Pendejo Cave, New Mexico. *American Antiquity* **61**(2):357–376.

Ciolek-Torrello, Richard 1995. The Houghton Road Site, the Agua Caliente Phase, and the Early Formative Period in the Tucson Basin. *The Kiva* **60**(4):531–574.

Clark, D. L. 1961. The Obsidian Dating Method. *Current Anthropology* **2**:111–114.

Clark, Jeoffrey A. 1969. A Preliminary Analysis of Burial Clusters at the Grasshopper Site, East-Central Arizona. *The Kiva* **35**(2):57–86.

Classen, M. M., and R. H. Shaw 1970. Water Deficit Effects on Corn (Part II: Grain Component). *Agronomy Journal* **62**:652–655.

Coe, M. D., and K. V. Flannery 1964. Microenvironments and Mesoamerican Prehistory. *Science* **143**:605–654.

Cohen, Mark Nathan 1977. "The Food Crisis in Prehistory: Overpopulation and the Origins of Agriculture." Yale University Press, New Haven.

Colbert, E. W. 1973. Further Evidence Concerning the Presence of Horse at Ventana Cave. *The Kiva* **39**(1):25–33.

Collins, G. N. 1914. Pueblo Indian Maize Breeding. *Journal of Heredity* **5**:255–267.

Collins, M. B. 1991. Rockshelters and the Early Archaeological Record of the Americas. *In* "The First Americans: Search and Research," pp. 157–182. CRC Press, Boca Raton.

Colson, E. 1979. In Good Years and in Bad: Food Strategies of Self-Reliant Societies. *Journal of Anthropological Research* **35**:18–29.

Colton, Harold S. 1939. Prehistoric Culture Units and Their Relationships in Northern Arizona. *Museum of Northern Arizona Bulletin* **17**.

Colton, Harold S. 1945. The Patayan Problem in the Colorado River Valley. *Southwestern Journal of Anthropology* **1**(1):114–121.

Colton, Harold S. 1946. "The Sinagua: A Summary of the Archaeology of the Region of Flagstaff, Arizona," Bulletin 22. Museum of Northern Arizona, Flagstaff.

Colton, Harold S. 1956. "Pottery Types of the Southwest," Ceramic Series 3C. Museum of Northern Arizona, Flagstaff.

Colton, Harold S. 1958. "Pottery Types of the Southwest: Wares 14, 15, 16, 17, 18," Ceramic Series 3D. Museum of Northern Arizona, Flagstaff.

Colton, Harold S. 1960. "Black Sand: Prehistory of Northern Arizona." University of New Mexico Press, Albuquerque.

Colton, Harold S., and Lyndon L. Hargrave 1937. "Handbook of Northern Arizona Pottery Wares," Museum of Northern Arizona Bulletin No. 11. Northern Arizona Society of Science and Art, Flagstaff.

Comeaux, M. L. 1981. "Arizona Geography." Westview Press, Boulder.

Cooke, R. U., and R. W. Reeves 1976. "Arroyos and Environmental Changes." Clarendon, Oxford.

Cordell, Linda S. 1975. Predicting Site Abandonment at Wetherill Mesa. *The Kiva* **40**(3): 189–202.

Cordell, Linda S. 1979. "Cultural Resources Overview of the Middle Rio Grande Valley, New Mexico." U.S. Government Printing Office, Washington, DC.

Cordell, Linda S. 1981. The Wetherill Mesa Simulation: A Retrospective. *In* "Simulations in Archaeology," edited by Jeremy A. Sabloff, pp. 119–141. University of New Mexico Press, Albuquerque.

Cordell, Linda S. 1982. The Pueblo Period in the San Juan Basin: An Overview and Some Research Problems. *In* "The San Juan Tomorrow," edited by Fred Plog and Walter Wait, pp. 59–83. National Park Service, Southwest Region, Santa Fe, and School of American Research, Santa Fe.

Cordell, Linda S. 1984 "Prehistory of the Southwest." Academic Press, Orlando.

Cordell, Linda S. 1989a. Durango to Durango: An Overview of the Southwest Heartland. *In* "Columbian Consequences: Archeological and Historical Perspectives on the Spanish Borderlands West," edited by David Hurst Thomas, pp. 17–40. Smithsonian Institution Press, Washington, DC.

Cordell, Linda S. 1989b. History and Theory in Reconstructing Southwestern Sociopolitical Organization. *In* "The Sociopolitical Structure of Prehistoric Southwestern Societies," edited by Steadman Upham, Kent G. Lightfoot, and Roberta A. Jewett, pp. 33–54. Westview Press, Boulder.

Cordell, Linda S. 1994. The Nature of Explanation in Archaeology: A Position Paper. *In* "Understanding Complexity in the Prehistoric Southwest," edited by George J. Gumerman and Murray Gell-Mann, Vol. XIV, pp. 149–162. Santa Fe Institute, Studies in the Sciences of Complexity, Addison Wesley, Reading.

Cordell, Linda S. 1995. Tracing Migration Pathways from the Receiving End. *Journal of Anthropological Archaeology* **14**(2):203–211.

Cordell, Linda S. 1996. Big Sites, Big Questions: Pueblos in Transition. *In* "The Prehistoric Pueblo World, AD 1150–1350," edited by Michael A. Adler, pp. 228–240. University of Arizona Press, Tucson.

Cordell, Linda S. 1997. "Before Pecos: Settlement Aggregation at Rowe, New Mexico. Including the 1917 Rowe Field Diary of Carl C. Guthe," transcribed by Jean Bagalah, Anthropological Papers No. 7. Maxwell Museum of Anthropology, University of New Mexico, Albuquerque.

Cordell, Linda S. (editor) 1980. "Tijeras Canyon: Analyses of the Past." University of New Mexico Press, Albuquerque.

Cordell, Linda S., David E. Doyel, and Keith W. Kintigh 1994. Processes of Aggregation in the Prehistoric Southwest. *In* "Themes in Southwest Prehistory," edited by George J. Gumerman, pp. 109–134. School of American Research Press, Santa Fe.

Cordell, Linda S., and Amy C. Earls 1982a. Mountains and Rivers: Resource Use at Three Sites. Paper presented at the 2nd Mogollon Conference, Las Cruces.

Cordell, Linda S., and Amy C. Earls 1982b. The Rio Grande Glaze "Sequence" and the Mogollon. Paper presented at the 2nd Mogollon Conference, Las Cruces.

Cordell, Linda S., and George J. Gumerman 1989. Cultural Interaction in the Prehistoric Southwest. *In* "Dynamics of Southwest Prehistory," edited by L. S. Cordell and G. J. Gumerman, pp. 1–18. Smithsonian Institution Press, Washington, DC.

Cordell, Linda S., and Mindy H. Halpern 1975. Anasazi Nucleation for Defense: Reasons to Doubt an Obvious Solution. *Rocky Mountain Social Science Journal* **12**(2):41–48.

Cordell, Linda S., and Fred Plog 1979. Escaping the Confines of Normative Thought: A Reevaluation of Puebloan Prehistory. *American Antiquity* **44**:405–429.

Cosgrove, H. S., and C. B. Cosgrove 1932. The Swarts Ruin: A Typical Mimbres Site in Southwestern New Mexico. *Papers of the Peabody Museum of American Archaeology and Ethnology* **15**(1).

Cowgill, George L. 1975. Population Pressure as a Non-Explanation. *American Antiquity* **40**(2): 127–131, Society for American Archaeology, Memoir 30.

Crabtree, Donald E. 1975. Experiments in Replicating Hohokam Points. *Tebiwa* **16**(1):10–45.

Crane, H. R. 1955. Antiquity of the Sandia Culture: Carbon 14 Measurements. *Science* **122**: 689–690.

Creamer, Winifred 1993. "The Architecture of Arroyo Hondo Pueblo, New Mexico." School of American Research Press, Santa Fe.

Creamer, Winifred, and Lisa Renken 1994. Testing Conventional Wisdom: Protohistoric Ceramics And Chronology in the Northern Rio Grande. Paper presented at the 59th Annual Meeting of the Society for American Archaeology, Anaheim.

Creel, D., and B. Adams 1985. Investigation of Water Control Features at NAN-20. *In* "The NAN Ranch Archaeology Project: 1985 Interim Report," edited by H. J. Shafer, Special Report 7, pp. 50–66. Anthropology Laboratory, Texas A&M University, College Station.

Crotty, Helen K. 1995. Anasazi Mural Art of the Pueblo IV Period, AD 1300–1600: Influences, Selective Adaptation, and Cultural Diversity in the Prehistoric Southwest. Unpublished Ph.D. dissertation in Art History, University of California, Los Angeles.

Crown, Patricia L. 1981. Variability in Ceramic Manufacture at the Chodistaas Site, East-Central Arizona. Ph.D. dissertation, University of Michigan, University Microfilms, Ann Arbor.

Crown, Patricia L. 1983. Design Variability on Hohokam Red-on-buff Ceramics. *In* "Hohokam Archaeology along the Salt-Gila Aqueduct, Central Arizona Project," edited by L. S. Teague and P. L. Crown. Archaeological Series No. 150, Vol. 8, pp. 205–247. Arizona State Museum, Tucson.

Crown, Patricia L. 1990. The Hohokam of the American Southwest. *Journal of World Prehistory* **4**(2):223–255.

Crown, Patricia L. 1991. The Hohokam: Current Views of Prehistory and the Regional System. *In* "Chaco and Hohokam: Prehistoric Regional Systems in the American Southwest," edited by P. L. Crown and W. J. Judge, pp. 135–158. School of American Research Press, Santa Fe.

Crown, Patricia L. 1994. "Ceramics and Ideology: Salado Polychrome Pottery." University of New Mexico Press, Albuquerque.

Crown, Patricia L. 1995. The Production of the Salado Polychromes in the American Southwest. *In* "Ceramic Production in the American Southwest," edited by Barbara J. Mills and Patricia L. Crown, pp. 142–166. University of Arizona Press, Tucson.

Crown, Patricia L., and Timothy A. Kohler 1994. Community Dynamics, Site Structure, and Aggregation in the Northern Rio Grande. *In* "The Ancient Southwestern Community: Models and Methods for the Study of Prehistoric Social Organization," edited by W. H. Wills and Robert D. Leonard, pp. 103–118. University of New Mexico Press, Albuquerque.

Crown, Patricia L., and W. James Judge (editors) 1991. "Chaco and Hohokam: Prehistoric Regional Systems in the American Southwest." School of American Research Press, Santa Fe.

Crown, Patricia L., Janet D. Orcutt, and Timothy A. Kohler 1996. Pueblo Cultures in Transition: The Northern Rio Grande. *In* "The Prehistoric Pueblo World, AD 1150–1350," edited by Michael A. Adler, pp. 188–204. University of Arizona Press, Tucson.

Crown, Patricia L., and W. H. Wills 1995. The Origins of Southwestern Ceramic Containers: Women's Time Allocation and Economic Intensification. *Journal of Anthropological Research* **51**(2):173–186.

Culbert, T. P. 1978. Mesoamerica. *In* "Ancient Native Americans," edited by J. D. Jennings, pp. 403–454. Freeman, San Francisco.

Cully, Anne C. 1979. Some Aspects of Pollen Analysis in Relation to Archaeology. *The Kiva* **44**: 95–100.

Cummings, Byron 1915. Kivas of the San Juan Drainage. *American Anthropologist* **17**:272–282.

Cummings, Byron 1937. Excavations at Kinishba Pueblo. *The Kiva* **3**:1–4.

Cummings, Byron 1940. "Kinishba, a Prehistoric Pueblo of the Great Pueblo Period." Hohokam Museum Association and the University of Arizona, Tucson.

Cushing, Frank H. 1890. Preliminary Notes on the Origin, Working Hypothesis, and Primary Researches of the Hemenway Southwestern Archaeological Expedition. *Comptes-Rendus de la Septieme Session, Congres International des Americanistes, Berlin, 1888*, pp. 152–194.

Dall, W. H. 1912. On the Geological Aspects of the Possible Human Immigration between Asia and America. *American Anthropologist* **14**:14–17.

Davis, Emma Lou 1965. Small Pressures and Cultural Drift as Explanations for Abandonment of the San Juan Area, New Mexico. *American Antiquity* **30**:353–355.

Dawson, Jerry, and W. James Judge 1969. Paleo-Indian Sites and Topography in the Middle Rio Grande Valley of New Mexico. *Plains Anthropologist* **14**(1):149–163.

Dean, Jeffrey S. 1969. Chronological Analysis of Tsegi Phase Sites in Northeastern Arizona. *Papers of the Laboratory of Tree-Ring Research* **3.**

Dean, Jeffrey S. 1970. Aspects of Tsegi Phase Social Organization: A Trial Reconstruction. *In* "Reconstructing Prehistoric Pueblo Societies," edited by William A. Longacre, pp. 140–174. School of American Research, Santa Fe, and University of New Mexico Press, Albuquerque.

Dean, Jeffrey S. 1983. Environmental Aspects of Modeling. *In* "Theory and Model Building: Refining Survey Strategies for Locating Prehistoric Resources, Trial Formulations for Southwestern Forests," edited by Linda S. Cordell and Dee F. Green, Cultural Resources Document 3, pp. 11–27. USDA Forest Service, Southwestern Region, Albuquerque.

Dean, Jeffrey S. 1988a. A Model of Anasazi Behavioral Adaptation. *In* "The Anasazi in a Changing Environment," edited by George J. Gumerman, pp. 25–44. Cambridge University Press, Cambridge.

Dean, Jeffrey S. 1988b. Dendrochronology and Paleoenvironmental Reconstruction on the Colorado Plateaus. *In* "The Anasazi in a Changing Environment," edited by George J. Gumerman, pp. 119–167. Cambridge University Press, Cambridge.

Dean, Jeffrey S. 1990. Intensive Archaeological Survey of Long House Valley, Northeastern Arizona. *In* "The Archaeology of Regions: A Case for Full-Coverage Surveys," edited by Suzanne K. Fish and Stephen A. Kowalewski, pp. 173–188. Smithsonian Institution Press, Washington, DC.

Dean, Jeffrey S. 1991. Thoughts on Hohokam Chronology. *In* "Exploring the Hohokam: Prehistoric Desert Peoples of the American Southwest," edited by George J. Gumerman, pp. 61–150. University of New Mexico Press, Albuquerque.

Dean, Jeffrey S. 1996a. Demography, Environment, and Subsistence Stress. *In* "Evolving Complexity and Environmental Risk in the Prehistoric Southwest, Proceedings Volume XXIV, Santa Fe Institute Studies in the Sciences of Complexity," edited by Joseph A. Tainter and Bonnie Bagley Tainter, pp. 25–56. Addison-Wesley Publishing Company, Reading.

Dean, Jeffrey S. 1996b. Kayenta Anasazi Settlement Transformations in Northeastern Arizona: A.D. 1150–1350. *In* "The Prehistoric Pueblo World, AD 1150–1350," edited by Michael A. Adler, pp. 29–47. University of Arizona Press, Tucson.

Dean, Jeffrey S., William H. Doelle, and Janet Orcutt 1994. Adaptive Stress, Environment, and Demography. *In* "Themes in Southwest Prehistory," edited by George J. Gumerman, pp. 53–86. School of American Research Press, Santa Fe.

Dean, Jeffrey S., Robert C. Euler, George J. Gumerman, Fred Plog, Richard H. Hevly, and Thor N. V. Karlstrom 1985. Human Behavior, Demography, and Paleoenvironment on the Colorado Plateaus. *American Antiquity* **50**:537–554.

Dean, Jeffrey S., Alexander J. Lindsay, Jr., and William J. Robinson 1978. Prehistoric Settlement in Long House Valley, Northeastern Arizona. *In* "Investigations of the Southwestern Anthropological Research Group: An Experiment in Archaeological Cooperation: The Preceedings of 1976 Conferences," edited by Robert C. Euler and George J. Gumerman, pp. 25–44. Museum of Northern Arizona, Flagstaff.

Dean, Jeffrey S., and John C. Ravesloot 1993. The Chronology of Cultural Interaction in the Gran Chichimeca. *In* "Culture and Contact: Charles C. Di Peso's Gran Chichimeca," edited by Anne I. Woosley and John C. Ravesloot, pp. 83–104. University of New Mexico Press, Albuquerque.

Dean, Jeffrey S., and William J. Robinson 1978. "Expanded Tree-Ring Chronologies for the Southwestern United States," Laboratory of Tree-Ring Research, University of Arizona, Tucson.

Dean, Jeffrey S., Mark C. Slaughter, and Dennie O. Bowden, III 1996. Desert Dendrochronology: Tree-Ring Dating Prehistoric Sites in the Tucson Basin. *The Kiva* **62**(1):7–26.

Dean, Jeffrey S., and Richard L. Warren 1983. Dendrochronology. *In* "The Architecture and Dendrochronology of Chetro Ketl," edited by S. H. Lekson, Reports of the Chaco Center No. 6, pp. 105–240. Division of Cultural Research, National Park Service, Albuquerque.

Deetz, James F. 1972. Archaeology as a Social Science. *In* "Contemporary Archaeology," edited by Mark P. Leone, pp. 108–117. Southern Illinois University Press, Carbondale.

Dick, Herbert W. 1965a. "Bat Cave," School of American Research Monograph 27. University of New Mexico Press, Albuquerque.

Dick, Herbert W. 1965b. Picuris Pueblo Excavations. *Clearinghouse for Federal Scientific and Technical Information* No. PB-177047, Springfield.

Dickson, Bruce D. 1979. "Prehistoric Pueblo Settlement Patterns: The Arroyo Hondo, New Mexico, Site Survey," Arroyo Hondo Archaeological Series, Vol. 2. School of American Research Press, Santa Fe.

Diehl, Michael 1996. The Intensity of Maize Processing and Production in Upland Mogollon Pithouse Villages, A.D. 200–1000. *American Antiquity* **61**(1):102–115.

Dillehay, T. D., G. A. Calderon, G. Politis, and M. C. Beltrao 1992. Earliest Hunters and Gatherers of South America. *Journal of World Prehistory* **6**:145–204.

Di Peso, Charles C. 1956. "The Upper Pima of San Cayetano Del Tumacacori: An Archeohistorical Reconstruction of the Ootam of Primeria Alta," Publication 8. Amerind Foundation, Dragoon.

Di Peso, Charles C. 1974. "Casas Grandes: A Fallen Trading Center of the Gran Chichimeca," Vols. 1–3, Series 9. Amerind Foundation, Dragoon.

Di Peso, Charles C. 1976. Gila Polychrome in the Casas Grandes Region. *The Kiva* **42**:57–63.

Di Peso, Charles C. 1979. Prehistory: Southern Periphery. *In* "Southwest," edited by Alfonso A. Ortiz, Handbook of North American Indians, Vol. 9, pp. 152–161. Smithsonian Institution, Washington, DC.

Di Peso, C. C. 1984. The Structure of the 11th Century Casas Grandes Agricultural System. *In* "Prehistoric Agricultural Strategies in the Southwest," edited by S. K. Fish and P. R. Fish, Anthropological Research Papers No. 33, pp. 261–269. Arizona State University, Tempe.

Di Peso, Charles C., J. B. Rinaldo, and G. Fenner 1974. "Casas Grandes: A Fallen Trading Center of the Gran Chichimeca," Vol. 4. Amerind Foundation, Dragoon, and Northland Press, Flagstaff.

Dittert, A. E., Jr. 1958a. "Preliminary Archaeological Investigations in the Navajo Project Area of Northwestern New Mexico," Papers in Anthropology No. 1, Navajo Project Studies No. 1. Museum of New Mexico and School of American Research, Santa Fe.

Dittert, A. E., Jr. 1958b. Salvage Archaeology and the Navajo Project: A Progress Report. *El Palacio* **65**(2):61–72.

Doebley, John 1990. Molecular Evidence and the Evolution of Maize. *Economic Botany* **44:**6–27.

Doebley, John, and Vorsila L. Bohrer 1983. Maize Variability and Cultural Selection at Salmon Ruin, New Mexico. *The Kiva* **49**(1–2):19–38.

Doelle, William H., Frederick W. Huntington, and Henry D. Wallace 1987. Rincon Phase Community Reorganization in the Tucson Basin. *In* "The Hohokam Village: Site Structure and Organization," edited by David E. Doyel, pp. 71–96. American Association for the Advancement of Science, Denver.

Doelle, William H., and Henry D. Wallace 1991. The Changing Role of the Tucson Basin in the Hohokam Regional System. *In* "Exploring The Hohokam: Prehistoric Desert Peoples of the American Southwest," edited by George J. Gumerman, pp. 279–346. University of New Mexico Press, Albuquerque.

Doleman, William H. 1994. Sites, Sampling and Cultural Landscapes: Problems in Defining Assemblages for Analysis. *In* "Archaic Hunter-Gatherer Archaeology in the American Southwest," edited by Bradley J. Vierra, Contributions in Anthropology 13(1), pp. 405–455. Eastern New Mexico University, Portales.

Doolittle, William E. 1984. Agricultural Change as an Incremental Process. *Annals of the Association of American Geographers* **74**:124–137.

Doolittle, William E. 1990. "Canal Irrigation in Prehistoric Mexico: The Sequence of Technological Change." University of Texas Press, Austin.

Doolittle, William E. 1991. A Finger on the Hohokam Pulse. *In* "Prehistoric Irrigation in Arizona: Symposium 1988," edited by Cory Dale Breternitz, No. 17, pp. 139–154. Soil Systems Publications in Archaeology, Phoenix.

Doolittle, William E. 1992. House-Lot Gardens in the Gran Chichimeca. *In* "Gardens of Prehistory," edited by Thomas W. Killion, pp. 69–91. University of Alabama Press, Tuscaloosa.

Douglass, Andrew E. 1929. The Secret of the Southwest Solved by Talkative Tree Rings. *National Geographic Magazine* **56**(6):736–770.

Douglas, C. L., D. L. Jenkins, and C. N. Warren 1988. Spatial and Temporal Variability in Faunal Remains from Four Lake Mojave-Pinto Period Sites in the Mojave Desert. *In* "Early Human Occupation in Far Western North America: The Clovis-Archaic Interface," edited by J. A. Willig, C. M. Aikens, and J. L. Fagan, Anthropological Papers No. 21, pp. 131–144. Nevada State Museum, Carson.

Dove, Donald E. 1982. Prehistoric Subsistence and Population Change along the Lower Agua Fria River, Arizona: A Model Simulation. Unpublished M.A. thesis, Department of Anthropology, Arizona State University, Tempe.

Downum, Christian E. 1990. From Myths to Methods: Intellectual Transitions in Flagstaff Archaeology, 1883–1930. *In* "Perspectives on Southwestern Prehistory," edited by Paul E. Minnis and Charles L. Redman, pp. 351–366. Westview Press, Boulder.

Downum, Christian E. 1993. "Between Desert and River: Hohokam Settlement and Land Use in the Los Robles Community," Anthropological Papers No. 57. University of Arizona Press, Tucson.

Doyel, David E. (assembler) 1975. "Excavations in the Escalante Ruin Group, Southern Arizona," Archaeological Series 37. Arizona State Museum, University of Arizona, Tucson.

Doyel, David E. 1976a. Classic Period Hohokam in the Gila River Basin, Arizona. *The Kiva* **42**(1):27–38.

Doyel, David E. 1976b. Salado Cultural Development in the Tonto Basin and Globe-Miami Areas, Central Arizona. *The Kiva* **42**:5–16.

Doyel, David E. 1980. Hohokam Social Organization and the Sedentary to Classic Transition. *In* "Current Issues in Hohokam Prehistory: Proceedings of a Symposium," edited by David E. Doyel and Fred T. Plog, Anthropological Research Papers 23, pp. 23–40. Arizona State University, Tempe.

Doyel, David E. 1983. The Evolution of Regional Diversity in the Prehistoric Southwest: Hohokam and Anasazi Pueblo. *In* "Proceedings of the 1981 Anasazi Conference," edited by J. Smith, pp. 43–48. Mesa Verde Museum Association, Mesa Verde National Park.

Doyel, David E. (editor) 1987. "The Hohokam Village: Site Structure and Organization." Southwestern and Rocky Mountain Division of the American Association for the Advancement of Science, Glenwood.

Doyel, David E. 1989. The Transition to History in Northern Pimeria Alta. *In* "Columbian Consequences," edited by David Hurst Thomas, Vol. 1, pp. 139–158. Smithsonian Institution Press, Washington, DC.

Doyel, David E. 1990. Hohokam Cultural Dynamics in the Phoenix Basin. *In* "Exploring the Hohokam: Prehistoric Desert Peoples of the American Southwest," edited by G. J. Gumerman. University of New Mexico Press, Albuquerque.

Doyel, David E. 1991a. Hohokam Cultural Evolution in the Phoenix Basin. *In* "Exploring The Hohokam: Prehistoric Desert Peoples of the American Southwest," edited by George J. Gumerman, pp. 231–278. University of New Mexico Press, Albuquerque.

Doyel, David E. 1991b. Hohokam Exchange and Interaction. *In* "Chaco and Hohokam: Prehistoric Regional Systems in the American Southwest," edited by Patricia L. Crown and W. James Judge, pp. 225–252. School of American Research Press, Santa Fe.

Doyel, David E. (editor) 1992. "Anasazi Regional Organization and the Chaco System," Anthropological Papers No. 5. Maxwell Museum of Anthropology, University of New Mexico, Albuquerque.

Doyel, David E. 1993. Interpreting Prehistoric Cultural Diversity in the Arizona Desert. *In* "Culture and Contact," edited by Anne I. Woosley and John C. Ravesloot, pp. 39–64. University of New Mexico Press, Albuquerque.

Doyel, David E., and Emil H. Haury (editors) 1976. The 1976 Salado Conference. *The Kiva* **42**(1).

Doyel, David E., and Fred T. Plog (editors) 1980. "Current Issues in Hohokam Prehistory: Proceedings of a Symposium," Anthropological Research Papers 23. Arizona State University, Tempe.

Dozier, Edward P. 1961. The Rio Grande Pueblos. *In* "Perspectives in American Indian Culture Change," edited by E. H. Spicer, pp. 94–186. University of Chicago Press, Chicago.

Dozier, Edward P. 1970. "The Pueblo Indians of North America." Holt, Rinehart, and Winston, New York.

Duncan, Roselind 1971. The "Cochise Culture": Analysis and Explanation of Archeological Remains. Unpublished M.A. thesis, University of California at Los Angeles.

Dutton, Bertha P. 1963. "Sun Father's Way: The Kiva Murals of Kuaua." University of New Mexico Press, Albuquerque.

Dutton, Bertha P. 1975. "Navajos and Apaches: The Athabascan Peoples. Indians of the American Southwest." Prentice-Hall, Englewood Cliffs.

Dutton, Bertha P. 1983. "American Indians of the Southwest." University of New Mexico Press, Albuquerque.

Earls, Amy C. 1987. "An Archaeological Assessment of "Las Huertas," Socorro, New Mexico," Paper No. 3. Maxwell Museum of Anthropology, Albuquerque.

Ebert, James I., and Thomas R. Lyons 1980. Prehistoric Irrigation Canals Identified from Skylab III and Landsat Imagery in Phoenix, Arizona. *In* "Cultural Resources Remote Sensing," edited by Thomas R. Lyons and Frances Joan Mathien, pp. 209–228. National Park Service and University of New Mexico, Albuquerque.

Eddy, Frank W. 1966. "Prehistory in the Navajo Reservoir District (2 parts)," Papers in Anthropology 15. Museum of New Mexico, Santa Fe.

Eddy, Frank W. 1977. "Archaeological Investigations at Chimney Rock Mesa: 1970–1972," Memoir No. 1. Colorado Archaeological Societies, Boulder.

Eddy, Frank W., and Maurice E. Cooley 1983. "Cultural and Environmental History of Cienega Valley Southeastern Arizona," Anthropological Papers, No. 43. University of Arizona, Tucson.

Eggan, Fred 1950. "Social Organization of the Western Pueblos." Aldine, Chicago. (Reprinted in 1970 by University of Chicago Press.)

Eighmy, Jeffrey L., and Randall H. McGuire 1989. Dating the Hohokam Phase Sequence: Analysis of Archaeomagnetic Dates. *Journal of Field Archaeology* **16**:215–231.

Eighmy, J. L., and F. Plog (editors) 1980. "Current Issues in Hohokam Prehistory," Anthropological Research Papers 23. Arizona State University, Tempe.

Elias, Scott A. 1994. "Quaternary Insects and their Environments." Smithsonian Institution Press, Washington, DC

Ellis, Florence Hawley 1934. The Significance of the Dated Prehistory of Chetro Ketl, Chaco Canyon, New Mexico. *University of New Mexico Bulletin, Monograph Series* **1**(1).

Ellis, Florence Hawley 1937. Pueblo Social Organization as a Lead to Pueblo History. *American Anthropologist* **39**:504–522.

Ellis, Florence Hawley 1951. Patterns of Aggression and the War Cult in Southwestern Pueblos. *Southwestern Journal of Anthropology* **7**:177–201.

Ellis, Florence Hawley 1967. Where Did the People Come From? *El Palacio* **74**(3):35–43.

Ellis, Florence Hawley 1970. Irrigation and Water Works in the Rio Grande Valley. Paper presented at the 33rd Annual Pecos Conference, Symposium on Water Control, Santa Fe.

Ellis, Florence Hawley 1974a. Anthropology of Laguna Pueblo Land Claims. *In* "Pueblo Indians," compiled and edited by David Agee Horr, Vol III, pp. 9–120. Garland, New York.

Ellis, Florence Hawley 1974b. Anthropological Data Pertaining to the Taos Land Claim. *In* "Indians of the Southwest," compiled and edited by David Agee Horr, American Indian Ethnohistory, Vol. I, pp. 29–150. Garland, New York.

Ellis, Florence Hawley 1974c. An Anthropological Study of the Navajo Indians. *In* "Navajo Indians," Vol. I. Garland, New York.

Ellis, Florence Hawley, and J. J. Brody 1964. Ceramic Stratigraphy and Tribal History at Taos Pueblo. *American Antiquity* **29**:316–327.

Ellis, Lain 1995. An Interpretive Framework for Radiocarbon Dates from Soil Organic Matter from Prehistoric Water Control Features. *In* "Soil, Water, Biology, and Belief in Prehistoric and Traditional Southwestern Agriculture, edited by J. Wolcott Toll, Special Publication No. 2, pp. 155–186. New Mexico Archaeological Council, Albuquerque.

Elsen, M. D., and J. J. Clark 1995. "The Roosevelt Community Development Study," Vol 1, Anthropological Papers No. 14. Center for Desert Archaeology, Tucson.

Emory, W. H. 1848. Notes of a Military Reconnaissance from Fort Leavenworth in Missouri to San Diego in California, etc. U.S. Senate Document 7, 30th Congress, 1st Session. Washington, DC.

Emslie, Steven D. 1981. Prehistoric Agricultural Ecosystems: Avifauna from Pottery Mound, New Mexico. *American Antiquity* **46**:853–860.

El-Najjar, M. Y. 1974. People of Canyon de Chelly: A Study of Their Biology and Culture. Unpublished Ph.D. dissertation, Department of Anthropology, Arizona State University, Tempe.

El-Najjar, M. Y., D. J. Ryan, C. G. Turner, II, and B. Lozoff 1976. The Etiology of Porotic Hyperostosis among the Prehistoric and Historic Anasazi Indians of the Southwestern United States. *American Journal of Physical Anthropology* **44**:477–488.

Erikson, Winston 1994. "Sharing the Desert: The Tohono O'odham in History." University of Arizona Press, Tucson.

Euler, Robert C. 1954. Environmental Adaptation at Sia Pueblo. *Human Organization* **12**:27–30.

Euler, Robert C. 1964. Southern Paiute Archaeology. *American Antiquity* **29**:379–381.

Euler, Robert C. 1975. The Pai: Cultural Conservation in Environmental Diversity. *In* "Collected Papers in Honor of Florence Hawley Ellis," edited by Theodore R. Frisbie, Paper No. 2, pp. 80–88. Archaeological Society of New Mexico, Albuquerque.

Euler, Robert C., and H. F. Dobyns 1962. Excavations West of Prescott, Arizona. *Plateau* **34**(3): 69–84.

Euler, Robert C., and Dee F. Green 1978. "An Archeological Reconnaissance of Middle Havasu Canyon, Arizona," Cultural Resources Report 22. U.S. Forest Service, Southwestern Region, Albuquerque.

Euler, Robert C., and George J. Gumerman (editors) 1978. "Investigations of the Southwestern Anthropological Research Group: An Experiment in Archaeological Cooperation," Proceedings of the 1976 Conference. Museum of Northern Arizona, Flagstaff.

Euler, Robert C., George J. Gumerman, Thor N. V. Karlstrom, Jeffrey S. Dean, and Richard H. Hevly 1979. Colorado Plateaus: Cultural Dynamics and Paleoenvironment. *Science* **205**: 1089–1101.

Ezell, Paul H. 1983. History of the Pima. *In* "Southwest," edited by Alfonso A. Ortiz, Handbook of North American Indians, Vol. 10, pp. 149–160. Smithsonian Institution, Washington, DC.

Ezzo, Joseph A., and William L. Deaver 1996. Data Recovery at the Costello-King Site (AZ AA: 12:503 [ASM]), a Late Archaic Site in the Northern Tucson Basin," Draft report prepared for Waste Management of Southern Arizona, Inc., Marana, AZ. Statistical Research, Inc., Tucson.

Farwell, Robin E. 1981. Pit Houses: Prehistoric Energy Conservation? *El Palacio* **87**(3):43–47.

Ferdon, E. N., Jr. 1955. "A Trial Survey of Mexican-Southwestern Architectural Parallels," Monograph No. 21. School of American Research, Santa Fe.

Ferdon, Edwin N., Jr. 1967. The Hohokam "Ball Court": An Alternative View of its Function. *The Kiva* **33**(1):1–14.

Ferguson, T. J. 1983. Towards Understanding the Role and Function of Aggregated Communities in the North American Southwest: A Proposal for Investigation of the Changing Structure of Regional Settlement in the Zuni Area after A.D. 900. Unpublished paper, Department of Anthropology, University of New Mexico, Albuquerque.

Fewkes, Jesse W. 1893. A-Wa'-tobi: An Archaeological Verification of a Tusayan Legend. *American Anthropologist* **6**:363–375.

Fewkes, Jesse W. 1896. The Prehistoric Culture of Tusayan. *American Anthropologist* **9**:151–174.

Fewkes, Jesse W. 1904. Two Summers' Work in Pueblo Ruins. In "22nd Annual Report, 1900–1901," Smithsonian Institution, Bureau of American Ethnology, pp. 3–195. Washington, DC.

Fewkes, Jesse W. 1909. "Antiquities of the Mesa Verde National Park—Spruce Tree House," Bureau of American Ethnology Bulletin 41. Smithsonian Institution, Washington, DC.

Fewkes, Jesse W. 1911a. "Preliminary Report on a Visit to the Navaho National Monument, Arizona," Bureau of American Ethnology Bulletin 50. Smithsonian Institution, Washington, DC.

Fewkes, Jesse W. 1911b. "Antiquities of the Mesa Verde National Park—Cliff Palace," Bureau of American Ethnology Bulletin 51. Smithsonian Institution, Washington, DC.

Fewkes, Jesse Walter 1912. Casa Grande, Arizona. *In* "Twenty-eighth Annual Report of the Bureau of American Ethnology," pp. 25–180. U.S. Government Printing Office, Washington, DC.

Fewkes, Jesse W. 1923. Archaeological Field-Work on the Mesa Verde National Park, Colorado. Explorations and Field-Work of the Smithsonian Institution in 1922. *Smithsonian Miscellaneous Collections* **74**(5):89–115.

Figgens, J.D. 1993. A Further Contribution to the Antiquity of Man in America. *Proceedings of the Colorado Museum of Natural History* **12**(2).

Fish, Paul R., and Suzanne K. Fish 1989. Hohokam Warfare from a Regional Perspective. *In* "Cultures in Conflict: Current Archaeological Perspectives," edited by D. C. Tkaczuk and B. C. Vivian, Proceedings of the Twentieth Chacmool Conference, pp. 112–128. Department of Archaeology, University of Calgary, Alberta.

Fish, Paul R., and Suzanne K. Fish 1991. Hohokam Political and Social Organization. *In* "Exploring the Hohokam: Prehistoric Desert Peoples of the American Southwest," edited by George J. Gumerman, pp. 151–176. University of New Mexico Press, Albuquerque.

Fish, Paul, and Suzanne K. Fish 1994. Southwest and Northwest: Recent Research at the Juncture of the United States and Mexico. *Journal of Archaeological Research* **2**(1):3–44.

Fish, Paul R., Suzanne K. Fish, and George J. Gumerman 1994. Toward an Explanation for Southwestern "Abandonments." *In* "Themes in Southwest Prehistory," edited by George J. Gumerman, pp. 135–165. School of American Research Press, Santa Fe.

Fish, Paul, Suzanne K. Fish, Austin Long, and Charles Miksicek 1986. Early Corn Remains from Tumamoc Hill, Southern Arizona. *American Antiquity* **51**:563–572.

Fish, Paul R., Suzanne K. Fish, John H. Madsen, Charles H. Miksicek, and Christine R. Szuter 1992. The Dairy Site: Occupational Continuity on an Alluvial Fan. *In* "The Marana Community in the Hohokam World," edited by Suzanne K. Fish, Paul R. Fish, and John Madsen, Anthropological Papers, No. 56, pp. 64–72. University of Arizona Press, Tucson.

Fish, Paul R., Peter Pilles, and Suzanne K. Fish 1980. Colonies, Traders, and Traits: The Hohokam in the North. *In* "Current Issues in Hohokam Prehistory: Proceedings of a Symposium," edited by David Doyel and Fred Plog, Anthropological Research Papers 23, pp. 151–175. Arizona State Museum, Tempe.

Fish, Suzanne K., Paul R. Fish, and Christian E. Downum 1984. Hohokam Terraces and Agricultural Production in the Tucson Basin, Arizona. *In* "Prehistoric Agricultural Strategies in the Southwest," edited by S. K. Fish and P. R. Fish, Anthropological Research Paper No. 33, pp. 55–71. Department of Anthropology, Arizona State University, Tempe.

Fish, Suzanne K., Paul R. Fish, and John Madsen 1985. Prehistoric Agave Cultivation in Southern Arizona. *Desert Plants* **7**:107–113.

Fish, Suzanne K., Paul R. Fish, and John Madsen 1990. Sedentism and Mobility in the Tucson Basin prior to A.D. 1000. *In* "Perspectives on Southwestern Prehistory," edited by P. Minnis and C. Redman, pp. 76–91. Westview Press, Boulder.

Fish, Suzanne K., Paul R. Fish, and John Madsen (editors) 1992a. "The Marana Community in the Hohokam World," Anthropological Papers, No. 56. University of Arizona, Tucson.

Fish, Suzanne K., Paul R. Fish, and John H. Madsen 1992b. Early Sedentism and Agriculture In The Northern Tucson Basin. *In* "Marana Community in the Hohokam World," edited by Suzanne K. Fish, Paul R. Fish, and John H. Madsen, Anthropological Papers No. 56, pp. 11–19. University of Arizona Press, Tucson.

Fish, Suzanne K., and Gary P. Nabhan 1991. Desert as Context: The Hohokam Environment. *In* "Exploring the Hohokam, Prehistoric Desert Peoples of the American Southwest," edited by George J. Gumerman, pp. 29–60. Amerind Foundation, Dragoon, and University of New Mexico Press, Albuquerque.

Fladmarck, M. R. 1979. Routes: Alternate Migration Corridors for Early Man in North America. *American Antiquity* **44**:55–69.

Flannery, Kent V. 1968. Archeological Systems Theory and Early Mesoamerica. *In* "Anthropological Archeology in the Americas," edited by B. J. Meggars, pp. 67–87. Anthropological Society of Washington, Washington, DC.

Flannery, Kent V. 1972. The Origins of the Village as a Settlement Type in Mesoamerica and the Near East: A Comparative Study. *In* "Man, Settlement and Urbanism," edited by P. Ucko, Ruth Trigham, and George Dimbleby, pp. 1–31. Duckworth, London.

Flannery, Kent V. 1973. The Origins of Agriculture. *Annual Review of Anthropology* **2**: 271–310.

Folsom, Franklin 1973. "The Life and Legend of George McJunkin: Black Cowboy." T. Nelson, Nashville.

Folsom, F., and George A. Agogino 1975. New Light on an Old Site: Events Leading up to the Discovery of the Folsom Type Site. *Anthropological Journal of Canada* **13**(3):2–5.

Forbes, J. D. 1960. "Apache, Navajo, and Spaniard." University of Oklahoma Press, Norman.

Ford, Richard I. 1972. An Ecological Perspective on the Eastern Pueblos. *In* "New Perspectives on the Pueblos," edited by Alfonso A. Ortiz, pp. 1–18. University of New Mexico Press, Albuquerque.

Ford, Richard I. 1975. Re-excavation of Jemez Cave, New Mexico. *Awanyu* **3**(3):13–27.

Ford, Richard I. 1980. Gardening and Farming before A.D. 1000: Patterns of Prehistoric Cultivation North of Mexico. Paper presented at the Advanced Seminar on the Origins of Plant Husbandry in North America, School of American Research, Santa Fe.

Ford, Richard I. 1981. Gardening and Farming before A.D. 1000: Patterns of Prehistoric Cultivation North of Mexico. *Journal of Ethnobiology* **1**(1):6–27.

Ford, Richard I. 1985. Patterns of Prehistoric Food Production in North America. *In* "Prehistoric Food Produciton in North America," edited by Richard I. Ford, Anthropological Papers, No. 75, pp. 341–364. University of Michigan, Ann Arbor.

Ford, Richard I., Albert H. Schroeder, and Stewart L. Peckham 1972. Three Perspectives on Puebloan Prehistory. *In* "New Perspectives on the Pueblos," edited by Alfonso A. Ortiz, pp. 22–40. School of American Research, Santa Fe, and University of New Mexico Press, Albuquerque.

Forde, Daryll, and Mary Douglas 1956. Primitive Economies. *In* "Man, Culture, and Society," edited by Harry L. Shapiro, pp. 330–344. Oxford University Press, Oxford.

Fosberg, S. 1979. Geologic Controls of Anasazi Settlement Patterns. *In* "Archeological Investigations in Cochiti Reservoir, New Mexico," edited by Jan V. Biella and Richard C. Chapman, Vol. 4, pp. 145–168. Office of Contract Archeology, University of New Mexico, Albuquerque.

Fosberg, S., and J. Hussler 1979. Pedology in the Service of Archeology: Soil Testing at LA 13086. *In* "Archeological Investigations in Cochiti Reservoir, New Mexico," edited by Jan V. Biella and Richard C. Chapman, Vol. 4, pp. 307–318. Office of Contract Archeology, University of New Mexico, Albuquerque.

Foster, M. S. 1985. The Loma San Gabriel Occupation of Zacatecas and Durango, Mexico. *In* "The Archaeology of West and Northwest Mesoamerica," edited by M. S. Foster and P. C. Weigand, pp. 327–351. Westview Press, Boulder.

Foster, M. S., and P. C. Weigand (editors) 1985. "The Archaeology of West and Northwest Mesoamerica." Westview Press, Boulder.

Fowler, Andrew P., and John R. Stein 1992. The Anasazi Great House in Space, Time, and Paradigm. *In* "Anasazi Regional Organization and the Chaco System," edited by David E. Doyel, Anthropological Papers No. 5, pp. 101–122. Maxwell Museum of Anthropology, Albuquerque.

Fowler, Andrew P., John R. Stein, and Roger Anyon 1987. "An Archaeological Reconnaissance of West-central New Mexico: The Anasazi Monuments Project," Draft report. New Mexico Historic Preservation Division, Office of Cultural Affairs, Santa Fe.

Fowler, Don D., and Jesse D. Jennings 1982. Great Basin Archaeology: A Historical Overview. *In* "Man and Environment in the Great Basin," edited by D. Madsen and J. O'Connell, Memoir No. 2, pp. 105–120. Society for American Archaeology.

Franklin, Hayward H., and W. Bruce Masse 1976. The San Pedro Salado: A Case of Prehistoric Migration. *The Kiva* **42**:47–55.

Friedman, I., and Robert L. Smith 1960. A New Dating Method Using Obsidian: The Development of the Method (Part 1). *American Antiquity* **25**:476–522.

Frisbie, Theodore R. 1967. The Excavation and Interpretation of the Artificial Leg Basketmaker III—Pueblo I Site near Corrales, New Mexico. Unpublished M.A. thesis, Department of Anthropology, University of New Mexico, Albuquerque.

Frisbie, Theodore R. 1978. High Status Burials in the Greater Southwest: An Interpretive Synthesis. *In* "Across the Chichimec Sea: Papers in Honor of J. Charles Kelley," edited by Carroll L. Riley and Basil C. Hedrick, pp. 202–228. Southern Illinois University Press, Carbondale.

Frisch, R. E. 1977. Population, Food Intake, and Fertility. *Science* **199**:22–30.

Frison, George C. (editor) 1974. "The Casper Site: A Hell Gap Bison Kill on the High Plains." Academic Press, New York.

Frison, George C. 1978. "Prehistoric Hunters of the High Plains." Academic Press, New York.

Frison, George C. 1980. Man and Bison Relationships in North America. *Canadian Journal of Anthropology* **1**(1):75–76.

Frison, George C. 1982. Paleoindian Winter Subsistence Strategies on the High Plains. *Smithsonian Contributions to Anthropology* **30**:194–201.

Frison, George C. 1988. Paleo-Indian Subsistence and Settlement During Post-Clovis Times on the Northwestern Plains, the Adjacent Mountain Ranges, and Intermontane Basins. *Ethnology Monographs* **12**:83–106.

Frison, George C. 1991. "Prehistoric Hunters of the High Plains," 2nd ed. Academic Press, New York.

Frison, George C. 1993. North American High Plains Paleo-Indian Hunting Strategies and Weaponry Assemblages. *In* "Kostenki to Clovis: Upper Paleolithic-Paleo-Indian Adaptations," edited by Olga Soffer and N. D. Praslov, pp. 237–249. Plenum Press, New York.

Frison, G. C. (editor) 1996. "The Iron Site." University of New Mexico Press, Albuquerque.

Frison, George C., and B. A. Bradley 1980. "Folsom Tools and Technology at the Hanson Site, Wyoming." University of New Mexico Press, Albuquerque.

Frison, G. C., and D. J. Stanford 1982. "The Agate Basin Site." Academic Press, New York.

Fritts, Harold C. 1976. "Tree Rings and Climate." Academic Press, New York.

Fritts, Harold C., David G. Smith, and Marvin A. Stokes 1965. The Biological Model for Paleoclimatic Interpretation of Mesa Verde Tree-Ring Series. *In* "Contributions of the Wetherill Mesa Archeological Project," edited by D. Osborne, Memoir No. 19, pp. 101–121. Society for American Archaeology, Salt Lake City.

Fritz, John M. 1978. Paleopsychology Today: Ideational Systems and Human Adaptation in Prehistory. *In* "Social Archaeology: Beyond Subsistence and Dating," edited by Charles L. Redman, Mary J. Berman, E. V. Curtin, W. T. Longhorne, Jr., N. M. Versaggi, and J. C. Wanser, pp. 37–60. Academic Press, New York.

Galinat, W. C., and James H. Gunnerson 1963. Spread of Eight-Rowed Maize from the Prehistoric Southwest. *Harvard University Botanical Museum Leaflets* **20**(5):117–160.

Garber, Emily 1979. Analysis of Plant Remains. *In* "Tijeras Canyon: Analyses of the Past," edited by Linda S. Cordell, pp. 71–87. Maxwell Museum of Anthropology and University of New Mexico Press, Albuquerque.

Gasser, Robert E. 1976. Hohokam Subsistence: A 2,000 Year Continuum in the Indigenous Exploitation of the Lower Sonoran Desert. *USDA Forest Service, Southwest Region, Archeological Report* **11.**

Gasser, Robert E. 1980. Gu Achi: Seeds, Seasons, and Ecosystems. *In* "Excavations at Gu Achi: A Reappraisal of Hohokam Settlement and Subsistence in the Arizona Papaqueria," by W. Bruce Masse, Publications in Anthropology No. 12, pp. 313–342. Western Archaeological Center, Tucson.

Gasser, Robert E. 1981. Appendix IV: Hohokam Plant Use at La Ciudad and Other Riverine Sites: The Flotation Evidence. *In* "Final Report for Archaeological Testing at La Ciudad (Group III), West Papago Inner Loop (I-10), Maricopa County, Arizona, prepared by Ronald K. Yablon." Department of Anthropology, Museum of Northern Arizona, Flagstaff.

Gasser, Robert E., and E. C. Adams 1981. Aspects of Deterioration of Plant Remains in Archaeological Sites: The Walpi Archaeological Project. *Journal of Ethnobiology* **1**:182–192.

Gasser, Robert E., and S. M. Kwiatkowski 1991. Regional Signatures of Hohokam Plant Use. *The Kiva* **56**(3):207–226.

Gilman, Patricia Ann 1983. Changing Architectural Forms in the Prehistoric Southwest. Unpublished Ph.D. dissertation. Department of Anthropology, University of New Mexico, Albuquerque.

Gilman, Patricia A. 1987. Architecture as Artifact: Pit Structures and Pueblos in the American Southwest. *American Antiquity* **52**(3):538–564.

Gilman, Patricia A. 1995. Multiple Dimensions of the Archaic-to-Pit Structure Period Transition in Southeastern Arizona. *The Kiva* **60**(4):619–632.

Gilpin, Dennis 1992. Salina Springs and Lukachukai: Late Archaic/Early Basketmaker Habitation Sites in the Chinle Valley, Northeastern Arizona. Paper presented at the 57th Annual Meeting of the Society for American Archaeology, Pittsburgh.

Gish, Jennifer 1991. Current Perceptions, Recent Discoveries, and Future Directions in Hohokam Palynology. *The Kiva* **56**(3):237–255.

Gladwin, Harold S. 1928. Excavations at Casa Grande, Arizona, February 12–May 1, 1927. *Southwest Museum Paper* **2**:7–30.

Gladwin, Harold S. 1945. "The Chaco Branch, Excavations at White Mound and in the Red Mesa Valley," Medallion Papers 33. Gila Pueblo, Globe.

Gladwin, Harold S. 1948. "Excavations at Snaketown IV: Review and Conclusions," Medallion Papers No. 38. Gila Pueblo, Globe.

Gladwin, Harold S. 1957. "A History of the Ancient Southwest." Bond Wheelwright, Portland.

Gladwin, Harold S., Emil W. Haury, Edwin B. Sayles, and Nora Gladwin 1938. "Excavations at Snaketown I: Material Culture," Medallion Papers 25. Gila Pueblo, Globe. (Reprinted in 1965 by Arizona State Museum, Tucson.)

Gladwin, Winifred, and Harold S. Gladwin 1930. "Some Southwestern Pottery Types," Series I, Medallion Papers 8. Gila Pueblo, Globe.

Gladwin, Winifred, and Harold S. Gladwin 1933. "Some Southwestern Pottery Types," Series III, Medallion Papers 13. Gila Pueblo, Globe.

Gladwin, Winifred, and Harold S. Gladwin 1934. "A Method for Designation of Cultures and Their Variations," Medallion Papers 15. Gila Pueblo, Globe.

Gladwin, Winifred, and Harold S. Gladwin 1935. "The Eastern Range of the Red-on-Buff Culture," Medallion Papers 16. Gila Pueblo, Globe.

Glassow, Michael A. 1972. Changes in the Adaptations of Southwestern Basketmakers: A Systems Perspective. *In* "Contemporary Archaeology," edited by Mark P. Leone, pp. 289–302. Southern Illinois University Press, Carbondale.

Glassow, Michael A. 1980. "Prehistoric Agricultural Development in the Northern Southwest: A Study in Changing Patterns of Land Use," Anthropological Papers No. 16. Ballena Press, Socorro.

Goldstein, Lynne 1992. The Potential for Future Relationships between Archaeologists and Native Americans. *In* "Quandries and Quests: Visions of Archaeology's Future," edited by LuAnn Wandsnider, pp. 59–71. Center for Archaeological Investigations, Carbondale.

Goodyear, Albert C. 1975. "Hecla II and III: An Interpretive Study of Archaeological Remains from the Lakeshore Project, Papago Indian Reservation, South-Central Arizona," Anthropological Papers No. 9, Arizona State University, Tempe.

Goodyear, Albert C. 1989. A Hypothesis for the Use of Cryptocrystalline Raw Materials among Paleo-Indian Groups of North America. *In* "Eastern Paleo-Indian Lithic Resource Use," edited by Christopher J. Ellis and Jonathan C. Lothrop, pp. 1–9. Westview Press, Boulder.

Gorman, Frederick J. E., and S. Terry Childs 1981. Is Prudden's Unit Type of Anasazi Settlement Valid and Reliable? *North American Archaeologist* **2**(3):153–192.

Goss, J. A. 1965. Ute Linguistics and Anasazi Abandonment of the Four Corners Area. *In* "Contributions of the Wetherill Mesa Archaeological Project," edited by D. Osborne, Memoir No. 19, pp. 73–81. Society for American Archaeology, Salt Lake City.

Graves, Michael W., and William A. Longacre 1982. Aggregation and Abandonment at Grasshopper Pueblo, Arizona. *Journal of Field Archaeology* **9**:193–206.

Graves, Michael W., Sally J. Holbrook, and William A. Longacre 1982. Aggregation and Abandonment at Grasshopper Pueblo: Evolutionary Trends in the Late Prehistory of East-Central Arizona. *In* "Multidisciplinary Research at Grasshopper Pueblo, Arizona," edited by William A. Longacre, Sally J. Holbrook, and Michael W. Graves, Anthropological Papers No. 40, pp. 110–121. University of Arizona, Tucson.

Graybill, Donald A. 1973. Prehistoric Settlement Pattern Analysis in the Mimbres Region, New Mexico. Ph.D. dissertation, Department of Anthropology, University of Arizona, Tucson (University Microfilms, Ann Arbor).

Graybill, Donald A. 1989. The Reconstruction of Salt River Streamflow. *In* "Environment and Subsistence, The 1982–1984 Excavations at Las Colinas," Vol. 5, by David Gregory and others. Archaeological Series No. 162, pp. 25–38. Arizona State Museum, University of Arizona, Tucson.

Graybill, Donald A., David A. Gregory, Fred L. Nials, Suzanne K. Fish, Robert E. Gasser, Charles H. Miksicek, and Christine R. Szuter 1989. "The 1982–1984 Excavations at Las Colinas: Environment and Subsistence," Archaeological Series No. 162(5). Arizona State Museum, Tucson.

Grayson, Donald K. 1988. Perspectives on the Archaeology of the First Americans. *Ethnology Monographs* **12**:107–123.

Grayson, Donald K. 1993. "The Desert's Past: A Natural Prehistory of the Great Basin." Smithsonian Institution Press, Washington, DC.

Grebinger, Paul 1971. Hohokam Cultural Development in the Middle Santa Cruz River Valley, Arizona. Unpublished Ph.D. dissertation, Department of Anthropology, University of Arizona, Tucson.

Grebinger, Paul. 1976. Salado—Perspective from the Middle Santa Cruz Valley. *The Kiva* **42**: 39–46.

Green, Ernestine L. 1976. "Valdez Phase Occupation near Taos, New Mexico," Fort Burgwin Research Center 10. Southern Methodist University, Dallas.

Green, Jesse (editor) 1990. "Cushing at Zuni: The Correspondence and Journals of Frank Hamilton Cushing, 1879–1884." University of New Mexico Press, Albuquerque.

Greenleaf, J. C. 1975. "Excavations at Punto de Agua in the Santa Cruz River Basin, Southeastern Arizona." Anthropological Papers No. 26. University of Arizona, Tucson.

Gregory, David A. 1991. Form and Variation in Hohokam Settlement Patterns. *In* "Chaco and Hohokam: Prehistoric Regional Systems in the American Southwest," edited by Patricia L. Crown and W. James Judge, pp. 159–194. School of American Research Press, Santa Fe.

Guernsey, S. J., and A. V. Kidder 1921. Basketmaker Caves of Northeastern Arizona. *Peabody Museum Papers in American Archaeology and Ethnology* **8**(2).

Guilday, J. E. 1967. Differential Extinction during Late Pleistocene and Recent Times. *In* "Pleistocene Extinctions, The Search for a Cause," edited by P. S. Martin and H. E. Wright, pp. 121–140. Yale University Press, New Haven.

Gumerman, George J. (editor) 1971. "The Distribution of Prehistoric Population Aggregates," Anthropological Reports 1. Prescott College, Prescott.

Gumerman, George J. (editor) 1988. "The Anasazi in a Changing Environment." Cambridge University Press, Cambridge.

Gumerman, George J. (editor) 1994. "Themes in Southwest Prehistory." School of American Research Press, Santa Fe.

Gumerman, George J., and Jeffrey S. Dean 1989. Prehistoric Cooperation and Competition in the Western Anasazi Area. *In* "Dynamics of Southwest Prehistory," edited by Linda S. Cordell, and G. J. Gumerman, pp. 99–148. Smithsonian Institution Press, Washington, DC.

Gumerman, George J., and Robert C. Euler 1976. Black Mesa: Retrospect. *In* "Papers on the Archaeology of Black Mesa, Arizona," edited by George J. Gumerman and Robert C. Euler, pp. 162–170. Southern Illinois University Press, Carbondale.

Gumerman, George J., and Murray Gell-Mann (editors) 1994. "Understanding Complexity in the Southwest, Proceedings Volume XVI, Santa Fe Institute Studies in the Sciences of Complexity." Addison-Wesley Publishing Company, Reading.

Gumerman, George J., and Emil W. Haury 1979. Prehistory: Hohokam. *In* "Southwest," edited by Alfonso A. Ortiz, Handbook of North American Indians, Vol. 9, pp. 75–90. Smithsonian Institution, Washington, DC.

Gumerman, George J., and Carol S. Weed 1976. The Question of Salado in the Agua Fria and New River Drainages of Central Arizona. *The Kiva* **42**:105–112.

Gunnerson, James H. 1969. Apache Archaeology in Northeastern New Mexico. *American Antiquity* **34**:23–39.

Gunnerson, James H., and D. A. Gunnerson 1971. Apachean Culture: A Study in Unity and Diversity. *In* "Apachean Culture History and Ethnology," edited by Keith Basso and Morris E. Opler, Anthropological Papers No. 21, pp. 7–27. University of Arizona, Tucson.

Guthrie, R. D. 1980. Bison and Man in North America. *Canadian Journal of Anthropology* **1**(1): 55–74.

Haas, Jonathan, and Winifred Creamer 1993. "Stress and Warfare Among the Kayenta Anasazi of the Thirteenth Century AD." *Fieldiana: Anthropology* **N.S. 21.** Field Museum of Natural History, Chicago.

Haas, Jonathan, and Winifred Creamer 1996. The Role of Warfare in the Pueblo II Period. *In* "The Prehistoric Pueblo World, AD 1150–1350," edited by Michael A. Adler, pp. 205–213. University of Arizona Press, Tucson.

Habicht-Mauche, Judith A. 1987. Southwestern-Style Culinary Ceramics on the Southern Plains: A Case Study of Technological Innovation and Cross-Cultural Interaction. *Plains Anthropologist* **32**(116):175–191.

Habicht-Mauche, Judith A. 1991. Evidence for the Manufacture of Southwestern-Style Culinary Ceramics on the Southern Plains. *In* "Farmers, Hunters, and Colonists: Interaction between the Southwest and the Southern Plains," edited by Katherine A. Spielmann, pp. 51–70. University of Arizona Press, Tucson.

Habicht-Mauche, Judith A. 1993. "The Pottery from Arroyo Hondo Pueblo, New Mexico: Tribalization and Trade in the Northern Rio Grande," Arroyo Hondo Archaeological Series Vol. 8. School of American Research Press, Santa Fe.

Habicht-Mauche, Judith A. 1995. Changing Patterns of Pottery Manufacture and Trade in the Northern Rio Grande Region. *In* "Ceramic Production in the American Southwest," edited by Barbara J. Mills and Patricia L. Crown, pp. 167–199. University of Arizona Press, Tucson.

Hack, John T. 1942. The Changing Physical Environment of the Hopi Indians of Arizona. *Papers of the Peabody Museum of American Archaeology and Ethnology* **35**(1).

Hackenberg, Robert A. 1964. "Aboriginal Land Use and Occupancy of the Papago Indians," Ms. on file. Arizona State Museum, Tucson.

Hafsten, U. 1961. Pleistocene Development of Vegetation and Climate in the Southern High Plains as Evidenced by Pollen Analysis. *In* "Paleoecology of the Llano Estacado," edited by Fred Wendorf, Fort Burgwin Research Center Publications 1, pp. 55–91. Southern Methodist University, Dallas.

Hall, Don Alan 1996. Aubrey Site A Deep, Undisturbed Camp. *Mammoth Trumpet* **11**(1):5–9.

Hall, Edward T., Jr. 1944. Recent Clues to Athabascan Prehistory in the Southwest. *American Anthropologist* **46**:98–105.

Hall, Stephen A. 1977. Late Quaternary Sedimentation and Paleoecologic History of Chaco Canyon, New Mexico. *Geological Society of America Bulletin* **88**:1593–1618.

Hammack, Nancy S. 1992. The Oven Site, LA 4169: A Reevaluation Based on Recent Excavations. *In* "Cultural Diversity and Adaptation: The Archaic, Anasazi, and Navajo Occupation of the Upper San Juan Basin," edited by Lori Stephens Reed and Paul F. Reed, pp. 37–54. Bureau of Land Management, New Mexico State Office, Santa Fe.

Hammond, George P., and Agapito Rey (translators) 1940. "Narratives of the Coronado Expedition, 1540–1542." University of New Mexico Press, Albuquerque.

Hancock, P. M. 1992. Evidence of the Dinetah Phase in the La Plata River Valley, San Juan County, New Mexico. *In* "Current Research on the Late Prehistory and Early History of Northern New Mexico," edited by Bradley J. Vierra, Special Publication No. 1, pp. 287–297. New Mexico Archaeological Council, Albuquerque.

Hantman, Jeffrey L. 1983. Social Networks and Stylistic Distributions in the Prehistoric Plateau Southwest. Unpublished Ph.D. dissertation, Department of Anthropology, Arizona State University, Tempe.

Hard, Robert J. 1990. Agriculture Dependence in the Mountain Mogollon. *In* "Perspectives on Southwestern Prehistory," edited by Paul E. Minnis and Charles L. Redman, pp. 135–149. Westview Press, Boulder.

Hardy, Karen 1996. The Preceramic Sequence from the Tehuacan Valley: A Reevaluation. *Current Anthropology* **37**(4):700–716.

Harlan, Jack 1967. A Wild Wheat Harvest in Turkey. *Archaeology* **20**:197–201.

Harrington, H. D. 1967. "Edible Native Plants of the Rocky Mountains." University of New Mexico Press, Albuquerque.

Harrington, M. R. 1957. "A Pinto Site at Little Lake, California," Paper No. 17. Southwest Museum, Los Angeles.

Hassan, Fekri A. 1981. "Demographic Archaeology." Academic Press, New York.

Hatch, Elvin 1973. "Theories of Man and Culture." Columbia University Press, New York.

Haury, Emil W. 1934. "The Canyon Creek Ruin and Cliff Dwellings of the Sierra Ancha," Medallion Papers 14. Gila Pueblo, Globe.

Haury, Emil W. 1936. "The Mogollon Culture of Southwestern New Mexico," Medallion Papers 20. Gila Pueblo, Globe.

Haury, Emil W. 1937. A Pre-Spanish Rubber Ball from Arizona. *American Antiquity* **2**:282–288.

Haury, Emil W. 1940. "Excavations in the Forestdale Valley, East-central Arizona," University of Arizona Bulletin 11(4), Social Science Bulletin 12. University of Arizona, Tucson.

Haury, Emil W. 1950. "The Stratigraphy and Archaeology of Ventana Cave." University of Arizona Press, Tucson.

Haury, Emil W. 1956. The Lehner Mammoth Site. *The Kiva* **21**(3–4):23–24.

Haury, Emil W. 1957. An Alluvial Site on the San Carlos Indian Reservation, Arizona. *American Antiquity* **23**:2–27.

Haury, Emil W. 1958. Evidence at Point of Pines for a Prehistoric Migration from Northern Arizona. *In* "Migrations in New World Culture History," edited by R. H. Thompson, pp. 1–7. University of Arizona Press, Tucson.

Haury, Emil W. 1960. Association of Fossil Fauna and Artifacts at the Sulpher Springs Stage, Cochise Culture. *American Antiquity* **25**:609–610.

Haury, Emil W. 1962a. HH-39: Recollections of a Dramatic Moment in Southwestern Archaeology. *Tree-Ring Bulletin* **24**(3–4):11–14.

Haury, Emil W. 1962b. The Greater American Southwest. *In* "Courses toward Urban Life: Some Archaeological Considerations of Cultural Alternates," edited by Robert J. Braidwood and Gordon R. Willey, pp. 106–131. Viking Fund Publications in Anthropology, New York.

Haury, Emil W. 1976. "The Hohokam, Desert Farmers and Craftsmen: Excavations at Snaketown, 1964–1965." University of Arizona Press, Tucson.

Haury, Emil W. 1985. "Mogollon Culture in the Forestdale Valley, East-Central Arizona." University of Arizona Press, Tucson.

Haury, Emil W. 1988. Recent Thoughts of the Mogollon. *The Kiva.* **53**(2):195–196.

Haury, Emil W., Ernst Antevs, and John F. Lance 1953. Artifacts with Mammoth Remains. Naco, Arizona. *American Antiquity* **19**(1):1–24.

Haury, Emil W., and J. D. Hayden 1975. Preface. *In* "The Stratigraphy and Archaeology of Ventana Cave," by Emil W. Haury, pp. v–vi. University of Arizona Press, Tucson.

Haury, Emil W., and E. B. Sayles 1947. "An Early Pit House Village of the Mogollon Culture, Forestdale Valley, Arizona," Social Science Bulletin 16. University of Arizona, Tucson.

Haury, Emil W., E. B. Sayles, and W. W. Wasley 1959. The Lehner Mammoth Site, Southeastern Arizona. *American Antiquity* **25**:2–30.

Hawley, Florence M. 1932. The Bead Mountain Pueblos of Southern Arizona. *Art and Archaeology* **33**:227–236.

Hawley, Florence M. 1934. The Significance of Dated Prehistory of Chetro Ketl, Chaco Canyon, New Mexico. *University of New Mexico Bulletin, Monograph Series* **1**(1).

Hawley, Florence M. 1936. Field Manual of Prehistoric Southwestern Pottery Types. *University of New Mexico Bulletin* **291.**

Hayden, Julian D. 1970. Of Hohokam Origins and Other Matters. *American Antiquity* **35**: 87–93.

Hayes, Alden C. 1964. "The Archaeological Survey of Wetherill Mesa," Archaeological Research Series 7A. National Park Service, Washington, DC.

Hayes, Alden C. 1981a. A Survey of Chaco Canyon. *In* "Archaeological Surveys of Chaco Canyon, New Mexico," by Alden C. Hayes, David M. Brugge, and W. James Judge, Publications in Archaeology 18A, Chaco Canyon Studies, pp. 1–68. National Park Service, Washington, DC.

Hayes, Alden C. 1981b. "Contributions to Gran Quivira Archaeology." National Park Service, Washington, DC.

Hayes, Alden C., David M. Brugge, and W. James Judge 1981. "Archaeological Surveys of Chaco Canyon, New Mexico," Publications in Archaeology 18A. National Park Service, Washington, DC.

Haynes, C. Vance, Jr. 1969. The Earliest Americans. *Science* **166**:709–715.

Haynes, C. Vance, Jr. 1970. Geochronology of Man-Mammoth Sites and Their Bearing on the Origin of the Llano Complex. *In* "Pleistocene and Recent Environments of the Central Plains," edited by Wakefield Dort, Jr. and J. Knox Jones, Jr., Special Publication 3, pp. 78–92. Department of Geology, University of Kansas, Lawrence.

Haynes, C. Vance, Jr. 1975. Pleistocene and Recent Stratigraphy. *In* "Pleistocene and Recent Environments of the Southern High Plains," edited by Fred Wendorf and James J. Hester, Fort Burgwin Research Center Publications 9, pp. 57–96. Southern Methodist University, Dallas.

Haynes, C. Vance, Jr. 1980. The Clovis Culture. *Canadian Journal of Anthropology* **1**(1):115–121.

Haynes, C. V., Jr. 1987. Clovis Origins Update. *The Kiva* **52**:83–94.

Haynes, C. Vance, Jr. 1993. Clovis-Folsom Geochronology and Climatic Change. *In* "Kostenki to Clovis: Upper Paleolithic–Paleo-Indian Adaptations," edited by Olga Soffer and N. D. Praslov, pp. 219–236. Plenum Press, New York.

Haynes, C. Vance, Jr., and E. T. Hemmings 1968. Mammoth Bone Shaft Wrench from Murray Springs, Arizona. *Science* **159**:186–187.

Haynes, C. Vance, Jr., and Austin Long 1976. Radiocarbon Dating at Snaketown. *In* "The Hohokam, Desert Farmers and Craftsmen: Excavations at Snaketown, 1964–1965," by Emil W. Haury, pp. 333–338. University of Arizona Press, Tucson.

Hays, Kelley Ann 1994. Kachina Depictions on Prehistoric Pueblo Pottery. *In* "Kachinas in the Pueblo World," edited by Polly Schaafsma, pp. 47–62. University of New Mexico Press, Albuquerque.

Hegmon, Michelle 1989. Risk Reduction and Variation in Agricultural Economies: A Computer Simulation of Hopi Agriculture. *Research in Economic Anthropology* **11**:89–121.

Hegmon, Michelle 1994. Boundary-Making Strategies in Early Pueblo Societies: Style and Architecture in the Kayenta and Mesa Verde Regions. *In* "The Prehistoric Southwestern Community: Models and Methods for the Study of Prehistoric Social Organization," edited by W. H. Wills and Robert D. Leonard, pp. 171–190. University of New Mexico Press, Albuquerque.

Hegmon, Michelle 1996. Variability in Food Production, Strategies of Storage and Sharing, and the Pithouse-to-Pueblo Transition in the Northern Southwest. *In* "Evolving Complexity and Environmental Risk in the Prehistoric Southwest," edited by Joseph A. Tainter and Bonnie Bagley Tainter, pp. 223–250. Santa Fe Institute Studies in the Sciences of Complexity. Addison-Wesley Publishing Company, Reading.

Hegmon, Michelle, and Wenda R. Trevathan 1996. Gender, Anatomical Knowledge, and Pottery Production: Implications of an Anatomically Unusual Birth Depicted on Mimbres Pottery from Southwestern New Mexico. *American Antiquity* **61**(4):747–754.

Heller, M. M. 1976. Zoo-archaeology of Tularosa Cave, Catron County, New Mexico. M.A. thesis, University of Texas, El Paso.

Herrington, LaVerne 1982. Water-Control Systems of the Mimbres Classic Phase. *In* "Mogollon Archaeology: Proceedings of the 1980 Mogollon Conference," edited by P. Beckett, pp. 75–90. Acoma Books, Ramona.

Hester, James J. 1962. "Navajo Migrations and Acculturation in the Southwest," Papers in Anthropology 6. Museum of New Mexico, Santa Fe.

Hester, James J. 1972. "Blackwater Locality No. 1." Fort Burgwin Research Center, Southern Methodist University, Dallas.

Hester, James J. 1975. Paleoarchaeology of the Llano Estacado. *In* "Late Pleistocene Environments of the Southern High Plains," edited by Fred Wendorf and James J. Hester, Fort Burgwin Research Center Publications 9, pp. 247–256. Southern Methodist University, Dallas.

Hevly, Richard H. 1964. Pollen Analysis of Quaternary Archaeological and Lacustrine Sediments from the Colorado Plateau. Unpublished Ph.D. dissertation, University of Arizona, Tucson.

Hewett, Edgar L. 1906. "Antiquities of the Jemez Plateau, New Mexico," Bureau of American Ethnology Bulletin 32. Smithsonian Institution, Washington, DC.

Hewett, Edgar L. 1909. The Excavations at Tyounyi, New Mexico, in 1908. *American Anthropologist* **11**:434–455.

Hewett, Edgar L., Junius Henderson, and Wilfred William Robbins 1913. "The Physiography of the Rio Grande Valley, New Mexico, in Relation to Pueblo Culture," Bureau of American Ethnology Bulletin 54. Smithsonian Institution, Washington, DC.

Hibben, Frank C. 1941. Evidences of Early Occupation in Sandia Cave, New Mexico, and Other Sites in the Sandia-Manzano Region. *Smithsonian Institution Miscellaneous Collections* **99**(3): 1–44.

Hibben, Frank C. 1946. The First Thirty-Eight Sandia Points. *American Antiquity* **11**:257–258.

Hibben, Frank C. 1948. The Gallina Architectural Forms. *American Antiquity* **14**:32–36.

Hibben, Frank C. 1955. Specimens from Sandia Cave and Their Possible Significance. *Science* **122**:688–689.

Hibben, Frank C. 1966. A Possible Pyramidal Structure and Other Mexican Influences at Pottery Mound, New Mexico. *American Antiquity* **31**(4):522–529.

Hibben, Frank C. 1967. Mexican Features of Mural Painting at Pottery Mound. *Archaeology* **20**(2):84–87.

Hibben, Frank C. 1975. "Kiva Art of the Anasazi at Pottery Mound." K.C. Publications, Las Vegas.

Hill, James N. 1970. "Broken K Pueblo: Prehistoric Social Organization in the American Southwest," Anthropological Papers 18. University of Arizona, Tucson.

Hill, W. W. 1938. "Navaho Agricultural and Hunting Methods," Publications in Anthropology 18. Yale University, New Haven.

Hillerud, J. M. 1980. Bison as Indicators of Geologic Age. *Canadian Journal of Anthropology* **1**(1): 77–80.

Hinsley, Curtis M., Jr. 1983. Ethnographic Charisma and Scientific Routine: Cushing and Fewkes in the American Southwest, 1879–1893. *In* "Observers Observed: Essays on Ethnographic Fieldwork, History of Anthropology," edited by G. W. Stocking, Jr., Vol. 1, pp. 53–69. University of Wisconsin Press, Madison.

Hitchcock, R. K., and James I. Ebert, in press. Foraging and Food Production among Kalahari Hunter-Gatherers. *In* "The Causes and Consequences of Food Production in Africa," edited by J. D. Clark and S. A. Brandt. University of California Press, Berkeley and Los Angeles.

Hodge, F. W. 1893. Prehistoric Irrigation in Arizona. *American Anthropologist* **6**:323–330.

Hodge, Frederick Webb 1937. "History of Hawikuh, New Mexico: One of the So-called Cities of Cibola," Frederick Webb Hodge Anniversary Publication Fund 1. Southwest Museum. Ward Ritchie Press, Los Angeles.

Hogan, Patrick 1989. Dinetah: A Reevaluation of Pre-Revolt Navajo Occupation in Northwest New Mexico. *Journal of Anthropological Research* **45**:53–66.

Hogan, Patrick 1994a. Archaic Hunter-Gatherer Mobility Strategies in Northwestern New Mexico. *In* "Archaic Hunter-Gatherer Archaeology in the American Southwest," edited by Bradley J. Vierra, Contributions in Anthropology 13(1), pp. 121–154. Eastern New Mexico University, Portales.

Hogan, Patrick 1994b. Foragers to Farmers II: A Second Look at the Adoption of Agriculture in Northwestern New Mexico. *In* "Archaic Hunter-Gatherer Archaeology in the American Southwest," edited by Bradley J. Vierra, Contributions in Anthropology 13(1), pp. 155–184. Eastern New Mexico University, Portales.

Hohmann, John W. 1990. "A Master Stabilization and Development Plan for the Casa Malpais National Historic Landmark Site," Studies in Western Archaeology No. 3. Cultural Resource Group, Louis Berger & Associates, Inc.

Hohmann, John W. 1992. An Overview of Salado Heartland Archaeology. *In* "Proceedings of the Second Salado Conference," edited by Richard C. Lange and Stephen Germick, pp. 1–16. Arizona Archaeological Society, Phoenix.

Hoijer, Harry 1956. The Chronology of the Athapaskan Languages. *International Journal of American Linguistics* **22**(4):219–232.

Holbrook, Sally J., and James C. Mackey 1976. Prehistoric Environmental Change in Northern New Mexico: Evidence from a Gallina Phase Archaeological Site. *The Kiva* **41**: 309–317.

Holden, Jane 1955. A Preliminary Report on Arrowhead Ruin. *El Palacio* **62**(4):102–119.

Holliday, V. T. 1985. Archaeological Geology of the Lubbock Lake Site, Southern High Plains of Texas. *Geological Society of America Bulletin* **96**:1483–1492.

Holsinger, S. J. 1901. "Report on Prehistoric Ruins of Chaco Canyon National Monument. General Land Office," Ms. on file. Division of Cultural Research, National Park Service, Albuquerque.

Honea, Kenneth 1969. The Rio Grande Complex and the Northern Plains. *Plains Anthropologist* **14**(43):57–70.

Hopkins, D. M. 1967. Quaternary Marine Transgressions in Alaska. *In* "The Bering Land Bridge," edited by D. M. Hopkins, pp. 47–90. Stanford University Press, Stanford.

Hough, Walter 1914. "Culture of the Ancient Pueblos of the Upper Gila," Bulletin 87. Smithsonian Institution, Washington, DC.

Hough, Walter 1920. Explorations of a Pit House Village at Luna, New Mexico. *Proceedings of the U.S. National Museum* **35**:409–431.

Houghton, Frank E. 1959. "Climate of New Mexico." U.S. Department of Commerce, National Oceanic and Atmospheric Administration, Environmental Data Service, Silver Spring.

Howard, Jerry B. 1982. Hohokam Community Patterns at La Ciudad de los Hornos. *In* "The Archaeology of La Ciudad de los Hornos," edited by David Wilcox and Jerry Howard, manuscript on file. Arizona State University, Tempe.

Howard, Jerry B. 1985. Courtyard Groups and Domestic Cycling: A Hypothetical Model of Growth. *In* "Proceedings of the 1983 Hohokam Symposium," edited by A. E. Dittert, Jr. and D. E. Dove, Occasional Paper No. 2, pp. 311–326. Arizona Archaeological Society, Phoenix.

Hrdlicka, A. 1926. The Race and Antiquity of the American Indian. *Scientific American* **135**:7–10.

Huckell, Bruce B. 1984a. The Paleo-Indian and Archaic Occupation of the Tucson Basin: An Overview. *The Kiva* **49**(3–4):133–145.

Huckell, Bruce B. 1988. Late Archaic Archaeology of the Tucson Basin: A Status Report. *In* "Recent Research on Tucson Basin Prehistory: Proceedings of the Second Tucson Basin Conference," edited by William H. Doelle and Paul R. Fish, Anthropological Papers, Vol. 10, pp. 57–80. Institute for American Research, Tucson.

Huckell, Bruce B. 1990. Late Preceramic Farmer-Foragers in Southeastern Arizona: A Cultural and Ecological Consideration of the Spread of Agriculture in the Arid Southwestern United States. Ph.D. dissertation, Arid Lands Resource Sciences, University of Arizona, Tucson. University Microfilms, Ann Arbor.

Huckell, Bruce B. 1993. "Archaeological Testing of the Pima Community College New Campus Property: The Valencia North Project," Technical Report No. 92-13. Center for Desert Archaeology, Tucson.

Huckell, Bruce B. 1995. "Of Marshes and Maize: Preceramic Agricultural Settlements in the Cienega Valley, Southeastern Arizona," Anthropological Papers No. 59. University of Arizona, Tucson.

Huckell, Bruce B. 1996. The Southwestern Archaic: Scale and Perception of Preceramic Hunter-Gatherers. *In* "Interpreting Southwestern Diversity: Underlying Principles and Overarching Patterns," edited by P. R. Fish and J. J. Reid, Anthropological Research Papers No. 48, pp. 7–16. Arizona State University, Tempe.

Huckell, Bruce B., and Lisa W. Huckell 1988. Crops Come to the Desert: Late Preceramic Agriculture in Southeastern Arizona. Paper presented at the 53rd Annual Meeting of the Society for American Archaeology, Phoenix.

Huckell, Bruce B., Lisa W. Huckell, and Suzanne K. Fish 1994. "Investigations at Milagro, a Late Preceramic Site in the Eastern Tucson Basin," Technical Report 94-5. Center for Desert Archaeology, Tucson.

Hunt, Charles B. 1967. "Physiography of the United States." Freeman, San Francisco.

Hunter-Anderson, Rosalind 1979. Explaining Residential Aggregation in the Northern Rio Grande: A Competition Reduction Model. *In* "Adaptive Change in the Northern Rio Grande. Archeological Investigations in Cochiti Reservoir," edited by Jan V. Biella and Richard C. Chapman, Vol. 4, pp. 169–175. Office of Contract Archeology, University of New Mexico, Albuquerque.

Hunter-Anderson, Rosalind L. 1986. "Prehistoric Adaptation in the American Southwest." Cambridge University, Cambridge Press.

Huscher, B. H., and H. A. Huscher 1942. Athapaskan Migration via the Intermontane Region. *American Antiquity* **8**:80–88.

Iltis, Hugh H. 1983. From Teosinte to Maize: The Catastrophic Sexual Transmutation. *Science* **222**:886–894.

Irwin, Henry J. 1971. Developments in Early Man Studies in Western North America, 1960–1970. *Arctic Anthropology* **8**(2):42–67.

Irwin, Henry J., and Cynthia C. Irwin 1959. Excavations at the LoDaisKa Site in the Denver, Colorado Area. *Denver Museum of Natural History Proceedings No.* **8**.

Irwin, Henry J., and H. M. Wormington 1970. Paleo-Indian Tool Types in the Great Plains. *American Antiquity* **35**:24–34.

Irwin-Williams, Cynthia n.d. Paleo-Indian and Archaic Cultural Systems in the Southwestern United States. Ms. prepared for the Handbook of North American Indians, Smithsonian Institution, Washington, DC.

Irwin-Williams, Cynthia 1967. Picosa: The Elementary Southwestern Culture. *American Antiquity* **32**:441–456.

Irwin-Williams, Cynthia 1973. "The Oshara Tradition: Origins of Anasazi Culture," Contributions in Anthropology 5(1). Eastern New Mexico University, Portales.

Irwin-Williams, Cynthia 1979. Post-Pleistocene Archeology, 7000–2000 B.C. *In* "Southwest," edited by Alfonso A. Ortiz, Handbook of North American Indians, Vol. 9, pp. 31–42. Smithsonian Institution, Washington, DC.

Irwin-Williams, Cynthia 1980a. Investigations at Salmon Ruin: Methodology and Overview. *In* "Investigations at the Salmon Site: The Structure of Chacoan Society in the Northern Southwest," edited by Cynthia Irwin-Williams and Phillip H. Shelley, pp. 107–170. Eastern New Mexico University, Portales.

Irwin-Williams, Cynthia 1980b. San Juan Valley Archaeological Project: Synthesis, 1980. Part 12. *In* "Investigations at the Salmon Site: The Structure of Chacoan Society in the Northern Southwest," edited by Cynthia Irwin-Williams and Phillip H. Shelley, pp. 135–211. Eastern New Mexico University, Portales.

Irwin-Williams, Cynthia 1994. The Archaic of the Southwestern United States: Changing Goals and Research Strategies in the Last Twenty Five Years, 1964–1989. *In* "Archaic Hunter-Gatherer Archaeology in the American Southwest," edited by Bradley J. Vierra, Contributions in Anthropology 13(1), pp. 566–670. Eastern New Mexico University, Portales.

Irwin-Williams, Cynthia (editor) 1972. "The Structure of Chacoan Society in the Northern Southwest: Investigations at the Salmon Site, 1972," Contributions to Anthropology 4(3). Eastern New Mexico University, Portales.

Irwin-Williams, Cnythia, and P. Beckett 1973. "Excavations at the Moquino Site: A Cochise Culture Locality in Northern New Mexico," Ms. on file. Department of Anthropology, Eastern New Mexico University, Portales.

Irwin-Williams, Cynthia, and C. Vance Haynes, Jr. 1970. Climatic change and early population dynamics in the southwestern United States. *Quaternary Research* **1**:59–71.

Irwin-Williams, Cynthia, and Henry J. Irwin 1966. Excavations at Magic Mountain: A Diachronic Study of Plains-Southwest Relations. *Denver Museum of Natural History Proceedings No.* **12.**

Irwin-Williams, Cynthia, and S. Tompkins 1968. "Excavations at En Medio Shelter, New Mexico," Interim Report of the Anasazi Origins Project of Eastern New Mexico University, Contributions in Anthropology 1(2). Eastern New Mexico University, Portales.

Irwin-Williams, Cynthia, Henry J. Irwin, George Agogino, and C. Vance Haynes, Jr. 1973. Hell Gap: A Paleo-Indian Occupation on the High Plains. *Plains Anthropologist* **18**(59):40–53.

Jackson, William H. 1878. Report on the Ancient Ruins Examined in 1875 and 1877. *In* "Tenth Annual Report of the U.S. Geological and Geographical Survey," U.S. Government Printing Office, Washington, DC.

Jennings, Calvin H. 1971. Early Prehistory of the Coconino Plateau, Northwestern Arizona. Ph.D. dissertation, University of Colorado, Boulder.

Jennings, Jesse D. 1957. "Danger Cave," Anthropological Papers No. 27. University of Utah, Salt Lake City.

Jennings, Jesse D. 1963. "Anthropology and the World of Science," Bulletin 54(18). University of Utah, Salt Lake City.

Jennings, Jesse D. 1964. The Desert West. *In* "Prehistoric Man in the New World," edited by J. D. Jennings and E. Norbeck, pp. 149–174. University of Chicago Press, Chicago.

Jennings, Jesse D. 1966. "Glen Canyon: A Summary," Anthropological Papers No. 81, Glen Canyon Series 31. University of Utah, Salt Lake City.

Jennings, Jesse D. 1973. The Short Simple Life of a Useful Hypothesis. *Tebiwa* **16**(1):1–19.

Jennings, Jesse D. 1978. "Prehistory of Utah and the Eastern Great Basin," Anthropological Papers No. 98. University of Utah, Salt Lake City.

Jennings, Jesse D. 1980. "Cowboy Cave," Anthropological Papers No. 104. University of Utah, Salt Lake City.

Johnson, A. E. 1966. Archaeology of Sonora, Mexico. *In* "Archaeological Frontiers and External Connections," edited by Gordon F. Ekholm and Gordon R. Willey. Handbook of Middle American Indians, Vol. 4, pp. 26–37. University of Texas Press, Austin.

Johnson, E. 1987. "Lubbock Lake: Late Quaternary Studies on the Southern High Plains." Texas A&M University Press, College Station.

Johnson, E., and V. T. Holliday 1980. A Plainview Kill/Butchering Locale on the Llano Estacado—The Lubbock Lake Site. *Plains Anthropologist* **25**(88, Part 1):89–111.

Johnson, E., and V. T. Holliday 1981. Late Paleoindian Activity at the Lubbock Lake Site. *Plains Anthropologist* **26**:173–193.

Johnson, E., and V. T. Holliday 1986. The Archaic Record at Lubbock Lake. *Plains Anthropologist* **31**(114, Part 2):7–54.

Jorde, Lynn B. 1977. Precipitation Cycles and Cultural Buffering in the Prehistoric Southwest. *In* "For Theory Building in Archaeology: Essays on Faunal Remains, Aquatic Resources, and Systematic Modeling," edited by Lewis R. Binford, pp. 385–396. Academic Press, New York.

Judd, Neil M. 1922. Archaeological Investigations at Pueblo Bonito. *Smithsonian Miscellaneous Collections* **72**(15):106–117.

Judd, Neil Merton 1924. "Two Chaco Canyon Pit Houses," Annual Report. Smithsonian Institution, Washington, DC.

Judd, Neil Merton 1927. The Architectural Evolution of Pueblo Bonito. *Proceedings of the National Academy of Sciences* **13**(7):561–563.

Judd, Neil M. 1954. The Material Culture of Pueblo Bonito. *Smithsonian Miscellaneous Collections* **124.**

Judd, Neil M. 1964. The Architecture of Pueblo Bonito. *Smithsonian Miscellaneous Collections* **147**(1).

Judge, W. James 1970. Systems Analysis and the Folsom-Midland Question. *Southwestern Journal of Anthropology* **26**(1):40–51.

Judge, W. James 1973. "The Paleo-Indian Occupation of the Central Rio Grande Valley, New Mexico." University of New Mexico Press, Albuquerque.

Judge, W. James 1979. The Development of a Complex Cultural Ecosystem in the Chaco Basin, New Mexico. *In* "Proceedings of the First Conference on Scientific Research in the National Parks," edited by Robert M. Linn, pp. 901–905. U.S. Government Printing Office, Washington, DC.

Judge, W. James 1982. The Paleo-Indian and Basketmaker Periods: An Overview and Some Research Problems. *In* "The San Juan Tomorrow," edited by Fred Plog and Walter Wait, pp. 5–57. National Park Service, Southwest Region, Santa Fe.

Judge, W. James 1989. Chaco Canyon-San Juan Basin. *In* "Dynamics of Southwestern Prehistory," edited by L. S. Cordell and G. J. Gumerman, pp. 209–262. Smithsonian Institution, Washington, DC.

Judge, W. James 1991. Chaco: Current Views of Prehistory and the Regional System. *In* "Chaco and Hohokam: Prehistoric Regional Systems in the American Southwest," edited by Patricia L. Crown and W. James Judge, pp. 11–30. School of American Research Press, Santa Fe.

Judge, W. James n.d. "Early Man: Plains and Southwest. An Interpretive Summary of the Paleoindian Occupation of the Plains and Southwest," Ms. prepared for the Handbook of North American Indians, Vol. 3. Smithsonian Institution, Washington, DC.

Judge, W. James, and J. Dawson 1972. Paleoindian Settlement Technology in New Mexico. *Science* **176**:1210–1216.

Judge, W. James, and John D. Schelberg (editors) 1984. "Recent Research on Chaco Prehistory," Report of the Chaco Center No. 8. Division of Cultural Research, National Park Service, Albuquerque.

Judge, W. James, W. B. Gillespie, Stephen H. Lekson, and H. W. Toll 1981. "Tenth Century Developments in Chaco Canyon," Anthropological Papers 6. Archaeological Society of New Mexico, Santa Fe.

Kaplan, Lawrence 1963. The Archaeoethnobotany of Cordova Cave. *Economic Botany* **18**(4): 350–356.

Kaplan, Lawrence 1965. Beans of the Wetherill Mesa. *In* "Contributions of the Wetherill Mesa Archaeological Project," edited by D. Osborne, Memoirs 19, pp. 153–155. Society of American Archaeology, Salt Lake City.

Karlstrom, Thor N. V. 1988. Alluvial Chronology and Hydrological Change of Black Mesa and Nearby Regions. *In* "The Anasazi in a Changing Environment," edited by George J. Gumerman, pp. 45–91. Cambridge University Press, Cambridge.

Kelley, J. Charles 1952. Factors Involved in the Abandonment of Certain Peripheral Southwestern Settlements. *American Anthropologist* **54**:356–387.

Kelley, J. Charles 1971. Archaeology of the Northern Frontier: Zacatecas and Durango. *In* "Archaeology of Northern Mesoamerica," edited by Gordon F. Ekholm and Ignacio Bernal. Handbook of Middle American Indians, Vol. 11, Part 2, pp. 768–801. University of Texas Press, Austin.

Kelley, J. Charles 1985. The chronology of the Chalchihuites culture. *In* "The Archaeology of West and Northwest Mesoamerica," edited by M.S. Foster and P. C. Weigand, pp. 269–288. Westview Press, Boulder.

Kelley, J. Charles 1992. La Cuenca del Rio Conchos: Historia, Arqueologia y Significado. *In* "Historia General de Chihuahua I. Geologia, Geografia y Arqueologia," edited by Ruben Lau Rojo, pp. 131–136. Universidad Autonoma de Ciudad Juarez, Ciudad Juarez.

Kelley, J. Charles, and Ellen Abbott Kelley 1975. An Alternative Hypothesis for the Explanation of Anasazi Culture History. *In* "Collected Papers in Honor of Florence Hawley Ellis," edited by Theodore R. Frisbie, Paper No. 2, pp. 178–223. Archaeological Society of New Mexico, Santa Fe.

Kelley, Jane H. 1966. The Archaeology of the Sierra Blanca Region of Southwestern New Mexico. Unpublished Ph.D. dissertation, Department of Anthropology, Harvard University, Cambridge.

Kelley, Jane H. 1984. "The Archaeology of the Sierra Blanca Region of Southeastern New Mexico." Anthropological Papers No. 74. Museum of Anthropology, University of Michigan, Ann Arbor.

Kelley, Jane H., and Joe D. Stewart 1992. El Projecto Arqueologico de Chihuahua: Informe de la Temporada 1990. *In* "Tercer Congreso Internacional de Historia Regional Comparada, 1991," edited by Ricardo Leon Garcia, pp. 47–50. Universidad Autonoma de Ciudad Juarez, Ciudad Juarez.

Kelley, Jane H., and Maria Elisa Villalpando 1996. An Overview of the Mexican Northwest. *In* "Interpreting Southwestern Diversity: Underlying Principles and Overarching Patterns," edited by P. R. Fish and J. Jefferson Reid, Anthropological Research Papers No. 48, pp. 69–77. Arizona State University, Tempe.

Kessell, John L. 1979. "Kiva, Cross, and Crown: The Pecos Indians of New Mexico, 1540–1840." National Park Service, U.S. Government Printing Office, Washington, DC.

Kessell, John L. 1989. Spaniards and Pueblos: From Crusading Intolerance to Pragmatic Accommodation. *In* "Columbian Consequences," edited by David Hurst Thomas, Vol. 1, pp. 127–138. Smithsonian Institution Press, Washington, DC.

Kidder, Alfred Vincent 1917. "The Old North Pueblo of Pecos: the Condition of the Main Pecos Ruin." Archaeological Institute of America Paper No. 38. School of American Research, Santa Fe.

Kidder, Alfred Vincent 1924. "An Introduction to the Study of Southwestern Archaeology, with a Preliminary Account of the Excavations at Pecos," Papers of the Southwest Expedition 1. (Reprinted in 1962 by Yale University Press, New Haven.)

Kidder, Alfred Vincent 1927. Southwestern Archaeological Conference. *Science* **68**:489–491.

Kidder, Alfred Vincent 1931. "The Pottery of Pecos, Vol. 1." Papers of the Phillips Academy Southwestern Expedition 5. Yale University Press, New Haven.

Kidder, Alfred Vincent 1936a. Discussion. *In* "The Pottery of Pecos, Vol. 2, The Glaze-Paint, Culinary, and Other Wares," by Alfred Vincent Kidder and Anna O. Shepard, pp. 589–628. Papers of the Phillips Academy Southwest Expedition 7. Yale University Press, New Haven.

Kidder, Alfred Vincent 1936b. Speculations on New World Prehistory. *In* "Essays in Anthropology Presented to A. L. Kroeber," pp. 143–152. University of California Press, Berkeley.

Kidder, Alfred Vincent 1958. "Pecos, New Mexico: Archaeological Notes." Papers of the Robert S. Peabody Foundation for Archaeology, Volume 5. Phillips Academy, Andover.

Kidder, Alfred Vincent 1962. "An Introduction to the Study of Southwestern Archaeology with a Preliminary Account of the Excavations at Pecos, and a Summary of Southwestern Archaeology Today." Yale University Press, New Haven.

Kidder, Alfred Vincent, and S. J. Guernsey 1919. "Archaeological Exploration in Northeastern Arizona," Bureau of American Ethnology 65. Smithsonian Institution, Washington, DC.

Kidder, Alfred Vincent, and Anna O. Shepard 1936. "The Pottery of Pecos, Vol. 2, The Glaze-Paint, Culinary, and Other Wares." Papers of the Phillips Academy Southwest Expedition 7. Yale University Press, New Haven.

Kincaid, Chris (editor) 1983. "Chaco Roads Project Phase I: A Reappraisal of Prehistoric Roads in the San Juan Basin." Bureau of Land Management, Albuquerque.

Kintigh, Keith W. 1980. "An Archaeological Clearance Survey of Miller Canyon and the Southwest Boundary Fenceline, Zuni Indian Reservation, McKinley County, New Mexico," Ms. on file. Zuni Archaeology Program, Pueblo of Zuni.

Kintigh, Keith W. 1985. "Settlement, Subsistence, and Society in Late Zuni Prehistory," Anthropological Papers No. 44. University of Arizona Press, Tucson.

Kintigh, Keith W. 1994. Chaco, Communal Architecture, and Cibolan Aggregation. *In* "The Ancient Southwestern Community: Models and Methods for the Study of Prehistoric Social Organization," edited by W. H. Wills and Robert D. Leonard, pp. 131–140. University of New Mexico Press, Albuquerque.

Kintigh, Keith W. 1996. The Cibola Region in the Post-Chacoan Era. *In* "The Prehistoric Pueblo World, AD 1150–1350," edited by Michael A. Adler, pp. 131–144. University of Arizona Press, Tucson.

Knight, Paul J. 1978. The Role of Seed Morphology in Identification of Archeological Remains. Unpublished M.S. thesis, Department of Biology, University of New Mexico, Albuquerque.

Knudson, R. 1973. Organizational Variability in Late Paleoindian Assemblages. Ph.D. dissertation, Washington State University, Pullman.

Kohler, Timothy A. 1992. Field Houses, Villages, and the Tragedy of the Commons in the Early Northern Anasazi Southwest. *American Antiquity* **57**:617–635.

Kohler, Timothy A., and M. H. Matthews 1988. Long-Term Anasazi Land Use and Forest Reduction: A Case Study from Southwest Colorado. *American Antiquity* **53**:537–564.

Kohler, Timothy A., and Carla R. Van West 1996. The Calculus of Self-Interest in the Development of Cooperation: Sociopolitical Development and Risk Among the Northern Anasazi. *In* "Evolving Complexity and Environmental Risk in the Prehistoric Southwest," edited by Joseph A. Tainter and Bonnie Bagley Tainter, pp. 169–196. Santa Fe Institute Studies in the Sciences of Complexity, Addison-Wesley Publishing Company, Reading.

Kohler, Timothy A., William D. Lipe, and Allen E. Kane (compilers) 1986. "Dolores Archaeological Program: Anasazi Communities at Dolores: Early Small Settlements in the Dolores River Canyon and Western Sagehen Flats Area." U.S. Dept. of the Interior, Bureau of Reclamation, Engineering and Research Center, Denver.

Kroeber, Alfred L. 1916. Zuni Potsherds. *Anthropological Papers of the American Museum of Natural History* **18**(Part 1).

Lahren, L., and R. Bonnichsen 1974. Bone Foreshafts from A Clovis Burial in Southwestern Montana. *Science* **186**:147–150.

Laird, W. D. 1977. "Hopi Bibliography." University of Arizona Press, Tucson.

Lambert, Marjorie F. 1954. "Paa-Ko: Archaeological Chronicle of an Indian Village in North Central New Mexico," School of American Research Monograph 19. University of New Mexico Press, Albuquerque.

Lance, J. F. 1959. Faunal Remains from the Lehner Mammoth Site. *American Antiquity* **25**: 35–59.

Lang, Richard W. 1977a. "An Archaeological Survey of Certain State Lands within the Drainages of Arroyo de la Vega de los Tanos and Arroyo Tonque de los Tanos and Arroyo Tonque, Sandoval County, New Mexico," Archaeology Contract Program. School of American Research, Santa Fe.

Lang, Richard W. 1977b. "Archeological Survey of the Upper San Cristobal Arroyo Drainage, Galisteo Basin, Santa Fe County, New Mexico," Archaeology Contract Program. School of American Research, Santa Fe.

Lange, Richard C., and Stephen Germick, (editors) 1992. "Proceedings of the Second Salado Conference, Globe, Arizona, 1992." Arizona Archaeological Society, Phoenix.

Larson, Clark Spencer 1995. Biological Changes in the Human Populations with Agriculture. *Annual Review of Anthropology* **24**:185–213.

LeBlanc, Steven A. 1982. The Advent of Pottery in the Southwest. *In* "Southwestern Ceramics: A Comparative Review," edited by Albert H. Schroeder, 15: 27–51. *The Arizona Archaeologist.*

LeBlanc, Steven A. 1983. "The Mimbres People: Ancient Pueblo Potters of the American Southwest." Thames and Hudson, London.

LeBlanc, Steven A. 1989a. Cultural Dynamics in the Southern Mogollon Area. *In* "Dynamics of Southwest Prehistory," edited by L. S. Cordell and G. J. Gumerman, pp. 179–208. Smithsonian Institution Press, Washington, DC.

LeBlanc, Steven A. 1989b. Cibola: Shifting Cultural Boundaries. *In* "Dynamics of Southwest Prehistory," edited by L. S. Cordell and G. J. Gumerman, pp. 337–370. Smithsonian Institution Press, Washington, DC.

Lee, Richard B. 1968. What Hunters Do for a Living, or How to Make Out on Scarce Resources. *In* "Man the Hunter," edited by Richard B. Lee and I. DeVore, pp. 30–48. Aldine, Chicago.

Lee, Richard B., and I. DeVore (editors) 1968. "Man the Hunter." Aldine, Chicago.

Lehmer, D. J. 1948. "The Jornada Branch of the Mogollon," Bulletin 19(2). University of Arizona, Tucson.

Lekson, Stephen H. (editor) 1984. "The Architecture and Dendrochronology of Chetro Ketl, Chaco Canyon, New Mexico," Reports of the Chaco Center No. 6. Division of Cultural Research, National Park Service, Albuquerque.

Lekson, Stephen H. 1986. "Great Pueblo Architecutre of Chaco Canyon, New Mexico." University of New Mexico Press, Albuquerque (Originally published in 1984 as Publications in Archeology No. 18B, Chaco Canyon Studies, National Park Service, Albuquerque.

Lekson, Stephen H. 1991. Settlement Patterns and the Chaco Region. *In* "Chaco and Hohokam: Prehistoric Regional Systems in the American Southwest," edited by Patricia L. Crown and W. James Judge, pp. 31–56. School of American Research Press, Santa Fe.

Lekson, Stephen H. 1992. Salado of the East. *In* "Proceedings of the Second Salado Conference," Globe, Arizona, 1992, edited by Richard C. Lange and Stephen Germick, pp. 17–21. Arizona Archaeological Society, Phoenix.

Lekson, Stephen H. 1996a. Scale and Process in the Southwest. *In* "Interpreting Southwestern Diversity: Underlying Principles and Overarching Patterns," edited by P. R. Fish and J. Jefferson Reid, Anthropological Research Papers No. 48, pp. 81–86. Arizona State University, Tempe.

Lekson, Stephen H. 1996b. Southwestern New Mexico and Southeastern Arizona, AD 900. *In* "The Prehistoric Pueblo World, AD 1150–1350," edited by Michael A. Adler, pp. 170–176. University of Arizona Press, Tucson.

Lekson, Stephen H., Thomas C. Windes, John R. Stein, and W. James Judge 1988. The Chaco Canyon Community. *Scientific American* **256**(7):100–109.

Lenihan, Daniel J., Toni L. Correll, Thomas S. Hopkins, A. Wayne Prokopetz, Sandra L. Rayl, and Cathryn S. Tarasovic 1977. "The Preliminary Report of the National Reservoir Inundation Study." National Park Service, Santa Fe.

Levine, Frances 1991. Economic Perspectives on the Comanchero Trade. *In* "Farmers, Hunters, and Colonists: Interaction between the Southwest and the Southern Plains," edited by Katherine A. Spielmann, pp. 155–170. University of Arizona Press, Tucson.

Levy, Jerrold E. 1992. "Orayvi Revisited: Social Stratification in an "Egalitarian" Society." School of American Research Press, Santa Fe.

Lightfoot, Dale R. 1993. The Landscape Context of Anasazi Pebble-Mulched Fields in the Galisteo Basin, Northern New Mexico. *Geoarchaeology* **8**:349–370.

Lightfoot, Dale R., and Frank W. Eddy 1995. The Construction and Configuration of Anasazi Pebble-Mulch Gardens) in the Northern Rio Grande. *American Antiquity* **60**(3):459–470.

Lightfoot, Kent G. 1984. "Prehistoric Political Dynamics: A Case Study from the American Southwest." Northern Illinois University Press, Dekalb.

Lightfoot, Kent G., and Gary M. Feinman 1982. Social Differentiation and Leadership Development in Early Pithouse Villages in the Mogollon Region of the American Southwest. *American Antiquity* **47**:64–86.

Lightfoot, Ricky R. 1992. Architecture and Tree-Ring Dating at the Duckfoot Site in Southwestern Colorado. *The Kiva* **57**:213–236.

Lindsay, Alexander J., and Calvin H. Jennings 1968. "Salado Red Ware Conference: Ninth Southwestern Ceramic Seminar," Ceramic Series 4. Museum of Northern Arizona, Flagstaff.

Lindsay, Alexander J., J. Richard Ambler, Mary Anne Stein, and Phillip M. Hobler 1968. "Survey and Excavations North and East of Navajo Mountain, Utah. 1959–1962," Bulletin 45. Museum of Northern Arizona, Flagstaff.

Linton, Ralph 1944. Nomadic Raids and Fortified Pueblos. *American Antiquity* **10**:28–32.

Lipe, William D. 1978. The Southwest. *In* "Ancient Native Americans," edited by Jesse D. Jennings, pp. 403–454. Freeman, San Francisco.

Lipe, William D. 1992. Summary and Concluding Comments. *In* "The Sand Canyon Archaeological Project: A Progress Report," edited by William D. Lipe, Occasional Papers No. W, pp. 121–133. Crow Canyon Archaeological Center, Cortez.

Lipe, William D. 1994. Comments on Population Aggregation and Community Organization. *In* "The Ancient Southwestern Community: Models and Methods for the Study of Prehistoric Social Organization," edited by W. H. Wills and Robert D. Leonard, pp. 141–143. University of New Mexico Press, Albuquerque.

Lipe, William D., and Cory D. Breternitz 1980. Approaches to Analyzing Variability among Dolores Structures, A.D. 600–950. *Contract Abstracts and CRM Archeology* **1**(2):21–28.

Lipe, William D., and Timothy A. Kohler 1988. Introduction. *In* "Dolores Archaeological Program: Anasazi Communities at Dolores: Grass Mesa Village," compiled by W. D. Lipe, J. N. Morris, and T. A. Kohler, pp. 1–29. U.S. Dept. of the Interior, Bureau of Reclamation, Engineering and Research Center, Denver.

Lipe, William D., and R. G. Matson 1971. Human Settlement and Resources in the Cedar Mesa Area, Southeast Utah. *In* "The Distribution of Population Aggregates," edited by George J. Gumerman, Anthropological Reports 1, pp. 116–151. Prescott College, Prescott.

Lipe, William D., James N. Morris, and Timothy A. Kohler 1988. "Dolores Archaeological Program: Anasazi Communities at Dolores: Grass Mesa Village." U.S. Dept. of the Interior, Bureau of Reclamation, Engineering and Research Center, Denver.

Lister, Robert H. 1958. "Archaeological Excavations in the Northern Sierra Madre Occidental, Chihuahua and Sonora, Mexico," Series in Anthropology No. 7, University of Colorado Studies, Boulder.

Lister, Robert H. 1966. "Contributions to Mesa Verde Archaeology III: Site 866 and the Cultural Sequence at Four Villages in the Far View Group, Mesa Verde National Park, Colorado," Series in Anthropology 12. University of Colorado Studies, Boulder.

Lister, Robert H., and Florence C. Lister 1981. "Chaco Canyon: Archaeology and Archaeologists." University of New Mexico Press, Albuquerque.

Lomawaima, Hartman H. 1989. Hopification, a Strategy for Cultural Preservation. *In* "Columbian Consequences," edited by David Hurst Thomas, Vol. 1, pp. 93–99. Smithsonian Institution Press, Washington, DC, and London.

Long, A., and Bruce Rippeteau 1974. Testing Contemporaneity and Averaging Radiocarbon Dates. *American Antiquity* **39**:205–215.

Long, A., R. I. Ford, D. J. Donahue, A. T. Jull, T. W. Linick, and T. Zabel 1986. Tandem Accelerator Dating of Archaeological Cultigens. Paper delivered at the 51st Annual Meeting of the Society for American Archaeology, New Orleans.

Longacre, William A. 1964. A Synthesis of Upper Little Colorado Prehistory, Eastern Arizona. *Fieldiana: Anthropology* **55**:201–215.

Longacre, William A. 1968. Some Aspects of Prehistoric Society in East-Central Arizona. *In* "New Perspectives in Archaeology," edited by Sally R. Binford and Lewis R. Binford, pp. 89–102. Aldine, Chicago.

Longacre, William A. 1970. "Archaeology as Anthropology: A Case Study," Anthropological Papers No. 17. University of Arizona, Tucson.

Longacre, William A., and Michael W. Graves 1976. Probability Sampling Applied to an Early Multi-component Surface Site in East-Central Arizona. *The Kiva* **41**(3–4):277–288.

Longacre, William A., and J. Jefferson Reid 1974. The University of Arizona Archaeological Field School at Grasshopper: 11 Years of Multidisciplinary Research and Teaching. *The Kiva* **40**:3–38.

Longacre, William A., Sally J. Holbrook, and Michael W. Graves 1982. "Multidisciplinary Research at Grasshopper Pueblo, Arizona," Anthropological Papers No. 40. University of Arizona, Tucson.

Loose, Richard W., and Thomas R. Lyons 1976. The Chetro Ketl Field: A Planned Water Control System in Chaco Canyon. In "Remote Sensing Experiments in Cultural Resource Studies: Non-destructive Methods of Archeological Exploration, Survey and Analysis," assembled by Thomas R. Lyons, Reports of the Chaco Center No. 1, pp. 133–156. Division of Cultural Research, National Park Service, Albuquerque.

Lösch, A. 1954. "The Economics of Location." Yale University Press, New Haven.

Love, David W. 1980. Quaternary Geology of Chaco Canyon, Northwestern New Mexico. Unpublished Ph.D. dissertation, Department of Geology, University of New Mexico, Albuquerque.

Love, Marian F. 1975. A Survey of the Distribution of T-Shaped Doorways in the Greater Southwest. *In* "Collected Papers in Honor of Florence Hawley Ellis," edited by Theodore R. Frisbie, Paper No. 2. pp. 296–311. Archaeological Society of New Mexico, Santa Fe.

Lowell, Julie C. 1991. "Prehistoric Households at Turkey Creek Pueblo, Arizona," Anthropological Papers No. 54, University of Arizona Press, Tucson.

Lyneis, Margaret M. 1995. The Virgin Anasazi, Far Western Puebloans. *Journal of World Prehistory* **9**:199–241.

Lyneis, Margaret M. 1996. Pueblo II-Pueblo III Change in Southwestern Utah, the Arizona Strip, and Southern Nevada. *In* "The Prehistoric Pueblo World, AD 1150–1350," edited by Michael A. Adler, pp. 11–28. University of Arizona Press, Tucson.

Lyons, Thomas R. and Robert K. Hitchcock 1977. Remote Sensing Interpretation of Anasazi Land Route System. *In* "Aerial Remote Sensing Techniques in Archeology," edited by Thomas R. Lyons and Robert K. Hitchcock, Reports of the Chaco Center 2, pp. 111–134. National Park Service, Southwest Cultural Resource Center, and University of New Mexico, Albuquerque.

Mackey, James C., and Sally J. Holbrook 1978. Environmental Reconstruction and the Abandonment of the Largo-Gallina Area. *Journal of Field Archaeology* **5**(1):29–49.

MacNeish, Richard S. 1958. Preliminary Archaeological Investigations in the Sierra de Tamaulipas, Mexico. *Transactions of the American Philosophical Society* [N.S.] **44**(5).

MacNeish, Richard S. 1964. Ancient Mesoamerican Civilization. *Science* **143**:531–537.

MacNeish, Richard S. 1967. A Summary of the Subsistence. *In* "Environment and Subsistence: The Prehistory of the Tehuacan Valley," edited by Douglas S. Byers, Vol. 1, pp. 290–309. University of Texas Press, Austin.

MacNeish, Richard S. 1971. Speculation about How and Why Food Production and Village Life Developed in the Tehuacan Valley, Mexico. *Archaeology* **24**(4):307–315.

MacNeish, Richard S. (editor) 1980. "Prehistory of the Ayacucho Basin, Peru." University of Michigan Press, Ann Arbor.

MacNeish, Richard S., Geoffrey Cunnar, Gary Jessop, and Peggy Wilner 1994. "A Summary of the Paleo-Indian Discoveries in Pendejo Cave near Orogrande, New Mexico," Annual Report for 1993. Andover Foundation for Archaeological Research, Andover.

Malville, J. McKim, and Gary Matlock (editors) 1993. "Chimney Rock Archaeological Symposium (1990: Durango, CO). The Chimney Rock Archaeological Symposium: October 20–21, 1990, Durango, CO." Rocky Mountain Forest and Range Experiment Station, U.S. Dept. of Agriculture, Fort Collins.

Madsen, David B., and Michael S. Berry 1975. A Reassessment of Northeastern Great Basin Prehistory. *American Antiquity* **40**:82–86.

Mangelsdorf, Paul C. 1954. New Evidence on the Origin and Ancestry of Maize. *American Antiquity* **19**:409–410.

Mangelsdorf, Paul C. 1974. "Corn, Its Origin, Evolution, and Improvement." Harvard University Press, Cambridge.

Mangelsdorf, Paul C., and Robert H. Lister 1956. Archaeological Evidence on the Diffusion and Evolution of Maize in Northern Mexico. *Harvard University Botanical Museum Leaflets* **17**:151–178.

Mangelsdorf, Paul C., H. W. Dick, and J. Camera-Hernandez 1967. Bat Cave Revisited. *Harvard University Botanical Museum Leaflets* **22**:213–260.

Marshall, Michael P. 1991. Ceramic Analysis. *In* "The Prehistoric Cebolla Canyon Community: An Archeological Class III Inventory of 320 Acres of BLM Land at the Mouth of Cebolla Canyon," edited by Frank E. Wozniak and Michael P. Marshall. Office of Contract Archeology, Albuquerque.

Marshall, Michael P., and David E. Doyel 1981. "An Interim Report on Bi sa' ani Pueblo, with Notes on the Chacoan Regional System," Ms. on file. Navajo Nation Cultural Resource Management Program, Window Rock.

Marshall, Michael P., and Henry J. Walt 1984. "Rio Abajo: The Prehistory and History of a Rio Grande Province." New Mexico Historic Preservation Division, Santa Fe.

Marshall, Michael P., John R. Stein, Richard W. Loose, and Judith E. Novotny 1979. "Anasazi Communities of the San Juan Basin." Public Service Company of New Mexico, Albuquerque, and New Mexico Historic Preservation Bureau, Santa Fe.

Martin, Debra L. 1994. Stress Profiles for the Prehistoric Southwest. *In* "Themes in Southwest Prehistory," edited by George J. Gumerman, pp. 87–108. School of American Research Press, Santa Fe.

Martin, Paul S. 1929. The 1928 Archaeological Expedition of the State Historical Society of Colorado. *Colorado Magazine* **6**(1):1–35.

Martin, Paul Schultz 1963. "The Last 10,000 Years." University of Arizona Press, Tucson.

Martin, P. S. 1967. Pleistocene Overkill. *Natural History* **76**:32–38.

Martin, Paul Schultz, and William Byers 1965. Pollen and Archaeology at Wetherill Mesa. *In* "Contributions of the Wetherill Mesa Archaeological Project," edited by D. Osborne, Memoir No. 10, pp. 5–13. Society for American Archaeology, Salt Lake City.

Martin, Paul Schultz, and James Schoenwetter 1960. Arizona's Oldest Cornfield. *Science* **132**: 33–34.

Martin, Paul Schultz, and H. E. Wright (editors) 1967. "Pleistocene Extinctions: The Search for Cause." Yale University Press, New Haven.

Martin, Paul Sidney 1950. Conjectures Concerning the Social Organization of the Mogollon Indians. *Fieldiana: Anthropology* **38**(3):556–569.

Martin, Paul Sidney 1973. The Desert Culture: A Hunting and Gathering Adaptation. *In* "The Archaeology of Arizona, A Study of the Southwest Region," by P. S. Martin and F. Plog, pp. 69–80. Doubleday/Natural History Press, Garden City.

Martin, Paul Sidney 1979. Prehistory: Mogollon. *In* "Southwest," edited by Alfonso A. Ortiz, Handbook of North American Indians, Vol. 9, pp. 61–74. Smithsonian Institution, Washington, DC.

Martin, Paul S., and Richard G. Klein (editors) 1984. "Quaternary Extinctions: A Prehistoric Revolution." University of Arizona Press, Tucson.

Martin, Paul Sidney, and Fred Plog 1973. "The Archaeology of Arizona." Doubleday/Natural History Press, Garden City.

Martin, Paul Sidney, and John B. Rinaldo 1939. Modified Basketmaker Sites, Ackman-Lowry Area, Southwestern Colorado, 1938. *Anthropological Series, Field Museum of Natural History* **23**(3).

Martin, Paul S., and John B. Rinaldo 1947. The Su Site Excavations at a Mogollon Village Western New Mexico: Third Season. *Anthropological Series Field Museum of Natural History* **32,** No. 3.

Martin, Paul Sidney, and John B. Rinaldo 1951. The Southwestern Co tradition. *Southwestern Journal of Anthropology* **7**:215–229.

Martin, Paul Sidney, and John B. Rinaldo 1960. Table Rock Pueblo, Arizona. *Fieldiana: Anthropology* **51**(2).

Martin, Paul Sidney, John B. Rinaldo, and Ernst Antevs 1949. Cochise and Mogollon Sites in Pine Lawn Valley, Western New Mexico. *Fieldiana: Anthropology* **38**(1).

Martin, Paul Sidney, John B. Rinaldo, E. Bluhm, H. C. Cutler, and R. Grange, Jr. 1952. Mogollon Cultural Continuity and Change: The Stratigraphic Analysis of Tularosa and Cordova Caves. *Fieldiana: Anthropology* **40.**

Martin, Paul Sidney, John B. Rinaldo, and Elaine A. Bluhm 1954. Caves of the Reserve Area. *Fieldiana. Anthropology* **42.**

Martin, Paul Sidney, John B. Rinaldo, and William A. Longacre 1961. Mineral Creek Site and Hooper Ranch Pueblo. *Fieldiana: Anthropology* **52.**

Martin, Paul S., John B. Rinaldo, William A. Longacre, Constance Cronin, Leslie G. Freeman, Jr., and James Schoenwetter 1962. Chapters in the Prehistory of Arizona, 1. *Fieldiana: Anthropology* **53.**

Masse, W. Bruce 1980. "Excavations at Gu Achi: A Reappraisal of Hohokam Settlement and Subsistence in the Arizona Papagueria," Publications in Anthropology No. 12. Western Archeological Center, Tucson.

Masse, W. Bruce 1981. Prehistoric Irrigation Systems in the Salt River Valley, Arizona. *Science* **214**:408–415.

Masse, W. Bruce 1991. The Quest for Subsistence Sufficiency and Civilization in the Sonoran Desert. *In* "Chaco and Hohokam: Prehistoric Regional Systems in the American Southwest," edited by Patricia L. Crown and W. James Judge, pp. 195–224. School of American Research Press, Santa Fe.

Mathien, Frances Joan 1990. Three Months on the Jemez Plateau: An Account of Edgar Lee Hewett's 1905 Field Season. *In* "Clues to the Past: Papers in Honor of William M. Sundt," edited by Meliha S. Duran and David T. Kirkpatrick, Papers of the Archaeological Society of New Mexico No. 16, pp. 185–202. Archaeological Society of New Mexico, Albuquerque.

Matson, R. G. 1991. "The Origins of Southwestern Agriculture." University of Arizona Press, Tucson.

Matson, R. G., and Brian Chisholm 1986. Basketmaker II Subsistence: Carbon Isotopes and Other Dietary Indicators from Cedar Mesa, Utah. Paper presented at the 3rd Annual Anasazi Symposium, Monument Valley.

Matson, R. G., and Brian Chisholm 1991. Basketmaker II Subsistence: Carbon Isotopes and Other Dietary Indicators from Cedar Mesa, Utah. *American Antiquity* **56**:444–459.

Matson, R. G., and William D. Lipe 1978. Settlement Patterns on Cedar Mesa: Boom and Bust on the Northern Periphery. *In* "Investigations of the Southwestern Anthropological Research Group: The Proceedings of the 1976 Conference," edited by Robert C. Euler and George J. Gumerman, pp. 1–12. Museum of Northern Arizona, Flagstaff.

Mauldin, Raymond 1993. The Relationship Between Ground Stone and Agricultural Intensification in Western New Mexico. *The Kiva* **58**:317–330.

Maxwell, T. D., and K. F. Anschuetz 1992. The Southwestern Ethnographic Record and Prehistoric Agricultural Diversity. *In* "Gardens in Prehistory: The Archaeology of Settlement Agriculture in Greater Mesoamerica," edited by T. W. Killion, pp. 35–68. University of Alabama Press, Tuscaloosa.

McGregor, John C. 1936. Dating the Eruption of Sunset Crater, Arizona. *American Antiquity* **2**: 15–26.

McGregor, John C. 1937. "Winona Village," Bulletin 12. Museum of Northern Arizona, Flagstaff.

McGregor, John C. 1941. "Architecture and Material Culture. Winona and Ridge Ruin," Part 1, Bulletin 18. Museum of Northern Arizona, Flagstaff.

McGregor, John C. 1943. Burial of an Early American Magician. *Proceedings of the American Philosophical Society* **86**(2):270–298.

McGregor, John C. 1951. "The Cohonina Culture of Northwestern Arizona." University of Illinois Press, Urbana.

McGregor, John C. 1965. "Southwestern Archaeology." University of Illinois Press, Urbana.

McGuire, Randall H. 1980. The Mesoamerican Connection in the Southwest. *The Kiva* **46** (1–2):3–38.

McGuire, Randall H. 1982. Problems in Culture History. *In* "Hohokam and Patayan, Prehistory of Southwestern Arizona," edited by Randall H. McGuire and Michael B. Schiffer, pp. 153–222. Academic Press, New York.

McGuire, Randall H. 1993. Charles Di Peso and the Mesoamerican Connection. *In* "Culture and Contact," edited by Anne I. Woosley and John C. Ravesloot, pp. 23–38. University of New Mexico Press, Albuquerque.

McGuire, Randall H., and Michael B. Schiffer (editors) 1982. "Hohokam and Patayan, Prehistory of Southwestern Arizona." Academic Press, New York.

McGuire, Randall H., and M. E. Villalpando 1989. Prehistory and the making of history in Sonora. *In* "Columbian Consequences. Vol. I. Archaeological and Historical Perspectives on the Spanish Borderlands West," edited by David Hurst Thomas, pp. 159–177. Smithsonian Institution Press, Washington, DC.

McGuire, Randall H., E. Charles Adams, Ben A. Nelson, and Katherine Spielmann 1994. Drawing the Southwest to Scale: Perspectives on Macroregional Relations. *In* "Themes in Southwest Prehistory," edited by George J. Gumerman, pp. 239–266. School of American Research Press, Santa Fe.

McKenna, Peter J. 1984. "The Architecture and Material Culture of 29SJ1360," Reports of the Chaco Center No. 7. Division of Cultural Research, National Park Service, Albuquerque.

McKern, William C. 1939. The Midwestern Taxonomic Method as an Aid to Archaeological Study. *American Antiquity* **4**:301–313.

McManamon, Francis P. 1992. Managing America's Archaeological Resources. *In* "Quandries and Quests: Visions of Archaeology's Future," edited by LuAnn Wandsnider, pp. 25–40. Center for Archaeological Investigations, Carbondale.

Mehringer, P. J., Jr. 1967. Pollen Analysis and Alluvial Chronology. *The Kiva* **32**(3):96–101.

Mehringer, P. J., Jr., and C. Vance Haynes, Jr. 1965. The Pollen Evidence for the Environment of Early Man and Extinct Mammals at the Lehner Mammoth Site, Southeastern Arizona. *American Antiquity* **31**:17–23.

Meltzer, David J. 1991. Altithermal Archaeology and Paleoecology at Mustang Springs, on the Southern High Plains of Texas. *American Antiquity* **52**:236–267.

Meltzer, David J. 1993. Is There a Clovis Adaptation? *In* "Kostenki to Clovis: Upper Paleolithic-Paleo-Indian Adaptations," edited by Olga Soffer and N. D. Praslov, pp. 293–310. Plenum Press, New York.

Meltzer, David J. 1995. Clocking the First Americans. *Annual Review of Anthropology* **24**:21–45.

Merbs, Charles, F. 1989. Patterns of Health and Sickness in the Precontact Southwest. *In* "Columbian Consequences," edited by David Hurst Thomas, Vol. 1, pp. 41–56. Smithsonian Institution Press, Washington, DC.

Merriam, C. Hart 1980. Results of a Biological Survey of the San Francisco Mountain Region and the Desert of the Little Colorado, Arizona. *North American Fauna* **3**:1–113.

Michels, Joseph W., and Carl A. Bebrich 1971. Obsidian Hydration Dating. *In* "Dating Techniques for the Archaeologist," edited by H. N. Michael and Elizabeth K. Ralph, pp. 164–223. MIT Press, Cambridge.

Michels, Joseph W., and Ignatius S. T. Tsong 1980. Obsidian Hydration Dating: Coming of Age. *In* "Advances in Archaeological Method and Theory," edited by Michael B. Schiffer, Vol. 3, pp. 405–439. Academic Press, New York.

Mills, Barbara J. 1996. The Social Context of Production. *In* "Interpreting Southwestern Diversity: Underlying Principles and Overarching Patterns," edited by Paul Fish and J. Jefferson Reid, Anthropological Research Papers No. 48, pp. 121–124. Arizona State University, Tempe.

Mills, Barbara J., and Patricia L. Crown (editors) 1995. "Ceramic Production in the American Southwest." University of Arizona Press, Tucson.

Mindeleff, Cosmos 1896. Aboriginal Remains in Verde Valley, Arizona. *In* 13th Annual Report of the Bureau of American Ethnology, pp. 176–261. Smithsonian Institution, Washington, DC.

Mindeleff, Victor. 1891. A Study of Pueblo Architecture in Tusayan and Cibola. *In* "Eighth Annual Report of the Bureau of American Ethnology for the Years 1886–1887," pp. 3–228. U.S. Government Printing Office, Washington, DC.

Minnis, Paul E. 1980. Domesticating Plants and People in the Greater Southwest. Paper presented at the Advanced Seminar on the Origins of Plant Husbandry in North America, School of American Research, Santa Fe.

Minnis, Paul E. 1981. Economic and Organizational Responses to Food Stress by Non-Stratified Societies: An Example from Prehistoric New Mexico. Unpublished Ph.D. dissertation, Department of Anthropology, University of Michigan, Ann Arbor.

Minnis, Paul E. 1984. Peeking under the Tortilla Curtain: Regional Interaction and Integration on the Northern Periphery of Casas Grandes. *American Archaeology* **4**:181–193.

Minnis, Paul E. 1985. "Social Adaptation to Food Stress: A Prehistoric Southwestern Example." University of Chicago Press, Chicago.

Minnis, Paul E. 1988. Four Examples of Specialized Production at Casas Grandes, Northwestern Chihuahua. *The Kiva* **53**:181–193.

Minnis, Paul E. 1989. Prehistoric Diet in the Northern Southwest, Macroplant Remains from Four Corners Feces. *American Antiquity* **54**:543–563.

Minnis, Paul E. 1991. Famine Foods of the Northern American Desert Borderlands in Historical Perspective. *Journal of Ethnobiology* **11**:231–257.

Minnis, Paul E. 1992. Early Plant Cultivation in the Desert Borderlands of the American West. *In* "The Origins of Agriculture: An International Perspective," edited by C. W. Cowan and P. J. Watson, pp. 121–141. Smithsonian Institution Press, Washington, DC.

Minnis, Paul E. 1996. Notes on Economic Uncertainty and Human Behavior in the Prehistoric North American Southwest. *In* "Evolving Complexity and Environmental Risk in the Prehistoric Southwest," edited by Joseph A. Tainter and Bonnie Bagley Tainter, pp. 57–78. Santa Fe Institute Studies in the Sciences of Complexity, Addison-Wesley Publishing Company, Reading.

Minnis, Paul E., and Charles L. Redman (editors) 1990. "Perspectives on Southwestern Prehistory." Westview Press, Boulder.

Montgomery, R. G., W. Smith, and J. O. Brew 1949. "Franciscan Awatovi: The Excavation and Conjectural Reconstruction of a 17th Century Spanish Mission Establishment at a Hopi Indian Town in Northeastern Arizona," *Papers of the Peabody Museum of American Archaeology and Ethnology*. Harvard University, Cambridge.

Morgan, J. R. 1977. Were Chaco's Great Kivas Ancient Computers of Astronomy? *El Palacio* **83**(1):28–41.

Morris, Donald H. 1969. Red Mountain: An Early Pioneer Period Hohokam Site in the Salt River Valley of Central Arizona. *American Antiquity* **34**:40–53.

Morris, Earl H. 1915. The Excavation of a Ruin near Aztec, San Juan County, New Mexico. *American Anthropologist* **17**:656–684.

Morris, Earl H. 1924. Burials in the Aztec Ruin. The Aztec Ruin Annex. *Anthropological Papers of the American Museum of Natural History* **26**(3,4).

Morris, Earl H. 1928. "Notes on Excavations in the Aztec Ruin," Anthropological Papers No. 26, Part 5. American Museum of Natural History, New York.

Morris, Earl H. 1938. Mummy Cave: Repairing the Watch Tower of the Oldest Consecutively Occupied Cliff Dwelling in North America. *Natural History* **42**(2):127–138.

Morris, Earl H., and Robert F. Burgh 1954. Basket Maker sites near Durango, Colorado. *Carnegie Institution of Washington Publication* **604.**

Moriss, Noel 1931. "The Ancient Culture of the Fremont River in Utah" *Peabody Museum Papers* **12**(3).

Moulard, Barbara 1981. "Within an Underworld Sky: Mimbres Ceramic Art in Context." Twelvetrees Press, Pasadena.

Munson, Patrick J., Paul H. Parmalee, and Richard A. Yarnell 1971. Subsistence Ecology of Scovill, A Terminal Middle Woodland Village. *American Antiquity* **36**:410–431.

Murdock, George Peter 1949. "Social Structure." Macmillan, New York.

Musil, Robert R. 1988. Functional Efficiency and Technological Change: A Hafting Tradition Model for Prehistoric North America. *In* "Early Human Occupation in Far Western North America: The Clovis Archaic Interface," edited by J. A. Willig, C. M. Aikens, and J. L. Fagan, Anthropological Papers, Vol. 21, pp. 373–388. Nevada State Museum, Carson.

Nabhan, Gary Paul 1977. Viable Seeds from Prehistoric Caches? Archaeobotanical Remains in Southwestern Folklore. *The Kiva* **43**(3):143–159.

Nabhan, Gary Paul 1985. "Gathering the Desert." University of Arizona Press, Tucson.

Nabhan, Gary Paul 1989. "Enduring Seeds, Native American Agriculture and Wild Plant Conservation." North Point Press, Berkeley.

Nagata, Shuichi 1970. "Modern Transformations of Moenkopi Pueblo," Illinois Studies in Anthropology 6. University of Illinois Press, Urbana.

Neitzel, Jill 1991. Hohokam Material Culture and Behavior: The Dimensions of Organizational Change. *In* "Exploring The Hohokam: Prehistoric Desert Peoples of the American Southwest," edited by George J. Gumerman, pp. 177–231. University of New Mexico Press, Albuquerque.

Neitzel, Jill (editor) In Press. "Great Towns and Regional Polities: Late Prehistoric Sociopolitical Organization in the U.S. Southwest and Southeast," Amerind New World Studies Series, Vol. 3. Amerind Foundation and University of New Mexico Press, Albuquerque.

Neller, E. 1976. "Botanical Analysis in Atlatl Cave," Ms. on file. Southwest Cultural Resources Center, National Park Service, Albuquerque.

Nelson, Ben A., and Linda S. Cordell 1982. Dynamics of the Anasazi Adaptation. *In* "Anasazi and Navajo Land Use in the McKinley Mine Area near Gallup, New Mexico," edited by Christina G. Allen and Ben A. Nelson, Vol. 1, Part 1, pp. 867–893. Office of Contract Archeology, University of New Mexico, Albuquerque.

Nelson, Ben A., and Steven A. LeBlanc 1986. "Short-Term Sedentism in the American Southwest, The Mimbres Valley Salado." Maxwell Museum of Anthropology and the University of New Mexico Press, Albuquerque.

Nelson, Ben A., Debra L. Martin, Alan C. Swedlund, Paul R. Fish, and George J. Armelagos 1994. Studies in Disruption: Demography and Health in the Prehistoric Southwest. *In* "Understanding Complexity in the Prehistoric Southwest," edited by George J. Gumerman and Murray Gell-Mann, pp. 59–112. Addison-Wesley Publishing Company, Reading.

Nelson, Margaret C. 1981. Chipped Stone Analysis in the Reconstruction of Prehistoric Subsistence Practice: An Example From Southwestern New Mexico. Unpublished Ph.D. dissertation, Department of Anthropology, University of California, Santa Barbara.

Nelson, Nels C. 1914. Pueblo Ruins of the Galisteo Basin, New Mexico. *Anthropological Papers of the American Museum of Natural History* **15**(Part 1).

Nelson, Nels C. 1916. Chronology of the Tano Ruins, New Mexico. *American Anthropologist* **18**: 159–180.

Nelson, Richard S. 1981. The Role of a Pochteca System in Hohokam Exchange. Ph.D. dissertation, Department of Anthropology, New York University, New York.

Nesbitt, Paul 1931. "The Ancient Mimbrenos, Based on Investigations at the Mattocks Ruin," Bulletin 4. Logan Museum, Mimbres Valley.

Nials, Fred, David Gregory, and Donald Graybill 1989. Salt River Streamflow and Hohokam Irrigation Systems. *In* "The 1982–1984 Excavations at Las Clinas: Environment and Subsistence," edited by C. Heathington and D. Gregory, Archaeological Series 162, pp. 59–78. Arizona State University, Tempe.

Nicholas, L. M., and J. E. Neitzel 1984. Canal Irrigation and Sociopolitical Organization in the Lower Salt River Valley: A Diachronic Analysis. *In* "Prehistoric Agricultural Strategies in the Southwest," edited by S. K. Fish and P. R. Fish, Anthropological Research Papers No. 33, pp. 161–178. Arizona State University, Tempe.

Nicholas, Linda M. 1981. Irrigation and Sociopolitical Development—The Salt River Valley, Arizona: An Examination of Three Prehistoric Canal Systems. M.A. thesis, Department of Anthropology, Arizona State University, Tempe.

Nichols, Deborah L., and F. E. Smiley 1985. An Overview of Northern Black Mesa. *In* "Excavations on Black Mesa, 1983, A Descriptive Report, edited by A. L. Christenson and W. J. Perry, Center for Archaeological Investigations Research Paper 46, pp. 47–82. Southern Illinois University, Carbondale.

North, Douglass C., and Robert Paul Thomas 1973. "The Rise of the Western World: A New Economic History." Cambridge University Press, Cambridge.

Noy-Meir, I. 1973. Desert Ecosystems: Environment and Producers. *Annual Review of Ecology and Systematics* **4**:25–51.

Noy-Meir, I. 1974. Desert Ecosystems: Higher Trophic Levels. *Annual Review of Ecology and Systematics* **5**:195–214.

Obenauf, Margaret 1980. The Chacoan Roadway System. Unpublished M.A. thesis, Department of Anthropology, University of New Mexico, Albuquerque.

O'Bryan, Deric 1950. "Excavations in Mesa Verde National Park, 1947–1948," Medallion Papers 39. Gila Pueblo, Globe.

O'Laughlin, Thomas C. 1980. "The Keystone Dam Site and Other Archaic and Formative Sites in Northwest El Paso, Texas," Publication No. 8. El Paso Centennial Museum, University of Texas at El Paso.

Oldfield, F., and James Schoenwetter 1975. Discussion of the Pollen Analytical Evidence. *In* "Late Pleistocene Environments of the Southern High Plains," edited by Fred Wendorf and James J. Hester, Fort Burgwin Research Center Publication 9, pp. 149–171. Southern Methodist University, Dallas.

Olson, A. P. 1966. A Mass Secondary Burial from Northern Arizona. *American Antiquity* **31**: 822–826.

Opler, Morris E. 1983. The Apachean Culture Pattern and its Origins. *In* "Southwest," edited by Alfonso A. Ortiz, Handbook of North American Indians, Vol. 10, pp. 368–392. Smithsonian Institution, Washington, DC.

Orcutt, Janet D. 1991. Environmental Variability and Settlement Changes on the Pajarito Plateau, New Mexico. *American Antiquity* **56**(2):315–332.

Ortiz, Alfonso A. (editor) 1979. "Southwest," Handbook of North American Indians, Vol. 9. Smithsonian Institution, Washington, DC.

Ortiz, Alfonso A. (editor) 1983. "Southwest," Handbook of North American Indians, Vol. 10. Smithsonian Institution, Washington, DC.

Osborn, Alan J. 1993. Snowblind in the Desert Southwest: Moisture Islands, Ungulate Ecology, and Alternative Prehistoric Overwintering Strategies. *Journal of Anthropological Research* **49**: 135–164.

Pailes, Richard A. 1963. An Analysis of the Fitch Site and its Relationship to the Hohokam Classic Period. M.A. thesis, Department of Anthropology, Arizona State University, Tempe.

Pailes, Richard A. 1990. Elite Formation and Interregional Exchanges in Peripheries. *In* "Perspectives on Southwestern Prehistory," edited by Paul E. Minnis and Charles L. Redman, pp. 213–222. Westview Press, Boulder.

Parry, William, F. E. Smiley, and Galen Burgett 1994. The Archaic Occupation of Black Mesa, Arizona. *In* "Archaic Hunter-Gatherer Archaeology in the American Southwest," edited by Bradley J. Vierra, Contributions in Anthropology 13(1). pp. 185–230. Eastern New Mexico University, Portales.

Parsons, Elsie C. 1939. "Pueblo Indian Religion." University of Chicago Press, Chicago.

Pepper, George H. 1920. Pueblo Bonito. *Anthropological Papers of the American Museum of Natural History* **27**.

Phillips, David A. 1989. Prehistory of Chihuahua and Sonora, Mexico. *Journal of World Prehistory* **3**(4):373–401.

Pilles, Peter J., Jr. 1979. Sunset Crater and the Sinagua: A New Interpretation. *In* "Volcanic Activity and Human Ecology," edited by Payson D. Sheets and Donald K. Grayson, pp. 459–485. Academic Press, New York.

Pilles, Peter J., Jr. 1996. The Pueblo II Period along the Mogollon Rim: The Honanki, Elden, and Turkey Hill Phases of the Sinagua. *In* "The Prehistoric Pueblo World, AD 1150–1350," edited by Michael A. Adler, pp. 59–72. University of Arizona Press, Tucson.

Pippin, Lonnie C. 1987. "Prehistory and Paleoecology of Guadalupe Ruin, New Mexico." University of Utah Press, Salt Lake City.

Plog, Fred T. 1974. "The Study of Prehistoric Change." Academic Press, New York.

Plog, Fred T. 1978. The Keresan Bridge: an Ecological and Archaeological Analysis. *In* "Social Archaeology: Beyond Subsistence and Dating," edited by Charles L. Redman, E. B. Curtin, N. M. Versaggi, and J. L. Wagner, pp. 349–372. Academic Press, New York.

Plog, Fred 1979. Alternative Models of Prehistoric Change. *In* "Transformations, Mathematical Approaches to Culture Change," edited by Colin Renfrew and Kenneth L. Cooke, pp. 221–236. Academic Press, New York.

Plog, Fred 1980. Explaining Culture Change in the Hohokam Preclassic. *In* "Current Issues in Hohokam Prehistory: Proceedings of a Symposium," edited by David Doyel and Fred Plog, Anthropological Research Papers 23, pp. 4–22. Arizona State University, Tempe.

Plog, Fred 1983. Political and Economic Alliances on the Colorado Plateaus, AD 400 to 1450. *World Archaeology* 2:289–330.

Plog, Fred 1983a. The Sinagua and Their Relations. Paper presented at the School of American Research Advanced Seminar on Dynamics of Southwest Prehistory, October 1983, Santa Fe.

Plog, Fred 1983b. Political and Economic Alliances on the Colorado Plateaus, A.D. 400–1450. *In* "Advances in World Archaeology," edited by Fred Wendorf and A. Close, Vol. 2, pp. 289–330. Academic Press, New York.

Plog, Fred, and Cheryl K. Garrett 1972. Explaining Variability in Prehistoric Southwestern Water Systems. *In* "Contemporary Archaeology: A Guide to Theory and Contributions," edited by Mark P. Leone, pp. 280–288. Southern Illinois University Press, Carbondale.

Plog, Fred, Richard Effland, and Dee F. Green 1978. Inferences Using the SARG Data Bank. *In* "Investigations of the Southwestern Anthropological Research Group: An Experiment in Cooperation," edited by Robert C. Euler and George J. Gumerman, pp. 139–148. Museum of Northern Arizona, Flagstaff.

Plog, Fred, George J. Gumerman, Robert C. Euler, Jeffrey S. Dean, Richard H. Hevley, and Thor N. V. Karlstrom 1988. Anasazi Adaptive Strategies: The Model, Predictions, and Results. *In* "The Anasazi in a Changing Environment," edited by George J. Gumerman, pp. 230–276. Cambridge University Press, Cambridge.

Plog, Fred, and Walter Wait (editors) 1979. "The San Juan Tomorrow. Planning for the Conservation of Cultural Resources in the San Juan Basin." Published by the National Park Service, Southwest Region, in cooperation with the School of American Research, Santa Fe.

Plog, Stephen E. 1980. "Stylistic Variation in Prehistoric Ceramics: Design Analysis in the American Southwest." Cambridge University Press, New York.

Powell, Shirley L. 1983. "Mobility and Adaptation: the Anasazi of Black Mesa, Arizona." Southern Illinois University Press, Carbondale.

Powell, Shirley 1988. Anasazi Demographic Patterns and Organizational Responses: Assumptions and Interpretive Difficulties. *In* "The Anasazi in a Changing Environment," edited by George J. Gumerman, pp. 168–191. Cambridge University Press, Cambridge.

Powers, Robert P., William B. Gillespie, and Stephen H. Lekson 1983. "The Outlier Survey: A Regional View of Settlement in the San Juan Basin," Reports of the Chaco Center No. 3. Division of Cultural Research, National Park Service, Albuquerque.

Powers, W. E. 1939. Basin and Shore Features of the Extinct Lake San Agustin, New Mexico. *Journal of Geomorphology* **2**:345–356.

Propper, Judith G. 1988. The Program: Managing Cultural Resources in the Southwestern Region. *In* "Tools to Manage the Past: Research Priorities for Cultural Resources Management in the Southwest," edited by Joseph A. Tainter and R. H. Hamre, pp. 12–16. *USDA Forest Service General Technical Report* **RM-164.** Symposium Proceedings, Grand Canyon, AZ, 1988.

Prudden, T. Mitchell 1903. The Prehistoric Ruins of the San Juan Watershed of Utah, Arizona, Colorado, and New Mexico. *American Anthropologist* **5**:224–228.

Prudden, T. Mitchell 1914. The Circular Kivas of Small Ruins in the San Juan Watershed. *American Anthropologist* **16**:33–58.

Prudden, T. Mitchell 1918. A Further Study of Prehistoric Small House Ruins in the San Juan Watershed. *Memoirs of the American Anthropological Association* **5**(1).

Raab, M. L. 1977. The Santa Rosa Wash Project: Notes on Archaeological Research Design under Contract. *In* "Conservation Archaeology," edited by Michael B. Schiffer and George J. Gumerman, pp. 167–182. Academic Press, New York.

Raish, Carol 1992. "Domestic Animals and Stability in Pre-State Farming Societies," BAR International Series No. 579. Tempvs Repartvm, Oxford.

Ralph, Elizabeth K. 1971. Carbon-14 Dating. *In* "Dating Techniques for the Archaeologist," edited by H. N. Michael and Elizabeth K. Ralph, pp. 1–48. MIT Press, Cambridge.

Rautman, Alison E. 1993. Resource Variability, Risk, and the Structure of Social Networks: An Example from the Prehistoric Southwest. *American Antiquity* **58**:403–424.

Rautman, Alison E. 1996. Risk, Reciprocity, and the Operation of Social Networks. *In* "Evolving Complexity and Environmental Risk in the Prehistoric Southwest," edited by J. A. Tainter and B. Bagley Tainter, pp. 197–222. Santa Fe Institute Studies in the Sciences of Complexity, Addison-Wesley Publishing Company, Reading.

Reed, Erik K. 1946. The Distinctive Features of the San Juan Anasazi Culture. *Southwestern Journal of Anthropology* **2**:295–305.

Reed, Erik K. 1948. The Western Pueblo Archaeological Complex. *El Palacio* **55**(1):9–15.

Reed, Erik K. 1949. Sources of Upper Rio Grande Pueblo Culture and Population. *El Palacio* **56**:163–184.

Reed, Erik K. 1956. Types of Village-Plan Layouts in the Southwest. *In* "Prehistoric Settlement Patterns in the New World," edited by Gordon R. Willey, Viking Fund Publications in Anthropology 23, pp. 11–17.

Reed, Erik K. 1964. The Greater Southwest. *In* "Prehistoric Man in the New World," edited by Jesse D. Jennings and Edward Norbeck, pp. 175–193. University of Chicago Press, Chicago.

Reed, Lori Stephens, and Paul F. Reed 1992a. "Cultural Diversity and Adaptation: The Archaic, Anasazi, and Navajo Occupation of the Upper San Juan Basin," Cultural Resources Series No. 9. New Mexico Bureau of Land Management, Santa Fe.

Reed, Lori Stephens, and Paul F. Reed 1992b. The Protohistoric Navajo: Implications of Interaction, Exchange, and Alliance Formation with the Eastern and Western Pueblos. *In* "Cultural Diversity and Adaptation: The Archaic, Anasazi, and Navajo Occupation of The Upper San Juan Basin," Cultural Resources Series No. 9, pp. 91–104. New Mexico Bureau of Land Management, Santa Fe.

Reher, Charles A. 1977a. Adaptive Processes on the Shortgrass Plains. *In* "For Theory Building in Archaeology," edited by Lewis R. Binford, pp. 13–40. Academic Press, New York.

Reher, Charles A. (editor) 1977b. "Settlement and Subsistence along the Lower Chaco River: The CGP Survey." University of New Mexico Press, Albuquerque.

Reher, Charles A., and D. C. Witter 1977. Archaic Settlement and Vegetative Diversity. *In* "Settlement and Subsistence along the Lower Chaco River: The CGP Survey," edited by Charles A. Reher, pp. 113–126. University of New Mexico Press, Albuquerque.

Reid, J. Jefferson 1986. Emil W. Haury: The Archaeologist as Humanist and Scientist. *In* "Emil W. Haury's Prehistory of the American Southwest," edited by J. Jefferson Reid and David E. Doyel, pp. 3–17. University of Arizona Press, Tucson.

Reid, J. Jefferson 1989. A Grasshopper Perspective on the Mogollon of the Arizona Mountains. *In* "Dynamics of Southwest Prehistory," edited by Linda S. Cordell and George J. Gumerman, pp. 65–98. Smithsonian Institution Press, Washington, DC.

Reid, J. Jefferson, and Stephanie M. Whittlesey 1990. The Complicated and the Complex: Observations on the Archaeological Record of Large Pueblos. *In* "Perspectives on Southwestern Prehistory," edited by Paul E. Minnis and Charles L. Redman, pp. 184–195. Westview Press, Boulder.

Reid, J. Jefferson, John R. Welch, Barbara Montgomery, and Maria Nieves Zedeño 1996. A Demographic Overview of the Late Pueblo II Period in the Mountains of East-Central Arizona. *In* "The Prehistoric Pueblo World, AD 1150–1350," edited by Michael A. Adler, pp. 73–85. University of Arizona Press, Tucson.

Reiter, Paul 1938. "The Jemez Pueblo of Unshagi, New Mexico, with Notes on the Earlier Excavations at "Amoxiumqua" and Giusewa," Bulletin 326, Monograph Series 1(4). University of New Mexico, Albuquerque.

Renfrew, Colin 1977. Alternative Models for Exchange and Spatial Distribution. *In* "Exchange Systems in Prehistory," edited by T. K. Earle and J. E. Erickson, pp. 71–90. Academic Press, New York.

Renfrew, Colin 1978. The Simulator as Demiurge. Paper presented at the Symposium on Simulating the Past, School of American Research, Santa Fe.

Reyman, Jonathan E. 1976. Astronomy, Architecture, and Adaptation at Pueblo Bonito. *Science* **193**:957–962.

Reyman, Jonathan E. 1978. Pochteca Burial at Anasazi Sites. *In* "Across the Chichimec Sea: Papers in Honor of J. Charles Kelley," edited by Carroll L. Riley and Basil C. Hedrick, pp. 242–259. Southern Illinois University Press, Carbondale.

Reyman, Jonathan E. 1980. An Anasazi Solar Marker? *Science* **209**:858–859.

Rice, Glen E. 1980. An Analytical Overview of the Mogollon Tradition. *In* "Studies in the Prehistory of the Forestdale Region, Arizona," edited by C. R. Stafford and Glen E. Rice, Anthropological Field Studies 1, pp. 9–40. Office of Cultural Resource Management, Department of Anthropology, Arizona State University, Tempe.

Riley, Carroll L. 1987. "The Frontier People, the Greater Southwest in the Protohistoric Period," Revised and expanded edition. University of New Mexico Press, Albuquerque.

Rinaldo, John B. 1974. Projectile Points. *In* "Casas Grandes: A Fallen Trading Center of the Gran Chichimeca," by Charles Di Peso, John B. Rinaldo, and G. J. Fenner, Vol. 7, pp. 389–398. The Amerind Foundation, Dragoon, and Northland Press, Flagstaff.

Roberts, Frank H. H., Jr. 1929. "Shabik'eschee Village: A Late Basketmaker Site in the Chaco Canyon, New Mexico," Bulletin 92. Bureau of American Ethnology, Smithsonian Institution, Washington, DC.

Roberts, Frank H. H., Jr. 1935a. A Folsom Complex: Preliminary Report on Investigations at the Lindenmeier Site in Northern Colorado. *Smithsonian Institution Miscellaneous Collections* **49.**

Roberts, Frank H. H., Jr. 1935b. A Survey of Southwestern Archaeology. *American Anthropologist* **37**:1–33.

Roberts, Frank H. H., Jr. 1936. Additional Information on the Folsom Complex: Report on the Second Season's Investigations at the Lindenmeier Site in Northern Colorado. *Smithsonian Institution Miscellaneous Collections* **95**(10).

Roberts, Frank H. H., Jr. 1938. "The Folsom Problem in American Archaeology," Annual Report of the Smithsonian Institution, pp. 531–546. U.S. Government Printing Office, Washington, DC.

Roberts, Frank H. H., Jr. 1939. "Archaeological Remains in the Whitewater District, Eastern Arizona," Part I—House Types, Bulletin 121. Bureau of American Ethnology, Washington, DC.

Robertson, Benjamin P. 1983. Other New World Roads and Trails. *In* "Chaco Roads Project," assembled and edited by Chris Kincaid, pp. 2.1–2.23. Draft ms. on file. Bureau of Land Management, State Office, Santa Fe.

Robinson, David G. 1980. Ceramic Technology and Later Pine Lawn/Reserve Branch Exchange Systems. Paper presented at the 45th Annual Meeting of the Society for American Archaeology, Philadelphia.

Robinson, William J. 1979. "Preliminary Report to the Chaco Center," Ms. on file. Southwest Cultural Resource Center, National Park Service, Albuquerque.

Robinson, William J., and Catherine M. Cameron 1991. "A Directory of Tree-Ring Dated Prehistoric Sites in the American Southwest." Laboratory of Tree-Ring Research, University of Arizona, Tucson.

Rogers, Malcom J. 1939. "Early Lithic Industries of the Lower Basin of the Colorado River and Adjacent Desert Areas," San Diego Museum Papers 3. Museum of Man, San Diego.

Rogers, Malcom J. 1945. An Outline of Yuman Prehistory. *Southwestern Journal of Anthropology* **1**:167–198.

Rogers, M. J. 1958. San Dieguito Implements from the Terraces of the Rincon-Patano and Rillito Drainage System. *The Kiva* **24**(1):1–23.

Rohn, Arthur H. 1971. "Mug House, Mesa Verde National Park, Colorado," Archaeological Research Series 7D. National Park Service, Washington, DC.

Rohn, Arthur H. 1977. "Cultural Change and Continuity on Chapin Mesa." The Regents Press of Kansas, Lawrence.

Rohn, Arthur H. 1989. Northern San Juan Prehistory. *In* "Dynamics of Southwest Prehistory," edited by Linda S. Cordell and George J. Gumerman, pp. 149–178. Smithsonian Institution Press, Washington, DC.

Roney, John R. 1995. Mesa Verdean Manifestations South of the San Juan River. *Journal of Anthropological Archaeology* **14**(2):170–183.

Roney, John R. 1996. The Pueblo II Period in the Eastern San Juan Basin and Acoma-Laguna Areas. *In* "The Prehistoric Pueblo World, AD 1150–1350," edited by Michael A. Adler, pp. 73–85. University of Arizona Press, Tucson.

Roosa, William B. 1956a. Preliminary Report on the Lucy Site. *El Palacio* **63**:36–49.

Roosa, William B. 1956b. The Lucy Site in Central New Mexico. *American Antiquity* **21**:310.

Rose, Martin R., Jeffrey S. Dean, and William J. Robinson 1981. "The Past Climate of Arroyo Hondo, New Mexico, Reconstructed from Tree Rings," Arroyo Hondo Archaeological Series 4. School of American Research, Santa Fe.

Rosenthal, E. J., D. R. Brown, M. Severson, and J. B. Clonts 1978. "The Quijota Valley Project." National Park Service, Western Archaeological Center, Tucson.

Rouse, Irving 1958. The Inference of Migration from Anthropological Evidence. *In* "Migrations in New World Cultural History," edited by R. H. Thompson, Social Science Bulletin 27, Bulletin 29, pp. 63–68. University of Arizona, Tucson.

Ruppé, Reynold J., Jr. 1953. The Acoma Culture Province: An Archaeological Concept. Unpublished Ph.D. dissertation, Department of Anthropology, Harvard University, Cambridge.

Ruppé, Reynold J., Jr. 1966. The Archaeological Survey: A Defense. *American Antiquity* **31**: 313–333.

Russell, G. S. 1981. Preliminary Results of the Redondo Valley Obsidian Study. *In* "High Altitude Adaptations along Redondo Creek: The Baca Geothermal Project," edited by Craig Baker and Joseph C. Winter, pp. 363–370. Office of Contract Archeology, University of New Mexico, Albuquerque.

Rutter, N. W. 1980. Late Pleistocene History of the Western Canadian Ice-Free Corridor. *Canadian Journal of Anthropology* **1**(1):1–8.

Sahagun, Fray Bernardino de 1959. Florentine Codex: General History of the Things of New Spain. *In* "Book 9: The Merchants," edited and translated by A. J. O. Anderson and C. E. Dibble. School of American Research, Santa Fe, and University of Utah, Salt Lake City.

Saitta, Dean J. 1994. Class and Community in the Prehistoric Southwest. *In* "The Ancient Southwestern Community: Models and Methods for the Study of Prehistoric Social Organization," edited by W. H. Wills and Robert D. Leonard, pp. 25–44. University of New Mexico Press, Albuquerque.

Sanders, William T., Jeffrey R. Parsons, and Robert S. Santley 1979. "The Basin of Mexico: Ecological Processes in the Evolution of a Civilization." Academic Press, New York.

Sanders, William T., and Robert S. Santley 1978. Review of Monte Alban, Settlement Patterns at the Ancient Zapotec Capital by R. E. Blanton. *Science* **202**:303–304.

Sanders, William T., and D. Webster 1978. Unilinealism, Multilinealism, and the Evolution of Complex Societies. *In* "Social Archaeology: Beyond Subsistence and Dating," edited by Charles L. Redman, Mary J. Berman, E. B. Curtin, N. M. Versaggi, and J. L. Wagner, pp. 249–302. Academic Press, New York.

Sando, Joe S. 1992. "Pueblo Nations Eight Centuries of Pueblo Indian History." Clear Light Publishers, Santa Fe.

Sandor, J. A., P. L. Gersper, and J. W. Hawley 1990. Prehistoric Agricultural Terraces and Soils in the Mimbres Area, New Mexico. *World Archaeology* **22**(1):70–86.

Saunders, J. J. 1980. A Model for Man-Mammoth Relationships in Late Pleistocene North America. *Canadian Journal of Anthropology* **1**(1)87–98.

Saunders, Lyle 1944. "A Guide to Materials Bearing on Cultural Relations in New Mexico." University of New Mexico Press, Albuquerque.

Saxe, Arthur 1970. Social Dimensions of Mortuary Practices. Ph.D. dissertation, University of Michigan, Ann Arbor.

Sayles, E. B. 1945. "The San Simon Branch, Excavations at Cave Creek and in the San Simon Valley. I. Material Culture," Medallion Papers 34. Gila Pueblo, Globe.

Sayles, E. B. 1983. "The Cochise Cultural Sequence in Southeastern Arizona," Anthropological Papers No. 42. University of Arizona, Tucson.

Sayles, E. B., and A. Antevs 1941. "The Cochise Culture," Medallion Papers 29. Gila Pueblo, Globe.

Scarborough, Vernon, L., and David R. Wilcox (editors) 1991. "The Mesoamerican Ballgame." University of Arizona Press, Tucson.

Schaafsma, Curtis F. 1976. "Archaeological Survey of Maximum Pool and Navajo Excavations at Abiquiu Reservoir, Rio Arriba County, New Mexico." School of American Research, Santa Fe.

Schaafsma, Polly 1971. "The Rock Art of Utah from the Donald Scott Collection" *Papers of the Peabody Museum of Archaeology and Ethnology* **65**.

Schaafsma, Polly 1980. "Indian Rock Art of the Southwest." School of American Research, Santa Fe, and University of New Mexico Press, Albuquerque.

Schaafsma, Polly (editor) 1994a. "Kachinas in the Pueblo World." University of New Mexico Press, Albuquerque.

Schaafsma, Polly (editor) 1994b. The Prehistoric Kachina Cult and Its Origins as Suggested by Southwestern Rock Art. *In* "Kachinas in the Pueblo World," edited by Polly Schaafsma, pp. 63–80. University of New Mexico Press, Albuquerque.

Schaafsma, Polly, and Curtis F. Schaafsma 1974. Evidence for the Origins of Pueblo Katchina Cult as Suggested by Southwestern Rock Art. *American Antiquity* **39**:535–545.

Schelberg, John D. 1992. Hierarchical Organization as a Short-Term Buffering Strategy in Chaco Canyon. *In* "Anasazi Regional Organization and the Chaco System," edited by David E. Doyel, Anthropological Papers No. 5, pp. 59–74. Maxwell Museum of Anthropology, Albuquerque.

Schiffer, Michael B. 1972. Cultural Laws and Reconstruction of Past Lifeways. *The Kiva* **37**: 148–157.

Schiffer, Michael B. 1976. "Behavioral Archaeology." Academic Press, New York.

Schiffer, Michael B. 1982. Hohokam Chronology: An Essay on History and Method. *In* "Hohokam and Patayan: Prehistory of Southwestern Arizona," edited by Randall H. McGuire and Michael B. Schiffer, pp. 299–344. Academic Press, New York.

Schiffer, Michael B. 1983. Toward the Identification of Formation Processes. *American Antiquity* **48**:675–706.

Schmidt, E. F. 1926. The Mrs. William Boyce Thompson Expedition. *Natural History* (Nov.–Dec.):635–644.

Schmidt, E. F. 1928. Time-Relations of Prehistory Pottery in Southern Arizona. *Anthropological Papers of the American Museum of Natural History* **30**:245–302.

Schoenwetter, James 1966. A Re-evaluation of the Navajo Reservoir Pollen Chronology. *El Palacio* **73**(1):19–26.

Schoenwetter, James, and Alfred E. Dittert, Jr. 1968. An Ecological Interpretation of Anasazi Settlement Patterns. *In* "Anthropological Archaeology in the Americas," edited by Betty J. Meggers, pp. 41–66. Anthropological Society of Washington, Washington, DC.

Schroeder, Albert H. 1952. "The Excavations at Willow Beach, Arizona, 1950." National Park Service, Santa Fe.

Schroeder, Albert H. 1953a. Brief History of the Chama Basin. In "Salvage Archaeology in the Chama Valley, New Mexico," edited by Fred Wendorf, Monograph No. 17, pp. 5–8. School of American Research, Santa Fe.

Schroeder, Albert H. 1953b. The Problem of Hohokam, Sinagua, and Salado Relations in Southern Arizona. *Plateau* **26**(2):75–83.

Schroeder, Albert H. 1957. The Hakataya Cultural Tradition. *American Antiquity* **23**:176–178.

Schroeder, Albert H. 1958. Ware 16: Lower Colorado Buffware. *In* "Pottery Types of the Southwest," edited by Harold S. Colton, Ceramic Series 3D. Museum of Northern Arizona, Flagstaff.

Schroeder, Albert H. 1960. "The Hohokam, Sinagua, and Hakataya," Archives of Archaeology 5. Society for American Archaeology.

Schroeder, Albert H. 1965. Unregulated Diffusion from Mexico into the Southwest prior to AD 700. *American Antiquity* **30**:297–309.

Schroeder, Albert H. 1979a. Prehistory: Hakataya. *In* "Southwest," edited by Alfonso A. Ortiz, Handbook of North American Indians, Vol. 9, pp. 100–107. Smithsonian Institution, Washington, DC.

Schroeder, Albert H. 1979b. Pueblos Abandoned in Historic Times. *In* "Southwest," edited by Alfonso A. Ortiz, Handbook of North American Indians, Vol. 9, pp. 236–254. Smithsonian Institution, Washington, DC.

Schroeder, Albert H. 1982. "Southwestern Ceramics: A Comparative Review." *The Arizona Archaeologist* No. 15, Phoenix.

Schulman, Edmund 1956. "Dendroclimatic Changes in Semiarid America." University of Arizona Press, Tucson.

Schwartz, Douglas W. 1956. The Havasupai, 600 AD–1955 AD: A Short Culture History. *Plateau* **28**(4):77–85.

Schwartz, Douglas W. 1959. Culture Area and Time Depth: The Four Worlds of the Havasupai. *American Anthropologist* **61**:1060–1070.

Schwartz, Douglas W., and Richard W. Lang 1972. "Archaeological Investigations at the Arroyo Hondo Site, Third Field Report, 1972." School of American Research, Santa Fe.

Scudder, T. 1962. "The Ecology of the Gwembe Tonga." Rhodes-Livingstone Institute, Manchester.

Scudder, Thayer 1971. "Gathering Among African Woodland Savannah Cultivators. A Case Study: The Gwembe Tonga." Manchester University Press, Manchester.

Sebastian, Lynne 1991. Chaco Canyon and the Anasazi Southwest: Changing View of Sociopolitical Organization. *In* "Anasazi Regional Organization and the Chaco System," edited by David E. Doyel, Anthropological Papers No. 5, pp. 23–34. Maxwell Museum of Anthropology, Albuquerque.

Sebastian, Lynne 1992. "The Chaco Anasazi: Sociopolitical Evolution in the Prehistoric Southwest." Cambridge University Press, Cambridge.

Sellards, E. H. 1940. Early Man in America: Index to Localities, and Selected Bibliography. *Bulletin of the Geological Society of America* **51**:373–432.

Sellards, E. H. 1952. "Early Man in America: A Study in Prehistory." University of Texas Press, Austin.

Sellards, E. H., G. L. Evans, and G. E. Meade 1947. Fossil Bison and Associated Artifacts from Plainview, Texas. *Bulletin of the Geological Society of America* **58**:927–954.

Shafer, Harry J. 1982. Classic Mimbres Phase Households and Room Use Pattern. *The Kiva* **489**(1–2):17–38.

Shafer, Harry J. 1991. Archaeology at the NAN Ruin: 1986 Interim Report. *The Artifact* **29**(2): 1–42.

Shafer, Harry J. 1993. Transitional Pueblo Development in the Mimbres Valley: The NAN Ruin Evidence. Paper presented at the 58th Annual Meeting of the Society for American Archaeology, St. Louis.

Shafer, Harry J. 1995. Architecture and Symbolism in Transitional Pueblo Development in Mimbres Valley, S. W. New Mexico. *Journal of Field Archaeology* **22**(1):23–47.

Shafer, Harry J. 1996. The Classic Mimbres Phenomenon and Some New Interpretations. Paper presented at the 9th Mogollon Archaeology Conference, Silver City.

Shafer, Harry J., and Anna J. Taylor 1986. Mimbres Mogollon Pueblo Dynamics and Ceramic Style Change. *Journal of Field Archaeology* **13**(1):33–68.

Shelley, Phillip H. 1994. Review of the Archaic Archaeology of the Llano Estacado and Adjacent Areas of New Mexico. *In* "Archaic Hunter-Gatherer Archaeology in the American Southwest," edited by Bradley J. Vierra, Contributions in Anthropology 13(1), pp. 372–404. Eastern New Mexico University, Portales.

Shepard, Anna O. 1939. Technology of La Plata Pottery. *In* "Archaeological Studies in the La Plata District," by Earl H. Morris, Publication 519, pp. 249–287. Carnegie Institute of Washington, Washington, DC.

Shepard, Anna O. 1942. Rio Grande Glaze Paint Ware. Contributions to American Anthropology and History 39. *Carnegie Institute of Washington Publication* **528**.

Shepard, Anna O. 1954. Ceramics for the Archaeologist. *Carnegie Institute of Washington Publication* **609.**

Sheridan, Thomas E. and Nancy J. Parezo (editors) 1996. "Paths of Life: American Indians of the Southwest and Northern Mexico." University of Arizona Press, Tucson.

Shott, Michael J. 1992. Commerce or Service: Models of Practice in Archaeology. *In* "Quandries and Quests: Visions of Archaeology's Future," edited by LuAnn Wandsnider, pp. 9–24. Center for Archaeological Investigations, Carbondale.

Simmons, Alan H. 1986. New Evidence for the Early Use of Cultigens in the American Southwest. *American Antiquity* **51**:73–89.

Simmons, Marc 1969. Settlement Patterns and Village Plans in Colonial New Mexico. *Journal of the West* **8**:7–21.

Simmons, Marc 1979. History of Pueblo-Spanish Relations to 1821. *In* "Southwest," edited by Alfonso A. Ortiz, Handbook of North American Indians, Vol. 9, pp. 170–177. Smithsonian Institution, Washington, DC.

Simon, Arleyn W., and John C. Ravesloot 1995. Salado Ceramic Burial Offerings: A Consideration of Gender and Social Organization. *Journal of Anthropological Research* **51**(2):103–124.

Simpson, James H. 1850. Journal of a Military Reconnaissance from Santa Fe, New Mexico, to the Navaho Country. Report of the Secretary of War to the 31st Congress, 1st Session, Senate. Executive Document 64. Washington, DC.

Slatter, Edwin D. 1973. Climate in Pueblo Abandonment of the Chevelon Drainage, Arizona. Paper presented at the 38th Annual Meeting of the American Anthropological Association, New Orleans.

Slaughter, B. H. 1967. Animal Range as a Clue to Late Pleistocene Extinction. *In* "Pleistocene Extinctions, the Search for a Cause," edited by Paul S. Martin and H. E. Wright, Jr., pp. 98–120. Yale University Press, New Haven.

Smiley, Francis E. 1985. The Chronometrics of Early Agricultural Sites in Northeastern Arizona: Approaches to the Interpretation of Radiocarbon Dates. Ph.D. dissertation, University of Michigan, Ann Arbor. University Microfilms, Ann Arbor.

Smiley, Francis E. 1994. The Agricultural Transition in the Northern Southwest: Patterns in the Current Chronometric Data. *The Kiva* **60**(2):165–186.

Smiley, Francis E., William J. Parry, and George J. Gumerman 1986. Early Agriculture in the Black Mesa/Marsh Pass Region of Arizona: New Chronometric Data and Recent Excavations at Three Fir Shelter. Paper presented at the 51st Annual Meeting of the Society for American Archaeology, New Orleans.

Smith, C. E., Jr. 1950. Prehistoric Plant Remains from Bat Cave. *Harvard University Botanical Museum Leaflets* **14**:157–180.

Smith, Watson 1952. "Kiva Mural Decorations at Awatovi and Kawaika-a," *Peabody Museum of Archaeology and Ethnology Papers* 37.

Smith, Watson 1971. "Painted Ceramics of the Western Mound at Awatovi," *Papers of the Peabody Museum of Archaeology and Ethnology* 38.

Smith, Watson, R. B. Woodbury, and N. F. S. Woodbury (editors) 1966. "The Excavation of Hawikuh by Frederick Webb Hodge," Contributions of Museum of the American Indian, Heye Foundation, New York.

Snow, David H. 1982. The Rio Grande Glaze, Matte-Paint, and Plainware Tradition. *In* "Southwestern Ceramics: A Comparative Review," edited by Albert H. Schroeder, *The Arizona Archaeologist* No. 15, pp. 235–278.

Snow, David H. 1991. Upland Prehistoric Maize Agriculture in the Eastern Rio Grande and its Peripheries. *In* "Farmers, Hunters, and Colonists: Interaction between the Southwest and the Southern Plains," edited by Katherine A. Spielmann, pp. 71–89. University of Arizona Press, Tucson.

Sofaer, A., V. Zinser, and R. M. Sinclair 1979. A Unique Solar Marking Construct. *Science* **206**: 283–291.

Spaulding, Albert C. 1953. Statistical Techniques for the Discovery of Artifact Types. *American Antiquity* **18**:305–313.

Spaulding, Albert C. 1960. The Dimensions of Archaeology. *In* "Essays in the Science of Culture," edited by G. E. Dole and Robert L. Carneiro, pp. 437–456. Crowell, New York.

Spaulding, W. G., J. L. Betancourt, L. K. Croft, and K. L. Cole 1990. Packrat Middens: Their Composition and Methods of Analysis. *In* "Packrat Middens: The Last 40,000 Years of Biotic Change," edited by J. L. Betancourt, T. R. Van Devender, and P. S. Martin, pp. 71–89. University of Arizona Press, Tucson.

Spaulding, W. G., E. B. Leopold, and T. R. Van Devender 1983. Late Wisconsin Paleoecology of the American Southwest. *In* "Late Quaternary Environments of the United States," edited by S. Porter, Vol. 1, pp. 259–293. University of Minnesota Press, Minneapolis.

Speth, John D. 1990. Seasonality, Resource Stress, and Food Sharing in So-called Egalitarian Foraging Societies. *Journal of Anthropological Archaeology* **9**:148–188.

Speth, John D. 1991. Some Unexplored Aspects of Mutualistic Plains-Pueblo Food Exchange. *In* "Farmers, Hunters, and Colonists: Interaction between the Southwest and the Southern Plains," edited by Katherine A. Spielmann, pp. 18–35. University of Arizona Press, Tucson.

Spicer, Edward H. 1962. "Cycles of Conquest." University of Arizona Press, Tucson.

Spicer, Edward H. 1969. The Yaqui and Mayo. *In* "Handbook of Middle American Indians," edited by Evon Z. Vogt, Vol. 8, Part 2, pp. 830–845. University of Texas Press, Austin.

Spielmann, Katherine A. 1983. Late Prehistoric Exchange between the Southwest and Southern Plains. *Plains Anthropologist* **28**(102):257–272.

Spielmann, K. A. 1986. Interdependence among Egalitarian Societies. *Journal of Anthropological Archaeology* **5**:279–312.

Spielmann, Katherine A. 1989. Colonists, Hunters, and Farmers: Plains-Pueblo Interaction in the Seventeenth Century. *In* "Columbian Consequences," edited by David Hurst Thomas, Vol. 1, pp. 101–114. Smithsonian Institution Press, Washington, DC.

Spielmann, Katherine A. 1991a. Coercion or Cooperation? Plains-Pueblo Interactions in the Protohistoric Period. *In* "Farmers, Hunters, and Colonists: Interaction between the Southwest and the Southern Plains," edited by Katherine A. Spielmann, pp. 36–50. University of Arizona Press, Tucson.

Spielmann, Katherine A. 1991b. "Interdependence in the Prehistoric Southwest." Garland Publishing, New York.

Spielmann, Katherine A. (editor) 1991c. "Farmers, Hunters, and Colonists: Interactions between the Southwest and the Southern Plains." University of Arizona Press, Tucson.

Spielmann, K. A. 1994. Clustered Confederacies: Sociopolitical Organization in the Protohistoric Rio Grande. *In* "The Ancient Southwestern Community: Models and Methods for the Study of Prehistoric Social Organization," edited by W. H. Wills and Robert D. Leonard, pp. 45–54. University of New Mexico Press, Albuquerque.

Spielmann, Katherine A. 1995. Glimpses of Gender in the Prehistoric Southwest. *Journal of Anthropological Research* **51**(2):91–102.

Spielmann, Katherine A. 1996. Impressions of Pueblo III Settlement Trends among the Rio Abajo and Eastern Border Pueblos. *In* "The Prehistoric Pueblo World, AD 1150–1350, edited by Michael A. Adler, pp. 177–187. University of Arizona Press, Tucson.

Spielmann, Katherine A., and Eric A. Angstadt-Leto 1995. Hunting, Gathering, and Health in the Prehistoric Southwest. *In* "Evolving Complexity and Environmental Risk in the Prehistoric Southwest," edited by Joseph A. Tainter and Bonnie Bagley Tainter, pp. 79–106. Santa Fe Institute Studies in the Sciences of Complexity, Addison-Wesley Publishing Company, Reading.

Spier, Leslie 1917. "An Outline for a Chronology of Zuni Ruins," Anthropological Papers No. 18(Part 4). American Museum of Natural History, New York.

Spoerl, Patricia M. and George J. Gumerman (editors) 1984. "Prehistoric Cultural Development in Central Arizona: Archaeology of the Upper New River Region," Center for Archaeological Investigations, Carbondale.

Spooner, Brian (editor) 1972. "Population Growth: Anthropological Implications." MIT Press, Cambridge.

Stafford, C. R., and G. E. Rice (editors) 1980. "Studies in the Prehistory of the Forestdale Region, Arizona," Anthropological Field Studies 1. Office of Cultural Resource Management, Department of Anthropology, Arizona State University, Tempe.

Stalker, A. MacS. 1980. The Geology of the Ice-Free Corridor: the Southern Half. *Canadian Journal of Anthropology* **1**(1):11–14.

Stanislawski, Michael B. 1969. The Ethnoarchaeology of Hopi Pottery Making. *Plateau* **42**(1): 27–33.

Steen, Charles R. 1977. "Pajarito Plateau Archaeological Survey and Excavation." Los Alamos Scientific Laboratories, Los Alamos.

Steen, Charles R., Lloyd M. Pierson, Vorsila L. Bohrer, and Kate Peck Kent 1962. "Archaeological Studies at Tonto National Monument, Arizona," Technical Series 2. Southwestern Monuments Association, Globe.

Stein, John R., and Andrew P. Fowler 1996. Looking Beyond Chaco in the San Juan Basin and Its Peripheries. *In* "The Prehistoric Pueblo World, AD 1150–1350," edited by Michael A. Adler, pp. 114–131. University of Arizona Press, Tucson.

Stein, John R., and Chris Kincaid 1983. Archaeological Inventory Methodology. *In* "Chaco Roads Project Phase I: A Reappraisal of Prehistoric Roads in the San Juan Basin 1983," edited by Chris Kincaid, pp. 7-1 to 7-9. U.S. Dept. of the Interior, Bureau of Land Management, New Mexico State Office, Albuquerque District Office.

Stein, John R., and Peter J. McKenna 1988. An Archaeological Reconnaissance of a Late Bonito Phase Occupation Near Aztec Ruins National Monument, New Mexico." Southwest Cultural Resources Center, National Park Service, Santa Fe.

Stevens, Dominique E., and George Agogino 1975. "Sandia Cave: A Study in Controversy," Contributions in Anthropology 7(1). Eastern New Mexico University, Portales.

Steward, Julian H. 1938. "Basin Plateau Socio-Political Groups," Bulletin 120. Bureau of American Ethnology, Washington, DC.

Steward, Julian H. 1955. "Theory of Culture Change." University of Illinois Press, Urbana.

Stiger, Mark A. 1979. Mesa Verde Subsistence Patterns from Basketmaker to Pueblo III. *The Kiva* **44**(2):133–145.

Stone, Connie L. 1987. "People of the Desert, Canyons and Pines: Prehistory of the Patayan Country in West Central Arizona," Cultural Resource Series No. 5. Bureau of Land Management, Arizona State Office, Phoenix.

Strong, William D., W. E. Schenck, and J. Steward 1930. Archaeology of the Dalles-Deschutes Region. *University of California, Berkeley, Publications in American Archaeology and Ethnology* **29**:1–154.

Struever, Mollie 1979. "Evidence of Ancient and Modern Human Behavior in Flotation Remains from Howiri Pueblo," Ms. on file. Museum of New Mexico, Santa Fe.

Stuart, David E., and Robin E. Farwell 1983. Out of Phase: Late Pithouse Occupations in the Highlands of New Mexico. *In* "High Altitude Adaptations in the Southwest," edited by Joseph C. Winter, Cultural Resources Management Report 2, pp. 115–158. USDA Forest Service, Southwestern Region, Albuquerque.

Stuart, David E., and Rory P. Gauthier 1981. "Prehistoric New Mexico: Background for Survey." New Mexico Historic Preservation Bureau, Santa Fe.

Stubbs, Stanley A., and W. S. Stallings, Jr. 1953. "The Excavation of Pindi Pueblo, New Mexico," Monograph No. 18. Laboratory of Anthropology and School of American Research, Santa Fe.

Sullivan, Alan P., III 1995. Risk, Anthropogenic Environments and Western Anasazi Subsistence. *In* "Evolving Complexity and Environmental Risk in the Prehistoric Southwest," edited by Joseph A. Tainter and Bonnie Bagley Tainter, pp. 145–167. Santa Fe Institute Studies in the Sciences of Complexity, Addison-Wesley Publishing Company, Reading.

Swadesh, Frances Leon 1974. "Los Primeros Pobladores: Hispanic Americans of the Ute Frontier." University of Notre Dame Press, South Bend.

Swedlund, Alan C. 1994. Issues in Demography and Health. *In* "Understanding Complexity in the Prehistoric Southwest," edited by G. J. Gumerman and Murray Gell-Mann, Vol. 16, pp. 39–58. Santa Fe Institute Studies in the Sciences of Complexity, Addison-Wesley Publishing Company, Reading.

Szuter, Christine 1991. Hunting by Hohokam Desert Farmers. *The Kiva* **56**(3):277–293.

Szuter, Christine R., and Frank E. Bayham 1989. Sedentism and Animal Procurement among Desert Horticulturalists of the North American Southwest. *In* "Farmers as Hunters: The Implications of Sedentism," edited by Susan Kent, pp. 80–95. Cambridge University Press, Cambridge.

Tainter, Joseph A., and David A. Gillio 1980. "Cultural Resources Overview, Mount Taylor Area, New Mexico." U.S. Government Printing Office, Washington, DC.

Tanner, Clara Lee 1976. "Prehistoric Southwestern Craft Arts." University of Arizona Press, Tucson.

Taylor, Walter W. 1966. Archaic Cultures Adjacent to the Northeastern Frontiers of Mesoamerica. *In* "Archaeological Frontiers and External Connections," edited by Gordon F. Ekholm and Gordon R. Willey, Handbook of Middle American Indians, Vol. 4, pp. 59–94. University of Texas Press, Austin.

Teague, Lynn S. 1993. Prehistory and the Traditions of the O'Odham and Hopi. *The Kiva* **58**(4): 435–455.

Thom, R. 1975. "Structural Stability and Morphogenesis." Benjamin, Reading.

Thomas, David Hurst 1971. On Distinguishing Natural from Cultural Bone in Archaeological Sites. *American Antiquity* **36**:366–371.

Tichy, Marjorie F. 1938. The Archaeology of Puaray. *El Palacio* **46**(7):145–162.

Titiev, Mischa 1944. "Old Oraibi: A Study of the Hopi Indians of Third Mesa." *Papers of the Peabody Museum of American Archaeology and Ethnology* **22**(1).

Todd, L. J. Hofman, and C. B. Schultz 1990. Seasonality of the Scottsbluff and Lipscomb Bison Bonebeds: Implications for Modeling Paleoindian Subsistence. *American Antiquity* **55**: 813–827.

Toll, H. Wolcott 1991. Material Distributions and Exchange in the Chaco Systems. *In* "Chaco and Hohokam: Prehistoric Regional Systems in the American Southwest," edited by Patricia L. Crown and W. James Judge, pp. 77–108. School of American Research Press, Santa Fe.

Toll, H. Wolcott, Thomas C. Windes, and Peter J. McKenna 1980. Late Ceramic Patterns in Chaco Canyon: The Pragmatics of Modeling Ceramic Exchange. *In* "Models and Methods in Regional Exchange," edited by Robert E. Fry, Paper 1, pp. 95–118. Society for American Archaeology.

Toll, Mollie S., and Anne C. Cully 1983. Archaic Subsistence and Seasonal Round. *In* "Economy and Interaction Along the Lower Chaco River: The Navajo Mine Archaeological Program, Mining Area III," edited by P. Hogan and J. Winter, pp. 385–392. Office of Contract Archeology, University of New Mexico, Albuquerque.

Toll, Mollie S., and Anne C. Cully 1994. Archaic Subsistence and Seasonal Population Flow in Northwest New Mexico. *In* "Archaic Hunter-Gatherer Archaeology in the American Southwest," edited by Bradley J. Vierra, Contributions in Anthropology 13(1), pp. 103–120. Eastern New Mexico University, Portales.

Towner, Ronald H., and Jeffrey S. Dean 1996. Questions and Problems in Pre-Fort Sumner Navajo Archaeology. *In* "The Archaeology of Navajo Origins," edited by Ronald H. Towner, pp. 3–18. University of Utah Press, Salt Lake City.

Traylor, Diane, Nancy Wood, Lyndi Hubbell, Robert Scaife, and Sue Waber 1977. "Bandelier: Excavations in the Flood Pool of Cochiti Lake, New Mexico," Ms. on file. Southwest Cultural Resource Center, National Park Service, Santa Fe.

Trewartha, G. T. 1966. "The Earth's Problem Climates." Methuen, London, and University of Wisconsin Press, Madison.

Truell, Marcia L. 1986. A Summary of Small Site Architecture in Chaco Canyon, New Mexico. *In* "Small Site Architecture of Chaco Canyon," by P. J. McKenna and M. L. Truell, Publications in Archaeology No. 18D, Chaco Canyon Studies, pp. 115–502. National Park Service, Santa Fe.

Tuan, Yi-Fu, Cyril E. Everard, Jerold G. Widdison, and Ivan Bennett 1973. "The Climate of New Mexico." New Mexico State Planning Office, Santa Fe.

Turnbull, Colin M. 1978. Rethinking the Ik: A Functional Non-social System. *In* "Extinction and Survival in Human Populations," edited by Charles D. Loughlin, Jr., and Ivan A. Brady, pp. 49–75. Columbia University Press, New York.

Turner, Christy G., II 1983. Taphonomic Reconstructions of Human Violence and Cannibalism Based on Mass Burials in the American Southwest. *In* "Carnivores, Human Scavengers and Predators: A Question of Bone Technology," edited by G. M. LeMoine and A. S. Mac-Eachem, Proceedings of the Fifteenth Annual Conference, pp. 219–240. Archaeological Association of the University of Calgary, Alberta.

Turner, Christy G., II 1989. Teec Nos Pos: More Possible Cannibalism in Northeastern Arizona. *The Kiva* **54**:147–152.

Turner, Christy G., II, and N. T. Morris 1970. A Massacre at Hopi. *American Antiquity* **35**: 320–331.

Turner, Christy G., II, and Jacqueline A. Turner 1990. Perimortem Damage to Human Skeletal Remains from Wupatki National Monument, Northern Arizona. *The Kiva* **55**:187–212.

Tyler, Hamilton A., and Lawrence Ormsby (illustrator) 1991. "Pueblo Birds & Myths." Northland Press, Flagstaff.

Upham, Steadman 1982. "Polities and Power: An Economic and Political History of the Western Pueblo." Academic Press, New York.

Upham, Steadman 1984. Adaptive Diversity and Southwestern Abandonment. *Journal of Anthropological Research* **40**(2):235–256.

Upham, Steadman 1987. The Tyranny of Ethnographic Analogy in Southwestern Archaeology. *In* "Coasts, Plains and Deserts: Essays in Honor of Reynold J. Ruppe," edited by S. W. Gaines, Anthropological Research Papers No. 38, pp. 265–281. Arizona State University, Tempe.

Upham, Steadman, Kent G. Lightfoot, and Roberta A. Jewett (editors) 1989. "The Sociopolitical Structure of Prehistoric Southwestern Societies." Westview Press, Boulder.

Upham, Steadman, Richard S. MacNeish, Walton Galinat, and Christopher M. Stevenson 1987. Evidence Concerning the Origin of Maiz de Ocho. *American Anthropologist* **89**:410–419.

Upham, Steadman, and Fred Plog 1986. The Interpretation of Prehistoric Political Complexity in Central and Northern Southwest: Toward a Mending of the Models. *Journal of Field Archaeology* **13**:223–238.

Upham, Steadman, and Lori Stephens Reed 1989. Regional Systems in the Central and Northern Southwest: Demography, Economy, and Sociopolitics Preceding Contact. *In* "Columbian Consequences," edited by David Hurst Thomas, Vol. 1, pp. 57–76. Smithsonian Institution Press, Washington, DC.

Van Devender, Thomas R. 1990. Late Quaternary Vegetation and Climate of the Sonoran Desert, United States and Mexico. *In* "Packrat Middens: The Last 40,000 Years of Biotic Change," edited by Julio Betancourt, T. R. Van Devender, and P. S. Martin, pp. 134–165. University of Arizona Press, Tucson.

Van Devender, T. R., and W. G. Spaulding 1979. Development of Vegetation and Climate in the Southwestern United States. *Science* **204**:701–710.

Van Devender, T. R., R. S. Thompson, and J. L. Betancourt 1987. Vegetation History of the Deserts of Southwestern North America: The Nature and Time of the Late Wisconsin-Holocene Transition. *In* "The Geology of North America," edited by W. F. Ruddiman and H. E. Wright, Jr., Vol. K-3, pp. 323–352. Geological Society of America, Boulder.

Van Devender, T. R., D. E. Wiseman, and J. G. Gallagher 1978. "Holocene Environments and Archeology in Rocky Arroyo and Last Chance Canyon, Eddy County, New Mexico," Ms. on file. Office of Contract Archeology, University of New Mexico, Albuquerque.

Van West, Carla R. 1994. Reconstructing Prehistoric Climatic Variability and Agricultural Production in Southwestern Colorado, AD 901–1300: A GIS Approach. *In* "Proceedings of the Second Anasazi Symposium," compiled by A. Hutchinson and Jack E. Smith, pp. 25–33. Mesa Verde Museum Association, Mesa Verde National Park.

Van West, Carla R. 1996. Agricultural Potential and Carrying Capacity in Southwestern Colorado, AD 901 to 1300. *In* "The Prehistoric Pueblo World, AD 1150–1350," edited by Michael A. Adler, pp. 214–227. University of Arizona Press, Tucson.

Van West, C. R., and T. A. Kohler 1992. "A Time to Rend, A Time to Sew: New Perspectives on Northern Anasazi Sociopolitical Development," Ms. on file. Department of Anthropology, Washington State University, Pullman.

Vargas, Victoria D. 1995. "Copper Bell Trade Patterns in the Prehispanic U.S. Southwest and Northwest Mexico," Archaeological Series 187. Arizona State Museum, Tucson.

Varien, Mark D., William D. Lipe, Michael A. Adler, Ian M. Thompson, and Bruce A. Bradley 1996. Southwestern Colorado and Southeastern Utah Settlement Patterns: AD 1100–1300. *In* "The Prehistoric Pueblo World, AD 1150–1350," edited by Michael A. Adler, pp. 86–113. University of Arizona Press, Tucson.

Vickery, Irene 1939. Besh-ba-gowah. *The Kiva* **4**(5):19–21.

Vierra, Bradley J. (editor) 1994a. "Archaic Hunter-Gatherer Archaeology in the American Southwest." Contributions in Anthropology 13(1). Eastern New Mexico University, Portales.

Vierra, Bradley J. 1994b. Introduction. *In* "Archaic Hunter-Gatherer Archaeology in the American Southwest," edited by Bradley J. Vierra, Contributions in Anthropology 13(1): 5–61. Eastern New Mexico University, Portales.

Vierra, Bradley J. 1994c. Archaic Hunter-Gatherer Mobility Strategies in Northwestern New Mexico. *In* "Archaic Hunter-Gatherer Archaeology in the American Southwest," edited by Bradley J. Vierra, Contributions in Archaeology 13(1) pp. 121–154. Eastern New Mexico University, Portales.

Vierra, Bradley J., and William H. Doleman 1994. The Organization of Archaic Settlement-Subsistence Systems in the Northern Southwest. *In* "Archaic Hunter-Gatherer Archaeology in the American Southwest," edited by Bradley J. Vierra, Contributions in Anthropology 13(1), pp. 76–102. Eastern New Mexico University, Portales.

Vivian, Gordon 1959. "The Hubbard Site and Other Tri-Wall Structures in New Mexico and Colorado." Archaeological Research Series 5. National Park Service, Washington, DC.

Vivian, Gordon, and Tom W. Mathews 1965. "Kin Kletso, a Pueblo III Community in Chaco Canyon, New Mexico," Technical Series 6. Southwestern Monuments Association, Globe.

Vivian, Gordon, and Paul Reiter 1965. "The Great Kivas of Chaco Canyon and Their Relationships," Monograph 22. School of American Research, Santa Fe.

Vivian, R. G. 1964. "Gran Quivira: Excavations in a 17th-century Jumano Pueblo," Archaeological Research Series No. 8, U.S. Dept. of the Interior, National Park Service, Washington, DC.

Vivian, R. Gwinn 1970. Aspects of Prehistoric Society in Chaco Canyon, New Mexico. Unpublished Ph.D. dissertation, Department of Anthropology, University of Arizona, Tucson.

Vivian, R. Gwinn 1972. "Prehistoric Water Conservation in Chaco Canyon: Final Technical Letter Report," On file. Division of Cultural Resources. National Park Service, Albuquerque.

Vivian, R. Gwinn 1974. Conservation and Diversion: Water-Control Systems in the Anasazi Southwest. *In* "Irrigation's Impact on Society," edited by Theodore Downing and McGuire Gibson, Anthropological Papers 25, pp. 95–112. University of Arizona, Tucson.

Vivian, R. Gwinn 1989. Kluckhohn Reappraised: The Chacoan System as an Egalitarian Enterprise. *Journal of Anthropological Research* **45**:101–113.

Vivian, R. Gwinn 1990. "The Chacoan Prehistory of the San Juan Basin." Academic Press, San Diego.

Vivian, R. Gwinn 1995. Agricultural Strategies of the Chacoan Anasazi. Paper presented at the 60th Annual Meeting of the Society for American Archaeology, Minneapolis.

Vogt, Evon Z. 1969. Introduction. *In* "Handbook of Middle American Indians," Vol. 7, Part 1, pp. 3–17. University of Texas Press, Austin.

Wait, Walter K. 1976. "An Archaeological Survey of Star Lake: A Report on the Prehistoric, Historic, and Current Cultural Resources of the Star Lake Area, Northwestern New Mexico." Southern Illinois University Press, Carbondale.

Wait, Walter K. 1981. Some Old Problems and a New Model for the Paleo/Archaic Transition in the San Juan Basin, New Mexico. Paper presented at the 54th Pecos Conference, Fort Burgwin Research Center, Taos.

Wallace, W. J. 1978. Post-Pleistocene Archaeology, 9000 to 2000 BC *In* "California," edited by Robert F. Heizer, Handbook of North American Indians, Vol. 8, pp. 25–36. Smithsonian Institution, Washington, DC.

Wallerstein, I. 1974. "The Modern World System." Academic Press, New York.

Wallerstein, I. 1979. "The Capitalist World Economy." Cambridge University Press, New York.

Wandsnider, LuAnn (editor) 1992. "Quandaries and Quests: Visions of Archaeology's Future," Occasional Paper No. 20. Center for Archaeological Investigations, Southern Illinois University, Carbondale.

Warburton, Miranda, and Donna K. Graves 1992. Navajo Springs, Arizona: Frontier Outlier or Autonomous Great House? *Journal of Field Archaeology* **19**(1):51–70.

Ware, John A. 1992. "The Ojo Caliente Project: Archaeological Test Excavations and a Data Recovery Plan for Cultural Resources Along U.S. 285, Rio Arriba County, New Mexico," Archaeology Notes No. 99. Museum of New Mexico, Office of Archaeological Studies, Santa Fe.

Warren, A. Helene 1977. Prehistoric and Historic Ceramic Analyses. *In* "Excavation and Analysis, 1975 Season. Archaeological Investigations in Cochiti Reservoir," edited by Richard C. Chapman and Jan V. Biella, Vol. 2, pp. 97–101. Office of Contract Archeology, University of New Mexico, Albuquerque.

Warren, C. N. 1967. The San Dieguito Complex: A Review and Hypothesis. *American Antiquity* **32**:168–185.

Warren, Claude N. 1984. Obsidian Hydration and the Chronology of Lake Mojave and Pinto Period Occupations at Fort Irwin, California. Paper presented at the Great Basin Anthropological Conference, Boise.

Wasley, William W. 1960. Salvage Archaeology on Highway 66 in Eastern Arizona. *American Antiquity* **26**:30–43.

Wasley, William W., and David E. Doyel 1980. Classic Period Hohokam. *The Kiva* **45**(4): 337–352.

Wasley, William W., and A. Johnson 1965. "Salvage Archaeology in Painted Rocks Reservoir, Western Arizona," Anthropological Papers 9. University of Arizona, Tucson.

Waters, Michael R. 1982. The Lowland Patayan Tradition. *In* "Hohokam and Patayan: Prehistory of Southwestern Arizona," edited by Randall H. McGuire and Michael B. Schiffer, pp. 275–297. Academic Press, New York.

Waters, Michael R. 1986. The Geoarchaeology of Whitewater Draw, Arizona. Anthropological Papers of the University of Arizona No. 45. University of Arizona Press, Tucson.

Watson, Patty Jo 1976. In Pursuit of Prehistoric Subsistence: A Comparative Account of Some Contemporary Flotation Techniques. *Mid-Continental Journal of Archaeology* **1**(1)77–100.

Weaver, David S. 1981. An Osteological Test of Changes in Subsistence and Settlement Patterns at Casas Grandes, Chihuahua, Mexico. *American Antiquity* **46**:361–363.

Weaver, Donald E., Jr. 1972. A Cultural Ecological Model for the Classic Hohokam Period in the Lower Salt River Valley, Arizona. *The Kiva* **38**(1):43–52.

Weaver, Donald E., Jr. 1976. Salado Influences in the Lower Salt River Valley. *The Kiva* **42**(1): 17–26.

Weaver, Kenneth F. 1967. Magnetic Clues Help Date the Past. *National Geographic* **131**: 696–701.

Webb, R. H., and J. L. Betancourt 1990. The Spatial and Temporal Distribution of Radiocarbon Ages from Packrat Middens. *In* "Packrat Middens: The Last 40,000 Years of Biotic Change," edited by Julio Betancourt, T. R. Van Devender, and P. S. Martin, pp. 85–102. University of Arizona Press, Tucson.

Weber, Robert H., and George A. Agogino 1968. Mockingbird Gap Paleo-Indian Site: Excavations in 1967. Paper presented at the 33rd Annual Meeting of the Society for American Archaeology, Santa Fe.

Weissner, Polly 1983. Style and Social Information in Kalahari San Projectile Points. *American Antiquity* **48**:253–276.

Wendorf, Fred 1953a. "Archaeological Studies in the Petrified Forest National Monument," Bulletin 27. Museum of Northern Arizona, Flagstaff.

Wendorf, Fred 1953b. Excavations at Te'ewi. *In* "Salvage Archaeology in the Chama Valley, New Mexico," assembled by Fred Wendorf, Monograph No. 17, pp. 34–100. School of American Research, Santa Fe.

Wendorf, Fred 1970. The Lubbock Subpluvial. *In* "Pleistocene and Recent Environment of the Central Plains," edited by W. Dort, Jr. and J. K. Jones, Jr., Special Publication 3, pp. 23–35. Department of Geology, University of Kansas, Regents Press of Kansas, Lawrence.

Wendorf, Fred 1975. The Modern Environment. *In* "Late Pleistocene Environments of the Southern High Plains," edited by Fred Wendorf and James J. Hester, Fort Burgwin Research Center Publication 9, pp. 1–12. Southern Methodist University, Dallas.

Wendorf, Fred (editor) 1961. "Paleoecology of the Llano Estacado," Fort Burgwin Research Paper 1. Museum of New Mexico Press, Santa Fe.

Wendorf, Fred, and James J. Hester (editors) 1975. "Late Pleistocene Environments on the Southern High Plains," Fort Burgwin Research Center Publication 9. Southern Methodist University, Dallas.

Wendorf, Fred, and John P. Miller 1959. Artifacts from High Mountain Sites in the Sangre de Cristo Range, New Mexico. *El Palacio* **66**(2):37–52.

Wendorf, Fred, and Erik Reed 1955. An Alternative Reconstruction of Northern Rio Grande Prehistory. *El Palacio* **62**(5–6):131–173.

Wendorf, Fred, Nancy Fox, and Orian L. Lewis (editors) 1956. "Pipeline Archaeology." Laboratory of Anthropology, Santa Fe and Museum of Northern Arizona, Flagstaff.

Wetherington, Ronald Knox 1964. Early Occupation in the Taos District in the Context of Northern Rio Grande Culture History. Unpublished Ph.D. dissertation, Department of Anthropology, University of Michigan, Ann Arbor.

Wetherington, Ronald Knox 1968. "Excavations at Pot Creek Pueblo," Fort Burgwin Research Center Report 6. Southern Methodist University, Dallas.

Wetterstrom, Wilma 1986. "Food, Diet, and Population at Prehistoric Arroyo Hondo Pueblo, New Mexico." Arroyo Hondo Archaeological Series No. 6. School of American Research Press, Santa Fe.

Whalen, Michael E. 1981. Cultural-Ecological Aspects of the Pithouse-To-Pueblo Transition in a Portion of the Southwest. *American Antiquity* **46**:75–92.

Whalen, Michael E. 1994. Moving Out of the Archaic on the Edge of the Southwest. *American Antiquity* **59**:622–638.

Whalen, Michael E., and Paul E. Minnis 1996. Ball Courts and Political Centralization in the Casas Grandes Region. *American Antiquity* **61**(4):732–746.

Whalen, Norman M. 1971. Cochise Culture Sites in the Central San Pedro Drainage, Arizona. Ph.D. dissertation, Arizona State University, Tempe. University Microfilms, Ann Arbor.

Whalen, Norman M. 1975. Cochise Site Distribution in the San Pedro River Valley. *The Kiva* **40**(3):203–211.

Wheat, Joe Ben 1954. "Crooked Ridge Valley (Arizona W:10:15)," Social Science Bulletin 24. University of Arizona, Tucson.

Wheat, Joe Ben 1955. "Mogollon Culture prior to AD 1000," Memoirs of the Society for American Archaeology 10, Memoirs of the American Anthropological Association 82.

Wheat, Joe Ben 1972. "The Olsen-Chubbock Site: A PaleoIndian Bison Kill." *Society for American Archaeology Memoir* **26**:1–179.

Wheat, Joe Ben 1983. Anasazi Who? *In* "Proceedings of the 1981 Anasazi Symposium," edited by J. E. Smith, pp. 11–15. Mesa Verde Museum Association, Mesa Verde National Park.

White, Leslie A. 1969. "The Science of Culture," revised edition. Farrar, Straus, and Giroux, New York.

Whiteley, Peter Michael 1982. Third Mesa Hopi Social Structural Dynamics and Sociocultural Change: The View from Bacavi. Unpublished Ph.D. dissertation, Department of Anthropology, University of New Mexico, Albuquerque.

Whiteley, Peter Michael 1988. "Deliberate Acts, Changing Hopi Culture Through the Oraibi Split." University of Arizona Press, Tucson.

Whiting, Alfred J. 1937. "Hopi Indian Agriculture, II," Museum Notes 10, pp. 11–16. Museum of Northern Arizona, Flagstaff.

Whittlesey, Stephanie M., and J. Jefferson Reid 1982. Cholla Project Perspectives on Salado. *In* "Introduction and Special Studies," edited by J. Jefferson Reid, Arizona State Museum Archaeological Series No. 161, Cholla Project Archaeology, Vol. 1, pp. 63–80. University of Arizona, Tucson.

Whittlesey, Stephanie M. 1995. Mogollon, Hohokam, and O'Odham: Rethinking the Early Formative Period in Southern Arizona. *The Kiva* **60**(4):465–480.

Wilcox, David R. 1978. The Theoretical Significance of Fieldhouses. *In* "Limited Activity and Occupation Sites: A Collection of Conference Papers," edited by Albert E. Ward, Contributions to Anthropological Studies 1, pp. 25–32. Center for Anthropological Studies, Albuquerque.

Wilcox, David R. 1980. The Current Status of the Hohokam Concept. *In* "Current Issues in Hohokam Prehistory: Proceedings of a Symposium," edited by David E. Doyel and Fred T. Plog, Anthropological Research Papers 23, pp. 236–242. Arizona State University, Tempe.

Wilcox, David R. 1981. Changing Perspectives on the Protohistoric Pueblos, AD 1450–1700. *In* "The Protohistoric Periods in the North American Southwest, AD 1450–1700," edited by David R. Wilcox and W. Bruce Masse, Anthropological Research Papers 24, pp. 378–409. Arizona State University, Tempe.

Wilcox, David R. 1987. The Evolution of Hohokam Ceremonial Systems. *Papers of the Maxwell Museum of Anthropology* **2**:149–168.

Wilcox, David R. 1991. The Mesoamerican Ballgame in the American Southwest. *In* "The Mesoamerican Ballgame," edited by V. L. Scarborough and D. R. Wilcox, pp. 101–128. University of Arizona Press, Tucson.

Wilcox, David R. 1996. Pueblo III People and Polity in Relational Context. *In* "The Prehistoric Pueblo World, AD 1150–1350," edited by Michael A. Adler, pp. 241–254. University of Arizona Press, Tucson.

Wilcox, David R., and Jonathan Haas 1994. The Scream of the Butterfly: Competition and Conflict in the Prehistoric Southwest. *In* "Themes in Southwest Prehistory," edited by George J. Gumerman, pp. 211–238. School of American Research Press, Santa Fe.

Wilcox, David R., and W. Bruce Masse (editors) 1981. "The Protohistoric Period in the North American Southwest, AD 1450–1700," Anthropological Research Papers 24. Arizona State University, Tempe.

Wilcox, David, and Charles Sternberg 1983. "Hohokam Ballcourts and Their Interpretation," Archaeological Series No. 160. Arizona State Museum, Tucson.

Wilcox, David R., Thomas R. McGuire, and Charles Sternberg 1981. "Snaketown Revisited: A Partial Cultural Resource Survey, Analysis of Site Structure, and an Ethnohistoric Study of the Proposed Hohokam-Pima National Monument," Archaeological Series 155. Arizona State Museum, Tucson.

Willey, Gordon R. 1966. "North and Middle America. An Introduction to American Archaeology," Vol. 1. Prentice-Hall, Englewood Cliffs.

Willey, Gordon R. 1979. The Concept of the "Disembedded Capital" in Comparative Perspective. *Journal of Anthropological Research* **35**:123–137.

Willey, Gordon R., and Philip Phillips; 1958. "Method and Theory in American Archaeology." University of Chicago Press, Chicago.

Williamsen, R. A., J. Fisher, and D. O'Flynn 1977. Anasazi Solar Observatories. *In* "Native American Astronomy," edited by A. Aveni, pp. 204–217. University of Texas Press, Austin.

Willig, Judith A., and C. Melvin Aikens 1988. The Clovis-Archaic Interface in Far Western North America. *In* "Early Human Occupation In Far Western North America: The Clovis Archaic Interface," edited by J. A. Willig, C. M. Aikens, and J. L. Fagan, Anthropological Papers, Vol. 21, pp 1–41. Nevada State Museum, Carson.

Wills, Wirt H. 1988a. "Early Prehistoric Agriculture in the American Southwest." School of American Research Press, Santa Fe.

Wills, Wirt H. 1988b. Early Agriculture and Sedentism in the American Southwest: Evidence and Interpretations. *Journal of World Prehistory* **2**(4):445–488.

Wills, Wirt H. 1990. Cultivating Ideas: The Changing Intellectual History of the Introduction of Agriculture in the American Southwest. *In* "Perspectives on Southwestern Prehistory," edited by Paul Minnis and Charles L. Redman, pp. 319–332. Westview Press, Boulder.

Wills, Wirt H. 1991. Organizational Strategies and the Emergence of Prehistoric Villages in the American Southwest. *In* "Between Bands and States," edited by Susan A. Gregg, Occasional Paper No. 9, pp. 161–180. Center for Archaeological Investigations, Southern Illinois University, Carbondale.

Wills, Wirt H. 1994. Economic Implications of Changing Land Use Patterns in the Late Archaic. *In* "Themes in Southwest Prehistory," edited by George J. Gumerman, pp. 33–52. School of American Research Press, Santa Fe.

Wills, Wirt H. 1995. Archaic Foraging and the Beginning of Food Production in the American Southwest. *In* "Last Hunters, First Farmers," edited by Douglas Price and Anne Birgitte Gebauer, pp. 215–242. School of American Research Press, Santa Fe.

Wills, Wirt H., and Bruce B. Huckell 1994. Economic Implications of Changing Land-use Patterns in the Late Archaic. *In* "Themes in Southwest Prehistory," edited by G. J. Gumerman, pp. 33–52. School of American Research Press, Santa Fe.

Wills, W. H., and Robert D. Leonard (editors) 1994. "The Ancient Southwestern Community: Models and Methods for the Study of Prehistoric Social Organization." University of New Mexico Press, Albuquerque.

Wills, Wirt H., F. E. Smiley, and Bruce Huckell 1989. Economic Implications of Changing Land Use Patterns in the Late Archaic. Paper presented at the School of American Research Advanced Seminar: The Organization of Prehistoric Southwestern Society, Santa Fe.

Wills, W. H., and Thomas C. Windes 1989. Evidence for Population Aggregation and Dispersal during the Basketmaker III Period in Chaco Canyon, New Mexico. *American Antiquity* **54**: 347–369.

Wilmsen, Edwin N. 1965. An Outline of Early Man Studies in the United States. *American Antiquity* **31**:172–192.

Wilmsen, Edwin N. 1974. "Lindenmeier: A Pleistocene Hunting Society." Harper & Row, New York.

Wilshusen, R. H., and E. Blinman 1992. Pueblo I Village Formation: A Reevaluation of Sites Recorded by Earl Morris on the Ute Mountain Tribal Lands. *The Kiva* **57**:251–269.

Wilson, C. Dean, and Eric Blinman 1995. Changing Specialization of White Ware Manufacture in the Northern San Juan Region. *In* "Ceramic Production in the American Southwest," edited by Barbara J. Mills and Patricia L. Crown, pp. 63–87. University of Arizona Press, Tucson.

Wilson, M. 1980. Morphological Dating of the Late Quaternary Bison on the Northern Plains. *Canadian Journal of Anthropology* **1**(1):81–86.

Wimberly, Mark 1972. "Training Bulletin for the Tularosa Valley Project," Ms. on file. Human Systems Research, Tularosa.

Wimberly, Mark, and Peter Eidenbach 1980. "Reconnaissance Study of the Archaeological and Related Sources of the Lower Puerco and Salado Drainages, Central New Mexico." Human Systems Research, Tularosa.

Windes, Thomas C. 1980. Archeomagnetic Dating: Lessons from Chaco Canyon, New Mexico. Paper presented at the 45th Annual Meeting of the Society for American Archaeology, Philadelphia.

Windes, Thomas C., and Dabney Ford 1992. The Nature of the Early Bonito Phase. *In* "Anasazi Regional Organization and the Chaco System," edited by David E. Doyel, Anthropological Papers No. 5, pp. 75–86. Maxwell Museum of Anthropology, University of New Mexico, Albuquerque.

Wing, E. S., and A. B. Brown 1979. "Paleonutrition, Method and Theory in Prehistoric Foodways." Academic Press, New York.

Winship, G. P. (editor) 1904. "The Journey of Coronado: 1540–1542." Aberton, New York (University Microfilms, Ann Arbor, 1966).

Winter, Joseph 1991. "Summary of Archaeological Survey and Test Excavations, and Preliminary Ethnological Studies—A Phase 2 Management Report, Vol. 1 in Across the Colorado Plateau: Anthropological Studies for Transwestern Pipeline Expansion Project." Office of Contract Archeology, University of New Mexico, Albuquerque.

Winter, Joseph C. 1976. The Process of Farming Diffusion in the Southwest and Great Basin. *American Antiquity* **41**:421–429.

Wittfogel, K. 1957. "Oriental Despotism." Yale University Press, New Haven.

Wittfogel, K., and E. Goldfrank 1943. Some Aspects of Pueblo Mythology and Society. *Journal of American Folklore* **56**:17–30.

Wolf, Eric R. 1982. "Europe and the People Without History." University of California Press, Berkeley.

Wood, S., and M. McAllister 1980. Foundation and Empire: The Colonization of the Northeastern Hohokam Periphery. *In* "Current Issues in Hohokam Prehistory: Proceedings of a Symposium," edited by David E. Doyel and Fred T. Plog, Anthropological Research Papers 23, pp. 180–200. Arizona State University, Tempe.

Woodbury, Richard B. 1961. Prehistoric Agriculture at Point of Pines, Arizona. Memoirs of the Society for American Archaeology 17. *American Antiquity* **26**(3, Part 2).

Woodbury, Richard B. 1973. "Alfred V. Kidder." Columbia University Press, New York.

Woodbury, Richard B. 1993. "Sixty Years of Southwestern Archaeology." University of New Mexico Press, Albuquerque.

Woodbury, Richard B., and Ezra B. W. Zubrow 1979. Agricultural Beginnings, 2000 BC–AD 500. *In* "Southwest," edited by Alfonso A. Ortiz, Handbook of North American Indians, Vol. 9, pp. 43–60. Smithsonian Institution, Washington, DC.

Woosley, Anne I. 1980. "Taos Archaeology." Fort Burgwin Research Center, Southern Methodist University, Dallas.

Woosley, Anne I., and Bart Olinger 1993. The Casas Grandes Ceramic Tradition: Production and Interregional Exchange of Ramos Polychrome. *In* "Culture and Contact," edited by Anne I. Woosley and John C. Ravesloot, pp. 105–132. University of New Mexico Press, Albuquerque.

Wormington, H. M. 1957. "Ancient Man in North America," Popular Series 4. Museum of Natural History, Denver.

Wormington, H. M. 1961. "Prehistoric Indians of the Southwest," Popular Series 7. Museum of Natural History, Denver.

Zedeño, Maria Nieves 1994. "Sourcing Prehistoric Ceramics at Chodistaas Pueblo, Arizona: The Circulation of People and Pots in the Grasshopper Region," Anthropological Papers No. 58. University of Arizona Press, Tucson.

Zubrow, Ezra B. W. 1972. Carrying Capacity and Dynamic Equilibrium in the Prehistoric Southwest. *In* "Contemporary Archaeology," edited by Mark P. Leone, pp. 268–279. Southern Illinois University Press, Carbondale.

Zubrow, Ezra B. W. 1974. "Population, Contact, and Climate in New Mexican Pueblos," Anthropological Papers No. 24. University of Arizona, Tucson.

INDEX[1]

Note:[1] Page numbers ending in "f" refer to a figure on the cited page; those ending in "m" refer to a map on the cited page; those ending in "t" refer to a table on the cited page.